Introduction to Automotive Service

James D. Halderman
Darrell Deeter

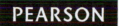

Boston Columbus Indianapolis New York San Francisco Upper Saddle River Amsterdam
Cape Town Dubai London Madrid Milan Munich Paris Montreal Toronto Delhi
Mexico City São Paulo Sydney Hong Kong Seoul Singapore Taipei Tokyo

Vice President and Executive Publisher: Vernon Anthony
Senior Acquisitions Editor: Lindsey Prudhomme
Development Editor: Dan Trudden
Editorial Assistant: Yvette Schlarman
Project Manager: Jessica H. Sykes
Media Project Manager: Karen Bretz
Director of Marketing: David Gesell
Senior Marketing Manager: Harper Coles
Senior Marketing Coordinator: Alicia Wozniak
Production Manager: Holly Shufeldt
Creative Director: Jayne Conte
Cover Designer: Bruce Kenselaar
Full-Service Project Management/Composition: Abinaya Rajendran,
 Integra Software Services, Ltd.
Printer/Binder: LSC Communications, Inc.
Cover Printer: LSC Communications, Inc.

Library of Congress Cataloging-in-Publication Data
Halderman, James D.,
  Introduction to automotive service/James D. Halderman, Darrell Deeter.—1 [edition].
    pages cm
  ISBN-13: 978-0-13-254008-7
  ISBN-10: 0-13-254008-8
  1. Automobiles—Maintenance and repair—Textbooks.   I. Title.
TL152.H19 2013
629.28'72—dc23

2011048644

PEARSON

ISBN-10:   0-13-254008-8
ISBN-13: 978-0-13-254008-7

PREFACE

This new book is designed to meet the needs of a typical beginning or introductory automotive course. The book is designed to fulfill the needs for the three types of students who usually take an introductory course in automotive service:

- Preparation for entry into an automotive program of study
- Survey course for those wanting to know how to maintain their vehicles
- Preparation for an entry-level position in the automotive service field

DEPTH OF CONTENT AND FORMAT

Automotive instructors have asked for the following in a beginning-level textbook:

1. The content should be **"an ankle deep and a mile wide"**
2. Easy to read
3. Many short chapters instead of a few longer chapters
4. Each new term defined at first use
5. Many full-color illustrations to help bring the topics to life

Scope: The scope of this title includes the duties and skills needed to function at an entry-level service technician position.

This means, for example, that when dealing with brakes, the topic is limited to removing the wheels and performing a *visual inspection* and does *not* include disassembly or replacement of brake parts. The reasoning behind this level of coverage is that once the brake parts are removed, all of the precautions and service issues must also be included to be sure that the service is performed correctly. The actual servicing of the brake system or other systems should be done by a technician who has been trained or has extensive and informed experience with the system.

Content: The content includes the basics needed by all service technicians and includes the following for most systems:

1. Purpose and function of the system
2. Parts involved and how it works (operation)
3. Basic visual diagnosis with the objective being:

Is it working as designed or must further service or diagnosis be required?

Depth: The key to a good introductory textbook is to include useful technical information but limit the information in depth. This means that the topics could and should include those areas where information is needed to perform the entry-level service or inspection service. For example, oil, lubricants, and coolants should be covered in detail to make sure that the reader understands the importance of using the specified fluid.

IN-TEXT FEATURES

chapter 1 — AUTOMOTIVE BACKGROUND AND OVERVIEW

OBJECTIVES: After studying Chapter 1, the reader will be able to: • Explain the evolution of the automobile. • Discuss the major components of a vehicle. • Describe the evolution of engines. • List the common components of most vehicles. • List the eight areas of automotive service according to ASE/NATEF.

KEY TERMS: • Air filter 5 • Body 2 • Body-on-frame (BOF) 3 • Carbon monoxide (CO) 5 • Catalytic converter 5 • Chassis 2 • Coolant 5 • Drive shaft 6 • Double overhead camshaft (DOHC) 4 • Evaporative emission system (EVAP) 5 • Exhaust gas recirculation (EGR) 5 • Flathead 4 • Frames 3 • Hydrocarbon (HC) 5 • Ignition control module (ICM) 5 • Inline engine 4 • Intake manifold 5 • Internal combustion engine 4 • Malfunction indicator light (MIL) 6 • Manufacturer's suggested retail price (MSRP) 4 • OBD-II 6 • Oil filter 5 • Oil galleries 5 • Oil pan 5 • Oil pump 5 • Oil sump 5 • Overhead camshaft (OHC) 4 • Overhead valve (OHV) 4 • Oxides of nitrogen (NOX) 5 • PCV valve 5 • Pillars 3 • Positive crankcase ventilation (PCV) 5 • Propeller shaft 6 • Radiator 5 • Scan tool 6 • Self-propelled vehicle 1 • Single overhead camshaft (SOHC) 4 • Thermostat 5 • Transaxle 6 • Transfer case 6 • Unibody 3 • Universal joints (U-joints) 6 • Water jackets 5 • Water pump 5

HISTORICAL BACKGROUND

For centuries, man either walked or used animals to provide power for transportation. After the invention of electric, steam, and gasoline propulsion systems, people used **self-propelled vehicles**, which are vehicles that moved under their own power.

Major milestones in vehicle development include:

1876	The OTTO four-stroke cycle engine was developed by a German engineer, Nikolaus Otto.
1885	The first automobile was powered by an OTTO cycle gasoline engine designed by Karl Friedrich Beary (1844–1929).
1892	Rudolf Diesel (1858–1913) received a patent for a compression ignition engine. The first diesel engine was built in 1897.
1896	Henry Ford (1863–1947) built his first car, called the Quadricycle. ● **SEE FIGURE 1–1.**
1900	About 4,200 total automobiles were sold, including: • 40% were steam powered • 38% were battery/electric powered • 22% were gasoline engine powered
1902	Oldsmobile, founded by Ransom E. Olds (1864–1950), produced the first large-scale, affordable vehicle.
1908	William Durant (1861–1947) formed General Motors.
1908	The Ford Model T was introduced.
1912	The electric starter was invented by Charles F. Kettering (1876–1958) of Dayton, Ohio, first used on a Cadillac. The starter was produced by a new company called Delco, which stood for Dayton Engineering Laboratories Company.
1914	First car with a 100% steel body was made by the Budd Corporation for Dodge. Before 1914, all car bodies had wood components in them.
1922	The first vehicle to have four-wheel hydraulically operated brakes was a Duesenberg built in Indianapolis, Indiana.
1940	The first fully automatic transmission was introduced by Oldsmobile.
1973	Airbags were offered as an option on some General Motors vehicles.
1985	Lincoln offers the first four-wheel antilock braking system.
1997	The first vehicle with electronic stability control was offered by Cadillac.

AUTOMOTIVE BACKGROUND AND OVERVIEW   1

OBJECTIVES AND KEY TERMS appear at the beginning of each chapter to help students and instructors focus on the most important material in each chapter. The chapter objectives are based on specific ASE and NATEF tasks.

TECH TIP

Treat a Vehicle Body with Respect

Do not sit on a vehicle. The metal can easily be distorted, which could cost hundreds of dollars to repair. This includes sitting on the hood, roof, and deck (trunk) lid, as well as fenders. Also, do not hang on any opened door as this can distort the hinge area causing the door not to close properly.

TECH TIP feature real-world advice and "tricks of the trade" from ASE-certified master technicians.

SAFETY TIP

Compressed Air Safety

Improper use of an air nozzle can cause blindness or deafness. Compressed air must be reduced to less than 30 PSI (206 kPa). **SEE FIGURE 6–11.** If an air nozzle is used to dry and clean parts, make sure the air stream is directed away from anyone else in the immediate area. Always use an OSHA-approved nozzle with side slits that limit the maximum pressure at the nozzle to 30 PSI. Coil and store air hoses when they are not in use.

SAFETY TIP alert students to possible hazards on the job and how to avoid them.

REAL-WORLD FIX

The Toyota Truck Story

The owner of a Toyota truck complained that several electrical problems plagued the truck, including the following:

1. The cruise (speed) control would kick out intermittently.
2. The red brake warning lamp would come on, especially during cold weather.

The owner had replaced the parking brake switch, thinking that was the cause of the red brake warning lamp coming on. An experienced technician checked the wiring diagram found in service information. Checking the warning lamp circuit, the technician noticed that the same wire went to the brake fluid–level sensor. The brake fluid was at the minimum level. Filling the master cylinder to the maximum level with clean brake fluid solved both problems. The electronics of the cruise control stopped operation when the red brake warning lamp was on as a safety measure.

REAL-WORLD FIX present students with actual automotive service scenarios and show how these common (and sometimes uncommon) problems were diagnosed and repaired.

FREQUENTLY ASKED QUESTION

Employee or Contract Labor?

Most shops and dealerships hire service technicians as employees. However, some shops or businesses will pay a technician for services performed on a contract basis. This means that they are not hiring you as an employee, but simply paying for a service similar to having a plumber repair a toilet. The plumber is performing a service and is paid for the job rather than as an employee of the shop. An employer/employee relationship exists if the shop meets two factors:

1. **Direction**—This means that the employer can direct the technician to report to work to perform service work.
2. **Control**—This means that the employer can direct the hours and days when the work is to be performed and at the employer's location.

A contract labor association exists if the repairs are performed without both direction and control of the shop.

If a contract labor basis is established, then no taxes are withheld. It is then the responsibility of the technician to make the necessary and required general tax payments and pay all taxes on time.

FREQUENTLY ASKED QUESTIONS are based on the author's own experience and provide answers to many of the most common questions asked by students and beginning service technicians.

NOTE: A claw hammer has a claw used to remove nails and is not used for automotive service.

NOTE provide students with additional technical information to give them a greater understanding of a specific task or procedure.

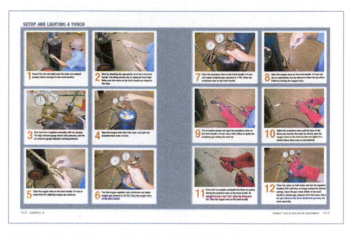

STEP-BY-STEP PHOTO SEQUENCES show in detail the steps involved in performing a specific task or service procedure.

CAUTION: Do not use penetrating oil as a lubricating oil because it is volatile and will evaporate soon after usage leaving little lubricant behind for protection.

CAUTION alert students about potential damage to the vehicle that can occur during a specific task or service procedure.

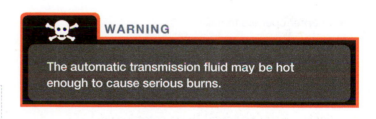

WARNING

The automatic transmission fluid may be hot enough to cause serious burns.

WARNING alert students to potential dangers to themselves during a specific task or service procedure.

REVIEW QUESTIONS AND CHAPTER QUIZ at the end of each chapter help students review the material presented in the chapter and test themselves to see how much they've learned.

SUPPLEMENTS

INSTRUCTOR SUPPLEMENTS The instructor supplement package has been completely revamped to reflect the needs of today's instructors. The Annotated Instructor's Guide (ISBN: 0-13-254017-7) is the cornerstone of the package and includes:

- Chapter openers that list:
  - NATEF/ASE tasks covered in the chapter
  - All key terms
  - All chapter objectives
- The entire text (matching page numbers with student edition) with margin notes. These notes include:
  - Tips for in-class demonstrations
  - Suggested hands-on activities
  - Cross-curricular activities
  - Internet search tips
  - Assessments
  - Safety tips
  - Classroom discussion questions
- A guide to using MyAutomotiveLab in the course Also included in the supplement package are:
- PowerPoint presentations
- Image Library containing every image in the book for use in class or customized PowerPoints

- TestGen software and test bank
- Chapter Quizzes
- Chapter Review Questions
- English glossary
- NATEF Correlated Task Sheets
- NATEF/ASE Correlation Charts

To access supplementary materials online, instructors need to request an instructor access code. Go to www.pearsonhighered.com/irc to register for an instructor access code. Within 48 hours of registering, you will receive a confirming e-mail, including an instructor access code. Once you have received your code, go to the site and log on for full instructions on downloading the materials you wish to use.

STUDENT SUPPLEMENTS A full compliment of student resources are available with *Introduction to Automotive Service*, including:

- MyAutomotiveLab: Combining an Ebook, video, animations, diagnostic simulations, and pre- and post-tests aligned with the chapters in the textbook, MyAutomotiveLab engages students and gives them the tools they need to enhance their performance in and outside of the classroom. Additional features include ASE Test Prep and practice tests, virtual toolbook, and new automotive professionalism modules. Visit www.myautomotivelab.com <http://www.myautomotivelab.com> for more information.

- Student study guide: This printed resource contains a chapter by chapter guide to help students understand the textbook material. Includes key terms, chapter objectives, and study questions. (ISBN: 0-13-298827-5)
- NATEF Correlated Task Sheets: Printed activity manual with correlated NATEF Automobile Standards to chapters and page numbers in the text. (ISBN: 0-13-254991-3)

ACKNOWLEDGMENTS

A large number of people and organizations have cooperated in providing the reference material and technical information used in this text. The authors wish to express sincere thanks to the following persons for their special contributions:

Dan Avery

John Kershaw

Gary DeCombs–WPAFB

Steve Cartwright–Federal Mogul Training Center

Elizabeth Rickard–Honda

Tim Jones–Honda

Kevin Boden–Consulab

Steve Ash–Sinclair Community College

Chuck Taylor–Sinclair Community College

Mike Garblik–Sinclair Community College

Jimmy Dinsmore–Cox Media

Tom Birch

Brad Halderman–Goodyear

Gale Halderman–Ford

Steve Goad–Sinclair Community College

Jim Sherritt

Jerry Million–North Pole Alaska

David Norman–San Jacinto College

Jeff Trick

Jim Linder–Linder Technical Services

Joe Palazzolo–GKN Driveline

Doug Poteet–Elizabethtown Community and Technical College

Justin Morgan–Sinclair Community College

Ken-Yon Hardy–Cox Media

Nathan Banke–Consulab

Richard Reaves

Tom Freels–Sinclair Community College

Tom Broxholm–Skyline College

Mick Williams

TECHNICAL AND CONTENT REVIEWERS The following people reviewed the manuscript before production and checked it for technical accuracy and clarity of presentation. Their suggestions and recommendations were included in the final draft of the manuscript. Their input helped make this textbook clear and technically accurate while maintaining the easy-to-read style that has made other books from the same authors so popular.

Jim Anderson
Greenville High School

Rankin E. Barnes
Guilford Technical Community College

Victor Bridges
Umpqua Community College

Bill Brown
Fred C. Beyer High School

Dave Crowley
College of Southern Nevada

Lance David
College of Lake County

Greg Del Vecchio
California State University, Long Beach

Matt Dixon
Southern Illinois University

Dr. Roger Donovan
Illinois Central College

A.C. Durdin
Moraine Park Technical College

Roger Duvall
Grayson County Technology Center

Herbert Ellinger
Western Michigan University

Al Engledahl
College of DuPage

Patrick English
Ferris State University

Robert M. Frantz
Ivy Tech Community College, Richmond

Christopher Fry
Harry S Truman College

Dr. David Gilbert
Southern Illinois University

Aaron Gregory
Merced College

Mario R. Guerrero
Frenship High School

Larry Hagelberger
Upper Valley Joint Vocational School

Oldrick Hajzler
Red River College

Gary F. Ham
South Plains College

Betsy Hoffman
Vermont Technical College

Curtis Jones
Bell-Brown Career Tech Center

Marty Kamimoto
Fresno City College

Joan Kelly
Automotive Training Center

Richard Krieger
Michigan Institute of Technology

Chad Lewis
Lassen College

Carlton H. Mabe, Sr.
Virginia Western Community College

Roy Marks
Owens Community College

Tony Martin
University of Alaska Southeast

Kerry Meier
San Juan College

Clifford G. Meyer
Saddleback College

Kevin Murphy
Stark State College of Technology

Fritz Peacock
Indiana Vocational Technical College

Dennis Peter
NAIT (Canada)

Jeff Rehkopf
Florida State College

Kenneth Redick
Hudson Valley Community College

Matt Roda
Mott Community College

Frank D. Russo
Northern Virginia Community College

Stewart Sikora
Triton College

Omar Trinidad
Southern Illinois University

Mitchell Walker
St. Louis Community College at Forest Park

Fred Werner
Temple High School

Jennifer Wise
Sinclair Community College

Special thanks to instructional designer
Alexis I. Skriloff James.

PHOTOS The authors wish to thank Blaine Heeter, Mike Garblik, and Chuck Taylor of Sinclair Community College in Dayton, Ohio, and James (Mike) Watson, who helped with many of the photos. A special thanks to Dick Krieger for his detailed and thorough review of the manuscript before publication. Most of all, we wish to thank Michelle Halderman for her assistance in all phases of manuscript preparation.

—James D. Halderman
—Darrell Deeter

JIM HALDERMAN brings a world of experience, knowledge, and talent to his work. His automotive service experience includes working as a flat-rate technician, a business owner, and a professor of automotive technology at a leading U.S. community college for more than 20 years.

He has a Bachelor of Science degree from Ohio Northern University and a Master's degree in Education from Miami University in Oxford, Ohio. Jim also holds a U.S. patent for an electronic transmission control device. He is an ASE-certified Master Automotive Technician and is also Advanced Engine Performance (L1) ASE certified. Jim is the author of many automotive textbooks, all published by Pearson Prentice Hall Publishing Company. Jim has presented numerous technical seminars to national audiences, including the California Automotive Teachers (CAT) and the Illinois College Automotive Instructor Association (ICAIA). He is also a member and presenter at the North American Council of Automotive Teachers (NACAT). Jim was also named Regional Teacher of the Year by General Motors Corporation and outstanding alumni of Ohio Northern University. Jim and his wife, Michelle, live in Dayton, Ohio. They have two children. You can reach Jim at

jim@jameshalderman.com

DARRELL DEETER has been an automotive machinist, an automotive technician, and a shop owner, and is currently a Professor of Automotive Technology at Saddleback College in Mission Viejo, California. Darrell has a Bachelor's degree from California State University, Long Beach, and a Master's in Vocational Education from the University of Alaska, Anchorage. Darrell is an ASE-certified Master Auto, Master Medium/Heavy Vehicle, M1-M3 Machinist, plus L1 and L2. Darrell has also presented technical seminars at the North American Council of Automotive Teachers (NACAT) and at the California Automotive Teachers (CAT) conferences. Darrell was named by CAT as the Outstanding College Instructor for 2009 and by NACAT as its MVP in 2010. When not working on cars, Darrell and his wife Beth can be found touring the continent on their motorcycle.

BRIEF CONTENTS

CONTENTS

chapter 10
POWER TOOLS AND SHOP EQUIPMENT 96

chapter 11
MEASURING SYSTEMS AND TOOLS 107

chapter 12
SERVICE INFORMATION 116

chapter 13
VEHICLE IDENTIFICATION AND EMISSION RATINGS 124

chapter 1

AUTOMOTIVE BACKGROUND AND OVERVIEW

OBJECTIVES: **After studying Chapter 1, the reader will be able to:** • Explain the evolution of the automobile. • Discuss the major components of a vehicle. • Describe the evolution of engines. • List the common components of most vehicles. • List the eight areas of automotive service according to ASE/NATEF.

KEY TERMS: • Air filter 5 • Body 2 • Body-on-frame (BOF) 3 • Carbon monoxide (CO) 5 • Catalytic converter 5 • Chassis 2 • Coolant 5 • Drive shaft 6 • Double overhead camshaft (DOHC) 4 • Evaporative emission system (EVAP) 5 • Exhaust gas recirculation (EGR) 5 • Flathead 4 • Frames 3 • Hydrocarbon (HC) 5 • Ignition control module (ICM) 5 • Inline engine 4 • Intake manifold 5 • Internal combustion engine 4 • Malfunction indicator light (MIL) 6 • Manufacturer's suggested retail price (MSRP) 4 • OBD-II 6 • Oil filter 5 • Oil galleries 5 • Oil pan 5 • Oil pump 5 • Oil sump 5 • Overhead camshaft (OHC) 4 • Overhead valve (OHV) 4 • Oxides of nitrogen (NOX) 5 • PCV valve 5 • Pillars 3 • Positive crankcase ventilation (PCV) 5 • Propeller shaft 6 • Radiator 5 • Scan tool 6 • Self-propelled vehicle 1 • Single overhead camshaft (SOHC) 4 • Thermostat 5 • Transaxle 6 • Transfer case 6 • Unibody 3 • Universal joints (U-joints) 6 • Water jackets 5 • Water pump 5

HISTORICAL BACKGROUND

For centuries, man either walked or used animals to provide power for transportation. After the invention of electric, steam, and gasoline propulsion systems, people used **self-propelled vehicles**, which are vehicles that moved under their own power.

Major milestones in vehicle development include:

1876	The OTTO four-stroke cycle engine was developed by a German engineer, Nikolaus Otto.
1885	The first automobile was powered by an OTTO cycle gasoline engine designed by Karl Friedrick Beary (1844–1929).
1892	Rudolf Diesel (1858–1913) received a patent for a compression ignition engine. The first diesel engine was built in 1897.
1896	Henry Ford (1863–1947) built his first car, called the Quadricycle. ● **SEE FIGURE 1–1.**
1900	About 4,200 total automobiles were sold, including:

- 40% were steam powered
- 38% were battery/electric powered
- 22% were gasoline engine powered

1902	Oldsmobile, founded by Ransom E. Olds (1864–1950), produced the first large-scale, affordable vehicle.
1908	William Durant (1861–1947) formed General Motors.
1908	The Ford Model T was introduced.
1912	The electric starter was invented by Charles F. Kettering (1876–1958) of Dayton, Ohio, first used on a Cadillac. The starter was produced by a new company called Delco, which stood for Dayton Engineering Laboratories Company.
1914	First car with a 100% steel body was made by the Budd Corporation for Dodge. Before 1914, all car bodies had wood components in them.
1922	The first vehicle to have four-wheel hydraulically operated brakes was a Duesenberg built in Indianapolis, Indiana.
1940	The first fully automatic transmission was introduced by Oldsmobile.
1973	Airbags were offered as an option on some General Motors vehicles.
1985	Lincoln offers the first four-wheel antilock braking system.
1997	The first vehicle with electronic stability control was offered by Cadillac.

FIGURE 1–1 A Ford Quadricycle built by Henry Ford.

FIGURE 1–2 Most vehicle bodies were constructed with a wood framework until the 1920s.

BODIES

Early motor vehicles evolved from horse-drawn carriages. The engine and powertrain were attached to a modified carriage leading to the term "horseless carriage".

The bodies evolved until in the 1930s, all-steel-enclosed bodies became the most used type. All bodies depended on a frame of wood or steel to support the chassis components. ● SEE FIGURE 1–2.

CHASSIS SYSTEMS OVERVIEW

The **chassis** system of the vehicle includes the following components:

1. Frame or **body** of the vehicle, which is used to provide the support for the suspension and steering components as well as the powertrain.

2. The suspension system of the vehicle, which provides a smooth ride to the driver and passengers and helps the tires remain on the road even when the vehicle is traveling over rough roads. The suspension system includes springs and control arms which allow the wheels to move up and down and keep the tires on the road.

3. The braking system of the vehicle is used to slow and stop the rotation of the wheels, which in turn stops the vehicle. The braking system includes the brake pedal, master cylinder, plus wheel brakes at each wheel. Two types of wheel brakes are used. Disc brakes include a caliper, which applies force to brake pads on both sides of a rotating disc or rotor. Drum brakes use brake shoes which are applied by hydraulic pressure outward against a rotating brake drum. The brake drum is attached to and stops the rotation of the wheels. Drum brakes are often used on the rear of most vehicles.

4. Wheels and tires—The wheels are attached to the bearing hubs on the axles. The tires must provide traction for accelerating, braking, and cornering, as well as provide a comfortable ride. Wheels are constructed of steel or aluminum alloy and mount to the hubs of the vehicle using lug nuts, which must be tightened correctly to the proper torque.

The chassis components include:

- Front and rear suspension
- Axles and hubs (to support the wheels and tires)
- Steering mechanism
- Engine and transmission
- Final drive differential and axles

Often, these chassis were so complete that they could be driven without a body. ● FIGURE 1–3.

Many of the expensive automakers in the 1920s and 1930s had bodies built by another company. Eventually, most bodies were constructed of steel and many without the need for a frame to support the drivetrain and suspension.

FIGURE 1–3 A chassis of a 1950s era vehicle showing the engine, drivetrain, frame, and suspension.

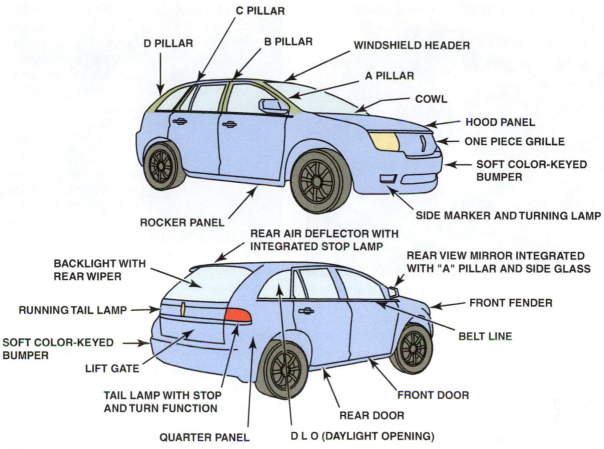

FIGURE 1–4 Body and terms.

BODY TERMS The roof of a vehicle is supported by **pillars** and they are labeled A, B, C, and D from the front to the rear of the vehicle. All vehicles have an A pillar at the windshield but many, such as a hardtop, do not have a B pillar. Station wagons and sport utility vehicles (SUVs) often have a D pillar at the rear of the vehicle. ● **SEE FIGURE 1–4.**

FRAMES

Frame construction usually consists of channel-shaped steel beams welded and/or fastened together. Vehicles with a separate frame and body are usually called **body-on-frame** vehicles (**BOF**). Many terms are used to label or describe the frame of a vehicle, including:

UNIT-BODY CONSTRUCTION Unit-body construction (sometimes called **unibody**) is a design that combines the body with the structure of the frame. The body is composed of many individual stamped-steel panels welded together. The strength of this type of construction lies in the *shape* of the assembly. The typical vehicle uses 300 separate stamped-steel panels that are spot-welded together to form a vehicle's body. ● **SEE FIGURE 1–5.**

NOTE: A typical vehicle contains about 10,000 separate individual parts.

FIGURE 1–5 Note the ribbing and the many different pieces of sheet metal used in the construction of this body.

SPACE-FRAME CONSTRUCTION Space-frame construction consists of formed sheet steel used to construct a framework of the entire vehicle. The vehicle is drivable without the body, which uses plastic or steel panels to cover the steel framework. ● **SEE FIGURE 1–6.**

FIGURE 1–6 A Corvette without the body. Notice that the vehicle is complete enough to be driven. This photo was taken at the Corvette Museum in Bowling Green, Kentucky.

FIGURE 1–7 A Ford flathead V-8 engine. This engine design was used by Ford Motor Company from 1932 through 1953. In a flathead design, the valves located next to (beside) the cylinders.

ENGINE DESIGN EVOLUTION

All gasoline and diesel engines are called **internal combustion engines** and were designed to compress an ignitable mixture. This mixture was ignited by using a spark (gasoline) or by heat of compression (diesel). Early engines used valves that were in the engine block, which also contained the round cylinders where pistons were fitted. The pistons are connected to a crankshaft, which converts the up and down motion of the pistons to a rotary force which is used to propel the vehicle.

INLINE VERSUS V-TYPE DESIGN
Most early engines used four or six cylinders arranged inline. These were called **inline engines** and are still produced today. Some engines with 4, 6, 8, 10, 12, or 16 cylinders were arranged with half of the cylinders on each set of a "V" and connected to a common crankshaft in the bottom of the "V." The crankshaft changed the up-and-down motion of the piston to rotary motion, allowing the engine to power the drive wheels.

VALVE LOCATION DESIGN
The design where the valves were located in the engine block is called **flathead** design because the cylinder head simply covered the combustion chamber and included a hole for the spark plug. The engine block contains passages for coolant as well as lubricating oil and is the support for all other engine systems. ● SEE FIGURE 1–7.

By the 1950s, most engine designs placed the valves in the cylinder head. This is called an **overhead valve or OHV** design.

Even newer engine designs feature **overhead camshafts (OHC)**, called **single overhead camshaft (SOHC)** designs and engines that use two overhead camshafts per bank of cylinders called **double overhead camshaft (DOHC)** designs. The placement of the camshaft, which results in better flow of intake air into and exhaust out of the engine.

FIGURE 1–8 A Monroney label as shown on the side window of a new vehicle.

The need for reduced emissions and greater fuel economy led to advances in engine design. These changes included:

- Electronic ignition systems
- Electronic fuel injection
- Computerized engine controls
- Emission control devices, including the catalytic converter used in the exhaust system to reduce emissions
- Improved engine oils that help reduce friction and reduce emissions

ENGINE SYSTEMS OVERVIEW

Every engine requires many systems to function correctly.

COOLING SYSTEM   While some older engines were air cooled, all engines currently in production are liquid cooled. Coolant is circulated by a **water pump** through passages in the cylinder block and head called **water jackets**. The **coolant** is a mixture of antifreeze and water to provide corrosion and freezing protection. After the coolant picks up the heat from the engine, it flows through a **radiator**, which cools the coolant by releasing the heat into the air. The temperature of the coolant is maintained by using a **thermostat** located in the coolant passage, which opens to allow coolant to flow to the radiator or closes until the coolant is hot enough to need cooling.

LUBRICATION SYSTEM   All engines need a supply of lubricating oil to reduce friction and help to cool the engine. Most engines are equipped with an **oil pan**, also called an **oil sump**, containing 3 to 7 quarts (liters) of oil. An engine driven **oil pump** forces the oil under pressure through an **oil filter**, then to passages in the block and head called **oil galleries**, and then to all of the moving parts.

AIR INTAKE SYSTEM   All engines, both gasoline and diesel engines, draw air from the atmosphere. It requires about 9,000 gallons of air for each gallon of gasoline used. The air must be drawn where deep water in the road cannot be drawn into the engine. The air is then filtered by a replaceable **air filter**. After the air is filtered, it passes through a throttle valve and then into the engine through an **intake manifold**.

FUEL SYSTEM   The fuel system includes the following components and systems:

- Fuel tank
- Fuel lines and filter(s)
- Fuel injectors
- Electronic control of the fuel pump and fuel injection

The fuel injectors are designed to atomize the liquid gasoline into small droplets so they can be mixed with the air entering the engine. This mixture of fuel and air is then ignited by the spark plug.

STARTING AND CHARGING SYSTEM   Engine starting and charging systems, which include the battery, starting (cranking) system and charging system components and circuits.

IGNITION SYSTEM   The ignition system includes the ignition coil(s), which creates a high voltage spark by stepping up battery voltage using an **ignition control module (ICM)**. The arc across the electrodes of the spark plug ignites the air-fuel mixture in the combustion chamber and the resulting pressure pushes the piston down on the power stroke.

EMISSION CONTROL SYSTEM   The control of vehicle emissions includes controlling gasoline vapors from being released into the atmosphere in addition to reducing the emissions from the exhaust. Unburned gasoline emissions are called **hydrocarbon (HC)** emissions and exhaust gases that are controlled include **carbon monoxide (CO)** and **oxides of nitrogen (NOX)**. The **evaporative emission control system**, usually called the **EVAP system**, is designed to prevent gasoline fumes and vapors from being released. Other emission control systems include:

- **Positive crankcase ventilation (PCV)**. This system uses a valve called a **PCV valve** to regulate the flow of gases created in the crankcase of a running engine, which are routed back into the intake manifold. The engine will then draw these gases into the combustion chamber where they are burned to help prevent the release of the gases into the atmosphere.
- **Exhaust gas recirculation (EGR)**. The EGR system meters about 3% to 7% of the exhaust gases back into the intake where the gases reduce the peak combustion temperature and prevent the oxygen (O2) and nitrogen (NO) from the air from combining to form oxides of nitrogen.
- **Catalytic converter**. The catalytic converter is a unit located in the exhaust system usually close to the engine, which causes chemical changes in the exhaust gases.

- On-board diagnostics means that the engine as well as the engine management systems can test itself for proper operation and alert the driver if a fault is detected. The warning lamp is called the **malfunction indicator light (MIL)** and is labeled "Check Engine" or "Service Engine Soon." The on-board diagnostic system is currently in the second generation and is called **OBD-II**. Electronic hand-held testers, called **scan tools**, are needed to access (retrieve) stored diagnostic trouble codes (DTCs) and view sensor and system data.

POWERTRAIN OVERVIEW

The purpose of the powertrain is to transfer the torque output of the engine to the drive wheels.

REAR-WHEEL-DRIVE POWERTRAIN

A rear-wheel-drive vehicle uses the following components to transfer engine torque to the rear drive wheels:

- Transmission. An automatic transmission usually uses planetary gear sets and electronic controls to change gear ratios. In a manually shifted transmission, the drivetrain contains a clutch assembly, which allows the driver to disengage engine torque from the transmission to allow the driver to shift from one gear ratio to another. The transmission contains gears and other assemblies that provide high torque output at low speeds for acceleration and lower torque output but at higher speeds for maximum fuel economy at highway speeds.
- Drive Shaft. A **drive shaft**, also called a **propeller shaft**, is used to connect and transmit engine torque from the transmission to the rear differential. **Universal joints (U-joints)** are used to allow the rear differential to move up and down on the rear suspension and still be able to transmit engine torque.
- Differential. A differential is used at the rear of the vehicle and performs three functions:
  - Allows different axle speeds for cornering.
  - The differential increases the torque applied to the rear drive wheels by reducing the speed.
  - The differential also changes the direction of the applied engine torque and uses axle shafts to transfer the torque to the drive wheels.

FRONT-WHEEL-DRIVE POWERTRAIN

A front-wheel-drive vehicle uses a **transaxle**, which is a combination of a transmission and differential in one assembly. Drive axle shafts then transfer the engine torque to the front drive wheels from the output of the transaxle.

FOUR-WHEEL-DRIVE SYSTEM

There are many types of methods of powering all four wheels. Many include a

FIGURE 1–9 A dash control panel used by the driver to control the four-wheel-drive system.

transfer case to split engine torque to both the front and the rear wheels. ● **SEE FIGURE 1–9.**

ELECTRICAL/ELECTRONIC SYSTEMS OVERVIEW

Early vehicles did not have an electrical system because even the ignition did not require a battery. Early engines used a magneto to create a spark instead of using electrical power from a battery as used today.

The first electrical components on vehicles were battery-powered lights, not only for the driver to see the road, but also so others could see an approaching vehicle at night.

Only after 1912 and the invention of the self-starter did the use of a battery become commonplace. Charles F. Kettering also invented the point-type ignition system about the same time as the self-starter. Therefore, the early batteries were often referred to as SLI batteries meaning starting, lighting, and ignition. From the 1920s into the 1950s other electrical components were added, such as radios, defroster fans, and horns. It was not until the 1960s that electrical accessories, such as air conditioning, power seats, and power windows, became common.

Today's vehicles require alternators that are capable of producing a higher amount of electricity than was needed in the past, and the number of electronic components has grown to include every system in the vehicle, including:

- A tire pressure monitoring system for the tires
- Heated and cooled seats
- Automatic climate control
- Power windows
- Security systems
- Electric power steering
- Electronic suspension

● **SEE FIGURE 1–10.**

FIGURE 1–10 The alternator is in the heart of the electrical system.

FIGURE 1–11 Test registration booklet that includes details on all vehicle-related certification tests given by ASE.

HEATING, VENTILATION, AND AIR CONDITIONING OVERVIEW

Early model vehicles did not include any heaters or other methods to provide comfort for the driver and passengers. Most early vehicles were open with a simple removable top. Some had optional side curtains that provided all-weather protection. In the 1930s and 1940s when fully enclosed bodies became common, the vehicle manufacturers started to include heaters, which were small radiators with engine coolant flowing through them. About the same time and into the 1950s, about the only options that many vehicles had were a radio and heater, abbreviated R & H.

Today, air conditioning systems are on most vehicles and incorporate defrosters and passenger compartment heating, often in two zones for maximum comfort of the driver and passenger. Additional related comfort options today include heated and cooled seats and heated steering wheels.

EIGHT AREAS OF AUTOMOTIVE SERVICE

In 1972, the National Institute for Automotive Service Excellence, a non-profit organization known as simply ASE, created a series of eight tests that cover the major vehicle systems. ● **SEE FIGURE 1–11**.

ENGINE REPAIR (A1) This content area includes questions related to engine block and cylinder head diagnosis and service, as well as the lubrication, cooling, fuel, ignition, and exhaust systems inspection and service.

AUTOMATIC TRANSMISSION (A2) This content area includes general automatic transmission/transaxle diagnosis, including hydraulic and electronic related systems.

MANUAL DRIVE TRAIN AND AXLES (A3) This content area includes clutch diagnosis and repair, manual transmission diagnosis and repair, as well as drive shaft, universal, and constant velocity joint diagnosis and service. Also included in this content area are rear differential diagnosis and repair plus four-wheel-drive component diagnosis and repair.

SUSPENSION AND STEERING (A4) This content area includes steering and suspension system diagnosis and repair, including wheel alignment diagnosis and adjustments plus wheel and tire diagnosis and repair procedures.

BRAKES (A5) The brake content area includes the diagnosis and repair of the hydraulic system, drum and disc brake systems, plus power assist units, antilock braking, and traction control systems.

ELECTRICAL/ELECTRONIC SYSTEMS (A6) This content area includes many systems, including the battery, starting, charging, lighting, gauges, and accessory circuit diagnosis and repair.

HEATING AND AIR CONDITIONING (A7) The heating and air conditioning content area includes air conditioning service, refrigeration systems, heating and engine cooling systems diagnosis and repair, as well as refrigerant recovery, recycling, handling, and retrofit.

ENGINE PERFORMANCE (A8) The engine performance content area includes diagnosis and testing of those systems responsible for the proper running and operation of the engine. Included in this area are general engine diagnosis, ignition and fuel systems, as well as emission control and computerized engine control diagnosis and repair.

This textbook covers the content of all eight ASE areas plus all of the background and fundamental information needed by technicians.

SUMMARY

1. Major automobile milestones include: the OTTO cycle engine (1876), the first diesel engine (1892), Henry Ford's first car (1896), Oldsmobile's large-scale production (1902), the first Model T Ford (1908), the first car with four-wheel hydraulic brakes (1922), the first automatic transmission (1940), the first vehicle to use a four-wheel antilock braking system (1985), and the first vehicle with electronic stability control (1997).

2. The chassis of the vehicle consists of a frame or body, which has attached to it the front and rear suspension, the brake system, the engine and transmission, as well as the steering system.

3. A vehicle frame is the main structural support for the body.

4. Engine design has changed from inline flathead 4-, 6-, and 8-cylinder engines to new double-overhead camshaft designs, which are computer controlled.

5. The engine consists of the following systems: air intake, cooling, lubrication, fuel, ignition, and emission control.

6. Major advances have also been made to electrical systems and controls from no electrical circuits in the early days of self-propelled vehicles to computer-controlled accessory and climate control systems today.

7. The eight areas of automotive service include: engine repair (A1), automatic transmission/transaxle (A2), manual transmission/transaxle (A3), suspension and steering (A4), brakes (A5), electrical and electronic systems (A6), heating and air conditioning (A7), and engine performance (A8).

REVIEW QUESTIONS

1. In 1900, what was the most produced vehicle powered by?

2. What parts are included in the vehicle chassis?

3. Why were early engines called flat heads?

4. What is the difference between a unit-body and body-on-frame vehicle?

5. The powertrain consists of what components?

6. What are the eight ASE automotive service content areas?

CHAPTER QUIZ

1. The first self-propelled vehicle that used an OTTO cycle four-stroke gasoline engine was produced in _____.
   - **a.** 1885
   - **b.** 1900
   - **c.** 1902
   - **d.** 1908

2. Early vehicles were constructed mostly of what material?
   - **a.** Steel
   - **b.** Cast iron
   - **c.** Wood
   - **d.** Tin

3. Which component is *not* part of the chassis system?
   - **a.** Frame
   - **b.** Electrical system
   - **c.** Suspension
   - **d.** Brakes

4. Early engines were called flat head design because they_____.
   - **a.** Were only inline engines
   - **b.** Did not include valves
   - **c.** Used valves beside the cylinder
   - **d.** Used spark plugs at the top of the cylinders

5. A V-type engine could have how many cylinders?
   - **a.** 4
   - **b.** 6
   - **c.** 8
   - **d.** All of the above

6. What component regulates the temperature of the coolant in an engine?
   - **a.** Cooling (water) jackets
   - **b.** Thermostat
   - **c.** Cooling fan(s)
   - **d.** Radiator

7. A malfunction indicator light (MIL) on the dash may be labeled _____.
   - **a.** Check engine
   - **b.** Service vehicle soon
   - **c.** MIL
   - **d.** MAL

8. To retrieve stored diagnostic trouble codes, a service technician needs a _____.
   - **a.** Paper clip
   - **b.** Desktop computer
   - **c.** Wireless connection to an electronic tester
   - **d.** Scan tool

9. A four-wheel drive vehicle often uses a _____ to transmit torque to all four wheels.
   - **a.** Drive shaft
   - **b.** U-joint
   - **c.** Transaxle
   - **d.** Transfer case

10. Automotive service systems are generally separated into how many content areas?
    - **a.** 4
    - **b.** 6
    - **c.** 8
    - **d.** 10

chapter 2

CAREERS IN THE AUTOMOTIVE SERVICE INDUSTRY

OBJECTIVES: After studying Chapter 2, the reader will be able to: • Describe automotive service-related positions. • Discuss the level of training and experience needed for each position. • Describe the technical skills needed for each position. • Explain the relationship of the service manager to others in a shop and company. • Prepare and complete a work order. • Discuss vehicle warranty policies.

KEY TERMS: • Entrepreneur 16 • On-the-job training (OJT) 11 • Parts counter person 15 • Service advisor 13 • Service consultant 13 • Service manager 14 • Service writer 13 • Shop foreman 13 • Team leader 13 • Technician (tech) 9 • Vehicle Identification Number (VIN) 12 • Work order 12

THE NEED FOR AUTOMOTIVE TECHNICIANS

The need for trained and skilled automotive **technicians** is greater than ever for several reasons, including:

- Vehicles are becoming more complex and require a higher level of knowledge and skills.
- Electrical and electronic components and sensors are included throughout the vehicle.
- Construction of parts and materials being used has changed over the last few years, meaning that all service work must be done to specified procedures to help avoid damage being done to the vehicle.
- Increasing numbers of different types of lubricants and coolants make even routine service challenging.

All of the above issues require proper training and the ability to follow factory specified procedures to ensure customer satisfaction. The number of service technicians needed is increasing due to more vehicles on the road. A good service technician can find work in almost any city or town in the country, making the career as a professional service technician an excellent choice.

THE NEED FOR CONTINUOUS VEHICLE SERVICE

Vehicles are lasting longer due to improved materials and more exacting tolerances. Every year, vehicles are being driven farther than ever before. It used to be (in the 1950s) that the life of a vehicle was considered to be 100,000 miles or 10 years. Now achieving 200,000 miles without a major repair is common with proper maintenance and routine service. However, even the amount of needed routine service has been reduced due to changes in the vehicles, such as radial tires that now last 40,000 miles instead of older tires which were worn out and needed to be replaced every 15,000 miles.

WARRANTIES A warranty is a guarantee to the purchaser of a vehicle that it will function as specified. The warranty covers the quality and performance of the product and states the conditions under which the warranty will be honored. Vehicle warranties vary but all warranties indicate a time and mileage restriction. The expressed warranties often include the following areas:

- New vehicle limited warranty that covers most components and is commonly called a bumper-to-bumper policy.
- Powertrain warranty covers the engine, transmission/transaxle, and final drive units. This coverage usually is longer than the bumper-to-bumper coverage.
- Sheet metal rust through warranty is usually longer than the bumper-to-bumper and powertrain warranty and covers rust if a hole occurs starting from inside the outer metal surface of the body.
- Emission control device warranties depend on the emission rating, the warranty coverage of the powertrain control module (PCM), and the catalytic converter and are covered for 8 years and 80,000 miles up to 10 years and 150,000 miles.

Vehicle warranties, unless an emergency repair, must be performed at a dealership, which is certified by the vehicle manufacturer to perform the repairs. At the dealership, the technician performing the repair must also be certified by the vehicle manufacturer.

All technicians should be familiar with what may be covered by the factory warranties to help ensure that the customer does not have to pay for a repair that may be covered. While warranties do cover many components of the vehicle, wear and service items are not covered by a warranty in most cases and therefore, offer excellent opportunity for additional service work for trained automotive technicians.

INCREASING AGE OF A VEHICLE The average age of a vehicle on the road today has increased to older than nine years. This trend means that more vehicles than ever are not covered by a factory warranty and are often in need of repair. Aftermarket warranties also can be used at most repair facilities, making it very convenient for vehicle owners.

TECHNICIAN WORK SITES

Service technician work takes place in a variety of work sites, including:

NEW VEHICLE DEALERSHIPS Most dealerships handle one or more brands of vehicle, and the technician employed at dealerships usually has to meet minimum training standards. The training is usually provided at no cost online or at regional training centers. The dealer usually pays the service technician for the day(s) spent in training as well as provides or pays for transportation, meals, and lodging. Most dealerships offer in house on-line training with minimum off-site training. ● **SEE FIGURE 2-1.**

INDEPENDENT SERVICE FACILITIES These small- to medium-size repair facilities usually work on a variety of vehicles. Technicians employed at independent service facilities usually have to depend on aftermarket manufacturers' seminars or the local vocational school or college to keep technically up-to-date. ● **SEE FIGURE 2-2.**

FIGURE 2-1 A service technician checking for a noise of a vehicle in a new-vehicle dealership service department.

FIGURE 2-2 A typical independent service facility. Independent garages often work on a variety of vehicles and perform many different types of vehicle repairs and service. Some independent garages specialize in just one or two areas of service work or in just one or two makes of vehicles.

FIGURE 2-3 This NAPA parts store also performs service work from the garage area on the side of the building.

MASS MERCHANDISER Large national chains of vehicle repair facilities are common in most medium- and large-size cities. Some examples of these chains include Sears, Goodyear, Firestone, and NAPA, as shown in the figure. ● **SEE FIGURE 2-3.** Technicians employed by these chains usually work on a wide variety of vehicles. Many of the companies have their own local or regional training sites designed to train beginning service technicians and to provide update training for existing technicians.

SPECIALTY SERVICE FACILITIES Specialty service facilities usually limit their service work to selected systems or components of the vehicle and/or to a particular brand of vehicle. Examples of specialty service facilities include Midas, Speedy, and AAMCO Transmissions. Many of the franchised specialty facilities have their own technician training for both beginning and advanced technicians. ● **SEE FIGURE 2-4.**

FLEET FACILITIES Many city, county, and state governments have their own vehicle service facilities for the maintenance and repair of their vehicles. Service technicians are usually employees of the city, county, or state and are usually paid by the hour rather than on a commission basis. ● **SEE FIGURE 2-5.**

FIGURE 2–4 Midas is considered to be a specialty service shop.

TECHNICIAN JOB CLASSIFICATIONS

There are many positions and jobs in the vehicle service industry. In smaller service facilities (shops), the duties of many positions may be combined in one job. A large city dealership may have all of the following vehicle service positions. A technician is often referred to as a tech.

LUBE TECH/QUICK SERVICE TECHNICIAN A lubrication technician should be trained in the proper use of hand tools and instructed how to properly service various types of vehicles. The training could be **on-the-job (OTJ)** or could be the result of high school or college automotive training. Some larger companies provide in-house training for new technicians and as a result they are trained to perform according to a specified standard. It is important that the lubrication technician double-check the work to be certain that the correct viscosity oil has been installed and to the specified level. The oil plug and oil filter must also be checked for leakage.

Lubrication technicians are trained to perform routine services, including:

- Oil and oil filter change
- Chassis lubrication
- Fluids check and refill
- Tire inflation checks
- Accessory drive belt inspection
- Air filter check and replacement
- Cabin filter replacement
- Windshield wiper blade replacement

FIGURE 2–5 A school bus garage is a typical fleet operation shop that needs skilled service technicians.

As a result of these tasks the lubrication technician should be skilled in hoisting the vehicle and able to handle the tasks efficiently and in minimum time.

NEW VEHICLE PREPARATION FOR DELIVERY An entry-level position at a dealership often includes preparing new vehicles for delivery to the customer. This is often referred to as "new car prep." The duties performed for new vehicle preparation are generally learned on the job. The vehicle manufacturer publishes guidelines that should be followed and it is the responsibility of the new vehicle preparation person to see that all items are checked and serviced, and all associated paperwork is completed. The activities normally associated with preparing a new vehicle for delivery include:

- Installing wheel center caps or wheel covers (if used)
- Installing roof racks, running boards, and other dealer-installed options
- Checking and correcting tire pressures

   NOTE: Many vehicle manufacturers ship the vehicles to the dealer with the tires overinflated to help prevent movement of the vehicle during shipping.

- Checking all fluids
- Checking that everything works, including the remote key fob and all accessories
- Ordering any parts found to be broken, missing, and damaged in transit
- Removing all protective covering and plastic from the seats, carpet, and steering wheel
- Washing the vehicle

GENERAL SERVICE TECHNICIAN A general service technician usually has training as an automotive technician either in one or more of the following:

- High school—Technical or vocational school or a comprehensive high school that has an Automotive Youth Education System (AYES) program or NATEF certification.
- College or technical school—Usually a two-year program that can earn the student an associate's degree.
- Career college or institute—Usually a 6-month to 12-month program earning the graduate a certificate.

Automotive service technicians perform preventative maintenance, diagnose faults, and repair automotive vehicles and light trucks.

Automotive service technicians adjust, test, and repair engines, steering systems, braking systems, drivetrains, vehicle suspensions, electrical systems and air conditioning systems, and perform wheel alignments. In large shops, some technicians specialize in repairing, rebuilding, and servicing specific parts, such as braking systems, suspension, and steering systems. In smaller shops, automotive service technicians may work on a wider variety of repair jobs.

Automotive service technicians begin by reading the work order and examining the vehicle. To locate the cause of faulty operation and repair it, a technician will:

- Verify customer concern
- Use testing equipment, take the vehicle for a test-drive, and/or refer to manufacturer's specifications and manuals
- Dismantle faulty assemblies, repair, or replace worn or damaged parts
- Reassemble, adjust, and test the repaired mechanism

Automotive service technicians also may:

- Perform scheduled maintenance services, such as oil changes, lubrications, and filter replacement
- Advise customers on work performed, general vehicle conditions, and future repair requirements

WORKING CONDITIONS. Most automotive service technicians work a 40-hour, five-day week. Some evening, weekend, or holiday work may be required. The work is sometimes noisy and dirty. There is some risk of injury involved in working with power tools and near exhaust gases.

SKILLS AND ABILITIES. The work is most rewarding for those who enjoy doing precise work that is varied and challenging. Also, technicians usually achieve job security and a feeling of independence.

To be successful in the trade, automotive service technicians need:

- Good hearing, eyesight, and manual dexterity (ability to work with hands)
- Mechanical aptitude and interest

- The ability to lift between 25 and 50 pounds (11 and 25 kilograms)
- The willingness to keep up-to-date with changing technology

A working knowledge of electricity, electronics, and computers is also required for many service procedures.

EMPLOYMENT AND ADVANCEMENT. Automotive service technicians are employed by automotive repair shops, specialty repair shops, service facilities, car and truck dealerships, and by large organizations that own fleets of vehicles.

Experienced automotive service technicians may advance to service manager or shop foreman. Some automotive service technicians open their own repair facilities.

Many technicians can also start work in a shop or dealership and learn on the job. Most technicians keep up-to-date by attending update seminars or training classes on specific topics throughout the year.

Specific tasks performed by a general service technician can include the following:

- All of the tasks performed by the lubrication technician.
- Engine repairs, including intake manifold gasket replacement; cylinder head replacement; and oil and water pump replacement plus other engine-related tasks.
- Brake system service and repair, including disc brakes; drum brakes; parking brake; and antilock brake (ABS) diagnosis and service.
- Suspension-related service, including tire inspection and replacement; shock and strut replacement; servicing or replacing wheel bearings; performing steering component inspection and parts replacement; and performing wheel alignment and vibration diagnosis.
- Electrical-related diagnosis and repair, including starting and charging problems; correcting lighting and accessory faults; and general service such as light bulb replacement and key fob reprogramming.
- Heating, ventilation, and air conditioning work usually involves the use of diagnostic and service equipment that requires special training and certification if working with refrigerants.
- Engine performance-related diagnosis and repair, including replacing fuel pumps and filters; cleaning or replacing fuel injectors; service ignition system components; solving emissions-related failures; and determining the cause and correcting "Check Engine" lights.
- Manual transmission service and repairs, including replacing clutches; adjusting, or replacing clutch linkage; servicing differentials and performing four-wheel drive diagnosis and service procedures.
- Automatic transmission service and repairs, including performing routine automatic transmission service; removing and replacing automatic transmissions; transmissions/transaxles and performing diagnosis and service checks, including fluid pressure and scan tool diagnosis.

The vehicle is then driven by the service technician to verify the repair.

TECHNICIAN TEAM LEADER   A **team leader** is an experienced service technician who is capable of performing most if not all of the work that the shop normally handles. The team leader then assigns work to others in the group based on the experience or competency of the technician. The team leader then checks the work after it has been completed to be sure that it has been correctly performed. The number of hours of labor for each member of the team is totaled each pay period. Each member of the team is paid an equal share of the time but at different rates. The team leader gets a higher per hour rate than the others on the team. The rate of pay per hour is based on the level of training and experience. A beginning technician may or may not be paid as part of the total team hours depending on how the team system is organized. While some shops do not use teams, many large shops or dealerships have two or more teams. The advantage of a team-type organization is that everyone on the team looks out and helps each other if needed because they are all paid based on the number of hours the team generates. The team leader performs the duties of a shop foreman but only for those members on the team and not the entire shop. The team leader is under the direction and control of the service manager.

SHOP FOREMAN   A **shop foreman** (usually employed in larger dealerships and vehicle repair facilities) is an experienced service technician who is usually paid a salary (so much a week, month, or year). A shop foreman is a knowledgeable and experienced service technician who keeps up-to-date with the latest vehicle systems, tools, and equipment. Typical shop foreman's duties include:

- Test-driving the customer's vehicle to verify the customer concern (complaint)
- Assigning work to the service technicians
- Assisting the service technicians
- Helps maintain the shop and shop equipment
- Assisting the service manager
- Verifying that the repair is completed satisfactorily

The shop foreman is under the direction and control of the service manager.

SERVICE ADVISOR   A **service advisor**, also called a **service writer** or **service consultant**, is the person at the dealership or shop designated to communicate the needs of the customer and accurately complete a work order.

A service advisor should:

- Have a professional appearance
- Be able to speak clearly
- Be able to listen carefully to the customer
- Write neatly and/or type accurately
- Be familiar with industry and shop standards and procedures

Most service advisors would benefit from taking a short course on service advising skill development and

HOME TOWN CHEVROLET
100 N. MAIN ST.
8993

Customer's Description of Problem/Repair:

This accurately describes the problem or symptom I am experiencing with my motor vehicle. Customer's Initials _____

COST	QUAN.	PART NUMBER / DESCRIPTION		PRICE	
	1	Battery	Interstate 60 Month Battery	74	00
	1	Oil filter		11	25
	1	Air filter		36	59
	1	Seal Ring			25
	1	Ant Mast		67	97
				190	06

SUBLET REPAIRS

ALL PARTS ARE NEW UNLESS SPECIFIED OTHERWISE.

This Facility charges _____ % of the Total _____ Charges, up to a Maximum of $ _____ , for Shop Materials.

WE WILL OFFER TO RETURN TO YOU ALL REPLACED PARTS, AS REQUIRED BY LAW, UNLESS THEY ARE TO BE REBUILT, SOLD, OR RETURNED TO THE MANUFACTURER.

I hereby authorize the repair work herein set forth to be done by you, together with the furnishing by you of the necessary parts and other material for such repair, and agree: that you are not responsible for any delays caused by unavailability or delayed availability of parts or material for any reason; that you neither assume nor authorize any other person to assume for you any liability in connection with such repair; that you shall not be responsible for loss of or damage to the above vehicle, or articles left therein, in case of fire, theft or other cause beyond your control; that an express mechanic's lien is hereby acknowledged on the above vehicle to secure the amount of repairs thereto; that your employees may operate the above vehicle on streets, highways or elsewhere for the purpose of testing and/or inspecting such vehicle.
I HEREBY ACKNOWLEDGE RECEIPT OF A COPY HEREOF.

X _____

NAME: MR CUSTOMER
ADDRESS: 444 W. 3rd St.
CITY: STATE: ZIP:
DATE RECEIVED: 9/18/11
COMPLETION DATE:
MILEAGE IN: 45.105
MILEAGE OUT:

VIN: 1G2NW51AA6S6201
ENGINE NO.: 3.9 V-6
MAKE: CHEVY

TYPE OR MODEL: IMPALA
YEAR: 06
LICENSE NUMBER: BQU449
PHONE WHEN READY: YES ☐ NO ☐

TERMS:
ORDER ACCEPTED BY:
PHONE:

OPER. NO.	INSTRUCTIONS:		
1.0	45 K Service	450	00
.6	Check Battery Replace	22	50
.5	Ant Mast	22	50
.5	Check left front Headlight	22	50

	TECH ID # / INIT.	LABOR CHARGE
LUBRICATE ☐		
CHANGE OIL ☐		
CHANGE OIL FILTER CART. ☐		
CHANGE TRANS. OIL ☐		
CHANGE DIFF. OIL ☐		
PACK FRONT WHEEL BRGS. ☐		
ADJUST BRAKES ☐		
X TIRES ☐		
WASH ☐		
SAFETY INSPECTION ☐		

ESTIMATE
(UNDER OHIO LAW) YOU HAVE THE RIGHT TO AN ESTIMATE IF THE EXPECTED COST OF REPAIRS OR SERVICES WILL BE MORE THAN TWENTY-FIVE DOLLARS. INITIAL YOUR CHOICE.
WRITTEN _____ ORAL _____ ESTIMATE
I DO NOT REQUEST _____ AN ESTIMATE

WARRANTY STATEMENT AND DISCLAIMER: THE DEALER HEREBY DISCLAIMS ALL WARRANTIES EXPRESS OR IMPLIED, INCLUDING ANY IMPLIED WARRANTIES OF MERCHANTABILITY OR FITNESS FOR A PARTICULAR PURPOSE, AND NEITHER ASSUMES NOR AUTHORIZES ANY OTHER PERSON TO ASSUME FOR IT ANY LIABILITY IN CONNECTION WITH THE SALE OF SAID PARTS OR THIS REPAIR. THIS DISCLAIMER IN NO WAY AFFECTS THE PROVISIONS OF ANY MANUFACTURER OR OTHER SUPPLIER WARRANTIES. IF DEALER PROVIDES A WRITTEN WARRANTY, ANY IMPLIED WARRANTIES ARE EXPRESSLY LIMITED TO THE TERM OF THE WRITTEN WARRANTY.

ORIGINAL ESTIMATE
CUSTOMERS ACCEPTANCE
$ _____
AUTHORIZED ADDITIONS
DATE _____
TIME _____
$ _____ BY _____

In the event that you, the customer, authorize commencement but do not authorize completion of a repair or service, a charge will be imposed for disassembly, reassembly or partially completed work. Such charge will be directly related to the actual amount of labor or parts involved in the inspection, repair or service.

	SALE	
TOTAL LABOR	517	50
TOTAL PARTS	190	06
GAS, OIL & GREASE	18	75
SUBLET REPAIRS		
	726	31
TAX 6.5%	47	21
TOTAL	773	52

FIGURE 2–6 Typical work order. *(Courtesy of Reynolds and Reynolds Company)*

interpersonal relationship building. A service advisor should be familiar with the operation of the vehicle, but not to the same level as a service technician. A service advisor should not diagnose the problem, but rather state clearly on the work order what, when, and where the problem occurs so that the service technician has all the needed information to make an accurate diagnosis. ● **SEE FIGURE 2–6** for an example of a typical work order.

The service advisor's duties include:

1. Recording the vehicle identification number (VIN) of the vehicle on the work order
2. Recording the make, model, year, and mileage on the work order
3. Carefully recording what the customer's complaint (concern) is so that the service technician can verify the complaint and make the proper repair
4. Reviewing the customer's vehicle history file and identifying additional required service
5. Keeping the customer informed as to the progress of the service work

A service advisor must be at the shop early in the morning to greet the customers and often needs to stay after the shop closes for business to be available when the customer returns at the end of the day.

SERVICE MANAGER The **service manager** rarely works on a vehicle but instead organizes the service facility and keeps it operating smoothly. A service manager can be a former service technician or in many larger dealerships, a business major graduate who is skilled at organization and record keeping. The service manager typically handles all of the paperwork associated with operating a service department.

NOTE: In a small shop, the shop owner usually performs all of the duties of a shop foreman and service manager, as well as the lead technician in many cases.

Typical duties of a service manager include:

- Establishing guidelines to determine the technicians' efficiency
- Supervising any warranty claims submitted to the vehicle manufacturer or independent insurer
- Evaluating and budgeting for shop tools and equipment
- Establishing service department hours of operation and employee schedules

Check the Vehicle before Work Is Started

As part of the work order writing process, the service advisor should look over the vehicle and make a written note of any body damage that may already exist. If any damage is noted it should be mentioned to the customer and noted on the work order. Often the customer is not aware of any damage especially on the passenger side and thus would blame the shop for the damage after the service work was performed.

FIGURE 2–7 Parts counter people need to know many aspects of automotive repair to be effective with customers.

- Assigning working hours and pay for technicians and others in the service department
- Establishing procedures and policies to keep the service area clean and properly maintained

PARTS-RELATED POSITIONS

The parts manager at the service facility or other parts personnel such as the **parts counter person** are responsible for getting the correct part for the service technician.

PARTS COUNTER PERSON   A parts counter person often learns job skills by on-the-job training. A good parts counter person must be able to greet and easily talk to customers and technicians. A parts counter person must also have computer skills and the willingness to help others.

The parts counter person usually has the following duties:

- Greet the customer or technician
- Locate the correct parts for the service technician or customer
- Suggest related parts (retail customers)
- Stock shelves
- Check in delivered parts
- Take inventory
- Keep the parts department clean
- Help the parts manager
- ● **SEE FIGURE 2–7.**

PARTS MANAGER   The specific duties of a parts manager usually include:

- Ordering parts from the vehicle manufacturers and aftermarket companies
- Stocking parts
- Organizing the parts department in a clear and orderly fashion

- Locating parts quickly within the parts department
- Developing contacts with parts departments in other local dealerships so that parts that are not in stock can be purchased quickly and at a reasonable cost

SALES JOBS—USED VEHICLES; NEW VEHICLES

SALESPERSON   When a vehicle is sold, it generates a potential customer for the service department. New and many used vehicle sales dealerships employ salespeople to help the customer select and purchase a vehicle. The salesperson should have excellent interpersonal skills, as well as be familiar with the local and regional laws and taxes to be able to complete all of the paperwork associated with the sale of a vehicle. The usual duties of a vehicle salesperson include:

- Greet the customer
- Introduce yourself and welcome the customer to the store
- Qualify the customer as to the ability to purchase a vehicle
- Demonstrate and ride with the customer on a test-drive
- Be able to find the answer to any question the customer may ask about the vehicle and/or financing
- Be able to complete the necessary paperwork
- Follow up the sale with a telephone call or card

SALES MANAGER   A sales manager is an experienced salesperson who is able to organize and manage several individual salespeople. The duties of a sales manager include:

- Establish a schedule where salespeople will be available during all hours of operation

- Consult with salespeople as needed on individual sales
- Train new salespeople
- Conduct sales promotion activities
- Attend or assign someone to attend vehicle auctions to sell and/or purchase vehicles
- Keep up-to-date with the automotive market
- Purchase vehicles that sell well in the local market
- Answer to the general manager or dealership principal

OTHER CAREERS IN THE AUTOMOTIVE INDUSTRY

Other careers in the automotive industry include:

- Sales representative for automotive tools and equipment
- Technical trainers
- Technical school instructors
- Wholesale parts warehouse management
- Insurance adjuster
- Automotive technical writer
- Warranty claim examiner

TYPICAL AUTOMOTIVE ORGANIZATION ARRANGEMENT

LARGE COMPREHENSIVE NEW VEHICLE DEALER A typical dealership includes many levels because there are many departments such as sales (new and used) as well

as the service, parts and body shops to manage. ● **SEE FIGURE 2–8.**

INDEPENDENT SHOP An independent shop may or may not have a shop foreman depending on the number of technicians and the volume of work. Larger independent shops have a shop foreman, whereas at smaller shops, the owner is the shop foreman. ● **SEE FIGURE 2–9.**

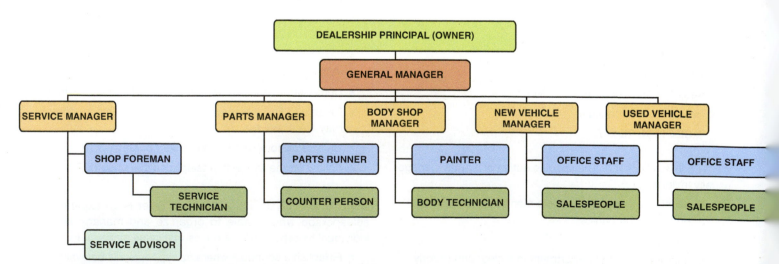

FIGURE 2–8 A typical large new vehicle dealership organizational chart.

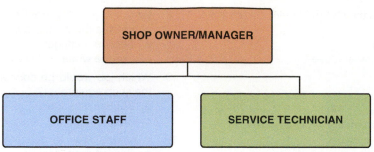

FIGURE 2–9 A typical independent shop organizational chart.

SUMMARY

1. A service advisor is the person at a dealership or shop who greets the customer and writes the work order stating what repairs and service the customer wants.

2. A lube or quick service technician performs routine service, such as oil change, cabin and air filter replacement, and other common service procedures.

3. A new vehicle preparation technician is a person who prepares a new vehicle for delivery to the customer.

4. A general service technician has training and experience in a wide range of automotive systems, including engines, brakes, suspensions, manual transmissions, electrical, heat, air conditioning, engine performance, and automatic transmissions.

5. A shop foreman is an experienced service technician who performs diagnosis, as well as helping other technicians.

6. A service manager handles financial responsibilities associated with the proper operation of the service department or shop, including budgets, equipment purchases, and maintenance arrangement, as well as working hours, pay rate determination, and efficiency ratings.

7. Parts departments are a key part of a dealership and parts delivery and/or inventory is a large part of any shop operation.

8. Vehicle sales, both new and used, generate the need for vehicle service, and the salespeople must have good interpersonal skills.

REVIEW QUESTIONS

1. What should be included on a work order?

2. Why should a vehicle be inspected when the work order is being written?

3. What tasks are usually performed by a general service technician?

4. What duties are performed by the shop foreman and service manager?

5. What duties are performed by a parts counter person?

6. What duties are performed by vehicle salespeople?

CHAPTER QUIZ

1. A service advisor is called a _____
   a. Shop foreman
   b. Service manager
   c. Service writer
   d. Technician

2. What is *not* included on a work order?
   a. Customer's mother's maiden name
   b. VIN
   c. Mileage
   d. Description of work requested

3. All of the following are usual duties of a lube technician *except* _____
   a. Oil change
   b. Air filter replacement
   c. Water pump replacement
   d. Accessory drive belt inspection

4. New vehicle preparation is usually an entry-level vehicle service position and usually involves what duties?
   a. Installing dealer-installed options
   b. Correcting tire pressures
   c. Removal of all protective coverings and plastic
   d. All of the above

5. What is *not* a duty of a general service technician?
   a. Have the customer sign the work order
   b. Order the parts needed
   c. Diagnose the customer's concern
   d. Perform vehicle repair procedures

6. Which description best fits the role of a service advisor?
   a. A skilled technician
   b. A beginning technician
   c. A customer service representative
   d. A money manager

7. Two technicians are discussing the duties of a shop fore-man and a service manager. Technician A says that a shop foreman diagnoses vehicle problems. Technician B says that the service manager usually repairs vehicles. Which technician is correct?
   a. Technician A only
   b. Technician B only
   c. Both Technicians A and B
   d. Neither Technician A nor B

8. Who is the person that greets the service customer and completes the work order?
   a. Service manager
   b. Service advisor
   c. Service writer
   d. Either b or c

9. Which job would be concerned with the maintenance of the shop equipment?
   a. Service manager
   b. Shop foreman
   c. Shop owner
   d. Any of the above

10. Which job would be concerned with working hours and pay?
    a. Service manager
    b. Shop foreman
    c. Service advisor
    d. Service technician

chapter 3

STARTING A CAREER IN THE AUTOMOTIVE INDUSTRY

OBJECTIVES: **After studying Chapter 3, the reader will be able to:** • Explain the steps and processes for applying for a job. • Describe what the resume should include. • Explain why having a good driving record is important to a shop owner. • Discuss how to prepare for a career in the automotive industry.

KEY TERMS: • Apprentice program 20 • Clock-in 22 • Clock time 22 • Commission pay 23 • Cooperative education 20 • Entrepreneur 25 • Federal tax 23 • FICA 23 • Flat-rate 23 • Gross 23 • Housing expense 24 • Incentive pay 23 • Job shadowing 20 • Net 23 • Part-time employment 20 • Reference 21 • Resume 21 • Soft skills 20 • State tax 23 • Straight time 22

PREPARING FOR AN AUTOMOTIVE SERVICE CAREER

DESIRE AND INTEREST If a person has an interest in automobiles and trucks and likes computers, the automotive service field may be a good career choice. Computer skills are needed in addition to hands-on skills for several reasons, including:

- Service information, such as diagnostic procedures and specifications, is commonly available in electronic format.
- Work orders are commonly written and sent to the technician electronically. The technician therefore needs typing skills to type the steps taken during the service or repair procedures.
- Warranty claims are often submitted by the Internet and computer skills are needed to quickly and accurately submit claims and answer questions from the insurance company.

Interest in vehicles is also very important toward being successful as a professional service technician. Most technicians enjoy working on vehicles, not only professionally, but also during their spare time. Many technicians own a project vehicle, which could include:

- Drag race vehicle
- Race vehicle used in road racing
- A fun vehicle used on sunny weekend days and evenings
- Motorcycle
- Snowmobile or jet ski
- Truck for rock crawling

TECHNICAL KNOWLEDGE AND SKILLS The enjoyment of being involved with vehicles is very important because the job of servicing and repairing automobiles and trucks can be hard and dirty work. Many men and women enjoy being around and learning about the details of vehicle operation. With these desires and interest, working in the automotive service field is a great career. Technical information, skills, and tools needed include:

- **Hand tools and tool usage.** Owning and experience using hand tools is important for a service technician. All service technicians are expected to be able to remove and replace parts and components as needed in a timely manner using proper tools and techniques.
- **Technical knowledge.** While knowing how all aspects of the vehicle works is not expected of a beginning service technician, it is important that the technician have a basic understanding of the parts and procedures needed at least for routine service procedures.

 **TECH TIP**

If in Doubt, Ask

No one expects a beginning service technician to know everything, but other technicians do not know what you do or do not know. It is usually assumed that the beginning technician will ask for help if they think they need the help. However, asking for help is very rare and requires the beginning technician to admit that they do not know something. Not asking for help can cause harm to the vehicle or the service technician. If in doubt—always ask. No one will be upset and learning the answer to your question will help in the learning experience.

JOB SHADOWING

A great way to see what it is really like to work as a service technician is to follow a professional around for a day or more. **Job shadowing** is usually arranged through an automotive program, and the shop or dealership has agreed to allow someone into the shop area to observe.

While it does allow the student to observe, job shadowing does not allow the person to perform any work or help the technician in any way. During the day, the person who is job shadowing has to wear all personal protective equipment as required by the technician and must observe all safety regulations. The advantages of job shadowing include:

- Being able to observe a typical day in the life of an automotive technician
- Being able to talk to the working technician about what is being done and why
- Being able to observe other technicians and seeing the various skill levels that often exist in a shop

COOPERATIVE EDUCATION PROGRAMS

Cooperative education programs are formal programs of study at a high school or college where the student attends classes at the school, and also works at a local shop or dealership.

If a cooperative education program is held at the high school level, the work at the shop or dealership occurs during the afternoon or evening and during the summer between the junior and senior year. The most common high school cooperative program is called AYES, which means Automotive Youth Education System (see www.ayes.org). The vehicle manufacturers involved in this program include:

- General Motors
- Chrysler
- Toyota
- Honda
- Nissan
- BMW
- Kia
- Subaru
- Hyundai

If the cooperative education program is held at a community college, the work at the dealership occurs around the training sessions, usually the first or second half of a semester or on alternative semesters. The most common college programs include:

- General Motors ASEP (Automotive Service Educational Program) (see www.gmasepbsep.com)
- Ford ASSET (Automotive Student Service Educational Program) (see www.fordasset.com)
- Chrysler CAP (College Automotive Program) (see www.chryslercap.com)
- Toyota T-TEN (Toyota Technician Education Network) (see www.toyota.com/about/tten/index.html)

Another factory sponsored program open to those who have already completed a postsecondary automotive program is BMW STEP (Service Technician Education Program) (see www.bmwusa.com/about/techtraining.html).

APPRENTICE PROGRAMS

An **apprentice program** involves a beginning service technician working at a shop or dealership during the day and attending training classes in the evening. The key advantage to this type of program is that money is being earned due to full-time employment and getting on-the-job training (OJT) during the day. Often the shop or dealership will help pay for training. While this program usually takes more than two years to complete, the work performed at the shop or dealership usually becomes more technical as the apprentice becomes more knowledgeable and gets more experienced.

PART-TIME EMPLOYMENT

Working part time in the automotive service industry is an excellent way to get hands-on experience, which makes it easier to relate classroom knowledge to everyday problems and service issues. Working part time gives the student technician some flexibility as to college schedules and provides an income needed for expenses. Often **part-time employment** becomes full-time employment so it is important to keep attending technical classes toward becoming an asset to the company.

DEVELOPING AN EMPLOYMENT PLAN

An employment plan is an evaluation of your skills, interest, and talents. Selecting a career is different than getting a job. A typical job, while it does involve some training, usually can be learned in a few days to several months. However, a career requires many years to achieve competence. Therefore, selecting a career should require a thorough self-examination to determine what your true interest is in a particular career field. Some items that you should enjoy or would be willing and able to learn include:

- Working with your hands, using tools and equipment
- Computer usage, including typing skills
- Working in an area where lifting is often required
- Being able to read, understand, and follow service information, technical service bulletins, and work orders
- Being able to perform diagnostic work and figure out the root cause of a problem

SOFT SKILLS

In addition, any career, including being a service technician, requires many people skills, often called **soft skills**. These people-related skills include:

- Working cooperatively with other people
- Communicating effectively with others verbally (speech) and in writing
- Working as a member of a team for the benefit of all

- Being able to work by yourself to achieve a goal or complete a job assignment
- Being able to lead or supervise others
- Willingness to work with others with a different background or country of origin

While it is almost impossible to be able to answer all of these questions, just looking at these items and trying to identify your interests and talents will help in your selection of a career that gives you lifelong satisfaction.

LOCATING EMPLOYMENT POSSIBILITIES Locating where you wish to` work is a very important part of your career. Of course, where you would like to work may not have an opening and you may have to work hard to locate a suitable employer. First, try to select a shop or dealership where you think you would like to work because of location, vehicles serviced, or other factors. Ask other technicians who have worked or are presently working there to be sure that the location would meet your needs.

If looking for employment through a want ad in a newspaper or employment website, check the following:

- **Job description.** Is this a position that could advance into a more technical position?
- **Tools needed.** Most professional service technician positions require that the technician provide their own tools. (The shop or dealership provides the shop equipment.) Do you have the tools needed to do the job?
- **Hours needed.** Are you available during the hours specified in the ad?
- **Drug testing.** Is a drug test needed for employment and are you prepared to pass?

PREPARING A RESUME

A **resume** is usually a one-page description of your skills, talents, and education. It is used by prospective employers to help narrow the field of applicants for a job or position. The number one purpose of a resume is to obtain a job interview. A good resume should include the following items:

Personal Information

- Full given name (avoid nicknames)
- Mailing address (do not use a post office [PO] box)
- Telephone and/or cell phone number
- E-mail address
- Avoid using dates which could indicate your age

Educational Information

- Highest education level achieved
- Major, if in a college or in a training program

Experience and Skills

- Work or volunteer experience that may be helpful or useful to an employer. For example, if you took a course

in welding, this may be useful to a shop owner who is looking for a service technician who could do welding, even though this fact was not included in the job posting.

- A valid driver's license is a must for most professional service technicians.
- A good driving record. Often the shop insurance company will not allow a shop owner to hire a technician with a poor driving record.

REFERENCES A **reference** is someone who is willing to tell a possible employer about you, including your skills and talents, as well as your truthfulness and work habits.

Most employers would like to see someone who is familiar with you and your family, such as a priest, minister, or elder in your church. Some teachers or coaches also can be asked to be a reference. Always ask the person for approval before including the person on your list of references. Ask the reference to supply you with a written recommendation. Some references prefer to simply fill out a reference questionnaire sent by many companies. If a reference sends you a written recommendation, have copies made so they can be included with your resume.

PREPARING A COVER LETTER

When answering an advertisement in a newspaper or magazine, be sure to include the details of where you saw the ad in your cover letter to the employer. For example: "I am applying for the position as an entry-level service technician as published in the August 15 edition of the Daily News."

If the requirements for the position are listed, be sure to include that you do have the specified training and/or experience and the tools needed for the job.

If calling about a position, be sure to state that you are applying for the position posted and ask to speak to the correct person or to the person mentioned in the ad.

CONTACTING POTENTIAL EMPLOYERS

When a job opening is posted in a newspaper or it is mentioned by a friend, most experts recommend that you visit the shop or dealership in person to see where the job is located, the condition of the buildings, and the surrounding areas. This trip could also be used for you to submit your resume and cover letter in person unless the company indicates otherwise. Be prepared to be interviewed when submitting your resume. Even if the position has already been filled, the trip gives you experience in meeting people and seeing the shop, which helps increase your

Always Be Truthful

No one is smart enough to be a liar. If you say something that is not true, then you have to remember what was said forever or your lie will often be discovered. If asked about your experience or knowledge, try to be as truthful as possible. Facts and skills can be learned and not knowing how to do everything that a shop may be involved with is not an indication that you will be rejected from the job opening.

confidence during the job search. Searching for a job is a full-time job in itself. Be prepared every day to answer ads, search employment websites and travel to shops or dealerships.

COMPLETING THE EMPLOYMENT APPLICATION

Most businesses require that an employment application be completed because it not only asks for all necessary personal information needed, but also references and emergency contacts. Most employment application forms ask for previous employers, the names and telephone numbers of contact people, and other information which you may not remember. It is wise to have all of the information written down ahead of time and take it with you for reference when completing the application. Always answer questions honestly and as thoroughly as possible. Never lie on an employment application.

THE INTERVIEW

When meeting for the job interview, be sure to dress appropriately for the position. For example, a suit and tie would not be appropriate for an interview for a service technician position. However, the following may be a helpful guide:

- Wear shoes that are not sneakers and be sure they are clean
- Wear slacks, not jeans
- Wear a shirt with a collar
- Do not wear a hat
- Be clean shaven or have beard/mustache neatly trimmed
- Have clean hair
- Avoid facial jewelry

During the interview, try to answer every question honestly. Emphasize what you are capable of providing to the shop, including:

- Enthusiasm
- Experience

- Willingness to work
- Willingness to work long hours and/or long weeks

AFTER THE INTERVIEW

After the interview, follow up with a letter thanking the shop for the interview. In the letter include when the interview occurred and that from the information you received, that you are very interested in becoming a part of the organization (shop or dealership). Also include contact information such as your cell phone number and e-mail address so the service manager can easily get in contact with you. A quick review of your skills and talent will also be helpful to the shop owner or service manager.

ACCEPTING EMPLOYMENT

When a job is offered, there will likely be some paperwork that needs to be filled out and decisions made. Some of the requested information could include:

- Social security number (social insurance number in Canada)
- W-4 tax withholding form
- Emergency contact people
- Retirement plan selection (This is usually given to you to study and return at a later date.)
- Other information that may be unique to the shop or dealership

After accepting the employment position, be sure to determine exactly what day and time you should report to work and try to determine where your tools should be placed. Most places will show you around and introduce you to others you will work with.

TECHNICIAN PAY METHODS

STRAIGHT-TIME PAY METHODS When the particular service or repair is not covered or mentioned in a flat-rate guide, it is common practice for the technician to **clock-in** and use the actual time spent on the repair as a basis for payment. The technician uses a flat-rate time ticket and a time clock to record the actual time. Being paid for the actual time spent is often called **straight time** or **clock time**. Difficult engine performance repairs are often calculated using the technician's straight time.

FLAT-RATE PAY METHODS Beginning service technicians are usually paid by the hour. The hourly rate can vary greatly depending on the experience of the technician and type of work being performed. Most experienced service technicians are paid by a method called **flat-rate**. The flat-rate method of pay is also called **incentive** or **commission pay**. "Flat-rate" means that the technician is paid a set amount of time (flat-rate) for every service operation. The amount of time allocated is published in a flat-rate manual. For example, if a bumper requires replacement, the flat-rate manual may call for 1.0 hour (time is always expressed in tenths of an hour). Each hour has 60 minutes. Each tenth of an hour is 1/10 of 60 or 6 minutes.

0.1 hour = 6 minutes
0.2 hour = 12 minutes
0.3 hour = 18 minutes
0.4 hour = 24 minutes
0.5 hour = 30 minutes
0.6 hour = 36 minutes
0.7 hour = 42 minutes
0.8 hour = 48 minutes
0.9 hour = 54 minutes
1.0 hour = 60 minutes

Many service operations are greater than 1 hour and are expressed as such:

2.4 hours = 2 hours and 24 minutes
3.6 hours = 3 hours and 36 minutes

The service technician would therefore get paid the flat-rate time regardless of how long it actually took to complete the job. Often, the technician can "beat flat-rate" by performing the operation in less time than the published time. It is therefore important that the technician not waste time and work efficiently to get paid the most for a day's work. The technician also has to be careful to perform the service procedure correctly because if the job needs to be done again due to an error, the technician does the repair at no pay. Therefore, the technician needs to be fast and careful at the same time.

The vehicle manufacturer determines the flat-rate for each labor operation by having a team of technicians perform the operation several times. The average of all of these times is often published as the allocated time. The flat-rate method was originally developed to determine a fair and equitable way to pay dealerships for covered warranty repairs. Because the labor rate differs throughout the country, a fixed dollar amount would not be fair compensation. However, if a time could be established for each operation, then the vehicle manufacturer could reimburse the dealership for the set number of hours multiplied by the labor rate approved for that dealership. For example, if the approved labor rate is $60.00 per hour and:

Technician A performed 6.2 hours × $60.00 = $372.00
Technician B performed 4.8 hours × $60.00 = $288.00
The total paid to the dealership by the manufacturer = $660.00

This does not mean that the service technician gets paid $60.00 per hour. Sorry, no! This means that the dealership gets reimbursed for labor at the $60.00 per hour rate. The service technician usually gets paid a lot less than half of the total labor charge.

Depending on the part of the country and the size of the dealership and community, the technician's flat-rate per hour income can vary from $7.00 to $20.00 or more per flat-rate hour. Remember, a high pay rate ($20 for example) does not necessarily mean that the service technician will be earning $800.00 per week (40 hours × $20.00 per hour = $800.00). If the dealership is not busy or it is a slow time of year, maybe the technician will only have the opportunity to "turn" 20 hours per week. So it is not really the pay rate that determines what a technician will earn but rather a combination of all of the following:

- Pay rate
- Number of service repairs performed
- Skill and speed of the service technician
- Type of service work (a routine brake service may be completed faster and easier than a difficult engine performance problem)

A service technician earns more at a busy dealership with a lower pay rate than at a smaller or less busy dealership with a higher pay rate.

PAYROLL DEDUCTIONS

GROSS VERSUS NET COMPENSATION Most beginning technicians start by receiving a certain amount of money per hours worked. **Gross** earnings are the total amount you earned during the pay period. The paycheck you receive will be for an amount called **net** earnings. Taxes and deductions that are taken from your paycheck may include all or most of the following:

- **Federal** income **tax**
- **State** income **tax** (not all states)
- Social Security taxes (labeled **FICA**, which stands for Federal Insurance Contribution Act)
- Health/dental/eye insurance deductions

In addition to the above, uniform costs, savings plan deductions, parts account deductions, as well as weekly payments for tools, may also reduce the amount of your net or "take-home" pay.

RETIREMENT INFORMATION AND PAYMENTS

Some shops or dealerships offer some retirement savings plan but the most commonly used is an employer-sponsored 401(k) account named after a section of the U.S. Internal Revenue Code. A 401(k) account allows a worker to save for retirement while deferring taxes on the saved money and earnings until withdrawal. Most 401(k) plans allow the employer to select from stock mutual funds or other investments. A 401(k) retirement plan offers two advantages compared to a simple savings account.

- The contributions (money deposited into the account) are tax deferred. The amount will increase due to interest and no taxes are due until the money is withdrawn.
- Many employers provide matching contributions to your 401(k) account, which can range from 0% (no matching contributions) to 100%.

TECH TIP

Hourly Rate to Annual Income

To calculate the amount of income that will be earned using an hourly rate, do the following:

Multiply the hourly rate times 2 and then times 1000. For example: $10 per hour × 2 × 1000 = $20,000 per year.

This easy-to-use formula assumes working 8 hours a day, 5 days a week for 50 weeks (instead of 52 weeks in the year).

The reverse can also be easily calculated:

Divide the yearly income by 2 and then by 1000 = hourly rate

For example: $36,000 per year ÷ 2 = $18,000 ÷ 1000 = $18 per hour

The savings really add up over time. For example, if you start saving at age 25 and your income averages $3,000 per month ($36,000 per year) and you contribute 6% of your pay and the employer contributes 3%, after 40 years at age 65, the account will be worth $1,700,000 (one million, seven hundred thousand dollars) assuming a 10% average return.

In retirement, most experts agree that 4% of the total can be withdrawn each year and not reduce the capital investment. Four percent of $1,700,000 is $68,000 per year or over $5,600 per month every month for the rest of your life.

ADDITIONAL SERVICE TECHNICIAN BENEFITS Many larger dealerships and service facilities often offer some or all of the following:

- Paid uniforms/cleaning
- Vacation time
- Update training (especially new vehicle dealerships)
- Some sort of retirement (usually a contributing 401(k) program
- Health and dental insurance (usually not fully paid)
- Discounts on parts and vehicles purchased at the dealership or shop

Not all service facilities offer all of these additional benefits.

HOUSING AND LIVING EXPENSES

As a general guideline, **housing expenses** such as rent or a mortgage payment should not exceed 30% of the gross monthly income. For example,

Ten dollars per hour times 40 hours per week = $400 per week times 4 weeks in a month = $1600 per month. Thirty percent of $1600 is $480 per month for rent or a mortgage payment.

A vehicle payment should not exceed 25% of the gross earnings. In the example where the pay was $10 per hour, the maximum recommended vehicle payment should be $400 per month.

BECOMING A SHOP OWNER

Many service technicians want to start and operate their own shop. Becoming a shop owner results in handling many non-automotive-related duties that some technicians do not feel qualified to handle, including:

- Handling customers
- Ordering and paying for shop equipment and supplies
- Bookkeeping, including payroll
- Budgeting for and paying for garage owner's insurance and workers' compensation
- Paying rent, as well as heat/air conditioning bills
- Advertising expenses
- Hiring and firing employees

? FREQUENTLY ASKED QUESTION

Where Does All the Money Go?

Money earned does seem to quickly disappear. For example, if a soft drink and a bag of chips were purchased every day at work for $2.50, this amounts to $12.50 per week or $50 per month, which is $600 per year. Use the following chart to see where the money goes.

Income

Labor rate per hour × number of hours worked = _____
Overtime pay, if applicable = _____
Part-time work on weekends = _____
TOTAL WEEKLY INCOME = _____
Multiply by 4.3 to get the **MONTHLY INCOME** = _____

Monthly Expenses

Car/truck payment = _____
Rent/mortgage = _____
Gasoline = _____
Food (groceries) = _____
Fast food or restaurants = _____
Heat and electric (heat/air conditioning) = _____
Water and sewer = _____
Telephone (cell) = _____
Cable TV/Internet access = _____
Clothing (including cleaning) = _____
Credit card payment = _____
TOTAL MONTHLY EXPENSES = _____

Hopefully, the total income is more than the total expenses!

Employee or Contract Labor?

Most shops and dealerships hire service technicians as employees. However, some shops or businesses will pay a technician for services performed on a contract basis. This means that they are not hiring you as an employee, but simply paying for a service similar to having a plumber repair a toilet. The plumber is performing a service and is paid for the job rather than as an employee of the shop. An employer–employee relationship exists if the shop meets two factors:

1. **Direction**—This means that the employer can direct the technician to report to work to perform service work.
2. **Control**—This means that the employer can direct the hours and days when the work is to be performed and at the employer's location.

A contract labor association exists if the repairs are performed without both direction and control of the shop.

If a contract labor basis is established, then no taxes are withheld. It is then the responsibility of the technician to make the necessary and required general tax payments and pay all taxes on time.

Find Three Key People

An **entrepreneur** is a person who organizes and manages their own business assuming the risk for the sake of a profit. Many service technicians have the desire to own their own repair facility. The wise business owner (entrepreneur) seeks the advice of the following people when starting and operating their own business.

1. **Attorney (lawyer)**—This professional will help guide you to make sure that your employees and your customers are protected by the laws of your community, state, and federal regulations.
2. **Accountant**—This professional will help you with the journals and records that must be kept by all businesses and to help with elements such as payroll taxes, unemployment taxes, and workmen's compensation that all businesses have to pay.
3. **Insurance Agent**—This professional will help you select the coverage needed to protect you and your business from major losses.

SUMMARY

1. When applying for a job, list in your cover letter where you saw the opening and also mention that you meet all of the requirements for the position.
2. A resume is a brief description of your education and experience.
3. Present a professional appearance during an interview.
4. Net pay is gross pay minus all deductions, such as federal taxes and FICA.
5. Housing and vehicle payments each should not exceed 25% of your monthly income.
6. Becoming a shop owner involves more paperwork than most service technicians realize.

REVIEW QUESTIONS

1. What facts should be included on the resume?
2. What are five interviewing tips?
3. What is the difference between gross pay and net pay?
4. What taxes are usually withheld from a paycheck?
5. What are five duties of a shop owner?

CHAPTER QUIZ

1. A resume should be how many pages long?
   - **a.** 1
   - **b.** 2
   - **c.** 3
   - **d.** 4 or more

2. What personal information should *not* be included on the resume?
   - **a.** Address
   - **b.** Cell or telephone number
   - **c.** Age
   - **d.** Work experience

3. Why is having a good driving record good for the shop?
   a. Allows the use of a company vehicle
   b. Lowers insurance costs
   c. Allows you to drive customers' vehicles
   d. Permits you to use your vehicle to get parts

4. Which is *not* recommended during an interview?
   a. Wear shoes that are not sneakers
   b. Wear a shirt with a collar
   c. Have clean hair
   d. Wear jeans

5. During an interview, try to _____.
   a. Show enthusiasm
   b. Explain your work experience
   c. State your willingness to work
   d. All of the above

6. Ten dollars per hour is about how much income per year?
   a. $20,000   b. $25,000
   c. $30,000   d. $35,000

7. One of the deductions from a paycheck is for Social Security. This item is usually shown on the pay stub as_____.
   a. Social Security
   b. SSA
   c. FICA
   d. U.S. government deduction

8. Technician A says that the net pay amount is usually higher than the gross pay amount. Technician B says that the gross pay amount is usually higher than the net pay. Which technician is correct?
   a. Technician A only
   b. Technician B only
   c. Both Technicians A and B
   d. Neither Technician A nor B

9. A beginning service technician earns $400 per week. How much should the technician spend on a vehicle payment?
   a. $400 per month
   c. $800 per month
   b. $500 per month
   d. $1000 per month

10. Which activity does not allow a person to perform any work while at the shop?
    a. Cooperative education program
    b. Apprenticeship program
    c. Job shadowing
    d. Part-time employment

chapter 4

WORKING AS A PROFESSIONAL SERVICE TECHNICIAN

OBJECTIVES: After studying Chapter 4, the reader will be able to: • Discuss how to start a new job. • Describe the advantages of having a mentor. • Explain how a mentor can improve on-the-job learning. • Discuss the role of the trainee with a mentor. • Explain formal and informal evaluations. • Describe the role of a service technician. • Explain how the flat-rate pay plan works. • Describe the type and pricing of parts.

KEY TERMS: • Advisor 35 • Advocate 35 • Aftermarket parts 33 • Coach 35 • Core 33 • Core charge 33 • Counselor 35 • Critical thinking 36 • Customer pay (CP) 32 • Flagging 33 • Formal evaluation 37 • Informal evaluation 37 • Jobber 33 • Mentor 34 • Original equipment (OE) 33 • Rebuilt 34 • Remove and inspect (R & I) 33 • Remove and replace (R & R) 33 • Renewal parts 33 • Repair order (RO) 30 • Role model 35 • Service bay 30 • Stall 30 • Teacher 35 • Three Cs (concern, cause, correction) 30 • Trainee 34 • Warehouse distributor 33

PROFESSIONALISM

Professionalism and personal credibility are important and can determine success as a service technician or as a customer service provider. A true professional does the following on a regular basis.

1. **Practice consistency.** Be positive, professional, and warm at all times.

2. **Keep your word.** Follow through with the commitments that you make. People will not have faith in you if you break your promises.

3. **Develop technical expertise.** Become very knowledgeable about the vehicles being serviced. Attend regular update training classes to keep up with the latest technical information and equipment.

4. **Become a teammate with your coworkers.** Working successfully with others shows that you have common goals and can benefit from the specific skills of others.

5. **Be accountable.** Practice honesty all of the time, admit mistakes, and take responsibility for actions. Apologize if you are wrong.

ETHICS   Ethics are a set of principles that govern the conduct of an individual or group. Sometimes ethical decisions are easy to recognize and are perceived as popular choices of behavior by the people around us. At times the range of

 **TECH TIP**

Clean Clothes Are a Must
Anyone who meets the public in any business must not only be dressed appropriately, but the clothing should be clean. Service advisors and others that greet the public should also be sure that their shoes are shined. Dull, dirty, or scuffed shoes or messy appearance reflects an unprofessional look.

possible choices falls into choices falls into gray areas in which the "right" or "wrong" course of action is difficult or nearly impossible to identify. When faced with an ethically challenging situation, ask yourself the following questions:

- Is it legal? (Is it against local, state, or federal laws?)

- Is it fair? (Is it harmful to me or to others?)

- How do I feel about it? (Is it against the teachings of my parents or my religion?)

- Would public opinion find my behavior incorrect? (Would it disappoint my family?)

- Am I fearful of what those I trust would say about my actions? (Would I be hurt or upset if someone did this to me?)

The above questions can be quite revealing when attempting to choose an ethical course of action.

COMMUNICATIONS

The five main methods of communication used in effective customer service interaction include listening, talking, nonverbal communications, reading, and writing.

LISTENING Active listening is the ability to hear and understand what the speaker is saying. To listen to your customers or other technicians is to show them that you care about and respect their questions and concerns. It is not easy to be a good listener; it takes practice and dedication to improve your listening techniques. Listening is a skill that must continuously be developed.

Several barriers to good listening exist. A listener may be distracted from what is being said, have a closed mind to the speaker and the message, won't stop talking, or is lazy and unwilling to make the commitment to be a good listener.

Listening requires the listener to stop talking and to hear what the speaker is saying. It has been said that humans were given two ears and one mouth because we are supposed to listen twice as much as we speak. The best way to keep your mind focused on the speaker and to avoid becoming distracted is to pay attention. We can think about 10 times faster than we can speak, so frequently we have processed what speakers have said and are waiting for them to catch up with us. By focusing on speakers and on what is being said we are less likely to miss the messages being delivered. Putting that into practice is not as easy as it sounds.

A good listener does the following:

- Focuses on the speaker and what is being said.
- Looks at the speaker and makes eye contact when possible.
- Listens with an open mind.
- Rephrases what was said to clarify that the intended message is understood.
- A good listener knows the joy of sharing and communicating with others. Work to become the best listener you can be.

VERBAL Verbal means speaking, using words and terminology that others can comprehend. Eye contact is always important when we are communicating with others.

Eye contact is allowing our eyes to make visual contact with someone else's. In our culture, eye contact conveys sincerity and interest. Avoiding eye contact may suggest a lack of concern or lack of honesty. Customers may perceive that a customer service provider is not interested in what they are saying if they do not periodically make eye contact with the customer.

When dealing with people from other cultures, customer service providers should be aware of cultural differences. In many other cultures eye avoidance is a sign of respect. Be sensitive to others but use eye contact whenever possible.

NONVERBAL COMMUNICATION The tone and inflection of the voice, facial expressions, posture, hand movements, and eye contact are all forms of nonverbal communications. These nonverbal indicators can contradict the message conveyed through another method of communication.

Nonverbal communication includes body posture such as having the arms crossed. When a person crosses his or her arms, or looks at other things rather than paying attention to what you are discussing, these actions could indicate one of several things, including:

1. They are not interested in what you are saying
2. They don't believe what you are saying
3. They are not listening

If this type of nonverbal communication is noticed, there are several things that could be done to overcome this barrier, including:

1. Ask questions, which would require them to pay attention plus it shows that you are interested in what they think.
2. Give the customer options rather than just ask them what they want such as saying "would you prefer to have this work done all at the same time or spread out over several weeks?"

TELEPHONE COMMUNICATION A large percentage of customers make first contact with a shop or dealer service department by telephone. Service technicians normally do not talk to customers directly but may be asked to help clarify a repair or a service procedure.

TECH TIP

Never Use Profanity

Regardless of the situation, a true professional never resorts to the use of profanity. If tensions are high and the discussion becomes heated, try to defuse the situation by turning the situation over to someone else.

TECH TIP

Always Have Paper and a Pen When on the Telephone

When talking to a customer, whether in person or on the telephone, have paper and a pencil or pen to record the necessary information. In this case, the customer service representative at a dealer is using a preprinted form to record the service procedures to be performed on a customer's vehicle while talking on the phone. ● **SEE FIGURE 4–1.**

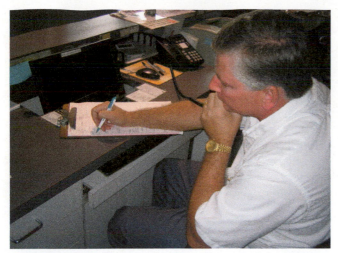

FIGURE 4–1 When answering the telephone, be sure to have paper and pen or pencil handy to record the customer information.

FIGURE 4–2 If you smile while talking on the telephone, your attitude will be transmitted to the customer.

Some suggestions when talking on the telephone include:

- Use proper titles for the people with whom you communicate. If in doubt about whether to use a first name, call the person by the more formal *Mr.* or *Ms.* If they prefer the more informal first name, they will say so. It is better to be a little too formal than overly familiar.

- Thank people for calling. "Thank you" is the most powerful phrase in human relations and it reassures customers that you are interested in serving.

- Try to avoid technical terms and abbreviations such as EGR and other terms commonly used in the trade but will not be understood by the customer. Try to phrase the technical description by saying that you replaced or serviced a part in the emission control system and include the entire name of the part such as the "exhaust gas recirculation valve."

- Keep your comments positive and focused toward solving the problem or concern.

- Avoid saying anything that makes people or your shop look unprofessional or uncaring. When dealing with customers, some words are more positive and appropriate to use. Some customer service providers find it helpful to list words to use and words to avoid on a card so that it is available for easy reference.

 **TECH TIP**

Smile While You Talk

If you smile while talking on the telephone, your voice will reflect a positive and helpful attitude, which customers or vendors will easily recognize over the telephone. ● **SEE FIGURE 4–2**.

- Speak clearly and distinctly. Hold the telephone mouthpiece about a half-inch from your lips. Speak naturally and comfortably. Talk to your caller as you would to a friend.

- Move to a quiet area if background noise level is high.

WRITING   Writing is communicating by using the written word so that others can understand the intended message. Service technicians are required to document the work that was performed on a vehicle. For some technicians this is the most difficult part of the service. If writing, be sure it is legible and if not, then print all messages and information. Writing or typing in the description of the steps performed during the diagnosis and repair of the vehicle should be worded as if the technician is talking to the customer. For example, if a coolant leak was repaired by replacing the water pump the technician should write out the following steps and operations on the work order:

1. Visually verified coolant leaking.

2. Performed a pressure test of the cooling system and located the leak as coming from the water pump.

3. Replaced the water pump and added new coolant and bled the system of trapped air.

4. Pressure tested the cooling system to verify that the leak was corrected—no leaks found.

READING   Reading means the ability to read and comprehend the written word. All service technicians need to be able to read, understand, and follow written instructions and repair procedures. If some words are not understood use a dictionary or ask another technician for help. For example, a beginning technician read in the service information that the wiring connector was "adjacent to the coolant reservoir." The technician did not understand what the word adjacent meant and found out from another technician that it meant "next or close to."

If reading a note from a customer written in another language you do not understand try to ask if someone else in the shop can read it for you.

Use Internet Translation

If the customer is non-English speaking, type the information into a text document and search for a translation on the Internet. Give the copy of the translated document to the customer. The customer request could also be translated into English if needed to help the shop understand exactly what the customer is requesting and needs.

 **TECH TIP**

Google Is Your Friend

If unsure as to how something works or if you need more detailed information about something, go to *www.google.com*® and search for the topic. Using the Internet can help with locating hard-to-find facts and can even be used to help with a service procedure that you have not done before. For a link to all factory service information, go to the website of National Automotive Service Task Force at *www. nastf.org*. Look at the work scheduled for the next day and try to determine as much about the job as possible so you can be prepared the next day to tackle the procedure. Using the International Automotive Technicians Network at *www.iatn.net* is also very helpful for technical information and can help pin down hard-to-find problems.

 **TECH TIP**

Don't Touch Other Technician's Tools

A beginning technician seldom has all of the tools needed to perform all of the service and repair tasks. A technician's tools are very important. If a tool needs to be borrowed, the beginning technician should ask for permission to borrow a tool. Then when the tool is returned , it should be clean and replaced back exactly where the technician asks for it to be returned.

 **TECH TIP**

Regulated Terms to Use

In some states or areas where automotive service is regulated, such as in California or Michigan, it is important that the term used to describe a labor operation is the term defined by the state agency. This means that some terms used in parts and time guides may not be the same terms used by the state. Always check that the terms used are in compliance with all regulations. Some terms that could be affected include rebuild, repair, overhaul, inspection and R & R (remove and replace), and safety inspection.

WHAT HAPPENS THE FIRST DAY?

The first day on the job, someone, usually the shop owner or shop foreman, should:

- Introduce the new technician to key people at the shop.
- Show the new technician the facility, parking, rules, and regulations of the organization.
- Establish the new technician's work area.
- Ask questions of the new technician regarding their skills and talents.

The shop owner or foreman should:

- Review the training tasks that were completed in school.
- Try to direct work to the new technician that covers their training or experience.

The first day on the job the beginning technician should:

- Smile and ask questions if needed to clarify procedures and regulations.

- Be prepared to take and pass a drug test.
- Assure the service manager or shop owner that you are serious about a career as an automotive technician.

A work order, also called a **repair order** or **RO** is assigned to a technician who is best qualified to perform the work. The technician gets the keys and drives the vehicle to an assigned **service bay** (also called a **stall**), performs the proper diagnosis, gets the necessary parts from the parts department, and completes the repair.

After the service work has been performed, the service technician should then fill out the work order and describe what work was performed. These are called the "**three Cs.**"

1. **Concern**—Write on the work order what was done to confirm the customer's concern. For example, "Drove the vehicle at highway speed and verified a vibration."

2. **Cause**—The service technician should write the cause of the problem. For example, "Used a scan tool and discovered that cylinder #3 was misfiring."

3. **Correction**—The service technician should write what was done to correct the problem. For example, "Removed the spark plug wire from cylinder number three and by visual inspection found that the boot had been arcing to the cylinder head. Replaced the spark plug wire and verified that the misfire was corrected."

DUTIES OF A SERVICE TECHNICIAN

READING THE WORK ORDER   A work order is selected or assigned to a service technician who then performs the listed tasks. The work order should be written so that the technician knows exactly what needs to be done. However, if there is any doubt, the technician should clarify the needed task with the service advisor or the person who spoke to the customer.

TALKING TO CUSTOMERS   The typical service technician usually does not talk directly to a customer except in some smaller shops. However, there may be causes where the technician will be asked to clarify a procedure or repair to a customer. Many technicians do not like to talk to the customers and fear that they may say too much or not enough. If a technician is asked to talk to a customer, try to keep the discussion to the following without being too technical.

- The service technician should repeat the original concern. This is to simply verify to the customer and the technician the goal of the service or repair.

 **TECH TIP**

If Late—Call

When running late, you may know that you will be just a few minutes late but your boss does not how late you will be. If you are going to be late, even by a few minutes, call the shop and let them know. This does not eliminate your being late from your record, but does demonstrate your concern to your service manager and other technicians who are counting on you to being on time to work every day.

 **TECH TIP**

Ask Me about This

A good service advisor will document what the customer wants done on the work order. However, there are times when the explanation and description would take too long and too much space to be practical. In these cases, the wise service advisor simply states on the work order for the service technician to see the service advisor to discuss the situation. The service advisor can write the basic request to document what is needed.

- The cause of the fault should be mentioned. If further diagnostic steps needed to find the cause are requested, discuss the steps followed and the equipment or tools used.
- Discuss what was done to solve the concern, including what part or parts were replaced. This step may also include what other service operations were needed to complete the repair, such as reprogramming the computer.

NOTE: If the customer speaks a foreign language that you do not understand, excuse yourself and locate someone in the shop who can assist you with communicating with the customer. Avoid using slang or abbreviation of technical terms. Ask the person if they understand and be willing to restate, if needed, until the situation is understood. This can often be difficult if discussing technical situations to persons of another language or culture.

ESTIMATING A REPAIR   Sometimes a service technician is asked to help create an estimate for the customer. It is usually the responsibility of the service advisor or shop owner to create estimates. The technician may be helpful by pointing out all of the operations that need to be performed to achieve a repair. The estimate for a repair includes:

- **Parts needed**—This list would also include any gaskets and/or supplies needed. The technician can help identify if extra supplies may be needed.
- **Labor**—A published time guide is usually used but many times options such as rear air conditioning or four-wheel drive may add substantial time to the operation. The technician can help with the estimate by making sure that the options are pointed out to the service advisor or shop owner.

DOCUMENTING THE WORK ORDER   The service technician must document the work order. This means that the service technician must write (or type) what all was done to the vehicle, including documenting defective components or conditions that were found in the course of the diagnosis. The documentation is often called "telling the story" and should include the following:

- The test equipment used to diagnose the problem. For example: Used a Tech 2 scan tool to retrieve P0300 random misfire diagnostic trouble code.

 **TECH TIP**

Car, Truck, or Vehicle?

When discussing a vehicle with a customer, it is best to avoid creating problems. For example, if a technician asked about a customer's "car", the customer could become concerned because they drive a truck and many owners of trucks do not want their vehicle called a car. Use of the term "vehicle," a generic term, is often recommended when talking to customers to avoid possible concerns.

- Used a digital multimeter to determine a spark plug wire was defective.
- List what parts or service operations were performed. For example: Replaced the spark plug wire on cylinder number 3. Used a scan tool to clear the diagnostic trouble codes and verify that the engine is operating correctly.

FOLLOWING RECOMMENDED PROCEDURES

All service technicians should follow the diagnostic and service procedures specified by the vehicle manufacturer. Service information procedures to be followed include the following:

- Follow and document the diagnostic procedure. Writing down the test results helps the customer see all that was involved in the procedure and creates the proper paper trail for future reference, if needed.
- Follow the recommended removal and reinstallation (R & R) procedures. This step helps prevent the possibility of doing harm to the vehicle if an alternative method is attempted.
- Always torque fasteners to factory specifications. This step is very important because under- or overtightened fasteners can cause problems that were not present until after the repair. The wise technician will document torque specifications on the work order.

CUSTOMER PAY

Customer pay (CP) means that the customer will be paying for the service work at a dealership rather than the warranty. Often the same factory flat-rate number of hours is used to calculate the technician's pay, but customer pay often pays the service technician at a higher rate.

For example, a service technician earning $15.00 per flat-rate hour for warranty work may be paid $18.00 per hour for customer-pay work. Obviously, service technicians prefer to work on vehicles that require customer-pay service work rather than factory-warranty service work.

NONDEALERSHIP FLAT-RATE Technicians who work for independent service facilities or at other nondealership locations use one or both of the following to set rates of pay:

- Mitchell, Motors, or Chilton parts and time guides
- Alldata, Shop-Key, Car-Quest, Auto Value, Mitchell, AC Delco, or other shop management software program.

These guides contain service operation and flat-rate times. Generally, these are about 20% higher (longer) than those specified by the factory flat-rate to compensate for rust or corrosion and other factors of time and mileage that often lengthen the time necessary to complete a repair. Again, the service technician is usually paid a dollar amount per flat-rate hour based on one of these aftermarket flat-rate guides. The guides also provide a list price for the parts for each vehicle. This information allows the service advisor to accurately estimate the total cost of the repair.

FLAGGING A WORK ORDER

When a service technician completes a service procedure or repair, a sticker or notification on the work order indicates the following:

- Technician number (number rather than a name is often used not only to shorten the identification but also to shield the actual identity of the technician from the customer)

FREQUENTLY ASKED QUESTION

What Can a Service Technician Do to Earn More Money?

Because most service technicians are paid on a commission basis (flat-rate), the more work that is completed, the more hours the technician can "turn." Therefore, to earn the most money, the service technician could do the following to increase the amount of work performed:

- Keep up-to-date and learn the latest technical information
- Practice good habits that help avoid errors or incomplete repairs
- Learn from experienced and successful fellow technicians and try to approach the repair the same way the successful technician does
- Purchase the proper tools to do the work efficiently

NOTE: This does not mean that every technician needs to purchase all possible tools. Purchase only those tools that you know you will need and use.

TECH TIP

Technician Skill Level and Severe Service

Most aftermarket service information includes a guideline for the relative level of the technician's skill required to perform the listed service procedures. These include:

A = Highly skilled and experienced technician
B = Skilled technician who is capable of performing diagnosis of vehicle systems
C = Semiskilled technician who is capable of performing routine service work without direct supervision

Many time guides provide additional time for vehicles that may be excessively rusted due to climate conditions or have been subjected to abuse. Be sure to quote the higher rate if any of these conditions are present on the customer's vehicle.
● **SEE FIGURE 4–3.**

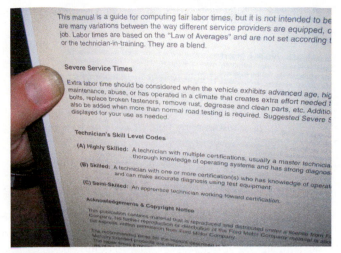

FIGURE 4–3 Note the skill levels of the technician and the extra time that should be added if work is being performed on a vehicle that has excessive rust or other factors as stated in the time guide.

- Work order number
- Actual clock time from a time clock record for certain jobs as needed
- Amount of time allocated to the repair expressed in hours and tenths of an hour

The application of the service technician's sticker to the back of the work order or completing the details of the repair into the electronic service record is called **flagging the work order.**

NOTE: The actual assignment of the time is often done by another person at the dealership or service facility. This procedure assures that the correct number of hours is posted to the work order and to the technician's ticket.

SUBLET REPAIRS

Often a repair (or a part of a repair) is performed by another person or company outside of the dealership or service facility. For example, an engine needing repair that also has a defective or leaking radiator would be repaired by the original repair facility, but the radiator may be sent to a specialty radiator repair shop. The radiator repair cost is then entered on the work order as a sublet repair.

PARTS REPLACEMENT

Parts replacement is often called **R & R,** meaning **remove and replace.**

NOTE: R & R can also mean **remove and repair,** but this meaning is generally not used as much now as it used to

be when components such as starters and air conditioning compressors were repaired rather than replaced as an assembly.

R & I is often used to indicate **remove and inspect** to check a component for damage. The old replaced part is often returned for remanufacturing and is called a **core.** A **core charge** is often charged by parts stores when a new (or remanufactured) part is purchased. This core charge usually represents the value of the old component. Because it is needed by the remanufacturer as a starting point for the remanufacturing process, the core charge is also an incentive to return the old part for credit (or refund) of the core charge.

NOTE: Most parts stores today require that all cores be returned in the original boxes. Be sure to place the defective part into the same box that was used for the new or remanufactured part to be sure that the shop gets the proper credit for the core.

ORIGINAL EQUIPMENT PARTS Parts at a new vehicle dealership come either directly from the vehicle manufacturer or a regional dealership. If one dealership purchases from another dealership, the cost of the part is higher, but no waiting is required. If a dealership orders a part from the manufacturer directly, the cost is lower, but there is often a 7- to 10-day waiting period. **Original equipment** parts, abbreviated **OE,** are generally of the highest quality because they have to meet performance and durability standards not required of replacement parts manufacturers.

NOTE: Many service technicians will use only OE parts for certain critical systems such as fuel injection and ignition system components because, in their experience, even though the price is often higher, the extra quality seems to be worth the cost not only to the owner of the vehicle but also to the service technician who does not have to worry about having to replace the same part twice.

AFTERMARKET PARTS Parts manufactured to be sold for use after the vehicle is made are often referred to as **aftermarket parts** or **renewal parts.** Most aftermarket parts are sold at automotive parts stores or **jobbers.** A jobber or parts retailer usually gets parts from a large regional **warehouse distributor.** The warehouse distributor can either purchase parts directly from the manufacturer or from an even larger central warehouse. Because each business needs to make a profit (typically, 35%), the cost to the end user may not be lower than it is for the same part purchased at a dealership (two-step process instead of the typical three-step process) even though it costs more to manufacture the original equipment part. To determine what a 35% margin increase is for any product, simply divide the cost by 0.65. To illustrate how this works, compare the end cost of a part (part A) from a dealership and a parts store.

Retail Parts Store	New Vehicle Dealership
Manufacturer's selling price = $17.00	Manufacturer's selling price = $25.00
Warehouse distributor's selling price = $26.15 ($17.00 ÷ 0.65 = $26.15)	Parts department selling price = $38.46 ($25.00 ÷ 0.65 = $38.46)
Retail store selling price = $40.23 ($26.15 ÷ 0.65 = $40.23)	

NOTE: The cost of the part to the customer where service work is performed is increased about 35% over the base cost of the part. For example, a part from a parts store that costs the repair facility $40.23 will be billed to the customer at about $61.00. The retail service customer at the dealer may pay $59.17 ($38.46 ÷ 0.65 = $59.17).

NEW VERSUS REMANUFACTURED PARTS New parts are manufactured from raw materials and have never been used on a vehicle. A remanufactured component (also called **rebuilt**) has been used on a vehicle until the component wore out or failed. A remanufacturer totally disassembles the component, cleans, machines, and performs all the necessary steps to restore the part to a "like new" look and function. If properly remanufactured, the component can be expected to deliver the same length of service as a new component part.

The cost of a remanufactured component is often less than the cost of a new part.

CAUTION: Do not always assume that a remanufactured component is less expensive than a new component. Due to the three-step distribution process, the final cost to the end user (you) may be close to the same!

USED PARTS Used parts offer another alternative to either new or remanufactured parts. The cost of a used component is typically one-half the cost of the component if purchased new. Wrecking and salvage yards use a Hollander manual that lists original equipment part numbers and cost and cross-references them to other parts that are the same.

WORKING WITH A MENTOR

A mentor is a person at the job site who helps the beginning service technician, also called the **trainee.** The word **mentor** comes from Greek mythology. In Homer's *The Odyssey,* Mentor was the faithful companion and friend of Ulysses (Odysseus), the King of Ithaca. Before Ulysses went to the Trojan Wars, he instructed Mentor to stay and take full charge of the royal household. This meant that Mentor had to be father figure,

TECH TIP

Work Habit Hints

The following statements reflect the expectations of service managers or shop owners for their technicians:

1. Report to work every day on time. Being several minutes early every day is an easy way to show your service manager and fellow technicians that you are serious about your job and career.
2. If you *must* be late or absent, call your service manager as soon as possible.
3. Keep busy. If not assigned to a specific job, ask what activities the service manager or supervisor wants you to do.
4. Report any mistakes or accidents *immediately* to your supervisor or team leader. *Never* allow a customer to be the first to discover a mistake.
5. Never lie to your employer or to a customer.
6. Always return any borrowed tools as soon as you are done with them and in *clean* condition. *Show* the person you borrowed the tools from that you are returning them to the toolbox or workbench.
7. Keep your work area neat and orderly.
8. Always use fender covers when working under the hood.
9. Double-check your work to be sure that everything is correct.
   a. Remember: "If you are forcing something, you are probably doing something wrong."
   b. Ask for help if unclear as to what to do or how to do it.
10. Do not smoke in a customer's vehicle.
11. Avoid profanity.
12. DO NOT TOUCH THE RADIO! If the radio is turned on and prevents you from hearing noises, turn the volume down. Try to return the vehicle to the owner with the radio at the same volume as originally set.

NOTE: Some shops have a policy that requires employees to turn the radio off.

13. Keep yourself neatly groomed, including:
    a. Shirttail tucked into pants (unless shirt is designed to be worn outside)
    b. Daily bathing and use of deodorant
    c. Clean hair, regular haircuts, and hair tied back if long
    d. Men: daily shave or keep beard and/or mustache neatly trimmed
    e. Women: makeup and jewelry kept to a minimum

teacher, role model, counselor, trusted advisor, challenger, and encourager to the King's son in order that he become a wise and good ruler.

Therefore, a good definition of a mentor would be, "A highly qualified individual who is entrusted with the protection and development of an inexperienced technician."

A mentor therefore fulfills many roles, such as:

- **Teacher**—helps teach information and procedures
- **Coach**—has trainee practice service procedures
- **Counselor**—concerned about, but not trained to offer advice on personal life decisions.
- **Advisor**—helps with career-type decisions, such as what tools are needed
- **Advocate** (stands up for the trainee)—represents and helps the trainee's concerns be expressed to others
- **Role model**—presents a positive role model every day

QUALIFICATIONS OF A GOOD MENTOR
A good mentor should be assigned to a new technician. Qualifications of a good mentor include:

- **Trade proficiency**—The person selected should be a highly skilled technician.
- **Good coaching/mentoring skills and techniques**—The mentor has to have patience and be willing to help the trainee by explaining each step needed to complete a service procedure.

TECH TIP

Adhere to the Times

When starting a new job at a shop or dealership, be sure to ask about the following:

- **What time should I arrive at work?** This may be different than the scheduled work starting time. For example, the work day could start at 8 a.m. but the shop owner or service manager may want all technicians to arrive and start to get ready to work at 7:50 a.m.
- **When is break time?** Breaks may or may not be regularly scheduled and it is important for the beginning technician to know and adhere to break times.
- **When is lunch time?** In some busy shops, the lunch period is staggered to be sure that some technicians are always available for work. Always be willing to adhere to the requested lunch period.

- **Leadership/role model**—The mentor should take pride in being a professional service technician and have high ethical and professional standards.

Mentoring a trainee can be frustrating for an experienced technician. This occurs because the mentor needs to verify almost everything the trainee does until satisfied that competence has been achieved. Even very basic procedures need to be watched, such as hoisting the vehicle, changing the oil and oil filter, plus many other operations. As a result, the time taken to help the beginning technician will reduce the efficiency, and therefore, the pay of the mentor. However, after several weeks, the trainee can start helping the mentor, thereby increasing efficiency.

TEAMWORK

TEAM BUILDING   A team is a group of individuals working together to achieve a common goal. Even shops or service departments that do not use a team system with a group of technicians is still a team. All members of the service department are really part of a team effort working together to achieve efficient vehicle service and customer satisfaction. The key to building a team that works together is selecting employees that are willing to work together. While the shop owner or service manager at a dealership has hiring authority, every technician should consider what is best for the entire group to help increase repeat business and satisfied customers.

LEADERSHIP ROLES   As a technician gains experience, he or she often asks for guidance, not only for technical answers, but also for how to handle other issues in the shop, such as paperwork, use of aftermarket parts, and other issues. Therefore, the more experience the technician has, the more likely he or she will be placed in a leadership and role model position.

GOAL SETTING AND BUSINESS MEETINGS

GOAL SETTING   The wise service technician sets goals to achieve during a career and life. The purpose of goal setting is to focus efforts on improving your personal and professional life. Goals can include:

Career, physical, family, education, financial, and public service. There are many helpful websites that can be used to help set and track progress toward achieving goals. The hardest part of any goal is to write it down. Until it is written down, a goal is not real.

BUSINESS MEETINGS All service technicians attend business (shop) meetings. A good business meeting will have the following features:

1. An agenda (list of topics to be discussed) will be given out or displayed.

2. The meeting should start on time and end on time.

3. If someone is to give a report or be asked to do a project, this topic should be discussed with the designated person before the meeting to avoid that person from being surprised and made to feel uncomfortable.

4. The meeting should be held following the "Robert's Rule of Order" guidelines.

5. Often meetings include others from inside or outside the company or shop, so try to look your best and smile to make the best impression.

ADVANCEMENT SKILLS

The job of a service technician becomes more valuable to the shop or dealership if work can be accomplished quickly and without any mistakes. Therefore, being careful to avoid errors is the first consideration for any service technician. Then, with experience, the speed of accomplishing tasks can and will increase.

More than speed is needed to become a master technician. It requires problem solving and critical thinking skills, too. While beginning technicians are usually not required to diagnose problems, troubleshooting skills are very important toward becoming a master technician. Most master technicians follow a plan that includes:

1. Always verify the customer concern.

2. Perform a thorough visual inspection and check for possible causes of the problem, including damage from road debris or accidents.

3. Use a scan tool and check for stored diagnostic trouble codes (DTCs).

4. Check service information for technical service bulletins (TSBs).

5. Check service information and follow all diagnostic trouble charts.

6. Locate and correct the root cause of the problem.

7. Verify the repair and document the work order.

The hardest part of the diagnostic process is to locate the root cause of the problem. The process of analyzing and evaluating information and making a conclusion is called **critical thinking.**

HOUSEKEEPING DUTIES

A professional service technician is usually responsible for keeping his or her work area clean and tidy. Good housekeeping includes all of the following:

- **Clean floor**—If coolant or oil is spilled on the floor during a repair procedure, it should be cleaned before starting another job.

- **Tool box**—Keep work area and tool box clean and organized.

TECH TIP

Keeping "Things" off the Floor

To make cleaning easier and for a more professional shop appearance, keep only those items on the floor that have to be on the floor and find a place off the floor for all other items.

TECH TIP

Look at the Shop from a Customer's Point of View

To determine if the shop and other technicians look professional, step outside and enter the shop through the same door as a customer. Now look around. Look at the shop and the other technicians. Does the shop give the appearance of a professional service facility? If not, try to improve the look by asking the shop owner or service manager to do the same thing in an attempt to create a more professional-looking shop.

- **Items kept off the floor**—It is easy to allow parts and other items to be stored in and around the toolbox and in corners. However, having items on the floor makes keeping the area clean and neat looking very difficult.

- **Keep areas around exits and fire extinguishers clear.** Do not store or place parts, boxes, or shop equipment, such as floor jacks and testers, near exits and fire extinguishers. This helps ensure that people can have easy access to exits or the fire extinguishers in the event of an emergency.

- **Avoid spraying chemicals in the air.** To help keep the air in the shop clean, keep the use of spray chemicals, such as brake cleaner, to a minimum and avoid spraying where it could result in affecting the air others breathe.

SELF-MANAGEMENT

A professional service technician should try to maintain a professional appearance at all times. For example, if coolant or automatic transmission fluid (ATF) gets onto a shirt or pants, the wise technician would change into a clean uniform before working on another vehicle. Many shop owners and service managers recommend that shirttails always be tucked into pants to ensure a more professional appearance.

 **TECH TIP**

Write It Down

If a technician needs to have another technician finish a repair due to illness or some other reason, be sure to write down exactly what was done and what needs to be done. Verbal communication, while very effective, is often not a good way to explain multiple steps or processes. For example, the other technician could easily forget that the oil had not yet been added to the engine, which could cause a serious problem if the engine were to be started. If in doubt, write it down.

 **TECH TIP**

Don't Cover Up Mistakes

Everyone makes mistakes. While a damaged component or vehicle is never a good thing to have happen, the wise technician should notify the service manager or other person in charge as soon as a problem or accident occurs. Only then can work begin to correct the problem. If a mistake is hidden, eventually someone will learn about the error and then people will not think it was wise to ignore or to cover up the situation.

JOB EVALUATION

In most jobs, there is an evaluation of performance. A beginning technician is not expected to perform at the same level as an experienced master technician but should be able to do the following:

- **Follow instructions.** The trainee should follow the instructions of the mentor or service manager. This includes making sure that the person is notified when the job has been completed and if there were any problems.

- **Do no harm.** Avoid exerting a lot of force to door panels or other components to help avoid breaking clips or components. Always use the right tool for the job. For example, never use pliers to remove a bolt or nut, which could round off the flats of the fastener. Always think before acting, "Am I going to hurt something by doing this?"

- **Keep a neat and clean appearance.** It is normal to get dirty while performing service work on a vehicle. However, after each job is completed or even during the repair, try to keep as clean as possible.

- **Ask that your work be checked.** Even though the trainee thinks that the service or repair was done correctly, until confidence has been established, it is wise to ask to have all work double-checked.

CAUTION: Never allow a mistake to reach the customer. It is only a problem if it cannot be corrected.

FORMAL EVALUATION   The mentor and/or service manager may or may not conduct a written evaluation on a regular basis. If a written evaluation is performed, this is called a **formal evaluation.** A formal evaluation usually includes many points of discussion. See the sample evaluation form.

INFORMAL EVALUATION   In many cases, a beginning technician's activities are simply observed and noted, which is a type of **informal evaluation.** Both are usually done and both can influence the technician's pay.

NOTE: Most employees are fired from a job as the result of not being able to get along with others, rather than a lack of technical skills.

Technician Evaluation

Please check one of the spaces to the left of each characteristic which best expresses your judgment of the technician:

ATTITUDE-APPLICATION TO WORK
_____ outstanding in enthusiasm
_____ very interested and industrious
_____ average in diligence and interest
_____ somewhat indifferent
_____ definitely not interested

DEPENDABILITY
_____ completely dependable
_____ above average in dependability
_____ usually dependable
_____ sometimes neglectful or careless
_____ unreliable

QUALITY OF WORK
_____ excellent
_____ very good
_____ average
_____ below average
_____ very poor

MATURITY
_____ shows confidence
_____ has good self-assurance
_____ average maturity
_____ seldom assertive
_____ timid
_____ brash

ABILITY TO LEARN
_____ learned work exceptionally well
_____ learned work readily
_____ average in understanding work
_____ rather slow in learning
_____ very slow to learn

INITIATIVE
_____ proceeds well on his or her own
_____ proceeds independently at times
_____ does all assigned work
_____ hesitates
_____ must be pushed frequently

RELATIONS WITH OTHERS
_____ exceptionally well accepted
_____ works well with others
_____ gets along satisfactorily
_____ has difficulty working with others
_____ works very poorly with others

QUANTITY OF WORK
_____ usually high output
_____ more than average
_____ normal amount
_____ below average
_____ low output, slow

JUDGMENT
_____ exceptionally mature
_____ above average
_____ usually makes the right decision
_____ often uses poor judgment

ATTENDANCE
_____ regular
_____ irregular

PUNCTUALITY
_____ regular
_____ irregular

SUMMARY

1. Professionalism and personal credibility are important to the success of any service technician.

2. A mentor is an experienced technician who helps a beginning technician in all aspects of the trade.

3. A mentor can help a beginning service technician to not only quickly learn how to perform automotive service and repair procedures but also can provide career and personal development guidance.

4. The beginning service technician (trainee) has the responsibility to ask questions and act in a professional manner.

5. Evaluations can be formal or informal.

6. Before a technician starts to work on a vehicle, the work order should be read carefully to determine exactly what service needs to be performed.

7. If a technician is asked to talk to a customer about a repair, discuss the original problem (concern), what was found (cause), and what was done to correct the fault (correction).

8. A technician should always document the work order and follow the vehicle manufacturer's recommended procedures.

REVIEW QUESTIONS

1. What factors are part of being a professional service technician?

2. What is a mentor?

3. What are the roles of a mentor?

4. What are the responsibilities the beginning technician has to the shop and/or mentor?

5. A formal evaluation could include what items?

6. What are the three Cs?

7. What should be included on the work order after the repair has been completed?

CHAPTER QUIZ

1. Professionalism includes which factor?
  a. Keeping your word
  b. Becoming a teammate with your coworkers
  c. Apologizing if you are wrong
  d. All of the above

2. Types of communications include _____
  a. Verbal
  b. Written
  c. Nonverbal
  d. All of the above

3. The three Cs include _____
  a. Correction, correct torque, and customer name
  b. Concern, cause, and correction
  c. Cause, cost, and caller name
  d. Captured data, cause, and cost (of the repair)

4. When documenting the work order, what things should be listed?
  a. The test equipment used in the diagnosis
  b. The test procedure that was followed
  c. The parts that were replaced
  d. All of the above

5. Technician A says that customer-pay rate is sometimes higher than the factory flat-rate. Technician B says that the factory flat-rate times are usually longer (given more time) compared to aftermarket flat-rate time guides. Which technician is correct?
  a. Technician A only
  b. Technician B only
  c. Both Technicians A and B
  d. Neither Technician A nor B

6. Housekeeping duties of a technician can include_____
  a. Cleaning the floor
  b. Keeping the work area clean and organized
  c. Keeping items off the floor whenever possible
  d. All of the above

7. If running late, the wise technician should_____
  a. Call the shop and let them know you will be late
  b. Speed up
  c. Call the shop and take the day off
  d. Stop and eat a good breakfast before going to the shop

8. Flat-rate pay means_____
  a. The same pay (flat-rate) every week
  b. The same number of hours every week
  c. The technician is paid according to the job, not by the number of hours worked
  d. The technician is paid overtime

9. Customer pay (CP) means_____
  a. Customer pays for the repair or service
  b. Warranty does not pay for the repair or service
  c. The technician often gets paid more for each job
  d. All of the above

10. A mentor performs all of the following *except* _____
  a. Helps guide diagnosis of a problem
  b. Signs paychecks
  c. Offers advice on how to do a job
  d. Advises on professional behavior

chapter 5

TECHNICIAN CERTIFICATION

OBJECTIVES: **After studying Chapter 5, the reader will be able to:** • Explain the requirements for becoming an ASE certified technician. • Describe the type of test questions asked on the certification tests. • Explain how to prepare to take the ASE certification tests. • Describe test taking skills needed to help pass the certification tests. • Explain how to register and take the ASE certification tests.

KEY TERMS: • Except-type questions 42 • ASE (National Institute for Automotive service Excellence) 40 • Distracter 41 • Experience-based questions 41 • IP certification 46 • Key 41 • Least-likely-type question 42 • ASE certified master 40 • Most-likely-type question 42 • Multiple-choice question 41 • Technician A and B question 42 • Work experience 41

AUTOMOBILE TECHNICIAN CERTIFICATION TESTS

Even though individual franchises and companies often certify their own technicians, there is a nationally recognized certification organization, the **National Institute for Automotive Service Excellence,** better known by its abbreviation, **ASE.** ● **SEE FIGURE 5–1.**

ASE is a nonprofit association founded in 1972, and its main goal is to improve the quality of vehicle service through standardized testing and volunteer certification.

WHAT AREAS OF VEHICLE SERVICE ARE COVERED BY THE ASE TESTS? Automobile test service areas include:

A1 Engine Repair

A2 Automatic Transmission/Transaxle

A3 Manual Drivetrain and Axles

A4 Suspension and Steering

A5 Brakes

A6 Electrical/Electronic Systems

A7 Heating and Air Conditioning

A8 Engine Performance

If a technician takes and passes all eight of the automobile tests and has achieved two or more years of work experience, ASE will award the designation of **ASE Certified Master Automobile Technician.** Contact ASE for other certification areas.

FIGURE 5–1 The ASE logo. *(Courtesy of ASE)*

HOW CAN I CONTACT ASE?

ASE

101 Blue Seal Drive, SE

Suite 101

Leesburg, VA 20175

Toll-free: 1-800-390-6789

1-703-669-6600

website: www.ase.com

WHEN ARE THE TESTS GIVEN AND WHERE?

The ASE written tests are given at hundreds of test sites throughout the year for online testing.

NOTE: ASE offers tests at various times of the year electronically. Go to the ASE website for details.

Consult the ASE registration booklet or website for details and locations of the test sites.

WHAT DO I HAVE TO DO TO REGISTER?

You can register for the ASE tests in three ways:

1. Mail in the registration form that is in the registration booklet.
2. Register online at www.ase.com
3. Telephone at (866) 427-3273

Call ASE toll-free at 1-888-ASE-TEST or visit the website for details about cost and dates.

HOW MANY YEARS OF WORK EXPERIENCE ARE NEEDED?

ASE requires that you have two or more years of full-time, hands-on **working experience** either as an automobile, truck, truck equipment, or school bus technician, engine machinist, or in collision repair, refinishing, or damage analysis and estimating for certification, except as noted below. If you have *not* previously provided work experience information, you will receive a Work Experience Report Form with your admission ticket. You *must* complete and return this form to receive a certificate.

SUBSTITUTIONS FOR WORK EXPERIENCE. You may receive credit for up to one year of the two-year work experience requirement by substituting relevant formal training in one, or a combination, of the following:

High School Training: Three full years of training, either in automobile/truck/school bus repair or in ollision repair, refinishing, or damage estimating, may be substituted for one year of work experience.

Post-High School Training: Two full years of post-high school training in a public or private trade school, technical institute, community or four-year college, or in an apprenticeship program may be counted as one year of work experience.

Short Courses: For shorter periods of post-high school training, you may substitute two months of training for one month of work experience.

You may receive full credit for the two-year work experience requirement with the following:

Completion of Apprenticeship: Satisfactory completion of either a three- or four-year bona fide apprenticeship program.

ARE THERE ANY HANDS-ON ACTIVITIES ON THE ASE TEST?

No. All ASE tests are written using objective-type questions, meaning that you must select the correct answer from four possible alternatives.

WHO WRITES THE ASE QUESTIONS?

All ASE test questions are written by a panel of industry experts, educators, and experienced ASE certified service technicians. Each question is reviewed by the committee and it is checked for the following:

- **Technically accurate.** All test questions use the correct terms and only test for vehicle manufacturer's recommended service procedures. Slang is not used nor are any aftermarket accessories included on the ASE test.
- **Manufacturer neutral.** All efforts are made to avoid using vehicle or procedures that are manufacturer specific such as to General Motors vehicles or to Toyotas. A service technician should feel comfortable about being able to answer the questions regardless of the type or brand of vehicle.
- **Logical answers.** All effort is made to be sure that all answers (not just the correct answers) are possible. While this may seem to make the test tricky, it is designed to test for real knowledge of the subject.
- **Random answer.** All efforts are made to be sure that the correct answers are not always the longest answer or that one letter, such as **c,** is not used more than any other letter.
- **Experience-based questions.** The questions asked are generally not knowledge-based questions, but rather require experience to answer correctly. Specifications are not asked for, but instead a question as to what would most likely occur if the unit is out-of-specifications could be asked.

KEY AND DISTRACTER

The **key** is the correct answer. As part of the test writing sessions, the committee is asked to create other answers that sound feasible but are not correct. These incorrect answers are called **distracters.**

WHAT TYPES OF QUESTIONS ARE ASKED ON THE ASE TEST?

All ASE test questions are objective. This means that there will not be questions where you will have to write an answer. Instead, all you have to do is select one of the four possible answers and place a mark in the correct place on the score sheet.

- **Multiple-choice questions.** This type of question has one correct (or mostly correct) answer (called the key) and three incorrect answers. A multiple-choice question example:

What part of an automotive engine does not move?

a. Piston
b. Connecting rod
c. Block
d. Valve

The correct answer is **c** (block). This type of question asks for a specific answer. Answer **a** (piston), **b** (connecting rod), and **d** (valve) all move during normal engine operation. The best answer is **c** (block) because even though it may vibrate, it does not move as the other parts do.

- **Technician A and Technician B questions.** This type of question is generally considered to be the most difficult according to service technicians who take the ASE test. A situation or condition is usually stated and two technicians (A and B) say what they think could be the correct answer and you must decide which technician is correct.

  a. Technician A only
  b. Technician B only
  c. Both Technicians A and B
  d. Neither Technician A nor B

The best way to answer this type of question is to carefully read the question and consider Technician A and Technician B answers to be solutions to a true or false question. If Technician A is correct, mark on the test by Technician A the letter T for true. If Technician B is also correct, write the letter T for true by Technician B. Then mark **c** on your test score sheet, for both technicians are correct.

Example:

Two technicians are discussing an engine that has lower than specified fuel pressure. Technician A says that the fuel pump could be the cause. Technician B says that the fuel pressure regulator could be the cause.

　　Which technician is correct?

a. Technician A only
b. Technician B only
c. Both Technicians A and B
d. Neither Technician A nor B

Analysis:

Is Technician A correct? The answer is yes because if the fuel pump was defective, the pump pressure could be lower than specified by the vehicle manufacturer. Is Technician B correct? The answer is yes because a stuck open regulator with a weak spring could be the cause of lower than specified fuel pressure. The correct answer is therefore **c** (Both Technicians A and B are correct).

- **Most-likely-type questions.** This type of question asks which of the four possible items listed is the most likely to cause the problem or symptom. This type of question is often considered to be difficult because recent experience may lead you to answer the question incorrectly because even though it is possible, it is not the "most likely."

Example:

Which of the items below is the most likely to cause blue exhaust at engine start?

a. Valve stem seals
b. Piston rings
c. Clogged PCV valve
d. A stuck oil pump regulator valve

Analysis:

The correct answer is **a** because valve stem seals are the most likely to cause this problem. Answer **b** is not correct because even though worn piston rings can cause the engine to burn oil and produce blue exhaust smoke, it is not the most likely cause of blue smoke at engine start. Answers **c** and **d** are not correct because even though these items could contribute to the engine burning oil and producing blue exhaust smoke, they are not the most likely.

- **Except-type questions.** ASE will sometimes use a question that includes answers that are all correct except one. You have to determine which of the four answers is not correct.

Example:

A radiator is being pressure tested using a hand-operated tester. This test will check for leaks in all except:

a. Radiator
b. Heater core
c. Water pump
d. Evaporator

Analysis:

The correct answer is **d** because the evaporator is not included in the cooling system and will not be pressurized during this test. Answers **a** (radiator), **b** (heater core), and **c** (water pump) are all being tested under pressure exerted on the cooling system by the pressure tester.

- **Least-likely-type questions.** Another type of question asked on many ASE tests is a question that asks which of the following is least likely to be the cause of a problem or symptom. In other words, all of the answers are possible, but it is up to the reader to determine which answer is the least likely to be correct.

Example:

Which of the following is the least likely cause of low oil pressure?

a. Clogged oil pump screen
b. Worn main bearing
c. Worn camshaft bearing
d. Worn oil pump

Analysis:

The correct answer is **c** because even though worn camshaft bearings can cause low oil pressure, the other answers are more likely to be the cause.

QUESTIONS OFTEN ASKED

SHOULD I GUESS IF I DON'T KNOW THE ANSWER?
Yes. ASE tests simply record the correct answers, and by guessing, you will have at least a 25% (1 out of 4) chance. If you leave the answer blank, it will be scored as being incorrect. Instead of guessing entirely, try to eliminate as many of the answers as possible as not being very likely. If you can eliminate two out of the four, you have increased your chance of guessing to 50% (two out of four).

IS EACH TEST THE SAME EVERY TIME I TAKE IT?
No. ASE writes many questions for each area and selects from this "test bank" for each test session. You may

see some of the same questions if you take the same test in the spring and then again in the fall, but you will also see many different questions.

CAN I SKIP QUESTIONS I DON'T KNOW AND COME BACK TO ANSWER LATER?
Yes. You may skip a question if you wish, but be sure to mark the question and return to answer the question later. It is often recommended to answer the question or guess and go on with the test so that you do not run out of time to go back over the questions.

HOW MUCH TIME DO I HAVE TO TAKE THE TESTS?
Each computer-based test will allow enough time for completion, usually between one and two hours for each test. The time allowed for each test is available on the ASE website.

WILL I HAVE TO KNOW SPECIFICATIONS AND GAUGE READINGS?
Yes and no. You will be asked the correct range for a particular component or operation and you must know about what the specification should be. Otherwise, the questions will state that the value is less than or greater than the allowable specification. The question will deal with how the service technician should proceed or what action should be taken.

CAN I TAKE A BREAK DURING THE TEST?
Yes, you may use the restroom after receiving permission from the proctor of the test site.

CAN I LEAVE EARLY IF I HAVE COMPLETED THE TEST(S)?
Yes, you may leave quietly after you have completed the test(s).

HOW ARE THE TESTS SCORED?
The ASE tests are machine scored and the results tabulated by American College Testing (ACT).

WHAT PERCENTAGE DO I NEED TO ACHIEVE TO PASS THE ASE TEST?
While there is no exact number of questions that must be answered correctly in each area, an analysis of the test results indicate that the percentage needed to pass varies from 61% to 69%. Therefore, in order to pass the Engine Repair (A1) ASE certification test, you will have to answer about 39 questions correct out of 60. In other words, you can miss about 21 questions and still pass.

WHAT HAPPENS IF I DO NOT PASS? DO I HAVE TO WAIT A YEAR BEFORE TRYING AGAIN?
No. If you fail to achieve a passing score on any ASE test, you can take the test again at the next testing session.

DO I HAVE TO PAY ANOTHER REGISTRATION FEE IF I ALREADY PAID IT ONCE?
Yes. The registration fee is due at every test session whether you select to take one or more ASE tests. Therefore, it is wise to take as many tests as you can at each test session.

WILL I RECEIVE NOTICE OF WHICH QUESTIONS I MISSED?
ASE sends out a summary of your test results, which shows how many questions you missed in each category, but not individual questions.

WILL ASE SEND ME THE CORRECT ANSWERS TO THE QUESTIONS I MISSED SO I WILL KNOW HOW TO ANSWER THEM IN THE FUTURE?
No. ASE will not send you the answers to test questions.

TEST-TAKING TIPS

START NOW Even if you have been working on vehicles for a long time, taking an ASE certification test can be difficult. The questions will not include how things work or other "textbook" knowledge. The questions are based on "real-world" diagnosis and service. The tests may seem tricky to some because the wrong answers are designed to be similar to the correct answer.

If this is your first time taking the test or you are going to recertify, start now to prepare. Allocate time each day to study.

PRACTICE IS IMPORTANT Many service technicians do not like taking tests. As a result, many technicians rush through the test to get the pain over with quickly. Also, many service technicians have lots of experience on many different vehicles. This is what makes them good at what they do, but when an everyday problem is put into a question format (multiple choice), the answer may not be as clear as your experience has taught you.

KEYS TO SUCCESS

The keys to successful test taking include:

- Practice answering similar-type questions.
- Carefully read each question two times to make sure you understand the question.
- Read each answer.
- Pick the best answer.
- Avoid reading too much into each question.
- Do not change an answer unless you are sure that the answer is definitely wrong.
- Look over the glossary of automotive terms for words that are not familiar to you.

The best preparation is practice, practice, and more practice. This is where using the ASE Test Prep practice tests can help.

PREPARE MENTALLY

Practicing also helps relieve another potential problem many people have called "chronic test syndrome." This condition is basically an inability to concentrate or focus during a test. The slightest noise, fear of failure, and worries about other things all contribute. The best medicine is practice, practice, and more practice. With practice, test taking becomes almost second nature.

PREPARE PHYSICALLY

Be prepared physically. Get enough sleep and eat right.

ONE MONTH BEFORE THE TEST

- Budget your time for studying. On average you will need four to six hours of study for each test that you are taking.
- Use the ASE Test Prep Online test preparation service three or more times a week for your practice.
- Study with a friend or a group if possible.

THE WEEK BEFORE THE TEST

- Studying should consist of about two hours of reviewing for each test being taken.
- Make sure you know how to get to the testing center. If possible, drive to the test site and locate the room.
- Get plenty of rest.

THE DAY OF THE TEST

- Study time is over.
- Keep your work schedule light or get the day off if possible.
- Eat a small, light meal the evening of the test.
- Drink a large glass of water one to two hours before the test. (The brain and body work on electrical impulses, and water is used as a conductor.)
- Arrive at least 30 minutes early at the test center. Be ready to start on time.

WHAT TO BRING TO THE TEST

- A photo ID.
- Your Entry Ticket that came with your ASE packet.

DURING THE TEST

- BREATHE (oxygen is the most important nutrient for the brain).
- Read every question TWICE.
- Read ALL the ANSWERS.
- If you have trouble with a question, leave it blank and continue. At the end of the test, go back and try any skipped questions. (Frequently, you will get a hint in another question that follows.)

There are eight automotive certifications including:

1. **Engine Repair (A1) ASE Task List**

Content Area	Questions in Test	Percentage of Test
A. General Engine Diagnosis	15	28%
B. Cylinder Head and Valve Train Diagnosis and Repair	10	23%
C. Engine Block Diagnosis and Repair	10	23%
D. Lubrication and Cooling Systems Diagnosis and Repair	8	14%
E. Fuel, Electrical, Ignition, and Exhaust Systems Inspection and Service	7	12%
Total	**50**	**100%**

2. **Automatic Transmission/Transaxles (A2) ASE Task List**

Content Area	Questions in Test	Percentage of Test
A. General Transmission/Transaxle Diagnosis **1.** Mechanical/Hydraulic Systems (11) **2.** Electronic Systems (14)	25	50%
B. In-Vehicle Transmission/Transaxle Repair	12	16%
C. Off-Vehicle Transmission/Transaxle Repair **1.** Removal, Disassembly, and Assembly (3) **2.** Gear Train, Shafts, Bushings, Oil Pump, and Case (4) **3.** Friction and Reaction Units (4)	13	26%
Total	**50**	**100%**

3. Manual Drivetrain and Axles (A3) ASE Task List

Content Area	Questions in Test	Percentage of Test
A. Clutch Diagnosis and Repair	6	15%
B. Transmission Diagnosis and Repair	7	18%
C. Transaxle Diagnosis and Repair	7	20%
D. Drive (Half) Shaft and Universal Joint/Constant Velocity (CV) Joint Diagnosis and Repair (Front- and Rear-wheel Drive)	5	13%
E. Rear Axle Diagnosis and Repair 1. Ring and Pinion Gears (3) 2. Differential Case Assembly (2) 3. Limited Slip Differential (1) 4. Axle Shafts (1)	7	17%
F. Four-Wheel Drive Component Diagnosis and Repair	8	17%
Total	**40**	**100%**

4. Suspension and Steering (A4) ASE Task List

Content Area	Questions in Test	Percentage of Test
A. Steering Systems Diagnosis and Repair 1. Steering Columns and Manual Steering Gears (3) 2. Power-Assisted Steering Units (4) 3. Steering Linkage (3)	10	25%
B. Suspension Systems Diagnosis and Repair 1. Front Suspensions (6) 2. Rear Suspensions (5) 3. Miscellaneous Service (2)	11	28%
C. Related Suspension and Steering Service	2	5%
D. Wheel Alignment Diagnosis, Adjustment, and Repair	12	30%
E. Wheel and Tire Diagnosis and Repair	5	12%
Total	**40**	**100%**

5. Brakes (A5) ASE Task List

Content Area	Questions in Test	Percentage of Test
A. Hydraulic Systems Diagnosis and Repair 1. Master Cylinders (non-ABS) (3) 2. Fluids, Lines, and Hoses (3) 3. Valves and Switches (non-ABS) (4) 4. Bleeding, Flushing, and Leak Testing (non-ABS) (4)	12	27%
B. Drum Brake Diagnosis and Repair	5	11%
C. Disc Brake Diagnosis and Repair	10	22%
D. Power Assist Units Diagnosis and Repair	4	8%
E. Miscellaneous Diagnosis and Repair	7	16%
F. Antilock Brake System Diagnosis and Repair	7	16%
Total	**45**	**100%**

6. Electrical Systems (A6) ASE Task List

Content Area	Questions in Test	Percentage of Test
A. General Electrical/Electronic System Diagnosis	13	26%
B. Battery Diagnosis and Service	4	8%
C. Starting System Diagnosis and Repair	5	10%
D. Charging System Diagnosis and Repair	5	10%
E. Lighting Systems Diagnosis and Repair 1. Headlights, Parking Lights, Taillights, Dash Lights, and Courtesy Lights (3) 2. Stoplights, Turn Signals, Hazard Lights, and Back-up Lights (3)	6	12%
F. Gauges, Warning Devices, and Driver Information Systems Diagnosis and Repair	6	12%
G. Horn and Wiper/Washer Diagnosis and Repair	3	6%
H. Accessories Diagnosis and Repair 1. Body (4) 2. Miscellaneous (4)	8	16%
Total	**50**	**100%**

7. Heating and Air Conditioning (A7) ASE Task List

Content Area	Questions in Test	Percentage of Test
A. A/C System Diagnosis and Repair	13	24%
B. Refrigeration System Component Diagnosis and Repair 1. Compressor and Clutch (5) 2. Evaporator, Condenser, and Related Components (5)	10	20%
C. Heating and Engine Cooling Systems Diagnosis and Repair	4	10%
D. Operating Systems and Related Controls Diagnosis and Repair 1. Electrical (9) 2. Vacuum/Mechanical (3) 3. Automatic and Semi-Automatic Heating, Ventilating, and A/C Systems (5)	19	34%
E. Refrigerant Recover, Recycling, and Handling	4	12%
Total	**50**	**100%**

8. Engine Performance (A8) ASE Task List

Content Area	Questions in Test	Percentage of Test
A. General Engine Diagnosis	12	17%
B. Ignition System Diagnosis and Repair	8	17%
C. Fuel, Air Induction, and Exhaust Systems Diagnosis and Repair	9	18%
D. Emissions Control Systems Diagnosis and Repair 1. Positive Crankcase Ventilation (1) 2. Exhaust Gas Recirculation (3) 3. Secondary Air Injector (AIR) and Catalytic Converter (2) 4. Evaporative Emissions Controls (3)	8	15%
E. Computerized Engine Controls Diagnosis and Repair (Including OBD II)	13	27%
Total	**50**	**100%**

To become certified by ASE, the service technician must have two years of experience and pass a test in each area. If a technician passes all eight automotive certification tests, then the technician is considered a master certified automobile service technician.

CANADA'S AUTOMOTIVE APPRENTICESHIP PROGRAM (RED SEAL)

In Canada, in all provinces and territories but Quebec and British Columbia, an **Inter-Provincial (IP) Certificate** is required. An apprenticeship program is in place that takes a minimum of four years, combining ten months in a shop and about two months in school training in each of the four years. Most apprentices must undergo 7200 hours of training before they can complete the IP examination. ASE certifications are currently used on a voluntary basis since 1993, however an IP Certificate is still required. Other licensing of automotive technicians may be required in some cases, such as environmental substances, liquefied petroleum gas, or steam operators.

NOTE: A valid driver's license is a must for any automotive service technician.

RE CERTIFICATION

All ASE certifications expire after five years and the technician needs to take a recertification test to remain certified. As vehicles and technology change, it is important that all technicians attend update classes. Most experts recommend that each technician should have at least 40 hours (one full week) of update training every year. Update training classes can be found through many sources, including:

1. Many parts stores and warehouse distributors provide training classes throughout the year.

2. State or regional associations, such as the Automotive Service Association (www.asashop.org), offer update conferences.

3. Local colleges or training companies offer update training. Other training can be found listed on the International Automotive Technicians Network (www.iatn.net).

SUMMARY

1. ASE is an abbreviation for the National Institute for Automotive Service Excellence, a nonprofit association founded in 1972.

2. The eight ASE test content areas include: A1—Engine Repair, A2—Automatic Transmission, A3—Manual Drivetrain and Axles, A4—Suspension and Steering, A5—Brakes, A6— electrical/ Electronic Systems, A7—Heating and Air Conditioning, and A8—Engine Performance.

3. To become an ASE certified technician, two years of experience are required plus achieving a passing test score on one or more ASE certification tests.

4. The types of questions used on an ASE certification test include: multiple-choice questions, Technician A and Technician B questions, most-likely-type questions, except-type questions, and least-likely-type questions.

REVIEW QUESTIONS

1. What are the eight ASE test areas?
2. When are the written ASE tests given?
3. What types of questions are asked on the ASE certification tests?
4. What can a technician do to help prepare to take the certification tests?

CHAPTER QUIZ

1. Which ASE certification test would cover experience in lighting system diagnosis?
   a. A6
   b. A7
   c. A8
   d. All of the above are possible

2. How many ASE tests must be passed to become a master automotive technician?
   a. 8
   b. 6
   c. 4
   d. 2

3. How many years of experience are required to achieve ASE certification?
   a. 8
   b. 6
   c. 4
   d. 2

4. Credit for how many years of work experience can be substituted by attending automotive service training?
   a. None —no substitution for work experience is permitted
   b. 1 year
   c. 2 years
   d. 3 years

5. When taking an ASE certification test, _____.
   a. You can take a break after receiving permission
   b. The correct answers will be shown after you finish
   c. Only one test can be taken
   d. Some hands-on activities may be required

6. A type of test question *not* asked on the ASE certification test is_____.
   a. Most likely
   b. Least likely
   c. Fill in the blank
   d. Multiple choice

7. Which type of question is the same as two true-and-false-type questions?
   a. All except type
   b. Technician A and Technician B
   c. Least likely type
   d. Most likely type

8. Technician A says that you should guess if you do not know the correct answer. Technician B says that ASE will send you the correct answers to the questions you missed with your test results. Which technician is correct?
   a. Technician A only
   b. Technician B only
   c. Both Technicians A and B
   d. Neither Technician A nor B

9. ASE tests require knowledge of vehicle specifications for spark plug gap.
   a. True
   b. False

10. A technician should do all of the following to prepare to take the ASE certification test *except* _____.
    a. Get a good night's sleep the night before the test
    b. Try to keep work schedule light the day of the test
    c. Eat a big meal
    d. Have photo ID and entry ticket

OBJECTIVES: **After studying Chapter 6, the reader should be able to:** • Identify situations where hearing protection should be worn. • Discuss how to safely handle tools and shop equipment. • Describe how to properly use a fire extinguisher. • Discuss shop safety procedures.

KEY TERMS: • ANSI 48 • Bump cap 49 • Decibel (dB) 49 • Eye wash station 54 • Fire blankets 53 • Microbes 51 • "PASS" 52 • Personal protective equipment (PPE) 48 • Spontaneous combustion 50

PERSONAL PROTECTIVE EQUIPMENT

Safety is not just a buzzword on a poster in the work area. Safe work habits can reduce accidents and injuries, ease the workload, and keep employees pain free.

SAFETY GLASSES The most important **personal protective equipment (PPE)** a technician should wear all the time are safety glasses, which meet standard **ANSI** Z87.1. ● **SEE FIGURE 6–1**.

STEEL-TOED SHOES Steel-toed safety shoes are also a good investment. ● **SEE FIGURE 6–2**. If safety shoes are not available, then leather-topped shoes offer more protection than canvas or cloth covered shoes.

GLOVES Wear gloves to protect your hands from rough or sharp surfaces. Thin rubber gloves are recommended when working around automotive liquids such as engine oil, antifreeze,

transmission fluid, or any other liquids that may be hazardous. Several types of gloves and their characteristics include:

- **Latex surgical gloves.** These gloves are relatively inexpensive, but tend to stretch, swell, and weaken when exposed to gas, oil, or solvents.
- **Vinyl gloves.** These gloves are also inexpensive and are not affected by gas, oil, or solvents. ● **SEE FIGURE 6–3**.
- **Polyurethane gloves.** These gloves are more expensive, yet very strong. Even though these gloves are also not affected by gas, oil, or solvents, they tend to be slippery.
- **Nitrile gloves.** These gloves are exactly like latex gloves, but are not affected by gas, oil, or solvents, yet they tend to be expensive.
- **Mechanic's gloves.** These gloves are usually made of synthetic leather and spandex and provide thermo protection, as well as protection from dirt and grime.

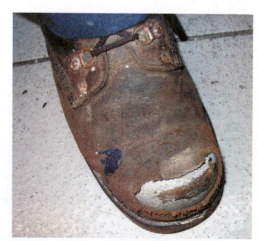

FIGURE 6–2 Steel-toed shoes are a worthwhile investment to help prevent foot injury due to falling objects. Even these well-worn shoes can protect the feet of this service technician.

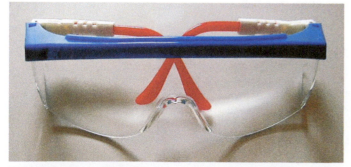

FIGURE 6–1 Safety glasses should be worn at all times when working on or around any vehicle or servicing any component.

FIGURE 6–3 Protective gloves such as these vinyl gloves are available in several sizes. Select the size that allows the gloves to fit snugly. Vinyl gloves last a long time and often can be worn all day to help protect your hands from dirt and possible hazardous materials.

FIGURE 6–4 One version of a bump cap is this padded plastic insert that is worn inside a regular cloth cap.

BUMP CAP Service technicians working under a vehicle should wear a **bump cap** to protect the head against under-vehicle objects and the pads of the hoist. ● SEE FIGURE 6–4.

HANDS, JEWELRY, AND CLOTHING Remove jewelry that may get caught on something or act as a conductor to an exposed electrical circuit. ● SEE FIGURE 6–5.

Take care of your hands. Keep your hands clean by washing with soap and hot water that is at least 110°F (43°C). Avoid loose or dangling clothing. Also, ear protection should be worn if the sound around you requires that you raise your voice (sound level higher than 90 **decibels [dB]**).

NOTE: A typical lawnmower produces noise at a level of about 110 dB. This means that everyone who uses a lawnmower or other lawn or garden equipment should wear ear protection.

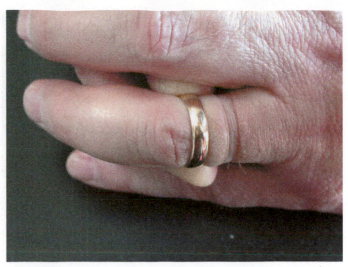

FIGURE 6–5 Remove all jewelry before performing service work on any vehicle.

TECH TIP

Professional Behavior in the Shop Is a Must

To be respected as a professional service techni-cian and for safety, always behave in a professional manner. These behaviors include, but are not limited to the following:

- Show respect to other technicians and employees. For example, the shop owner or service manager may not always be right, but they are always the boss.
- Avoid horseplay or practical jokes.
- Act as if a customer is observing your behavior at all times because this is often the case.

SAFETY TIPS FOR TECHNICIANS

- When lifting any object, get a secure grip with solid footing. Keep the load close to your body to minimize the strain. Lift with your legs and arms, not your back.
- Do not twist your body when carrying a load. Instead, pivot your feet to help prevent strain on the spine.
- Ask for help when moving or lifting heavy objects.
- Push a heavy object rather than pull it. (This is oppo-site to the way you should work with tools—never push a wrench! If you do and a bolt or nut loosens,

FIGURE 6–6 Always connect an exhaust hose to the tailpipe of the engine of a vehicle to be run inside a building.

FIGURE 6–7 A magnetic tray is a helpful item to keep tools needed up where they can be easily reached without having to bend over saving time and energy over the course of a long day in the shop.

your entire weight is used to propel your hand(s) forward. This usually results in cuts, bruises, or other painful injury.)

- Always connect an exhaust hose to the tailpipe of any running vehicle to help prevent the buildup of carbon monoxide inside a closed garage space. ● SEE FIGURE 6–6.

- When standing, keep objects, parts, and tools with which you are working between chest height and waist height. If seated, work at tasks that are at elbow height. ● SEE FIGURE 6–7.

- Always be sure the hood is securely held open.

- Ask for help when pushing a vehicle or use a motorized pusher. ● SEE FIGURE 6–8.

FIGURE 6–8 An electric pusher used to push vehicles into or around the shop.

+ SAFETY TIP

Shop Cloth Disposal

Always dispose of oily shop cloths in an enclosed container to prevent a fire. ● SEE FIGURE 6–9. Whenever oily cloths are thrown together on the floor or workbench, a chemical reaction can occur which can ignite the cloth even without an open flame. This process of ignition without an open flame is called **spontaneous combustion.**

FIGURE 6–9 All oily shop cloths should be stored in a metal container equipped with a lid to help prevent spontaneous combustion.

Pound with Something Softer

If you must pound on something, be sure to use a tool that is softer than what you are about to pound on to avoid damage. Examples are given in the following table.

The Material Being Pounded	What to Pound With
Steel or cast iron	Brass or aluminum hammer or punch
Aluminum	Plastic or rawhide mallet or plastic-covered dead-blow hammer
Plastic	Rawhide mallet or plastic dead-blow hammer

CLEANING METHODS AND PROCESSES

There are four basic types of cleaning methods and processes used in vehicle service.

POWER WASHING   Power washing uses an electric- or gasoline-powered compressor to increase the pressure of water and force it out of a nozzle. The pressure of the water itself is usually enough to remove dirt, grease, and grime from vehicle components. Sometimes a chemical cleaner, such as a detergent, is added to the water to help with cleaning.

SAFE USE OF POWER WASHERS.   Because water is being sprayed at high pressure, a face shield should be worn when using a power washer to protect not only the eyes but also the face in the event of the spray being splashed back toward the technician. Also use a pressure washer in an area where the runoff from the cleaning will not contaminate local groundwater or cause harm to plants or animals.

CHEMICAL/MICROBE CLEANING   Chemical cleaning involves one of several cleaning solutions, including detergent, solvents, or small, living microorganisms called **microbes** that eat oil and grease. The microbes live in water and eat the hydrocarbons that are the basis of grease and oil.

SAFE USE OF CHEMICAL CLEANING.   A face shield should be worn when cleaning parts using a chemical cleaner. Avoid spilling the cleaner on the floor to help prevent slipping accidents. Clean and replace the chemical cleaner regularly.

ABRASIVE CLEANING   Abrasive cleaning is used to clean disassembled parts, such as engine blocks. The abrasives used include steel shot, ground walnut shells, or in the case of cleaning paint from a vehicle body, baking soda can be used.

SAFE USE OF ABRASIVE CLEANERS.   Always wear a protective face shield and protective clothing, including gloves, long sleeves, and long pants.

THERMAL OVENS   Thermal cleaning uses heat to bake off grease and dirt with special high-temperature ovens. This method of cleaning requires the use of expensive equipment but does not use any hazardous chemicals and is environmentally safe.

SAFE USE OF THERMAL OVENS.   Because thermal ovens operate at high temperatures, often exceeding 600°F (315°C), the oven should be turned off and allowed to cool overnight before removing the parts from the oven to avoid being exposed to the high temperature.

ELECTRICAL CORD SAFETY

Use correctly grounded three-prong sockets and extension cords to operate power tools. Some tools use only two-prong plugs. Make sure these are double insulated and repair or replace any electrical cords that are cut or damaged to prevent the possibility of an electrical shock. When not in use, keep electrical cords off the floor to prevent tripping over them. Tape the cords down if they are placed in high foot traffic areas.

JUMP-STARTING AND BATTERY SAFETY

To jump-start another vehicle with a dead battery, connect good-quality copper jumper cables as indicated in ● **FIGURE 6–10** or use a jump box. The last connection made should always be on the engine block or an engine bracket as far from the battery as possible. It is normal for a spark to be created when the jumper cables finally complete the jumper cable connections, and this spark could cause an explosion of the gases around the battery. Many newer vehicles have special ground connections built away from the battery just for the purpose of jump-starting. Check the owner manual or service information for the exact location.

SAFETY TIP

Compressed Air Safety

Improper use of an air nozzle can cause blindness or deafness. Compressed air must be reduced to less than 30 PSI (206 kPa). ● **SEE FIGURE 6–11.** If an air nozzle is used to dry and clean parts, make sure the air stream is directed away from anyone else in the immediate area. Always use an OSHA-approved nozzle with side slits that limit the maximum pressure at the nozzle to 30 PSI. Coil and store air hoses when they are not in use.

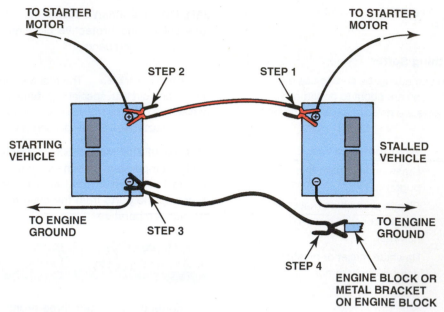

FIGURE 6–10 Jumper cable usage guide.

FIGURE 6–11 The air pressure going to the nozzle should be reduced to 30 PSI or less.

FIGURE 6–12 A typical fire extinguisher designed to be used on type class A, B, or C fires.

Batteries contain acid and should be handled with care to avoid tipping them greater than a 45-degree angle. Always remove jewelry when working around a battery to avoid the possibility of electrical shock or burns, which can occur when the metal comes in contact with a 12 volt circuit and ground, such as the body of the vehicle.

FIRE EXTINGUISHERS

There are four classes of fire extinguishers. Each class should be used on specific fires only.

- *Class A* is designed for use on general combustibles, such as cloth, paper, and wood.

- *Class B* is designed for use on flammable liquids and greases, including gasoline, oil, thinners, and solvents.

- *Class C* is used only on electrical fires.

- *Class D* is effective only on combustible metals such as powdered aluminum, sodium, or magnesium.

The class rating is clearly marked on the side of every fire extinguisher. Many extinguishers are good for multiple types of fires. ● SEE FIGURE 6–12.

When using a fire extinguisher, remember the word **"PASS."**

P = Pull the safety pin.

A = Aim the nozzle of the extinguisher at the base of the fire.

S = Squeeze the lever to actuate the extinguisher.

S = Sweep the nozzle from side to side.

● SEE FIGURE 6–13.

FIGURE 6–13 A CO_2 fire extinguisher being used on a fire set in an open steel drum during a demonstration at a fire department training center.

FIGURE 6–14 A treated wool blanket is kept in this easy-to-open wall-mounted holder and should be placed in a centralized location in the shop.

TYPES OF FIRE EXTINGUISHERS Types of fire extinguishers include the following:

- **Water.** A water fire extinguisher, usually in a pressurized container, is good to use on Class A fires by reducing the temperature to the point where a fire cannot be sustained.
- **Carbon dioxide (CO_2).** A carbon dioxide fire extinguisher is good for almost any type of fire, especially Class B or Class C materials. A CO_2 fire extinguisher works by removing the oxygen from the fire and the cold CO_2 also helps reduce the temperature of the fire.
- **Dry chemical (yellow).** A dry chemical fire extinguisher is good for Class A, B, or C fires by coating the flammable materials, which eliminates the oxygen from the fire. A dry chemical fire extinguisher tends to be very corrosive and will cause damage to electronic devices.

FIRE BLANKETS

Fire blankets are required to be available in the shop areas. If a person is on fire, a fire blanket should be removed from its storage bag and thrown over and around the victim to smother the fire. ● **SEE FIGURE 6–14** showing a typical fire blanket.

FIRST AID AND EYE WASH STATIONS

All shop areas must be equipped with a first aid kit and an eye wash station centrally located and kept stocked with emergency supplies.

FIGURE 6–15 A first aid box should be centrally located in the shop and kept stocked with the recommended supplies.

FIRST AID KIT A first aid kit should include:

- Bandages (variety)
- Gauze pads
- Roll gauze
- Iodine swab sticks
- Antibiotic ointment
- Hydrocortisone cream
- Burn gel packets
- Eye wash solution
- Scissors
- Tweezers
- Gloves
- First aid guide

● **SEE FIGURE 6–15.** Every shop should have a person trained in first aid. If there is an accident, call for help immediately.

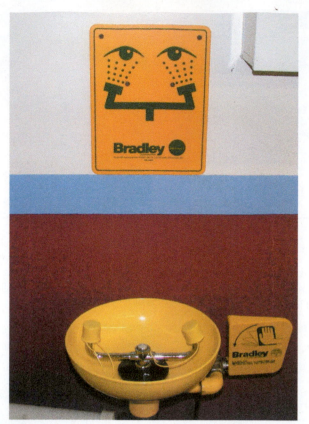

FIGURE 6–16 A typical eye wash station. Often a thorough flushing of the eyes with water is the best treatment in the event of eye contamination.

EYE WASH STATION An **eye wash station** should be centrally located and used whenever any liquid or chemical gets into the eyes. If such an emergency does occur, keep eyes in a constant stream of water and call for professional assistance. ● **SEE FIGURE 6–16**.

FIGURE 6–17 This area has been blocked off to help keep visitors from the dangerous work area.

🔧 **TECH TIP**

Mark Off the Service Area

Some shops rope off the service bay area to help keep traffic and distractions to a minimum, which could prevent personal injury. ● **SEE FIGURE 6–17**.

SUMMARY

1. All service technicians should wear safety glasses that meet standard ANSI Z87.1.

2. Ear protection should be worn anytime the noise level is at 90 decibels (dB) or higher.

3. Safety should be exercised when working with electrical cords or when jump-starting another vehicle.

4. If a fire extinguisher is needed, remember: Pull the safety pin, aim the nozzle, squeeze the lever, and sweep the nozzle from side-to-side.

REVIEW QUESTIONS

1. List four items that are personal protective equipment (PPE).

2. What are the types of fire extinguishers and their usage?

3. What items are included in a typical first aid box?

CHAPTER QUIZ

1. What do you call the service technician's protective head cover?
   - **a.** Cap
   - **b.** Hat
   - **c.** Bump cap
   - **d.** Helmet

2. All safety glasses should meet the standards set by _____.
   - **a.** ANSI
   - **b.** SAE
   - **c.** ASE
   - **d.** DOT

3. When washing hands, the water should be at what temperature?
   - **a.** 98°F (37°C)
   - **b.** 110°F (43°C)
   - **c.** 125°F (52°C)
   - **d.** 135°F (57°C)

4. Hearing protection should be worn anytime the noise level exceeds _____.
   - **a.** 60 dB
   - **b.** 70 dB
   - **c.** 80 dB
   - **d.** 90 dB

5. Two technicians are discussing the safe use of a wrench. Technician A says that a wrench should be pulled toward you. Technician B says that a wrench should be pushed away from you. Which technician is correct?
   - **a.** Technician A only
   - **b.** Technician B only
   - **c.** Both Technicians A and B
   - **d.** Neither Technician A nor B

6. Exhaust hoses should be used because one of the exhaust gases is deadly in high concentration. This gas is _____.
   - **a.** Carbon monoxide (CO)
   - **b.** Carbon dioxide (CO_2)
   - **c.** Hydrocarbons (HC)
   - **d.** Oxides of nitrogen (NO_X)

7. The process of combustion occurring without an open flame is called _____.
   - **a.** Direct ignition
   - **b.** Non-open flame combustion
   - **c.** Spontaneous combustion
   - **d.** Cold fusion

8. When using a fire extinguisher, what word can be used to remember what to do?
   - **a.** PASS
   - **b.** FIRE
   - **c.** RED
   - **d.** LEVER

9. Which type of fire extinguisher can create a corrosive compound when discharged?
   - **a.** CO_2
   - **b.** Dry chemical
   - **c.** Water
   - **d.** CO

10. Which item is usually *not* included in a first aid kit?
    - **a.** Eye wash solution
    - **b.** Antibiotic cream
    - **c.** Fire blanket
    - **d.** Bandages

chapter
7

ENVIRONMENTAL AND HAZARDOUS MATERIALS

OBJECTIVES: **After studying Chapter 7, the reader should be able to:** • Prepare for the ASE assumed knowledge content required by all service technicians to adhere to environmentally appropriate actions and behavior. • Define the Occupational Safety and Health Act (OSHA). • Explain what is contained in the material safety data sheet (MSDS). • Identify hazardous waste materials in accordance with state and federal regulations and follow proper safety precautions while handling hazardous waste materials. • Define the steps required to safely handle and store automotive chemicals and waste.

KEYTERMS: • Aboveground storage tank (AGST) 59 • Asbestosis 58 • BCI 62 • CAA 57 • CFR 56 • EPA 56 • Hazardous waste material 56 • HEPA vacuum 58 • Mercury 64 • MSDS 57 • OSHA 56 • RCRA 57 • Right-to-know laws 57 • Solvent 58 • Underground storage tank (UST) 59 • Used oil 59 • WHMIS 57

HAZARDOUS WASTE

DEFINITION OF HAZARDOUS WASTE **Hazardous waste materials** are chemicals, or components, that the shop no longer needs that pose a danger to the environment and people if they are disposed of in ordinary garbage cans or sewers. However, no material is considered hazardous waste until the shop has finished using it and is ready to dispose of it.

PERSONAL PROTECTIVE EQUIPMENT (PPE) When handling hazardous waste material, one must always wear the proper protective clothing and equipment detailed in the right-to-know laws. This includes respirator equipment. All recommended procedures must be followed accurately. Personal injury may result from improper clothing, equipment, and procedures when handling hazardous materials.

FEDERAL AND STATE LAWS

OCCUPATIONAL SAFETY AND HEALTH ACT The United States Congress passed the **Occupational Safety and Health Act (OSHA)** in 1970. This legislation was designed to assist and encourage the citizens of the United States in their efforts to assure:

- Safe and healthful working conditions by providing research, information, education, and training in the field of occupational safety and health.

- Safe and healthful working conditions for working men and women by authorizing enforcement of the standards developed under the Act.

Because about 25% of workers are exposed to health and safety hazards on the job, the OSHA standards are necessary to monitor, control, and educate workers regarding health and safety in the workplace.

EPA The **Environmental Protection Agency (EPA)** publishes a list of hazardous materials that is included in the **Code of Federal Regulations (CFR)**. The EPA considers waste hazardous if it is included on the EPA list of hazardous materials, or it has one or more of the following characteristics:

- **Reactive.** Any material that reacts violently with water or other chemicals is considered hazardous.

- **Corrosive.** If a material burns the skin, or dissolves metals and other materials, a technician should consider it hazardous. A pH scale is used, with the number 7 indicating neutral. Pure water has a pH of 7. Lower numbers indicate an acidic solution and higher numbers indicate a caustic solution. If a material releases cyanide gas, hydrogen sulfide gas, or similar gases when exposed to low pH acid solutions, it is considered hazardous.

 WARNING

Hazardous waste disposal laws include serious penalties for anyone responsible for breaking these laws.

- **Toxic.** Materials are hazardous if they leak one or more of eight different heavy metals in concentrations greater than 100 times the primary drinking water standard.
- **Ignitable.** A liquid is hazardous if it has a flash point below 140°F (60°C), and a solid is hazardous if it ignites spontaneously.
- **Radioactive.** Any substance that emits measurable levels of radiation is radioactive. When individuals bring containers of a highly radioactive substance into the shop environment, qualified personnel with the appropriate equipment must test them.

RIGHT-TO-KNOW LAWS   The **right-to-know laws** state that employees have a right to know when the materials they use at work are hazardous. The right-to-know laws started with the Hazard Communication Standard published by OSHA in 1983. Originally, this document was intended for chemical companies and manufacturers that required employees to handle hazardous materials in their work situation but the federal courts have decided to apply these laws to all companies, including automotive service shops. Under the right-to-know laws, the employer has responsibilities regarding the handling of hazardous materials by their employees. All employees must be trained about the types of hazardous materials they will encounter in the workplace. The employees must be informed about their rights under legislation regarding the handling of hazardous materials.

MATERIAL SAFETY DATA SHEETS (MSDS).   All hazardous materials must be properly labeled, and information about each hazardous material must be posted on **material safety data sheets (MSDS)** available from the manufacturer. In Canada, MSDS information is called **Workplace Hazardous Materials Information Systems (WHMIS).**

The employer has a responsibility to place MSDS information where they are easily accessible by all employees. The MSDS information provide the following information about the hazardous material: chemical name, physical characteristics, protective handling equipment, explosion/fire hazards, incompatible materials, health hazards, medical conditions aggravated by exposure, emergency and first aid procedures, safe handling, and spill/leak procedures.

The employer also has a responsibility to make sure that all hazardous materials are properly labeled. The label information must include health, fire, and reactivity hazards posed by the material, as well as the protective equipment necessary to handle the material. The manufacturer must supply all warning and precautionary information about hazardous materials. This information must be read and understood by the employee before handling the material. ● **SEE FIGURE 7–1.**

RESOURCE CONSERVATION AND RECOVERY ACT (RCRA)   Federal and state laws control the disposal of hazardous waste materials and every shop employee must be familiar with these laws. Hazardous waste disposal laws include the **Resource Conservation and Recovery Act (RCRA).** This law states that hazardous material users are responsible for hazardous materials from the time they become

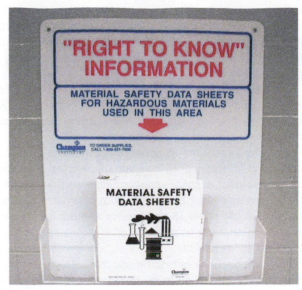

FIGURE 7–1 Material safety data sheets (MSDS) should be readily available for use by anyone in the area who may come into contact with hazardous materials.

a waste until the proper waste disposal is completed. Many shops hire an independent hazardous waste hauler to dispose of hazardous waste material. The shop owner, or manager, should have a written contract with the hazardous waste hauler. Rather than have hazardous waste material hauled to an approved hazardous waste disposal site, a shop may choose to recycle the material in the shop. Therefore, the user must store hazardous waste material properly and safely, and be responsible for the transportation of this material until it arrives at an approved hazardous waste disposal site, where it can be processed according to the law. The RCRA controls the following types of automotive waste:

- Paint and body repair products waste
- Solvents for parts and equipment cleaning
- Batteries and battery acid
- Mild acids used for metal cleaning and preparation
- Waste oil, and engine coolants or antifreeze
- Air conditioning refrigerants and oils
- Engine oil filters

CLEAN AIR ACT   Air conditioning (A/C) systems and refrigerants are regulated by the **Clean Air Act (CAA),** Title VI, Section 609. Technician certification and service equipment is also regulated. Any technician working on automotive air conditioning systems must be certified. Air conditioning refrigerants must not be released or vented into the atmosphere, and used refrigerants must be recovered.

ASBESTOS HAZARDS

Friction materials such as brake and clutch linings often contain asbestos. While asbestos has been eliminated from most original equipment friction materials, the automotive service technician cannot know whether the vehicle being serviced is or is not equipped with friction materials containing asbestos. It is important that all friction materials be handled as if they do contain asbestos.

Asbestos exposure can cause scar tissue to form in the lungs. This condition is called **asbestosis.** It gradually causes increasing shortness of breath, and the scarring to the lungs is permanent.

Even low exposures to asbestos can cause *mesothelioma*, a type of fatal cancer of the lining of the chest or abdominal cavity. Asbestos exposure can also increase the risk of *lung cancer* as well as cancer of the voice box, stomach, and large intestine. It usually takes 15 to 30 years or more for cancer or asbestos lung scarring to show up after exposure. Scientists call this the *latency period*.

Government agencies recommend that asbestos exposure be eliminated or controlled to the lowest level possible. These agencies have developed recommendations and standards that the automotive service technician and equipment manufacturer should follow. These U.S. federal agencies include the National Institute for Occupational Safety and Health (NIOSH), Occupational Safety and Health Administration (OSHA), and Environmental Protection Agency (EPA).

ASBESTOS OSHA STANDARDS
The Occupational Safety and Health Administration (OSHA) has established three levels of asbestos exposure. Any vehicle service establishment that does either brake or clutch work must limit employee exposure to asbestos to less than 0.2 fibers per cubic centimeter (cc) as determined by an air sample.

If the level of exposure to employees is greater than specified, corrective measures must be performed and a large fine may be imposed.

NOTE: Research has found that worn asbestos fibers such as those from automotive brakes or clutches may not be as hazardous as first believed. Worn asbestos fibers do not have sharp flared ends that can latch onto tissue, but rather are worn down to a dust form that resembles talc. Grinding or sawing operations on unworn brake shoes or clutch discs *will* contain *harmful* asbestos fibers. To limit health damage, always use proper handling procedures while working around any component that may contain asbestos.

ASBESTOS EPA REGULATIONS
The federal Environmental Protection Agency (EPA) has established procedures for the removal and disposal of asbestos. The EPA procedures require that products containing asbestos be "wetted" to prevent the asbestos fibers from becoming airborne. According to the EPA, asbestos-containing materials can be disposed of as regular waste. Only when asbestos becomes airborne is it considered to be hazardous.

ASBESTOS HANDLING GUIDELINES
The air in the shop area can be tested by a testing laboratory, but this can

FIGURE 7–2 All brakes should be moistened with water or solvent to help prevent brake dust from becoming airborne.

be expensive. Tests have determined that asbestos levels can easily be kept below the recommended levels by using a liquid, like water, or a special vacuum.

NOTE: The service technician cannot tell whether the old brake pads, shoes, or clutch discs contain asbestos. Therefore, to be safe, the technician should assume that all brake pads, shoes, or clutch discs contain asbestos.

HEPA VACUUM. A special **high-efficiency particulate air (HEPA) vacuum** system has been proven to be effective in keeping asbestos exposure levels below 0.1 fibers per cubic centimeter.

SOLVENT SPRAY. Many technicians use an aerosol can of brake cleaning solvent to wet the brake dust and prevent it from becoming airborne. A **solvent** is a liquid that is used to dissolve dirt, grime, or solid particles. Commercial brake cleaners are available that use a concentrated cleaner that is mixed with water. ● **SEE FIGURE 7–2.** The waste liquid is filtered, and when dry, the filter can be disposed of as solid waste.

DISPOSAL OF BRAKE DUST AND BRAKE SHOE. The hazard of asbestos occurs when asbestos fibers are airborne. Once the asbestos has been wetted down, it is then considered to be solid waste, rather than hazardous waste. Old brake shoes and pads should be enclosed, preferably in a plastic bag, to help prevent any of the brake material from becoming airborne. *Always follow current federal and local laws concerning disposal of all waste.*

 WARNING

Never use compressed air to blow brake dust. The fine talclike brake dust can create a health hazard even if asbestos is not present or is present in dust rather than fiber form.

USED BRAKE FLUID

Most brake fluid is made from polyglycol, is water soluble, and can be considered hazardous if it has absorbed metals from the brake system.

STORAGE AND DISPOSAL OF BRAKE FLUID

- Collect brake fluid in a container clearly marked to indicate that it is designated for that purpose.
- If the waste brake fluid is hazardous, be sure to manage it appropriately and use only an authorized waste receiver for its disposal.
- If the waste brake fluid is nonhazardous (such as old, but unused), determine from your local solid waste collection provider what should be done for its proper disposal.
- Do not mix brake fluid with used engine oil.
- Do not pour brake fluid down drains or onto the ground.
- Recycle brake fluid through a registered recycler.

USED OIL

Used oil is any petroleum-based or synthetic oil that has been used. During normal use, impurities such as dirt, metal scrapings, water, or chemicals can get mixed in with the oil. Eventually, this used oil must be replaced with virgin or re-refined oil. The EPA's used oil management standards include a three-pronged approach to determine if a substance meets the definition of *used oil*. To meet the EPA's definition of used oil, a substance must meet each of the following three criteria.

- **Origin.** The first criterion for identifying used oil is based on the oil's origin. Used oil must have been refined from crude oil or made from synthetic materials. Animal and vegetable oils are excluded from the EPA's definition of used oil.
- **Use.** The second criterion is based on whether and how the oil is used. Oils used as lubricants, hydraulic fluids, heat transfer fluids, and for other similar purposes are considered used oil. The EPA's definition also excludes products used as cleaning agents, as well as certain petroleum-derived products like antifreeze and kerosene.
- **Contaminants.** The third criterion is based on whether the oil is contaminated with either physical or chemical impurities. In other words, to meet the EPA's definition, used oil must become contaminated as a result of being used. This aspect of the EPA's definition includes residues and contaminants generated from handling, storing, and processing used oil.

NOTE: The release of only 1 gallon of used oil (a typical oil change) can make 1 million gallons of fresh water undrinkable.

If used oil is dumped down the drain and enters a sewage treatment plant, concentrations as small as 50 to 100 parts per million (ppm) in the wastewater can foul sewage treatment processes. Never mix a listed hazardous waste, gasoline, wastewater, halogenated solvent, antifreeze, or an unknown waste material with used oil. Adding any of these substances will cause the used oil to become contaminated, which classifies it as hazardous waste.

STORAGE AND DISPOSAL OF USED OIL   Once oil has been used, it can be collected, recycled, and used over and over again. An estimated 380 million gallons of used oil are recycled each year. Recycled used oil can sometimes be used again for the same job or can take on a completely different task. For example, used engine oil can be re-refined and sold at some discount stores as engine oil or processed for furnace fuel oil. After collecting used oil in an appropriate container such as a 55 gallon steel drum, the material must be disposed of in one of two ways.

- Shipped offsite for recycling
- Burned in an onsite or offsite EPA-approved heater for energy recovery

Used oil must be stored in compliance with an existing **underground storage tank (UST)** or an **aboveground storage tank (AGST)** standard, or kept in separate containers. ● **SEE FIGURE 7–3.** Containers are portable receptacles, such as a 55 gallon steel drum.

KEEP USED OIL STORAGE DRUMS IN GOOD CONDITION.   This means that they should be covered, secured from vandals, properly labeled, and maintained in compliance with local fire codes. Frequent inspections for leaks, corrosion, and spillage are an essential part of container maintenance.

NEVER STORE USED OIL IN ANYTHING OTHER THAN TANKS AND STORAGE CONTAINERS.   Used oil may also be stored in units that are permitted to store regulated hazardous waste.

FIGURE 7–3 A typical aboveground oil storage tank.

USED OIL FILTER DISPOSAL REGULATIONS. Used oil filters contain used engine oil that may be hazardous. Before an oil filter is placed into the trash or sent to be recycled, it must be drained using one of the following hot-draining methods approved by the EPA.

- Puncture the filter antidrainback valve or filter dome end and hot drain for at least 12 hours
- Hot draining and crushing
- Dismantling and hot draining
- Any other hot-draining method, which will remove all the used oil from the filter

After the oil has been drained from the oil filter, the filter housing can be disposed of in any of the following ways.

- Sent for recycling
- Picked up by a service contract company
- Disposed of in regular trash

SOLVENTS

The major sources of chemical danger are liquid and aerosol brake cleaning fluids that contain chlorinated hydrocarbon solvents. Several other chemicals that do not deplete the ozone, such as heptane, hexane, and xylene, are now being used in nonchlorinated brake cleaning solvents. Some manufacturers are also producing solvents they describe as environmentally responsible, which are biodegradable and noncarcinogenic (not cancer causing).

There is no specific standard for physical contact with chlorinated hydrocarbon solvents or the chemicals replacing them. All contact should be avoided whenever possible. The law requires an employer to provide appropriate protective equipment and ensure proper work practices by an employee handling these chemicals.

EFFECTS OF CHEMICAL POISONING The effects of exposure to chlorinated hydrocarbon and other types of solvents can take many forms. Short-term exposure at low levels can cause symptoms such as:

- Headache
- Nausea

FIGURE 7–4 Washing hands and removing jewelry are two important safety habits all service technicians should practice.

- Drowsiness
- Dizziness
- Lack of coordination
- Unconsciousness

It may also cause irritation of the eyes, nose, and throat, and flushing of the face and neck. Short-term exposure to higher concentrations can cause liver damage with symptoms such as yellow jaundice or dark urine. Liver damage may not become evident until several weeks after the exposure.

HAZARDOUS SOLVENTS AND REGULATORY STATUS Most solvents are classified as hazardous wastes. Other characteristics of solvents include the following:

- Solvents with flash points below 140°F (60°C) are considered flammable and, like gasoline, are federally regulated by the Department of Transportation (DOT).
- Solvents and oils with flash points above 60°C are considered combustible and, like engine oil, are also regulated by the DOT. All flammable items must be stored in a fireproof container. ● **SEE FIGURE 7–5.**

 FREQUENTLY ASKED QUESTION

How Can You Tell If a Solvent Is Hazardous?
If a solvent or any of the ingredients of a product contains "fluor" or "chlor" then it is likely to be hazardous. Check the instructions on the label for proper use and disposal procedures.

It is the responsibility of the repair shop to determine if its spent solvent is hazardous waste. Solvent reclaimers are available that clean and restore the solvent so it lasts indefinitely.

 **SAFETY TIP**

Hand Safety
Service technicians should wash their hands with soap and water after handling engine oil, differential oil, or transmission fluids or wear protective rubber gloves. Another safety hint is that the service technician should not wear watches, rings, or other jewelry that could come in contact with electrical or moving parts of a vehicle. ● **SEE FIGURE 7–4.**

FIGURE 7–5 Typical fireproof flammable storage cabinet.

FIGURE 7–6 Using a water-based cleaning system helps reduce the hazards from using strong chemicals.

USED SOLVENTS Used or spent solvents are liquid materials that have been generated as waste and may contain xylene, methanol, ethyl ether, and methyl isobutyl ketone (MIBK). These materials must be stored in OSHA-approved safety containers with the lids or caps closed tightly. Additional requirements include the following:

- Containers should be clearly labeled "Hazardous Waste" and the date the material was first placed into the storage receptacle should be noted.

- Labeling is not required for solvents being used in a parts washer.

- Used solvents will not be counted toward a facility's monthly output of hazardous waste if the vendor under contract removes the material.

- Used solvents may be disposed of by recycling with a local vendor, such as SafetyKleen®, to have the used solvent removed according to specific terms in the vendor agreement.

- Use aqueous-based (nonsolvent) cleaning systems to help avoid the problems associated with chemical solvents. ● SEE FIGURE 7–6.

FIGURE 7–7 Used antifreeze coolant should be kept separate and stored in a leakproof container until it can be recycled or disposed of according to federal, state, and local laws. Note that the storage barrel is placed inside another container to catch any coolant that may spill out of the inside barrel.

COOLANT DISPOSAL

Coolant is a mixture of antifreeze and water. New antifreeze is not considered to be hazardous even though it can cause death if ingested. Used antifreeze may be hazardous due to dissolved metals from the engine and other components of the cooling system. These metals can include iron, steel, aluminum, copper, brass, and lead (from older radiators and

heater cores). Coolant should be disposed of in one of the following ways:

- Coolant should be recycled either onsite or offsite.

- Used coolant should be stored in a sealed and labeled container. ● SEE FIGURE 7–7.

- Used coolant can often be disposed of into municipal sewers with a permit. Check with local authorities and obtain a permit before discharging used coolant into sanitary sewers.

LEAD-ACID BATTERY WASTE

About 70 million spent lead-acid batteries are generated each year in the United States alone. Lead is classified as a toxic metal and the acid used in lead-acid batteries is highly corrosive. The vast majority (95% to 98%) of these batteries are recycled through lead reclamation operations and secondary lead smelters for use in the manufacture of new batteries.

BATTERY DISPOSAL   Used lead-acid batteries must be reclaimed or recycled in order to be exempt from hazardous waste regulations. Leaking batteries must be stored and transported as hazardous waste. Some states have more strict regulations, which require special handling procedures and transportation. According to the **Battery Council International (BCI),** battery laws usually include the following rules.

1. Lead-acid battery disposal is prohibited in landfills or incinerators. Batteries are required to be delivered to a battery retailer, wholesaler, recycling center, or lead smelter.

2. All retailers of automotive batteries are required to post a sign that displays the universal recycling symbol and indicates the retailer's specific requirements for accepting used batteries.

3. Battery electrolyte contains sulfuric acid, which is a very corrosive substance capable of causing serious personal injury, such as skin burns and eye damage. In addition, the battery plates contain lead, which is highly poisonous. For this reason, disposing of batteries improperly can cause environmental contamination and lead to severe health problems.

BATTERY HANDLING AND STORAGE   Batteries, whether new or used, should be kept indoors if possible. The storage location should be an area specifically designated for battery storage and must be well ventilated (to the outside). If outdoor storage is the only alternative, a sheltered and secured area with acid-resistant secondary containment is strongly recommended. It is also advisable that acid-resistant secondary containment be used for indoor storage. In addition, batteries should be placed on acid-resistant pallets and never stacked.

FUEL SAFETY AND STORAGE

Gasoline is a very explosive liquid. The expanding vapors that come from gasoline are extremely dangerous. These vapors are present even in cold temperatures. Vapors formed in gasoline

tanks on many vehicles are controlled, but vapors from gasoline storage may escape from the can, resulting in a hazardous situation. Therefore, place gasoline storage containers in a well-ventilated space. Although diesel fuel is not as volatile as gasoline, the same basic rules apply to diesel fuel and gasoline storage. These rules include the following:

1. Use storage cans that have a flash-arresting screen at the outlet. These screens prevent external ignition sources from igniting the gasoline within the can when someone pours the gasoline or diesel fuel.

2. Use only a red approved gasoline container to allow for proper hazardous substance identification. ● **SEE FIGURE 7–8.**

3. Do not fill gasoline containers completely full. Always leave the level of gasoline at least 1 in. from the top of the container. This action allows expansion of the gasoline at higher temperatures. If gasoline containers are completely full, the gasoline will expand when the temperature increases. This expansion forces gasoline from the can and creates a dangerous spill. If gasoline or diesel fuel containers must be stored, place them in a designated storage locker or facility.

4. Never leave gasoline containers open, except while filling or pouring gasoline from the container.

5. Never use gasoline as a cleaning agent.

FIGURE 7–8 This red gasoline container holds about 30 gallons of gasoline and is used to fill vehicles used for training.

6. Always connect a ground strap to containers when filling or transferring fuel or other flammable products from one container to another to prevent static electricity that could result in explosion and fire. These ground wires prevent the buildup of a static electric charge, which could result in a spark and disastrous explosion.

AIRBAG HANDLING

Airbag modules are pyrotechnic devices that can be ignited if exposed to an electrical charge or if the body of the vehicle is subjected to a shock. Airbag safety should include the following precautions.

1. Disarm the airbag(s) if you will be working in the area where a discharged bag could make contact with any part of your body. Consult service information for the exact procedure to follow for the vehicle being serviced.

2. If disposing of an airbag, the usual procedure is to deploy the airbag using a 12 volt power supply, such as a jump-start box, using long wires to connect to the module to ensure a safe deployment.

3. Do not expose an airbag to extreme heat or fire.

4. Always carry an airbag pointing away from your body.

5. Place an airbag module facing upward.

6. Always follow the manufacturer's recommended procedure for airbag disposal or recycling, including the proper packaging to use during shipment.

7. Wear protective gloves if handling a deployed airbag.

8. Always wash your hands or body well if exposed to a deployed airbag. The chemicals involved can cause skin irritation and possible rash development.

USED TIRE DISPOSAL

Used tires are an environmental concern because of several reasons, including the following:

1. In a landfill, they tend to "float" up through the other trash and rise to the surface.

2. The inside of tires traps and holds rainwater, which is a breeding ground for mosquitoes. Mosquito-borne diseases include encephalitis, malaria and dengue fever.

3. Used tires present a fire hazard and, when burned, create a large amount of black smoke that contaminates the air.

Used tires should be disposed of in one of the following ways.

1. Used tires can be reused until the end of their useful life.

2. Tires can be retreaded.

3. Tires can be recycled or shredded for use in asphalt.

4. Derimmed tires can be sent to a landfill (most landfill operators will shred the tires because it is illegal in many states to landfill whole tires).

5. Tires can be burned in cement kilns or other power plants where the smoke can be controlled.

6. A registered scrap tire handler should be used to transport tires for disposal or recycling.

AIR CONDITIONING REFRIGERANT OIL DISPOSAL

Air conditioning refrigerant oil contains dissolved refrigerant and is therefore considered to be hazardous waste. This oil must be kept separated from other waste oil or the entire amount of oil must be treated as hazardous. Used refrigerant oil must be sent to a licensed hazardous waste disposal company for recycling or disposal. ● **SEE FIGURE 7–9**.

WASTE CHART All automotive service facilities create some waste and while most of it is handled properly, it is important that all hazardous and nonhazardous waste be accounted for and properly disposed. ● **SEE CHART 7–1** for a list of typical wastes generated at automotive shops, plus a checklist for keeping track of how these wastes are handled.

FIGURE 7–9 Air conditioning refrigerant oil must be kept separated from other oils because it contains traces of refrigerant and must be treated as hazardous waste.

WASTE STREAM	TYPICAL CATEGORY IF NOT MIXED WITH OTHER HAZARDOUS WASTE	IF DISPOSED IN LANDFILL AND NOT MIXED WITH A HAZARDOUS WASTE	IF RECYCLED
Used oil	Used oil	Hazardous waste	Used oil
Used oil filters	Nonhazardous solid waste, if completely drained	Nonhazardous solid waste, if completely drained	Used oil, if not drained
Used transmission fluid	Used oil	Hazardous waste	Used oil
Used brake fluid	Used oil	Hazardous waste	Used oil
Used antifreeze	Depends on characterization	Depends on characterization	Depends on characterization
Used solvents	Hazardous waste	Hazardous waste	Hazardous waste
Used citric solvents	Nonhazardous solid waste	Nonhazardous solid waste	Hazardous waste
Lead-acid automotive batteries	Not a solid waste if returned to supplier	Hazardous waste	Hazardous waste
Shop rags used for oil	Used oil	Depends on used oil characterization	Used oil
Shop rags used for solvent or gasoline spills	Hazardous waste	Hazardous waste	Hazardous waste
Oil spill absorbent material	Used oil	Depends on used oil characterization	Used oil
Spill material for solvent and gasoline	Hazardous waste	Hazardous waste	Hazardous waste
Catalytic converter	Not a solid waste if returned to supplier	Nonhazardous solid waste	Nonhazardous solid waste
Spilled or unused fuels	Hazardous waste	Hazardous waste	Hazardous waste
Spilled or unusable paints and thinners	Hazardous waste	Hazardous waste	Hazardous waste
Used tires	Nonhazardous solid waste	Nonhazardous solid waste	Nonhazardous solid waste

CHART 7–1

Typical wastes generated at auto repair shops and typical category (hazardous or nonhazardous) by disposal method.

 **TECH TIP**

Remove Components That Contain Mercury

Some vehicles have a placard near the driver's side door that lists the components that contain the heavy metal, mercury. **Mercury** can be absorbed through the skin and is a heavy metal that once absorbed by the body does not leave. ● **SEE FIGURE 7–10**.

These components should be removed from the vehicle before the rest of the body is sent to be recycled to help prevent releasing mercury into the environment.

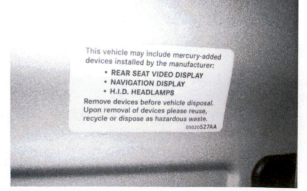

FIGURE 7–10 Placard near driver's door, including what devices in the vehicle contain mercury.

Hazardous Materials Identification Guide (HMIG)

TYPE HAZARD		DEGREE	
○	HEALTH	4 - Extreme	
○	FLAMMABILITY	3 - Serious	
○	REACTIVITY	2 - Moderate	
○	PROTECTIVE EQUIPMENT	1 - Slight	
		0 - Minimal	

HAZARD RATING AND PROTECTIVE EQUIPMENT

Health		Flammable		Reactive	
Type of Possible Injury		**Susceptibility of materials to burn**		**Susceptibility of materials to release energy**	
4	Highly Toxic. May be fatal on short-term exposure. Special protective equipment required.	4	Extremely flammable gas or liquid. Flash Point below 73°F.	4	Extreme. Explosive at room temperature.
3	Toxic. Avoid inhalation or skin contact.	3	Flammable. Flash Point 73°F to 100°F.	3	Serious. May explode if shocked, heated under confinement or mixed w/ water.
2	Moderately Toxic. May be harmful if inhaled or absorbed.	2	Combustible. Requires moderate heating to ignite. Flash Point 100°F to 200°F.	2	Moderate. Unstable, may react with water.
1	Slightly Toxic. May cause slight irritation.	1	Slightly Combustible. Requires strong heating to ignite.	1	Slight. May react if heated or mixed with water.
0	Minimal. All chemicals have a slight degree of toxicity.	0	Minimal. Will not burn under normal conditions.	0	Minimal. Normally stable, does not react with water.

Protective Equipment

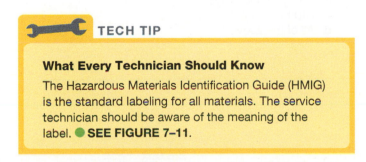

A	Safety Glasses	E	Safety Glasses + Gloves + Dust Respirator	I	Safety Glasses + Gloves + Combination Dust & Vapor Respirator
B	Safety Glasses + Gloves	F	Safety Glasses + Gloves + Apron + Dust Respirator	J	Chemical Goggles + Gloves + Apron + Combination Dust & Vapor Respirator
C	Safety Glasses + Gloves + Apron	G	Safety Glasses + Gloves + Vapor Respirator	K	Apron + Gloves + Full Protection Suit + Boots
D	Faceshield + Gloves + Apron	H	Chemical Goggles + Gloves + Apron + Vapor Respirator	X	Ask your supervisor for guidance.

FIGURE 7–11 The Environmental Protection Agency (EPA) Hazardous Materials Identification Guide is a standardized listing of the hazards and the protective equipment needed.

🔧 **TECH TIP**

What Every Technician Should Know

The Hazardous Materials Identification Guide (HMIG) is the standard labeling for all materials. The service technician should be aware of the meaning of the label. ● **SEE FIGURE 7–11.**

SUMMARY

1. Hazardous materials include common automotive chemicals, liquids, and lubricants, especially those whose ingredients contain *chlor* or *fluor* in their name.

2. Right-to-know laws require that all workers have access to material safety data sheets (MSDS).

3. Asbestos fibers should be avoided and removed according to current laws and regulations.

4. Used engine oil contains metals worn from parts and should be handled and disposed of properly.

5. Solvents represent a serious health risk and should be avoided as much as possible.

6. Coolant should be disposed of properly or recycled.

7. Batteries are considered to be hazardous waste and should be discarded to a recycling facility.

REVIEW QUESTIONS

1. List five common automotive chemicals or products that may be considered hazardous materials.

2. The Resource Conservation and Recovery Act (RCRA) controls what types of automotive waste?

CHAPTER QUIZ

1. Hazardous materials include all of the following *except* _____.
   - a. Engine oil
   - b. Asbestos
   - c. Water
   - d. Brake cleaner

2. To determine if a product or substance being used is hazardous, consult _____.
   - a. A dictionary
   - b. An MSDS
   - c. SAE standards
   - d. EPA guidelines

3. Exposure to asbestos dust can cause what condition?
   - a. Asbestosis
   - b. Mesothelioma
   - c. Lung cancer
   - d. All of the above

4. Wetted asbestos dust is considered to be _____.
   - a. Solid waste
   - b. Hazardous waste
   - c. Toxic
   - d. Poisonous

5. An oil filter should be hot drained for how long before disposing of the filter?
   - a. 30 to 60 minutes
   - b. 4 hours
   - c. 8 hours
   - d. 12 hours

6. Used engine oil should be disposed of by all *except* the following methods.
   - a. Disposed of in regular trash
   - b. Shipped offsite for recycling
   - c. Burned onsite in a waste oil-approved heater
   - d. Burned offsite in a waste oil-approved heater

7. All of the following are the proper ways to dispose of a *drained* oil filter *except* _____.
   - a. Sent for recycling
   - b. Picked up by a service contract company
   - c. Disposed of in regular trash
   - d. Considered to be hazardous waste and disposed of accordingly

8. Which act or organization regulates air conditioning refrigerant?
   - a. Clean Air Act (CAA)
   - b. MSDS
   - c. WHMIS
   - d. Code of Federal Regulations (CFR)

9. Gasoline should be stored in approved containers that include what color(s)?
   - a. A red container with yellow lettering
   - b. A red container
   - c. A yellow container
   - d. A yellow container with red lettering

10. What automotive devices may contain mercury?
    - a. Rear seat video displays
    - b. Navigation displays
    - c. HID headlights
    - d. All of the above

FASTENERS AND THREAD REPAIR

OBJECTIVES: After studying Chapter 8, the reader should be able to: • Explain the terms used to identify bolts and other threaded fasteners. • Explain the strength ratings of threaded fasteners. • Describe the proper use of nonthreaded fasteners. • Discuss how snap rings are used. • Discuss thread repair procedures • Describe use of nuts, washers and clips.

KEY TERMS: • Bolts 67 • Cap screws 67 • Capillary action 75 • Christmas tree clips 73 • Cotter pins 73 • Crest 67 • Die 70 • Grade 68 • Helical insert 75 • Heli-Coil® 75 • Jam nut 74 • Metric bolts 68 • Pal nut 74 • Penetrating oil 75 • Pitch 67 • Pop rivet 74 • Prevailing torque nuts 69 • Self-tapping screw 72 • Snap ring 73 • Stud 67 • Tap 70 • Tensile strength 69 • Threaded insert 76 • UNC (Unified National Coarse) 67 • UNF (Unified National Fine) 67 • Washers 72

THREADED FASTENERS

Most of the threaded fasteners used on vehicles are cap screws. They are called **cap screws** when they are threaded into a casting. Automotive service technicians usually refer to these fasteners as **bolts**, regardless of how they are used. In this chapter, they are called bolts. Sometimes, studs are used for threaded fasteners. A **stud** is a short rod with threads on both ends. Often, a stud will have coarse threads on one end and fine threads on the other end. The end of the stud with coarse threads is screwed into the casting. A nut is used on the opposite end to hold the parts together.

The fastener threads *must* match the threads in the casting or nut. The threads may be measured either in threads per inch (called fractional) or in metric units. The size is measured across the outside of the threads, called the **crest** of the thread. ● **SEE FIGURE 8–1.**

Fractional threads are either coarse or fine. The coarse threads are called **Unified National Coarse (UNC)**, and the fine threads are called **Unified National Fine (UNF)**. Standard combinations of sizes and number of threads per inch (called **pitch**) are used. Pitch can be measured with a thread pitch gauge as shown in ● **FIGURE 8–2.**

Bolts are identified by their diameter and length as measured from below the head, and not by the size of the head or the size of the wrench used to remove or install the bolt. Bolts and screws have many different-shaped heads. ● **SEE FIGURE 8–3.**

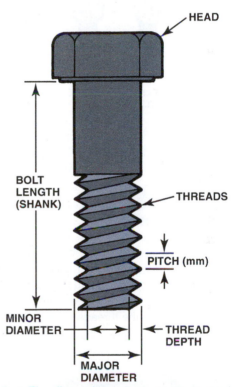

FIGURE 8–1 The dimensions of a typical bolt showing where sizes are measured. The major diameter is called the crest.

Fractional thread sizes are specified by the diameter in fractions of an inch and the number of threads per inch. Typical UNC thread sizes would be 5/16-18 and 1/2-13. Similar UNF thread sizes would be 5/16-24 and1/2-20. ● **SEE CHART 8–1.**

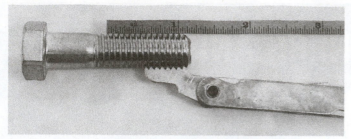

FIGURE 8–2 Thread pitch gauge used to measure the pitch of the thread. This bolt has 13 threads to the inch.

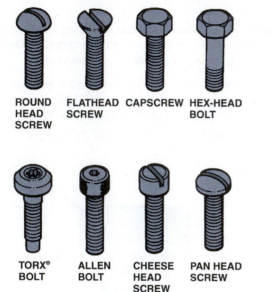

| ROUND HEAD SCREW | FLATHEAD SCREW | CAPSCREW | HEX-HEAD BOLT |

| TORX® BOLT | ALLEN BOLT | CHEESE HEAD SCREW | PAN HEAD SCREW |

FIGURE 8–3 Bolts and screws have many different heads, which determine what tool must be used.

METRIC BOLTS

The size of a **metric bolt** is specified by the letter *M* followed by the diameter in millimeters (mm) across the outside (crest) of the threads. Typical metric sizes would be M8 and M12. Metric threads are specified by the thread diameter followed by *X* and the distance between the threads measured in millimeters (M8 × 1.5). ● **SEE FIGURE 8–4.**

| | THREADS PER INCH | | OUTSIDE DIAMETER INCHES |
SIZE	NC UNC	NF UNF	
0	..	80	0.0600
1	64	..	0.0730
1	..	72	0.0730
2	56	..	0.0860
2	..	64	0.0860
3	48	..	0.0990
3	..	56	0.0990
4	40	..	0.1120
4	..	48	0.1120
5	40	..	0.1250
5	..	44	0.1250
6	32	..	0.1380
6	..	40	0.1380
8	32	..	0.1640
8	..	36	0.1640
10	24	..	0.1900
10	..	32	0.1900
12	24	..	0.2160
12	..	28	0.2160
1/4	20	..	0.2500
1/4	..	28	0.2500
5/16	18	..	0.3125
5/16	..	24	0.3125
3/8	16	..	0.3750
3/8	..	24	0.3750
7/16	14	..	0.4375
7/16	..	20	0.4375
1/2	13	..	0.5000
1/2	..	20	0.5000
9/16	12	..	0.5625
9/16	..	18	0.5625
5/8	11	..	0.6250
5/8	..	18	0.6250
3/4	10	..	0.7500
3/4	..	16	0.7500
7/8	9	..	0.8750
7/8	..	14	0.8750

CHART 8–1

The American National System is one method of sizing fasteners.

GRADES OF BOLTS

Bolts are made from many different types of steel, and for this reason some are stronger than others. The strength or classification of a bolt is called the **grade**. The bolt heads are marked to indicate their grade strength. Graded bolts are commonly used in the suspension parts of the vehicle but can be used almost anywhere in the vehicle.

The grade of fractional bolts is two more than the number of lines on the bolt head. Metric bolts have a decimal number to indicate the grade. More lines or a higher grade number indicate a stronger bolt. Higher grade bolts usually have threads that are rolled rather than cut, which also makes them stronger. ● **SEE FIGURE 8–5.** In some cases, nuts and machine screws have similar grade markings.

CAUTION: *Never* use hardware store (nongraded) bolts, studs, or nuts on any vehicle steering, suspension, or brake component. Always use the exact size and grade of hardware that is specified and used by the vehicle manufacturer.

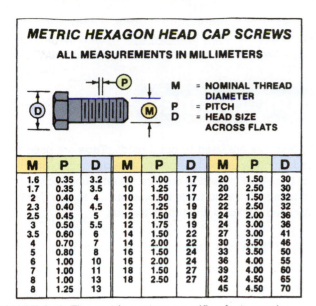

METRIC HEXAGON HEAD CAP SCREWS
ALL MEASUREMENTS IN MILLIMETERS

M = NOMINAL THREAD DIAMETER
P = PITCH
D = HEAD SIZE ACROSS FLATS

M	P	D	M	P	D	M	P	D
1.6	0.35	3.2	10	1.00	17	20	1.50	30
1.7	0.35	3.5	10	1.25	17	20	2.50	30
2	0.40	4	10	1.50	17	22	1.50	32
2.3	0.40	4.5	12	1.25	19	22	2.50	32
2.5	0.45	5	12	1.50	19	24	2.00	36
3	0.50	5.5	12	1.75	19	24	3.00	36
3.5	0.60	6	14	1.50	22	27	3.00	41
4	0.70	7	14	2.00	22	30	3.50	46
5	0.80	8	16	1.50	24	33	3.50	50
6	1.00	10	16	2.00	24	36	4.00	55
7	1.00	11	18	1.50	27	39	4.00	60
8	1.00	13	18	2.50	27	42	4.50	65
8	1.25	13				45	4.50	70

FIGURE 8–4 The metric system specifies fasteners by diameter, length, and pitch.

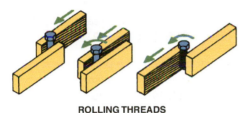

ROLLING THREADS

FIGURE 8–5 Stronger threads are created by cold-rolling a heat-treated bolt blank instead of cutting the threads using a die.

🔧 **TECH TIP**

A 1/2 In. Wrench Does Not Fit a 1/2 In. Bolt

A common mistake made by persons new to the automotive field is to think that the size of a bolt or nut is the size of the head. The size of the bolt or nut (outside diameter of the threads) is usually smaller than the size of the wrench or socket that fits the head of the bolt or nut. Examples are given in the following table.

Wrench Size	Thread Size
7/16 in.	1/4 in.
1/2 in.	5/16 in.
9/16 in.	3/8 in.
5/8 in.	7/16 in.
3/4 in.	1/2 in.
10 mm	6 mm
12 mm or 13 mm*	8 mm
14 mm or 17 mm*	10 mm

*European (Système International d'Unités-SI) metric.

HINT: An open-end wrench can be used to gauge bolt sizes. A 3/8 in. wrench will fit the threads of a 3/8 in. bolt.

4.6	8.8	9.8	10.9	METRIC CLASS
60,000	120,000	130,000	150,000	APPROXIMATE MAXIMUM POUND FORCE PER SQUARE INCH

FIGURE 8–6 Metric bolt (cap screw) grade markings and approximate tensile strength.

TENSILE STRENGTH

Graded fasteners have a higher tensile strength than nongraded fasteners. **Tensile strength** is the maximum stress used under tension (lengthwise force) without causing failure of the fastener. Tensile strength is specified in pounds per square inch (PSI). ● **SEE CHART 8–2** that shows the grade and specified tensile strength.

The strength and type of steel used in a bolt is supposed to be indicated by a raised mark on the head of the bolt. The type of mark depends on the standard to which the bolt was manufactured. Most often, bolts used in machinery are made to SAE Standard J429.

Metric bolt tensile strength property class is shown on the head of the bolt as a number, such as 4.6, 8.8, 9.8, and 10.9; the higher the number, the stronger the bolt. ● **SEE FIGURE 8–6**.

NUTS

Most nuts used on cap screws have the same hex size as the cap screw head. Some inexpensive nuts use a hex size larger than the cap screw head. Metric nuts are often marked with dimples to show their strength. More dimples indicate stronger nuts. Some nuts and cap screws use interference fit threads to keep them from accidentally loosening. This means that the shape of the nut is slightly distorted or that a section of the threads is deformed. Nuts can also be kept from loosening with a nylon washer fastened in the nut or with a nylon patch or strip on the threads. ● **SEE FIGURE 8–7**.

NOTE: Most of these "locking nuts" are grouped together and are commonly referred to as prevailing torque nuts. This means that the nut will hold its tightness or torque and not loosen with movement or vibration. Most prevailing torque nuts should be replaced whenever removed to ensure that the nut will not loosen during service. Always follow the

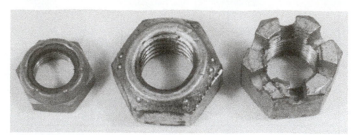

FIGURE 8–7 Types of lock nuts. On the left, a nylon ring; in the center, a distorted shape; and on the right, a castle for use with a cotter key.

SAE Bolt Designations				
SAE Grade No.	Size Range	Tensile Strength, PSI	Material	Head Marking
1	1/4 through 1-1/2	60,000	Low or medium carbon steel	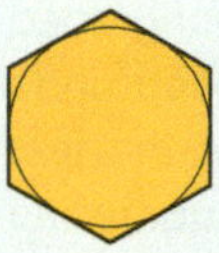
2	1/4 through 3/4 7/8 through 1-1/2	74,000 60,000		
5	1/4 through 1 1-1/8 through 1-1/2	120,000 105,000	Medium carbon steel, quenched & tempered	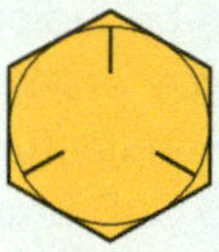
5.2	1/4 through 1	120,000	Low carbon martensite steel*, quenched & tempered	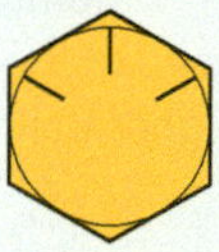
7	1/4 through 1-1/2	133,000	Medium carbon alloy steel, quenched & tempered	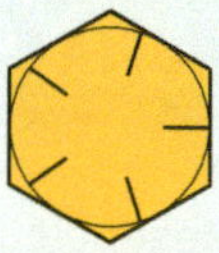
8	1/4 through 1-1/2	150,000	Medium carbon alloy steel, quenched & tempered	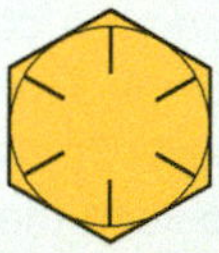
8.2	1/4 through 1	150,000	Low carbon Martensite steel*, quenched & tempered	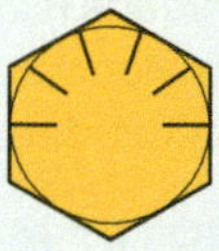

CHART 8–2

*Martensite steel is steel that has been cooled rapidly, thereby increasing its hardness. It is named after a German metallurgist, Adolf Martens.

manufacturer's recommendations. Anaerobic sealers, such as Loctite®, are used on the threads where the nut or cap screw must be both locked and sealed.

TAPS AND DIES

Taps and dies are used to cut threads. **Taps** are used to cut threads in holes drilled to an exact size depending on the size of the tap. A **die** is used to cut threads on round rods or studs. Most taps and dies come as a complete set for the most commonly used fractional and metric threads.

TAPS There are two commonly used types of taps, including:

- **Taper tap.** This is the most commonly used tap and is designed to cut threads by gradually enlarging the threaded hole.
- **Bottoming tap.** This tap has a flat bottom instead of a tapered tip to allow it to cut threads to the bottom of a drilled hole. ● **SEE FIGURE 8–8**.

All taps must be used in the proper size hole called a "tap drill size." This information is often stamped on the tap itself or in a chart that is included with a tap and die tool set. ● **SEE FIGURE 8–9**.

DIES A die is a hardened steel round cutter with teeth on the inside of the center hole. ● **SEE FIGURE 8–10**. A die is rotated using a die handle over a rod to create threads.

PROPER USE OF TAPS AND DIES Taps and dies are used to cut threads on rods in the case of a die or in a hole for a tap. A small tap can be held using a T-handle tap wrench but for larger taps a tap handle is needed to apply the needed force to cut threads. ● **SEE FIGURES 8–11A AND 8–11B**.

TAP USAGE. Be sure that the hole is the correct size for the tap and start by inserting the tap straight into the hole. Lubricate the tap using tapping lubricant. Rotate the tap about one full turn clockwise, then reverse the direction of the tap one-half turn to break the chip that was created. Repeat the procedure until the hole is completely threaded.

DIE USAGE. A die should be used on the specified diameter rod for the size of the thread. Install the die securely into the die handle. ● **SEE FIGURE 8–12**.
Lubricate the die and the rod and place the die onto the end of the rod to be threaded. Rotate the die handle one full turn clockwise, then reverse the direction and rotate the die handle about a half turn counterclockwise to break the chip that was created. Repeat the process until the threaded portion has been completed.

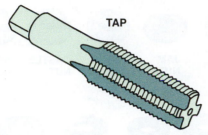

TAP

FIGURE 8–8 A typical bottoming tap used to create threads in holes that are not open, but stop in a casting, such as an engine block.

I/2-20
USA
DRILL
29/64

FIGURE 8–9 Many taps, especially larger ones, have the tap drill size printed on the top.

DIE

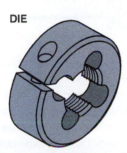

FIGURE 8–10 A die is used to cut threads on a metal rod.

THREAD PITCH GAUGE

A thread pitch gauge is a hand tool that has the outline of various thread sizes machined on stamped blades. To determine the thread pitch size of a fastener, the technician matches the thread of the thread pitch gauge to the threads of the fastener. ● **SEE FIGURE 8–13**.

**T-HANDLE
TAP WRENCH**

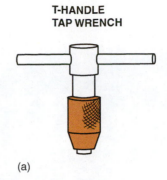

(a)

HAND TAP WRENCH

(b)

FIGURE 8–11 (a) A T-handle is used to hold and rotate small taps. (b) A tap wrench is used to hold and drive larger taps.

DIE HANDLE

FIGURE 8–12 A die handle used to rotate a die while cutting threads on a metal rod.

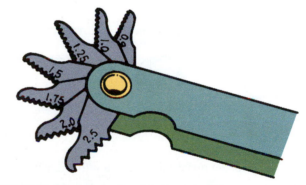

FIGURE 8–13 A typical metric thread pitch gauge.

? FREQUENTLY ASKED QUESTION

What Is the Difference Between a Tap and a Thread Chaser?

A tap is a cutting tool and is designed to cut new threads. A thread chaser has more rounded threads and is designed to clean dirty threads without removing metal. Therefore, when cleaning threads, it is best to use a thread chaser rather than a tap to prevent the possibility of removing metal, which would affect the fit of the bolt being installed. ● **SEE FIGURE 8–14.**

FIGURE 8–14 A thread chaser is shown at the top compared to a tap on the bottom. A thread chaser is used to clean threads without removing metal.

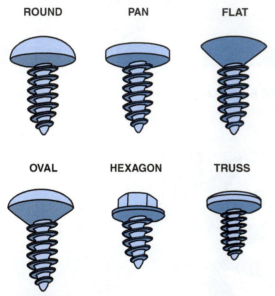

ROUND   PAN   FLAT

OVAL   HEXAGON   TRUSS

FIGURE 8–15 Sheet metal screws come with many head types.

SHEET METAL SCREWS

Sheet metal screws are fully threaded screws with a point for use in sheet metal. Also called **self-tapping screws**, they are used in many places on the vehicle, including fenders, trim, and door panels. ● SEE FIGURE 8–15.

These screws are used in unthreaded holes and the sharp threads cut threads as they are installed. This makes for a quick and easy installation when installing new parts, but the sheet metal screw can easily strip out the threads when used on the same part over and over, so care is needed.

When reinstalling self-tapping screws, first turn the screw lightly backwards until you feel the thread drop into the existing

HEX NUT   JAM NUT   NYLON LOCK NUT   CASTLE NUT   ACORN NUT

FLAT WASHER   LOCK WASHER   STAR WASHER   STAR WASHER

FIGURE 8–16 Various types of nuts (top) and washers (bottom) serve different purposes and all are used to secure bolts or cap screws.

thread in the screw hole. Then, turn the screw in; if it threads in easily, continue to tighten the screw. If the screw seems to turn hard, stop and turn it backwards about another half turn to locate the existing thread and try again. This technique can help prevent stripped holes in sheet metal and plastic parts.

Sheet metal screws are sized according to their major thread diameter.

Size	Diameter Decimal (inch)	Diameter Nearest Fraction Inch
4	0.11	7/64
6	0.14	9/64
8	0.17	11/64
10	0.19	3/16
12	0.22	7/32
14	0.25	1/4

WASHERS

Washers are often used under cap screw heads and under nuts. ● SEE FIGURE 8–16.

Plain flat washers are used to provide an even clamping load around the fastener. Lock washers are added to prevent accidental loosening. In some accessories, the washers are locked onto the nut to provide easy assembly.

Flat washers are placed underneath a nut to spread the load over a wide area and prevent gouging of the material. However, flat washers do not prevent a nut from loosening.

Lock washers are designed to prevent a nut from loosening. Spring-type lock washers resemble a loop out of a coil spring. As the nut or bolt is tightened, the washer is compressed. The tension of the compressed washer holds the fastener firmly against the threads to prevent it from loosening. Lock washers should not be used on soft metal such as aluminum. The sharp ends of the steel washers would gouge the aluminum badly, especially if they are removed and replaced often.

EXPANDING OR INTERNAL EXPANDING OR EXTERNAL E-CLIP EXPANDING OR INTERNAL CONTRACTING OR EXTERNAL C-CLIP

FIGURE 8–17 Some different types of snap rings. An internal snap ring fits inside of a housing or bore, into a groove. An external snap ring fits into a groove on the outside of a shaft or axle. An E-clip fits into a groove in the outside of a shaft. A C-clip shown is used to retain a window regulator handle on its shaft.

Another type of locking washer is the star washer. The teeth on a star washer can be external or internal, and they bite into the metal because they are twisted to expose their edges. Star washers are used often on sheet metal or body parts. They are seldom used on engines. The spring steel lock washer also uses the tension of the compressed washer to prevent the fastener from loosening. The waves in this washer make it look like a distorted flat washer.

SNAP RINGS AND CLIPS

SNAP RINGS **Snap rings** are not threaded fasteners, but instead attach with a springlike action. Snap rings are constructed of spring steel and are used to attach parts without using a threaded fastener. There are several different types of snap rings and most require the use of a special pair of pliers, called snap ring pliers, to release or install. The types of snap rings include:

- Expanding (internal)
- Contracting (external)
- E-clip
- C-clip
- Holeless snap rings in both expanding and contracting styles

● **SEE FIGURE 8–17.**

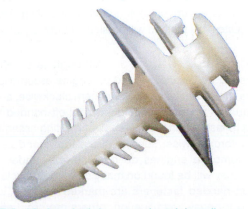

FIGURE 8–18 A typical door panel retaining clip.

DOOR PANEL CLIPS Interior door panels and other trim pieces are usually held in place with plastic clips. Due to the tapered and fluted shape, these clips are often called **Christmas tree clips**. ● **SEE FIGURE 8–18.**

A special tool is often used to remove interior door panels without causing any harm. ● **SEE FIGURE 8–19.**

CAUTION: Use extreme care when removing panels that use plastic or nylon clips. It is very easy to damage the door panel or clip during removal.

PINS **Cotter pins**, also called a cotter key, are used to keep linkage or a threaded nut in place or to keep it retained. The word *cotter* is an Old English verb meaning "to close or fasten." There are many other types of pins used in vehicles, including clevis pins, roll pins, and hair pins. ● **SEE FIGURE 8–20.**

Pins are used to hold together shafts and linkages, such as shift linkages and cable linkages. The clevis pin is held in place with a cotter pin, while the taper and roll pins are driven in and held by friction. The hair pin snaps into a groove on a shaft.

RIVETS Rivets are used in many locations to retain components, such as window mechanisms, that do not require routine removal and/or do not have access to the back side for

FIGURE 8–19 Plastic or metal trim tools are available to help the technician remove interior door panels and other trim without causing harm.

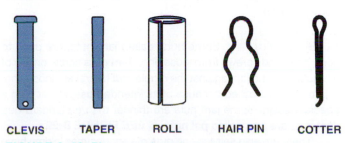

CLEVIS   TAPER   ROLL   HAIR PIN   COTTER

FIGURE 8–20 Pins come in various types.

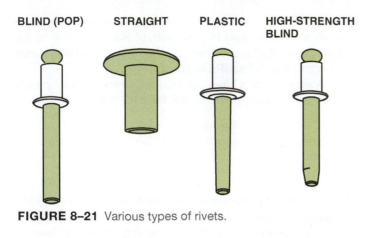

FIGURE 8–21 Various types of rivets.

BLIND (POP)   STRAIGHT   PLASTIC   HIGH-STRENGTH BLIND

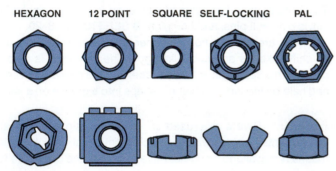

HEXAGON   12 POINT   SQUARE   SELF-LOCKING   PAL

SELF-THREADING   CAGE   CASTLE   WING   CAP

FIGURE 8–22 All of the nuts shown are used by themselves except for the pal nut, which is used to lock another nut to a threaded fastener so they will not be loosened by vibration.

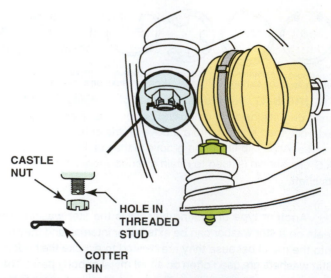

CASTLE NUT

HOLE IN THREADED STUD

COTTER PIN

FIGURE 8–23 A castle nut is locked in place with a cotter pin.

a nut. A drill is usually used to remove a rivet and a rivet gun is needed to properly install a rivet. Some rivets are plastic and are used to hold some body trim pieces. The most common type of rivet is called a **pop rivet** because as the rivet tool applies a force to the shaft of the pop rivet, it causes the rivet to expand and tighten the two pieces together. When the shaft of the rivet, which looks like a nail, is pulled to its maximum, the shaft breaks, causing a "pop" sound.

Rivets may be used in areas of the vehicle where a semi-permanent attachment is needed and in places where there is no access to the back side of the workpiece. They are installed using a rivet gun or by peening with a ball-peen hammer. ● **SEE FIGURE 8–21**.

Both types of blind rivets require the use of a rivet gun to install. The straight rivet is placed through the workpieces and then peened over with a ball-peen hammer or an air-operated tool. The plastic rivet is used with a rivet gun to install some body trim parts.

LOCKING NUTS Some nuts, called jam nuts, are used to keep bolts and screws from loosening. **Jam nuts** screw on top of a regular nut and jam against the regular nut to prevent loosening. A jam nut is so called because of its intended use, rather than a special design. Some jam nuts are thinner than a standard nut. Jam nuts are also called **pal nuts**. ● **SEE FIGURE 8–22**.

There are also self-locking nuts of various types. Some have threads that are bent inward to grip the threads of the bolt. Some

are oval-shaped at one end to fit tightly on a bolt. Fiber lock nuts have a fiber insert near the top of the nut or inside it; this type of nut is also made with a plastic or nylon insert. When the bolt turns through the nut, it cuts threads in the fiber or plastic. This puts a drag on the threads that prevents the bolt from loosening.

One of the oldest types of retaining nuts is the castle nut. It looks like a small castle, with slots for a cotter pin. A castellated nut is used on a bolt that has a hole for the cotter pin. ● **SEE FIGURE 8–23**.

HOW TO AVOID BROKEN FASTENERS

Try not to break, strip, or round off fasteners in the first place. There are several ways that you can minimize the number of fasteners you damage. First, never force fasteners loose during disassembly. Taking a few precautionary steps will often prevent damage. If a bolt or nut will not come loose with normal force, try tightening it in slightly and then backing it out. Sometimes turning the fastener the other way will break corrosion loose, and the fastener will then come out easily. Another method that works well is to rest a punch on the head of a stubborn bolt and strike it a sharp blow with a hammer. Often this method will break the corrosion loose.

LEFT-HANDED THREADS Although rare, left-handed fasteners are occasionally found on engine assemblies. These fasteners will loosen when you turn them clockwise, and tighten when you turn them counterclockwise. Left-handed fasteners are used to fasten parts to the ends of rotating assemblies that turn counterclockwise, such as crankshafts and camshafts. Most automobile engines do not use left-handed threads; however, they will be found on many older motorcycle engines. Some left-handed fasteners are marked with an "L" on the bolt head for easy identification, others are not. Left-handed threads are also found inside some transaxles.

PENETRATING OIL

Penetrating oil is a lightweight lubricant similar to kerosene, which soaks into small crevices in the threads by **capillary action**. The chemical action of penetrating oils helps to break up and dissolve rust and corrosion. The oil forms a layer of boundary lubrication on the threads to reduce friction and make the fastener easier to turn.

For best results, allow the oil time to soak in before removing the nuts and bolts. To increase the effectiveness of penetrating oil, tap on the bolt head or nut with a hammer, or alternately work the fastener back and forth with a wrench. This movement weakens the bond of the corrosion and lets more of the lubricant work down into the threads.

PROPER TIGHTENING

Proper tightening of bolts and nuts is critical for proper clamping force, as well as to prevent breakage. All fasteners should be tightened using a torque wrench. A torque wrench allows the technician to exert a known amount of torque to the fasteners. However, rotating torque on a fastener does not mean clamping force because up to 80% of the torque used to rotate a bolt or nut is absorbed by friction by the threads. Therefore, for accurate tightening, two things must be performed:

- The threads must be clean and lubricated if service information specifies that they be lubricated.
- Always use a torque wrench to not only ensure proper clamping force, but also to ensure that all fasteners are tightened the same.

THREAD REPAIR INSERTS

Thread repair inserts are used to replace the original threaded hole when it has become damaged beyond use. The original threaded hole is enlarged and tapped for threads and a threaded insert is installed to restore the threads to the original size.

HELICAL INSERTS

A **helical insert** looks like a small, stainless-steel spring. ● **SEE FIGURE 8–24**.

To install a helical insert, a hole must be drilled to a specified oversize, and then it is tapped with a special tap designed for the thread inserts. The insert is then screwed into the hole. ● **SEE FIGURE 8–25**.

The insert stays in the casting as a permanent repair and bolts can be removed and replaced without disturbing the insert. One advantage of a helical insert is that the original bolt can be used because the internal threads are the same size. When correctly installed, an insert is often stronger than the original threads, especially in aluminum castings. Some vehicle manufacturers, such as BMW, specify that the threads be renewed using an insert if the cylinder head has to be removed and reinstalled. Plus many high-performance engine rebuilders install inserts in blocks, manifolds, and cylinder heads as a precaution.

FIGURE 8–24 Helical inserts look like small, coiled springs. The outside is a thread to hold the coil in the hole, and the inside is threaded to fit the desired fastener.

FIGURE 8–25 The insert provides new, stock-size threads inside an oversize hole so that the original fastener can be used.

One of the best known of the helical fasteners is the **Heli-Coil**®, manufactured by Heli-Coil® Products. To install Heli-Coil® inserts, you will need to have a thread repair kit. The kit includes a drill bit, tap, installation mandrel, and inserts. Repair kits are available for a wide variety of diameters and pitch to fit both American Standard and metric threads. A simple kit contains the tooling for one specific thread size. Master kits that cover a range of sizes are also available. Installing an insert is similar to tapping new threads. A summary of the procedures includes:

1. Select the Heli-Coil® kit designed for the specific diameter and thread pitch of the hole to be repaired. ● **SEE FIGURE 8–26**.

2. Use the drill bit supplied with the kit. The drill size is also specified on the Heli-Coil® tap, to open up the hole to the necessary diameter and depth.

3. Tap the hole with the Heli-Coil® tap, being sure to lubricate the tap. Turn it in slowly and rotate counterclockwise occasionally to break the chip that is formed.

4. Thread an insert onto the installation mandrel until it seats firmly. Apply a light coating of the recommended thread locking compound to the external threads of the insert.

5. Use the mandrel to screw the insert into the tapped hole. Once started, spring tension prevents the insert from

FIGURE 8–26 Heli-Coil® kits, available in a wide variety of sizes, contain everything needed to repair a damaged hole back to its original size.

unscrewing. Stop when the top of the insert is 1/4 to 1/2 turn below the surface.

6. Remove the mandrel by unscrewing it from the insert, and then use a small punch or needle-nose pliers to break off the tang at the base of the insert. Never leave the tang in the bore. The finished thread is ready for use immediately.

THREADED INSERTS **Threaded inserts** are tubular, case-hardened, solid steel wall pieces that are threaded inside and outside. The inner thread of the insert is sized to fit the original fastener of the hole to be repaired. The outer thread design will vary. These may be self-tapping threads that are installed in a blank hole, or machine threads that require the hole to be tapped. Threaded inserts return a damaged hole to original size by replacing part of the surrounding casting so drilling is required. Most inserts fit into three categories.

- Self-tapping
- Solid-bushing
- Key-locking

SELF-TAPPING INSERTS The external threads of a self-tapping insert are designed to cut their own way into a casting. This eliminates the need of running a tap down the hole. To install a typical self-tapping insert, follow this procedure.

1. Drill out the damaged threads to open the hole to the proper size, using the specified size drill bit.
2. Select the proper insert and mandrel. As with Heli-Coils®, the drill bit, inserts, and mandrel are usually available as a kit.
3. Thread the insert onto the mandrel. Use a tap handle or wrench to drive the insert into the hole. Because the insert will cut its own path into the hole, it may require a considerable amount of force to drive the insert in.
4. Thread the insert in until the nut or flange at the bottom of the mandrel touches the surface of the workpiece. This is the depth stop to indicate the insert is seated.
5. Hold the nut or flange with a wrench, and turn the mandrel out of the insert. The threads are ready for immediate use.

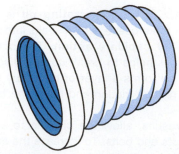

FIGURE 8–27 This solid-bushing insert is threaded on the outside, to grip the workpiece. The inner threads match the desired bolt size.

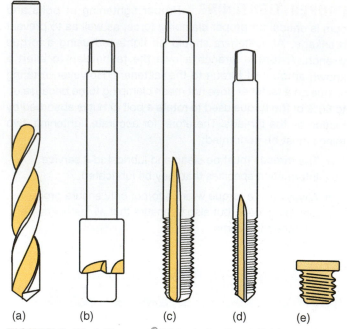

(a)   (b)   (c)   (d)   (e)

FIGURE 8–28 A Timesert® kit includes the drill (a), the recess cutter (b), a special tap (c), the installer (d), and the Timesert® threaded bushing (e).

SOLID-BUSHING INSERTS The external threads of solid-bushing inserts are ground to a specific thread pitch, so you will have to run a tap into the hole. ● **SEE FIGURE 8–27**.

Some inserts use a machine thread so a standard tap can be used; others have a unique thread and you have to use a special tap. The thread inserts come with a matching installation kit. ● **SEE FIGURE 8–28**.

To install threaded inserts, follow this procedure.

1. Drill out the damaged threads to open the hole to the proper size. The drill bit supplied with the kit must be the one used because it is properly sized to the tap. ● **SEE FIGURE 8–29**.
2. Cut the recess in the top of the hole with the special tool, then clean the hole with a brush or compressed air.
3. Use the previously detailed tapping procedures to thread the hole. ● **SEE FIGURE 8–30**. Be sure to tap deep enough; the top of the insert must be flush with the casting surface.

FIGURE 8-29 Drill out the damaged threads with the correct bit.

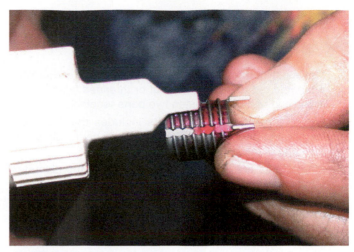

FIGURE 8-31 Put some thread-locking compound on the insert.

FIGURE 8-30 Use a special tap for the insert.

4. Thread the insert onto the installation driver, using the driver to screw the insert into the hole. Some inserts require that a thread-locking compound be applied; others go in dry.

5. Remove the installation driver, and the new threads are ready for service with the original fastener.

KEY-LOCKING INSERTS Key-locking inserts are similar to solid-bushing inserts, but are held in place by small keys. After the insert has been installed, the keys are driven into place—perpendicular to the threads—to keep the insert from turning out. A typical installation procedure includes the following steps.

1. Drill out the damaged thread with the specified drill size.

2. Tap the drilled hole with the specified tap.

3. After putting thread locking compound on the insert, use the mandrel to screw the insert into the tapped hole until it is slightly below the surface. ● **SEE FIGURE 8-31.** The keys act as a depth stop and prevent the insert from turning.

4. Drive the keys down using the driver supplied with the insert kit. Be sure the keys are flush with the top of the insert. ● **SEE FIGURES 8-32 AND 8-33.**

FIGURE 8-32 Use the driver to drive the keys down flush with the surface of the workpiece.

FIGURE 8-33 The insert and insert locks should be below the surface of the workpiece.

1. The most common type of fastener is a threaded one often referred to as a bolt. A nut or threaded hole is used at the end of a bolt to fasten two parts together.

2. The size of threaded fasteners includes the diameter, length, and pitch of the threads, as well as the shape of the head of the bolt.

3. Metric bolts are labeled with an "M," and the diameter across the threads is in millimeters followed by the distance between the threads measured in millimeters, such as M8 × 1.5.

4. Graded bolts are hardened and are capable of providing more holding force than nongraded bolts.

5. Many nuts are capable of remaining attached to the bolt regardless of vibration. These types of nuts are often called prevailing torque nuts.

6. Other commonly used fasteners in the automotive service industry include sheet metal screws, snap rings and clips, door panel clips, cotter pins, and rivets.

7. Damaged threads can be repaired using a Heli-Coil® or threaded insert.

REVIEW QUESTIONS

1. What is the difference between a bolt and a stud?
2. How is the size of a metric bolt expressed?
3. What is meant by the grade of a threaded fastener?
4. How do prevailing torque nuts work?
5. How are threaded inserts installed?

CHAPTER QUIZ

1. The thread pitch of a bolt is measured in what units?
   a. Millimeters
   b. Threads per inch
   c. Fractions of an inch
   d. Both a and b

2. Technician A says that the diameter of a bolt is the same as the wrench size used to remove or install the fastener. Technician B says that the length is measured from the top of the head of the bolt to the end of the bolt. Which technician is correct?
   a. Technician A only
   b. Technician B only
   c. Both Technicians A and B
   d. Neither Technician A nor B

3. The grade of a fastener, such as a bolt, is a measure of its _____.
   a. Tensile strength
   b. Hardness
   c. Finish
   d. Color

4. Which of the following is a metric bolt?
   a. 5/16 – 18
   b. 1/2 – 20
   c. M12 × 1.5
   d. 8 mm

5. A bolt that is threaded into a casting is often called a _____.
   a. Stud
   b. Cap screw
   c. Block bolt
   d. Crest bolt

6. The marks (lines) on the heads of bolts indicate _____.
   a. Size
   b. Grade
   c. Tensile strength
   d. Both b and c

7. A bolt that requires a 1/2 in. wrench to rotate is usually what size when measured across the threads?
   a. 1/2 in.
   b. 5/16 in.
   c. 3/8 in.
   d. 7/16 in.

8. A screw that can make its own threads when installed is called a _____ screw.
   a. Sheet metal
   b. Tapered
   c. Self-tapping
   d. Both a and c

9. All of the following are types of clips except _____.
   a. E-clip
   b. Cotter
   c. C-clip
   d. Internal

10. What type of fastener is commonly used to retain interior door panels?
    a. Christmas tree clips
    b. E-clips
    c. External clips
    d. Internal clips

OBJECTIVES: After studying Chapter 9, the reader should be able to: • Explain the types, proper name and classification of hand tools • Describe what tool is the best to use for each job. • Discuss how to safely use hand tools. • Explain the difference between the brand name (trade name) and the proper name for tools. • Explain how to maintain hand tools.

KEY TERMS: • Adjustable wrench 79 • Aviation tin snips 87 • Beam-type torque wrench 81 • Box-end wrench 79 • Breaker bar (flex handle) 80 • Cheater bar 93 • Chisel 88 • Clicker-type torque wrench 81 • Close end 79 • Cold chisel 88 • Combination wrench 79 • Crowfoot socket 81 • Dead-blow hammer 85 • Diagonal (side-cut or dike) pliers 85 • Double-cut file 87 • Drive size 81 • Easy out 89 • Extension 81 • Files 87 • Fitting wrench 80 • Flare-nut wrench 80 • Flat-tip (straight blade) screwdriver 83 • Hacksaw 90 • Locking pliers 86 • Multigroove adjustable pliers 85 • Needle-nose pliers 85 • Nut splitter 88 • Offset left aviation snip 87 • Offset right aviation snip 87 • Open-end wrench 79 • Punch 88 • Ratchet 80 • Removers 88 • Screwdriver 83 • Seal driver 92 • Seal puller 92 • Single-cut file 87 • Slip-joint pliers 85 • Snap-ring pliers 86 • Socket 80 • Socket adapter 83 • Straight cut aviation snip 87 • Stud removal tool 88 • Stud remover 88 • Tin snips 87 • Torque wrench 81 • Tube-nut wrench 80 • Universal joint 81 • Utility knife 87 • Vise-Grip® 86 • Water pump pliers 85 • Wrench 79

WRENCHES

Wrenches are the most used hand tool by service technicians. Most wrenches are constructed of forged alloy steel, usually chrome-vanadium steel. ● **SEE FIGURE 9–1**.

After the wrench is formed, it is hardened, tempered to reduce brittleness, and then chrome plated. Wrenches are available in both fractional and metric sizes. There are several types of wrenches.

FIGURE 9–1 A forged wrench after it has been forged but before the flashing, extra material around the wrench, has been removed.

OPEN-END WRENCH
An **open-end wrench** is often used to loosen or tighten bolts or nuts that do not require a lot of torque. An open-end wrench can be easily placed on a bolt or nut with an angle of 15 degrees, which allows the wrench to be flipped over and used again to continue to rotate the fastener. The major disadvantage of an open-end wrench is the lack of torque that can be applied due to the fact that the open jaws of the wrench only contact two flat surfaces of the fastener. An open-end wrench has two different sizes, one at each end. ● **SEE FIGURE 9–2**.

BOX-END WRENCH
A **box-end wrench** is placed over the top of the fastener and grips the points of the fastener. A box-end wrench is angled 15 degrees to allow it to clear nearby objects.

Therefore, a box-end wrench should be used to loosen or to tighten fasteners. A box-end wrench is also called a **close-end** wrench. A box-end wrench has two different sizes, one at each end. ● **SEE FIGURES 9–3 AND 9–4**.

COMBINATION WRENCH
Most service technicians purchase **combination wrenches**, which have the open end at one end and the same size box end on the other. ● **SEE FIGURE 9–5**.

A combination wrench allows the technician to loosen or tighten a fastener using the box end of the wrench, turn it around, and use the open end to increase the speed of rotating the fastener.

ADJUSTABLE WRENCH
An **adjustable wrench** is often used where the exact size wrench is not available or when a large nut, such as a wheel spindle nut, needs to be rotated but not tightened. An adjustable wrench should not be used to

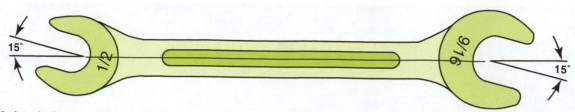

FIGURE 9–2 A typical open-end wrench. The size is different on each end and notice that the head is angled 15 degrees at each end.

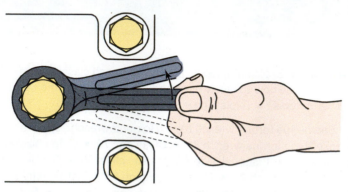

FIGURE 9–3 A typical box-end wrench is able to grip the bolt or nut at points completely around the fastener. Each end is a different size.

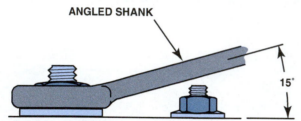

FIGURE 9–4 The end of a box-end wrench is angled 15 degrees to allow clearance for nearby objects or other fasteners.

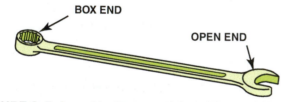

FIGURE 9–5 A combination wrench has an open end at one end and a box end at the other with the same size at each end.

loosen or tighten fasteners because the torque applied to the wrench can cause the movable jaws to loosen their grip on the fastener, causing it to become rounded. ● **SEE FIGURE 9–6**.

LINE WRENCHES Line wrenches are also called **flare-nut wrenches**, **fitting wrenches**, or **tube-nut wrenches** and are designed to grip almost all the way around a nut used to retain a fuel or refrigerant line, and yet be able to be installed over the line. ● **SEE FIGURE 9–7**.

SAFE USE OF WRENCHES. Wrenches should be inspected before use to be sure they are not cracked, bent, or damaged.

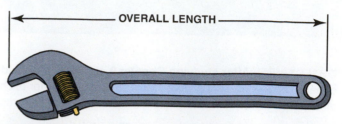

FIGURE 9–6 An adjustable wrench. Adjustable wrenches are sized by the overall length of the wrench and not by how far the jaws open. Common sizes of adjustable wrenches include 8, 10, and 12 in.

FIGURE 9–7 The end of a typical line wrench, which shows that it is capable of grasping most of the head of the fitting.

All wrenches should be cleaned after use before being returned to the toolbox. Always use the correct size of wrench for the fastener being loosened or tightened to help prevent the rounding of the flats of the fastener. When attempting to loosen a fastener, pull a wrench—do not push a wrench. If a wrench is pushed, your knuckles can be hurt when forced into another object if the fastener breaks loose.

RATCHETS, SOCKETS, AND EXTENSIONS

A **socket** fits over the fastener and grips the points and/or flats of the bolt or nut. The socket is rotated (driven) using either a long bar called a **breaker bar (flex handle)** or a **ratchet**. ● **SEE FIGURES 9–8 AND 9–9**.

A ratchet turns the socket in only one direction and allows the rotating of the ratchet handle back and forth in a narrow

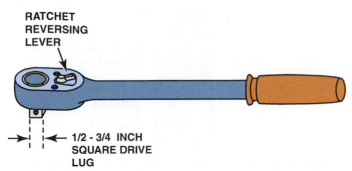

FIGURE 9–8 A typical ratchet used to rotate a socket. A ratchet makes a ratcheting noise when it is being rotated in the opposite direction from loosening or tightening. A knob or lever on the ratchet allows the user to switch directions.

FIGURE 9–9 A typical flex handle used to rotate a socket, also called a breaker bar because it usually has a longer handle than a ratchet and, therefore, can be used to apply more torque to a fastener than a ratchet.

space. Socket **extensions** and **universal joints** are also used with sockets to allow access to fasteners in restricted locations.

Sockets are available in various **drive sizes**, including 1/4 in., 3/8 in., and 1/2 in. sizes for most automotive use. ● **SEE FIGURES 9–10 AND 9–11**.

Many heavy-duty truck and/or industrial applications use 3/4 in. and 1 in. sizes. The drive size is the distance of each side of the square drive. Sockets and ratchets of the same size are designed to work together.

CROWFOOT SOCKETS
A **crowfoot socket** is a socket that is an open-end or line wrench to allow access to fasteners that cannot be reached using a conventional wrench. ● **SEE FIGURE 9–12**.

Crowfoot sockets are available in the following categories.

- Fractional inch open-end wrench
- Metric open-end wrench
- Fractional line wrench
- Metric line wrench

 **TECH TIP**

Right to Tighten

It is sometimes confusing which way to rotate a wrench or screwdriver, especially when the head of the fastener is pointing away from you. To help visualize while looking at the fastener, say "righty tighty, lefty loosey."

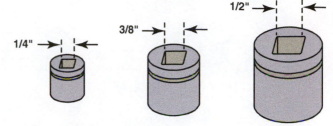

FIGURE 9–10 The most commonly used socket drive sizes include 1/4 in., 3/8 in., and 1/2 in. drive.

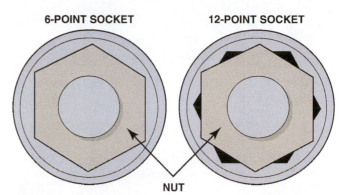

FIGURE 9–11 A 6-point socket fits the head of the bolt or nut on all sides. A 12-point socket can round off the head of a bolt or nut if a lot of force is applied.

FIGURE 9–12 A crowfoot socket is designed to reach fasteners using a ratchet or breaker bar with an extension.

TORQUE WRENCHES
Torque wrenches are socket turning handles that are designed to apply a known amount of force to the fastener. There are two basic types of torque wrenches.

1. A **clicker-type torque wrench** is first set to the specified torque and then it "clicks" when the set torque value has been reached. When force is removed from the torque wrench handle, another click is heard. The setting on a clicker-type torque wrench should be set back to zero after use and checked for proper calibration regularly. ● **SEE FIGURE 9–13**.

2. A **beam- or dial-type torque wrench** is used to measure torque, but instead of presetting the value, the actual torque is displayed on the scale or dial of the wrench as the fastener is being tightened. Beam-type torque wrenches are available in 1/4 in., 3/8 in., and 1/2 in. drives and both English and metric units. ● **SEE FIGURE 9–14**.

FIGURE 9–13 Using a torque wrench to tighten connecting rod nuts on an engine.

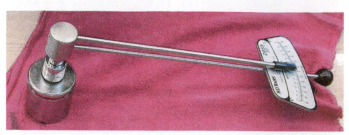

FIGURE 9–14 A beam-type torque wrench that displays the torque reading on the face of the dial. The beam display is read as the beam deflects, which is in proportion to the amount of torque applied to the fastener.

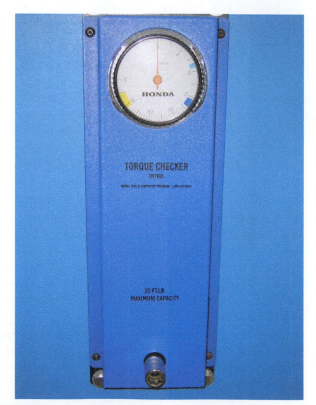

FIGURE 9–15 Torque wrench calibration checker.

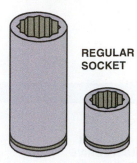

FIGURE 9–16 Deep sockets allow access to the nut that has a stud plus other locations needing great depth, such as spark plugs.

🔧 TECH TIP

Check Torque Wrench Calibration Regularly
Torque wrenches should be checked regularly. For example, Honda has a torque wrench calibration setup at each of their training centers. It is expected that a torque wrench be checked for accuracy before every use. Most experts recommend that torque wrenches be checked and adjusted as needed at least every year and more often if possible.
● SEE FIGURE 9–15.

SAFE USE OF SOCKETS AND RATCHETS. Always use the proper size socket that correctly fits the bolt or nut. All sockets and ratchets should be cleaned after use before being placed back into the toolbox. Sockets are available in short and deep well designs. ● SEE FIGURE 9–16.

Also select the appropriate drive size. For example, for small work, such as on the dash, select a 1/4 in. drive. For most general service work, use a 3/8 in. drive and for suspension and steering and other large fasteners, select a 1/2 in. drive. When loosening a fastener, always pull the ratchet toward you rather than push it outward.

? FREQUENTLY ASKED QUESTION

Is It Lb-Ft or Ft-Lb of Torque?
The unit for torque is expressed as a force times the distance (leverage) from the object. Therefore, the official unit for torque is lb-ft (pound-feet) or newton-meters (a force times a distance). However, it is commonly expressed in ft-lb and even some torque wrenches are labeled with this unit.

TECH TIP

Double-Check the Specifications

Misreading torque specifications is easy to do but can have serious damaging results. Specifications for fasteners are commonly expressed lb-ft. Many smaller fasteners are tightened to specifications expressed in lb-in.

1 lb-ft = 12 lb-in.

Therefore, if a fastener were to be accidentally tightened to 24 lb-ft instead of 24 lb-in., the actual torque applied to the fastener will be 288 lb-in. instead of the specified 24 lb-in.

This extra torque will likely break the fastener, but it could also warp or distort the part being tightened. Always double-check the torque specifications.

TECH TIP

Use Socket Adapters with Caution

Socket adapters are available and can be used for different drive size sockets on a ratchet. Combinations include:

- 1/4 in. drive—3/8 in. sockets
- 3/8 in. drive—1/4 in. sockets
- 3/8 in. drive—1/2 in. sockets
- 1/2 in. drive—3/8 in. sockets

Using a larger drive ratchet or breaker bar on a smaller size socket can cause the application of too much force to the socket, which could crack or shatter. Using a smaller size drive tool on a larger socket will usually not cause any harm, but would greatly reduce the amount of torque that can be applied to the bolt or nut.

TECH TIP

Avoid Using "Cheater Bars"

Whenever a fastener is difficult to remove, some technicians will insert the handle of a ratchet or a breaker bar into a length of steel pipe. The extra length of the pipe allows the technician to exert more torque than can be applied using the drive handle alone. However, the extra torque can easily overload the socket and ratchet, causing them to break or shatter, which could cause personal injury.

SCREWDRIVERS

Many smaller fasteners are removed and installed by using a **screwdriver**. Screwdrivers are available in many sizes and tip shapes. The most commonly used screwdriver is called a **flat tip** or **straight blade**.

Flat-tip screwdrivers are sized by the width of the blade and this width should match the width of the slot in the screw. ● **SEE FIGURE 9–17**.

CAUTION: Do not use a screwdriver as a pry tool or as a chisel. Always use the proper tool for each application.

Another type of commonly used screwdriver is called a Phillips screwdriver, named for Henry F. Phillips, who invented the crosshead screw in 1934. Due to the shape of the crosshead screw and screwdriver, a Phillips screw can be driven with more torque than can be achieved with a slotted screw.

A Phillips head screwdriver is specified by the length of the handle and the size of the point at the tip. A #1 tip has a sharp point, a #2 tip is the most commonly used, and a #3 tip is blunt and is only used for larger sizes of Phillips head fasteners. For example, a #2 × 3 in. Phillips screwdriver would typically measure 6 in. from the tip of the blade to the end of the handle (3 in. long handle and 3 in. long blade) with a #2 tip.

Both straight blade and Phillips screwdrivers are available with a short blade and handle for access to fasteners with limited room. ● **SEE FIGURE 9–18**.

OFFSET SCREWDRIVERS Offset screwdrivers are used in places where a conventional screwdriver cannot fit. An offset screwdriver is bent at the ends and is used similar to a wrench. Most offset screwdrivers have a straight blade at one end and a Phillips end at the opposite end. ● **SEE FIGURE 9–19**.

IMPACT SCREWDRIVER An impact screwdriver is used to break loose or tighten a screw. A hammer is used to strike the end after the screwdriver holder is placed in the head of the screw and rotated in the desired direction. The force

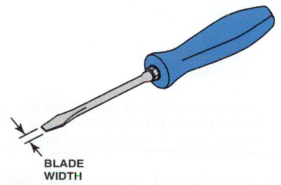

BLADE WIDTH

FIGURE 9–17 A flat-tip (straight blade) screwdriver. The width of the blade should match the width of the slot in the fastener being loosened or tightened.

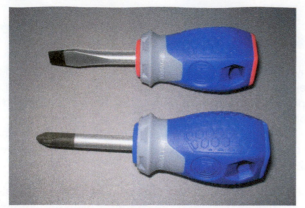

FIGURE 9–18 Two stubby screwdrivers that are used to access screws that have limited space above. A straight blade is on top and a #2 Phillips screwdriver is on the bottom.

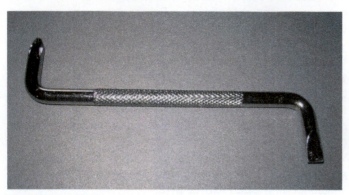

FIGURE 9–19 An offset screwdriver is used to install or remove fasteners that do not have enough space above to use a conventional screwdriver.

FIGURE 9–20 An impact screwdriver used to remove slotted or Phillips head fasteners that cannot be broken loose using a standard screwdriver.

from the hammer blow does two things: It applies a force downward holding the tip of the screwdriver in the slot and then applies a twisting force to loosen (or tighten) the screw. ● **SEE FIGURE 9–20.**

SAFE USE OF SCREWDRIVERS. Always use the proper type and size screwdriver that matches the fastener. Try to avoid pressing down on a screwdriver because if it slips, the screwdriver tip could go into your hand, causing serious

personal injury. All screwdrivers should be cleaned after use. Do not use a screwdriver as a pry bar; always use the correct tool for the job.

HAMMERS AND MALLETS

HAMMERS Hammers and mallets are used to force objects together or apart. The shape of the back part of the hammer head (called the *peen*) usually determines the name. For example, a ball-peen hammer has a rounded end like a ball and it is used to straighten oil pans and valve covers, using the hammer head, and for shaping metal, using the ball peen. ● **SEE FIGURE 9–21.**

NOTE: A claw hammer has a claw used to remove nails and is not used for automotive service.

A hammer is usually sized by the weight of the head of the hammer and the length of the handle. For example, a commonly used ball-peen hammer has an 8 oz head with an 11 in. handle.

MALLETS Mallets are a type of hammer with a large striking surface, which allows the technician to exert force over a larger area than a hammer, so as not to harm the part or component.

FIGURE 9–21 A typical ball-peen hammer.

FIGURE 9–22 A rubber mallet used to deliver a force to an object without harming the surface.

FIGURE 9–23 A dead-blow hammer that was left outside in freezing weather. The plastic covering was damaged, which destroyed this hammer. The lead shot is encased in the metal housing and then covered.

Mallets are made from a variety of materials including rubber, plastic, or wood. ● **SEE FIGURE 9–22.**

A shot-filled plastic hammer is called a **dead-blow hammer.** The small lead balls (shot) inside a plastic head prevent the hammer from bouncing off of the object when struck. ● **SEE FIGURE 9–23.**

SAFE USE OF HAMMERS AND MALLETS. All mallets and hammers should be cleaned after use and not exposed to extreme temperatures. Never use a hammer or mallet that is damaged in any way and always use caution to avoid doing damage to the components and the surrounding area. Always follow the hammer manufacturer's recommended procedures and practices.

PLIERS

SLIP-JOINT PLIERS Pliers are capable of holding, twisting, bending, and cutting objects and are an extremely useful classification of tools. The common household type of pliers is called the **slip-joint pliers.** There are two different positions where the junction of the handles meets to achieve a wide range of sizes of objects that can be gripped. ● **SEE FIGURE 9–24.**

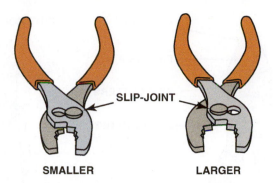

FIGURE 9–24 Typical slip-joint pliers, which are also common household pliers. The slip joint allows the jaws to be opened to two different settings.

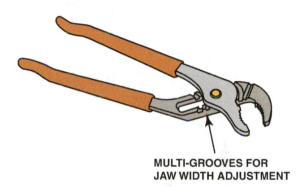

FIGURE 9–25 Multigroove adjustable pliers are known by many names, including the trade name Channel Locks.

MULTIGROOVE ADJUSTABLE PLIERS For gripping larger objects, a set of **multigroove adjustable pliers** is a commonly used tool of choice by many service technicians. Originally designed to remove the various size nuts holding rope seals used in water pumps, the name **water pump pliers** is also used. ● **SEE FIGURE 9–25.**

LINESMAN'S PLIERS Linesman's pliers are specifically designed for cutting, bending, and twisting wire. While commonly used by construction workers and electricians, linesman's pliers are very useful tools for the service technician who deals with wiring. The center parts of the jaws are designed to grasp round objects such as pipe or tubing without slipping. ● **SEE FIGURE 9–26.**

DIAGONAL PLIERS **Diagonal pliers** are designed for cutting only. The cutting jaws are set at an angle to make it easier to cut wires. Diagonal pliers are also called **side cuts** or **dikes.** These pliers are constructed of hardened steel and they are used mostly for cutting wire. ● **SEE FIGURE 9–27.**

NEEDLE-NOSE PLIERS **Needle-nose pliers** are designed to grip small objects or objects in tight locations. Needle-nose pliers have long, pointed jaws, which allow the tips to reach into narrow openings or groups of small objects. ● **SEE FIGURE 9–28.**

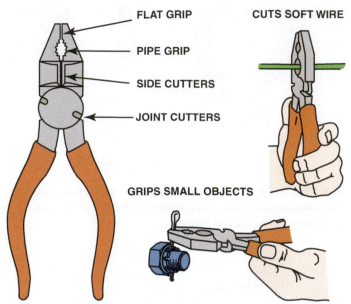

FLAT GRIP
PIPE GRIP
SIDE CUTTERS
JOINT CUTTERS

CUTS SOFT WIRE

GRIPS SMALL OBJECTS

FIGURE 9–26 A linesman's pliers are very useful because they can help perform many automotive service jobs.

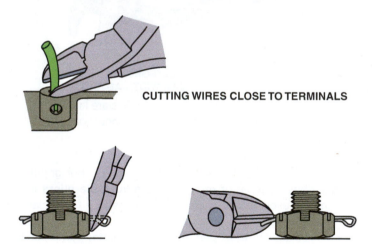

CUTTING WIRES CLOSE TO TERMINALS

PULLING OUT AND SPREADING COTTER PIN

FIGURE 9–27 Diagonal-cut pliers are another common tool that has many names.

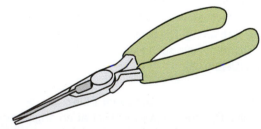

FIGURE 9–28 Needle-nose pliers are used where there is limited access to a wire or pin that needs to be installed or removed.

Most needle-nose pliers have a wire cutter located at the base of the jaws near the pivot. There are several variations of needle-nose pliers, including right angle jaws or slightly angled to allow access to certain cramped areas.

LOCKING PLIERS **Locking pliers** are adjustable pliers that can be locked to hold objects from moving. Most locking pliers also have wire cutters built into the jaws near the pivot point. Locking pliers come in a variety of styles and sizes and are commonly referred to by their trade name **Vise-Grip**®. The size is the length of the pliers, not how far the jaws open. ● SEE FIGURE 9–29.

SAFE USE OF PLIERS. Pliers should not be used to remove any bolt or other fastener. Pliers should only be used when specified for use by the vehicle manufacturer.

SNAP-RING PLIERS **Snap-ring pliers** are used to remove and install snap rings. Many snap-ring pliers are designed to be able to remove and install inward, as well as outward,

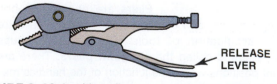

RELEASE LEVER

FIGURE 9–29 Locking pliers are best known by their trade name Vise-Grip®.

expanding snap rings. Snap-ring pliers can be equipped with serrated-tipped jaws for grasping the opening in the snap ring, while others are equipped with points, which are inserted into the holes in the snap ring. ● SEE FIGURE 9–30.

FILES Files are used to smooth metal and are constructed of hardened steel with diagonal rows of teeth. Files are available with a single row of teeth called a **single-cut file**, as well as two rows of teeth cut at an opposite angle called a **double-cut file**. Files are available in a variety of shapes and sizes from small flat files, half-round files, and triangular files. ● SEE FIGURE 9–31.

SAFE USE OF FILES. Always use a file with a handle. Because files cut only when moved forward, a handle must be attached to prevent possible personal injury. After making a forward strike, lift the file and return the file to the starting position; avoid dragging the file backward.

CUTTERS

SNIPS Service technicians are often asked to fabricate sheet metal brackets or heat shields and need to use one or more types of cutters available. The simplest is called **tin snips**, which are designed to make straight cuts in a variety of materials, such as sheet steel, aluminum, or even fabric. A variation of the tin snips is called **aviation tin snips**. There are three designs of aviation snips, including one designed to cut straight (called a **straight cut aviation snip**), one designed to cut left (called an **offset left aviation snip**), and one designed to cut right (called an **offset right aviation snip**). The handles are color coded for easy identification. These include yellow for straight, red for left, and green for right. ● SEE FIGURE 9–32.

UTILITY KNIFE A **utility knife** uses a replaceable blade and is used to cut a variety of materials such as carpet, plastic, wood, and paper products, such as cardboard. ● SEE FIGURE 9–33.

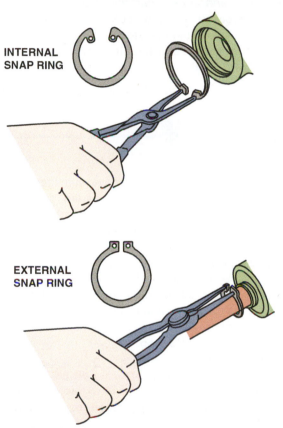

FIGURE 9–30 Snap-ring pliers are also called lock-ring pliers and are designed to remove internal and external snap rings (lock rings).

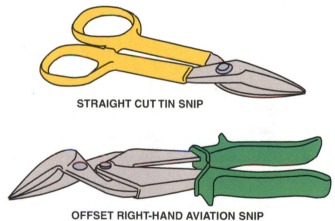

STRAIGHT CUT TIN SNIP

OFFSET RIGHT-HAND AVIATION SNIP

FIGURE 9–32 Tin snips are used to cut thin sheets of metal or carpet.

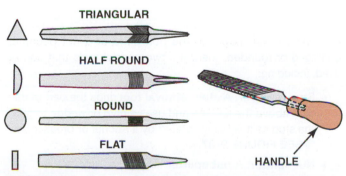

FIGURE 9–31 Files come in many different shapes and sizes. Never use a file without a handle.

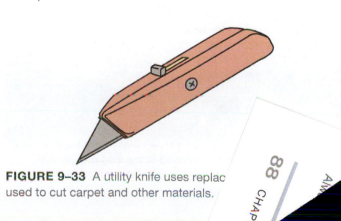

FIGURE 9–33 A utility knife uses replac[...] used to cut carpet and other materials.

SAFE USE OF CUTTERS. Whenever using cutters, always wear eye protection or a face shield to guard against the possibility of metal pieces being ejected during the cut. Always follow recommended procedures.

PUNCHES AND CHISELS

PUNCHES A **punch** is a small diameter steel rod that has a smaller diameter ground at one end. A punch is used to drive a pin out that is used to retain two components. Punches come in a variety of sizes, which are measured across the diameter of the machined end. Sizes include 1/16 in., 1/8 in., 3/16 in., and 1/4 in. ● **SEE FIGURE 9–34**.

CHISELS A **chisel** has a straight, sharp cutting end that is used for cutting off rivets or to separate two pieces of an assembly. The most common design of chisel used for automotive service work is called a **cold chisel**.

SAFE USE OF PUNCHES AND CHISELS. Always wear eye protection when using a punch or a chisel because the hardened steel is brittle and parts of the punch could fly off and cause serious personal injury. See the warning stamped on the side of this automotive punch in ● **SEE FIGURE 9–35**.

FIGURE 9–34 A punch used to drive pins from assembled components. This type of punch is also called a pin punch.

FIGURE 9–35 Warning stamped in the side of a punch warning that goggles should be worn when using this tool. Always follow safety warnings.

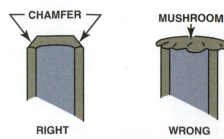

FIGURE 9–36 Use a grinder or a file to remove the mushroom material on the end of a punch or chisel.

Punches and chisels can also have the top rounded off, which is called "mushroomed." This material must be ground off to help avoid the possibility that the overhanging material is loosened and becomes airborne during use. ● **SEE FIGURE 9–36**.

REMOVERS

Removers are tools used to remove damaged fasteners. A remover tool is not normally needed during routine service unless the fastener is corroded or has been broken or damaged by a previous attempt to remove the bolt or nut.

To help prevent the need for a remover tool, all rusted and corroded fasteners should be sprayed with penetrating oil. Penetrating oil is a low viscosity oil that is designed to flow in between the threads of a fastener or other small separation between two parts. Commonly used penetrating oils include WD-40®, Kroil®, and CRC 5-56.

CAUTION: Do not use penetrating oil as a lubricating oil because it is volatile and will evaporate soon after usage leaving little lubricant behind for protection.

Over time, rust and corrosion can cause the threads of the fastener to be attached to the nut or the casting making it very difficult to remove. There are several special tools that can be used to remove damaged fasteners. Which one to use depends on the type of damage.

DAMAGED HEADS If the bolt head or a nut becomes damaged or rounded, there are two special tools that can be used, including:

- **Stud remover.** A **stud removal tool** grips the part of the stud above the surface and uses a cam or wedge to grip the stud as it is being rotated by a ratchet or breaker bar. ● **SEE FIGURE 9–37**.
- **Nut splitter.** A **nut splitter** is used to remove the nut by splitting it from the bolt. A nut splitter is used by inserting the cutter against a flat of the nut and

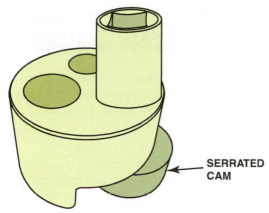

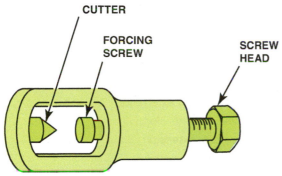

FIGURE 9–37 A stud remover uses an offset serrated wheel to grasp the stud so it will be rotated when a ratchet or breaker bar is used to rotate the assembly.

FIGURE 9–38 A nut splitter is used to split a nut that cannot be removed. After the nut has been split, a chisel is then used to remove the nut.

tightening the threaded bolt of the splitter. The nut will be split away from the bolt and can then be removed. ● **SEE FIGURE 9–38.**

CAUTION: Do not rotate the entire nut splitter or damage to the cutting wedge will occur.

BROKEN BOLTS, STUDS, OR SCREWS Often, bolts, studs, or screws break even with, or below the surface, making stud removal tools impossible to use. Bolt extractors are commonly called **easy outs**. An easy out is constructed of hardened steel with flutes or edges ground into the side in an opposite direction of most threads. ● **SEE FIGURE 9–39.**

NOTE: Always select the largest extractor that can be used to help avoid the possibility of breaking the extractor while attempting to remove the bolt.

A hole is drilled into the center of a broken bolt. Then, the extractor (easy out) is inserted into the hole and rotated counterclockwise using a wrench. As the extractor rotates, the grooves grip tighter into the wall of the hole drilled in the broken bolt. As a result, most extractors are capable of removing most broken bolts.

FIGURE 9–39 A set of bolt extractors, commonly called easy outs.

FIGURE 9–40 Removing plugs or bolts is easier if the plug is first heated to cherry red color, using a torch, and then applying wax. During cooling, the wax flows in between the threads, making it easier to remove.

 **TECH TIP**

The Wax Trick

Many times rusted fasteners can be removed by using heat to expand the metal and break the rust bond between the fastener and the nut or casting. Many technicians heat the fastener using a torch and then apply paraffin wax or a candle to the heated fastener. ● **SEE FIGURE 9–40.** The wax will melt and as the part cools, will draw the liquid wax down between the threads. After allowing the part to cool, attempt to remove the fastener. It will often be removed without any trouble.

I Broke Off an Easy Out—Now What?

An extractor (easy out) is hardened steel and removing this and the broken bolt is now a job for a professional machine shop. The part, which could be as large as an engine block, needs to be removed from the vehicle and taken to a machine shop that is equipped to handle this type of job. One method involves using an electrical discharge machine (EDM). An EDM uses a high amperage electrical current to produce thousands of arcs between the electrode and the broken tool. The part is submerged in a nonconducting liquid and each tiny spark vaporizes a small piece of the broken tool.

HACKSAWS

A **hacksaw** is used to cut metals, such as steel, aluminum, brass, or copper. The cutting blade of a hacksaw is replaceable and the sharpness and number of teeth can be varied to meet the needs of the job. Use 14 or 18 teeth per inch (tpi) for cutting plaster or soft metals, such as aluminum and copper. Use 24 or 32 teeth per inch for steel or pipe. Hacksaw blades should be installed with the teeth pointing away from the handle. This means that a hacksaw cuts while the blade is pushed in the forward direction, and then pressure should be released as the blade is pulled rearward before repeating the cutting operation. ● **SEE FIGURE 9–41.**

SAFE USE OF HACKSAWS. Check that the hacksaw is equipped with the correct blade for the job and that the teeth are pointed away from the handle. When using a hacksaw, move the hacksaw slowly away from you, then lift slightly and return for another cut.

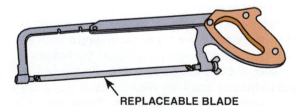

REPLACEABLE BLADE

FIGURE 9–41 A typical hacksaw that is used to cut metal. If cutting sheet metal or thin objects, a blade with more teeth should be used.

BASIC HAND TOOL LIST

Hand tools are used to turn fasteners (bolts, nuts, and screws). The following is a list of hand tools every automotive technician should possess. Specialty tools are not included.

Safety glasses

Tool chest

1/4 in. drive socket set (1/4 to 9/16 in. standard and deep sockets; 6 to 15 mm standard and deep sockets)

1/4 in. drive ratchet

1/4 in. drive 2 in. extension

1/4 in. drive 6 in. extension

1/4 in. drive handle

3/8 in. drive socket set (3/8 to 7/8 in. standard and deep sockets; 10 to 19 mm standard and deep sockets)

3/8 in. drive Torx set (T40, T45, T50, and T55)

3/8 in. drive 13/16 in. plug socket

3/8 in. drive 5/8 in. plug socket

3/8 in. drive ratchet

3/8 in. drive 1 1/2 in. extension

3/8 in. drive 3 in. extension

3/8 in. drive 6 in. extension

3/8 in. drive 18 in. extension

3/8 in. drive universal

1/2 in. drive socket set (1/2 to 1 in. standard and deep sockets; 9 to 19 mm standard and deep metric sockets)

1/2 in. drive ratchet

1/2 in. drive breaker bar

1/2 in. drive 5 in. extension

1/2 in. drive 10 in. extension

3/8 to 1/4 in. adapter

1/2 to 3/8 in. adapter

3/8 to 1/2 in. adapter

Crowfoot set (fractional inch)

Crowfoot set (metric)

3/8 through 1 in. combination wrench set

10 through 19 mm combination wrench set

1/16 through 1/4 in. hex (Allen) wrench set

2 through 12 mm hex (Allen) wrench set

3/8 in. hex socket

13 to 14 mm flare nut wrench

15 to 17 mm flare nut wrench

5/16 to 3/8 in. flare nut wrench

7/16 to 1/2 in. flare nut wrench

1/2 to 9/16 in. flare nut wrench

Diagonal pliers

Needle pliers

TECH TIP

Hide Those from the Boss

An apprentice technician started working for a dealership and put his top tool box on a workbench. Another technician observed that, along with a complete set of good-quality tools, the box contained several adjustable wrenches. The more experienced technician said, "Hide those from the boss." If any adjustable wrench is used on a bolt or nut, the movable jaw often moves or loosens and starts to round the head of the fastener. If the head of the bolt or nut becomes rounded, it becomes that much more difficult to remove.

TECH TIP

Need to Borrow a Tool More than Twice? Buy It!

Most service technicians agree that it is okay for a beginning technician to borrow a tool occasionally. However, if a tool has to be borrowed more than twice, then be sure to purchase it as soon as possible. Also, whenever a tool is borrowed, be sure that you clean the tool and let the technician you borrowed the tool from know that you are returning the tool. These actions will help in any future dealings with other technicians.

- Adjustable-jaw pliers
- Locking pliers
- Snap-ring pliers
- Stripping or crimping pliers
- Ball-peen hammer
- Rubber hammer
- Dead-blow hammer
- Five-piece standard screwdriver set
- Four-piece Phillips screwdriver set
- #15 Torx screwdriver
- #20 Torx screwdriver
- File
- Center punch
- Pin punches (assorted sizes)
- Chisel
- Utility knife
- Valve core tool
- Filter wrench (large filters)
- Filter wrench (smaller filters)
- Test light
- Feeler gauge
- Scraper
- Magnet

FIGURE 9–42 A typical beginning technician tool set that includes the basic tools to get started.

FIGURE 9–43 A typical large tool box, showing just one of many drawers.

TOOL SETS AND ACCESSORIES

A beginning service technician may wish to start with a small set of tools before spending a lot of money on an expensive, extensive tool box. See ● **SEE FIGURES 9–42 AND 9–43.**

 **TECH TIP**

The Valve Grinding Compound Trick

Apply a small amount of valve grinding compound to a Phillips or Torx screw or bolt head. The gritty valve grinding compound "grips" the screwdriver or tool bit and prevents the tool from slipping up and out of the screw head. Valve grinding compound is available in a tube from most automotive parts stores.

FIGURE 9–44 A seal puller being used to remove a seal from a rear axle.

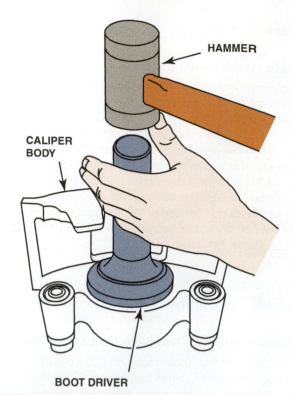

FIGURE 9–45 A seal (boot) driver or installer is usually plastic and is designed to seat the seal.

SEAL PULLERS AND DRIVERS

SEAL PULLERS Grease seals are located on many automotive components, including brake rotors, transmission housings, and differentials. A **seal puller** is used to properly remove grease seals, as shown in ● **SEE FIGURE 9–44.**

SEAL DRIVERS A **seal driver** can be either plastic or metal, usually aluminum, and is used to seat the outer lip of a grease seal into the grease seal pocket. A seal is usually driven into position using a plastic mallet and a seal driver that is the same size as the outside diameter of the grease seal retainer. ● **SEE FIGURE 9–45.**

ELECTRICAL HAND TOOLS

TEST LIGHTS A test light is used to test for electricity. A typical automotive test light consists of a clear plastic screwdriver-like handle that contains a light bulb. A wire is attached to one terminal of the bulb, which the technician connects to a clean metal part of the vehicle. The other end of the bulb is attached to a point that can be used to test for electricity at a connector or wire. When there is power at the point and a good connection at the other end, the light bulb lights. ● **SEE FIGURE 9–46.**

SOLDERING GUNS

- **Electric soldering gun.** This type of soldering gun is usually powered by 110 volt AC and often has two power settings expressed in watts. A typical electric

soldering gun will produce from 85 to 300 watts of heat at the tip, which is more than adequate for soldering. ● **SEE FIGURE 9–47.**

- **Electric soldering pencil.** This type of soldering iron is less expensive and creates less heat than an electric soldering gun. A typical electric soldering pencil (iron) creates 30 to 60 watts of heat and is suitable for soldering smaller wires and connections.

- **Butane-powered soldering iron.** A butane-powered soldering iron is portable and very useful for automotive service work because an electrical cord is not needed. Most butane-powered soldering irons produce about 60 watts of heat, which is enough for most automotive soldering.

FIGURE 9–46 A typical 12 volt test light.

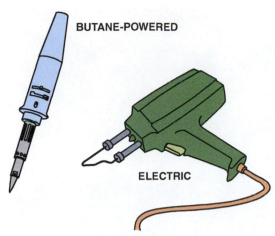

BUTANE-POWERED

ELECTRIC

FIGURE 9–47 An electric soldering gun used to make electrical repairs. Soldering guns are sold by the wattage rating. The higher the wattage, the greater amount of heat created. Most solder guns used for automotive electrical work usually fall within the 60 to 160 watt range.

In addition to a soldering iron, most service technicians who do electrical-related work should have the following:

- Wire cutters
- Wire strippers
- Wire crimpers
- Heat gun

A digital meter is a necessary tool for any electrical diagnosis and troubleshooting. A digital multimeter, abbreviated DMM, is usually capable of measuring the following units of electricity.

- DC volts
- AC volts
- Ohms
- Amperes

SAFETY TIPS FOR USING HAND TOOLS

The following safety tips should be kept in mind whenever you are working with hand tools.

- Always *pull* a wrench toward you for best control and safety. Never push a wrench.
- Keep wrenches and all hand tools clean to help prevent rust and to allow for a better, firmer grip.
- Always use a 6-point socket or a box-end wrench to break loose a tight bolt or nut.
- Use a box-end wrench for torque and an open-end wrench for speed.
- Never use a pipe extension or other type of "**cheater bar**" on a wrench or ratchet handle. If more force is required, use a larger tool or use penetrating oil and/or heat on the frozen fastener. (If heat is used on a bolt or nut to remove it, always replace it with a new part.)
- Always use the proper tool for the job. If a specialized tool is required, use the proper tool and do not try to use another tool improperly.
- Never expose any tool to excessive heat. High temperatures can reduce the strength ("draw the temper") of metal tools.
- Never use a hammer on any wrench or socket handle unless you are using a special "staking face" wrench designed to be used with a hammer.
- Replace any tools that are damaged or worn.

HAND TOOL MAINTENANCE

Most hand tools are constructed of rust-resistant metals but they can still rust or corrode if not properly maintained. For best results and long tool life, the following steps should be taken.

- Clean each tool before placing it back into the tool box.
- Keep tools separated. Moisture on metal tools will start to rust more readily if the tools are in contact with another metal tool.
- Line the drawers of the tool box with a material that will prevent the tools from moving as the drawers are opened and closed. This helps to quickly locate the proper tool and size.

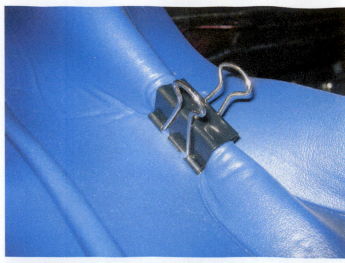

FIGURE 9–48 A binder clip being used to keep a fender cover from falling.

- Release the tension on all "clicker-type" torque wrenches after use.
- Keep the tool box secure.

SUMMARY

1. Wrenches are available in open end, box end, and combination open and box end.
2. An adjustable wrench should only be used where the proper size is not available.
3. Line wrenches are also called flare-nut wrenches, fitting wrenches, or tube-nut wrenches and are used to remove fuel or refrigerant lines.
4. Sockets are rotated by a ratchet or breaker bar, also called a flex handle.
5. Torque wrenches measure the amount of torque applied to a fastener.
6. Screwdriver types include straight blade (flat tip) Torx, and Phillips.
7. Hammers and mallets come in a variety of sizes and weights.
8. Pliers are a useful tool and are available in many different types, including slip-joint, multigroove, linesman's, diagonal, needle-nose, and locking pliers.
9. Other common hand tools include snap-ring pliers, files, cutters, punches, chisels, and hacksaws.

REVIEW QUESTIONS

1. Why are wrenches offset 15 degrees?
2. What are the other names for a line wrench?
3. What are the standard automotive drive sizes for sockets?
4. Which type of screwdriver requires the use of a hammer or mallet?
5. What is inside a dead-blow hammer?
6. What type of cutter is available in left and right cutters?

CHAPTER QUIZ

1. When working with hand tools, always _____.
   a. Push the wrench—don't pull toward you
   b. Pull a wrench—don't push a wrench
2. The proper term for Channel Locks is _____.
   a. Vise Grips
   b. Crescent wrench
   c. Locking pliers
   d. Multigroove adjustable pliers
3. The proper term for Vise Grips is _____.
   a. Locking pliers   c. Side cuts
   b. Slip-joint pliers   d. Multigroove adjustable pliers
4. Which tool listed is a brand name?
   a. Locking pliers
   b. Monkey wrench
   c. Side cutters
   d. Vise Grips

5. Two technicians are discussing torque wrenches. Technician A says that a torque wrench is capable of tightening a fastener with more torque than a conventional breaker bar or ratchet. Technician B says that a torque wrench should be calibrated regularly for the most accurate results. Which technician is correct?
   a. Technician A only
   b. Technician B only
   c. Both Technicians A and B
   d. Neither Technician A nor B

6. What type of screwdriver should be used if there is very limited space above the head of the fastener?
   a. Offset screwdriver
   b. Phillips screwdriver
   c. Impact screwdriver
   d. Robertson screwdriver

7. Where is the "peen" of the hammer?
   a. The striking face
   b. The handle
   c. The back part opposite the striking face
   d. The part that connects to the handle

8. What type of hammer is plastic coated, has a metal casing inside, and is filled with small lead balls?
   a. Dead-blow hammer
   b. Soft-blow hammer
   c. Sledge hammer
   d. Plastic hammer

9. Which type of pliers is capable of fitting over a large object?
   a. Slip-joint pliers
   b. Linesman's pliers
   c. Locking pliers
   d. Multigroove adjustable pliers

10. Which tool has a replaceable cutting edge?
   a. Side-cut pliers
   b. Tin snips
   c. Utility knife
   d. Aviation snips

POWER TOOLS AND SHOP EQUIPMENT

OBJECTIVES: **After studying Chapter 10, the reader should be able to:** • Identify commonly used power tools. • Identify commonly used shop equipment. • Discuss the proper use of power tools and shop equipment. • Describe the safety procedures that should be followed when working with power tools and shop equipment.

KEY TERMS: • Air-blow gun 98 • Air compressor 96 • Air drill 98 • Air ratchet 97 • Bearing splitter 100 • Bench grinder 99 • Bench vise 99 • Die grinder 97 • Engine stand 101 • Hydraulic press 100 • Impact wrench 97 • Incandescent light 98 • Light-emitting diode (LED) 99 • Portable crane 100 • Stone wheel 99 • Trouble light 98 • Wire brush wheel 99 • Work light 98

AIR COMPRESSOR

A shop air compressor is usually located in a separate room or an area away from the customer area of a shop. An **air compressor** is powered by a 220 V AC electric motor and includes a storage tank and the compressor itself, as well as the pressure switches, which are used to maintain a certain minimum level of air pressure in the system. The larger the storage tank, expressed in gallons, the longer an air tool can be operated in the shop without having the compressor start operating. ● **SEE FIGURE 10–1.**

SAFE USE OF COMPRESSED AIR. Air under pressure can create dangerous situations. For example, an object, such as a small piece of dirt, could be forced out of an air hose blow gun with enough force to cause serious personal injury. All OSHA-approved air nozzles have air vents drilled around the outside of the main discharge hole to help reduce the force of the air blast. Also, the air pressure used by an air nozzle (blow gun) must be kept to 30 PSI (207 kPa) or less. ● **SEE FIGURE 10–2.**

FIGURE 10–1 A typical shop compressor. It is usually placed out of the way, yet accessible to provide for maintenance to the unit.

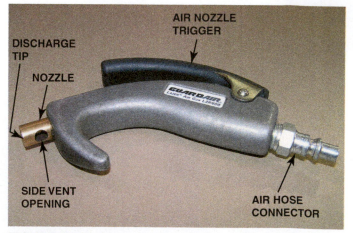

FIGURE 10–2 Always use an air nozzle that is OSHA approved. The openings in the side are used to allow air to escape if the nozzle tip were to become clogged.

FIGURE 10–3 A typical 1/2 in. drive impact wrench.

FIGURE 10–5 A typical battery-powered 3/8 in. drive impact wrench.

FIGURE 10–4 This impact wrench features a variable torque setting using a rotary knob. The direction of rotation can be changed by pressing the button at the bottom.

FIGURE 10–6 A black impact socket. Always use impact-type sockets whenever using an impact wrench to avoid the possibility of shattering the socket, which can cause personal injury.

AIR AND ELECTRICALLY OPERATED TOOLS

IMPACT WRENCH An **impact wrench**, either air (pneumatic) or electrically powered, is a tool that is used to remove and install fasteners. The air-operated 1/2 in. drive impact wrench is the most commonly used unit. ● **SEE FIGURE 10–3.**

The direction of rotation is controlled by a switch. ● **SEE FIGURE 10–4.**

Electrically powered impact wrenches commonly include:

- Battery-powered units. ● **SEE FIGURE 10–5.**

- 110-volt AC-powered units. This type of impact wrench is very useful, especially if compressed air is not readily available.

CAUTION: Always use impact sockets with impact wrenches, and be sure to wear eye protection in case the

socket or fastener shatters. Impact sockets are thicker walled and constructed with premium alloy steel. They are hardened with a black oxide finish to help prevent corrosion and distinguish them from regular sockets. ● **SEE FIGURE 10–6.**

AIR RATCHET An **air ratchet** is used to remove and install fasteners that would normally be removed or installed using a ratchet and a socket. An air ratchet is much faster, yet has an air hose attached, which reduces accessibility to certain places. ● **SEE FIGURE 10–7.**

DIE GRINDER A **die grinder** is a commonly used air-powered tool, which can also be used to sand or remove gaskets and rust. ● **SEE FIGURE 10–8.**

FIGURE 10–7 An air ratchet is a very useful tool that allows fast removal and installation of fasteners, especially in areas that are difficult to reach or do not have room enough to move a hand ratchet wrench.

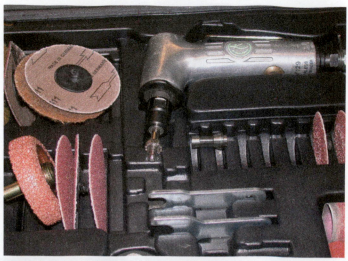

FIGURE 10–8 This typical die grinder surface preparation kit includes the air-operated die grinder, as well as a variety of sanding discs for smoothing surfaces or removing rust.

 REAL-WORLD FIX

The Case of the Rusty Air Impact Wrenches

In one busy shop, it was noticed by several technicians that water was being pumped through the air compressor lines and out of the vents of air impact wrenches whenever they were used. It is normal for moisture in the air to condense in the air storage tank of an air compressor. One of the routine service procedures is to drain the water from the air compressor. The water had been drained regularly from the air compressor at the rear of the shop, but the problem continued. Then someone remembered that there was a second air compressor mounted over the parts department. No one could remember ever draining the tank from that compressor. After that tank was drained, the problem of water in the lines was solved. The service manager assigned a person to drain the water from both compressors every day and to check the oil level. The oil in the compressor is changed every six months to help ensure long life of the expensive compressors.

AIR DRILL An **air drill** is a drill that rotates faster than electric drills (up to 20,000 RPM). Air drills are commonly used in auto body work when many holes need to be drilled for plug welding.

AIR-BLOW GUN An **air-blow gun** is used to clean equipment and other purposes where a stream of air would be needed. Automotive air-blow guns should meet OSHA requirements and include passages to allow air to escape outward at the nozzle, thereby relieving pressure if the nozzle were to become blocked.

AIR-OPERATED GREASE GUN An air-operated grease gun uses shop air to operate a plunger, which then applies a

force to the grease cartridge. Most air-operated grease guns use a 1/4 in. air inlet and operate on 90 PSI of air pressure.

BATTERY-POWERED GREASE GUN Battery-powered grease guns are more expensive than air-operated grease guns but offer the convenience of not having an air hose attached, making use easier. Many use rechargeable 14 to 18 volt batteries and use standard grease cartridges.

TROUBLE LIGHTS

INCANDESCENT **Incandescent lights** use a filament that produces light when electric current flows through the bulb. This was the standard **trouble light**, also called a **work light** for many years until safety issues caused most shops to switch to safer fluorescent or LED lights. If incandescent light bulbs are used, try to locate bulbs that are rated "rough service," which is designed to withstand shock and vibration more than conventional light bulbs.

FLUORESCENT A trouble light is an essential piece of shop equipment, and for safety, should be fluorescent rather than incandescent. Incandescent light bulbs can scatter or break if gasoline were to be splashed onto the bulb creating a serious fire hazard. Fluorescent light tubes are not as likely to be broken

 WARNING

Do not use incandescent trouble lights around gasoline or other flammable liquids. The liquids can cause the bulb to break and the hot filament can ignite the flammable liquid.

FIGURE 10–9 A fluorescent trouble light operates cooler and is safer to use in the shop because it is protected against accidental breakage where gasoline or other flammable liquids would happen to come in contact with the light.

and are usually protected by a clear plastic enclosure. Trouble lights are usually attached to a retractor, which can hold 20 to 50 ft of electrical cord. ● **SEE FIGURE 10–9.**

LED TROUBLE LIGHT **Light-emitting diode (LED)** trouble lights are excellent to use because they are shock resistant, long lasting, and do not represent a fire hazard. Some trouble lights are battery powered and therefore can be used in places where an attached electrical cord could present problems.

BENCH/PEDESTAL GRINDER

A grinder can be mounted on a workbench or on a stand-alone pedestal.

BENCH- OR PEDESTAL-MOUNTED GRINDER These high-powered grinders can be equipped with a wire brush wheel and/or a stone wheel.

- A **wire brush wheel** is used to clean steel or sheet metal parts.
- A **stone wheel** is used to grind metal or to remove the mushroom from the top of punches or chisels. ● **SEE FIGURE 10–10.**

CAUTION: Always wear a face shield when using a wire wheel or a grinder. Also keep the part support ledge (table), also called a throat plate, within 1/16 inch (2 mm) of the stone.

Most **bench grinders** are equipped with a grinding wheel (stone) on one side and a wire brush wheel on the other side. A bench grinder is a very useful piece of shop equipment and the wire wheel end can be used for the following:

FIGURE 10–10 A typical pedestal grinder with a wire wheel on the left side and a stone wheel on the right side. Even though this machine is equipped with guards, safety glasses or a face shield should always be worn when using a grinder or wire wheel.

- Cleaning threads of bolts
- Cleaning gaskets from sheet metal parts, such as steel valve covers

CAUTION: Use a steel wire brush only on steel or iron components. If a steel wire brush is used on aluminum or copper-based metal parts, it can remove metal from the part.

The grinding stone end of the bench grinder can be used for the following:

- Sharpening blades and drill bits
- Grinding off the heads of rivets or parts
- Sharpening sheet metal parts for custom fitting

BENCH VISE

A **bench vise** is used to hold components so that work can be performed on the unit. The size of a vise is determined by the width of the jaws. Two common sizes of vises are 4 in. and 6 in. models. The jaws of most vises are serrated and can cause damage to some components unless protected. Many types of protection can be used, including aluminum or copper jaw covers or by simply placing wood between the vise jaws and the component being held. ● **SEE FIGURE 10–11.**

SAFE USE OF VISES. The jaws of vises can cause damage to the part or component being held. Use pieces of wood or other soft material between the steel jaws and the workpiece to help avoid causing damage. Many vises are sold with optional aluminum jaw covers. When finished using a vise, be sure to close the jaws and place the handle straight up and down to help avoid personal injury to anyone walking near the vise.

FIGURE 10–11 A typical vise mounted to a workbench.

FIGURE 10–13 A typical portable crane used to lift and move heavy assemblies, such as engines and transmissions.

FIGURE 10–12 A hydraulic press is usually used to press bearings on and off on rear axles and transmissions.

HYDRAULIC PRESSES

Hydraulic presses are hand-operated hydraulic cylinders mounted to a stand and designed to press bearings on or off of shafts, as well as other components. To press off a bearing, a unit called a **bearing splitter** is often required to apply force to the inner race of a bearing. Hydraulic presses use a pressure gauge to show the pressure being applied. Always follow the operating instructions supplied by the manufacturer of the hydraulic press. ● **SEE FIGURE 10–12.**

PORTABLE CRANE AND CHAIN HOIST

A **portable crane** is used to remove and install engines and other heavy vehicle components. Most portable cranes use a hand-operated hydraulic cylinder to raise and lower a boom that is equipped with a nylon strap or steel chain. At the end of the strap or chain is a steel hook that is used to attach around a bracket or auxiliary lifting device. ● **SEE FIGURE 10–13.**

SAFE USE OF PORTABLE CRANES. Always be sure to attach the hook(s) of the portable crane to a secure location on the unit being lifted. The hook should also be attached to the center of the weight of the object so it can be lifted straight up without tilting.

CAUTION: Always keep feet and other body parts out from underneath the engine or unit being lifted. Always work around a portable crane as if the chain or strap could break at any time.

ENGINE STANDS

An **engine stand** is designed to safely hold an engine and to allow it to be rotated. This allows the technician to easily remove, install, and perform service work to the engine. ● **SEE FIGURE 10–14.**

Most engine stands are constructed of steel and supported by four casters to allow easy movement. There are two basic places where an engine stand attaches to the engine depending on the size of the engine. For most engines and stands, the retaining bolts attach to the same location as the bell housing at the rear of the engine.

On larger engines, such as the 5.9 Cummins inline 6-cylinder diesel engine, the engine mounts to the stand using the engine mounting holes in the block. ● **SEE FIGURE 10–15.**

SAFE OPERATION OF AN ENGINE STAND. When mounting an engine to an engine stand, be sure that the engine is being supported by a portable crane. Be sure the attaching bolts are grade 5 or 8 and the same thread size as the threaded holes in the block. Check that there is at least 1/2 inch (13 mm) of bolt thread engaged in the threaded holes in the engine block. Be sure that all attaching bolts are securely tightened before releasing the weight of the engine from the crane. Use caution when loosening the rotation retaining bolts because the engine could rotate rapidly, causing personal injury.

CARE AND MAINTENANCE OF SHOP EQUIPMENT

All shop equipment should be maintained in safe working order. Maintenance of shop equipment usually includes the following operations or procedures.

- **Keep equipment clean.** Dirt and grime can attract and hold moisture, which can lead to rust and corrosion. Oil or grease can attract dirt.

- **Keep equipment lubricated.** While many bearings are sealed and do not require lubrication, always check the instructions for the use of the equipment for suggested lubrication and other service procedures.

FIGURE 10–14 Two engines on engine stands. The plastic bags help keep dirt from getting onto the engines.

FIGURE 10–15 An engine stand that attaches to the engine from the sides rather than the end.

CAUTION: Always follow the instructions from the equipment manufacturer regarding proper use and care of the equipment.

1 Inspect the cart and make sure the tanks are chained properly before moving it to the work location.

2 Start by attaching the appropriate work tip to the torch handle. The fitting should only be tightened hand tight. Make sure the valves on the torch handle are closed at this time.

3 Each tank has a regulator assembly with two gauges. The high pressure gauge shows tank pressure, and the low pressure gauge indicates working pressure.

4 Open the oxygen tank valve fully open, and open the acetylene tank valve 1/2 turn.

5 Open the oxygen valve on the torch handle 1/4 turn in preparation for adjusting oxygen gas pressure.

6 Turn the oxygen regulator valve clockwise and adjust oxygen gas pressure to 20 PSI. Close the oxygen valve on the torch handle.

7 Open the acetylene valve on the torch handle 1/4 turn and adjust acetylene gas pressure to 7 PSI. Close the acetylene valve on the torch handle.

8 Open the oxygen valve on the torch handle 1/4 turn and use an appropriate size tip cleaner to clean the tip orifice. Finish by closing the oxygen valve.

9 Put on leather gloves and open the acetylene valve on the torch handle 1/4 turn. Use a flint striker to ignite the acetylene gas exiting the torch tip.

10 Adjust the acetylene valve until the base of the flame just touches the torch tip. Slowly open the oxygen valve on the torch handle and adjust for a neutral flame (blue cone is well-defined).

11 Once work is complete, extinguish the flame by quickly closing the acetylene valve on the torch handle. Be prepared to hear a loud "pop" when the flame goes out. Close the oxygen valve on the torch handle.

12 Close the valves on both tanks and turn the regulator handles CCW until they no longer contact the internal springs. Open the gas valves briefly on the torch handle to release gas pressure from the hoses. Close the gas valves on the torch handle and put away the torch assembly.

1 Heating attachments include ordinary heating tips, middle and right and a "rosebud" (left). Ordinary heating tips work fine for most purposes, but occasionally the rosebud is utilized when a great deal of heat is needed.

2 Note that while acetylene tank pressures are relatively low, the oxygen tank can be filled to over 2,000 PSI. This can represent a serious hazard if precautions are not taken. Be absolutely certain that the tanks are chained properly to the cart before attempting to move it!

3 Any time heating or cutting operations are being performed, be sure that any flammables have been removed from the immediate area. A fire blanket may be placed over floor drains or other objects to prevent fires. A fire extinguisher should be on hand in case of an emergency.

4 Be sure to wear appropriate personal protective equipment during heating and cutting operations.

5 Note that heating operations should be performed over steel or firebrick. Never heat or cut steel close to concrete, as it could cause the concrete to explode.

6 When heating steel, move the torch in a circular pattern to prevent melting of the metal. Don't hold the torch too close to the work as this will cause a "snapping" or "backfire" that can extinguish the flame.

1 Affix the cutting attachment to the torch handle. Note that the cutting attachment has a cutting handle and a separate oxygen valve.

2 Fully open the oxygen valve on the torch handle. Oxygen flow will now be controlled with the valve on the cutting attachment.

3 Oxygen gas pressure should be adjusted to 30 PSI whenever using the cutting attachment. Acetylene pressure is kept at 7 PSI.

4 Open the acetylene valve on the torch handle 1/4 turn and light the torch. Adjust the flame until its base just touches the cutting tip. Slowly open the oxygen valve on the cutting attachment and adjust the flame until the blue cone is well-defined.

5 Direct the flame onto a thin spot or sharp edge of the metal to be cut. This will build the heat quicker in order to get the cut started.

6 When the metal glows red, depress the cutting handle and move the torch to advance the cut. You will need to move the torch faster when cutting thinner pieces of steel. On thicker pieces, point the cutting tip into the direction of the cut.

SUMMARY

1. Most shops are equipped with a large air compressor that supplies pressurized air to all stalls for use by the technician.

2. An air impact wrench is the most commonly used power tool in the shop. It is used mostly to remove fasteners.

3. Other air-operated tools include an air ratchet and a die grinder.

4. A bench or pedestal grinder usually has both a grinding stone and a wire brush wheel.

5. Trouble lights should be fluorescent or LED for maximum safety in the shop.

6. A hydraulic press is used to remove bearings from shafts and other similar operations.

7. A portable crane is used to remove and install engines or engine/transmission assemblies from vehicles.

8. Engine stands are designed to allow the technician to rotate the engine to get access to the various parts and components.

REVIEW QUESTIONS

1. List the tools used by service technicians that use compressed air?

2. Which trouble light design(s) is (are) the recommended type for maximum safety?

3. What safety precautions should be adhered to when working with a vise?

4. When using a blow gun, what precautions need to be taken?

CHAPTER QUIZ

1. When using compressed air and a blow gun, what is the maximum allowable air pressure?
   a. 10 PSI
   b. 20 PSI
   c. 30 PSI
   d. 40 PSI

2. Which air impact drive size is the most commonly used?
   a. 1/4 in.
   b. 3/8 in.
   c. 1/2 in.
   d. 3/4 in.

3. What type of socket should be used with an air impact wrench?
   a. Black
   b. Chrome
   c. 12 point
   d. Either a or b

4. What can be used to cover the jaws of a vise to help protect the object being held?
   a. Aluminum
   b. Wood
   c. Copper
   d. All of the above

5. Technician A says that impact sockets have thicker walls than conventional sockets. Technician B says that impact sockets have a black oxide finish. Which technician is correct?
   a. Technician A only
   b. Technician B only
   c. Both Technicians A and B
   d. Neither Technician A nor B

6. Two technicians are discussing the use of a typical bench/pedestal-mounted grinder. Technician A says that a wire brush wheel can be used to clean threads. Technician B says that the grinding stone can be used to clean threads. Which technician is correct?
   a. Technician A only
   b. Technician B only
   c. Both Technicians A and B
   d. Neither Technician A nor B

7. A hydraulic press is being used to separate a bearing from a shaft. What should be used to cover the bearing during the pressing operation?
   a. Shop cloth
   b. Brake drum
   c. Fender cover
   d. Paper towel

8. Which type of trouble light is recommended for use in the shop?
   a. Incandescent
   b. Fluorescent
   c. LED
   d. Either b or c

9. When mounting an engine to an engine stand, what grade of bolt should be used?
   a. 5 or 8
   b. 4 or 7
   c. 3 or 5
   d. 1 or 4

10. Proper care of shop equipment includes _____.
    a. Tuning up every six months
    b. Keeping equipment clean
    c. Keeping equipment lubricated
    d. Both b and c

chapter 11

MEASURING SYSTEMS AND TOOLS

OBJECTIVES: **After studying Chapter 11, the reader should be able to:** • Describe how to read a ruler. • Explain how to use a micrometer and vernier dial caliper. • Describe how to use a telescopic gauge and a micrometer to measure cylinder and lifter bores. • Discuss how to measure valve guides using a small-hole gauge.

KEY TERMS: • Feeler gauge 112 • Sleeve 108 • Small-hole gauge 111 • Spindle 108 • Split-ball gauge 111 • Straightedge 113 • Thickness gauge 112 • Thimble 108

ENGLISH CUSTOMARY MEASURING SYSTEM

The English customary measuring system was established about A.D. 1100 in England during the reign of Henry I. The foot was determined to be 12 inches and was taken from the length of a typical foot. The yard (36 inches) was determined to be the length from King Henry's nose to the end of his outstretched hand. The mile came from Roman days and was originally defined as the distance traveled by a soldier in 1,000 paces or steps. Other English units, such as the pound (weight) and volume (gallon), evolved over the years from Roman and English measurements.

The Fahrenheit temperature scale was created by Gabriel Fahrenheit (1686–1736) and he used 100°F as the temperature of the human body, which he missed by 1.4 degrees (98.6°F is considered now to be normal temperature). On the Fahrenheit scale, water freezes at 32°F and water boils at 212°F.

METRIC SYSTEM OF MEASURE

Most of the world uses the metric system of measure. The metric system was created in the late 1700s in France and used the physical world for the basis of the measurements. For example, the meter was defined as being 1/40,000,000 of the circumference of the earth (the distance around the earth at the poles). The Celsius temperature scale developed by Anders Celsius (1701–1744) used the freezing point of water as 0°C (32°F) and the boiling point of water as 100°C (212°F). Other units include a liter of water, which was then used as a standard of weight where 1 liter of water (about 1 quart) weighs 1 kilogram (1,000 grams). Units of measure are then divided or multiplied by 10,

100, or 1,000 to arrive at usable measurements. For example, a kilometer is 1,000 meters and is the most commonly used metric measurement for distance for travel. Other prefixes include:

m = milli = 1/1,000

k = kilo = 1,000

M = mega = 1,000,000

LINEAR METRIC MEASUREMENTS

1 kilometer = 0.62 mile

1 meter = 39.37 inches

1 centimeter (1/100 meter) = 0.39 inch

1 millimeter (1/1,000 meter) = 0.039 inch

VOLUME MEASUREMENT

1 cc (cubic centimeter) = 0.06 cubic inch

1 liter = 0.26 U.S. gallon (about 1 quart)

WEIGHT MEASUREMENT

1 gram = 0.035 ounce

1 kilogram (1,000 grams) = 2.2 pounds

PRESSURE MEASUREMENTS

1 kilopascal (kPa) = 0.14 pound per square inch
    (6.9 kPa = 1 PSI)

1 bar = 14.5 pounds per square inch

DERIVED UNITS   All units of measure, except for the base units, are a combination of units that are referred to as derived units of measure. Some examples of derived units include:

Torque

Velocity

Density

Energy

Power

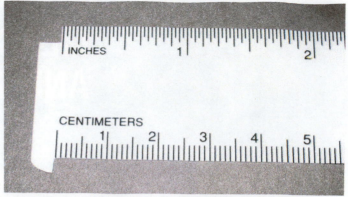

FIGURE 11–2 A plastic rule that has both inches and centimeters. Each line between the numbers on the centimeters represents 1 millimeter because there are 10 millimeters in 1 centimeter.

LINEAR MEASUREMENTS (TAPE MEASURE/RULE)

A tape measure or machinist rule divides inches into smaller units. Each smaller unit is drawn with a line shorter than the longer unit. The units of measure starting with the largest include:

1 inch

1/2 inch

1/4 inch

1/8 inch

1/16 inch

Some rules show 1/32 of an inch. ●**SEE FIGURE 11–1.**

A metric scale is also included on many tape measures and machinists rules. ●**SEE FIGURE 11–2.**

MICROMETER

A micrometer is the most used measuring instrument in engine-service and repair. ●**SEE FIGURE 11–3.**

The **thimble** rotates over the **sleeve** on a screw that has 40 threads per inch. Every revolution of the thimble moves the **spindle** 0.025 in. The thimble is graduated into 25 equally spaced lines; therefore, each line represents 0.001 in. Every micrometer should be checked for calibration on a regular basis. ●**SEE FIGURES 11–4 THROUGH 11–6.**

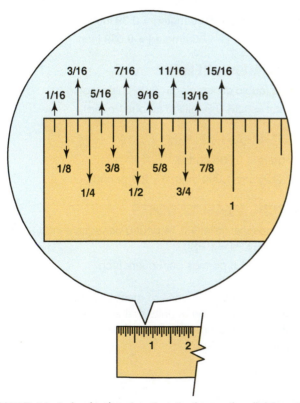

FIGURE 11–1 A rule showing that the larger the division, the longer the line.

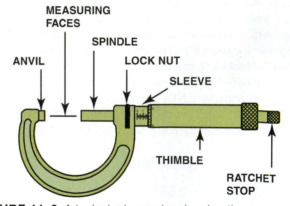

FIGURE 11–3 A typical micrometer showing the names of the parts. The sleeve may also be called the *barrel* or *stock*.

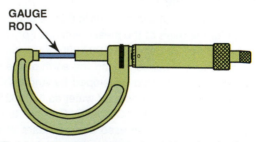

FIGURE 11–4 All micrometers should be checked and calibrated as needed using a gauge rod.

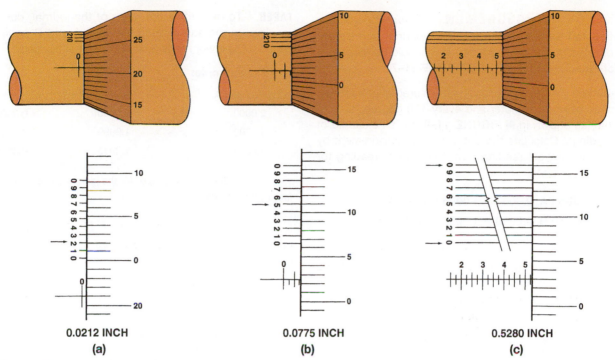

FIGURE 11–5 The three micrometer readings are (a) 0.0212 in.; (b) 0.0775 in.; and (c) 0.5280 in. These measurements used the vernier scale on the sleeve to arrive at the ten-thousandth measurement. The number that is aligned represents the digit in the ten-thousandth place.

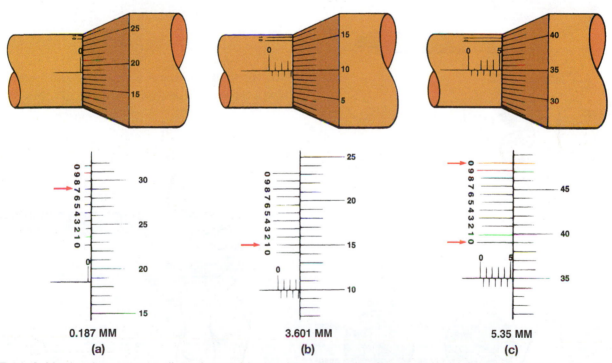

FIGURE 11–6 Metric micrometer readings that use the vernier scale on the sleeve to read to the nearest 0.001 millimeter. The arrows point to the final reading for each of the three examples.

CRANKSHAFT MEASUREMENT
Even though the connecting rod journals and the main bearing journals are usually different sizes, they both can and should be measured for out-of-round and taper. ● SEE FIGURE 11–7.

OUT-OF-ROUND. A journal should be measured in at least two positions across the diameter and every 120 degrees around the journal, as shown in ● FIGURE 11–8, for an example of the six readings. Calculate the out-of-round measurement by subtracting the lowest reading from the highest reading for both A and B positions.

Position A: 2.0000 − 1.9995 = 0.0005 in.

Position B: 2.0000 − 1.9989 = 0.0011 in.

The maximum out-of-round measurement occurs in position B (0.0011 in.), which is the measurement that should be used to compare against factory specifications to determine if any machining will be necessary.

TAPER. To determine the taper of the journal, compare the readings in the same place between A and B positions and subtract the lower reading from the higher reading.

For example:

Position A		Position B	
2.0000	−	2.0000	= 0.0000
1.9999	−	1.9999	= 0.0000
1.9995	−	1.9989	= 0.0006

Use 0.0006 in. as the taper for the journal and compare with factory specifications.

CAMSHAFT MEASUREMENT
The journal of the camshaft(s) can also be measured using a micrometer and compared with factory specifications for taper and out-of-round. ● SEE FIGURE 11–9.

NOTE: On overhead valve (pushrod) engines, the camshaft journal diameter often decreases slightly toward the rear of the engine. Overhead camshaft engines usually have the same journal diameter.

The cam lift can also be measured with a micrometer and compared with factory specifications, as shown in ● FIGURE 11–10.

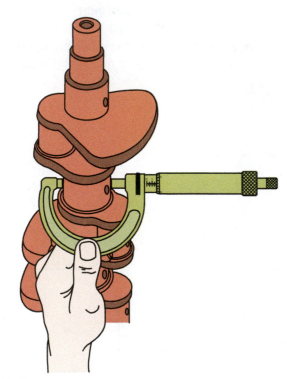

FIGURE 11–7 Using a micrometer to measure the connecting rod journal for out-of-round and taper.

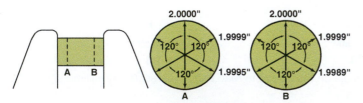

FIGURE 11–8 Crankshaft journal measurements. Each journal should be measured in at least six locations, but also in position A and position B and at 120-degree intervals around the journal.

FIGURE 11–9 Camshaft journals should be measured in three locations, 120 degrees apart, to check for out-of-round.

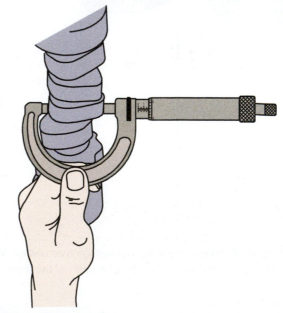

FIGURE 11–10 Checking a camshaft for wear by measuring the lobe height with a micrometer.

TELESCOPIC GAUGE

A telescopic gauge is used with a micrometer to measure the inside diameter of a hole or bore.

The cylinder bore can be measured by inserting a telescopic gauge into the bore and rotating the handle lock to allow the arms of the gauge to contact the inside bore of the cylinder. Tighten the handle lock and remove the gauge from the cylinder. Use a micrometer to measure the telescopic gauge. ● **SEE FIGURE 11–11.**

A telescopic gauge can also be used to measure the following:

- Camshaft bearing (● **SEE FIGURE 11–12.**)
- Main bearing bore (housing bore) measurement
- Connecting rod bore measurement

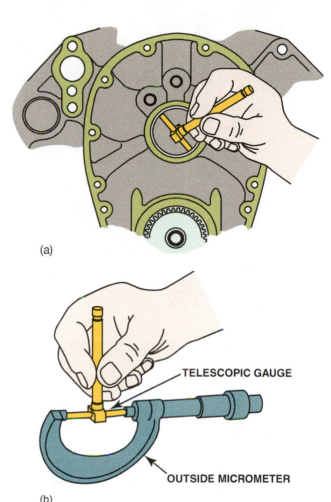

(a)

(b)

FIGURE 11–12 (a) A telescopic gauge being used to measure the inside diameter (ID) of a camshaft bearing. (b) An outside micrometer used to measure the telescopic gauge.

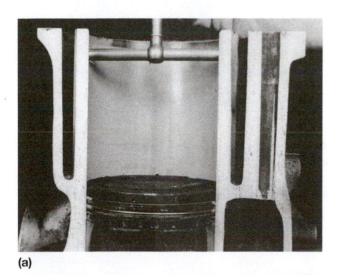

(a)

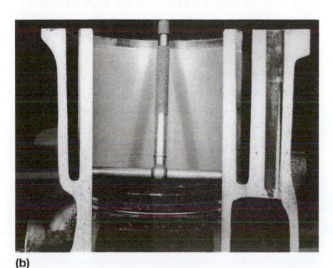

(b)

FIGURE 11–11 When the head is first removed, the cylinder taper and out-of-round should be checked below the ridge (a) and above the piston when it is at the bottom of the stroke (b).

SMALL-HOLE GAUGE

A **small-hole gauge** (also called a **split-ball gauge**) is used with a micrometer to measure the inside diameter of small holes such as a valve guide in a cylinder head. ● **SEE FIGURES 11–13 AND 11–14.**

VERNIER DIAL CALIPER

A vernier dial caliper is normally used to measure length, inside and outside diameters, and depth. ● **SEE FIGURE 11–15.**

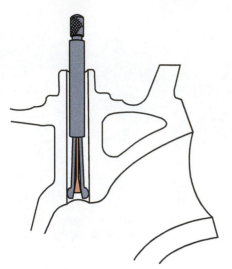

FIGURE 11–13 Cutaway of a valve guide with a hole gauge adjusted to the hole diameter.

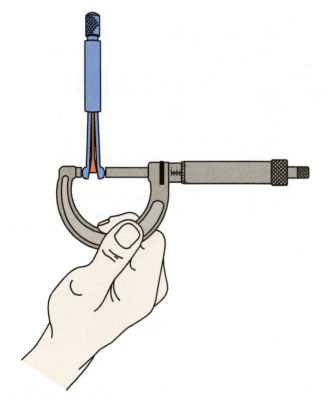

FIGURE 11–14 The outside of a hole gauge being measured with a micrometer.

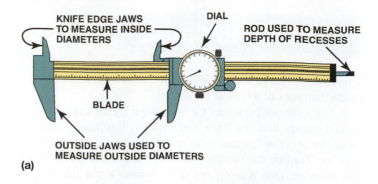

KNIFE EDGE JAWS TO MEASURE INSIDE DIAMETERS

DIAL

ROD USED TO MEASURE DEPTH OF RECESSES

BLADE

OUTSIDE JAWS USED TO MEASURE OUTSIDE DIAMETERS

(a)

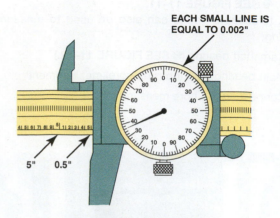

EACH SMALL LINE IS EQUAL TO 0.002"

5"   0.5"

ADD READING ON BLADE (5.5")
TO READING ON DIAL (0.036") TO
GET FINAL TOTAL MEASUREMENT (5.536")

(b)

FIGURE 11–15 (a) A typical vernier dial caliper. This is a very useful measuring tool for automotive engine work because it is capable of measuring inside, outside, and depth measurements. (b) To read a vernier dial caliper, simply add the reading on the blade to the reading on the dial.

FEELER GAUGE

A **feeler gauge** (also known as a **thickness gauge**) is an accurately manufactured strip of metal that is used to determine the gap or clearance between two components. ● **SEE FIGURE 11–16.**

? FREQUENTLY ASKED QUESTION

What Is the Difference Between the Word *Gage* and *Gauge*?

The word *gauge* means "measurement or dimension to a standard of reference." The word *gauge* can also be spelled *gage*. Therefore, in most cases, the words mean the same.

INTERESTING NOTE: One vehicle manufacturing representative told me that *gage* was used rather than *gauge* because even though it is the second acceptable spelling of the word, it is correct and it saved the company a lot of money in printing costs because the word *gage* has one less letter! One letter multiplied by millions of vehicles with gauges on the dash and the word *gauge* used in service manuals adds up to a big savings to the manufacturer.

FIGURE 11–16 A group of feeler gauges (also known as thickness gauges), used to measure between two parts. The long gauges on the bottom are used to measure the piston-to-cylinder wall clearance.

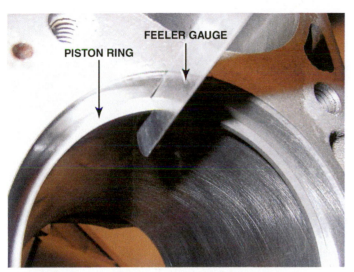

PISTON RING **FEELER GAUGE**

FIGURE 11–17 A feeler gauge, also called a thickness gauge, is used to measure the small clearances such as the end gap of a piston ring.

A feeler gauge can be used to check the following:

- Piston ring end gap (● SEE FIGURE 11–17.)
- Piston ring side clearance
- Connecting rod side clearance
- Piston-to-wall clearance

STRAIGHTEDGE

A **straightedge** is a precision ground metal measuring gauge that is used to check the flatness of engine components when used with a feeler gauge. A straightedge is used to check the flatness of the following:

- Cylinder heads (● SEE FIGURE 11–18.)
- Cylinder block deck
- Straightness of the main bearing bores (saddles)

FIGURE 11–18 A straightedge is used with a feeler gauge to determine if a cylinder head is warped or twisted.

DIAL INDICATOR

A dial indicator is a precision measuring instrument used to measure crankshaft end play, crankshaft runout, and valve guide wear. A dial indicator can be mounted three ways, including:

- **Magnetic mount.** This is a very useful method because a dial indicator can be attached to any steel or cast iron part.
- **Clamp mount.** A clamp-mounted dial indicator is used in many places where a mount could be clamped.
- **Threaded rod.** Using a threaded rod allows the dial indicator to be securely mounted, such as shown in ● FIGURE 11–19.

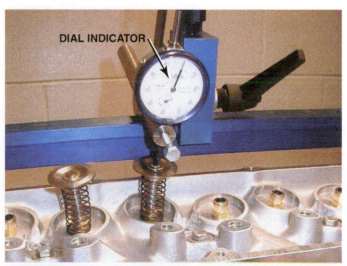

DIAL INDICATOR

FIGURE 11–19 A dial indicator is used to measure valve lift during flow testing of a high-performance cylinder head.

FIGURE 11–20 A dial bore gauge is used to measure cylinders and other engine parts for out-of-round and taper conditions.

DIAL BORE GAUGE

A dial bore gauge is an expensive, but important, gauge used to measure cylinder taper and out-of-round as well as main bearing (block housing) bore for taper and out-of-round.

●**SEE FIGURE 11–20.** A dial bore gauge has to be adjusted to a dimension, such as the factory specifications. The reading on the dial bore gauge then indicates plus (+) or minus (−) readings from the predetermined dimension. This is why a dial bore is best used to measure taper and out-of-round because it shows the difference in cylinder or bore rather than an actual measurement.

DEPTH MICROMETER

A depth micrometer is similar to a conventional micrometer except that it is designed to measure the depth from a flat surface. ●**SEE FIGURE 11–21.**

FIGURE 11–21 A depth micrometer being used to measure the height of the rotor of an oil pump from the surface of the housing.

SUMMARY

1. A tape measure or machinist rule can be used to measure linear distances.

2. A micrometer can measure 0.001 in. by using a thimble that has 40 threads per in. Each rotation of the thimble moves the thimble 0.025 in. The circumference of the thimble is graduated into 25 marks, each representing 0.001 in.

3. A micrometer is used to check the diameter of a crankshaft journal as well as the taper and out-of-round.

4. A camshaft bearing and lobe can be measured using a micrometer.

5. A telescopic gauge is used with a micrometer to measure the inside of a hole or bore, such as the big end of a connecting rod or a cylinder bore.

6. A small-hole gauge (also called a split-ball gauge) is used with a micrometer to measure small holes such as the inside diameter of a valve guide in a cylinder head.

7. A vernier dial caliper is used to measure the outside diameter of components such as pistons or crankshaft bearing journals as well as inside diameters and depth measurements.

8. A feeler gauge (also called a thickness gauge) is used to measure the gap or clearance between two components such as piston ring end gap, piston-ring side clearance, and connecting rod side clearance. A feeler gauge is also used with a precision straightedge to measure the flatness of blocks and cylinder heads.

9. A dial indicator and dial bore gauge are used to measure differences in a component such as crankshaft end play (dial indicator) or cylinder taper (dial bore gauge).

REVIEW QUESTIONS

1. Explain how a micrometer is read.
2. Describe how to check a crankshaft journal for out-of-round and taper.
3. List engine components that can be measured with the help of a telescopic gauge.
4. List the gaps or clearances that can be measured using a feeler (thickness) gauge.
5. Explain why a dial bore gauge has to be set to a dimension before using.

CHAPTER QUIZ

1. The threaded movable part that rotates on a micrometer is called the _____.
   - **a.** Sleeve
   - **b.** Thimble
   - **c.** Spindle
   - **d.** Anvil

2. To check a crankshaft journal for taper, the journal should be measured in at least how many locations?
   - **a.** One
   - **b.** Two
   - **c.** Four
   - **d.** Six

3. To check a crankshaft journal for out-of-round, the journal should be measured in at least how many locations?
   - **a.** Two
   - **b.** Four
   - **c.** Six
   - **d.** Eight

4. A telescopic gauge can be used to measure a cylinder bore if what other measuring device is used to measure the telescopic gauge?
   - **a.** Micrometer
   - **b.** Feeler gauge
   - **c.** Straightedge
   - **d.** Dial indicator

5. To directly measure the diameter of a valve guide in a cylinder head, use a micrometer and a _____.
   - **a.** Telescopic gauge
   - **c.** Small-hole gauge
   - **b.** Feeler gauge
   - **d.** Dial indicator

6. Which of the following *cannot* be measured using a feeler gauge?
   - **a.** Valve guide clearance
   - **b.** Piston-ring end gap
   - **c.** Piston-ring side clearance
   - **d.** Connecting rod side clearance

7. Which of the following *cannot* be measured using a straightedge and a feeler gauge?
   - **a.** Cylinder head flatness
   - **b.** Block deck flatness
   - **c.** Straightness of the main bearing bores
   - **d.** Straightness of the cylinder bore

8. Which measuring gauge needs to be set up (adjusted) to a fixed dimension before use?
   - **a.** Dial indicator
   - **b.** Dial bore gauge
   - **c.** Vernier dial gauge
   - **d.** Micrometer

9. A feeler gauge is also called a _____.
   - **a.** Dial gauge
   - **b.** Flat gauge
   - **c.** Straight gauge
   - **d.** Thickness gauge

10. Which metric unit of measure is used for volume measurement?
   - **a.** Meter
   - **b.** cc
   - **c.** Centimeter
   - **d.** Millimeter

chapter
12

SERVICE INFORMATION

OBJECTIVES: After studying Chapter 12, the reader should be able to: • Discuss the importance of vehicle history. • Retrieve vehicle service information. • Read and interpret service manuals and electronic service information. • Describe the use of the vehicle owner's manual.

KEY TERMS: • Julian date 121 • Labor guides 119 • Service information 117 • Technical service bulletin (TSB) 120

VEHICLE SERVICE HISTORY RECORDS

Whenever service work is performed, a record of what was done is usually kept on file by the shop or service department for a number of years. The wise service technician will check the vehicle service history if working on a vehicle with an unusual problem. Often, a previous repair may indicate the reason for the current problem or it could be related to the same circuit or components. For example, a collision could have caused hidden damage that can affect the operation of the vehicle. Knowing that a collision had been recently repaired may be helpful to the technician.

OWNER'S MANUALS

It has been said by many professional automotive technicians and service advisors that the owner's manual is not read by many vehicle owners. Most owner's manuals contain all or most of the following information.

1. How to reset the maintenance reminder light
2. Specifications, including viscosity of oil needed and number of quarts (liters)
3. Tire pressures for standard as well as optional tire sizes
4. Maintenance schedule for all fluids, including coolant, brake fluid, automatic transmission fluid, and differential fluid

FIGURE 12–1 The owner's manual has a lot of information pertaining to the operation as well as the maintenance and resetting procedures that technicians often need.

5. How to program the remote control as well as the power windows and door locks
6. How to reset the tire pressure monitoring system after a tire rotation

● **SEE FIGURE 12–1.**

LUBRICATION GUIDES

Lubrication guides, such as those published by Chek-Chart and Chilton, include all specifications for lubrication-related service, including:

■ Hoisting location
■ Lubrication points

Owner's Manual Is the Key to Proper Operation

A customer purchased a used Pontiac Vibe and complained to a shop that the cruise control would disengage and had to be reset if driven below 25 mph (40 km/h). The service technician was able to verify that in fact this occurred, but did not know if this feature was normal or not. The technician checked the owner's manual and discovered that this vehicle was designed to operate this way. Unlike other cruise control systems, those systems on Toyota-based vehicles are designed to shut off below 25 mph, requiring the driver to reset the desired speed. The customer was informed that nothing could be done to correct this concern and the technician also learned something. Vehicles that use the Toyota cruise control system include all Toyotas, plus Lexus, Pontiac Vibe, and Chevrolet Prism.

HINT: Some vehicle manufacturers offer owner's manuals on their website for a free download.

Exploded Views

Exploded views of components such as engines and transmissions are available in shop manuals and electronic service information, as well as in parts and labor time guides. These views, showing all of the parts as if the assembly was blown apart, give the service technician a clear view of the various parts and their relationship to other parts in the assembly.

- Grease and oil specifications
- Capacities for engine oil, transmission fluid, coolant, and differential fluid

SERVICE MANUALS

Factory and aftermarket service manuals, also called shop manuals, contain specifications and service procedures. While factory service manuals cover just one year and one or more models of the same vehicle, most aftermarket service manuals cover multiple years and/or models in one manual.

Included in most service manuals are the following:

- Capacities and recommended specifications for all fluids
- Specifications, including engine and routine maintenance items
- Testing procedures
- Service procedures, including the use of special tools when needed
- Component location information

While some factory service manuals are printed in one volume, most factory **service information** is printed in several volumes due to the amount and depth of information presented. The typical factory service manual is divided into sections.

GENERAL INFORMATION   General information includes topics such as:

- Warnings and cautions
- Vehicle identification numbers on engine, transmission/ transaxle, and body parts
- Lock cylinder coding
- Fastener information
- Decimal and metric equivalents
- Abbreviations and standard nomenclature used
- Service parts identification label and process code information

MAINTENANCE AND LUBRICATION INFORMATION
Maintenance and lubrication information includes topics such as:

- Schedule for "normal" as well as "severe" usage time and mileage charts
- Specified oil and other lubricant specifications
- Chassis lubrication points
- Tire rotation methods
- Periodic vehicle inspection services (items to check and time/mileage intervals)
- Maintenance item part numbers, such as oil and air filter numbers, and specifications, such as oil capacity and tire pressures

ENGINES

- Engine electrical diagnosis (battery, charging, cranking, ignition, and wiring)
- Engine mechanical diagnosis
- Specific engine information for each engine that may be used in the vehicle(s) covered by the service manual, including:
  - Engine identification
  - On-vehicle service procedures
  - Description of the engine and the operation of the lubrication system
  - Exploded views showing all parts of the engine
  - Disassembly procedures

- Inspection procedures and specifications of the parts and subsystems
- Assembly procedures
- Torque specifications for all fasteners, including the torque sequence

AUTOMATIC TRANSMISSION/TRANSAXLE

- General information (identification and specifications)
- Diagnosis procedures, including preliminary checks and fluid level procedures
- General service, including leak detection and correction
- Cooler flushing procedures
- Unit removal procedures
- Unit disassembly procedures and precautions
- Unit assembly procedures and torque specifications

ELECTRICAL SYSTEMS

- Symbols used
- Troubleshooting procedures
- Repair procedures (wire repair, connectors, and terminals)
- Power distribution
- Ground distribution
- Component location views
- Harness routing views
- Individual electrical circuits, including circuit operation and schematics

HEATING, VENTILATION, AND AIR CONDITIONING

- Heater system
  - General description
  - Heater control assembly
  - Diagnosis, including heater electrical wiring and vacuum system

- Blower motor and fan assembly diagnosis and servicing procedures
- Air distribution values
- Fastener torque specifications
- Air conditioning system
  - General description and system components
  - Air conditioning system diagnosis, including leak detection
  - Air conditioning and heater function tests
  - Air conditioning service procedures
  - Refrigerant recovery, recycling, adding oil, evacuating procedures, and charging procedures
  - Troubleshooting guide

ENGINE PERFORMANCE (DRIVEABILITY AND EMISSIONS)

- Vehicle emission control information (VECI) label, visual/physical underhood inspection
- On-board diagnostic system
- Scan tool values
- Wiring harness service
- Symptom charts
- Diagnostic trouble code (DTC) information

ADVANTAGES OF HARD COPY VERSUS ELECTRONIC SERVICE INFORMATION

All forms of service information have some advantages, including:

Hard Copy	Electronic Service Information
• Easy to use—no hardware or expensive computers needed	• Information can be printed out and taken to the vehicle
• Can be taken to the vehicle for reference	• Has a search function for information
• Can view several pages easily for reference	• Internet or network access allows use at several locations in the shop

DISADVANTGES OF HARD COPY VERSUS ELECTRONIC SERVICE INFORMATION

All forms of service information have some disadvantages, including:

Hard Copy	Electronic Service Information
• Can be lost or left in the vehicle	• Requires a computer and printer
• Cost is high for each manual	• Internet or network access can be a challenge
• Can get dirty and unreadable	• Cost can be high

LABOR GUIDE MANUALS

Labor guides, also called *flat-rate manuals*, list vehicle service procedures and the time it should take an average technician to complete the task. This flat-rate time is then the basis for estimates and pay for technicians. Some manuals also include a parts list, including the price of the part to help service advisors create complete estimates for both labor and parts. These manuals are usually called "parts and time guides." Some guides include labor time only. ● **SEE FIGURE 12–2.**

ELECTRONIC SERVICE INFORMATION

There are many programs available that will provide electronic service information for the automotive industry. Sometimes the vehicle makers make information available on CDs or DVDs, but mostly it is available online. Most electronic service information has technical service bulletins (TSBs), wiring diagrams, and a main menu that includes the major components of the vehicle as a starting point. ● **SEE FIGURE 12–3.** ALLDATA and Mitchell On-Demand are commonly used software programs that include service information for many vehicles.

Service information and testing procedures should be closely followed, including any symptom charts or flow charts. A sample of a symptom information chart is shown ● **CHART 12–1.**

HOME SCREEN The home screen is the first screen displayed when you start. It displays buttons that represent the major sections of the program. Access to the home screen is available from anywhere within the program by clicking the home button on the toolbar.

TOOLBARS A main toolbar is displayed on most screens, providing quick access to certain functions. This toolbar varies somewhat, depending upon what information is being accessed.

ELECTRONIC SERVICE INFORMATION Electronic service information is available mostly by subscription and provides access to an Internet site where service

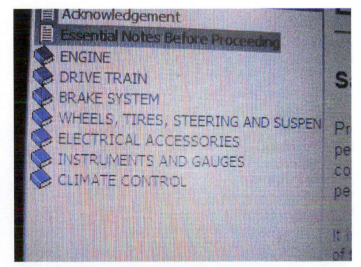

FIGURE 12–2 Some technical service bulletins also include the designated flat-rate time when specifying a repair procedure.

Description	Labor Time
Brake Burnish	0.2 hr
Pads, Front Disc Brake — Replace	Use Published Labor operation Time
Pads, Disc Brake — Rear R&R or Replace	Use published labor operation time
Rotor Asm — Front	Use published labor

FIGURE 12–3 A main menu showing the major systems of the vehicle. Clicking on one of these major topics opens up another menu showing more detailed information.

POSSIBLE CAUSE	REASON
Throttle-position (TP) sensor	• The TP sensor should be within the specified range at idle. If too high or too low, the computer may not provide a strong enough extra pulse to prevent a hesitation.
	• An open or short in the TP sensor can result in hesitation because the computer would not be receiving correct information regarding the position of the throttle.
Throttle-plate deposit buildup	An airflow restriction at the throttle plates creates not only less air reaching the engine but also swirling air due to the deposits. This swirling or uneven airflow can cause an uneven air-fuel mixture being supplied to the engine, causing poor idle quality and a sag or hesitation during acceleration.
Manifold absolute pressure (MAP) sensor fault	The MAP sensor detects changes in engine load and signals to the computer to increase the amount of fuel needed for proper operation. Check the vacuum hose and the sensor itself for proper operation.
Check the throttle linkage for binding	A kinked throttle cable or cruise (speed) control cable can cause the accelerator pedal to bind.
Contaminated fuel	Fuel contaminated with excessive amounts of alcohol or water can cause a hesitation or sag during acceleration. HINT: To easily check for the presence of alcohol in gasoline, simply get a sample of the fuel and place it in a clean container. Add some water and shake. If no alcohol is in the gasoline, the water will settle to the bottom and be clear. If there is alcohol in the gasoline, the alcohol will absorb the water. The alcohol-water combination will settle to the bottom of the container, but will be cloudy rather than clear.
Clogged, shorted, or leaking fuel injectors	Any injector problem that results in less than an ideal amount of fuel being delivered to the cylinders can result in a hesitation, a sag, or stumble during acceleration.
Spark plugs or spark plug wires	Any fault in the ignition system such as a defective spark plug wire or cracked spark plug can cause hesitation, a sag, or stumble during acceleration. At higher engine speeds, a defective spark plug wire is not as noticeable as it is at lower speeds, especially in vehicles equipped with a V-8 engine.
EGR valve operation	Hesitation, a sag, or stumble can occur if the EGR valve opens too soon or is stuck partially open.
False air	A loose or cracked intake hose between the mass airflow (MAF) sensor and the throttle plate can be the cause of hesitation.

CHART 12–1

A chart showing symptoms for hesitation while accelerating. These charts help the technician diagnose faults that do not set a diagnostic trouble code (DTC).

manual–type information is available. Most vehicle manufacturers also offer electronic service information to their dealers and to most schools and colleges that offer corporate training programs.

TECHNICAL SERVICE BULLETINS

Technical service bulletins, often abbreviated TSBs, are issued by the vehicle manufacturer to notify service technicians of a problem and include the necessary corrective action. Technical service bulletins are designed for dealership technicians but are republished by aftermarket companies and made available along with other service information to shops and vehicle repair facilities.

INTERNET

The Internet has opened the field for information exchange and access to technical advice. One of the most useful websites is the International Automotive Technician's network at **www.iatn.net**. This is a free site but service technicians need to register to join. For a small monthly sponsor fee, the shop or service technician can gain access to the archives, which include thousands of successful repairs in the searchable database.

RECALLS AND CAMPAIGNS

A recall or campaign is issued by a vehicle manufacturer and a notice is sent to all owners in the event of a safety- or emission-related fault or concern. While these faults may be repaired by independent shops, it is generally handled by a local dealer. Items that have created recalls in the past have included potential fuel system leakage problems, exhaust leakage, or electrical malfunctions that could cause a possible fire or the engine to stall. Unlike technical service bulletins whose cost is only covered when the vehicle is within the warranty period, a recall or campaign is always done at no cost to the vehicle owner.

FIGURE 12–4 Whenever calling a hot line service be sure that you have all of the vehicle information ready and are prepared to give answers regarding voltage readings or scan tool data when talking to the vehicle specialist.

HOTLINE SERVICES

A hotline service provider is a subscription-based helpline to assist service technicians solve technical problems. While services vary, most charge a monthly fee for a certain amount of time each month to talk to an experienced service technician who has a large amount of resource materials available for reference. Often, the technician hired by the hotline services specializes in one vehicle make and is familiar with many of the pattern failures that are seen by other technicians in the field. Hotline services are an efficient way to get information on an as-needed basis.

Some examples of hotline automotive service providers include:

- Identifix
- Autohotlineusa
- Taylor Automotive Tech-Line
- Aspire
- **SEE FIGURE 12–4.**

SPECIALITY REPAIR MANUALS

Examples of specialty repair manuals include unit repair for assembled components, such as automatic transmission/transaxle, manual transmission/transaxle, differentials, and engines. Some specialty repair manuals cover older or antique vehicles, which may include unit repair sections.

AFTERMARKET SUPPLIES GUIDES AND CATALOGS

Aftermarket supplies guides and catalogs are usually free and often include expanded views of assembled parts along with helpful hints and advice. Sometimes the only place where this information is available is at trade shows associated with automotive training conferences and expos. Go to the following websites for examples of training conferences with trade shows.

- **www.CARSevent.com**
- **www.avtechexpo.com**
- **www.visionkc.com** (Vision Expo)

SUMMARY

1. Vehicle history records are sometimes very helpful in determining problems that may be related to a previous fault or repair.

2. The vehicle owner's manual is very helpful to the service technician because it includes the procedures for resetting the maintenance reminder light (oil change light), as well as how to reset the tire pressure monitoring system after a tire rotation, and other important settings and specifications.

3. Lubrication guides provide information on the specified oil and lubricants needed along with the capacities and the location of lubrication points.

4. Factory service manuals or electronic service information include information that is vehicle and year specific and very detailed.

5. Other types of service information are labor and parts guides, wiring diagrams, component locator manuals, specialty manuals, and aftermarket supplies guides and catalogs.

6. Hotline services are subscription based and allow a technician to talk to an experienced technician who has many resources.

REVIEW QUESTIONS

1. What is included in the vehicle owner's manual that could be helpful for a service technician?

2. Lubrication service guides include what type of information?

3. Explain why factory service manuals or factory electronic service information are the most detailed of all service information.

4. Explain how flat-rate and parts guides are useful to customers.

5. List additional types of service manuals that are available.

6. Describe how hotline services and Internet sites assist service technicians.

CHAPTER QUIZ

1. What type of information is commonly included in the owner's manual that would be a benefit to service technicians?
   a. Maintenance reminder light reset procedures
   b. Tire pressure monitoring system reset procedures
   c. Maintenance items specifications
   d. All of the above

2. Two technicians are discussing the need for the history of the vehicle. Technician A says that an accident could cause faults due to hidden damage. Technician B says that some faults could be related to a previous repair. Which technician is correct?
   a. Technician A only
   b. Technician B only
   c. Both Technicians A and B
   d. Neither Technician A nor B

3. The viscosity of engine oil is found where?
   a. Owner's manual
   b. Factory service manual or service information
   c. Lubrication guide
   d. All of the above

4. Wiring diagrams are usually found where?
   a. Owner's manuals
   b. Factory service manuals
   c. Unit repair manuals
   d. Lubrication guides

5. What type of manual includes time needed to perform service procedures?
   a. Flat-rate manuals
   b. Owner's manuals
   c. Factory service manuals
   d. Parts guide

6. Component location can be found in _____.
   a. Factory service manuals
   b. Labor guide manuals
   c. Lubrication guides
   d. Both a and c

7. Aftermarket service information is available in what format?
   a. Manuals
   b. CDs or DVDs
   c. Internet
   d. All of the above

8. Hotline services are _____.
   a. Free
   b. Available for a service fee
   c. Available on CD or DVD format
   d. Accessed by the Internet

9. Aftermarket parts catalogs can be a useful source of information and they are usually _____.
   a. Free
   b. Available by paid subscription
   c. Available on CD or DVD
   d. Available for a fee on a secured Internet site

10. Which type of manual or service information includes the flat-rate time and the cost of parts?
   a. Parts and time guides
   b. Factory service manuals
   c. Component location guides
   d. Free Internet sites

chapter
13

VEHICLE IDENTIFICATION AND EMISSION RATINGS

OBJECTIVES: **After studying Chapter 13, the reader should be able to:** • Identify a vehicle. • Interpret vehicle identification numbers and placard information. • Interpret vehicle emissions and emission control information. • Read and interpret casting numbers. • Locate calibration codes.

KEY TERMS: • Bin number 126 • Calibration codes 128 • California Air Resources Board (CARB) 125 • Casting numbers 128 • Country of origin 124 • Environmental Protection Agency (EPA) 125 • Gross axle weight rating (GAWR) 125 • Gross vehicle weight rating (GVWR) 125 • Model year (MY) 124 • Tier 1 125 • Tier 2 126 • Vehicle emissions control information (VECI) 125 • Vehicle identification number (VIN) 124

PARTS OF A VEHICLE

The names of the parts of a vehicle are based on the location and purpose of the component.

LEFT SIDE OF THE VEHICLE—RIGHT SIDE OF THE VEHICLE
Both of these terms refer to the left and right as if the driver is sitting behind the steering wheel. Therefore, the left side (including components under the hood) is on the driver's left.

FRONT AND REAR
The proper term for the back portion of any vehicle is rear (for example, left rear tire).

FRONT-WHEEL DRIVE VERSUS REAR-WHEEL DRIVE

Front-wheel drive (FWD) means that the front wheels are being driven by the engine, as well as turned by the steering wheel. Rear-wheel drive (RWD) means that the rear wheels are driven by the engine. If the engine is in the front, it can be either front- or rear-wheel drive. In many cases, a front engine vehicle can also drive all four wheels called four-wheel drive (4WD) or all-wheel drive (AWD). If the engine is located at the rear of the vehicle, it can be rear-wheel drive or all-wheel-drive (AWD).

VEHICLE IDENTIFICATION

All service work requires that the vehicle, including the engine and accessories, be properly identified. The most common identification is the make, model, and year of the vehicle.

> **Make:** e.g., Chevrolet
>
> **Model:** e.g., Impala
>
> **Year:** e.g., 2007

The year of the vehicle is often difficult to determine exactly. A model may be introduced as the next year's model as soon as January of the previous year. Typically, a new **model year** (abbreviated **MY**) starts in September or October of the year prior to the actual new year, but not always. This is why the **vehicle identification number**, usually abbreviated **VIN**, is so important. ● SEE FIGURE 13–1.

Since 1981, all vehicle manufacturers have used a VIN that is 17 characters long. Although every vehicle manufacturer assigns various letters or numbers within these 17 characters, there are some constants, including:

- The first number or letter designates the **country of origin.** ● SEE CHART 13–1.
- The model of the vehicle is commonly the fourth and/or fifth character.
- The eighth character is often the engine code. (Some engines cannot be determined by the VIN number.)
- The tenth character represents represents the model year and not the calendar year (CY) on all vehicles. ● SEE CHART 13–2.

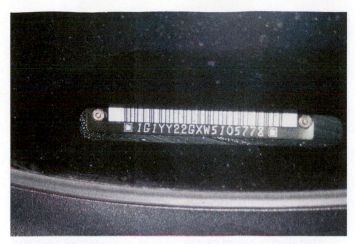

FIGURE 13–1 Typical vehicle identification number (VIN) as viewed through the windshield.

FIGURE 13–2 A VECI label on a 2008 Ford.

1 = United States	9 = Brazil	U = Romania
2 = Canada	J = Japan	V = France
3 = Mexico	K = Korea	W = Germany
4 = United States	L = China	X = Russia
5 = United States	R = Taiwan	Y = Sweden
6 = Australia	S = England	Z = Italy
8 = Argentina	T = Czechoslovakia	

CHART 13–1

A = 1980/2010	L = 1990/2020	Y = 2000/2030
B = 1981/2011	M = 1991/2021	1 = 2001/2031
C = 1982/2012	N = 1992/2022	2 = 2002/2032
D = 1983/2013	P = 1993/2023	3 = 2003/2033
E = 1984/2014	R = 1994/2024	4 = 2004/2034
F = 1985/2015	S = 1995/2025	5 = 2005/2035
G = 1986/2016	T = 1996/2026	6 = 2006/2036
H = 1987/2017	V = 1997/2027	7 = 2007/2037
J = 1988/2018	W = 1998/2028	8 = 2008/2038
K = 1989/2019	X = 1999/2029	9 = 2009/2039

CHART 13–2

VIN Year Chart *(The Pattern Repeats Every 30 Years)*

VEHICLE SAFETY CERTIFICATION LABEL

A vehicle safety certification label is attached to the left side pillar post on the rearward-facing section of the left front door. This label indicates the month and year of manufacture as well as the **gross vehicle weight rating (GVWR)**, the **gross axle weight rating (GAWR)**, and the vehicle identification number (VIN).

VECI LABEL

The **vehicle emissions control information (VECI)** label under the hood of the vehicle shows informative settings and emission hose routing information. ● **SEE FIGURE 13–2.**

The VECI label (sticker) can be located on the bottom side of the hood, the radiator fan shroud, the radiator core support, or the strut towers. The VECI label usually includes the following information.

- Engine identification
- Emissions standard that the vehicle meets
- Vacuum hose routing diagram
- Base ignition timing (if adjustable)
- Spark plug type and gap
- Valve lash
- Emission calibration code

EMISSION STANDARDS IN THE UNITED STATES

In the United States, emissions standards are managed by the **Environmental Protection Agency (EPA)** as well as some U.S. state governments. Some of the strictest standards in the world are formulated in California by the **California Air Resources Board (CARB)**.

TIER 1 AND TIER 2 Federal emission standards are set by the Clean Air Act Amendments (CAAA) of 1990 grouped by **tier**. All vehicles sold in the United States must meet

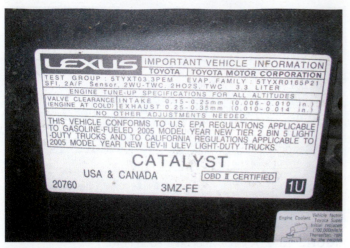

FIGURE 13–3 The underhood decal showing that this Lexus RX-330 meets both national (Tier 2; BIN 5) and California LEV-II (ULEV) regulation standards.

Tier 1 standards that went into effect in 1994 and are the least stringent. Additional **Tier** 2 standards have been optional since 2001, and were completely adopted in 2009. The current Tier 1 standards are different between automobiles and light trucks (SUVs, pickup trucks, and minivans), but Tier 2 standards are the same for both types.

There are several ratings that can be given to vehicles, and a certain percentage of a manufacturer's vehicles must meet different levels in order for the company to sell its products in affected regions. Beyond Tier 1, and in order by stringency, are the following levels.

- **TLEV—Transitional Low-Emission Vehicle.** More stringent for HC than Tier 1.

- **LEV—(also known as LEV I)—Low-Emission Vehicle.** An intermediate California standard about twice as stringent as Tier 1 for HC and NO_X.

- **ULEV—(also known as ULEV I).** Ultra-Low-Emission Vehicle. A stronger California standard emphasizing very low HC emissions.

- **ULEV II—Ultra-Low-Emission Vehicle.** A cleaner-than-average vehicle certified under the Phase II LEV standard. Hydrocarbon and carbon monoxide emissions levels are nearly 50% lower than those of a LEV II-certified vehicle. ● **SEE FIGURE 13–3.**

- **SULEV—Super-Ultra-Low-Emission Vehicle.** A California standard even tighter than ULEV, including much lower HC and NO_X emissions; roughly equivalent to Tier 2 Bin 2 vehicles.

- **ZEV—Zero-Emission Vehicle.** A California standard prohibiting any tailpipe emissions. The ZEV category is largely restricted to electric vehicles and hydrogen-fueled vehicles. In these cases, any emissions that are created are produced at another site, such as a power plant or hydrogen reforming center, unless such sites run on renewable energy.

NOTE: A battery-powered electric vehicle charged from the power grid will still be up to 10 times cleaner than even the cleanest gasoline vehicles over their respective lifetimes.

The current California ZEV regulation allows manufacturers a choice of two options for meeting the ZEV requirements.

1. Vehicle manufacturers can meet the ZEV obligations by meeting standards that are similar to the ZEV rule as it existed in 2001. This means using a formula allowing a vehicle mix of 2% pure ZEVs, 2% AT-PZEVs (vehicles earning advanced technology partial ZEV credits), and 6% PZEVs (extremely clean conventional vehicles). The ZEV obligation is based on the number of passenger cars and small trucks a manufacturer sells in California.

2. Manufacturers may also choose a new alternative ZEV compliance strategy of meeting part of the ZEV requirement by producing the sales-weighted market share of approximately 250 fuel-cell vehicles. The remainder of the ZEV requirements could be achieved by producing 4% AT-PZEVs and 6% PZEVs. The required number of fuel-cell vehicles will increase to 2,500 from 2009 to 2011, 25,000 from 2012 through 2020, and 50,000 from 2015 through 2017. Manufacturers can substitute battery electric vehicles for up to 50% of the fuel-cell vehicle requirements.

   - **PZEV—Partial-Zero-Emission Vehicle.** Compliant with the SULEV standard; additionally has near-zero evaporative emissions and a 15-year/150,000-mile warranty on its emission control equipment.

Tier 2 standards are even more stringent. Tier 2 variations are appended with "II," such as LEV II or SULEV II. Other categories have also been created.

- **ILEV—Inherently Low-Emission Vehicle.**

- **AT-PZEV—Advanced Technology Partial-Zero-Emission Vehicle.** If a vehicle meets the PZEV standards and is using high-technology features, such as an electric motor or high-pressure gaseous fuel tanks for compressed natural gas, it qualifies as an AT-PZEV. Hybrid electric vehicles such as the Toyota Prius can qualify, as can internal combustion engine vehicles that run on natural gas (CNG), such as the Honda Civic GX. These vehicles are classified as "partial" ZEV because they receive partial credit for the number of ZEV vehicles that automakers would otherwise be required to sell in California.

- **NLEV—National Low-Emission Vehicle.** All vehicles nationwide must meet this standard, which started in 2001. ● **SEE CHARTS 13–3 AND 13–4.**

FEDERAL EPA BIN NUMBER The higher the tier number, the newer the regulation; the lower the **bin number**, the cleaner

		NMOG GRAMS (MILE)	CO GRAMS (MILE)	NO$_X$ GRAMS (MILE)
LEV I (Cars)	TLEV	0.125 (0.156)	3.4 (4.2)	0.4 (0.6)
	LEV	0.075 (0.090)	3.4 (4.2)	0.2 (0.3)
	ULEV	0.040 (0.055)	1.7 (2.1)	0.2 (0.3)
LEV II (Cars and Trucks less than 8,500 lbs)	LEV	0.075 (0.090)	3.4 (4.2)	0.05 (0.07)
	ULEV	0.040 (0.055)	1.7 (2.1)	0.05 (0.07)
	SULEV	—(0.010)	—(1.0)	—(0.02)

CHART 13–3

LEV Standard Categories

NOTE: Numbers in parentheses are 100,000-mile standards for LEV I, and 120,000-mile standards for LEV II. NMOG means non-methane organic gases, which includes alcohol. CO means carbon monoxide. NO$_X$ means oxides of nitrogen. Data compiled from California Environmental Protection Agency—Air Resource Board (CARB) documents.

CERTIFICATION LEVEL	NMOG (g/ml)	CO (g/ml)	NO$_X$ (g/ml)
LEV II	0.090	4.2	0.07
ULEV II	0.055	2.1	0.07
SULEV II	0.010	1.0	0.02

CHART 13–4

California LEV II 120,000-Mile Tailpipe Emissions Limits

NOTE: Numbers in parentheses are 100,000-mile standards for LEV I, and 120,000-mile standards for LEV II. NMOG means non-methane organic gases, which includes alcohol. CO means carbon monoxide. NO$_X$ means oxides of nitrogen. The specification is in grams per mile (g/ml). Data compiled from California Environmental Protection Agency—Air Resources Board (CARB) documents.

the vehicle. The 2004 Toyota Prius is a very clean Bin 3, while the Hummer H2 is a dirty Bin 11. Examples include:

- Tier 1: The former federal standard; carried over to model year 2004 for those vehicles not yet subject to the phase-in.
- Tier 2, Bin 1: The cleanest federal Tier 2 standard; a zero-emission vehicle (ZEV).
- Tier 2, Bins 4–2: Cleaner than the average standard.
- Tier 2, Bin 5: "Average" of new Tier 2 standards, roughly equivalent to a LEV II vehicle.
- Tier 2, Bins 6–9: Not as clean as the average requirement for a Tier 2 vehicle.
- Tier 2, Bin 10: Least-clean Tier 2 bin applicable to passenger vehicles. ● SEE CHARTS 13–5 AND 13–6.

CERTIFICATION LEVEL	NMOG (g/ml)	CO (g/ml)	NO$_X$ (g/ml)
Bin 1	0.0	0.0	0.0
Bin 2	0.010	2.1	0.02
Bin 3	0.055	2.1	0.03
Bin 4	0.070	2.1	0.04
Bin 5	0.090	4.2	0.07
Bin 6	0.090	4.2	0.10
Bin 7	0.090	4.2	0.15
Bin 8a	0.125	4.2	0.20
Bin 8b	0.156	4.2	0.20
Bin 9a	0.090	4.2	0.30
Bin 9b	0.130	4.2	0.30
Bin 9c	0.180	4.2	0.30
Bin 10a	0.156	4.2	0.60
Bin 10b	0.230	6.4	0.60
Bin 10c	0.230	6.4	0.60
Bin 11	0.230	7.3	0.90

CHART 13–5

EPA Tier 2—120,000-Mile Tailpipe Emission Limits

NOTE: The bin number is determined by the type and weight of the vehicle. The highest bin allowed for vehicles built after January 1, 2007 is Bin 8. Data compiled from the Environmental Protection Agency (EPA).

U.S. EPA VEHICLE INFORMATION PROGRAM (THE HIGHER THE SCORE, THE LOWER THE EMISSIONS)	
SELECTED EMISSIONS STANDARDS	SCORE
Bin 1 and ZEV	10
PZEV	9.5
Bin 2	9
Bin 3	8
Bin 4	7
Bin 5 and LEV II cars	6
Bin 6	5
Bin 7	4
Bin 8	3
Bin 9a and LEV I cars	2
Bin 9b	2
Bin 10a	1
Bin 10b and Tier 1 cars	1
Bin 11	0

CHART 13–6

Air Pollution Score

Courtesy of the Environmental Protection Agency (EPA).

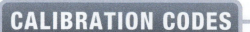

FIGURE 13–4 A typical computer calibration sticker on the case of the controller. The information on the sticker is often needed when ordering parts or a replacement controller.

FIGURE 13–5 Engine block identification number cast into the block is used for identification.

CALIBRATION CODES

Calibration codes are usually located on powertrain control modules (PCMs) or other controllers. Some calibration codes are only accessible with a scan tool. Whenever diagnosing an engine operating fault, it is often necessary to know the calibration code to be sure that the vehicle is the subject of a technical service bulletin or other service procedure. ● **SEE FIGURE 13–4.**

CASTING NUMBERS

Whenever an engine part such as a block is cast, a number is put into the mold to identify the casting. ● **SEE FIGURE 13–5.** These **casting numbers** can be used to check dimensions such as the cubic inch displacement and other information. Sometimes changes are made to the mold, yet the casting number is not changed. Most often the casting number is the best piece of identifying information that the service technician can use for identifying an engine.

SUMMARY

1. The front, rear, left, and right side of a vehicle are as viewed from the driver's seat.
2. The vehicle identification number (VIN) is very important as it includes when the vehicle was built, as well as the engine code and many other details about the vehicle.
3. The VECI label under the hood often needs to be checked by the technician to properly service the vehicle.
4. Other vehicle information that the technician may need for a service or repair include calibration codes, casting numbers, and emissions rating.

REVIEW QUESTIONS

1. From what position are the terms left and right determined?
2. What are the major pieces of information that are included in the vehicle identification number (VIN)?
3. What information is included on the VECI label under the hood?
4. What does Tier 2 Bin 5 mean?

CHAPTER QUIZ

1. The passenger side in the United States is the _____.
   a. Right side
   b. Left side
   c. Either right or left side, depending on how the vehicle is viewed
   d. Both a and b

2. A vehicle with the engine in the front can be _____.
   a. Front-wheel drive
   b. Rear-wheel drive
   c. Four-wheel drive
   d. All of the above

3. The vehicle identification number (VIN) since 1981, is how many characters long?
   a. 10
   b. 12
   c. 17
   d. 21

4. The tenth character represents the year of the vehicle. If the tenth character is a "Y," what year is the vehicle?
   a. 1998
   b. 2000
   c. 2002
   d. 2004

5. The first character of the vehicle identification number is the country of origin. Where was the vehicle built that has a "5" as the first character?
   a. United States
   b. Canada
   c. Mexico
   d. Japan

6. The VECI label includes all *except* _____.
   a. Engine identification
   b. Horsepower and torque rating of the engine
   c. Spark plug type and gap
   d. Valve lash

7. The vehicle safety certification label includes all *except* _____.
   a. VIN
   b. GVWR
   c. Tire pressure recommendation
   d. GAWR

8. What are the characters called that are embedded in most engine blocks and are used for identification?
   a. VIN
   b. Calibration codes
   c. Bin number
   d. Casting number

9. If the first character of the VIN is an "S," where was the vehicle made?
   a. United States
   b. Mexico
   c. Canada
   d. England

10. Technician A says that the lower the bin number is, the less emissions the vehicle produces. Technician B says that SULEV has cleaner standards than ULEV. Which technician is correct?
    a. Technician A only
    b. Technician B only
    c. Both Technicians A and B
    d. Neither Technician A nor B

chapter 14

GASOLINE ENGINE OPERATION

OBJECTIVES: **After studying Chapter 14, the reader should be able to:** • Explain how a four-stroke cycle gasoline engine operates. • List the various characteristics by which vehicle engines are classified. • Explain what a compression ratio is. • Explain how engine size is determined. • Describe how displacement is affected by the bore and stroke of the engine. • Discuss the difference between torque and power.

KEY TERMS: • Block 130 • Bore 137 • Bottom dead center (BDC) 133 • Boxer 133 • Cam-in-block design 135 • Camshaft 135 • Combustion 130 • Combustion chamber 130 • Compression ratio (CR) 138 • Connecting rod 133 • Crankshaft 133 • Cycle 133 • Cylinder 133 • Cylinder block 130 • Displacement 137 • Double overhead camshaft (DOHC) 135 • Exhaust valve 133 • External combustion engine 130 • Four-stroke cycle 133 • Intake valve 133 • Internal combustion engine 130 • Mechanical force 130 • Mechanical power 130 • Naturally aspirated 137 • Oil galleries 131 • Overhead valve (OHV) 135 • Pancake 133 • Piston stroke 133 • Pushrod engine 135 • Rotary engine 137 • Single overhead camshaft (SOHC) 135 • Stroke 137 • Supercharger 137 • Top dead center (TDC) 133 • Turbocharger 137 • Wankel engine 137

PURPOSE AND FUNCTION

The purpose and function of an engine is to convert the heat energy of burning fuel into mechanical energy. In a typical vehicle, mechanical energy is then used to perform the following:

- Propel the vehicle.
- Power the air conditioning and power steering systems.
- Produce electrical power for use throughout the vehicle.

ENERGY AND POWER

Engines use energy to produce power. The chemical energy in fuel is converted into heat energy by the burning of the fuel at a controlled rate. This process is called **combustion**. If engine combustion occurs within the power chamber, the engine is called an **internal combustion engine**.

NOTE: An external combustion engine burns fuel outside of the engine itself, such as a steam engine.

Engines convert the chemical energy of the gasoline into heat within a power chamber that is called a **combustion chamber**. Heat energy released in the combustion chamber raises the temperature of the combustion gases within the chamber. The increase in gas temperature causes the pressure of the gases to increase. The pressure developed within the combustion chamber is applied to the head of a piston to produce a usable **mechanical force**, which is then converted into useful **mechanical power**.

ENGINE CONSTRUCTION OVERVIEW

BLOCK All automotive and truck engines are constructed using a solid frame, called a **block** or **cylinder block**. A block is made of cast iron or aluminum and provides the foundation for most of the engine components and systems. The block is cast and then machined to very close tolerances to allow other parts to be installed.

ROTATING ASSEMBLY Pistons are installed in the block and they move up and down in the cylinders during engine operation. Pistons are connected to connecting rods, which connect the pistons to the crankshaft. The crankshaft converts the up-and-down motion of the piston to rotary motion, which is then transmitted to the drive wheels and propels the vehicle. ● **SEE FIGURE 14–1.**

FIGURE 14–1 The rotating assembly for a V-8 engine that has eight pistons and connecting rods and one crankshaft.

FIGURE 14–2 A Ford flathead V-8 engine. This engine design was used by Ford Motor Company from 1932 through 1953. In a flathead design, the valves located next to (beside) the cylinders.

 FREQUENTLY ASKED QUESTION

What Is a Flat-Head Engine?

A flat-head engine is an older type engine design that has the valves in the block. Because the valves are in the block, the heads are flat and, therefore, are called flat-head engines. The most commonly known was the Ford flat-head V-8 produced from 1932 until 1953. ● SEE FIGURE 14–2.

CYLINDER HEADS
All engines use a cylinder head to seal the top of the cylinders, which are in the engine block. The cylinder head also contains both intake valves, which allow air and fuel into the cylinder, and exhaust valves, which allow the hot gases left over to escape from the engine.

FIGURE 14–3 A cylinder head with four valves per cylinder, two intake valves (larger) and two exhaust valves (smaller).

Cylinder heads are made of cast iron or aluminum and are then machined for the valves and other valve-related components. ● SEE FIGURE 14–3.

ENGINE PARTS AND SYSTEMS

INTAKE AND EXHAUST MANIFOLDS Air and fuel enter the engine through the intake manifold and exit through the exhaust manifold. Intake manifolds operate at a cooler temperature than exhaust manifolds and are therefore constructed of nylon reinforced plastic or aluminum. Exhaust manifolds must be able to withstand hot exhaust gases, so most are made of cast iron or steel tubing.

COOLING SYSTEM All engines must have a cooling system to control engine temperatures. While some older engines were air cooled, all current production passenger vehicle engines are cooled by circulating antifreeze coolant through passages in the block and cylinder head. The coolant absorbs the heat from the engine and after the thermostat opens, the water pump circulates the coolant through the radiator, where the excess heat is released to the outside air, thereby cooling the coolant. The coolant is continuously circulated through the cooling system and the temperature is controlled by the thermostat. ● SEE FIGURE 14–4.

LUBRICATION SYSTEM All engines contain moving and sliding parts that must be kept lubricated to reduce wear and friction. The oil pan, bolted to the bottom of the engine block, holds 4 to 7 quarts (4 to 7 liters) of oil. An oil pump, which is driven by the engine, forces the oil through the oil filter and then into passages in the crankshaft and the block. These passages are called **oil galleries**. The oil is also forced up to the valves and then falls down through openings in the cylinder head and block, then back into the oil pan. ● SEE FIGURE 14–5.

FIGURE 14–4 The coolant temperature is controlled by the thermostat, which opens and allows coolant to flow to the radiator when the temperature reaches the rated temperature of the thermostat.

FUEL SYSTEM All engines require a fuel system to supply fuel to the cylinders. The fuel system includes the following components:

- Fuel tank, where fuel is stored
- Fuel pump, which is located inside the fuel tank in vehicles equipped with fuel injection
- Fuel filter and lines, which transfer the fuel for the fuel tank to the engine
- Fuel injectors, which spray fuel into the intake manifold or directly into the cylinder, depending on the type of system used

IGNITION SYSTEM The ignition system is designed to convert the 12 volts from the battery into 5,000 to 40,000 volts needed to jump the gap of a spark plug. Spark plugs are threaded into the cylinder head of each cylinder, and when the spark occurs, it ignites the air–fuel mixture in the cylinder, thus creating pressure and forcing the piston down in the cylinder. The following components are part of the ignition system:

- **Spark plugs.** Provide an air gap inside the cylinder where a spark occurs to start combustion
- **Sensor(s).** Includes crankshaft position (CKP) and camshaft position (CMP) sensors, used by the engine computer, called the powertrain control module (PCM), to trigger the ignition coil(s) and the fuel injectors

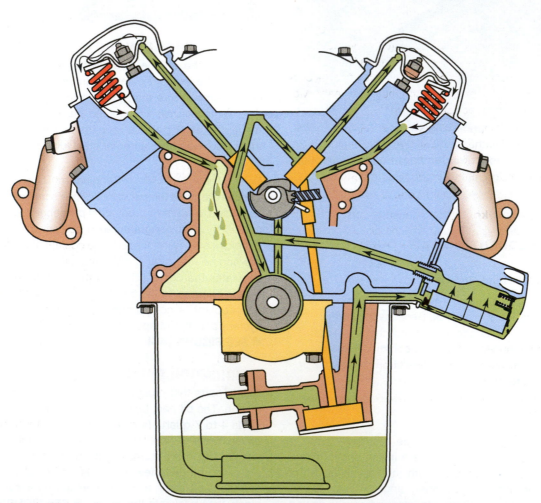

FIGURE 14–5 A typical lubrication system, showing the oil pan, oil pump, oil filter, and oil passages.

- **Ignition coils.** Increase battery voltage to 5,000 to 40,000 volts
- **Ignition control module (ICM).** Controls when the spark plug fires
- **Associated wiring.** Electrically connects the battery, ICM, coil, and spark plugs

FOUR-STROKE CYCLE OPERATION

HISTORY The first **four-stroke cycle** engine was developed by a German engineer, Nickolaus Otto, in 1876. The process begins by the starter motor rotating the engine until combustion takes place. The four-stroke cycle is repeated for each cylinder of the engine. ● **SEE FIGURE 14–6.**

A piston moves up and down, or reciprocates, in a **cylinder**. The piston is attached to a **crankshaft** with a **connecting rod**. This arrangement allows the piston to reciprocate (move up and down) in the cylinder as the crankshaft rotates. ● **SEE FIGURE 14–7.**

OPERATION The term **engine cycle** is defined by the number of piston strokes necessary to complete one cycle of events. A **piston stroke** is a one-way piston movement either from top to bottom or bottom to top of the cylinder. During one stroke, the crankshaft rotates 180° (1/2 revolution). A **cycle** is a complete series of events that continually repeats. Most automobile engines use a four-stroke cycle.

- **Intake stroke.** The **intake valve** is open and the piston inside the cylinder travels downward, drawing a mixture of air and fuel into the cylinder. The crankshaft rotates 180° from **top dead center (TDC)** to **bottom dead center (BDC)** and the camshaft rotates 90°.
- **Compression stroke.** As the crankshaft continues to rotate, the intake valve closes and the piston moves upward in the cylinder, compressing the air–fuel mixture. The combustion pressure developed in the combustion chamber at the correct time will push the piston downward to rotate the crankshaft. The crankshaft rotates 180° from BDC to TDC and the camshaft rotates 90°.
- **Power stroke.** When the piston gets near the top of the cylinder, the spark at the spark plug ignites the air–fuel mixture, which forces the piston downward. The crankshaft rotates 180° from TDC to BDC and the camshaft rotates 90°.
- **Exhaust stroke.** The crankshaft continues to rotate, and the piston again moves upward in the cylinder. The exhaust valve opens, and the piston forces the residual burned gases out of the combustion chamber through the **exhaust valve** and into the exhaust manifold and exhaust system.

The crankshaft rotates 180° from BDC to TDC and the camshaft rotates 90°. This sequence repeats as the engine rotates. To stop the engine, the electricity to the ignition system and fuel system is shut off by the ignition switch, which stops engine operation.

THE 720° CYCLE Each cycle (four strokes) of events requires that the engine crankshaft make two complete revolutions, or 720° (360° × 2 = 720°).

Each stroke of the cycle requires that the crankshaft rotate 180°. The greater the number of cylinders, the closer together the power strokes of the individual cylinders will occur.

The number of degrees that the crankshaft rotates between power strokes can be expressed as an angle. To find the angle between power strokes of an engine, divide 720° by the number of cylinders.

Angle with 3 cylinders: 720/3 = 240°

Angle with 4 cylinders: 720/4 = 180°

Angle with 5 cylinders: 720/5 = 144°

Angle with 6 cylinders: 720/6 = 120°

Angle with 8 cylinders: 720/8 = 90°

Angle with 10 cylinders: 720/10 = 72°

Angle with 12 cylinders: 720/12 = 60°

This means that in a 4-cylinder engine, a power stroke occurs at every 180° of the crankshaft rotation (every 1/2 rotation). A V-8 is a much smoother operating engine because a power stroke occurs twice as often (every 90° of crankshaft rotation).

ENGINE CLASSIFICATION AND CONSTRUCTION

Engines are classified by several characteristics, including:

- **Number of strokes.** Most automotive engines use the four-stroke cycle.
- **Cylinder arrangement.** An inline engine places all cylinders in a straight line. The 4-, 5-, and 6-cylinder engines are commonly manufactured inline engines. A V-type engine, such as a V-6 or V-8, has the number of cylinders split and built into a V shape. ● **SEE FIGURE 14–8.**

Horizontally opposed 4- and 6-cylinder engines have two banks of cylinders that are horizontal, resulting in a low engine. This style of engine is used in Porsche and Subaru engines, and is often called the **boxer** or **pancake** engine design. ● **SEE FIGURE 14–9.**

- **Longitudinal and transverse mounting.** Engines may be mounted in the vehicle either parallel with the length of the vehicle (longitudinally) or crosswise (transversely). ● **SEE FIGURES 14–10 AND 14–11.**

NOTE: The same engine may be mounted in various vehicles in either direction.

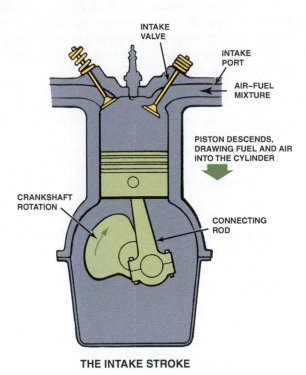

INTAKE VALVE

INTAKE PORT

AIR–FUEL MIXTURE

PISTON DESCENDS, DRAWING FUEL AND AIR INTO THE CYLINDER

CRANKSHAFT ROTATION

CONNECTING ROD

THE INTAKE STROKE

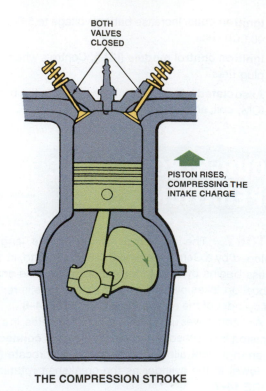

BOTH VALVES CLOSED

PISTON RISES, COMPRESSING THE INTAKE CHARGE

THE COMPRESSION STROKE

SPARK PLUG FIRES

AIR AND FUEL IGNITE

PISTON FORCED DOWN IN THE CYLINDER BY EXPANDING GASES

THE POWER STROKE

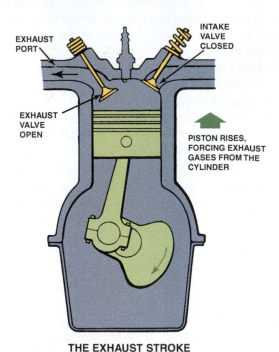

EXHAUST PORT

INTAKE VALVE CLOSED

EXHAUST VALVE OPEN

PISTON RISES, FORCING EXHAUST GASES FROM THE CYLINDER

THE EXHAUST STROKE

FIGURE 14–6 The downward movement of the piston draws the air–fuel mixture into the cylinder through the intake valve on the intake stroke. On the compression stroke, the mixture is compressed by the upward movement of the piston with both valves closed. Ignition occurs at the beginning of the power stroke, and combustion drives the piston downward to produce power. On the exhaust stroke, the upward-moving piston forces the burned gases out the open exhaust valve.

FIGURE 14–7 Cutaway of an engine showing the cylinder, piston, connecting rod, and crankshaft.

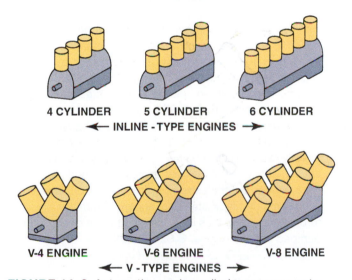

4 CYLINDER   **5 CYLINDER**   **6 CYLINDER**

← **INLINE - TYPE ENGINES** →

V-4 ENGINE   **V-6 ENGINE**   **V-8 ENGINE**

← **V - TYPE ENGINES** →

FIGURE 14–8 Automotive engine cylinder arrangements.

Although it might be possible to mount an engine in different vehicles both longitudinally and transversely, the engine component parts may not be interchangeable. Differences can include different engine blocks and crankshafts, as well as different water pumps.

■ **Valve and camshaft number and location.** The number of valves per cylinder and the number and location of camshafts are major factors in engine classification. A typical older-model engine uses one intake valve and one exhaust valve per cylinder. Many newer engines use two intake and two exhaust valves per cylinder. The valves

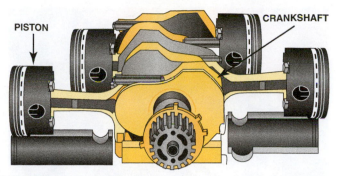

FIGURE 14–9 A horizontally opposed engine design helps to lower the vehicle's center of gravity.

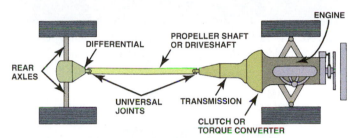

FIGURE 14–10 A longitudinally mounted engine drives the rear wheels through a transmission, driveshaft, and differential assembly.

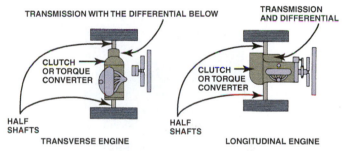

FIGURE 14–11 Two types of front-engine, front-wheel drive mountings.

are opened by a **camshaft.** Some engines use one camshaft for the intake valves and a separate camshaft for the exhaust valves. When the camshaft is located in the block, the valves are operated by lifters, pushrods, and rocker arms.

This type of engine is called:

■ A **pushrod engine**

■ **Cam-in-block design**

■ **Overhead valve (OHV),** because an overhead valve engine has the valves located in the cylinder head. ● **SEE FIGURE 14–12.**

When one overhead camshaft per cylinder head is used, the design is called a **single overhead camshaft (SOHC)** design. When two overhead camshafts per cylinder head are used, the design is called a **double overhead camshaft (DOHC)** design. ● **SEE FIGURES 14–13 AND 14–14.**

FIGURE 14–12 Cutaway of an overhead valve (OHV) V-8 engine showing the lifters, pushrods, roller rocker arms, and valves.

FIGURE 14–14 A DOHC engine uses a camshaft for the intake valve and a separate camshaft for the exhaust valves in each cylinder head.

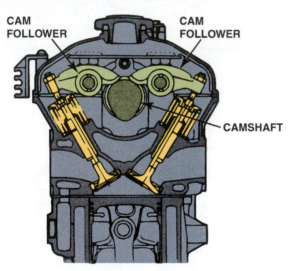

SINGLE OVERHEAD CAMSHAFT

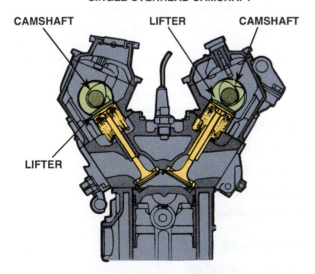

DOUBLE OVERHEAD CAMSHAFT

FIGURE 14–13 SOHC engines usually require additional components, such as a rocker arm, to operate all of the valves. DOHC engines often operate the valves directly.

? **FREQUENTLY ASKED QUESTION**

What Is the Difference Between a Turbocharger and a Supercharger?

A *supercharger* is an engine-driven air pump that supplies more than the normal amount of air into the intake manifold and boosts engine torque and power. A supercharger provides an instantaneous increase in power without any delay. However, a supercharger, because it is driven by the engine, requires horsepower to operate and is not as efficient as a turbocharger. ● **SEE FIGURE 14–15**.

A *turbocharger* uses the heat of the exhaust to power a turbine wheel and, therefore, does not directly reduce engine power. In a naturally aspirated engine, about half of the heat energy contained in the fuel goes out the exhaust system. A turbocharger uses some of this wasted heat energy to turn the turbine wheel and thus increase the amount of air pumped into the engine. ● **SEE FIGURE 14–16**.

NOTE: A V-type engine uses two banks or rows of cylinders. An SOHC design, therefore, uses two camshafts but only one camshaft per bank (row) of cylinders. A DOHC V-6, therefore, has four camshafts, two for each bank.

- **Type of fuel.** Most engines operate on gasoline, whereas some engines are designed to operate on ethanol (E85), methanol (M85), natural gas, propane, or diesel fuel.
- **Cooling method.** Most engines are liquid cooled, but some older models were air cooled. Air-cooled engines, such as the original VW Beatle, could not meet exhaust emission standards.

FIGURE 14–15 A supercharger on a Ford V-8.

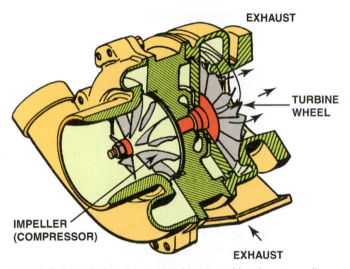

FIGURE 14–16 A turbine wheel is turned by the expanding exhaust gases.

? **FREQUENTLY ASKED QUESTION**

What Is a Rotary Engine?

A successful alternative engine design is the **rotary engine**, also called the **Wankel engine** after its German inventor, Felix Heinrich Wankel (1902–1988). The Mazda RX-7 and RX-8 represent the only long-term use of the rotary engine. The rotating combustion chamber engine runs very smoothly, and it produces high power for its size and weight. The basic rotating combustion chamber engine has a triangular rotor turning in a housing. The housing is in the shape of a geometric figure called a two-lobed epitrochoid. A seal on each corner, or apex, of the rotor is in constant contact with the housing, so the rotor must turn with an eccentric motion. This means that the center of the rotor moves around the center of the engine. The eccentric motion can be seen in ● **FIGURE 14–17.**

■ **Type of induction.** If atmospheric air pressure is used to force the air–fuel mixture into the cylinders, the engine is called **naturally aspirated.** Some engines use a **turbocharger** or **supercharger** to force the air–fuel mixture into the cylinder for even greater power.

ENGINE MEASUREMENT

BORE The diameter of a cylinder is called the **bore.** The larger the bore, the greater the area on the piston on which the gases have to work. Pressure is measured in units, such as pounds per square inch (PSI). The greater the area (in square inches), the higher the force exerted by the pistons to rotate the crankshaft. ● **SEE FIGURE 14–18.**

STROKE The **stroke** of an engine is the distance the piston travels from TDC to BDC. This distance is determined by the throw of the crankshaft. The throw is the distance from the centerline of the crankshaft to the centerline of the crankshaft rod journal. The throw is 1/2 of the stroke. ● **SEE FIGURE 14–19.**

The longer this distance, the greater the amount of air–fuel mixture that can be drawn into the cylinder. The more air–fuel mixture inside the cylinder, the more force will result when the mixture is ignited.

DISPLACEMENT Engine size is described as displacement. **Displacement** is the cubic inch (cu. in.) or cubic centimeter (cc) volume displaced or how much air is moved by all of the pistons. A liter (L) is equal to 1,000 cubic centimeters; therefore, most engines today are identified by their displacement in liters.

1 L = 1,000 cc

1 L = 61 cu. in.

1 cu. in. = 16.4 cc

CONVERSION

■ To convert cubic inches to liters, divide cubic inches by 61.02.

■ To convert liters into cubic inches, multiply by 61.02.

CALCULATING CUBIC INCH DISPLACEMENT The formula to calculate the displacement of an engine is basically the formula for determining the volume of a cylinder multiplied by the number of cylinders. The formula is

Cubic inch displacement = π **(pi)** × **R^2** × **Stroke** × **Number of cylinders**

where

R = Radius of the cylinder or 1/2 of the bore.

π = 3.14

The "πR^2" part is the formula for the area of a circle.

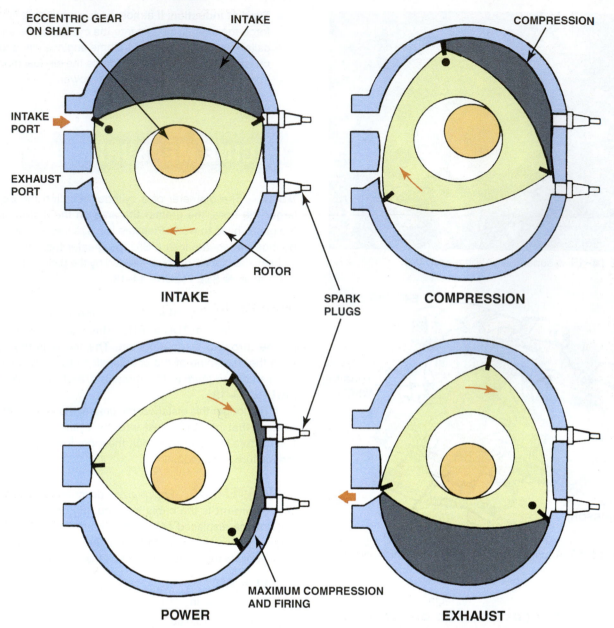

FIGURE 14–17 A rotary engine operates on the four-stroke cycle but uses a rotor instead of a piston and crankshaft to achieve intake, compression, power, and exhaust stroke.

Applying the formula to a 6-cylinder engine:

- Bore = 4.000 in.
- Stroke = 3.000 in.
- π = 3.14
- R = 2 in.
- R^2 = 4 (2^2 or 2×2)

Cubic inches = 3.14 × 4 (R^2) × 3 (stroke) × 6 (number of cylinders).

Cubic inches = 226 cubic inches

Because 1 cubic inch equals 16.4 cubic centimeters, this engine displacement equals 3,706 cubic centimeters or, rounded to 3,700 cubic centimeters or 3.7 liters.

COMPRESSION RATIO

DEFINITION Compression ratio (CR) is the ratio of the difference in the cylinder volume when the piston is at the bottom of the stroke to the volume in the cylinder above

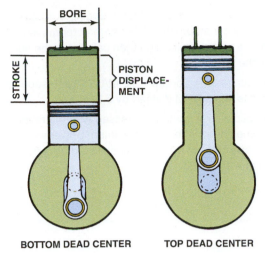

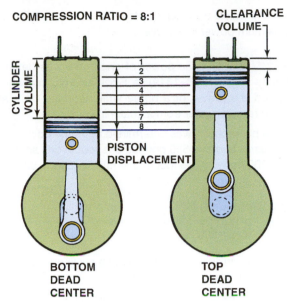

FIGURE 14–18 The bore and stroke of pistons are used to calculate an engine's displacement.

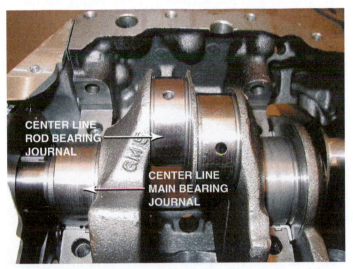

FIGURE 14–19 The distance between the centerline of the main bearing journal and the centerline of the connecting rod journal determines the stroke of the engine. This photo is a little unusual because it shows a V-6 with a splayed crankshaft used to even out the impulses on a 90°, V-6 engine design.

the piston when the piston is at the top of the stroke. The compression ratio of an engine is an important consideration when rebuilding or repairing an engine. ● **SEE FIGURE 14–20**.

TORQUE AND POWER

DEFINITION OF TORQUE *Torque* is the term used to describe a rotating force that may or may not result in motion.

Torque is measured as the amount of force multiplied by the length of the lever through which it acts. If you use a 1 ft-long wrench to apply 10 pounds (lb) of force to the end of the wrench to turn a bolt, then you are exerting 10 pound-feet (lb-ft) of torque. ● **SEE FIGURE 14–21**.

FIGURE 14–20 Compression ratio is the ratio of the total cylinder volume (when the piston is at the bottom of its stroke) to the clearance volume (when the piston is at the top of its stroke).

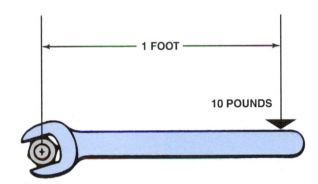

FIGURE 14–21 Torque is a twisting force equal to the distance from the pivot point times the force applied expressed in units called pound-feet (lb-ft) or Newton-meters (N-m).

Engine torque is the twisting force measured at the end of the crankshaft and measured on a dynamometer. Engine torque is always expressed at a specific engine speed (RPM) or range of engine speeds where the torque is at the maximum. For example, an engine may be listed as producing 275 lb-ft at 2,400 RPM. The metric unit for torque is Newton-meters (N-m), because the Newton is the metric unit for force and the distance is expressed in meters.

1 pound-foot = 1.3558 Newton-meters
1 Newton-meter = 0.7376 pound-foot

DEFINITION OF POWER The term *power* means the rate of doing work. Power equals work divided by time. Work is achieved when a certain amount of mass (weight) is moved a certain distance by a force. Whether the object is moved in 10 seconds or 10 minutes does not make a difference in the amount of work accomplished, but it does affect the amount of power needed. Power is expressed in units of foot-pounds per minute and power also includes the engine speed (RPM) where the maximum power is achieved.

HORSEPOWER The power of one horse was determined by James Watt (1736–1819), a Scottish inventor who first calculated the power of a horse while working on a steam engine to remove water from a coal mine.

- One horsepower was determined to be the power required to move 550 pounds one foot in one second or 33,000 pounds one foot in one minute (550 × 60 seconds = 33,000 pounds per minute). Engine output is measured using a dynamometer. A dynamometer measures the torque of the engine and then calculates the horsepower by the formula

- Horsepower = Torque × RPM/5,252 (Horsepower equals torque times RPM divided by 5,252)

- Horsepower is always expressed with the rating and the engine speed where the maximum power was achieved. For example, an engine may be listed as producing 280 hp at 4,400 RPM.

SUMMARY

1. The four strokes of the four-stroke cycle are intake, compression, power, and exhaust.

2. Engines are classified by the number and arrangement of cylinders and by the number and location of valves and camshafts, as well as by the type of mounting, fuel used, cooling method, and type of air induction.

3. Engine size is called displacement and represents the volume displaced by all of the pistons.

4. Engines are rated according to their torque and horsepower output.

REVIEW QUESTIONS

1. What are the strokes of a four-stroke cycle?
2. How are engines classified?

3. How is the size of an engine measured?

CHAPTER QUIZ

1. All overhead valve engines _____.
   a. Use an overhead camshaft
   b. Have the valves located in the cylinder head
   c. Operate using the Wankel cycle
   d. Use the camshaft to close the valves

2. An SOHC V-8 engine has how many camshafts?
   a. One   b. Two
   c. Three   d. Four

3. The coolant flow through the radiator is controlled by the _____.
   a. Size of the passages in the block
   b. Thermostat
   c. Cooling fan(s)
   d. Water pump

4. Torque is expressed in units of _____.
   a. Pound-feet   b. Pounds per minute
   c. Foot-pounds per minute d. Pound-feet per second

5. Horsepower is _____.
   a. Measurement of engine power
   b. Calculated as torque multiplied by engine speed (RPM) and then divided by 5,252
   c. Also called cubic inch displacement
   d. Both a and b

6. What part of an engine is considered to be the foundation of the engine?
   a. Block   b. Cylinder head(s)
   c. Crankshaft   d. Pistons

7. One cylinder of an automotive four-stroke cycle engine completes a cycle every _____.
   a. 90°   b. 180°
   c. 360°   d. 720°

8. How many rotations of the crankshaft are required to complete each stroke of a four-stroke cycle engine?
   a. One-fourth   b. One-half
   c. One   d. Two

9. A rotating force is called _____.
   a. Horsepower   b. Torque
   c. Combustion pressure d. Eccentric movement

10. Technician A says that a crankshaft determines the stroke of an engine. Technician B says that the length of the connecting rod determines the stroke of an engine. Which technician is correct?
   a. Technician A only
   b. Technician B only
   c. Both technicians A and B
   d. Neither technician A nor B

chapter 15

DIESEL ENGINE OPERATION

OBJECTIVES: After studying Chapter 15, the reader should be able to: • Prepare for ASE Engine Performance (A8) certification test content area "C" (Fuel, Air Induction, and Exhaust Systems Diagnosis and Repair). • Explain how a diesel engine operates. • Describe the difference between direct injection (DI) and indirect injection (IDI) diesel engines. • List the parts of the typical diesel engine fuel system. • Explain how glow plugs work. • List the advantages and disadvantages of a diesel engine.

KEY TERMS: • Diesel exhaust fluid (DEF) 149 • Diesel exhaust particulate filter (DPF) 148 • Diesel oxidation catalyst (DOC) 148 • Direct injection (DI) 142 • Glow plug 145 • Heat of compression 141 • High-pressure common rail (HPCR) 144 • Hydraulic electronic unit injection (HEUI) 144 • Indirect injection (IDI) 142 • Injection pump 141 • Lift pump 143 • Particulate matter (PM) 148 • Regeneration 148 • Selective catalytic reduction (SCR) 149 • Soot 148 • Urea 149 • Water–fuel separator 143

DIESEL ENGINES

FUNDAMENTALS In 1892, a German engineer named Rudolf Diesel perfected the compression ignition engine that bears his name. The diesel engine uses the heat generated by compression to ignite the fuel, so it requires no spark ignition system. The diesel engine requires compression ratios of 16:1 and higher. Incoming air is compressed until its temperature reaches about 1,000°F (540°C). This is called **heat of compression**. As the piston reaches the top of its compression stroke, fuel is injected into the cylinder, where it is ignited by the hot air. ● **SEE FIGURE 15–1.**

As the fuel burns, it expands and produces power. Because of the very high compression and torque output of a diesel engine, it is made heavier and stronger than the same size gasoline-powered engine. A diesel engine uses a fuel system with a precision **injection pump** and individual fuel injectors. The pump delivers fuel to the injectors at a high pressure and at timed intervals. Each injector sprays fuel into the combustion chamber at the precise moment required for efficient combustion. ● **SEE FIGURE 15–2.**

ADVANTAGES A diesel engine has several advantages compared to a similar size gasoline-powered engine, including the following:

1. More torque output
2. Greater fuel economy
3. Long service life

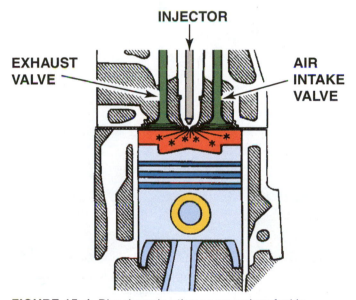

FIGURE 15–1 Diesel combustion occurs when fuel is injected into the hot, highly compressed air in the cylinder.

DISADVANTAGES A diesel engine has several disadvantages compared to a similar size gasoline-powered engine, including the following:

1. Engine noise, especially when cold and/or at idle speed
2. Exhaust smell
3. Poor cold weather starting
4. A vacuum pump is needed to supply the vacuum needs of the heat, ventilation, and air conditioning system

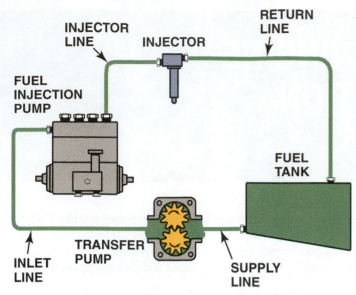

FIGURE 15–2 A typical injector pump type of automotive diesel fuel–injection system.

FIGURE 15–4 A rod/piston assembly from a 5.9 liter Cummins diesel engine used in a Dodge pickup truck.

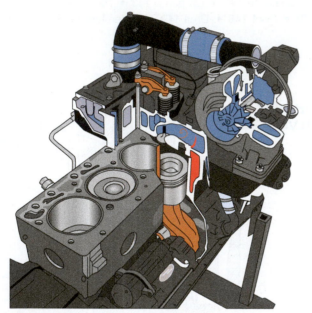

FIGURE 15–3 A Cummins diesel engine as found in a Dodge pickup truck. A high-pressure pump (up to 30,000 PSI) is used to supply diesel fuel to this common rail, which has tubes running to each injector. Note the thick cylinder walls and heavy duty construction.

5. Heavier than a gasoline engine
6. Fuel availability
7. Extra cost compared to a gasoline engine

CONSTRUCTION Diesel engines must be constructed heavier than gasoline engines because of the tremendous pressures that are created in the cylinders during operation. The torque output of a diesel engine is often double or more than that in same size gasoline-powered engines. ● **SEE FIGURE 15–3 AND 15–4.**

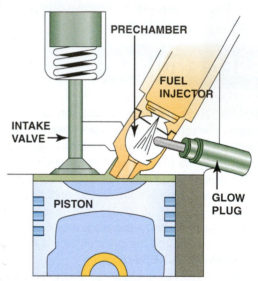

FIGURE 15–5 An indirect injection diesel engine uses a pre-chamber and a glow plug.

INDIRECT AND DIRECT FUEL INJECTION In an **indirect injection** (abbreviated **IDI**) diesel engine, fuel is injected into a small pre-chamber, which is connected to the cylinder by a narrow opening. The initial combustion takes place in this pre-chamber. This has the effect of slowing the rate of combustion, which tends to reduce noise. ● **SEE FIGURE 15–5.**

All indirect diesel injection engines require the use of a glow plug, which is an electrical heater that helps start the combustion process. In a **direct injection** (abbreviated **DI**) diesel engine, fuel is injected directly into the cylinder. The top of the piston has a small depression, where initial combustion takes place. Direct injection diesel engines are generally more efficient than indirect injection engines, but have a tendency to produce greater amounts of noise. ● **SEE FIGURE 15–6.**

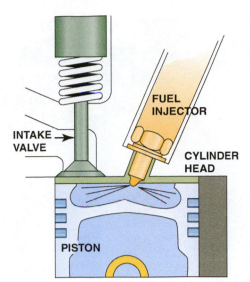

FIGURE 15–6 A direct injection diesel engine injects the fuel directly into the combustion chamber. Many designs do not use a glow plug.

Labels in figure: INTAKE VALVE, FUEL INJECTOR, CYLINDER HEAD, PISTON

While some direct injection diesel engines use glow plugs to help cold starting and to reduce emissions, many direct injection diesel engines do not use glow plugs.

DIESEL FUEL IGNITION Ignition occurs in a diesel engine by injecting fuel into the air charge, which has been heated by compression to a temperature greater than the ignition point of the fuel or about 1,000°F (538°C). The chemical reaction of burning the fuel generates heat, which causes the gases to expand, forcing the piston to rotate the crankshaft. A four-stroke diesel engine requires two rotations of the crankshaft to complete one cycle.

- During the intake stroke, as the piston passes TDC on the way down, the intake valve(s) opens, and filtered air enters the cylinder, while the exhaust valve(s) remains open for a few degrees to allow all of the exhaust gases to escape from the previous combustion event.
- During the compression stroke, after the piston passes BDC, the intake valve(s) closes and the piston travels up to TDC (completion of the first crankshaft rotation).
- During the power stroke, the piston nears TDC on the compression stroke and fuel is injected into the cylinder by the injectors. The fuel does not ignite immediately, but the heat of compression starts the combustion phases in the cylinder. During the power stroke, the piston passes TDC and the expanding gases force the piston down, rotating the crankshaft.
- During the exhaust stroke, as the piston passes BDC, the exhaust valve(s) opens and the exhaust gases start to flow out of the cylinder. This continues as the piston travels up to TDC, pumping the spent gases out of the cylinder. At TDC, the second crankshaft rotation is complete.

Why Are Diesel Engines Noisy?

There are three phases to the combustion in a diesel engine that are not found in gasoline engines and it is this combustion process that causes a diesel engine to sound different than a gasoline engine, especially at idle speed.

1. **Ignition delay.** Near the end of the compression stroke, fuel injection begins, but ignition does not begin immediately. This period is called ignition delay.
2. **Rapid combustion.** This phase of combustion occurs when the fuel first starts to burn, creating a sudden rise in cylinder pressure. It is this sudden and rapid rise in combustion chamber pressure that causes the characteristic diesel engine knock.
3. **Controlled combustion.** After the rapid combustion occurs, the rest of the fuel in the combustion chamber begins to burn and injection continues. This process occurs in an area near the injector that contains fuel surrounded by air. This fuel burns as it mixes with the air.

FUEL TANK AND LIFT PUMP

PARTS INVOLVED A fuel tank used on a vehicle equipped with a diesel engine differs from the one used with a gasoline engine in the following ways.

- The filler neck is larger for diesel fuel. The nozzle size is 15/16 in. (24 mm) instead of 13/16 in. (21 mm) for gasoline filler necks. Truck stop diesel nozzles for large over-the-road truck are usually larger, 1.25 in. or 1.5 in. (32 mm or 38 mm) to allow for faster fueling of large-capacity fuel tanks.
- There are no evaporative emission control devices or a charcoal (carbon) canister. Diesel fuel is not as volatile as gasoline and, therefore, diesel vehicles do not have evaporative emission control devices.

The diesel fuel is usually drawn from the fuel tank by a separate pump, called a **lift pump**, that delivers the fuel to the injection pump. The lift pump is a low-pressure but high-volume type pump.

WATER–FUEL SEPARATOR Between the fuel tank and the lift pump is a **water–fuel separator**. Water is heavier than diesel and sinks to the bottom of the separator. Part of normal routine maintenance on a vehicle equipped with a diesel engine is to drain the water from the water–fuel separator. A float is often used inside the separator, which is connected to a warning

FIGURE 15–7 A fuel filter attached to the frame rail on a Ford pickup truck equipped with a diesel engine. When the "water in fuel" warning lamp comes on, the water that is trapped in the filter-water separator assembly can be drained from the unit.

FIGURE 15–8 A typical distributor-type diesel injection pump showing the pump, lines, and fuel filter.

lamp on the dash that lights if the water reaches a level where it needs to be drained. The water separator is often part of the fuel filter assembly. Both the fuel filter and the water separator are common maintenance items. Many diesel engines also use a fuel temperature sensor. ● SEE FIGURE 15–7.

INJECTION PUMP

NEED FOR HIGH-PRESSURE DIESEL INJECTION PUMP
A diesel engine injection pump is used to increase the pressure of the diesel fuel from very low values in the lift pump to the extremely high pressures needed for injection.

- The lift pump is a low-pressure, high-volume pump.
- The high-pressure injection pump is a high-pressure, low-volume pump. Diesel injection pumps are usually driven by a gear off the camshaft at the front of the engine. ● SEE FIGURE 15–8.

NOTE: Because of the very tight tolerances in a diesel engine, the smallest amount of dirt can cause extensive damage to the engine and to the fuel-injection system.

DISTRIBUTOR INJECTION PUMP
A distributor diesel injection pump is a high-pressure pump assembly with steel lines leading to each individual injector. The high-pressure lines between the distributor and the injectors must be the exact same length to ensure proper injection timing. In this older-style diesel engine design, the high-pressure fuel actually opens the fuel injector when the fuel reaches the injector. ● SEE FIGURE 15–9.

HIGH-PRESSURE COMMON RAIL
Newer diesel engines use a fuel delivery system referred to as a high-pressure common rail (HPCR) design. Diesel fuel under high pressure, over 20,000 PSI (138,000 kPa), is applied to the injectors, which are opened by a solenoid controlled by the computer. Because the injectors are computer controlled, the combustion process can be precisely controlled to provide maximum engine efficiency with the lowest possible noise and exhaust emissions. ● SEE FIGURE 15–10.

HEUI SYSTEM

PRINCIPLES OF OPERATION
Ford (and Navistar) 7.3 and 6.0 liter diesels use a system called a hydraulic electronic unit injection system, or HEUI system. The components used include the following:

- High-pressure engine oil pump and reservoir
- Pressure regulator for the engine oil
- Passages in the cylinder head for flow of fuel to the injectors

OPERATION
The engine oil is pressurized to provide an opening pressure strong enough to overcome the fuel pressure when the solenoid is commanded to open by the power train control module (PCM). The system functions as follows:

- Diesel fuel is directed back to the fuel pump where fuel is pumped at high pressure into the cylinder head fuel galleries.
- The injectors are actuated by engine oil pressure from the high-pressure oil pump and are then fired by the PCM. ● SEE FIGURE 15–11.

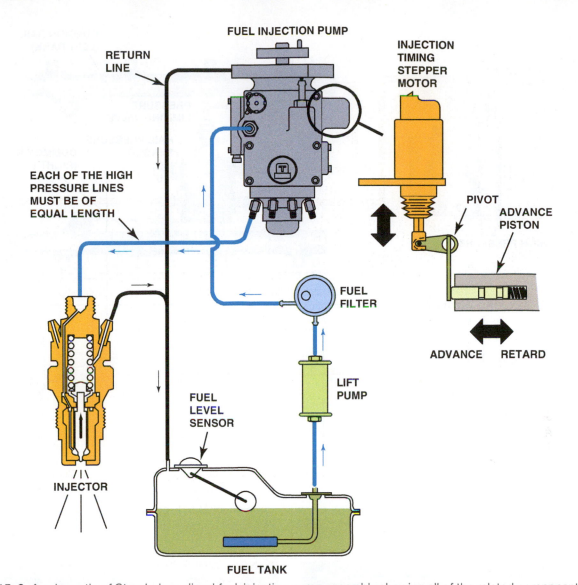

FIGURE 15–9 A schematic of Standadyne diesel fuel–injection pump assembly showing all of the related components.

DIESEL INJECTOR NOZZLES

PARTS INVOLVED Diesel injector nozzles are normally spring-loaded closed valves and spray fuel directly into the combustion chamber or precombustion chamber when the injector is opened. Injector nozzles are threaded or clamped into the cylinder head, one for each cylinder, and are replaceable as an assembly. The tip of the injector nozzle has many holes to deliver an atomized spray of diesel fuel into the cylinder.

DIESEL INJECTOR NOZZLE OPERATION The electric solenoid attached to the injector nozzle is computer controlled and opens to allow fuel to flow into the injector pressure chamber. ● SEE FIGURE 15–12.

The fuel flows down through a fuel passage in the injector body and into the pressure chamber. The high fuel pressure in the pressure chamber forces the needle valve upward, compressing the needle valve return spring and forcing the needle valve open. When the needle valve opens, diesel fuel is discharged into the combustion chamber in a hollow cone spray pattern. Any fuel that leaks past the needle valve returns to the fuel tank through a return passage and line. ● SEE FIGURE 15–13 on page 147.

GLOW PLUGS

PURPOSE AND FUNCTION Glow plugs are always used in diesel engines equipped with a precombustion chamber and may be used in direct injection diesel engines to aid starting. A **glow plug** is an electrical heating element that uses 12 volts from the battery and aids in the starting of a cold engine by providing heat to help the fuel to ignite. ● SEE FIGURE 15–14 on page 147.

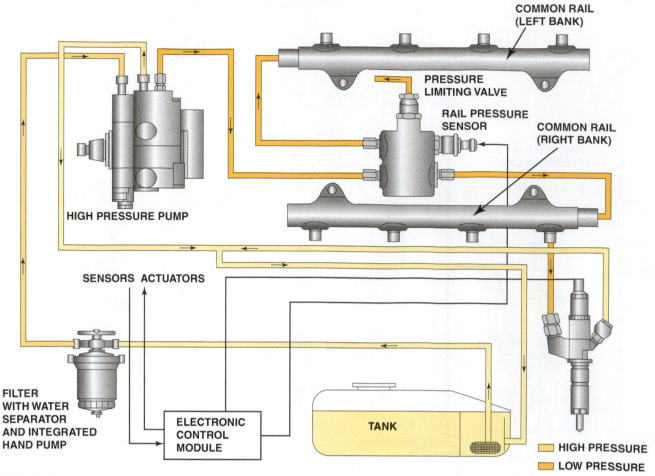

FIGURE 15–10 Overview of a computer-controlled high-pressure common rail V-8 diesel engine.

FIGURE 15–11 A HEUI injector from a Ford Power Stroke diesel engine. The O-ring grooves indicate the location of the O-rings that seal the fuel section of the injector from coolant and from the engine oil.

FIGURE 15–12 Typical computer-controlled diesel engine fuel injectors.

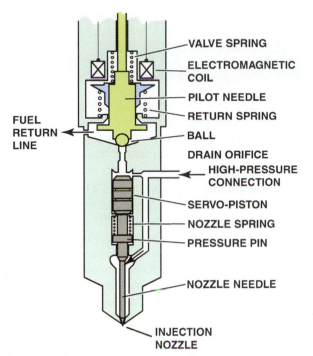

FIGURE 15–13 A Duramax injector showing all the internal parts.

FIGURE 15–14 A glow plug assortment showing the various types and sizes of glow plugs. Always use the specified glow plugs.

As the temperature of the glow plug increases, the resistance of the heating element inside increases, thereby reducing the current in amperes needed by the glow plugs.

OPERATION Most glow plugs used in newer vehicles are controlled by the PCM, which monitors coolant temperature and intake air temperature. The glow plugs are turned on or pulsed on or off depending on the temperature of the engine. The PCM will also keep the glow plug turned on after the engine starts, to reduce white exhaust smoke (unburned fuel) and to improve idle quality after starting. The "wait to start" lamp (if equipped) will come on when the engine and the outside temperatures are low to allow time for the glow plugs to get hot.

DIESEL FUEL HEATERS

Some diesel engines use fuel heaters to prevent power loss and stalling in cold weather. The fuel heater is placed in the fuel line between the tank and the primary fuel filter. Most fuel heaters use engine coolant to warm the diesel fuel. Some coolant heaters are thermostatically controlled, which allows fuel to bypass the heater once it has reached operating temperature.

DIESEL ENGINE TURBOCHARGERS

PURPOSE AND FUNCTION A turbocharger greatly increases engine power by pumping additional compressed air into the combustion chambers. This allows a greater quantity of fuel to be burned in the cylinders, resulting in greater power output. In a turbocharger, exhaust gases flow out of the engine

FIGURE 15–15 A Cummins diesel turbocharger is used to increase the power and torque of the engine.

and cause the blades of the turbocharger's turbine wheel to spin. The spinning turbine also rotates the compressor wheel at the opposite end of the turbine shaft, which pumps fresh air into the intake system. ● **SEE FIGURE 15–15.**

AIR CHARGE COOLER The first component in a typical turbocharger system is an air filter through which outside air passes before entering the compressor. The air is compressed, which raises its density (mass/unit volume) and also its temperature. All currently produced light-duty diesels use an air charge cooler, also called an *intercooler* or *after-cooler*, whose purpose is to cool the compressed air to further raise the air density. Cooler air entering the engine means more power can be produced by the engine. ● **SEE FIGURE 15–16.**

DIESEL EXHAUST EMISSION CONTROL SYSTEMS

NEED FOR DIESEL EMISSION CONTROL DEVICES Diesel engines are now required to meet very strict emission standards that require many different types of emission controls. Most of the major emission control devices are located in the exhaust system, including the following:

- **Diesel oxidation catalysts (DOC)** is a type of catalytic converter used in all light-duty diesel engines since 2007. They consist of a flow-through honeycomb-style substrate structure that is wash coated with a layer of catalyst materials, similar to those used in a gasoline engine catalytic converter. Catalysts chemically react with exhaust gas to convert harmful nitrogen oxide into nitrogen dioxide, and to oxidize absorbed hydrocarbons.

- **Diesel exhaust particulate filters (DPFs)** are used in all light-duty diesel vehicles since 2007 to meet the exhaust emissions standards for **particulate matter (PM)**, also called **soot**. The heated exhaust gas from the DOC flows into the DPF, which captures diesel exhaust gas particulates (soot) to prevent them from being released into the atmosphere. ● **SEE FIGURE 15–17.**

The filter must therefore be purged periodically to remove accumulated soot particles. The process of purging soot from the DPF is described as **regeneration**. When the temperature of the exhaust gas is increased, the heat incinerates the soot particles trapped in the filter and is effectively renewed. ● **SEE FIGURE 15–18.**

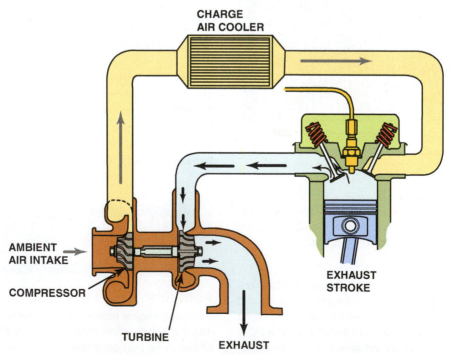

CHARGE AIR COOLER

AMBIENT AIR INTAKE

COMPRESSOR

TURBINE

EXHAUST

EXHAUST STROKE

FIGURE 15–16 An air charge cooler is used to cool the compressed air.

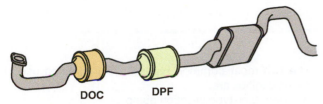

FIGURE 15–17 Aftertreatment of diesel exhaust is handled by the DOC and DPF.

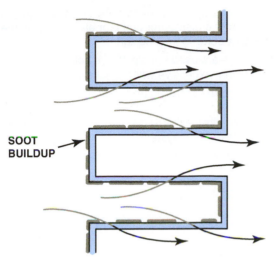

FIGURE 15–18 The soot is trapped in the passages of the DPF. The exhaust has to flow through the sides of the trap and exit.

FIGURE 15–19 Diesel exhaust fluid costs $3 to $4 a gallon and is housed in a separate container that holds from 5 to 10 gallons, or enough to last until the next scheduled oil change in most diesel vehicles that use SCR.

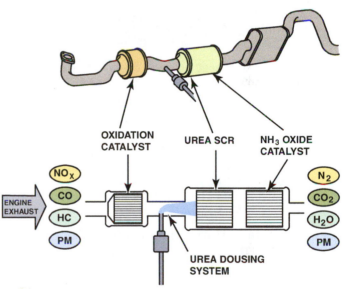

FIGURE 15–20 Urea (diesel exhaust fluid) injection is used to reduce NOx exhaust emissions. It is injected after the diesel oxidation catalyst (DOC) and before the diesel particulate filter (DPF) on this 6.7 liter Ford diesel engine.

TECH TIP

Always Use Cardboard to Check for High-Pressure Leaks

If diesel fuel is found on the engine, a high-pressure leak could be present. When checking for such a leak, wear protective clothing, including safety glasses, a face shield, gloves, and a long-sleeved shirt. Then use a piece of cardboard to locate the high-pressure leak. When a Duramax diesel is running, the pressure in the common rail and injector tubes can reach over 20,000 PSI. At these pressures, the diesel fuel is atomized and cannot be seen but can penetrate the skin and cause personal injury. A leak will be shown as a dark area on the cardboard. When a leak is found, shut off the engine and find the exact location of the leak without the engine running.

CAUTION: Sometimes a leak can actually cut through the cardboard, so use extreme care.

■ **Selective catalytic reduction (SCR)** is a method used to reduce NOx emissions by injecting urea into the exhaust stream. Instead of using large amounts of exhaust gas recirculation (EGR), the SCR system uses a

urea. **Urea** is used as a nitrogen fertilizer. It is colorless, odorless, and nontoxic. Urea is called **diesel exhaust fluid (DEF)** in North America and AdBlue in Europe.
● **SEE FIGURE 15–19.**

A warning light alerts the driver when the urea level needs to be refilled. If the warning light is ignored and the diesel exhaust fluid is not refilled, current EPA regulations require that the operation of the engine be restricted and may not start unless the fluid is refilled. This regulation is designed to prevent the engine from being operated without the fluid, which, if not used, would greatly increase exhaust emissions.
● **SEE FIGURE 15–20.**

1. A diesel engine uses heat of compression to ignite the diesel fuel when it is injected into the compressed air in the combustion chamber.

2. There are two basic designs of combustion chambers used in diesel engines. Indirect injection (IDI) uses a precombustion chamber, whereas direct injection (DI) occurs directly into the combustion chamber.

3. The three phases of diesel combustion include the following:
   a. Ignition delay
   b. Rapid combustion
   c. Controlled combustion

4. The typical diesel engine fuel system consists of the fuel tank, lift pump, water–fuel separator, and fuel filter.

5. The engine-driven injection pump supplies high-pressure diesel fuel to the injectors.

6. The two most common types of fuel injection used in diesel engines are:
   a. Distributor-type injection pump
   b. Common rail design, where all of the injectors are fed from the same fuel supply from a rail under high pressure

7. Injector nozzles are opened either by the high-pressure pulse from the distributor pump or electrically by the computer on a common rail design.

8. Glow plugs are used to help start a cold diesel engine and help prevent excessive white smoke during warm-up.

9. Emissions are controlled on newer diesel engines by using a diesel oxidation catalytic converter, a diesel exhaust particulate filter, exhaust gas recirculation, and a selective catalytic reduction system.

10. Diesel engines can be tested using a scan tool.

REVIEW QUESTIONS

1. What is the difference between direct injection and indirect injection?

2. What are the three phases of diesel ignition?

3. What are the two most commonly used types of diesel injection systems?

4. Why are glow plugs kept working after the engine starts?

5. What exhaust aftertreatment is needed to achieve exhaust emission standards for vehicles since 2007?

CHAPTER QUIZ

1. How is diesel fuel ignited in a warm diesel engine?
   a. Glow plugs
   b. Heat of compression
   c. Spark plugs
   d. Distributorless ignition system

2. Which type of diesel injection produces less noise?
   a. Indirect injection (IDI)   b. Direct injection
   c. Common rail   d. Distributor injection

3. Which diesel injection system requires the use of a glow plug?
   a. Indirect injection (IDI)
   b. High-pressure common rail
   c. Direct injection
   d. Distributor injection

4. The three phases of diesel ignition includes _____.
   a. Glow plug ignition, fast burn, slow burn
   b. Slow burn, fast burn, slow burn
   c. Ignition delay, rapid combustion, controlled combustion
   d. Glow plug ignition, ignition delay, controlled combustion

5. What fuel system component is used in a vehicle equipped with a diesel engine that is seldom used on the same vehicle when it is equipped with a gasoline engine?
   a. Fuel filter   b. Fuel supply line
   c. Fuel return line   d. Water–fuel separator

6. The diesel injection pump is usually driven by a _____.
   a. Gear off the camshaft
   b. Belt off the crankshaft
   c. Shaft drive off the crankshaft
   d. Chain drive off the camshaft

7. Which diesel system supplies high-pressure diesel fuel to all of the injectors all of the time?
   a. Distributor
   b. Inline
   c. High-pressure common rail
   d. Rotary

8. Glow plugs should have high resistance when _____ and lower resistance when _____.
   a. Cold/warm   b. Warm/cold
   c. Wet/dry   d. Dry/wet

9. Technician A says that glow plugs are used to help start a diesel engine and are shut off as soon as the engine starts. Technician B says that the glow plugs are turned off as soon as a flame is detected in the combustion chamber. Which technician is correct?
   a. Technician A only
   b. Technician B only
   c. Both technicians A and B
   d. Neither technician A nor B

10. What is the fluid called that has to be refilled regularly if the diesel engine is equipped with SCR?
    a. Urea
    b. AdBlue
    c. Diesel exhaust fluid (DEF)'
    d. All of the above

ENGINE LUBRICATION AND COOLING SYSTEMS

OBJECTIVES: After studying Chapter 16, the reader should be able to: • Prepare for ASE Engine Repair (A1) certification test content area "D" (Lubrication and Cooling Systems Diagnosis and Repair). • Describe how the oil pump works to provide engine lubrication. • Discuss how oil lubricates the internal engine parts. Describe how the cooling system works. List the types of coolant.

KEY TERMS: • DEX-COOL 157 • Ethylene glycol 157 • Gallery 154 • IAT coolant 157 • OAT coolant 157 • HOAT coolant 157 • Sump 155 • Windage tray 155

LUBRICATION

PURPOSE AND FUNCTION
Engine oil is the lifeblood of any engine. The purposes of a lubrication system include the following:

1. Lubricating all moving parts to prevent wear
2. Helping to cool the engine
3. Helping to seal piston rings
4. Cleaning and holding dirt in suspension in the oil until it can be drained from the engine
5. Neutralizing acids that are formed as a result of the combustion process
6. Reducing friction
7. Preventing rust and corrosion

Lubrication between two moving surfaces results from an oil film that separates the surfaces and supports the load. ● **SEE FIGURE 16–1.**

Although oil does not compress, it does leak out around the oil clearance between the shaft and the bearing. In most cases, the oil film is thick enough to keep the surfaces from seizing, but can allow some contact to occur.

NORMAL OIL PRESSURE
Engine oil pressure must be high enough to get the oil to the bearings with enough force to cause the oil flow that is required for proper cooling. The normal engine oil pressure range is from 10 to 60 PSI (200 to 400 kPa) or a minimum of 10 PSI per 1,000 engine RPM. It is normal to observe the following:

- Higher oil pressure when the engine is cold due to the oil being cold and thicker.

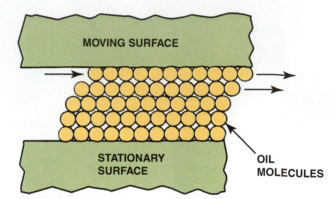

FIGURE 16–1 Oil molecules cling to metal surfaces but easily slide against each other.

- Lower oil pressure when the engine is at normal operating temperature due to the oil becoming thinner even though it is multiviscosity oil. ● **SEE FIGURE 16–2.**
- Oil pressure is lower when the engine is at idle speed and higher when the engine speed is high because the oil pump is rotating faster and is able to supply more oil at higher engine speeds up to a point where it is regulated. ● **SEE FIGURE 16–3.**

FACTORS AFFECTING OIL PRESSURE
Oil pressure can only be produced when the oil pump has a capacity larger than all the "leaks" inside the engine.

- **Leaks.** The leaks are the clearances at the end points of the lubrication system. The end points are at the edges of bearings, the rocker arms, the connecting rod spit holes, and so on. These clearances are designed into the engine and are necessary for its proper operation. As the engine parts wear and clearance becomes greater, more oil will

FIGURE 16–2 The dash oil pressure gauge may be a good indicator of engine oil pressure. If there is any concern about the oil pressure, always use a mechanical gauge to be sure.

leak out. In other words, worn main or rod bearings are often the cause of lower than normal oil pressure.

- **Oil pump capacity.** The oil pump must supply extra oil for all internal engine leaks. The capacity of the oil pump depends on its size, rotating speed, and physical condition. When the pump is rotating slowly as the engine idles, oil pump capacity is low. If the leaks are greater than the pump capacity, engine oil pressure is low. As the engine speed increases, the pump capacity increases and the pump tries

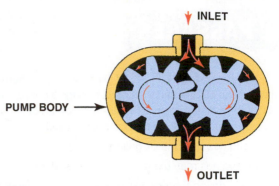

FIGURE 16–3 In an external gear-type oil pump, the oil flows through the pump around the outside of each gear. This is an example of a positive displacement pump, wherein everything entering the pump must leave the pump.

to force more oil out of the leaks. This causes the pressure to rise until it reaches the regulated maximum pressure.

NOTE: A clogged oil pump pickup screen will reduce the amount of oil delivered to the pump, which can cause lower than normal oil pressure.

- **Viscosity of the engine oil.** The viscosity (thickness) of the oil affects both the pump capacity and the oil leakage. Thin oil or oil of very low viscosity slips past the edges of the pump and flows freely from the leaks. Hot oil is thinner, and therefore, a hot engine often has low oil pressure. Cold oil is thicker than hot oil. This results in higher pressures, even with the cold engine idling. ● **SEE FIGURE 16–4.**

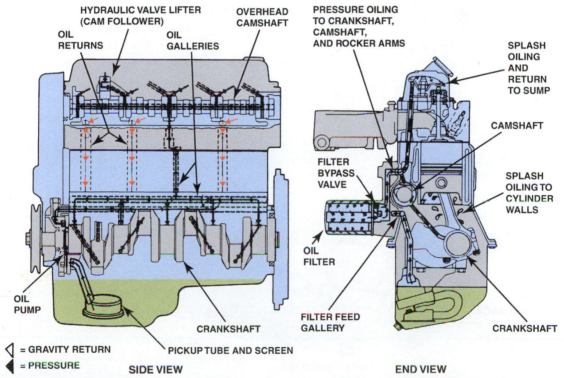

FIGURE 16–4 A typical engine design uses both pressure and splash lubrication. Oil travels under pressure through the galleries (passages) to reach the top of the engine. Other parts are lubricated as the oil flows back down into the oil pan or is splashed onto parts.

OIL PASSAGES

PURPOSE AND FUNCTION

Oil from the oil pump first flows through the oil filter and then goes through a drilled hole that intersects with a drilled main oil **gallery**, or longitudinal header. This is a long hole drilled from the front of the block to the back.

- Inline engines use one oil gallery.
- V-type engines may use two or three galleries.

Passages drilled through the block bulkheads allow the oil to go from the main oil gallery to the main and cam bearings. ● **SEE FIGURE 16–5.**

VALVE TRAIN LUBRICATION

The oil from the oil pump first flows to the main and rod bearings before being sent to the upper part of the engine to lubricate the valve train components such as:

- Rocker arms
- Valve springs (to carry heat away)
- Valve stem tips
- Rocker arm shaft
- Camshaft bearings and lobes

Oil drain holes can be either machined or cast into the cylinder heads and block. ● **SEE FIGURE 16–6.**

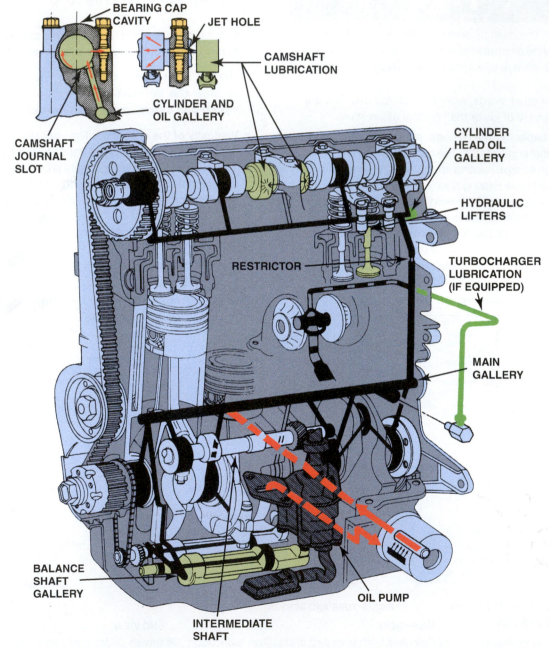

FIGURE 16–5 An intermediate shaft drives the oil pump on this overhead camshaft engine. Note the main gallery and other drilled passages in the block and cylinder head.

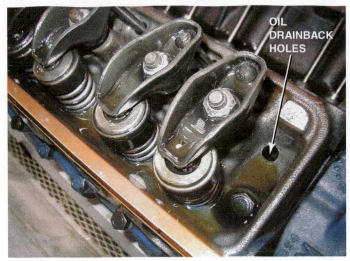

FIGURE 16–6 Oil is sent to the rocker arms on this Chevrolet V-8 engine through the hollow pushrods. The oil returns to the oil pan through the oil drain back holes in the cylinder head.

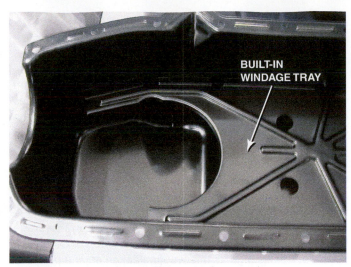

FIGURE 16–7 A typical oil pan with a built-in windage tray used to keep oil from being churned up by the rotating crankshaft.

FIGURE 16–8 Oil is cooled by the flow of coolant through the oil filter adaptor.

OIL PANS

PURPOSE AND FUNCTION The oil pan is where engine oil is stored for lubricating the engine. Another name for the oil pan is a **sump**. As the vehicle accelerates, brakes, or turns rapidly, the oil tends to move around in the pan. Pan baffles and oil pan shapes are often used to keep the oil inlet under the oil at all times. As the crankshaft rotates, it acts like a fan and causes air within the crankcase to rotate with it. This can cause a strong draft on the oil, churning it so that air bubbles enter the oil, which then causes oil foaming. Oil with air will not lubricate like liquid oil, so oil foaming can cause bearings to fail. A baffle or **windage tray** is sometimes installed in engines to eliminate the oil churning problem. This may be an added part or it may be a part of the oil pan.
● SEE FIGURE 16–7.

OIL COOLERS

PURPOSE AND FUNCTION Oil temperature must be controlled in many high-performance or turbocharged engines. A larger capacity oil pan helps to control oil temperature. Some engines use remote mounted oil coolers. Coolant flows through the oil cooler to help warm the oil when the engine is cold and cool the oil when the engine is hot.
● SEE FIGURE 16–8.

OIL TEMPERATURE Oil temperature should be:

- Above 212°F (100°C) to boil off any accumulated moisture
- Below 280°F to 300°F (138°C to 148°C)

COOLING SYSTEM

PURPOSE AND FUNCTION Satisfactory cooling system operation depends on the design and operating conditions of the system. The design is based on heat output of the engine, radiator size, type of coolant, size of water pump, type of fan, thermostat, and system pressure. The cooling system must allow the engine to warm up to the required operating temperature as rapidly as possible and then maintain that temperature. Peak combustion temperatures in the engine cycle run from 4,000°F to 6,000°F (2,200°C to 3,300°C). The combustion temperatures will average between 1,200°F and 1,700°F (650°C and 925°C). Continued temperatures as high as this would weaken engine parts, so heat must be removed from the engine. The cooling system keeps the head and cylinder walls at a temperature that is within the range for maximum efficiency. The cooling system removes about one-third of the heat generated in the engine. Another third escapes to the exhaust system, leaving only about a third to provide the power to move the vehicle. ● **SEE FIGURE 16–9.**

LOW-TEMPERATURE ENGINE PROBLEMS Engine operating temperatures must be above a minimum temperature for proper engine operation. If the coolant temperature does not reach the specified temperature as determined by the thermostat, then a P0128 diagnostic trouble code (DTC) can be set. This code indicates "coolant temperature below thermostat regulating temperature," which is usually caused by a defective thermostat staying open or partially open. ● **SEE FIGURE 16–10.**

COOLANT

PURPOSE AND FUNCTION Coolant is used in the cooling system because it:

1. Transfers heat from the engine to the radiator

2. Protects the engine and the cooling system from rust and corrosion

3. Prevents freezing in cold climates. Coolant is a mixture of antifreeze and water. Water is able to absorb more heat per gallon than any other liquid coolant. Under standard conditions, the following occur:

   ▪ Water boils at 212°F (100°C) at sea level.
   ▪ Water freezes at 32°F (0°C).
   ▪ When water freezes, it increases in volume by about 9%. The expansion of the freezing water can easily crack engine blocks, cylinder heads, and radiators.

FREEZING/BOILING TEMPERATURES The normal mixture of coolant is 50% antifreeze and 50% water. The freezing point of this 50-50 mixture is −34°F (−36°C). Ethylene glycol antifreeze contains:

▪ Anticorrosion additives
▪ Rust inhibitors
▪ Water pump lubricants

At the maximum level of protection, an ethylene glycol concentration of 60% will absorb about 85% as much heat as will water. Ethylene glycol–based antifreeze also has a higher boiling point than water.

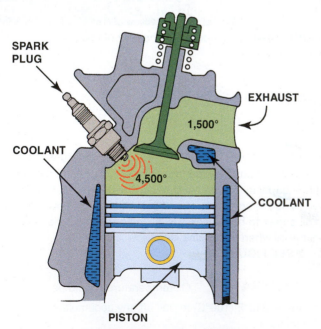

FIGURE 16–9 Typical combustion and exhaust temperatures.

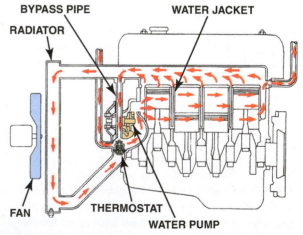

FIGURE 16–10 The engine cooling system includes the water jackets (passages) in the engine, plus the water pump and radiator. Hoses are used to move the coolant to and from the radiator and to and from the heater core inside the vehicle. The thermostat is used to control coolant temperature.

If the coolant boils, it vaporizes and does not act as a cooling agent because it is not in liquid form or in contact with the hot surface. All coolants have rust and corrosion inhibitors to help protect the metals in the engine and cooling systems.

COOLANT COMPOSITION All manufacturers recommend the use of ethylene glycol–based coolant, which contains:

- **Ethylene glycol** (EG): 47%
- Water: 50%
- Additives: 3%

Regardless of the type of coolant and its color, the only difference among all original equipment coolants is in the additives. This means that about 97% of all coolants are the same. The only difference is in the additive package and color used to help identify the coolant.

TYPES OF COOLANT

- **Inorganic additive technology (IAT)** coolants are conventional coolants that have been used for over 50 years. The color of an IAT coolant is green. Phosphates in these coolants can cause deposit formation if used with hard water (i.e., water with high mineral content). The use of IAT coolants in new vehicles was phased out in the mid-1990s.

- **Organic acid technology (OAT)** coolants contain ethylene glycol, but does not contain silicates or phosphates. The color of this type of coolant is usually orange. **DEX-COOL**, developed by Havoline, is just one brand of OAT coolant, which has been used in General Motors vehicles since 1996. ● SEE **FIGURE 16–11.**

Some other brands of OAT coolant that are orange are:

- Zerex G30 or G05 OAT
- Peak Global OAT

- **Hybrid organic acid technology (HOAT)** is a newer variation of OAT. An HOAT coolant is similar to the OAT-type antifreeze as it uses organic acid salts (carboxylates) that are not abrasive to water pumps. HOAT coolants can be green, orange, yellow, gold, pink, red, or blue.

- **Universal coolants** are usually HOAT coolants with extended life and are low-silicate and phosphate-free. They can be used in many vehicles, but cannot meet the needs of engines requiring a silicate-free formulation.

- **Premixed coolant** is a coolant that is mixed with the proper percentage of water and is ready for use. The water is demineralized and therefore does not include chlorine and other possible chemicals that could cause damage to the cooling system. Toyota and Honda are two vehicle manufacturers that specify the use of premixed coolant only. ● SEE **FIGURE 16–12.**

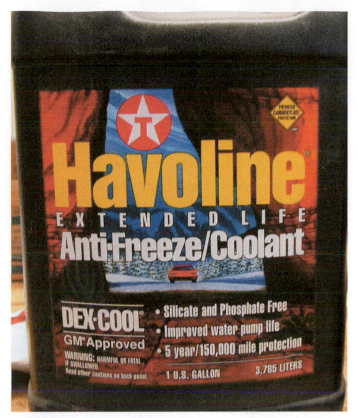

FIGURE 16–11 Havoline was the first company to make and market OAT coolants. General Motors uses the term "DEX-COOL."

FIGURE 16–12 Coolant used in Fords that use Mazda engines and in Mazda vehicles. It requires the use of an HOAT coolant, which is dark green and is premixed 55% antifreeze and 45% water in this example.

?

What Is "Pet Friendly" Antifreeze?

Conventional ethylene glycol antifreeze used by all vehicle manufacturers is attractive to pets and animals because it has a sweet taste. Ethylene glycol is fatal to any animal if swallowed, so any spill should be cleaned up quickly. There are two types of coolant that are safer for use around pets than the conventional type.

- **Propylene glycol (PG).** This type of antifreeze is less attractive to pets and animals because it is not as sweet, but it is still harmful if swallowed. This type of coolant, including the Sierra brand, should not be mixed with any other ethylene glycol–based coolant.

  CAUTION: Some vehicle manufacturers do not recommend the use of propylene glycol coolants. Check the recommendation in the owner manual or service information before using it in a vehicle.

- **Embittered coolant.** This coolant has a small amount of a substance that makes it taste bitter and therefore not appealing to animals. The embittering agent used in ethylene glycol (EG) antifreeze is usually denatonium benzoate, added at the rate of 30 parts per million (ppm). Oregon and California require all coolants sold in these states since 2004 to be embittered. ● **SEE FIGURE 16–13.**

FIGURE 16–13 Not all embittered coolants are labeled "embittered." Many states now require that all coolants sold in the state be embittered.

SUMMARY

1. Normal engine oil pump pressure ranges from 10 to 60 PSI (200 to 400 kPa) or a minimum of 10 PSI for every 1,000 engine RPM.

2. The oil pump supplies the internal parts of the engine with oil to reduce friction and wear to the moving parts.

3. Coolant is a mixture of antifreeze (ethylene glycol) and water and the various types of coolant are all determined by the additives used.

REVIEW QUESTIONS

1. Why does internal engine leakage affect oil pressure?

2. What are the last components to receive oil from the oil pump?

3. What type of coolant is sold as "universal" coolant?

1. Normal oil pump pressure in an engine is _____ PSI.
   a. 3 to 7
   b. 10 to 60
   c. 100 to 150
   d. 180 to 210

2. In typical engine lubrication systems, what components are the last to receive oil?
   a. Main bearings
   b. Rod bearings
   c. Valve train components
   d. Oil filters

3. Oil passages in an engine block are usually called _____.
   a. Galleries
   b. Holes
   c. Runners
   d. Pathways

4. Coolant is antifreeze plus _____.
   a. Water
   b. Methanol alcohol
   c. Ethanol alcohol
   d. Either b or c

5. DEX-COOL is what type of coolant?
   a. Propylene glycol
   b. Ethylene glycol
   c. OAT
   d. Both b and c

6. If coolant is mixed 50–50 with water, what is the freezing point?
   a. 0° F (−18° C)
   b. 32° F (0°C)
   c. −34° F (−37° C)
   d. −40°F (−40° C)

7. If a thermostat is not working, what diagnostic trouble code could be set?
   a. P0300
   b. P0128
   c. P0440
   d. P0700

8. The additives used in coolants such as the dye and anticorrosion additives are about what percentage of the coolant?
   a. 3%
   b. 6–10%
   c. 12–15%
   d. 20–25%

9. What type of water is used in premixed coolant?
   a. Distilled water
   b. Demineralized water
   c. Tap water
   d. Recycled water

10. An engine is operating at 2,000 RPM while the vehicle is traveling down the highway. The oil pressure should be about _____.
    a. 3–7 PSI
    b. 10–12 PSI
    c. 20 PSI or higher
    d. 50 PSI or higher

UNDER-HOOD VEHICLE INSPECTION

OBJECTIVES: **After studying Chapter 17, the reader should be able to:** • Prepare for ASE Engine Repair (A1) certification test content area "A" (General Engine Diagnosis) and content area "D" (Lubrication and Cooling Systems Diagnosis and Repair). • Perform routine fluid and service checks. • Discuss how to protect the vehicle during during service. • List the items that should be checked during a safety inspection. • Discuss the items that require routine (preventative) maintenance. • Explain how to replace a cabin and engine air filter. • Explain how to check brake fluid. • Discuss the types of automatic transmission fluids. • Explain how to check engine coolant. • Describe how to check accessory drive belts. • Explain how to check power steering fluid level.

KEY TERMS: • Air filter 163 • Automatic transmission fluid (ATF) 165 • Brake fluid 163 • Cabin filter 162 • Dipstick 165 • DOT 3 163 • DOT 4 164 • DOT 5 164 • DOT 5.1 164 • Polyglycol 163 • Preventative maintenance (PM) 161 • Serpentine (Poly V) 169 • Silicone brake fluid 164 • Viscosity 165

VEHICLE INSPECTION

PRESERVICE INSPECTION Prior to any service work, it is wise to check the vehicle for damage and document the work order if any damage is found. In most dealerships and shops, this is the responsibility of the following personnel.

- Service adviser (service writer) or
- Shop foreman or
- Shop owner

The designated person should check the vehicle for the following:

1. Body damage
2. Missing components such as wheel covers, mirrors, and radio antennas
3. Glass damage such as a cracked windshield
4. Any faults or scratches in the paint or trim
5. Valid license plates

PROTECT THE VEHICLE Before most service work is done, protect the inside of the vehicle by using commercially available plastic or paper protective coverings for the following areas.

- Seats
- Floor
- Steering wheel

● **SEE FIGURE 17-1**

PROTECT THE TECHNICIAN Before starting routine preventative maintenance on a vehicle, be sure to perform the following:

1. Open the hood (engine compartment cover). Often the struts that hold a hood open are weak or defective. Therefore, before starting to work under the hood, always make sure that the hood is securely held open using a prop rod if needed.
2. Connect an exhaust system hose to the tailpipe(s) before work is started that will involve operating the engine. ● **SEE FIGURE 17–2**.
3. Wear personal protective equipment (PPE), including:
   - Safety glasses
   - Hearing protection if around air tools or other loud noises
   - Gloves if handling hot objects or chemicals such as used engine oil
4. In hybrid vehicles, make sure that the technician has possession of the key transmitter and that the vehicle is *not* in the ready mode before starting any inspection or service procedure.

SAFETY INSPECTION A safety inspection is usually recommended anytime the vehicle is in the shop for service or repair. These inspections should include all of the following:

1. Exterior lights, including:
   a. Headlights (high and low beam)
   b. Tail lights
   c. Turn signals
   d. License plate light
   e. Parking lights
   f. Hazard warning lights

FIGURE 17–1 Before service begins, be sure to cover the seats, floor, and steering wheel with protective coverings.

2. Horn
3. Windshield wiper operation
4. Mirrors
5. Defroster fan operation
6. Turn the steering wheel and check for excessive looseness
7. Shock absorbers that allow excessive body sway
8. Tire tread depth, and proper inflation pressure.

NOTE: Checking, correcting, and indicating on the vehicle service invoice that a tire inflation service was completed and the tire pressure measurements after the service was performed is a law in some states.

9. Parking brake operation
10. Exhaust system for excessive noise or leaks

PREVENTATIVE MAINTENANCE

PURPOSE **Preventative maintenance (PM)** means periodic service work performed on a vehicle that will help keep it functioning correctly for a long time. All vehicle manufacturers publish a list of service work to be performed on a regular basis. Preventative maintenance is also called *routine maintenance*

FIGURE 17–2 An exhaust system hose should be connected to the tailpipe(s) whenever the engine is being run indoors.

because it is usually performed on a set scheduled routine. The interval specified for preventative maintenance is often expressed in time and miles (km), such as:

- Every six months (could be longer for many vehicles)
- Every 5,000 to 10,000 miles (8,000 to 16,000 km) depending on the vehicle and how it is being operated
- Either of the above, whichever occurs first

ITEMS REQUIRING MAINTENANCE The items or systems that require routine maintenance include:

1. Engine oil and oil filter replacement
2. Air and cabin filter replacement
3. Tire inflation pressure check, inspection, and rotation
4. Brake and suspension system inspection
5. Under-hood inspection and fluid checks
6. Under-vehicle inspection and fluid checks (See Chapter 19)
7. Air conditioning system inspection and service
8. Routine cleaning of vehicle both inside and out

WINDSHIELD WIPER AND WASHER FLUID SERVICE

WINDSHIELD WIPERS Windshield wiper blades are constructed of rubber and tend to become brittle due to age. Wiper blades should be cleaned whenever the vehicle is cleaned using water and a soft cloth. Wiper blade or wiper blade insert replacement includes the following steps.

- Turn the key on, engine off (KOEO).
- Turn the wiper switch on and operate the wipers.

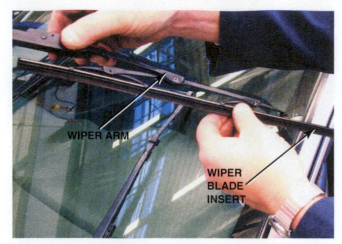

FIGURE 17–3 Installing a wiper blade insert into a wiper arm.

WIPER ARM

WIPER BLADE INSERT

(a)

(b)

FIGURE 17–4 (a) The windshield wiper fluid reservoir cap is usually labeled with a symbol showing a windshield washer. (b) Use only the recommended washer fluid. Never use antifreeze in the windshield washer reservoir.

■ When the wipers are located in an easy-to-reach location, turn the ignition switch off. The wipers should stop.

■ Remove the insert or the entire blade as per service information and/or the instructions on the replacement windshield wiper blade package.

■ After double-checking that the wiper is securely attached, turn the ignition switch on (run).

■ Turn the wiper switch off and allow the wipers to reach the park position. Check for proper operation. ● SEE FIGURE 17–3.

WINDSHIELD WASHER FLUID   Windshield washer fluid level should be checked regularly and refilled as necessary. Use only the fluid that is recommended for use in vehicle windshield washer systems. ● SEE FIGURE 17–4.

Most windshield washer fluid looks like blue water. It is actually water with an alcohol (methanol) additive to prevent freezing and to help clean the windshield by dissolving bugs. Be careful not to spill any washer fluid when filling the reservoir because the corrosiveness can harm wiring and electronic components.

CAUTION: Some mixed fluids are for summer-use only and do not contain antifreeze protection. Read the label carefully.

FILTER REPLACEMENT

CABIN FILTER   A **cabin filter** is used in the heating, ventilation, and air conditioning (HVAC) system to filter the outside air drawn into the passenger compartment. Some filters contain activated charcoal to help eliminate odors. The cabin air filter should be replaced often—every year or every 12,000 miles (19,000 km). The cabin air filter can be accessed from:

■ Under the hood at the cowl (bulkhead) or

■ Under the dash, usually behind the glove (instrument panel) compartment. (Check service information for the exact location and servicing procedures for the vehicle being serviced.) ● SEE FIGURE 17–5.

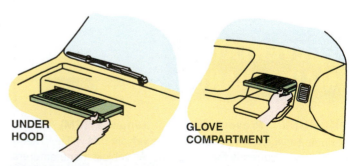

UNDER HOOD

GLOVE COMPARTMENT

FIGURE 17–5 A cabin filter can be accessed either through the glove compartment or under the hood.

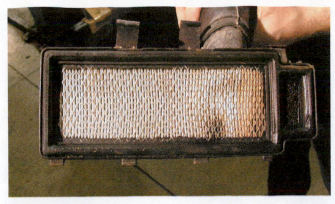

(a)

(b)

FIGURE 17–6 (a) A typical dirty air filter. (b) Always check the inlet passage leading to the air filter for debris that can reduce airflow to the engine.

ENGINE AIR FILTER An **air filter** filters dirt from the air before it enters the intake system of the engine. The air filter should be replaced according to the vehicle manufacturer's recommendations. Over time, the filter will start to get clogged and decrease the engine power. Many vehicle manufacturers recommend replacing the air filter every 30,000 miles (50,000 km), or more frequently under dusty conditions. Many service technicians recommend replacing the air filter every year. ● **SEE FIGURE 17–6.**

BRAKE FLUID

BRAKE FLUID LEVEL **Brake fluid** is used to transmit the force of the driver's foot on the brake pedal, called the service brake, to each individual wheel brake. The brake fluid should be checked at the same time the engine oil is changed, or every six months, whichever occurs first. It is normal for the brake fluid level to drop as the disc brake pads wear. Therefore, if the fluid level is low, check for two possible causes.

FIGURE 17–7 A master cylinder with a transparent reservoir. The brake fluid level should be between the MAX and the MIN levels as marked on the reservoir.

CAUSE 1 Normal disc brake pad wear. (Inspect the brakes if the fluid level is low.)

CAUSE 2 A leak somewhere in the hydraulic brake system. (Carefully inspect the entire brake system for leaks if the brakes are not worn and the brake fluid level is low.)

There are two types of brake master cylinder reservoirs.

- **Transparent reservoir.** This type of reservoir allows viewing of the brake fluid (and hydraulic clutch master cylinder if so equipped) without having to remove the cover of the reservoir. The proper level is between the MIN (minimum) and MAX (maximum) level indicated on the clear plastic reservoir. ● **SEE FIGURE 17–7.**

- **Metal or nontransparent plastic reservoir.** This type of reservoir used on older vehicles requires that the cover be removed to check the level of the brake fluid. The proper level of brake fluid should be 1/4 in. (6 mm) from the top.

CAUTION: Do not overfill a brake master cylinder. The brake fluid gets hotter as the brakes are used and there must be room in the master cylinder reservoir for the brake fluid to expand.

BRAKE FLUID TYPES Brake fluid is made from a combination of various types of glycol, a non-petroleum-based fluid. Brake fluid is a polyalkylene-glycol-ether mixture, called **polyglycol** for short. *All polyglycol brake fluids are clear to amber in color.*

CAUTION: DOT 3 brake fluid is a very strong solvent and can remove paint! Care is required when working with this type of brake fluid to avoid contact with the vehicle's painted surfaces. It also takes the color out of leather shoes.

All automotive brake fluids must meet Federal Motor Vehicle Safety Standard 116. The Society of Automotive Engineers (SAE) and the Department of Transportation (DOT) have established brake fluid specification standards.

- **DOT 3.** The **DOT 3** brake fluid is most often used. It absorbs moisture and, according to SAE, can absorb

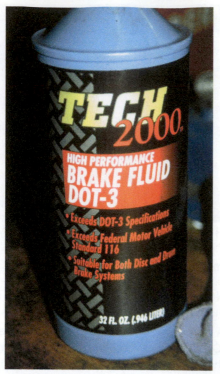

FIGURE 17–8 DOT 3 brake fluid. Always use fluid from a sealed container because brake fluid absorbs moisture from the air.

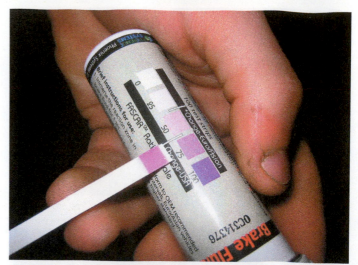

FIGURE 17–9 Brake fluid test strips are a convenient and easy-to-use method to determine if the brake fluid needs to be replaced.

CAUTION: Some vehicle manufacturers, such as Chrysler, do not recommend the use of or the mixing of other types of polyglycol brake fluids and specify the use of DOT 3 brake fluid only. Always follow the vehicle manufacturer's recommendation.

2% of its volume in water per year. Moisture is absorbed by the brake fluid through microscopic seams in the brake system and around seals. Over time, the water will corrode the system and thicken the brake fluid. Moisture can cause a spongy brake pedal because the increased concentration of water within the fluid boils at lower temperatures and can result in vapor lock. DOT 3 must be used from a sealed (capped) container. If allowed to remain open for any length of time, DOT 3 will absorb moisture from the surrounding air. ● **SEE FIGURE 17–8.**

■ **DOT 4.** The **DOT 4** brake fluid is formulated for use by all vehicles, imported or domestic. It is commonly called low moisture absorption (LMA) because it does not absorb water as fast as DOT 3. It is still affected by moisture, however, and should be used only from a sealed container. The cost of DOT 4 is approximately double the cost of DOT 3.

■ **DOT 5.** The **DOT 5** type is commonly called **silicone brake fluid.** Because it does not absorb water, it is called nonhygroscopic. DOT 5 brake fluid does not mix with and should not be used with DOT 3 or DOT 4 brake fluid. DOT 5 brake fluid is purple (violet), to distinguish it from DOT 3 or DOT 4 brake fluid.

■ **DOT 5.1.** The **DOT 5.1** brake fluid is a non-silicone-based polyglycol fluid that is clear to amber in color. This severe-duty fluid has a boiling point of over 500°F (260°C), equal to the boiling point of silicone-based DOT 5 fluid. Unlike DOT 5, the DOT 5.1 fluid can be mixed with either DOT 3 or DOT 4 according to the brake fluid manufacturer's recommendations.

BRAKE FLUID INSPECTION

■ **Visual inspection.** Check the color of the brake fluid. It should be clear or almost clear. If it is dark brown or black, it should be replaced.

■ **Test strips.** A quick and easy way to check the condition of the brake fluid is to use test strips. Always follow the instructions that come with the test strips for accurate results. ● **SEE FIGURE 17–9.**

■ **Boiling point.** The boiling point of brake fluid can be tested using a handheld tester. Follow the instructions that come with the tester.

? FREQUENTLY ASKED QUESTION

What Is Hydraulic Clutch Fluid?

The fluid used in hydraulic clutch master cylinders is DOT 3 brake fluid. It can be checked using the same procedures as those followed to check brake fluid. If the hydraulic clutch fluid is low, however, it has to be caused by a leak in the system. Therefore, do not fill the reservoir of the hydraulic clutch master cylinder without first finding and fixing the source of the leak. If the fluid gets too low, the clutch will not work and the transmission cannot be shifted. Always check service information for the exact procedure and fluid to use.

CAUTION: If any mineral oil such as engine oil, automatic transmission fluid (ATF), or power steering fluid gets into the brake fluid, the rubber seals will swell and cause damage to the entire braking system. Every part that includes a rubber seal will require replacement.

ENGINE OIL INSPECTION

OIL LEVEL The oil level should be checked when the vehicle is parked on level ground and after the engine has been off for at least several minutes. The *oil level indicator*, commonly called a **dipstick**, is clearly marked and is placed in a convenient location. ● **SEE FIGURE 17–10.**

To check the oil, remove the dipstick, wipe off the oil, and reinsert it all the way down. Once again remove the dipstick and check where the oil level touches the indicator. The "add" mark is usually at the 1 quart low point. ● **SEE FIGURE 17–11.**

If oil needs to be added, use the specified oil and add to the engine through the oil fill opening (not through the dipstick hole as is done with automatic transmission fluid).

FIGURE 17–10 A typical oil level indicator (dipstick).

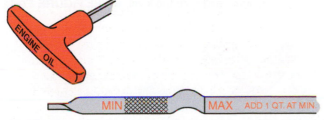

FIGURE 17–11 The oil level should be between the MAX and the MIN marks when the vehicle is on level ground and the oil has had time to drain into the oil pan.

OIL CONDITION When checking the engine oil, perform the following steps:

- Rub the oil from the end of the dipstick between your fingers. The oil should feel slippery. If it feels gritty, then the oil definitely needs to be changed.

- If the oil is black in color then it likely needs to be changed. Normal oil, even when near the scheduled oil change, is usually dark brown.

  NOTE: Diesel engine oil can turn black well before a scheduled oil change. This is normal and does not indicate that an oil change is necessary.

- If the oil has a "milky" appearance, it indicates potential coolant in the system or some other malfunction.

- Check the oil life monitor on the dash to see if there is a percentage of oil life remaining or a lamp on indicating that an oil change is due or almost due.

AUTOMATIC TRANSMISSION FLUID

TYPES OF AUTOMATIC TRANSMISSION FLUID

Automatic transmission fluid (ATF) is high-quality oil that has additives that resist oxidation, inhibit rust formation, and allow the fluid to flow easily at all temperatures. The automatic transmission fluid is dyed red for identification. Various vehicle manufacturers recommend a particular type of ATF based mainly on its friction characteristics. Friction is needed between the bands, plates, and clutches inside an automatic transmission/transaxle to make the shifts occur.

While the additive packages and **viscosity** (thickness) vary, ATF is grouped in three basic types, including:

1. Nonfriction modified (used in older types of automatic transmissions)

2. Friction modified

3. Highly friction modified (most used in current-type electrically controlled automatic transmissions/transaxles).

TYPICAL ATF APPLICATIONS ● **SEE CHART 17–1** for examples of the types and application of selected vehicle and fluids. Using the wrong type of ATF can cause the transmission to shift too harshly or cause a vibration when the transmission shifts.

PROCEDURE The **automatic transmission fluid (ATF)** should be checked regularly. The recommended procedure is usually stamped on the transmission dipstick or written in the owner's manual and/or service manual. Most automatic transmission fluid levels should be checked under the following conditions.

GENERAL MOTORS	DESCRIPTION
Type A	1949
Type A, Suffice A	1957 (friction modified)
Dexron	1967 (lower viscosity)
Dexron II	1978 (lower viscosity)
Dexron II-E	1990 (improved low temperature fluidity)
Dexron III	1993–2005 (improved low temperature fluidity)
Dexron VI	2005 (improved viscosity stability)
FORD/JAGUAR	**DESCRIPTION**
Type F	1967 (Nonfriction modified. Designed for older band-type automatic transmissions)
Mercon	1987 (Friction modified)
Mercon V	1997 (Highly friction modified)
Mercon SP	Used in the Ford 6 speeds such as the 6R60 6HP 26 and also the 2003 and up Torque Shift
Idemitsu K-17	Jaguar X-type
CHRYSLER	**DESCRIPTION**
Chrysler 7176	Designed for front-wheel drive transaxles
ATF+2	1997 (improved cold temperature flow)
ATF+3	1997 (designed for four-speed automatics)
ATF+4	Used in most 2000 and newer Chrysler vehicles
HONDA/TOYOTA	**DESCRIPTION**
Honda Z-1	For use in all Honda automatic transaxles
Toyota Type III	Specific vehicles and years
Toyota Type IV	Specific vehicles and years
Toyota WS	Lower viscosity than Type IV. Used in specific vehicles and years
MAZDA/NISSAN/ SUBARU	**DESCRIPTION**
Mazda ATF-III	Specific vehicles and years
Mazda ATF-MV	Specific vehicles and years
Nissan Matic D	Specific vehicles and years
Nissan Matic J	Specific vehicles and years
Nissan Matic K	Specific vehicles and years
Subaru ATF	Specific vehicles and years
Subaru ATF-HP	Specific vehicles and years

AUDI/BMW/ MERCEDES/VOLVO	DESCRIPTION
Audi G-052-025-A2	Specific vehicles and years
Audi G-052-162-A1	Specific vehicles and years
BMW LA2634	Specific vehicles and years
BMW LT1141	Lifetime fill (BMW warns to not use any other type of fluid)
Mercedes 236.1	Specific vehicles and years
Mercedes 236.2	Specific vehicles and years
Mercedes 236.5	Specific vehicles and years
Mercedes 236.6	Specific vehicles and years
Mercedes 236.7	Specific vehicles and years
Mercedes 236.9	Specific vehicles and years
Mercedes 236.10	Specific vehicles and years
Volvo 97340	Specific vehicles and years
Volvo JWS 3309	Specific vehicles and years
MITSUBISHI/ HYUNDAI/KIA	**DESCRIPTION**
Diamond SP II	Specific vehicles and years
Diamond SP III	Specific vehicles and years

CHART 17–1

Selected samples of automatic transmission fluid and some applications. Always check service information before using the specified fluid when servicing any automatic transmissions or transaxles.

- The vehicle should be parked on a level surface.
- The transmission fluid should be at normal operating temperature. This may require the vehicle to be driven several miles before the level is checked.
- The engine should be running with the transmission in neutral or park, as specified by the vehicle manufacturer.

NOTE: Honda and Acura manufacturers usually specify that the transmission fluid be checked with the engine off. Always follow the recommended checking procedure.

To check the automatic transmission fluid, perform the following steps.

STEP 1 Start the engine and move the gear selector to all gear positions and return to park or neutral as specified by the vehicle manufacturer.

STEP 2 Remove the transmission/transaxle dipstick (fluid level indicator) and wipe it off using a clean cloth.

STEP 3 Reinsert the dipstick until fully seated. Remove the dipstick again and note the level. ● **SEE FIGURE 17–12.**

Add 1 pt. or .5 L → ← Full hot

FIGURE 17–12 A typical automatic transmission dipstick.

NOTE: Some transmissions or transaxles do not use a dipstick. Check service information for the exact procedure to follow to check the fluid level. Some vehicles require the use of a scan tool to check the level of the fluid.

- **Do not overfill any automatic transmission/transaxle.** The "ADD" mark on most automatic transmissions indicates that it is down 1/2 quart (1/2 liter) instead of one quart as used when checking engine oil level. Even if just 1/2 quart too much was added by mistake, it could cause the fluid to foam. Foaming of the ATF is caused by the moving parts inside the transmission/transaxle, which stir up the fluid and introduce air into it. This foamy fluid cannot adequately lubricate or operate the hydraulic clutches that make the unit function correctly.

CAUTION: If the automatic transmission is overfilled, the extra fluid can be blown out through the vent tube at the top of the transmission/transaxle. This fluid could then be blown onto the exhaust system and catch fire.

- **Smell the ATF on the dipstick.** If it smells burned or rancid, further service of the automatic transmission/transaxle will be necessary.
- **Look at the color of the fluid.** It should be red or light brown. A dark brown or black color indicates severe oxidation usually caused by too high an operating temperature. Further service and diagnosis of the automatic transmission/transaxle will be required in that case.

NOTE: Chrysler warns that color and smell should not be used to determine the condition of ATF+4 used in most Chrysler-built vehicles since the 2000 model year. The dyes and additives can change during normal use and the change is not an indication of fluid contamination. This is true for most highly friction-modified ATF. Always follow the vehicle manufacturer's recommendation.

COOLING SYSTEM INSPECTION

STEPS INVOLVED Normal inspection/maintenance involves an occasional check of the following items.

1. Coolant level in the coolant recovery tank or in the surge tank. ● **SEE FIGURE 17–13.**
2. The front of the radiator should be carefully inspected and cleaned of bugs, dirt, or mud that can often restrict airflow.
3. Also included is a visual inspection for signs of coolant system leaks and for the condition of the coolant hoses and accessory drive belts.

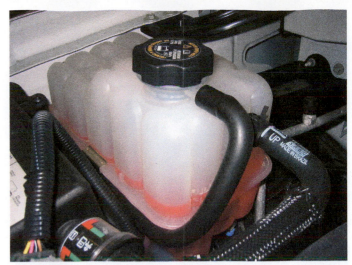

FIGURE 17–13 Visually check the level and color of coolant in the coolant recovery or surge tank.

The exact type of coolant to be used is often specific for each make, model, and year of vehicle, so check service information for the exact coolant to be used.

COOLANT TESTING

- **Visual inspection.** Coolant should be clean and close to the color when it was new. If dark or muddy, it should be replaced. Milky colored coolant is an indication of oil in the system that might be caused by a defective engine gasket. If the coolant is dark or muddy looking, it should be replaced.
- **Test strips.** Coolant test strips are available to test the condition of the coolant. Check to see that the test strips are being used on the specified type of coolant, as some will work only on the old green inorganic additive technology (IAT) coolant.
- **Boiling/freezing points (refractometer and hydrometer).** A hydrometer can be used to check the freezing and boiling temperatures of the coolant. A refractometer can be used to check the freezing temperature of the coolant. ● **SEE FIGURE 17–14.**
- **Proper reading.** A proper 50–50 mix of antifreeze and water should result in a freezing temperature of −34°F (−37°C).

1. If the freezing temperature is higher than −34°F (e.g., −20°F), there is too much water in the coolant.
2. If the freezing temperature is lower than −34°F (e.g., −46°F), there is too much antifreeze in the coolant.

NOTE: Many hybrid electric vehicles use two separate cooling systems—one for the internal combustion engine (ICE) and the other to cool the electronics. Check service information for the exact procedures to follow.

(a)

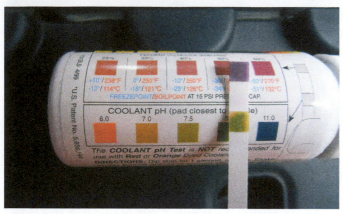

(b)

FIGURE 17–14 (a) A refractometer is used to measure the freezing point of coolant. A drop of coolant is added to a viewing screen, the lid is closed, and then held up to the light to view the display on the tool. (b) The use of test strips is a convenient and cost-effective method to check coolant condition and freezing temperature.

 **TECH TIP**

Ignore the Wind Chill Factor

The wind chill factor is a temperature that combines the actual temperature and the wind speed to determine the overall heat loss effect on open skin. Because it is the heat loss factor for open skin, the wind chill temperature is not to be considered when determining antifreeze protection levels. Although moving air makes it feel colder, the actual temperature is not changed by the wind, and the engine coolant will not be affected by the wind chill. If you are not convinced, try placing a thermometer in a room and wait until a stable reading is obtained. Now turn on a fan and have the air blow across the thermometer. The temperature will not change.

HOSE INSPECTION

RADIATOR AND HEATER HOSES Upper and lower radiator hoses must be pliable, yet not soft. The lower radiator hose will be reinforced or contain an inner spring to prevent the hose from being sucked closed, since the lower hose is attached to the suction side of the water pump. Heater hoses come in the following inside diameter sizes.

- 1/2 in.
- 5/8 in.
- 3/4 in.

The heater hoses connect the engine cooling system to the heater core. A heater core looks like a small radiator and is located inside the vehicle. All automotive hoses are made of rubber with reinforcing fabric weaving for strength. Sections of the coolant lines can be made from nylon-reinforced plastic or metal. All hoses should be inspected for leaks (especially near hose clamps), cracks, swollen areas indicating possible broken reinforcing material, and excessively brittle, soft, and swollen sections. Using a hand-operated pressure pump attached to the radiator opening is an excellent way to check for leaks. ● **SEE FIGURE 17–15.**

HOSE CLAMPS There are several types of hose clamps used depending on the make, model, and year of vehicle. The three basic types are as follows:

1. Worm drive (also called a screw band type)
2. Banded-type clamp
3. Wire clamp (spring type). **SEE FIGURE 17–16.**

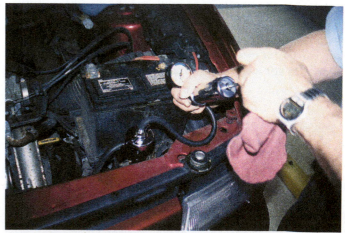

FIGURE 17–15 Pressure testing the cooling system. A typical hand-operated pressure tester applies pressure equal to the radiator cap pressure. The pressure should hold; if it drops, this indicates a leak somewhere in the cooling system. An adapter is used to attach the pump to the cap to determine if the radiator can hold pressure, and release it when pressure rises above its maximum rated pressure setting.

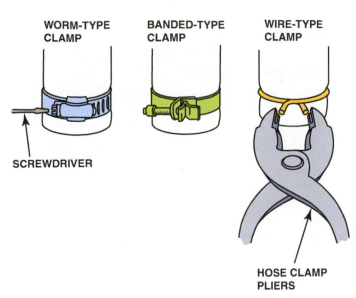

FIGURE 17–16 Hose clamps come in a variety of shapes and designs.

ACCESSORY DRIVE BELT INSPECTION

TYPES OF BELTS
Older V-belts (so-named because of their shape) are 34° at the V. The pulley they ride through is generally 36°. This 2° difference results in a wedging action and

FIGURE 17–17 A special tool is useful when installing a new accessory drive belt. The long-handled wrench fits in a hole of the belt tensioner.

FIGURE 17–18 A typical worn serpentine accessory drive belt. Newer belts made from ethylene propylene diene monomer (EPDM) do not crack like older belts that were made from neoprene rubber.

makes power transmission possible, but it is also the reason why V-belts must be closely inspected.

It is generally recommended that all belts, including the **serpentine (or Poly V)** belts be replaced every four to seven years. When a belt that turns the water pump breaks, the engine could rapidly overheat, causing serious engine damage, and if one belt breaks, it often causes the other belts to become tangled, causing them to break. ● **SEE FIGURES 17–17 AND 17–18.**

BELT INSPECTION
Check the belt(s) for cracks or other signs of wear such as shiny areas that could indicate where the belt has been slipping. Replace any serpentine belt that has more than three cracks in any one rib that appears in a 3-in. span.

BELT TENSION MEASUREMENT
There are four ways that vehicle manufacturers specify that the belt tension is within factory specifications.

1. **Belt tension gauge.** A belt tension gauge is needed to achieve the specified belt tension. Install the belt and operate the engine with all of the accessories turned on to "run-in" the belt for at least five minutes. Adjust the tension of the accessory drive belt to factory specifications. ● **SEE FIGURE 17–19.**

2. **Marks on a tensioner.** Many tensioners have marks that indicate the normal operating tension range for the accessory drive belt. Check service information for the preferred location of the tensioner mark. ● **SEE FIGURE 17–20.**

3. **Torque wrench reading.** Some vehicle manufacturers specify that a beam-type torque wrench be used to determine the torque needed to rotate the tensioner. If the torque reading is below specifications, the tensioner must be replaced.

4. **Deflection.** Depress the belt between the two pulleys that are the farthest apart, the flex or deflection should be 0.5 in.

FIGURE 17–19 A belt tension gauge displays the belt tension in pounds of force.

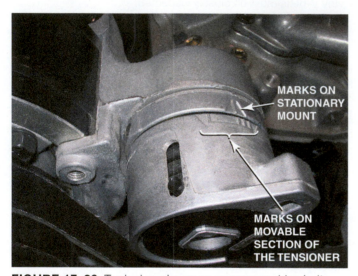

MARKS ON STATIONARY MOUNT

MARKS ON MOVABLE SECTION OF THE TENSIONER

FIGURE 17–20 Typical marks on an accessory drive belt tensioner.

BELT ROUTING GUIDE Always check the belt routing diagram located on the under-hood sticker or the service information for the proper routing when replacing an accessory drive belt. The belt routing can vary depending on engine size and accessories.

POWER STEERING FLUID

TYPES OF POWER STEERING FLUID The correct power steering fluid is *critical* to the operation and service life of the power steering system! The *exact* power steering fluid to use varies by vehicle manufacturer and sometimes

TECH TIP

The Water Spray Trick

Lower-than-normal alternator output could be the result of a loose or slipping drive belt. All belts (V and serpentine multigroove) use an interference angle between the angle of the Vs of the belt and the angle of the Vs on the pulley. Over time, this interference angle is worn off the edges of the V of the belt. As a result, the belt may start to slip and make a squealing sound even if tensioned properly. A fast method to determine if the noise is from the belt is to spray water from a squirt bottle at the belt with the engine running. If the noise stops, the belt is the cause of the noise. The water quickly evaporates; therefore, water simply reveals the problem, but it does not provide a short-term fix.
● **SEE FIGURE 17–21.**

between models made by the same vehicle manufacturer because of differences among various steering component manufacturers. Always check service information for the specified fluid to use. The types of power steering fluid can include the following:

- Automatic transmission fluid (check for the exact type)
- Power steering fluid
- Unique fluid that is specially designed for the vehicle

FIGURE 17–21 A water spray bottle is an excellent diagnostic tool to help determine if the noise is due to an accessory drive belt. If the noise goes away when the belt is sprayed with a mist of water, then the belt is the cause.

CHECKING POWER STEERING FLUID Check power steering fluid level with the engine off. The cap for the power steering reservoir is marked with an icon of a steering wheel or the words "power steering." Remove the cap by twisting it counterclockwise and use the level indicator as part of the cap to determine the level.

Often the level marks are for cold and hot fluid.

- *If too low*, check for leaks especially at the high-pressure lines and fittings. Add the specified fluid to the correct level.

- *If too high*, use a fluid siphon pump or a "turkey baster" and remove the excess fluid until the level is correct.

CAUTION: Do not use fluid that is labeled "for all vehicles" as this type may not be compatible with the seals used in the power steering system or provide the specified friction additives needed to provide the proper steering feel to the driver. ● SEE FIGURE 17–22.

FIGURE 17–22 Most vehicles use a combination filler cap and level indicator (dipstick) that shows the level of power steering fluid in the reservoir.

SUMMARY

1. Prior to servicing a vehicle, protective coverings should be used on the steering wheel, seats, and floor.
2. Brake fluid should be checked regularly and not filled above 0.25 in. from the top of the reservoir or above the "maximum" line imprinted on the side of the master cylinder.
3. Most vehicle manufacturers specify DOT 3 brake fluid.
4. The engine oil should be checked when the vehicle is parked on level ground and after the engine has been off for at least several minutes.
5. Always use the specified automatic transmission fluid when topping off or when changing the fluid. Using the wrong type of ATF can cause the transmission to shift too harshly or cause a vibration when the transmission shifts.

REVIEW QUESTIONS

1. What are the items that should be used to protect the vehicle before service work is begun?
2. Why should brake fluid not be filled above the full or MAX level as indicated on the master cylinder reservoir?
3. Why should brake fluid be kept in an airtight container?
4. What is hydraulic clutch fluid?
5. What does color mean in relation to the type of coolant?
6. What are the three basic classifications of ATF?

CHAPTER QUIZ

1. When inspecting engine oil what should be checked?
   a. Proper Level
   b. Color
   c. Feels slippery and not gritty
   d. All of the above
2. Most vehicle manufacturers specify brake fluid that meets what specification?
   a. DOT 2
   b. DOT 3
   c. DOT 4
   d. DOT 5
3. The cabin filter can be accessed from _____.
   a. Under the hood in some vehicles
   b. Under the dash in some vehicles
   c. From under the vehicle in some vehicles
   d. Either a or b
4. Coolant can be checked using _____.
   a. Boiling/freezing points using a refractometer and hydrometer
   b. Visual inspection
   c. Test strips
   d. All of the above

5. Dexron VI and Mercon V are examples of _____?
   a. Automatic transmission fluid (ATF)
   b. Power steering fluid
   c. Brake fluid
   d. Engine oil

6. What should be done to protect the vehicle during inspections and service?
   a. Cover the steering wheel
   b. Protect the floor of the vehicle
   c. Protect the seats
   d. All of the above

7. Windshield washer fluid is designed to _____.
   a. Clean the windshield
   b. Help remove bugs
   c. Contains alcohol to keep it from freezing
   d. All of the above

8. The fluid used in power steering systems is _____.
   a. Automatic transmission fluid or special power steering fluid
   b. Brake fluid
   c. Antifreeze (coolant)
   d. Gear oil

9. Accessory drive belts should be checked for proper tension by _____.
   a. Deflection
   b. Tensioner marks
   c. A torque wrench reading on the tensioner
   d. Any of the above may be specified

10. Spraying accessory drive belts with a fine mist of water from a spray bottle is used to _____.
   a. Provides increased gripping power to the belt.
   b. Is used to check if a noise is due to the belt.
   c. Lubricates the belt
   d. Cools the belt

chapter 18
VEHICLE LIFTING AND HOISTING

OBJECTIVES: **After studying Chapter 18, the reader should be able to:** • Identify vehicle hoisting and lifting equipment. • Discuss safety procedures related to hoisting or lifting a vehicle. • Describe the proper methods to follow to safely hoist a vehicle.

KEY TERMS: • Creeper 173 • Floor jack 173 • Jack stands 173 • Safety stands 173

FLOOR JACK

A **floor jack** is a hand-operated hydraulic device that is used to lift vehicles or components, such as engines, transmissions, and rear axle assemblies. Most floor jacks use four casters, which allow the jack to be easily moved around the shop. ● **SEE FIGURE 18–1.**

SAFE USE OF FLOOR JACKS. Floor jacks are used to lift a vehicle or major vehicle component, but they are not designed to hold a load. Therefore, **safety stands,** also called **jack stands,** should always be used to support the vehicle. After the floor jack has lifted the vehicle, safety stands should be placed under the vehicle, and then, using the floor jack, lowered onto the safety stands. The floor jack can be

FIGURE 18–2 Safety stands are being used to support the rear of this vehicle. Notice a creeper also.

left in position as another safety device but the load should be removed from the floor jack. If a load is retained on the floor jack, hydraulic fluid can leak past seals in the hydraulic cylinders, which would lower the vehicle, possibly causing personal injury or death. ● **SEE FIGURE 18–2.**

CREEPERS

When working underneath a vehicle, most service technicians use a **creeper,** which consists of a flat or concaved surface equipped with low-profile casters. A creeper allows the technician to maneuver under the vehicle easily.

SAFE USE OF CREEPERS Creepers can create a fall hazard if left on the floor. When a creeper is not being used, it should be picked up and placed vertically against a wall or tool box to help prevent accidental falls.

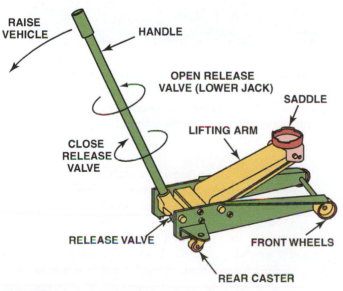

FIGURE 18–1 A hydraulic hand-operated floor jack.

RAISE VEHICLE
HANDLE
OPEN RELEASE VALVE (LOWER JACK)
SADDLE
LIFTING ARM
CLOSE RELEASE VALVE
RELEASE VALVE
FRONT WHEELS
REAR CASTER

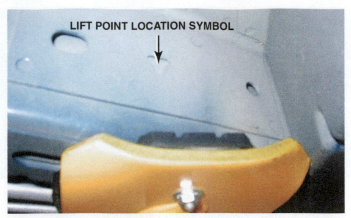

FIGURE 18–3 Most newer vehicles have a triangle symbol indicating the recommended hoisting lift points.

VEHICLE HOISTS

Vehicle hoists include older in ground pneumatic/hydraulic (air pressure over hydraulic) and above ground units. Most of the vehicle hoists used today use an electric motor to pressurize hydraulic fluid, which lifts the vehicle using hydraulic cylinders. Hoists are rated by the maximum weight that they can safely lift, such as 7,000 to 12,000 pounds (3200 to 5400 kg.) or more. Hoists can also have equal length arms or can be equipped with different length arms allowing the vehicle to be set so the doors can be opened and not hit the center support column. Many chassis and underbody service procedures require that the vehicle be hoisted or lifted off the ground. The simplest methods involve the use of drive-on ramps or a floor jack and safety (jack) stands, whereas in ground or surface-mounted lifts provide greater access.

SETTING THE PADS IS A CRITICAL PART OF THIS PROCEDURE
All automobile and light-truck service manuals include recommended locations to be used when hoisting (lifting) a vehicle. Some vehicles have a decal on the driver's door indicating the recommended lift points. The recommended standards for the lift points and lifting procedures are found in SAE Standard JRP-2184. ● **SEE FIGURE 18–3.**

These recommendations typically include the following points.

1. The vehicle should be centered on the lift or hoist so as not to overload one side or put too much force either forward or rearward. Use tall safety stands if a major component is going to be removed from the vehicle, such as the engine, to help support the vehicle. ● **SEE FIGURE 18–4.**

2. The pads of the lift should be spread as far apart as possible to provide a stable platform.

3. Each pad should be placed under a portion of the vehicle that is strong and capable of supporting the weight of the vehicle.
   a. Pinch welds at the bottom edge of the body are generally considered to be strong.

(a)

(b)

FIGURE 18–4 (a) Tall safety stands can be used to provide additional support for a vehicle while on a hoist. (b) A block of wood should be used to avoid the possibility of doing damage to components supported by the stand.

CAUTION: Even though pinch weld seams are the recommended location for hoisting many vehicles with unitized bodies (unit-body), care should be taken not to place the pad(s) too far forward or rearward. Incorrect placement of the vehicle on the lift could cause the vehicle to be imbalanced, and the vehicle could fall. This is exactly what happened to this vehicle. ● SEE FIGURE 18–5.

FIGURE 18–5 This training vehicle fell from the hoist when the pads were not set correctly. No one was hurt, but the vehicle was damaged.

b. Boxed areas of the body are the best places to position the pads on a vehicle without a frame. Be careful to note whether the arms of the lift might come into contact with other parts of the vehicle before the pad touches the intended location. Commonly damaged areas include the following:

1. Rocker panel moldings
2. Exhaust system (including catalytic converter)
3. Tires or body panels. ● **SEE FIGURES 18–6 AND 18–7.**

4. As soon as the pads touch the vehicle, check for proper pad placement. The vehicle should be raised about 1 ft (30 cm) off the floor, then stopped and shaken to check for stability. If the vehicle seems to be stable when checked at a short distance from the floor, continue raising the vehicle and continue to view the vehicle until it has reached the desired height. The hoist should be lowered onto the mechanical locks, and then raised off of the locks before lowering.

(a)

(a)

(b)

FIGURE 18–6 (a) An assortment of hoist pad adapters that are often necessary to safely hoist many pickup trucks, vans, and sport utility vehicles. (b) A view from underneath a Chevrolet pickup truck showing how the pad extensions are used to attach the hoist lifting pad to contact the frame.

(b)

FIGURE 18–7 (a) In this photo the pad arm is just contacting the rocker panel of the vehicle. (b) This photo shows what can occur if the technician places the pad too far inward underneath the vehicle. The arm of the hoist has dented the rocket panel.

CAUTION: Do not look away from the vehicle while it is being raised (or lowered) on a hoist. Often one side or one end of the hoist can stop or fail, resulting in the vehicle being slanted enough to slip or fall.

HINT: Most hoists can be safely placed at any desired height as long as it is high enough for the safety latches to engage. For ease while working, the area in which you are working should be at chest level. When working on brakes or suspension components, it is not necessary to work on them down near the floor or over your head. Raise the hoist so that the components are at chest level.

5. Before lowering the hoist, check that nothing is underneath the vehicle nor anyone near that may be injured when the vehicle is lowered. The safety latch(es) must be released and the direction of the controls reversed. The speed downward is often adjusted to be as slow as possible for additional safety.

DRIVE-ON RAMPS

Ramps are an inexpensive way to raise the front or rear of a vehicle. ● **SEE FIGURE 18–8.** Ramps are easy to store, but they can be dangerous because they can "kick out" when driving the vehicle onto the ramps.

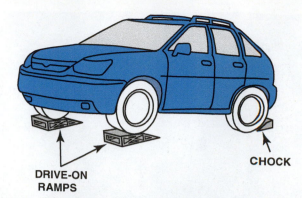

CHOCK

DRIVE-ON RAMPS

FIGURE 18–8 Drive-on-type ramps. The wheels on the ground level *must* be chocked (blocked) to prevent accidental movement down the ramp.

CAUTION: Professional repair shops do not use ramps because they are dangerous to use. Use only with extreme care.

1 The first step in hoisting a vehicle is to properly align the vehicle in the center of the stall.

2 Most vehicles will be correctly positioned when the left front tire is centered on the tire pad.

3 The arms can be moved in and out and most pads can be rotated to allow for many different types of vehicle construction.

4 Most lifts are equipped with short pad extensions that are often necessary to use to allow the pad to contact the frame of a vehicle without causing the arm of the lift to hit and damage parts of the body.

5 Tall pad extensions can also be used to gain access to the frame of a vehicle. This position is needed to safely hoist many pickup trucks, vans, and sport utility vehicles.

6 An additional extension may be necessary to hoist a truck or van equipped with running boards to give the necessary clearance.

CONTINUED ▶

7 Position the pads under the vehicle at the recommended locations.

8 After being sure all pads are correctly positioned, use the hoist controls to raise the vehicle.

9 With the vehicle raised one foot (30 cm) off the ground, push down on the vehicle to check to see if it is stable on the pads. If the vehicle rocks, lower the vehicle and reset the pads. The vehicle can be raised to any desired working level. Be sure the safety is engaged before working on or under the vehicle.

10 If raising a vehicle without a frame, place the flat pads under the pinch weld seam to spread the load. If additional clearance is necessary, the pads can be raised as shown.

11 When the service work is completed, the hoist should be raised slightly and the safety released before using the lever to lower the vehicle.

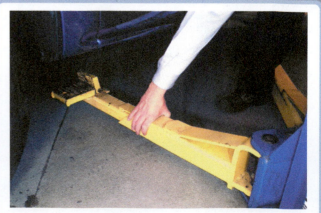

12 After lowering the vehicle, be sure all arms of the lift are moved out of the way before driving the vehicle out of the work stall.

SUMMARY

1. Whenever a vehicle is raised off the ground using a floor jack, it must be supported using safety stands.

2. Creepers should be stored vertically to prevent the possibility of stepping on it, which could cause a fall and personal injury.

3. Always adhere to the specified hoisting locations as found in service information.

4. Adapters or extensions are often needed when hoisting pickup trucks or vans.

REVIEW QUESTIONS

1. Why must safety stands be used after lifting a vehicle with a floor jack?

2. What precautions should be adhered to when storing a creeper?

3. What precautions should be adhered to when hoisting a vehicle?

CHAPTER QUIZ

1. A safety stand is also called a _____.
   a. Jack
   b. Jack stand
   c. Bottle jack
   d. Safety stool

2. Professional repair shops do not use ramps because _____.
   a. Can "kick out" and are dangerous to use
   b. Can be used to raise only the front of the vehicle
   c. Can be used to raise only the rear of the vehicle
   d. Can be used without having to block the wheels

3. The SAE standard for hoist location is _____.
   a. J-1980
   b. SAE-2009
   c. JRP-2184
   d. J-14302

4. Tall safety stands would be used to _____.
   a. Help support the vehicle when a major component is removed from the vehicle.
   b. Lift a vehicle
   c. Lift a component such as an engine high off the ground
   d. Both b and c

5. Commonly damaged areas of a vehicle during hoisting include _____.
   a. Rocker panels
   b. Exhaust systems
   c. Tires or body panels
   d. All of the above

6. Pad extensions may be needed when hoisting what type of vehicle?
   a. Small cars
   b. Pickup trucks
   c. Vans
   d. Either b or c

7. Technician A says that a hoist can be stopped at any level as long as the safety latch engages. Technician B says that the vehicle should be hoisted to the top of the hoist travel for safety. Which technician is correct?
   a. Technician A only
   b. Technician B only
   c. Both technicians A and B
   d. Neither technician A nor B

8. Before lowering the vehicle, what should the technician do?
   a. Be sure nothing is underneath the vehicle
   b. Raise the vehicle enough to release the safety latch
   c. Be sure no one will be walking under or near the vehicle
   d. All of the above

9. Technician A says that a creeper should be stored vertically. Technician B says that a creeper should be stored on its casters. Which technician is correct?
   a. Technician A only
   b. Technician B only
   c. Both technicians A and B
   d. Neither technician A nor B

10. When checking for stability, how high should the vehicle be raised?
    a. About 2 in. (5 cm)
    b. About 6 in. (15 cm)
    c. About 1 ft (30 cm)
    d. About 3 ft (91 cm)

OBJECTIVES: **After studying Chapter 19, the reader should be able to:** • Prepare for ASE Engine Repair (A1) certification test content area "A" (General Engine Diagnosis) and content area "D" (Lubrication and Cooling Systems Diagnosis and Repair). • Describe chassis system lubrication and under-vehicle inspection.

KEY TERMS: • Additive package 182 • Alemite fittings 187 • Algorithm 186 • American Petroleum Institute (API) 181 • Anti-drain-back valve 185 • Association des Constructeurs Européens d'Automobiles (ACEA) 182 • Bypass valve 185 • Endplay in any tie rod should be zero 188 • International Lubricant Standardization and Approval Committee (ILSAC) 181 • Miscible 183 • National Lubricating Grease Institute (NLGI) 187 • Pour point 180 • Society of Automotive Engineers (SAE) 181 • Steering stops 188 • Synchromesh transmission fluid (STF) 190 • Viscosity index (VI) 180 • Zerk fittings 187 • Zinc dialkyl dithiophosphate (ZDDP or ZDP) 185

INTRODUCTION

Lube oil and filter service, often abbreviated **LOF,** is the most often required automotive service. Regular oil changes are a must to keep the engine parts properly lubricated. When the vehicle is being serviced, it is also a great time to perform chassis lubrication and a visual inspection to make sure that no faults have occurred since the last service, and if so, to ensure that these can be taken care of before something wears out or fails due to lack of lubrication.

ENGINE OIL

PURPOSE AND FUNCTION   Engine oil has a major effect on the proper operation and life of any engine. Engine oil provides the following functions in every engine.

- Lubricates moving parts. ● **SEE FIGURE 19–1**
- Helps cool engine parts
- Helps seal piston rings
- Helps neutralize acids created as the by-products of combustion
- Reduces friction in the engine
- Helps prevent rust and corrosion

As a result of these many functions, only the specified engine oil must be used and it must be replaced at the specified mileage or time intervals.

OIL DRAINBACK HOLES

FIGURE 19–1 Clean engine oil is the life blood of any engine.

PROPERTIES OF ENGINE OIL   The most important engine oil property is its thickness or viscosity.

- As oil is cooled, it gets thicker.
- As oil is heated, it gets thinner.

That is, its viscosity changes with temperature. The oil must not be too thick at low temperatures to allow the engine to start. The lowest temperature at which oil will pour is called its **pour point.** An index of the change in viscosity between the cold and hot extremes is called the **viscosity index (VI).** Oils with a high viscosity index thin less with heat than do oils with a low viscosity index.

SAE RATING Engine oils are sold with a **Society of Automotive Engineers (SAE)** grade number, which indicates the viscosity range into which the oil fits. Oils tested at 212°F (100°C) have a number with no letter following. For example, SAE 30 indicates that the oil has only been checked at 212°F (100°C). This oil's viscosity falls within the SAE 30 grade number range when the oil is hot. Oils tested at a low temperature are rated with a number and the letter W, which means winter, such as SAE 20W.

MULTIGRADE ENGINE OIL An SAE 5W-30 multigrade oil meets the SAE 5W viscosity specification when cooled to 0°F (−18°C), and meets the SAE 30 viscosity specification when tested at 212°F (100°C).

Most vehicle manufacturers recommend the following multiviscosity engine oils.

- SAE 5W-30
- SAE 5W-20
  - ● **SEE FIGURE 19-2.**

API RATING The **American Petroleum Institute (API)**, working with the engine manufacturers and oil companies, has established an engine oil performance classification. Oils are tested and rated in production automotive engines. The oil container is printed with the API classification of the oil. The API performance or service classification and the SAE grade marking are the only information available to help determine which oil is satisfactory for use in an engine. ● **SEE FIGURE 19-3** for a typical API oil container "doughnut."

GASOLINE ENGINE RATINGS In gasoline engine ratings, the letter S means service, but can also indicate

FIGURE 19-3 API doughnut for an SAE 5W-30, SN engine oil. When compared to a reference oil, the "energy conserving" designation indicates a 1.1% better fuel economy for SAE 10W-30 oils and 0.5% better fuel economy for SAE 5W-30 oils.

spark ignition engines. The rating system is open ended so that newer, improved ratings can be readily added as necessary.

SL	2001–2003	
SM	2004–2010	
SN	2011+	

DIESEL ENGINE RATINGS Diesel classifications begin with the letter C, which stands for commercial, but can also indicate compression ignition or diesel engines.

CD	Minimum rating for use in a diesel engine service
CE	Designed for certain turbocharged or super-charged heavy-duty diesel engine service
CF	For off-road indirect injected diesel engine service
CF-2	Two-stroke diesel engine service
CF-4	High-speed four-stroke cycle diesel engine service
CG-4	Severe-duty high-speed four-stroke diesel engine service
CI-4	Severe-duty high-speed four-stroke diesel engine service
CJ-4	Required for use in all 2007 and newer diesels using ultra-low-sulfur diesel (ULSD) fuel

ILSAC OIL RATING

DEFINITION The **International Lubricant Standardization and Approval Committee (ILSAC)** developed an oil rating that consolidates the SAE viscosity rating and the API quality rating. If an engine oil meets the standards, a "starburst" symbol is displayed on the front of the oil container. If the

FIGURE 19-2 The SAE viscosity rating required is often printed on the engine oil filler cap.

FIGURE 19–4 The International Lubricant Standardization and Approval Committee (ILSAC) starburst symbol. If this symbol is on the front of the container of oil, then it is acceptable for use in almost any gasoline engine.

FIGURE 19–5 ACEA ratings are included on the back of the oil container if it meets any of the standards. ACEA ratings apply to European vehicles only such as BMW, Mercedes, Audi, and VW.

starburst is present, the vehicle owner and technician know that the oil is suitable for use in almost any gasoline engine. ● **SEE FIGURE 19–4.**

ILSAC RATINGS

- GF-4 -2004-2009
- GF-5 -2010+

For more information, visit www.gf-5.com.

EUROPEAN OIL RATING SYSTEM

DEFINITION The **Association des Constructeurs Européens d'Automobiles (ACEA)** rates the oil according to the following:

- Gasoline engine oils
  ACEA A1; A2; A3; A4 or A5
- Diesel engine oils
  ACEA B1; B2; B3; B4 or B5

ACEA C1, C2, C3 are oils that meet strict limits on the amount of sulfur, zinc, and other additives that could harm the catalytic converter. Starting in 2004, the ACEA began using combined ratings such as A1/B1, A3/B3, A3/B4, and A5/B5.

CAUTION: Do not use an API- or ILSAC-rated oil in an engine that requires an ACEA-rated oil. Some possible results include gelling (sludge) or even serous engine damage. The oil life monitor is calibrated for the ACEA-rated oil and the oil change interval can be as long as 18,000 miles (30,000 km), which is not possible without engine damage if API-rated oil is used. ● **SEE FIGURE 19–5.**

ENGINE OIL ADDITIVES

Oil producers are careful to check the compatibility of the oil additives they use. A number of chemicals that will help each other can be used for each of the additive requirements. The balanced additives are called an **additive package.**

ADDITIVES TO IMPROVE THE BASE OIL

- **Viscosity index (VI) improver.** Modifies the viscosity of the base fluid so that it changes less as the temperature rises; this allows the lubricant to operate over a wider temperature range. ● **SEE FIGURE 19–6.**
- **Pour point depressant.** Keeps the lubricant flowing at low temperatures.
- **Antifoam agents.** Foam reduces the effectiveness of a lubricant. The antifoam agents reduce/stop foaming when the oil is agitated or aerated.

ADDITIVES TO PROTECT THE BASE OIL

- **Antioxidants.** Slow the breakdown of the base fluid caused by oxygen (air) and heat. (Oxidation is the main cause of lubricant degradation in service.)
- **Oxidants.** Prevent acid formation (corrosion) in the form of sludges and varnishes.
- **Total base number (TBN).** The reserve alkalinity used to neutralize the acids created during the combustion process.

FIGURE 19–6 Viscosity index (VI) improver is a polymer and feels like finely ground foam rubber. When dissolved in the oil, it expands when hot to keep the oil from thinning.

ADDITIVES TO PROTECT THE ENGINE

- **Rust inhibitor.** Inhibits the action of water on ferrous metal such as steel.
- **Corrosion inhibitor.** Protects nonferrous metals such as copper.
- **Antiwear additive.** Forms a protective layer on metal surfaces to reduce friction and prevent wear when no lubricant film is present.
- **Extreme pressure additive.** Functions only when heavy loads and temperatures are occurring.

SYNTHETIC OIL

DEFINITION The term *synthetic* means that it is a manufactured product and not refined from a naturally occurring substance, as engine oil (petroleum base) is refined from crude oil. Synthetic oil is processed from several different base stocks using several different methods.

ADVANTAGES OF SYNTHETICS The major advantage of using synthetic engine oil is its ability to remain fluid at very low temperatures. This characteristic of synthetic oil makes it popular in colder climates where cold-engine cranking is important. ● SEE FIGURE 19–7.

DISADVANTAGES OF SYNTHETICS The major disadvantage is cost. The cost of synthetic engine oils can be four to five times the cost of petroleum-based engine oils.

SYNTHETIC BLENDS A synthetic blend indicates that some synthetic oil is mixed with petroleum base engine oil; however, the percentage of synthetic used in the blend is unknown.

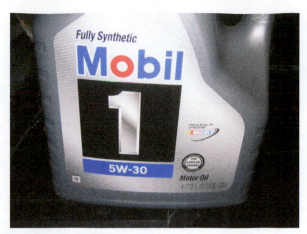

FIGURE 19–7 Mobil 1 synthetic engine oil is used by several vehicle manufacturers in new engines.

? FREQUENTLY ASKED QUESTION

Can I Go Back to Using Conventional Oil after I Use a Synthetic Oil?

Yes. Conventional oil can be used instead of synthetic oil even after synthetic oil has been used. This means that any oil that meets the specifications of the vehicle manufacturer can be used at any time. Oils must be **miscible,** meaning they are capable of mixing with other oils (of different brands, types, and viscosities, for example) without causing any problems such as sludge.

VEHICLE-SPECIFIC SPECIFICATIONS

BACKGROUND Some oils can meet industry specifications, such as SAE, API, and/or ILSAC ratings, but not pass the tests specified by the vehicle manufacturer. The oil used should meet the specifications of the vehicle manufacturer, which include the following:

- **BMW**
  Longlife-98 and longlife-01 (abbreviated LL-01), LL-04
- **General Motors**
  GM 6094M
  GM 4718M (synthetic oil specification)
  Dexos 1 (all GM gasoline engines, 2011+).
  ● SEE FIGURE 19–8.
  Dexos 2 (all GM diesel engines, 2011+)
- **Ford**
  WSS-M2C153-H
  WSS-M2C929-A
  WSS-M2C930-A

FIGURE 19–8 Dexos is the oil specified for use in all General Motors engines starting with the 2011 model year.

FIGURE 19–9 European vehicle manufacturers usually specify engine oil with a broad viscosity range, such as SAE 5W-40, and their own unique standards, such as the Mercedes specification 229.51. Always use the oil specified by the vehicle manufacturer.

WSS-M2C931-A

WSS-M2C934-A

- **Chrysler**

  MS-6395 (2005 + vehicles)

  MS-10725 (2004 and older)

- **Honda/Acura**

  HTO-06 (turbocharged engine only)

- **Mercedes**

  229.3, 229.5, 229.1, 229.3, 229.31, 229.5, and 229.51
  ● **SEE FIGURE 19–9.**

- **Volkswagen (VW and Audi)**

  502.00, 505.00, 505.01, 503, 503.01, 505 diesel, 506 diesel, 506.1 diesel, and 507 diesel

Be sure to use the oil that meets all of the specifications, especially during the warranty period.

EXAMPLES OF THE CORRECT OIL TO USE

2009 CHEVROLET IMPALA WITH A 5.3 LITER V-8

In this example, the owner's manual specifies the use of SAE 5W-30 and meeting the GM 6094M standard. Therefore, the oil should have the following on the label:

- SAE 5W-30
- API SM (or SN)
- ILSAC GF-4 (or GF-5)
- Meets GM 6094M

All of the above should be listed to be able to meet the standard for this vehicle as specified by the vehicle manufacturer. Dexos oil can be used in this application because while required for 2011 and newer General Motor's gasoline engines, it is backward compatible for use in any GM gasoline engine requiring SAE 5W-30 oil.

2008 HONDA ACCORD
The owner's manual does not specify Honda-specific oil but instead specifies the following:

- SAE 5W-20
- API SM (or SN)
- ILSAC GF-4 (or GF-5)

2007 VW JETTA
The owner's manual does specify VW-specific oil so the required oil should meet the following specifications:

- SAE 5W-40
- ACEA A3/B3 or A3/B4
- VW 505.01

Because of the unique viscosity (SAE 5W-40) and the need to meet the VW 505.01 standard and the ACEA standard, the oil usually cannot be found at most retail auto parts or larger discount stores, but instead can be found in a store that supplies parts for import vehicles.

HIGH MILEAGE OILS

DEFINITION A "high-mileage oil" is sold for use in vehicles that have over 75,000 miles. Usually, the oil has a higher viscosity and lacks friction-reducing additives, which means that most high-mileage oils cannot meet the ILSAC GF-4 or GF-5 rating and are, therefore, not recommended for use in most engines.

DIFFERENCES A high-mileage oil has the following differences compared to regular engine oil.

- Esters are added to swell oil seals (main and valve-stem seals).
- The oil is used only in engines with higher than 75,000 miles.
- The oil usually does not have the energy rating of conventional oils. This means that the oil will not meet the specifications for use according to the owner's manual in most cases.

OIL FILTERS

CONSTRUCTION The oil within the engine is pumped from the oil pan through the filter before entering the engine lubricating system passages. The filter is made from either:

- closely packed cloth fibers or
- porous paper. ● **SEE FIGURE 19–11**

Large particles are trapped by the filter. Microscopic particles will flow through the filter pores. These particles are so small that they can flow through the bearing oil film without touching the surfaces, so they do no damage.

OIL FILTER VALVES Many oil filters are equipped with an **anti-drain-back valve** that prevents oil from draining out of the filter when the engine is shut off. ● **SEE FIGURE 19–12.**

This valve keeps the oil in the filter and allows the engine to receive immediate lubrication as soon as the engine starts. Either the engine or the filter is provided with a **bypass valve** that will allow the oil to go around the filter element. The bypass allows the engine to be lubricated with dirty oil, rather than having no lubrication, if the filter becomes plugged. The oil also goes through the bypass when the oil is cold and thick.

OIL FILTER DISPOSAL Oil filters should be crushed and/or drained of oil before discarding. After the oil has been drained, the filter can usually be disposed of as regular metal scrap. Always check and follow local, state, or regional oil filter disposal rules, regulations, and procedures. ● **SEE FIGURE 19–13.**

FIGURE 19–10 Using a zinc additive is important when using SM or SN rated oil in an engine equipped with a flat-bottom lifter, especially during the break-in period.

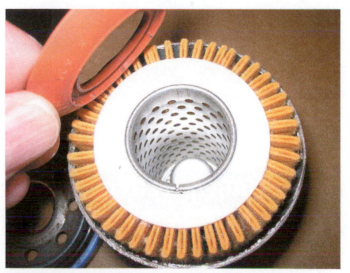

FIGURE 19–11 A cutaway of a typical spin-on oil filter. Engine oil enters the filter through the small holes around the center of the filter and flows through the pleated paper filtering media and out the large hole in the center of the filter. The center metal cylinder with holes is designed to keep the paper filter from collapsing under the pressure.

FIGURE 19–12 A rubber diaphragm acts as an anti-drain-back valve to keep the oil in the filter when the engine is stopped and the oil pressure drops to zero.

OIL DRAIN-BACK VALVE

FIGURE 19–13 A typical filter crusher. The hydraulic ram forces out most of the oil from the filter. The oil is trapped underneath the crusher and is recycled.

OIL CHANGE INTERVALS

All vehicle and engine manufacturers recommend a maximum oil change interval. The recommended intervals are almost always expressed in terms of mileage or elapsed time (or hours of operation), whichever milestone is reached first.

Most vehicle manufacturers recommend an oil change interval of 7,500 to 12,000 miles (12,000 to 19,000 km) or every six months. If, however, any one of the conditions in the following list exists, the oil change interval recommendation drops to a more reasonable 2,000 to 3,000 miles (3,000 to 5,000 km) or

every three months. The important thing to remember is that these are recommended maximum intervals and they should be shortened substantially if any of the following operating conditions exist.

1. Operating in dusty areas
2. Towing a trailer
3. Short-trip driving, especially during cold weather. (The definition of a *short trip* varies among manufacturers, but it is usually defined as 4 to 15 miles [6 to 24 km] each time the engine is started.)
4. Operating in temperatures below freezing (32°F, 0°C)
5. Operating at idle speed for extended periods of time (such as normally occurs in police or taxi service)

Because most vehicles driven during cold weather are driven on short trips, technicians and automotive experts recommend changing the oil every 5,000 to 7,500 miles or every six months, whichever occurs first.

OIL LIFE MONITORS Most vehicles built since the mid-1990s are equipped with a warning light that lets the driver know when the engine oil should be changed. The two basic types of oil change monitoring systems include:

- **Mileage only.** The service light will come on based on mileage only. The interval can be every 3,750 to 7,500 miles, or even longer in some cases.
- **Algorithm.** Computer programs contain algorithms that specify instructions a computer should perform (in a specific order) to carry out a task. This program uses the number of cold starts, the run time of the engine, and inputs from the engine coolant temperature (ECT) sensor to determine when the oil should be changed.
● **SEE FIGURE 19–14.**

FIGURE 19–14 Many vehicle manufacturers can display the percentage of oil life remaining, whereas others simply turn on a warning lamp when it has been determined that an oil change is required.

OIL CHANGE PROCEDURE

An oil change includes the following steps:

STEP 1 Start the engine (if cold) and allow it to reach operating temperature.

STEP 2 Check the oil level on the dipstick before hoisting the vehicle. Document the work order and notify the owner if the oil level is low before changing the oil.

STEP 3 Safely hoist the vehicle.

STEP 4 Position a drain pan under the drain plug, and then remove the plug with care to avoid contact with hot oil. ● **SEE FIGURE 19–15.**

CAUTION: Used engine oil has been determined to be harmful. Rubber gloves should be worn to protect the skin. If used engine oil gets on the skin, wash thoroughly with soap and water.

STEP 5 Allow the oil to drain freely so that the contaminants come out with the oil. It is not critically important to get every last drop of oil from the engine oil pan, because a quantity of used oil still remains in the engine oil passages and oil pump.

STEP 6 While the engine oil is draining, the oil plug gasket should be examined. If it appears to be damaged, it should be replaced.

NOTE: Honda/Acura recommends that the oil drain plug gasket be replaced at every oil change on many of their vehicles. The aluminum sealing gasket does not seal once it has been tightened. Always follow the vehicle manufacturer's recommendations.

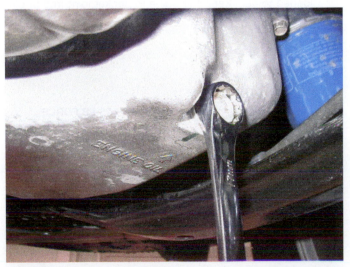

FIGURE 19–15 Always check to make sure that the oil drain plug is the plug being removed as some vehicles also have transmission or transfer cases that also have drain plugs. This oil pan has a label and an arrow pointing to the engine oil drain plug.

STEP 7 While the oil is draining, remove the oil filter, check that the old filter gasket has been removed from the engine block, and clean the gasket surface with a shop cloth.

STEP 8 Compare the new filter with the one that came off the vehicle to make sure that the replacement filter is the correct one.

STEP 9 When the oil stops running and starts to drip, reinstall and tighten the drain plug using a torque wrench to help prevent overtightening.

STEP 10 Apply a thin coating of engine oil on the gasket of the oil filter and install the oil filter and tighten hand tight only.

NOTE: Most experts recommend adding oil to the oil filter before installing it if it is mounted vertically so that oil will not drip out as it is being installed.

STEP 11 Refill the engine with the proper type, grade, and quantity of oil.

STEP 12 Clean any spilled oil from the exhaust system or frame of the vehicle using a shop cloth and brake cleaner.

STEP 13 Start the engine and allow the engine to idle until it develops oil pressure. The "Oil" light should go out or the oil pressure gauge should read pressure within 10 seconds after the engine is started. If not, stop the engine and investigate the reason for the lack of oil pressure.

STEP 14 Stop the engine and look under the vehicle for signs of leaks, especially at the oil filter. Check that the oil level is correct.

STEP 15 Reset the oil life monitor.

STEP 16 Return the vehicle to the customer in clean condition.

CHASSIS LUBRICATION

NEED FOR CHASSIS LUBRICATION Chassis lubrication refers to the greasing of parts that rub against each other or installing grease into a pivot (or ball joints) through a grease fitting. While many vehicles are using "sealed for life" low friction–type ball joints and steering linkage joints, there are still many vehicles that need to have routine chassis lubrication performed.

GREASE FITTINGS Grease fittings are also called **Zerk fittings** (named for Oscar U. Zerk) or **Alemite fittings** (named for the manufacturer of grease fittings). These fittings contain a one-way check valve that prevents the grease from escaping. Use chassis grease labeled NLGI #2 GC.

NLGI means the **National Lubricating Grease Institute** and the #2 means that it has the thickness specified for use in chassis parts.

Grease fittings are used on steering components, such as tie rod ends, and in the suspension ball joints, which

FIGURE 19–16 Greasing a tie rod end. Some joints do not have a hole for excessive grease to escape, and excessive grease can destroy the seal.

require lubrication to prevent wear and noise caused by the action of a ball rotating within a joint during vehicle operation. ● SEE FIGURE 19–16.

The procedure for greasing a grease fitting includes the following steps:

STEP 1   Wipe off the fitting with a shop cloth.

STEP 2   Make sure the grease gun coupler is fully seated on the fitting.

STEP 3   Apply grease only until the dust boot swells.

STEP 4   If the fitting will not accept grease, replace it with a new one and retry.

STEP 5   Remove the grease gun and wipe any spilled grease from the fitting.

CAUTION: If too much grease is forced into a sealed grease boot, the boot itself may rupture, requiring the entire joint to be replaced.

STEERING STOPS   During chassis lubrication, put grease on the *steering stop*, if so equipped. **Steering stops** are the projections or built-up areas on the control arms of the front suspension designed to limit the steering movement at full lock. ● SEE FIGURE 19–17.

If the steering stops are not lubricated, a metal-to-metal scraping sound can often be heard when turning the steering wheel all of the way and driving up a ramp or driveway approach at the same time.

STEERING SYSTEM INSPECTION   Hoist the vehicle and perform a thorough part-by-part inspection.

1.   Inspect each part for damage due to an accident or bent parts due to the vehicle's hitting an object in the roadway.

CAUTION: Never straighten a bent steering linkage; always replace with new parts.

FIGURE 19–17 Part of steering linkage lubrication is applying grease to the steering stops. If these stops are not lubricated, a grinding sound may be heard when the vehicle hits a bump when the wheels are turned all the way one direction or the other. This often occurs when driving into or out of a driveway that has a curb.

2.   Idler arm inspection is performed by using *hand* force of 25 lb (110 N-m) up and down on the arm. If the *total* movement exceeds 1/4 in. (6mm), the idler arm should be replaced. ● SEE FIGURE 19–18.

3.   All other steering linkages should be tested *by hand* for any vertical or side-to-side looseness. Tie rod ends use ball-and-socket joints to allow for freedom of movement for suspension travel and to transmit steering forces to the front wheels. It is therefore normal for tie rods to rotate in their sockets when the tie rod sleeve is rocked. **Endplay in any tie rod should be zero.** Many tie rods are spring loaded to help keep the ball-and-socket joint free of play

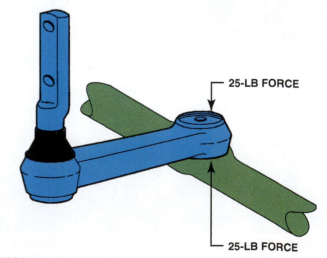

FIGURE 19–18 To check an idler arm, most vehicle manufacturers specify that 25 lb force be applied by hand up and down to the idler arm. The idler arm should be replaced if the total movement (up and down) exceeds 1/4 in. (6mm).

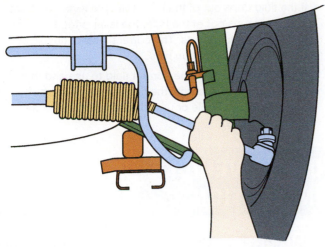

FIGURE 19–19 Steering system component(s) should be replaced if any noticeable looseness is detected when moved by hand.

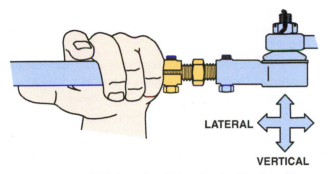

LATERAL

VERTICAL

FIGURE 19–20 All joints should be checked by hand for any lateral or vertical play.

as the joint wears. Eventually, the preloaded spring cannot compensate for the wear, and endplay occurs in the joint. ● **SEE FIGURES 19–19 AND 19–20.**

4. All steering components should be tested with the wheels in the straight-ahead position. If the wheels are turned, some apparent looseness may be noticed due to the angle of the steering linkage.

CAUTION: Do not turn the front wheels of the vehicle while suspended on a lift to check for looseness in the steering linkage. The extra leverage of the wheel and tire assembly can cause a much greater force to be applied to the steering components than can be exerted by hand alone. This extra force may cause some apparent movement in good components that may not need replacement.

DIFFERENTIAL FLUID CHECK

PROCEDURE FOR CHECKING Rear-wheel-drive vehicles use a differential in the rear of the vehicle to change the direction of power flow from the engine to the rear wheels.

FIGURE 19–21 This differential assembly has been leaking fluid. The root cause should be determined and the unit filled to the proper level using the specified lubricant, to help prevent early failure and an expensive repair later.

The differential also provides a gear reduction to increase engine torque applied to the drive wheels. Four-wheel-drive vehicles also use a differential at the front of the vehicle in addition to the differential at the rear. To check the differential fluid level and condition, perform the following steps.

STEP 1 Hoist the vehicle safely.

STEP 2 Visually check for any signs of leakage. ● **SEE FIGURE 19–21.**

STEP 3 Remove the inspection plug from the side or rear cover of the differential assembly.
- If fluid runs out, try to catch the fluid in a container so it can be disposed of and allow it to drain until it stops.
- The level should be only to the bottom of the fill plug and should not be overfilled.

STEP 4 Insert and remove your small finger into the hole in the housing and check for fluid on your finger.
- Rub the fluid between your fingers. If the fluid does not feel gritty, reinstall the inspection plug. If the fluid is gritty feeling, further service will be necessary to determine the cause and correct it.
- If the differential fluid is not on your finger, then the fluid level is too low.

NOTE: The reason for the low fluid level should be determined. Check items such as:
- axle side seals,
- spot welds, and
- differential cover gasket for leaks.

If repairs are not completed immediately, additional differential fluid should be added by pumping it into the differential through the inspection hole.

DIFFERENTIAL LUBRICANTS All differentials use hypoid gear sets; and a special lubricant is necessary because the gears both roll and slide between their meshed teeth. Gear lubes are specified by the API. Most differentials require:

1. SAE 80W-90 GL-5 *or*
2. SAE 75W-90 GL-5 *or*
3. SAE 80W GL-5

NOTE: Limited slip differentials (often abbreviated LSD) often require the use of an additive that modifies the friction characteristics of the rear axle lubricant to prevent chattering while cornering.

MANUAL TRANSMISSION/TRANSAXLE LUBRICANT CHECK

TYPES OF MANUAL TRANSMISSION FLUID Manual transmissions/transaxles may use any one of the following lubricants.

- Gear lube (usually SAE 80W-90)
- Automatic transmission fluid (ATF)
- Engine oil (usually SAE 5W-30)
- Manual transmission fluid (sometimes called **synchromesh transmission fluid**, or **STF**). This type of lubricant is similar to ATF, with special additives to ease shifting especially when cold.

PROCEDURE FOR CHECKING To check a manual transmission/transaxle lubricant, perform the following:

- Hoist the vehicle safely.
- Locate the transmission/transaxle inspection (fill) plug. Consult the factory service manual for the proper plug to remove to check the fluid level. ● **SEE FIGURE 19–22.**
- Some transaxles use manual transaxle dipstick for fluid level checking.

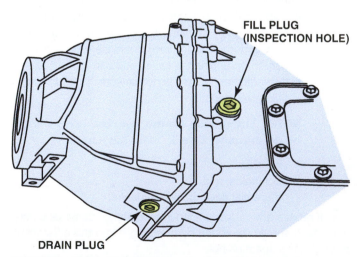

FIGURE 19–22 Always ensure that the fill plug can be accessed and removed *before* draining the fluid from a manual transmission.

- If the fluid drips out of the hole, then the level is correct. If the fluid runs out of the hole, the level is too full. Allow it to flow out until it stops. The correct level of fluid is at the bottom of the inspection hole.
- If low, first determine the correct fluid to use and then fill with the correct fluid until the fluid level is at the bottom of the inspection hole or until the fluid runs out of the inspection hole.

UNDER VEHICLE INSPECTION

VISUAL CHECKS Other items underneath the vehicle that may need checking or lubricating include:

- Shock absorbers and springs. Look for signs of wetness or damage. ● **SEE FIGURE 19–23.**
- Transmission/transaxle shift linkage (check service information for the correct lubricant to use if the linkage requires lubrication).
- Exhaust system including all pipes and hangers. Check for rusted components, leaks, and broken or missing clamps and hangers. ● **SEE FIGURE 19–24.**
- Brake lines for evidence of damage or leakage.
- Parking brake cable guides.
- Other abnormal conditions such as other broken or damaged parts.
- Check tire pressures as per driver's door placard pressure and tread condition (should be greater than 2/32 in.).
- Drive axle shaft U-joint boots. Check for a torn rubber boot or leaking grease. ● **SEE FIGURE 19–25.**

CAUTION: Do not lubricate plastic-coated parking brake cables. The lubricant can destroy the plastic coating.

FIGURE 19–23 A broken coil spring was found during an under-vehicle inspection. The owner was not aware of the problem and it did not make any noise, but the vehicle stability was affected.

FIGURE 19–24 This corroded muffler was found during a visual inspection, but was not detected by the driver because it was relatively quiet.

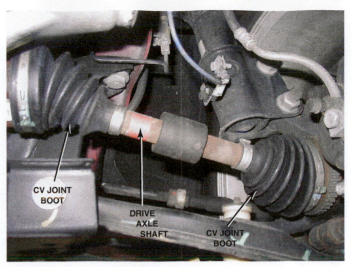

FIGURE 19–25 A drive axle shaft equipped with two flexible rubber grease boots at each of the axles. Look for signs of grease leaking from these boots.

FLUID LEAKS While under the vehicle look for any fluid leaks such as from:

1. The differential assembly (shows as being a moist area)

2. The transmission or transaxle assembly (red fluid color if automatic transmission fluid is used)

3. The power steering system (can be clear oily fluid or red ATF)

4. Engine oil leaks from the engine or oil filter area (can be brown or dark brown to black and oily)

5. Coolant leaks from the radiator or hoses (can be green, red, yellow, blue, or orange depending on the type of coolant)

6. Fuel tank and fuel lines for signs of wetness or excessive rust

If any leaks are discovered, document the leaks on the work order and ask that the customer be notified of the leaking fluid.

OIL CHANGE

1 Before entering the customer's car for the first time, be sure to install a seat cover as well as a steering wheel cover to protect the vehicle's interior.

2 Run the engine until it is close to operating temperature. This will help the used oil drain more quickly and thoroughly.

3 Raise the vehicle on a hoist, and place the oil drain container in position under the oil drain plug. Be sure to wear protective gloves.

4 Remove the plug and allow the hot oil to drain from the engine. Use caution during this step as hot oil can cause painful burns!

5 While the engine oil continues to drain, remove the engine oil filter using a filter wrench. Some oil will drain from the filter, so be sure to have the oil drain container underneath when removing it.

6 Compare the new oil filter with the old one to be sure that it is the correct replacement.

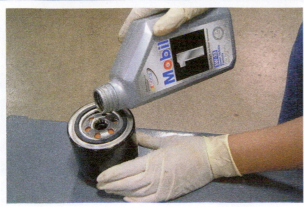

7 The wise service technician adds oil to the oil filter whenever possible. This provides faster filling of the filter during start-up and a reduced amount of time that the engine does not have oil pressure.

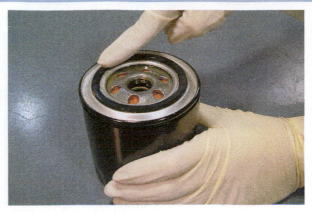

8 Apply a thin layer of clean engine oil to the gasket of the new filter. This oil film will allow the rubber gasket to slide and compress as the oil filter is being tightened.

9 Clean the area where the oil filter gasket seats to be sure that no part of the gasket remains that could cause an oil leak if not fully removed.

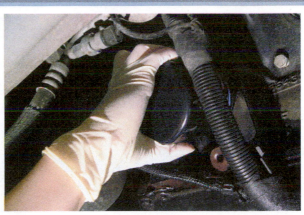

10 Install the new oil filter and tighten it by hand. Do not use an oil filter wrench to tighten the filter! Most filters should be tightened 3/4 of a turn after the gasket contacts the engine.

11 Carefully inspect the oil drain plug and gasket. Replace the gasket as needed. Install the drain plug and tighten firmly but do not overtighten!

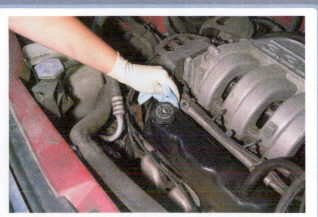

12 Lower the vehicle and clean around the oil fill cap before removing it.

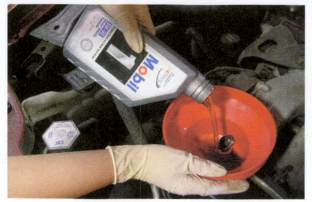

13 Use a funnel to add the specified amount of oil to the engine at the oil fill opening. When finished, replace the oil fill cap.

14 Start the engine and allow it to idle while watching the oil pressure gauge and/or oil pressure warning lamp. Oil pressure should be indicated within 15 seconds of starting the engine.

15 Stop the engine and let it sit for a few minutes to allow the oil to drain back into the oil pan. Look underneath the vehicle to check for any oil leaks at the oil drain plug(s) or oil filter.

16 Remove the oil-level dipstick and wipe it clean with a shop cloth.

17 Reinstall the oil-level dipstick. Remove the dipstick a second time and read the oil level.

18 The oil level should be between the MIN and the MAX lines. In this case, the oil level should be somewhere in the cross-hatched area of the dipstick

SUMMARY

1. Oil specifications include SAE (viscosity); API (quality standard); ILSAC (low friction requirements) as well as vehicle manufactures specified oil standard.

2. All grease fittings should be cleaned before using a grease gun to lubricate any greaseable joints under the vehicle.

3. Most differentials require a SAE 80W-90 GL-5 rated lubricant.

4. Manual transmissions/transaxles may require one of several different lubricants, including gear lube such as SAE 80W-90, ATF, engine oil (SAE 5W-30), or special manual transmission fluid.

REVIEW QUESTIONS

1. What oil specification is used to express the thickness (viscosity) of the oil?

2. Why do engines in vehicles built before about 1990 need an additive in the oil to help protect the engine?

3. How is the fluid level in a manual transmission checked?

CHAPTER QUIZ

1. Many vehicles do not require chassis lubrication if they are equipped with _____
   a. Low-friction suspension joints such as ball joints
   b. No grease fittings
   c. Sealed for life joints
   d. All of the above

2. A coolant leak will show as what color?
   a. Red
   b. Orange
   c. Green
   d. Any of the above depending on the type of coolant

3. Which oil specification stands for the thickness (viscosity)?
   a. SAE
   b. API
   c. ILSAC
   d. ACEA

4. Which oil standard is displayed on the front of the oil container?
   a. SAE
   b. API
   c. ILSAC
   d. ACEA

5. A service technician removed the inspection/fill plug from the differential of a rear-wheel-drive vehicle and gear lube started to flow out. Technician A says to quickly replace the plug to prevent any more loss of gear lube. Technician B says to catch the fluid and allow the fluid to continue to drain. Which technician is correct?
   a. Technician A only
   b. Technician B only
   c. Both technicians A and B
   d. Neither technician A nor B

6. A grease fitting can be called _____
   a. Grease fitting
   b. Alemite fitting
   c. Zerk fitting
   d. Any of the above

7. A red fluid is discovered under a vehicle. This could be due to a leaking _____
   a. Engine gasket (engine oil leak)
   b. Cooling hose (coolant leak)
   c. Transmission/transaxle (ATF leak)
   d. Either b or c

8. A Volkswagen Jetta is in the shop for an oil change. What specification is used for this European vehicle?
   a. SAE
   b. API
   c. ILSAC
   d. ACEA

9. Which is a typical lube used in rear-drive axle assemblies?
   a. SAE 80W-90 GL-5
   b. SAE 75W-90 GL-5
   c. SAE 80W GL-5
   d. Any of the above depending on the specification for the vehicle

10. An under vehicle inspection includes checking for _____
    a. Exhaust system faults such as broken hangers or leaks
    b. Torn drive axle shafts rubber boots
    c. Any fluid leaks
    d. All of the above

chapter 20

ELECTRICAL FUNDAMENTALS

OBJECTIVES: **After studying Chapter 20, the reader will be able to:** • Prepare for ASE Electrical/Electronic Systems (A6) certification test content area "A" (General Electrical/Electronic System Diagnosis). • Define electricity. • Explain the units of electrical measurement. • Discuss the relationship among volts, amperes, and ohms. • Discuss the principles of magnetism. • Discuss how electricity can be obtained from different sources.

KEY TERMS: • Ammeter 199 • Ampere 199 • Atom 196 • Conductors 197 • Conventional theory 198 • Coulomb 199 • Electrical potential 199 • Electricity 196 • Electromotive force (EMF) 200 • Electron theory 198 • Insulators 198 • Neutral charge 196 • Ohmmeter 200 • Ohms 200 • Resistance 200 • Semiconductor 198 • Valence ring 197 • Volt 199 • Voltmeter 200

INTRODUCTION

The electrical system is one of the most important systems in a vehicle today. Every year more and more vehicle components and systems use electricity. Those technicians who really know and understand automotive electrical and electronic systems will be in great demand.

Electricity may be difficult for some people to learn for the following reasons.

- It cannot be seen.
- Only the results of electricity can be seen.
- It has to be detected and measured.

ELECTRICITY

BACKGROUND   Our universe is composed of matter, which is *anything* that has mass and occupies space. All matter is made from slightly over 100 individual components called *elements*. The smallest particle that an *element* can be broken into and still retain the properties of that element is known as an **atom**. ● SEE FIGURE 20–1.

DEFINITION   **Electricity** is the movement of electrons from one atom to another. The dense center of each atom is called the nucleus. The nucleus contains

- *Protons*, which have a positive charge
- *Neutrons*, which are electrically neutral (have no charge)

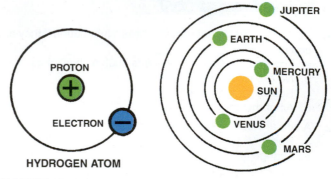

FIGURE 20–1 In an atom (left), electrons orbit protons in the nucleus just as planets orbit the sun in our solar system (right).

Electrons, which have a negative charge, orbit the nucleus. Each atom contains an equal *number* of electrons and protons. The physical aspect of the presence of protons, electrons, and neutrons is the same for all atoms. It is the number of electrons and protons in the atom that determines the material and how electricity is conducted. Because the number of negatively charged electrons is balanced with the same number of positively charged protons, an atom has a **neutral charge** (no charge).

NOTE: As an example of the relative sizes of the parts of an atom, consider that if an atom were magnified so that the nucleus were the size of the period at the end of this sentence, the whole atom would be bigger than a house.

POSITIVE AND NEGATIVE CHARGES   The parts of an atom have different charges. The orbiting electrons are negatively charged, while the protons are positively charged.

Positive charges are indicated by the "plus" sign (+), and negative charges by the "minus" sign (−). ● **SEE FIGURE 20–2.**

These same + and − signs are used to identify parts of an electrical circuit. Neutrons have no charge at all. They are neutral. In a normal, or balanced atom, the number of negative particles equals the number of positive particles. That is, there are as many electrons as there are protons. ● **SEE FIGURE 20–3.**

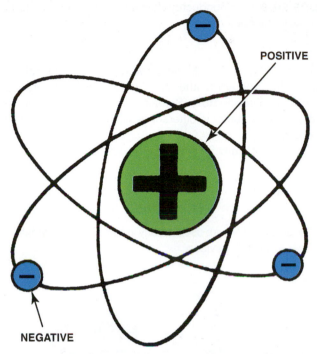

FIGURE 20–2 The nucleus of an atom has a positive (+) charge and the surrounding electrons have a negative (−) charge.

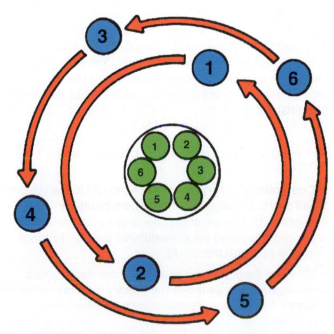

FIGURE 20–3 This figure shows a balanced atom. The number of electrons is the same as the number of protons in the nucleus.

MAGNETS AND ELECTRICAL CHARGE An ordinary magnet has two ends, or poles. One end is called the south pole, and the other is called the north pole. If two magnets are brought close to each other with like poles together (south to south or north to north), the magnets will push each other apart, because like poles repel each other. If the opposite poles of the magnets are brought close to each other, south to north, the magnets will snap together, because unlike poles attract each other. The positive and negative charges within an atom are like the north and south poles of a magnet. Charges that are alike will repel each other, similar to the poles of a magnet. ● **SEE FIGURE 20–4.**

That is why the negative electrons continue to orbit around the positive protons. They are attracted and held by the opposite charge of the protons. The electrons keep moving in orbit because they repel each other.

ELECTRON ORBITS Electrons orbit around the nucleus in *rings* and the outermost ring is called the **"valence ring."** Whether a material is a conductor or an insulator strictly depends on how many electrons are in the outer ring.

CONDUCTORS **Conductors** are materials with fewer than four electrons in their atom's outer orbit. ● **SEE FIGURE 20–5.**

Copper is an excellent conductor because it has only one electron in its outer orbit. This orbit is far enough away from the nucleus of the copper atom that the pull or force holding the outermost electron in orbit is relatively weak. ● **SEE FIGURE 20–6.**

Copper is the conductor most used in vehicles because the price of copper is reasonable compared to the relative cost of other conductors with similar properties. Examples of commonly used conductors include:

- Silver
- Copper
- Gold
- Aluminum
- Steel
- Cast iron

FIGURE 20–4 Unlike charges attract and like charges repel.

CONDUCTORS

FIGURE 20–5 A conductor is any element that has one to three electrons in its outer orbit.

COPPER

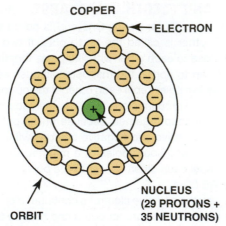

FIGURE 20–6 Copper is an excellent conductor of electricity because it has just one electron in its outer orbit, making it easy to be knocked out of its orbit and flow to other nearby atoms. This causes electron flow, which is the definition of electricity.

 FREQUENTLY ASKED QUESTION

Is Water a Conductor?

Pure water is an insulator; however, if anything is in the water, such as salt or dirt, then the water becomes conductive. Because it is difficult to keep it from becoming contaminated, water is usually thought of as being capable of conducting electricity, especially high-voltage household 110 or 220 volt outlets.

INSULATORS

Some materials hold their electrons very tightly; therefore, electrons do not move through them very well. These materials are called insulators. **Insulators** are materials with more than four electrons in their atom's outer orbit. Because they have more than four electrons in their outer orbit, it becomes easier for these materials to acquire (gain) electrons than to release electrons. ● SEE FIGURE 20–7.

Examples of insulators include:

- Rubber
- Plastic
- Nylon
- Porcelain
- Ceramic
- Fiberglass

INSULATORS

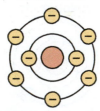

FIGURE 20–7 Insulators are elements with five to eight electrons in the outer orbit.

SEMICONDUCTORS

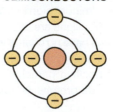

FIGURE 20–8 Semiconductor elements contain exactly four electrons in the outer orbit.

SEMICONDUCTORS

Materials with exactly four electrons in their outer orbit are neither conductors nor insulators, but are called **semiconductors.** Semiconductors can be either an insulator or a conductor in different design applications. ● SEE FIGURE 20–8.

Examples of semiconductors include:

- Silicon
- Germanium
- Carbon

Semiconductors are used mostly in transistors, computers, and other electronic devices.

HOW ELECTRONS MOVE THROUGH A CONDUCTOR

CURRENT FLOW The following events occur if a source of power, such as a battery, is connected to the ends of a conductor—a positive charge (lack of electrons) is placed on one end of the conductor and a negative charge (excess of electrons) is placed on the opposite end of the conductor. For current to flow, there *must* be an imbalance of excess electrons at one end of the circuit and a deficiency of electrons at the opposite end of the circuit. ● SEE FIGURE 20–9.

CONVENTIONAL THEORY VERSUS ELECTRON THEORY

- **Conventional theory.** It was once thought that electricity had only one charge and moved from positive to negative. This theory of the flow of electricity through a conductor is called the **conventional theory** of current flow. ● SEE FIGURE 20–10.
- **Electron theory.** The discovery of the electron and its negative charge led to the **electron theory,** which states that there is electron flow from negative to positive.

Most automotive applications use the conventional theory. This book will use the conventional theory (positive to negative) unless stated otherwise.

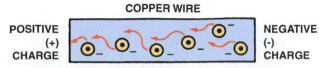

FIGURE 20–9 Current electricity is the movement of electrons through a conductor.

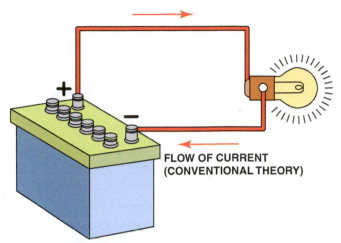

FIGURE 20–10 Conventional theory states that current flows through a circuit from positive (+) to negative (−). Automotive electricity uses the conventional theory in all electrical diagrams and schematics.

UNITS OF ELECTRICITY

Electricity is measured using meters or other test equipment. The three fundamentals of electricity-related units include the ampere, volt, and ohm.

AMPERE The **ampere** is the unit used throughout the world to measure current flow. When 6.28 billion billion electrons (the name for this large number of electrons is a **coulomb**) move past a certain point in 1 second, this represents 1 ampere of current. ● **SEE FIGURE 20–11.**

The ampere is the electrical unit for the amount of electron flow, just as "gallons per minute" is the unit that can be used to measure the quantity of water flow. It is named for the French electrician Andrè Marie Ampére (1775–1836). The conventional abbreviations and measurement for amperes are as follows:

1. The ampere is the unit of measurement for the amount of current flow.
2. *A* and *amps* are acceptable abbreviations for *amperes*.

FIGURE 20–11 One ampere is the movement of 1 coulomb (6.28 billion billion electrons) past a point in 1 second.

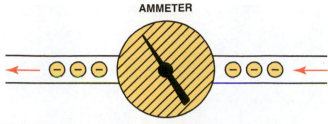

FIGURE 20–12 An ammeter is installed in the path of the electrons similar to a water meter used to measure the flow of water in gallons per minute. The ammeter displays current flow in amperes.

3. The capital letter *I*, for *intensity*, is used in mathematical calculations to represent amperes.
4. Amperes do the actual work in the circuit. It is the movement of the electrons through a light bulb or motor that actually makes the electrical device work. Without amperage through a device, it will not work at all.
5. Amperes are measured by an **ammeter** (not ampmeter). ● **SEE FIGURE 20–12.**

VOLTS The **volt** is the unit of measurement for electrical pressure. It is named for an Italian physicist, Alessandro Volta (1745–1827). The comparable unit using water pressure as an example would be pounds per square inch (PSI). It is possible to have very high pressures (volts) and low water flow (amperes). It is also possible to have high water flow (amperes) and low pressures (volts). Voltage is also called **electrical potential,** because if there is voltage present in a conductor, there is a potential (possibility) for current flow. This electrical pressure is a result of the following:

■ Excess electrons remain at one end of the wire or circuit.

■ There is a lack of electrons at the other end of the wire or circuit.

■ The natural effect is to equalize this imbalance, creating a pressure to allow the movement of electrons through a conductor.

■ It is possible to have pressure (volts) without any flow (amperes). For example, a fully charged 12 volt battery sitting on a workbench has 12 volts of pressure potential, but because there is not a conductor (circuit) connected between the positive and negative posts of the battery, there is no flow (amperes). Current will flow only when there is pressure and a circuit for the electrons to flow in order to "equalize" to a balanced state.

Voltage does *not* flow through conductors, but voltage does cause current (in amperes) to flow through conductors. ● **SEE FIGURE 20–13.**

FIGURE 20–13 Voltage is the electrical pressure that causes the electrons to flow through a conductor.

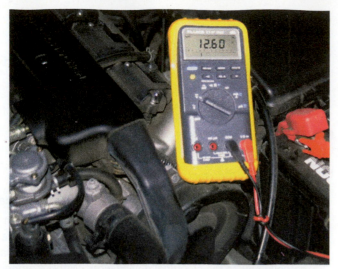

FIGURE 20–14 This digital multimeter set to read DC volts is being used to test the voltage of a vehicle battery. Most multimeters can also measure resistance (ohms) and current flow (amperes).

The conventional abbreviations and measurement for voltage are as follows:

1. The volt is the unit of measurement for the amount of electrical pressure.

2. **Electromotive force,** abbreviated **EMF,** is another way of indicating voltage.

3. *V* is the generally accepted abbreviation for *volts*.

4. The symbol used in calculations is *E*, for *electromotive force*.

5. Volts are measured by a **voltmeter.** ● **SEE FIGURE 20–14.**

OHMS **Resistance** to the flow of current through a conductor is measured in units called **ohms**, named after the German physicist George Simon Ohm (1787–1854). The resistance to the flow of free electrons through a conductor results from the countless collisions the electrons cause within the atoms of the conductor. ● **SEE FIGURE 20–15.**

Resistance can be:

- Desirable when it is part of how a circuit works, such as the resistance of a filament in a light bulb
- Undesirable, such as corrosion in a connection restricting the amount of current flow in a circuit

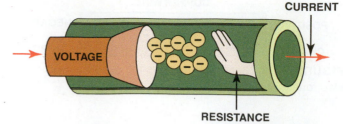

FIGURE 20–15 Resistance to the flow of electrons through a conductor is measured in ohms.

The conventional abbreviations and measurement for resistance are as follows:

1. The ohm is the unit of measurement for electrical resistance.

2. The symbol for ohms is Ω (Greek capital letter omega), the last letter of the Greek alphabet.

3. The symbol used in calculations is *R*, for *resistance*.

4. Ohms are measured by an **ohmmeter.**

5. Resistance to electron flow depends on the material used as a conductor.

CONDUCTORS AND RESISTANCE

All conductors have some resistance to current flow. The following are the principles of conductors and their resistance.

- **If the conductor length is doubled, its resistance doubles.** This is the reason why battery cables are designed to be as short as possible.

- **If the conductor diameter is increased, its resistance is reduced.** This is the reason starter motor cables are larger in diameter than other wiring in the vehicle.

- **As the temperature increases, the resistance of the conductor also increases.** This is the reason for installing heat shields on some starter motors. The heat shield helps to protect the conductors (copper wiring inside the starter) from excessive engine heat and so reduces the resistance of starter circuits.

SUMMARY

1. Electricity is the movement of electrons from one atom to another.

2. In order for current to flow in a circuit or wire, there must be an excess of electrons at one end and a deficiency of electrons at the other end.

3. Automotive electricity uses the conventional theory that electricity flows from positive to negative.

4. The ampere is the measure of the amount of current flow.

5. Voltage is the unit of electrical pressure.

6. The ohm is the unit of electrical resistance.

1. What is electricity?
2. Give three examples of conductors and three examples of insulators.
3. What are the ampere, volt, and ohm?

CHAPTER QUIZ

1. An electrical conductor is an element with _____ electrons in its outer orbit.
   - **a.** Less than 2
   - **b.** Less than 4
   - **c.** Exactly 4
   - **d.** More than 4

2. Like charges _____.
   - **a.** Attract
   - **b.** Repel
   - **c.** Neutralize each other
   - **d.** Add

3. Carbon and silicon are examples of _____.
   - **a.** Semiconductors
   - **b.** Insulators
   - **c.** Conductors
   - **d.** Photoelectric materials

4. Which unit of electricity actually measures the amount of current flow?
   - **a.** Volt
   - **b.** Ampere
   - **c.** Ohm
   - **d.** Coulomb

5. As temperature increases, _____.
   - **a.** The resistance of a conductor decreases
   - **b.** The resistance of a conductor increases
   - **c.** The resistance of a conductor remains the same
   - **d.** The voltage of the conductor decreases

6. The _____ is a unit of electrical pressure.
   - **a.** Coulomb
   - **b.** Volt
   - **c.** Ampere
   - **d.** Ohm

7. The _____ is a unit of electrical resistance.
   - **a.** Coulomb
   - **b.** Volt
   - **c.** Ampere
   - **d.** Ohm

8. Which of the following are conductors?
   - **a.** Gold
   - **b.** Silver
   - **c.** Copper
   - **d.** All of the above

9. The Greek letter Omega (Ω) represents what unit of electricity?
   - **a.** Coulomb
   - **b.** Volt
   - **c.** Ampere
   - **d.** Ohm

10. As the length of a wire increases, _____.
    - **a.** The resistance of the wire decreases
    - **b.** The resistance of the wire increases
    - **c.** The resistance of the wire remains the same
    - **d.** The voltage of the wire decreases

OBJECTIVES: **After studying Chapter 21, the reader will be able to:** • Prepare for ASE Electrical/Electronic Systems (A6) certification test content area "A" (General Electrical/Electronic Systems Diagnosis). • Explain Ohm's law. • Identify the parts of a complete circuit. • Describe the characteristics of an open, a short-to-ground, and a short-to-voltage.

KEY TERMS: • Circuit 202 • Complete circuit 202 • Continuity 202 • Electrical load 202 • Grounded 204 • High resistance 204 • Load 202 • Ohm's law 204 • Open circuit 203 • Power path 202 • Power source 202 • Protection 202 • Return path (ground) 202 • Shorted 203 • Short-to-ground 203 • Short-to-voltage 203 • Switches and controls 202

CIRCUITS

DEFINITION A **circuit** is a complete path that electrons travel from a power source (such as a battery) through a **load** such as a light bulb and back to the power source. It is called a *circuit* because the current must start and finish at the same place (power source). For *any* electrical circuit to work at all, it must be continuous from the battery (power), through all the wires and components, and back to the battery (ground). A circuit that is continuous throughout is said to have **continuity**.

PARTS OF A COMPLETE CIRCUIT Every **complete circuit** contains the following parts. ● **SEE FIGURE 21–1.**

1. A **power source**, such as a vehicle's battery.

2. **Protection** from harmful overloads (excessive current flow). (Fuses, circuit breakers, and fusible links are examples of electrical circuit protection devices.)

3. The **power path** for the current to flow through, from the power source to the resistance. (This path from a power source to the load—a light bulb in this example—is usually an insulated copper wire.)

4. The **electrical load** or resistance, which converts electrical energy into heat, light, or motion.

5. A **return path (ground)** for the electrical current from the load back to the power source so that there is a *complete* circuit. (This return, or ground, path is usually the metal body, frame, ground wires, and engine block of the vehicle.) ● **SEE FIGURE 21–2.**

6. **Switches and controls** that turn the circuit on and off. ● **SEE FIGURE 21–3.**

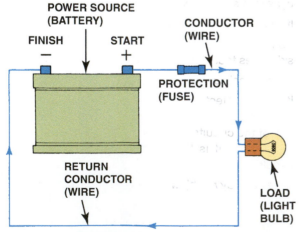

FIGURE 21–1 All complete circuits must have a power source, a power path, protection (fuse), an electrical load (light bulb in this case), and a return path back to the power source.

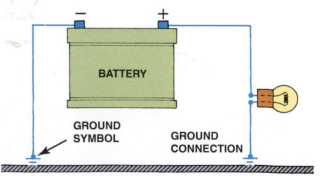

FIGURE 21–2 The return path back to the battery can be any electrical conductor, such as a copper wire or the metal frame or body of the vehicle.

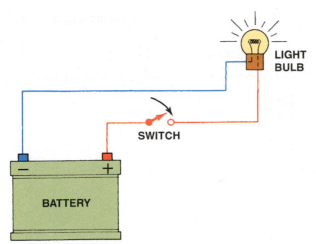

FIGURE 21–3 An electrical switch opens the circuit and no current flows. The switch could also be on the return (ground) path wire.

CIRCUIT FAULTS

Circuits can experience several different types of faults or problems, which often result in improper operation. The types of faults include opens, shorts, and high resistance.

OPEN CIRCUITS   An **open circuit** is any circuit that is *not* complete, or that lacks continuity, such as a broken wire. ● SEE **FIGURE 21–4.**

Open circuits have the following features.

1. *No current at all* will flow through an open circuit.
2. An open circuit may be created by a break in the circuit or by a switch that opens (turns off) the circuit and prevents the flow of current.

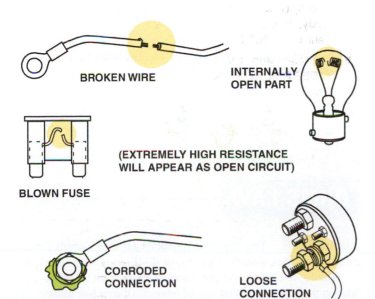

BROKEN WIRE

INTERNALLY OPEN PART

(EXTREMELY HIGH RESISTANCE WILL APPEAR AS OPEN CIRCUIT)

BLOWN FUSE

CORRODED CONNECTION

LOOSE CONNECTION

FIGURE 21–4 Examples of common causes of open circuits. Some of these causes are often difficult to find.

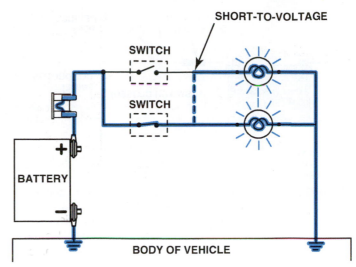

SHORT-TO-VOLTAGE

SWITCH

SWITCH

BATTERY

BODY OF VEHICLE

FIGURE 21–5 A short circuit permits electrical current to bypass some or all of the resistance in the circuit.

3. In any circuit containing a power load and ground, an opening anywhere in the circuit will cause the circuit not to work.
4. A light switch in a home and the headlight switch in a vehicle are examples of devices that open a circuit to control its operation.

NOTE: A blown fuse opens the circuit to prevent damage to the components or wiring in the circuit in the event of an overload caused by a fault in the circuit.

SHORT-TO-VOLTAGE   If a wire (conductor) or component is shorted to voltage, it is commonly referred to as being **shorted**. A **short-to-voltage** occurs when the power side of one circuit is electrically connected to the power side of another circuit. ● SEE **FIGURE 21–5.**

A short circuit has the following features.

1. It is a complete circuit in which the current usually bypasses *some* or *all* of the resistance in the circuit.
2. It involves the power side of the circuit.
3. It involves a copper-to-copper connection (two power-side wires touching together).
4. It is also called a *short-to-voltage.*
5. It usually affects more than one circuit. In this case, if one circuit is electrically connected to another circuit, one of the circuits may operate when it is not supposed to because it is being supplied power from another circuit.
6. It *may* or *may not* blow a fuse. ● SEE **FIGURE 21–6.**

SHORT-TO-GROUND   A **short-to-ground** is a type of short circuit that occurs when the current bypasses part of the normal circuit and flows directly to ground. A short-to-ground has the following features.

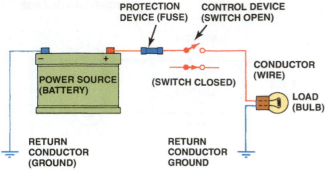

FIGURE 21–6 A fuse or circuit breaker opens the circuit to prevent possible overheating damage in the event of a short circuit.

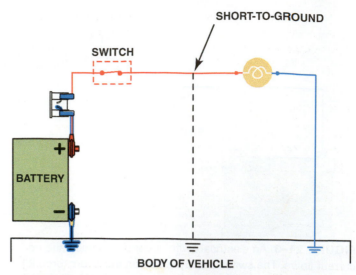

FIGURE 21–7 A short-to-ground affects the power side of the circuit. Current flows directly to the ground return, bypassing some or all of the electrical loads in the circuit. There is no current in the circuit past the short. A short-to-ground will also cause the fuse to blow.

 REAL-WORLD FIX

The Short-to-Voltage Story

A technician was working on a Chevrolet pickup truck with the following unusual electrical problems.

1. When the brake pedal was depressed, the dash light and the side marker lights would light.
2. The turn signals caused all lights to blink and the fuel gauge needle to bounce up and down.
3. When the brake lights were on, the front parking lights also came on.

　The technician tested all fuses using a conventional test light and found them to be okay. All body-to-engine block ground wires were clean and tight. All bulbs were of the correct trade number as specified in the owner's manual.

　Because most of the trouble occurred when the brake pedal was depressed, the technician decided to trace all the wires in the brake light circuit. The technician discovered the problem near the exhaust system. A small hole in the tailpipe (after the muffler) directed hot exhaust gases to the wiring harness containing all of the wires for circuits at the rear of the truck. The heat had melted the insulation and caused most of the wires to touch. Whenever one circuit was activated (such as when the brake pedal was applied), the current had a complete path to several other circuits. A fuse did not blow because there was enough resistance in the circuits being energized, so the current (in amperes) was too low to blow any fuses.

1. Because the ground return circuit is metal (vehicle frame, engine, or body), it is often identified as having current flowing from copper to steel.
2. A short-to-ground can occur at any place where a power path wire accidentally touches a return path wire or conductor. ● **SEE FIGURE 21–7.**

3. A defective component or circuit that is shorted to ground is commonly called **grounded.**
4. A short-to-ground almost always results in a blown fuse, damaged connectors, or melted wires.

HIGH RESISTANCE　　**High resistance** can be caused by any of the following:

- Corroded connections or sockets
- Loose terminals in a connector
- Loose ground connections

　If there is high resistance anywhere in a circuit, it may cause the following problems.

1. Slow operation of a motor-driven unit, such as the windshield wipers or blower motor
2. Dim lights
3. "Clicking" of relays or solenoids
4. No operation of a circuit or electrical component

OHMS LAW

DEFINITION　　The German physicist George Simon Ohm established that electrical pressure (EMF) in volts, electrical resistance in ohms, and the amount of current in amperes flowing through any circuit are all related. **Ohm's law** states:

It requires 1 volt to push 1 ampere through 1 ohm of resistance.

This means that if the voltage is doubled, then the number of amperes of current flowing through a circuit will also double if the resistance of the circuit remains the same.

$$I = \frac{E}{R}$$

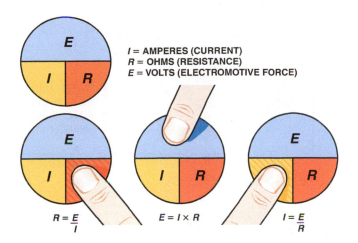

I = AMPERES (CURRENT)
R = OHMS (RESISTANCE)
E = VOLTS (ELECTROMOTIVE FORCE)

$R = \frac{E}{I}$ $E = I \times R$ $I = \frac{E}{R}$

FIGURE 21–8 To calculate one unit of electricity when the other two are known, simply use your finger and cover the unit you do not know. For example, if both voltage (E) and resistance (R) are known, cover the letter I (amperes). Note that the letter E is above the letter R, so divide the resistor's value into the voltage to determine the current in the circuit.

FORMULAS Ohm's law can also be stated as a simple formula used to calculate one value of an electrical circuit if the other two are known. ● **SEE FIGURE 21–8.**

I = Current in amperes (A)
E = Electromotive force (EMF) in volts (V)
R = Resistance in ohms (Ω)

1. Ohm's law can determine the resistance if the volts and amperes are known: $R = \dfrac{E}{I}$

2. Ohm's law can determine the *voltage* if the resistance (ohms) and amperes are known: $E = I \times R$

3. Ohm's law can determine the amperes if the resistance and voltage are known: $I = \dfrac{E}{R}$

NOTE: Before applying Ohm's law, be sure that each unit of electricity is converted into base units. For example, 10 KΩ should be converted to 10,000 ohms, and 10 mA should be converted into 0.010 A.

● **SEE CHART 21–1.**

OHM'S LAW APPLIED TO SIMPLE CIRCUITS
If a battery with 12 volts is connected to a resistor of 4 ohms, how many amperes will flow through the circuit? Using Ohm's law,

VOLTAGE	RESISTANCE	AMPERAGE
Up	Down	Up
Up	Same	Up
Up	Up	Same
Same	Down	Up
Same	Same	Same
Same	Up	Down
Down	Up	Down
Down	Same	Down

CHART 21–1

Ohm's law relationship with the three units of electricity.

🔧 TECH TIP

Think of a Waterwheel

A beginner technician cleaned the positive terminal of the battery when the starter was cranking the engine slowly. When questioned by the shop foreman as to why only the positive post had been cleaned, the technician responded that the negative terminal was "only a ground." The foreman reminded the technician that the current, in amperes, is constant throughout a series circuit (such as the cranking motor circuit). If 200 amperes leave the positive post of the battery, then 200 amperes must return to the battery through the negative post. The technician could not understand how electricity can do work (crank an engine), yet return the same amount of current, in amperes, as left the battery. The shop foreman explained that even though the current is constant throughout the circuit, the voltage (electrical pressure or potential) drops to zero in the circuit. To explain further, the shop foreman drew a waterwheel. ● **SEE FIGURE 21–9.**

As water drops from a higher level to a lower level, high potential energy (or voltage) is used to turn the waterwheel and results in low potential energy (or lower voltage). The same amount of water (or amperes) reaches the pond under the waterwheel as started the fall above the waterwheel. As current (amperes) flows through a conductor, it performs work in the circuit (turns the waterwheel) while its voltage (potential) drops.

we can calculate the number of amperes that will flow through the wires and the resistor.

Remember, if two factors are known (volts and ohms in this example), the remaining factor (amperes) can be calculated using Ohm's law.

$$I = \frac{E}{R} = \frac{12 \text{ V}}{4\Omega} = 3A$$

The values for the voltage (12) and the resistance (4) were substituted for the variables *E* and *R*, and *I* is thus 3 amperes. If we want to connect a 4 ohm resistor to a 12-volt battery, we now know that this simple circuit requires 3 amperes to operate. Knowing the current in the circuit can help determine two things:

1. The wire diameter needed for the circuit to function correctly.
2. The correct fuse rating to protect the circuit.

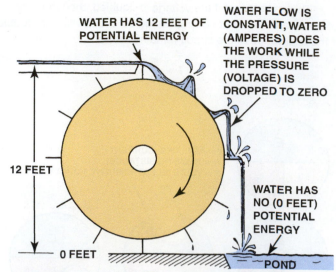

FIGURE 21–9 Electrical flow through a circuit is similar to water flowing over a waterwheel. The more the water (amperes in electricity), the greater the amount of work (waterwheel). The amount of water remains constant, yet the pressure (voltage in electricity) drops as the current flows through the circuit.

SUMMARY

1. All complete electrical circuits have a power source (such as a battery), a circuit protection device (such as a fuse), a power-side wire or path, an electrical load, a ground return path, and a switch or a control device.
2. A short-to-voltage involves a copper-to-copper connection and usually affects more than one circuit.
3. A short-to-ground usually involves a power path conductor coming in contact with a return (ground) path conductor and usually causes the fuse to blow.
4. An open is a break in the circuit resulting in absolutely no current flow through the circuit.
5. Ohm's Law can be used to determine one value of electricity if the other two are known.

REVIEW QUESTIONS

1. What is included in a complete electrical circuit?
2. What is the difference between a short-to-voltage and a short-to-ground?
3. What is the difference between an electrical open and a short?
4. What is Ohm's law?
5. What happens to current flow (amperes) and wattage if the resistance of a circuit is increased because of a corroded connection?

CHAPTER QUIZ

1. If an insulated wire rubbed through a part of the insulation, and the wire conductor touched the steel body of a vehicle, the type of failure would be called a(n) _____.
   a. Short-to-voltage
   b. Short-to-ground
   c. Open
   d. Chassis ground
2. If two insulated wires were to melt together where the copper conductors touched each other, the type of failure would be called a(n) _____.
   a. Short-to-voltage
   b. Short-to-ground
   c. Open
   d. Floating ground
3. If 12 volts are being applied to a resistance of 3 ohms, _____ amperes will flow.
   a. 12
   b. 3
   c. 4
   d. 36
4. A complete circuit has _____.
   a. A power side electrical path
   b. An electrical load device
   c. A return path
   d. All of the above

5. An electrical protection device is usually a _____.
   a. Fuse
   b. Wire
   c. Electrical load device
   d. Switch

6. High resistance in an electrical circuit can cause _____.
   a. Dim lights
   b. Slow motor operation
   c. Clicking of relays or solenoids
   d. All of the above

7. If the voltage increases in a circuit, what happens to the current (amperes) if the resistance remains the same?
   a. Increases
   b. Decreases
   c. Remains the same
   d. Cannot be determined

8. If 200 amperes flow from the positive terminal of a battery and operate the starter motor, how many amperes will flow back to the negative terminal of the battery?
   a. Cannot be determined
   b. Zero
   c. One half (about 100 amperes)
   d. 200 amperes

9. What is the symbol for voltage used in calculations?
   a. R
   b. E
   c. EMF
   d. I

10. Which circuit failure is most likely to cause the fuse to blow?
   a. Open
   b. Short-to-ground
   c. Short-to-voltage
   d. High resistance

CIRCUIT TESTERS AND DIGITAL METERS

OBJECTIVES: **After studying Chapter 22, the reader will be able to:** • Prepare for ASE Electrical/Electronic Systems (A6) certification test content area "A" (General Electrical/Electronic System Diagnosis). • Explain how to set up and use a digital meter to read voltage, resistance, and current. • Explain meter terms and readings. • Interpret meter readings and compare to factory specifications. • Discuss how to properly and safely use meters.

KEY TERMS: • AC/DC clamp-on DMM 213 • DMM 209 • DVOM 209 • Inductive ammeter 213 • OL 211 • Test light 209

INTRODUCTION

Electricity has to be measured and tested with testers or meters because it cannot be seen. Testers used to detect and measure electricity and electrical circuits include:

- Fused jumper wires
- Test lights
- Meters

FUSED JUMPER WIRE

PURPOSE AND FUNCTION A fuse jumper wire is used to check a circuit by bypassing the switch or to provide a power or ground to a component. A fused jumper wire, also called a lead, can be purchased or made by the service technician.
● **SEE FIGURE 22–1.**

It should include the following features:

- **Fuse.** A typical fused jumper wire has a blade-type fuse that can be easily replaced. A 10 ampere fuse (red color) is often the value used.

- **Alligator clip ends.** Alligator clips on the ends allow the fused jumper wire to be clipped to a ground or power source while the other end is attached to the power side or ground side of the unit being tested.

- **Good-quality insulated wire.** Most purchased jumper wire is about 14 gauge stranded copper wire with a flexible rubberized insulation to allow it to move easily even in cold weather.

USES OF A FUSED JUMPER WIRE A fused jumper wire can be used to help diagnose a component or circuit by performing the following procedures.

- **Supply power or ground.** If a component, such as a horn, does not work, a fused jumper wire can be used to supply power and/or ground. Start by unplugging the electrical connector from the device and connect a fused jumper lead to the power terminal. Another fused jumper wire may be needed to provide the ground. If the unit works, the problem is in the power-side or ground-side circuit.

FIGURE 22–1 A technician-made fused jumper lead, which is equipped with a red 10 ampere fuse. This fused jumper wire uses terminals for testing circuits at a connector instead of alligator clips.

TEST LIGHT

NON-POWERED TEST LIGHT

A 12-volt test light is one of the simplest testers that can be used to detect electricity. A **test light** is simply a light bulb with a probe and a ground wire attached. ● **SEE FIGURE 22–2.**

A test light is used to detect battery voltage potential at various test points. Battery voltage cannot be seen or felt, and can be detected only with test equipment. The ground clip is connected to a clean ground on either the negative terminal of the battery or a clean metal part of the body and the probe touched to terminals or components. If the test light comes on, this indicates that voltage is available. ● **SEE FIGURE 22–3.**

A purchased test light should be labeled a "12-volt test light." Do not purchase a test light designed for household current (110 or 220 volts), as it will not light with 12 to 14 volts.

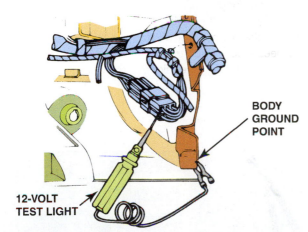

12-VOLT TEST LIGHT

BODY GROUND POINT

FIGURE 22–2 A 12-volt test light is attached to a good ground while probing for power.

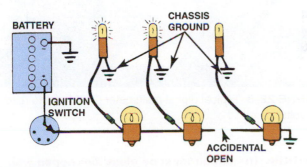

BATTERY

CHASSIS GROUND

IGNITION SWITCH

ACCIDENTAL OPEN

FIGURE 22–3 A test light can be used to locate an open in a circuit. Note that the test light is grounded at a different location than the circuit itself.

USES OF A 12-VOLT TEST LIGHT

A 12-volt test light can be used to check the following:

- **Electrical power.** If the test light lights, then there is power available. It will not, however, indicate the voltage level or if there is enough current available to operate an electrical load. It only indicates that there is enough voltage and current to light the test light (about 0.25A).

- **Grounds.** A test light can be used to check for grounds by attaching the clip of the test light to the positive terminal of the battery or any positive 12-volt electrical terminal. The tip of the test light can then be used to touch the ground wire. If there is a ground connection, the test light will light.

DIGITAL METERS

TERMINOLOGY

Digital multimeter (DMM) and **digital volt-ohm-meter (DVOM)** are terms commonly used to describe digital meters. ● **SEE FIGURE 22–4.**

The common abbreviations for the units that many meters can measure are often confusing. ● **SEE CHART 22–1** for the most commonly used symbols and their meanings.

MEASURING VOLTAGE

A voltmeter measures the *pressure* or potential of electricity in units of volts. A voltmeter is connected to a circuit in parallel. Voltage can be measured by selecting either AC or DC volts.

- **DC volts (DCV).** This setting is the most common for automotive use. Use this setting to measure battery voltage and voltage to all lighting and accessory circuits.

- **AC volts (ACV).** This setting is used to check some computer sensors and to check for unwanted AC voltage from alternators.

- **Range.** The range is automatically set for most meters but can be manually adjusted if needed. ● **SEE FIGURES 22–5 AND 22–6** on page 211.

MEASURING RESISTANCE

An ohmmeter measures the resistance in ohms of a component or circuit section when no current is flowing through the circuit. An ohmmeter contains a battery (or other power source) and is connected in series with the component or wire being measured. Note the following facts about using an ohmmeter.

- Zero ohms on the scale means that there is no resistance between the test leads, thus indicating continuity or a continuous path for the current to flow in a closed circuit.

- Infinity means no connection, as in an open circuit.

- Ohmmeters have no required polarity even though red and black test leads are used for resistance measurement.

FIGURE 22–4 Typical digital multimeter. The black meter lead is always placed in the COM terminal. The red meter test lead should be in the volt–ohm terminal except when measuring current in amperes.

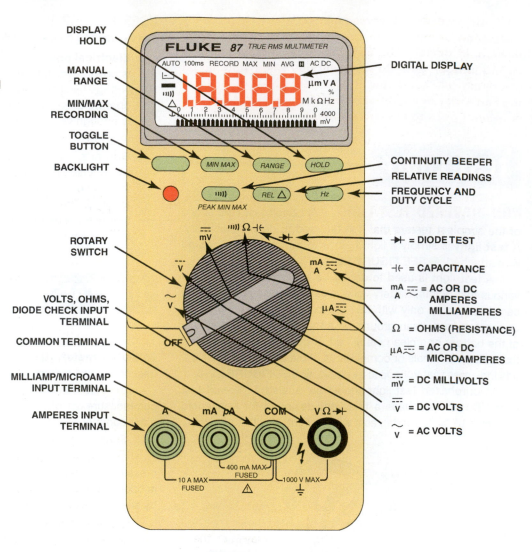

DISPLAY HOLD

MANUAL RANGE

MIN/MAX RECORDING

TOGGLE BUTTON

BACKLIGHT

DIGITAL DISPLAY

FLUKE 87 TRUE RMS MULTIMETER

AUTO 100ms RECORD MAX MIN AVG AC DC

μm V A %
M k Ω Hz
4000 mV

MIN MAX   RANGE   HOLD

CONTINUITY BEEPER
RELATIVE READINGS
FREQUENCY AND DUTY CYCLE

PEAK MIN MAX   REL △   Hz

ROTARY SWITCH

VOLTS, OHMS, DIODE CHECK INPUT TERMINAL

COMMON TERMINAL

MILLIAMP/MICROAMP INPUT TERMINAL

AMPERES INPUT TERMINAL

OFF

A   mA μA   COM   V Ω ➤⊦

10 A MAX FUSED

400 mA MAX FUSED

1000 V MAX

➤⊦ = DIODE TEST

⊣⊦ = CAPACITANCE

mA ⎓ = AC OR DC
A ∿   AMPERES
MILLIAMPERES

Ω = OHMS (RESISTANCE)

μA ⎓ = AC OR DC
MICROAMPERES

⎓ = DC MILLIVOLTS
mV

⎓ = DC VOLTS
V

∿ = AC VOLTS
V

SYMBOL	MEANING
AC	Alternating current or voltage
DC	Direct current or voltage
V	Volts
mV	Millivolts (1/1,000 volt)
A	Amperes (amps)
mA	Milliampers (1/1,000 amp)
%	Percentage (duty cycle)
Ω	Ohms
K Ω	Kilohm (1,000 ohms)
M Ω	Megohm (1,000,000 Ohm)
Hz	Hertz (frequency)
kHz	Kilohertz (1,000 cycles per second)
ms	Milliseconds

CHART 22–1

Common symbols and abbreviations used on digital meters.

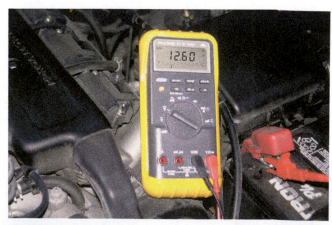

FIGURE 22–5 Typical digital multimeter (DMM) set to read DC volts.

CAUTION: The circuit must be electrically open with no voltage present when using an ohmmeter. If current is flowing when an ohmmeter is connected, the reading will be incorrect and the meter can be destroyed.

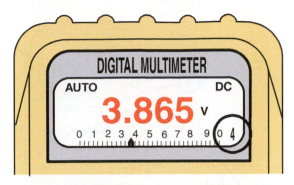

BECAUSE THE SIGNAL READING IS BELOW 4 VOLTS, THE METER AUTORANGES TO THE 4-VOLT SCALE. IN THE 4-VOLT SCALE, THIS METER PROVIDES THREE DECIMAL PLACES.

(a)

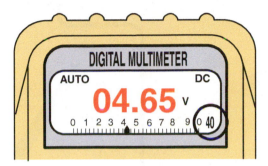

WHEN THE VOLTAGE EXCEEDED 4 VOLTS, THE METER AUTORANGES INTO THE 40-VOLT SCALE. THE DECIMAL POINT MOVES ONE PLACE TO THE RIGHT LEAVING ONLY TWO DECIMAL PLACES.

(b)

FIGURE 22–6 A typical auto-ranging digital multimeter automatically selects the proper scale to read the voltage being tested. The scale selected is usually displayed on the meter face. (a) Note that the display indicates "4," meaning that this range can read up to 4 volts. (b) The range is now set to the 40 volt scale, meaning that the meter can read up to 40 volts on the scale. Any reading above this level will cause the meter to reset to a higher scale. If not set on auto-ranging, the meter display would indicate OL if a reading exceeds the limit of the scale selected.

Different meters have different ways of indicating infinity resistance, or a reading higher than the scale allows. Examples of an over-limit display include:

- **OL, meaning over limit** or overload
- Flashing or solid number 1
- Flashing or solid number 3 on the left side of the display

Check the meter instructions for the exact display used to indicate an open circuit or over-range reading. ● **SEE FIGURES 22–7 AND 22–8.**

To summarize, open and zero readings are as follows:

0.00 Ω = Zero resistance (component or circuit has continuity)

OL = An open circuit (no current flows) or the reading is higher than the scale selected.

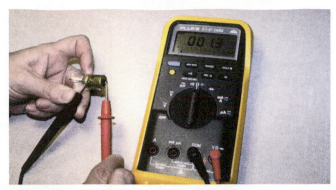

FIGURE 22–7 Using a digital multimeter set to read ohms (Ω) to test this light bulb. The meter reads the resistance of the filament.

MEASURING AMPERES An ammeter measures the flow of *current* through a complete circuit in units of amperes or milliamperes (1/1,000 of an ampere).

The ammeter has to be installed in the circuit (in series) so that it can measure all the current flow in that circuit, just as a water flow meter would measure the amount of water flow (cubic feet per minute, for example). ● **SEE FIGURE 22–9.**

TECH TIP

Fuse Your Meter Leads!

Most digital meters include an ammeter capability. When reading amperes, the leads of the meter must be changed from volts or ohms (V or Ω) to amperes (A), milliamperes (mA), or microamperes (μA). A common problem may then occur the next time voltage is measured. Although the technician may switch the selector to read volts, often the leads are not switched back to the volt or ohm position. Because the ammeter lead position results in zero ohms of resistance to current flow through the meter, the meter or the fuse inside the meter will be destroyed if the meter is connected to a battery. Many meter fuses are expensive and difficult to find. To avoid this problem, simply solder an inline 10 ampere blade-fuse holder into one meter lead. ● **SEE FIGURE 22–10.**

Do not think that this technique is for beginners only. Experienced technicians often get in a hurry and forget to switch the lead. A blade fuse is faster, easier, and less expensive to replace than a meter fuse or the meter itself. Also, if the soldering is done properly, the addition of an inline fuse holder and fuse does not increase the resistance of the meter leads. All meter leads have some resistance. If the meter is measuring very low resistance, touch the two leads together and read the resistance (usually no more than 0.2 ohm). Simply subtract the resistance of the leads from the resistance of the component being measured.

FIGURE 22–8 Many digital multimeters can have the display indicate zero to compensate for test lead resistance. (1) Connect leads in the V Ω and COM meter terminals. (2) Select the Ω scale. (3) Touch the two meter leads together. (4) Push the "zero" or "relative" button on the meter. (5) The meter display will now indicate zero ohms of resistance.

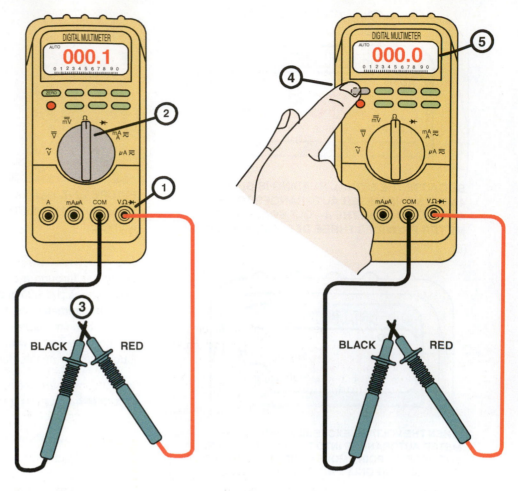

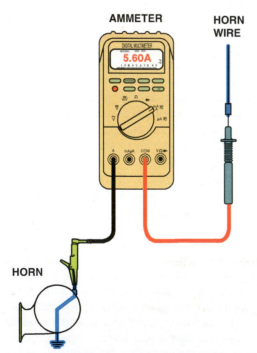

FIGURE 22–9 Measuring the current flow required by a horn requires that the ammeter be connected to the circuit in series and the horn button be depressed by an assistant.

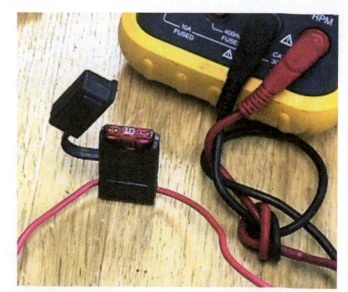

FIGURE 22–10 Note the blade-type fuse holder soldered in series with one of the meter leads. A 10 ampere fuse helps protect the internal meter fuse (if equipped) and the meter itself from damage that may result from excessive current flow if accidentally used incorrectly.

CAUTION: An ammeter must be installed in series with the circuit to measure the current flow in the circuit. If a meter set to read amperes is connected in parallel, such as across a battery, the meter or the leads may be destroyed, or the fuse will blow, by the current available across the battery. Some DMMs beep if the unit selection does not match the test lead connection on the meter. However, in a noisy shop, this beep sound may be inaudible.

Digital meters require that the meter leads be moved to the ammeter terminals. Most digital meters have an ampere scale that can accommodate a maximum of 10 amperes. See the Tech Tip "Fuse Your Meter Leads!"

INDUCTIVE AMMETERS

OPERATION   Inductive ammeters do not make physical contact with the circuit. Inductive ammeters have the advantage of being able to read much higher amperages than 10 amperes. A sensor is used to detect the strength of the magnetic field surrounding the wire carrying the current. The ammeter then uses the strength of the magnetic field to measure the electrical current. ● **SEE FIGURE 22–11.**

AC/DC CLAMP-ON DIGITAL MULTIMETERS   An **AC/DC clamp-on digital multimeter** is a useful meter for automotive diagnostic work. ● **SEE FIGURE 22–12.**

The major advantage of the clamp-on-type meter is that there is no need to break the circuit to measure current (amperes). Simply clamp the jaws of the meter around the power lead(s) or ground lead(s) of the component being measured and read the display. Most clamp-on meters can also measure alternating current, which is helpful in the diagnosis

FIGURE 22–11 An inductive ammeter clamp is used with all starting and charging testers to measure the current flow through the battery cables.

FIGURE 22–12 A typical mini clamp-on-type digital multimeter. This meter is capable of measuring alternating current (AC) and direct current (DC) without requiring that the circuit be disconnected to install the meter in series. The jaws are simply placed over the wire and current flow through the circuit is displayed.

of an alternator problem. Volts, ohms, frequency, and temperature can also be measured with the typical clamp-on DMM, but conventional meter leads should be used. The inductive clamp is used to measure only amperes.

TECH TIP

Over-Limit Display Does Not Mean the Meter Is Reading "Nothing"

The meaning of the over-limit display on a digital meter often confuses beginning technicians. When asked what the meter is reading when an over limit (OL) is displayed on the meter face, the response is often, "Nothing." Many meters indicate *over limit* or *over load*, which simply means that the reading is over the maximum that can be displayed for the selected range. For example, the meter will display OL if 12 volts are being measured but the meter has been set to read a maximum of 4 volts. Auto-ranging meters adjust the range to match what is being measured. Here OL means a value higher than the meter can read (unlikely on the voltage scale for automobile usage), or infinity when measuring resistance (ohms). Therefore, OL means infinity when measuring resistance or an open circuit is being indicated. The meter will read 00.0 if the resistance is zero, so "nothing" in this case indicates continuity (zero resistance), whereas OL indicates infinity resistance. Therefore, when talking with another technician about a meter reading, make sure you know exactly what the reading on the face of the meter means. Also be sure that you are connecting the meter leads correctly. ● **SEE FIGURE 22–13.**

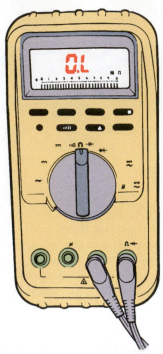

FIGURE 22–13 Typical digital multimeter showing OL (over limit) on the readout with the ohms (Ω) unit selected. This usually means that the unit being measured is open (infinity resistance) and has no continuity.

THINK OF MONEY Digital meter displays can often be confusing. The display for a battery measured as 12 1/2 volts would be 12.50 V, just as $12.50 is 12 dollars and 50 cents. A 1/2 volt reading on a digital meter will be displayed as 0.50 V, just as $0.50 is half of a dollar. It is more confusing when low values are displayed. For example, if a voltage reading is 0.063 volt, an auto-ranging meter will display 63 millivolts (63 mV), or 63/1,000 of a volt, or $63 of $1,000. (It takes 1,000 mV to equal 1 volt.) Think of millivolts as one-tenth of a cent, with 1 volt being $1.00. Therefore, 630 millivolts are equal to $0.63 of $1.00 (630 tenths of a cent, or 63 cents). To avoid confusion, try to manually range the meter to read base units (whole volts). If the meter is ranged to base unit volts, 63 millivolts would be displayed as 0.063 or maybe just 0.06, depending on the display capabilities of the meter.

HOW TO READ DIGITAL METERS

STEPS TO FOLLOW Getting to know and use a digital meter takes time and practice. The first step is to read, understand, and follow all safety and operational instructions that come with the meter. Use of the meter usually involves the following steps.

STEP 1 **Select the proper unit of electricity for what is being measured.** This unit could be volts, ohms (resistance), or amperes (amount of current flow). If the meter is not auto-ranging, select the proper scale for the anticipated reading. For example, if a 12-volt battery is being measured, select a meter reading range that is higher than the voltage but not too high. A 20- or 30 volt range will accurately show the voltage of a 12-volt battery. If a 1,000-volt scale is selected, a 12-volt reading may not be accurate.

STEP 2 **Place the meter leads into the proper input terminals.**

- The black lead is inserted into the common (COM) terminal. This meter lead usually stays in this location for all meter functions.
- The red lead is inserted into the volt, ohm, or diode check terminal usually labeled "VΩ" when voltage, resistance, or diodes are being measured.
- When current flow in amperes is being measured, most digital meters require that the red test lead be inserted in the ammeter terminal, usually labeled "A" or "mA."

CAUTION: If the meter leads are inserted into ammeter terminals, even though the selector is set to volts, the meter may be damaged or an internal fuse may blow if the test leads touch both terminals of a battery.

STEP 3 **Measure the component being tested.** Carefully note the decimal point and the unit on the face of the meter.

- **Meter lead connections.** If the meter leads are connected to a battery backward (red to the battery negative, for example), the display will still show the correct reading, but a negative sign (−) will be displayed in front of the number. The correct polarity is not important when measuring resistance (ohms) except where indicated, such as measuring a diode.
- **Auto-range.** Many meters automatically default to the auto-range position and the meter will display the value in the most readable scale. The meter can be manually ranged to select other levels or to lock in a scale for a value that is constantly changing. If a 12-volt battery is measured with an auto-ranging meter, the correct reading of 12.0 is given. "AUTO" and "V" should show on the face of the meter. For example, if a meter is manually set to the 2-kΩ (kilohm) scale, the highest that the meter will read is 2,000 ohms. If the reading is over 2,000 ohms, the meter will display OL. ● **SEE CHART 22–2.**

STEP 4 **Interpret the reading.** This is especially difficult on auto-ranging meters, where the meter itself selects the proper scale. The following are two examples of different readings.

Example 1: A voltage drop is being measured. The specifications indicate a maximum voltage drop of 0.2 volt. The meter reads "AUTO" and "43.6 mV." This reading means that the voltage drop is 0.0436 volt, or 43.6 mV, which is far lower than the 0.2 volt (200 millivolts). Because the number showing on the

	VOLTAGE BEING MEASURED					
	0.01 V (10 mV)	0.150 V (150 mV)	1.5 V	10.0 V	12.0 V	120 V
Scale Selected	Voltmeter will display:					
200 mV	10.0	150.0	OL	OL	OL	OL
2 V	0.100	0.150	1.500	OL	OL	OL
20 V	0.1	1.50	1.50	10.00	12.00	OL
200 V	00.0	01.5	01.5	10.0	12.0	120.0
2 kV	00.00	00.00	000.1	00.10	00.12	0.120
Auto-range	10.0 mV	15.0 mV	1.50	10.0	12.0	120.0
	RESISTANCE BEING MEASURED					
	10 ohms	100 ohms	470 ohms	1 kΩ	220 kΩ	1 MΩ
Scale Selected	Ohmmeter will display:					
400 ohms	10.0	100.0	OL	OL	OL	OL
4 kilohms	010	100	0.470 k	1000	OL	OL
40 kilohms	00.0	0.10 k	0.47 k	1.00 k	OL	OL
400 kilohms	000.0	00.1 k	00.5 k	0.10 k	220.0 k	OL
4 megohms	00.00	0.01 M	0.05 M	00.1 M	0.22 M	1.0 M
Auto-range	10.0	100.0	470.0	1.00 k	220 k	1.00 M
	CURRENT BEING MEASURED					
	50 mA	150 mA	1.0 A	7.5 A	15.0 A	25.0 A
Scale Selected	Ammeter will display:					
40 mA	OL	OL	OL	OL	OL	OL
400 mA	50.0	150	OL	OL	OL	OL
4 A	0.05	0.00	1.00	OL	OL	OL
40 A	0.00	0.000	01.0	7.5	15.0	25.0
Auto-range	50.0 mA	150.0 mA	1.00	7.5	15.0	25.0

CHART 22–2

Sample meter readings using manually set and auto-ranging selection on the digital meter control.

meter face is much larger than the specifications, many beginner technicians are led to believe that the voltage drop is excessive.

NOTE: Pay attention to the units displayed on the meter face and convert to whole units.

Example 2: A spark plug wire is being measured. The reading should be less than 10,000 ohms for each foot in length if the wire is okay. The wire being tested is 3-ft long (maximum allowable resistance is 30,000 ohms). The meter reads "AUTO" and "14.85 kΩ." This reading is equivalent to 14,850 ohms.

NOTE: When converting from kilohms to ohms, make the decimal point a comma.

Because this reading is well below the specified maximum allowable, the spark plug wire is okay.

PURCHASE A DIGITAL METER THAT WILL WORK FOR AUTOMOTIVE USE

Try to purchase a digital meter that is capable of reading the following:

- DC volts
- AC volts
- DC amperes (up to 10 A or more is helpful)
- Ohms (Ω) up to 40 MΩ (40 million ohms)
- Diode check

Additional features for advanced automotive diagnosis include:

- Frequency (hertz, abbreviated Hz)
- Temperature probe (°F and/or °C)
- Pulse width (millisecond, abbreviated ms)
- Duty cycle (%)

1. *Digital multimeter* (DMM) and *digital volt-ohm-milliammeter* (DVOM) are terms commonly used for electronic high impedance test meters.
2. Ammeters measure current and must be connected in series in the circuit.
3. Voltmeters measure voltage and are connected in parallel.
4. Ohmmeters measure resistance of a component and must be connected in series, with the circuit or component disconnected from power.

REVIEW QUESTIONS

1. How is a test light able to detect electricity?
2. How is an ammeter connected to an electrical circuit?
3. Why must an ohmmeter be connected to a disconnected circuit or component?

CHAPTER QUIZ

1. Inductive ammeters work because of what principle?
   a. Magic
   b. Electrostatic electricity
   c. A magnetic field surrounds any wire carrying a current
   d. Voltage drop as it flows through a conductor

2. A meter used to measure amperes is called a(n) _____.
   a. Amp meter
   b. Ampmeter
   c. Ammeter
   d. Coulomb meter

3. A voltmeter should be connected to the circuit being tested _____.
   a. In series
   b. In parallel
   c. Only when no power is flowing
   d. Both a and c

4. An ohmmeter should be connected to the circuit or component being tested _____.
   a. With current flowing in the circuit or through the component
   b. When connected to the battery of the vehicle to power the meter
   c. Only when no power is flowing (electrically open circuit)
   d. Both b and c

5. A meter set to read ohms and connected to light bulb terminals reads OL. This reading means that the bulb is _____.
   a. Bad
   b. Is reading what it should (good)
   c. Bulb filament is electrically open
   d. Both a and c

6. A meter is set to read DC volts on the 4-volt scale. The meter leads are connected at a 12-volt battery. The display will read _____.
   a. 0.00
   b. OL
   c. 12 V
   d. 0.012 V

7. What could happen if the meter leads were connected to the positive and negative terminals of the battery while the meter and leads were set to read amperes?
   a. Could blow an internal fuse or damage the meter
   b. Would read volts instead of amperes
   c. Would display OL
   d. Would display 0.00

8. The highest amount of resistance that can be read by a meter set to the 2-kΩ scale is _____.
   a. 2,000 ohms
   b. 200 ohms
   c. 200 kΩ (200,000 ohms)
   d. 20,000,000 ohms

9. If a digital meter face shows 0.93 when set to read kΩ, the reading means _____.
   a. 93 ohms
   b. 930 ohms
   c. 9,300 ohms
   d. 93,000 ohms

10. A reading of 432 shows on the face of the meter set to the millivolt scale. The reading means _____.
    a. 0.432 volt
    b. 4.32 volts
    c. 43.2 volts
    d. 4,320 volts

STARTING AND CHARGING SYSTEMS

OBJECTIVES: **After studying Chapter 23, the reader should be able to:** • Prepare for ASE Engine Performance (A8) certification test content area "F" (Engine Electrical Systems Diagnosis and Repair). Discuss methods that can be used to check the condition of a battery. • Discuss battery rating system. • Conduct a battery state-of-charge (SOC) test. • Conduct a battery load test. • Perform a charging voltage test. • Perform a battery conductance test. • Describe starting circuit components. • Perform routine battery service procedures. • Describe how to properly charge a battery. • Describe how to safely jump-start a vehicle. • Explain how to test the alternator.

KEY TERMS: • Alternator 217 • Ampere-hour 218 • Battery 217 • CA 217 • Capacity test 220 • CCA 217 • Charging circuit 222 • Conductance tester 220 • Cranking circuit 221 • DE 222 • Load test 220 • Marine cranking amperes (MCA) 218 • Neutral safety switch 222 • Open-circuit battery voltage test 219 • Reserve capacity 218 • SRE 222 • State of charge 219

BATTERIES

PURPOSE AND FUNCTION

The primary purpose of an automotive **battery** is to provide a source of electrical power for starting the vehicle and to meet electrical demands that exceed alternator output.

Just as in the old saying "If Mother isn't happy—no one is happy," the battery, the starter, and the charging system have to function correctly for the engine performance to be satisfactory.

The battery also acts as a voltage stabilizer for the entire electrical system. The battery is a voltage stabilizer because it acts as a reservoir where large amounts of current (amperes) can be removed quickly during starting and replaced gradually by the **alternator** during charging. The battery *must* be in good (serviceable) condition before the charging system and the cranking system can be tested. For example, if a battery is discharged, the **cranking circuit** (starter motor) could test as being defective because the battery voltage might drop below specifications.

The **charging circuit** could also test as being defective because of a weak or discharged battery. It is important to test the vehicle battery before further testing of the cranking or charging system.

BATTERY RATINGS

Batteries are rated according to the amount of current they can produce under specific conditions.

■ **Cold-Cranking Amperes** The cold-cranking power of a battery is the number of amperes that can be supplied at 0°F (−18°C) for 30 seconds while the battery still maintains a voltage of 1.2 volts per cell or higher. The cold-cranking performance rating is called **cold-cranking amperes (CCA).** ● SEE FIGURE 23–1.

■ **Cranking Amperes** Cranking amperes (CA) are not the same as CCA, but are often advertised and labeled on batteries. The designation "CA" refers to the number of amperes that can be supplied by the battery at 32°F (0°C).

FIGURE 23–1 The cold-cranking amperes (CCA) is the rating that is most commonly used to rate batteries.

This rating results in a higher number than the more stringent rating of CCA.

- **Marine Cranking Amperes** Marine cranking amperes **(MCA)** rating is similar to the CA rating and is tested at 32°F (0°C).

- **Ampere-Hour Rating** The **ampere-hour (Ah)** is how many amperes can be discharged from the battery over a 20-hour period before the battery voltage drops to 10.5 volts. A battery that is able to supply 3.75 amperes for 20 hours has a rating of 75 ampere hours ($3.75 \times 20 = 75$).

- **Reserve Capacity** The **reserve capacity (RC)** rating for batteries is *the number of minutes* for which the battery can produce 25 amperes and still have a battery voltage of 1.75 volts per cell (10.5 volts for a 12 volt battery). This rating is actually a measurement of the time for which a vehicle can be driven in the event of a charging system failure.

? FREQUENTLY ASKED QUESTION

Should Batteries Be Kept Off of Concrete Floors?

All batteries should be stored in a cool, dry place when not in use. Many technicians have been warned not to store or place a battery on concrete. According to battery experts, it is the temperature difference between the top and the bottom of the battery that causes a difference in the voltage potential between the top (warmer section) and the bottom (colder section). It is this difference in temperature that causes self-discharge to occur. In fact, submarines cycle seawater around their batteries to keep all sections of the battery at the same temperature to help prevent self-discharge. Therefore, always store or place batteries up off the floor and in a location where the entire battery can be kept at the same temperature, avoiding extreme heat and freezing temperatures. Concrete cannot drain the battery directly, because the case of the battery is a very good electrical insulator.

BATTERY SERVICE

SAFETY   Batteries contain acid and release explosive gases (hydrogen and oxygen) during normal charging and discharging cycles. To help prevent physical injury or damage to the vehicle, always adhere to the following safety procedures.

1. Whenever working on any electrical component of a vehicle, disconnect the negative battery cable from the battery. When the negative cable is disconnected, all electrical circuits in the vehicle will be open, which will prevent accidental electrical contact between an electrical component and ground. Any electrical spark has the potential to cause an explosion and personal injury.

2. Wear eye protection whenever working around any battery.

3. Wear protective clothing to avoid skin contact with battery acid.

SYMPTOMS OF A BAD BATTERY   There are several warning signs that may indicate that a battery is near the end of its useful life, including:

- **Excessive corrosion on battery cables or connections.** Corrosion is more likely to occur if the battery is sulfated, creating hot spots on the plates. When the battery is being charged, the acid fumes are forced out of the vent holes and get onto the battery cables, connections, and even on the tray underneath the battery.

- **Slower-than-normal engine cranking.** When the capacity of the battery is reduced due to damage or age, it is less likely to supply the necessary current for starting the engine, especially during cold weather.

VISUAL INSPECTION   The battery, battery tray, hold-down assembly, and battery cables should be included in the list of items checked during a thorough visual inspection. Check the battery cables for corrosion and tightness. ● **SEE FIGURE 23–2.**

NOTE: On side-post batteries, grasp the battery cable near the battery and tighten the cable in a clockwise direction in an attempt to tighten the battery connection.

If possible, remove the covers and observe the level of the electrolyte. ● **SEE FIGURE 23–3.**

ROUTINE BATTERY SERVICE   Check and service the following items as necessary.

1. Neutralize and clean any corrosion from the battery terminals with a solution of baking soda and water.

2. Conduct a careful visual inspection of the battery cables.

FIGURE 23–2 Corrosion on a battery cable could be an indication that the battery itself is either being overcharged or is sulfated, creating a lot of gassing of the electrolyte.

FIGURE 23–3 A visual inspection on this battery shows the electrolyte level was below the plates in all cells.

3. Check that the hold-down brackets or assembly and battery tray are secure and corrosion-free.

4. Check the tightness and cleanliness of all ground connections.

BATTERY VOLTAGE TEST Testing the battery voltage with a voltmeter is a simple method for determining the **state of charge (SOC)** of any battery. ● SEE FIGURE 23–4.

The voltage of a battery does not necessarily indicate whether the battery can perform satisfactorily, but it does indicate to the technician more about the battery's condition than a simple visual inspection. A battery that *looks* good may not be good. A commonly used test to determine the SOC is called an **open-circuit battery voltage test.** It is called an open circuit test because it is conducted with an open circuit—with no current flowing and no load applied to the battery.

1. Set the digital voltmeter to read DC volts. Connect a voltmeter to the positive (+) and negative (−) terminals of the battery.

2. If the battery has just been charged or the vehicle has recently been driven, it is necessary to remove the surface charge from the battery before testing. A surface charge is a charge of higher-than-normal voltage that is only on the surface of the battery plates. The surface charge is quickly removed whenever the battery is loaded and, therefore, does not accurately represent the true state of charge of the battery.

3. To remove the surface charge, turn the headlights on high beam (bright) for one minute, then turn the headlights off and wait two minutes.

4. Read the voltmeter and compare the results with the following state-of-charge chart. The voltages shown are for a battery at or near room temperature (70°F to 80°F, or 21°C to 27°C). ● SEE CHART 23–1.

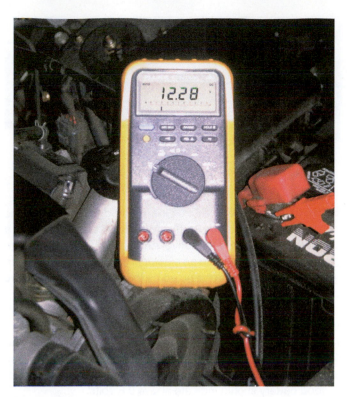

(a)

(b)

FIGURE 23–4 (a) A voltage reading of 12.28 volts indicates that the battery is not fully charged and should be charged before testing. (b) A battery that measures 12.6 volts or higher after the surface charge has been removed is 100% charged.

BATTERY VOLTAGE (V)	STATE OF CHARGE (%)
12.6	100
12.4	75
12.2	50
12.0	25

CHART 23–1

Battery voltage can indicate the state of charge (SOC) of a battery after the surface charge has been removed.

BATTERY LOAD TEST

One method to determine the condition of any battery is the **load test,** also known as a **capacity test.** Most automotive starting and charging testers use a carbon pile to create an electrical load on the battery. The amount of the load is determined by the original capacity of the battery being tested. The capacity is measured in CCA.

The proper electrical load to be used to test a battery is one-half of the CCA rating or three times the ampere-hour rating, with a minimum of a 150-ampere load. Apply the load for a full 15 seconds and observe the voltmeter at the end of the 15-second period while the battery is still under load. A good battery should indicate above 9.6 volts.

NOTE: This test is sometimes called the one-minute test, because many battery manufacturers recommend performing the load test twice, using the first load period (15 seconds) to remove the surface charge on the battery, then waiting for 30 seconds to allow time for the battery to recover, and then loading the battery again for 15 seconds. Total time required is 60 seconds (15 + 30 + 15 = 60 seconds or 1 minute). This method provides a true indication of the condition of the battery. ● SEE FIGURE 23–5.

If the battery fails the load test, recharge the battery and retest. If the battery fails the load test again, replace the battery.

BATTERY CONDUCTANCE TESTING

General Motors Corporation, Chrysler Corporation, Ford, and other vehicle manufacturers specify that a **conductance tester** be used to test batteries in vehicles still under factory warranty. The tester uses its internal electronic circuitry to determine the state of charge and capacity of the battery by measuring the voltage and conductance of the plates. A huge advantage of a conductance tester is that it can test a battery regardless of its state of charge whereas a "Load Tester," must have the battery at least 75% charged. Conductance testers will give a stated readout of how many CCAs the battery is capable of producing.● SEE FIGURE 23–6.

Connect the unit to the positive and negative terminals of the battery, and after entering the CCA rating (if known), push the arrow keys. The tester determines one of the following:

- **Good battery.** The battery can return to service.
- **Charge and retest.** Fully recharge the battery and return it to service.
- **Replace the battery.** The battery is not serviceable and should be replaced.
- **Bad cell—replace.** The battery is not serviceable and should be replaced.

CAUTION: Test results can be incorrectly reported on the display if proper, clean connections to the battery are not made. Also, be sure that all accessories and the ignition switch are in the off position. Inaccurate readings will occur if the tester is attached to the steel-side terminal battery bolts. Only lead connections must be used. The tester comes with lead-side terminal battery adapters, which must be used.

FIGURE 23–5 An alternator regulator battery starter tester (ARBST) automatically loads the battery with a fixed load for 15 seconds to remove the surface charge, then removes the load for 30 seconds to allow the battery to recover, and then reapplies the load for another 15 seconds. The results of the test are then displayed.

FIGURE 23–6 A conductance tester is very easy to use and has proved to accurately determine battery condition if the connections are properly made. Follow the instructions on the display exactly for best results.

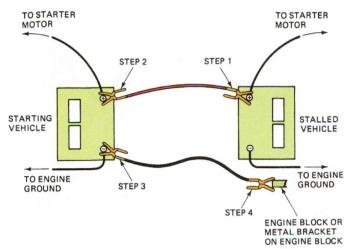

FIGURE 23–7 Jumper cable usage guide. Note that the last connection should be the engine block of the disabled vehicle to help prevent the spark that normally occurs from igniting the gases from the battery.

JUMP STARTING   To safely jump-start a vehicle without doing any harm, use the following procedure.

STEP 1   Be certain the ignition switch is off on both vehicles.

STEP 2   Connect good-quality copper jumper cables as indicated in ● **FIGURE 23–7.**

STEP 3   Start the vehicle with the good battery and allow it to run for 5 to 10 minutes. This allows the alternator of the good vehicle to charge the battery on the disabled vehicle.

STEP 4   Start the disabled vehicle and, after the engine is operating smoothly, disconnect the jumper cables in the reverse order of step 2.

NOTE: To help prevent accidental touching of the jumper cables, simply separate them into two cables and attach using wire (cable) ties or tape so that the clamps are offset from each other, making it impossible for them to touch.

BATTERY CHARGING   If the **state of charge** of a battery is low, it must be recharged. It is best to slow-charge any battery to prevent possible overheating damage to the battery. Remember, it may take eight hours or more to charge a fully discharged battery. The initial charge rate should be about 35 amperes for 30 minutes to help start the charging process. Fast-charging a battery increases the temperature of the battery and can cause warping of the plates inside the battery. Fast-charging also increases the amount of gassing (release of hydrogen and oxygen), which can create a health and fire hazard. The battery temperature should not exceed 125°F (hot to the touch). Most batteries should be charged at a rate equal to 1% of the battery's CCA rating. ● **SEE FIGURE 23–8.**

- Fast charge: 15 amperes maximum
- Slow charge: 5 amperes maximum

FIGURE 23–8 A typical industrial battery charger. Be sure that the ignition switch is in the off position before connecting any battery charger. Connect the cables of the charger to the battery before plugging the charger into the outlet. This helps prevent a voltage spike and spark that could occur if the charger happened to be accidentally left on. Always follow the battery charger manufacturer's instructions.

CRANKING CIRCUIT

PARTS INVOLVED   The cranking circuit includes the mechanical and electrical components required to crank the engine for starting. The cranking force in the early 1900s was the driver's arm. Cranking circuits include the following:

1. **Starter motor.** The starter is normally a 0.5 to 2.6 hp (0.4 to 2 kilowatts) electric motor that can develop nearly 8 hp (6 kilowatts) for a very short time when first cranking a cold engine. ● **SEE FIGURE 23–9.**

2. **Battery.** The battery must be of the correct capacity and be at least 75% charged to provide the necessary current and voltage for correct operation of the starter.

3. **Starter solenoid or relay.** The high current required by the starter must be able to be turned on and off. A large switch would be required if the current were controlled by the driver directly. Instead, a small current switch (ignition switch) operates a solenoid or relay that controls the high starter current.

FIGURE 23–9 A typical solenoid-operated starter.

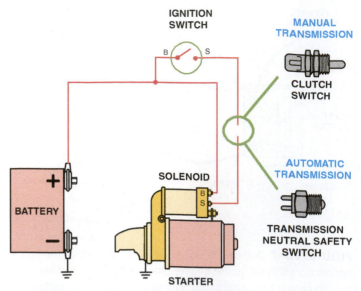

FIGURE 23–10 To prevent the engine from cranking, an electrical switch is usually installed to open the circuit between the ignition switch and the starter solenoid.

4. **Starter drive.** The starter drive uses a small gear that contacts the engine flywheel gear and transmits starter motor power to rotate the engine.

5. **Ignition switch.** The ignition switch and safety control switches control the starter motor operation.

The engine is cranked by an electric motor that is controlled by a key-operated ignition switch or the PCM on vehicles equipped with electronic starting. The ignition switch will not operate the starter unless the automatic transmission is in neutral or park or if the clutch pedal is not depressed on most vehicles equipped with a manual transmission. This is to prevent an accident that might result from the vehicle moving forward or backward when the engine is started. Many automobile manufacturers use a **neutral safety switch** or a **clutch switch** that opens the circuit between the ignition switch and the starter to prevent starter motor operation unless the gear selector is in neutral or park. The safety switch can be attached either to the steering column inside the vehicle near the floor or to the side of the transmission/transaxle. According to vehicle manufacturing engineers, starters can be expected to start an engine 25,000 times during the normal life of the vehicle. ● SEE FIGURE 23–10.

VISUAL INSPECTION For proper operation, all starters require that a known good battery is used and that both power-side and ground-side battery cables are clean and tight. ● SEE FIGURE 23–11.

- Check to see if the starter motor heat shield (if equipped) is in place.
- Check for any non-stock add-on accessories or equipment that may drain the battery, such as a cell phone charger.
- Crank the engine. It should crank and start normally. If the starter motor acts as if it is turning slower than normal, then additional tests may need to be performed to determine the root cause.

FIGURE 23–11 All battery cables and connections have to be clean and tight for the starter to be able to operate correctly.

CHARGING CIRCUIT

ALTERNATOR CONSTRUCTION An alternator is constructed of a two piece cast-aluminum housing. Aluminum is used because of its light weight, nonmagnetic properties, and heat transfer properties that are needed to help keep the alternator cool. A front ball bearing is pressed into the front housing (called the **drive-end [DE]** housing) to provide the support and friction reduction necessary for the belt-driven rotor assembly. The rear housing (called the **slip-ring-end [SRE]**) usually contains a bearing support for the rotor and mounting for the brushes, diodes, and internal voltage regulator (if the alternator is so equipped). ● SEE FIGURE 23–12.

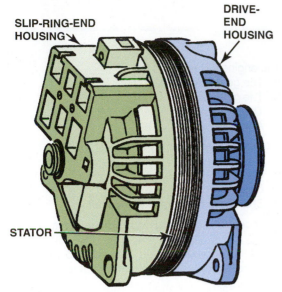

SLIP-RING-END
HOUSING

DRIVE-
END
HOUSING

STATOR

FIGURE 23–12 The end frame toward the drive belt is called the drive-end housing and the rear section is called the slip-ring-end housing.

CHARGING SYSTEM VOLTMETER TEST

- **Digital Multimeter Connections.** The charge indicator light on the dash should be on with the key on, engine off (KOEO), but should be off when the engine is running (KOER). If the charge light remains on with the engine running, check the charging system voltage. To measure charging system voltage, set the digital multimeter to read DC volts. Connect the test leads of a digital multimeter to the positive (+) and negative (−) terminals of the battery.

- **Charging System Voltage Specifications.** Most alternators are designed to supply between 13.5 and 15 volts at 2,000 engine RPM. Be sure to check the vehicle manufacturer's specifications.

- **Charging System Voltage Test Procedure.** Charging system voltage tests should be performed on a vehicle with a battery at least 75% charged. If the battery is discharged (or defective), the charging voltage may be below specifications. To measure charging system voltage, follow these steps.

1. Set the meter to read DC volts.
2. Connect the voltmeter to the positive and negative terminals of the battery.
3. Start the engine and raise to a fast idle (about 2,000 RPM).
4. Observe the voltmeter (a good reading should be between 13.5 and 15.0 volts). ● SEE FIGURE 23–13.

FIGURE 23–13 The digital multimeter should be set to read DC volts, with the red lead connected to the positive (+) battery terminal and the black meter lead connected to the negative (−) battery terminal.

SUMMARY

1. Batteries can be tested with a voltmeter to determine its state of charge. A battery load test loads the battery to one-half of its CCA rating. A good battery should be able to maintain above 9.6 volts for the entire 15-second test period.

2. Proper operation of the starter motor depends on the battery being at least 75% charged.

3. An open in the control circuit can prevent starter motor operation.

4. Charging system testing requires that the battery be at least 75% charged to be assured of accurate test results. The charge indicator light should be on with the ignition switch on, but should go out whenever the engine is running. Normal charging voltage (at 2,000 engine RPM) is 13.5 to 15 volts.

REVIEW QUESTIONS

1. What are the results of a voltmeter battery state-of-charge (SOC) test?

2. What are the steps for performing a battery load test?

3. How do you set the digital multimeter to read charging voltage?

1. Which battery rating is used mostly when testing a battery to see if it is performing normally?
   a. CA
   b. CCA
   c. MCA
   d. Reserve capacity

2. A battery high-rate discharge (load capacity) test is being performed on a 12-volt battery. Technician A says that a good battery should have a voltage reading higher than 9.6 volts while under load at the end of the 15-second test. Technician B says that the battery should be discharged (loaded to two times its CCA rating). Which technician is correct?
   a. Technician A only
   b. Technician B only
   c. Both technicians A and B
   d. Neither technician A nor B

3. When jump starting, _____.
   a. The last connection should be the positive post of the dead battery
   b. The last connection should be the engine block of the dead vehicle
   c. The alternator must be disconnected on both vehicles
   d. Both a and c

4. Starters rotate the engine by a _____.
   a. Drive belt
   b. Gear
   c. Chain
   d. Shaft from the engine crankshaft

5. The engine will not start if _____.
   a. The gear selector is in "D"
   b. The gear selector is in "R"
   c. The gear selector is in "L"
   d. Any of the above

6. Alternators are driven by a _____.
   a. Drive belt
   b. Gear
   c. Chain
   d. Shaft from the engine crankshaft

7. An acceptable charging circuit voltage on a 12-volt system is _____.
   a. 13.5 to 15 volts
   b. 12.6 to 15.6 volts
   c. 12 to 14 volts
   d. 14.9 to 16.1 volts

8. When measuring battery voltage, set the meter to read _____.
   a. DC volts
   b. AC volts
   c. Hertz (Hz)
   d. Amperes (A)

9. A type of electronic battery testing that does *not* place a load on the battery is called _____.
   a. VAT test
   b. Conductance tester
   c. Load tester
   d. Ammeter tester

10. A battery should be charged at what rate?
    a. High or fast depending on the capacity of the charger
    b. At a rate of 1% of the CCA rating of the battery
    c. At a rate that does not cause the battery to get hotter than 125°
    d. Both b and c are correct

chapter 24

DASH WARNING LIGHTS AND DRIVER INFORMATION SYSTEMS

OBJECTIVES: After studying Chapter 24, the reader will be able to: • Prepare for ASE Electrical/Electronic Systems (A6) certification test content area "F" (Gauges, Warning Devices, and Driver Information System Diagnosis and Repair). • Be able to identify the meaning of dash warning symbols. • Describe how a navigation system can display the location of the vehicle. • List the various types of dash instrument displays. • Describe how night vision, backup camera and warning systems, lane departure systems, network communications, and OnStar systems can make driving safer and easier.

KEY TERMS: • Backup camera 235 • GPS 233 • HUD 230 • IP 229 • LDWS 236 • PM generator 231 • RPA 235 • WOW display 229

DASH WARNING SYMBOLS

PURPOSE AND FUNCTION All vehicles are equipped with warning lights that are often confusing to drivers. Because many vehicles are sold throughout the world, symbols instead of words are being used as warning lights. The dash warning lights are often called *telltale* lights as they are used to notify the driver of a situation or fault.

BULB TEST When the ignition is first turned on, all of the warning lights come on as part of a self-test and to help the driver or technician spot any warning light that may be burned out. Technicians or drivers who are familiar with what indicator bulbs should light may be able to determine if one or more warning lights are not on when the ignition is first turned on. Most factory scan tools can be used to command all of the warning lights on to help determine if one is not working.

ENGINE FAULT WARNING Engine fault warning lights include the following:

- **Engine coolant temperature.** This warning lamp should come on when the ignition is first turned on as a bulb check and then if the coolant temperature reaches 248°F to 258°F (120°C to 126°C), depending on the make and model of the vehicle. ● SEE FIGURE 24–1.

If the engine coolant temperature warning lamp is on:

1. Turn on the heater.
2. If the hot light remains on, drive to a safe location and shut off the engine and allow it to cool to help avoid serious engine damage.

CAUTION: Do not open the radiator cap when the engine is hot as this can cause the coolant to boil rapidly, which can cause the coolant to escape and cause serious personal injury.

- **Engine oil pressure.** The oil pressure warning lamp should light when the ignition is first turned on as a bulb check. This indicator light operates through an oil pressure sensor unit, which is threaded into an oil passage in the engine block. The sensor grounds the electrical circuit and lights up the dash warning lamp in the event of low oil pressure, about 3 to 7 PSI (20 to 50 kilopascals [kPa]). Normal oil pressure is generally 10 PSI per 1,000 RPM or between 10 and 60 PSI (70 and 400 kPa). If the engine oil pressure light comes on while driving, perform the following steps:

1. Pull off the road as soon as possible.
2. Shut off the engine.
3. Check the oil level.
4. Do not drive the vehicle with the engine oil light on or severe engine damage can occur. ● SEE FIGURE 24–2.

- **Water in diesel fuel warning.** On vehicles equipped with a diesel engine, this warning lamp will turn on when the ignition is first turned on as a bulb check and when water

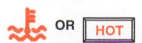 OR

FIGURE 24–1 Engine coolant temperature is too high.

 OR OIL

FIGURE 24–2 Engine oil pressure is too low.

is detected in the diesel fuel. If the *"water in diesel fuel"* warning lamp comes on, do the following:

1. Remove the water using the built-in drain, usually made as part of the fuel filter.
2. Check service information for the exact procedure to follow.

● **SEE FIGURE 24–3.**

- **Maintenance required warning.** The maintenance required lamp comes on when the ignition is first turned on as a bulb check and if the vehicle requires service. The services required could include:

1. Oil and oil filter change
2. Tire rotation
3. Inspection

Check service information for the exact service required.
● **SEE FIGURE 24–4.**

- **Malfunction indicator lamp (MIL), also called a check engine or service engine soon (SES) light.** This amber warning lamp comes on when the ignition is first turned on as a bulb test and then only if a fault in the powertrain control module (PCM) has been detected. If the MIL comes on when driving, it is not necessary to stop the vehicle, but the cause for why the warning lamp came on should be determined as soon as possible to avoid harming the engine or engine control systems. The MIL will come on if any of the following is detected:

1. A sensor or actuator is electrically open or shorted.
2. A sensor is out of range from expected values.
3. An emission control system failure occurs, such as a loose gas cap. If the MIL is on, a diagnostic trouble code has been set. Use a scan tool to retrieve the code(s) and follow service information for the exact procedure to follow. ● **SEE FIGURE 24–5.**

FIGURE 24–3 Water detected in fuel. Note the draining of water from the fuel filter assembly on a vehicle equipped with a diesel engine.

FIGURE 24–4 Maintenance required. This usually means that the engine oil is scheduled to be changed or other routine service items need to be replaced or checked.

FIGURE 24–5 Malfunction indicator lamp (MIL), also called a check engine light. The light means the engine control computer has detected a fault.

ELECTRICAL SYSTEM–RELATED WARNING LIGHTS

- **Charging system fault.** This warning lamp will come on when the ignition is first turned on as a bulb check and if a fault in the charging system has been detected. The lamp could include a fault with any of the following:

1. Battery SOC, electrical connections, or the battery itself.
2. Alternator or related wiring.

● **SEE FIGURE 24–6.**

If the charge system warning lamp comes on, continue to drive until it is safe to pull over. The vehicle can usually be driven for several miles using battery power alone. Check the following by visual inspection:

1. Alternator drive belt.
2. Loose or corroded electrical connections at the battery.
3. Loose or corroded wiring to the alternator.
4. Defective alternator.

SAFETY-RELATED WARNING LAMPS
Safety-related warning lamps include the following:

- **Safety belt warning lamp.** The safety belt warning lamp will light and sound an alarm to notify the driver if the driver's side or passenger's side safety belt is not fastened. It is also used to indicate a fault in the safety belt circuit. Check service information for the exact procedure to follow if the safety belt warning light remains on even when the belts are fastened.
● **SEE FIGURE 24–7.**

- **Airbag warning lamp.** The airbag warning lamp comes on and flashes when the ignition is first turned on as part of a self-test of the system. If the airbag warning lamp remains on after the self-test, then the airbag controller has detected a fault. Check service information for the exact procedure to follow if the airbag warning lamp is on. ● **SEE FIGURE 24–8.**

FIGURE 24–6 Charging system fault detected.

FIGURE 24–7 Fasten safety belt warning light.

FIGURE 24–8 Fault detected in the supplemental restraint system.

NOTE: The passenger side airbag light may indicate that it is on or off, depending on whether there is a passenger or an object heavy enough to trigger the seat sensor. Many vehicles that do not have a rear seat for a child are equipped with a switch that can be used to disconnect the passenger side airbag if a child seat is going to be used in the front seat.

■ **Red brake fault warning light.** All vehicles are equipped with a red brake warning (RBW) lamp that comes on if a fault in the base (hydraulic) brake system is detected. Three types of sensors are used to turn the brake warning light on.

1. A brake fluid–level sensor located in the master cylinder brake fluid reservoir.

2. A pressure switch located in the pressure differential switch, which detects a difference in pressure between the front and rear or diagonal brake systems.

3. A switch located on the parking brake to indicate that the parking brake could be applied. ● **SEE FIGURE 24–9.**

If the red brake warning light comes on, do not drive the vehicle until the cause is determined and corrected.

■ **Brake light bulb failure.** Some vehicles are able to detect if a brake light is burned out. The warning lamp will warn the driver when this situation occurs. ● **SEE FIGURE 24–10.**

■ **Exterior light bulb failure.** Many vehicles use the body control module (BCM) to monitor current flow through all of the exterior lights and, therefore, can detect if a bulb is not working. ● **SEE FIGURE 24–11.**

■ **Worn brake pads.** Some vehicles are equipped with sensors built into the disc brake pads that are used to trigger a dash warning light. The warning light often comes on when the ignition is first turned on as a bulb check and then goes out. If the brake pad warning lamp is on, check service information for the exact service procedure to follow. ● **SEE FIGURE 24–12.**

 OR

FIGURE 24–9 Fault detected in base brake system.

FIGURE 24–10 Brake light bulb failure detected.

FIGURE 24–11 Exterior light bulb failure detected.

FIGURE 24–12 Worn brake pads or linings detected.

The Toyota Truck Story

The owner of a Toyota truck complained that several electrical problems plagued the truck, including the following:

1. The cruise (speed) control would kick out intermittently.

2. The red brake warning lamp would come on, especially during cold weather.

The owner had replaced the parking brake switch, thinking that was the cause of the red brake warning lamp coming on. An experienced technician checked the wiring diagram found in service information. Checking the warning lamp circuit, the technician noticed that the same wire went to the brake fluid–level sensor. The brake fluid was at the minimum level. Filling the master cylinder to the maximum level with clean brake fluid solved both problems. The electronics of the cruise control stopped operation when the red brake warning lamp was on as a safety measure.

■ **Antilock brake system (ABS) fault.** The amber antilock brake system warning light comes on if the ABS controller detects a fault in the antilock braking system. Examples of what could trigger the warning light include:

1. Defective wheel speed sensor

2. Low brake fluid level in the hydraulic control unit assembly

3. Electrical fault detected anywhere in the system. ● **SEE FIGURE 24–13.**

If the amber ABS warning lamp is on, it is safe to drive the vehicle, but the antilock portion of the brake system may not function.

■ **Low tire pressure warning.** A tire pressure monitoring system (TPMS) warns the driver if the inflation pressure of a tire has decreased by 25% (about 8 PSI). If the warning lamp or message of a low tire is displayed, check the tire pressures before driving. If the inflation pressure is low, repair or replace the tire. ● **SEE FIGURE 24–14.**

 OR OR

FIGURE 24–13 Fault detected in antilock brake system.

 OR OR

FIGURE 24–14 Low tire pressure detected.

Check the Spare

Some vehicles that are equipped with a full-size spare tire also have a sensor in the spare. If the low tire pressure warning lamp is on and all four tires are properly inflated, check the spare.

DRIVER INFORMATION SYSTEM
A driver information system can be a screen that displays many functions or can just be warning lights depending on the vehicle.

- **Door open or ajar warning light.** If a door is open or ajar, a warning light is used to notify the driver. Check and close all doors and tailgates before driving. ● SEE FIGURE 24–15.

- **Windshield washer fluid low.** A sensor in the windshield washer fluid reservoir is used to turn on the low washer fluid warning lamp. ● SEE FIGURE 24–16.

- **Low fuel warning.** A low fuel indicator light is used to warn the driver that the fuel level is low. In most vehicles, the light comes on when there is between 1 and 3 gallons (3.8 and 11 liters) of fuel remaining. ● SEE FIGURE 24–17.

- **Headlights on light.** This dash indicator lights whenever the headlights are on. ● SEE FIGURE 24–18.

  The high beam indicator is usually a separate light from the headlights on indicator.

NOTE: This light may or may not indicate that the headlights are on if the headlight switch is set to the automatic position.

- **Low traction detected.** On a vehicle equipped with a traction control system (TCS), a dash indicator light is flashed whenever the system is working to restore traction. If the low traction warning light is flashing, reduce the rate of acceleration to help the system restore traction of the drive wheels with the road surface. ● SEE FIGURE 24–19.

- **Electronic stability control.** If a vehicle is equipped with electronic stability control (ESC), also called vehicle stability control (VSC), the dash indicator lamp will flash if the system is trying to restore vehicle stability. ● SEE FIGURE 24–20.

- **Traction off.** If the TCS is turned off by the driver, an indicator lamp lights to help remind the driver that this system has been turned off and will not be able to restore traction when lost. The driver must push the button to turn the system off. The system reverts to on, when the ignition is turned off so it is always on unless the traction off button is depressed. ● SEE FIGURE 24–21.

- **Cruise indicator lamp.** Most vehicles are equipped with a switch that turns on the cruise control. The cruise (speed) control system does not work unless it has been turned on to help prevent accidental engagement. When the cruise control has been turned on, the cruise indicator light is on. ● SEE FIGURE 24–22.

FIGURE 24–15 Door open or ajar.

FIGURE 24–16 Windshield washer fluid low.

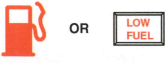

FIGURE 24–17 Low fuel level.

FIGURE 24–18 Headlights on.

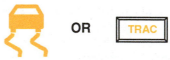

FIGURE 24–19 Low traction detected. Traction control system is functioning to restore traction (usually flashes when actively working to restore traction).

VSC

FIGURE 24–20 Vehicle stability control system either off or working if flashing.

TRAC
OFF

FIGURE 24–21 Traction control system has been turned off.

CRUISE

FIGURE 24–22 Indicates that the cruise control is on and able to maintain vehicle speed if set. Sometimes a symbol that looks like a small speedometer is used to indicate that the cruise control is on.

MAINTENANCE REMINDER LAMP

SERVICE NEEDED   Maintenance reminder lamps indicate that one or more of the following services may need to be performed:

- Oil changed
- Tires rotated
- Air filter replaced
- Cabin filter replaced

Check the owner's manual or service information for the exact services that should be done when the light comes on.

HOW TO PUT THE LIGHT OUT   There are numerous ways to extinguish a maintenance reminder lamp. Some require the use of a special tool. Always check the owner's manual or service information for the exact procedure for the vehicle being serviced. For example, to reset the oil service reminder light on many General Motors vehicles, you have to perform the following:

STEP 1   Turn the ignition key on (engine off).

STEP 2   Depress the accelerator pedal three times and hold it down on the fourth.

STEP 3   When the reminder light flashes, release the accelerator pedal.

STEP 4   Turn the ignition key to the off position.

STEP 5   Start the engine and the light should be off.

ANALOG DASH INSTRUMENTS

Needle-type or electromechanical dash instruments use cables, mechanical transducers, and sensors to operate a particular dash instrument. An analog display uses a needle to show the value, whereas a digital display uses numbers. Analog electromagnetic dash instruments use small electromagnetic coils that are connected to a sending unit for such things as fuel level, water temperature, and oil pressure. The sensors are the same regardless of the type of display used. The resistance of the sensor varies with what is being measured. ● **SEE FIGURE 24–23.**

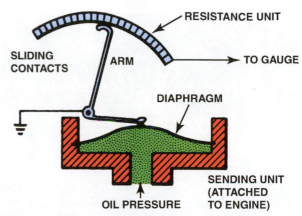

FIGURE 24–23 A typical oil pressure sending unit provides a varying amount of resistance as engine oil pressure changes. The output from the sensor is a variable voltage.

DIGITAL DASH INSTRUMENTS

TYPES

- Digital dash instruments use various electric and electronic sensors that activate segments or sections of an electronic display. Most electronic dash clusters use a computer chip and various electronic circuits to operate and control the internal power supply, sensor voltages, and display voltages.
- Electronic dash display systems may use one or more of several types of displays: light-emitting diode (LED), liquid crystal display (LCD), vacuum tube fluorescent (VTF), and cathode ray tube (CRT).

WOW DISPLAY   When a vehicle equipped with a digital dash is started, all segments of the electronic display are turned on at full brilliance for one or two seconds. This is commonly called the **WOW display,** and is used to show off the brilliance of the display. If numbers are part of the display, the number 8 is shown, because this number uses all segments of a number display. Technicians can also use the WOW display to determine if all segments of the electronic display are functioning correctly.

NETWORK COMMUNICATIONS

DESCRIPTION   Many instrument panels are operated by electronic control units that communicate with the powertrain control module (PCM) for engine data such as revolutions per minute (RPM) and engine temperature. These electronic **instrument panels (IPs)** use the voltage changes from variable-resistance sensors, such as that of the fuel gauge,

FIGURE 24–24 A temperature gauge showing normal operating temperature between 180°F and 215°F, depending on the specific vehicle and engine.

to determine fuel level. Therefore, even though the sensor in the fuel tank is the same, the display itself may be computer controlled. The data is transmitted to the instrument cluster as well as to the PCM through data lines. Because all sensor inputs are interconnected, the technician should always follow the factory-recommended diagnostic procedures. ● SEE FIGURE 24–24.

HEAD-UP DISPLAY

The **head-up display (HUD)** is a supplemental display that projects the vehicle speed and sometimes other data, such as turn signal information, onto the windshield. The projected

FIGURE 24–25 A typical head-up display showing zero miles per hour, which is actually projected on the windshield from the head-up display in the dash.

image looks as if it is some distance ahead, making it easy for the driver to see without having to refocus on a closer dash display. ● SEE FIGURES 24–25 AND 24–26.

The head-up display can also have the brightness controlled on most vehicles that use this type of display. The HUD unit is installed in the instrument panel and uses a mirror to project vehicle information onto the inside surface of the windshield. ● SEE FIGURE 24–27.

Follow the vehicle manufacturer's recommended diagnostic and testing procedures if any faults are found with the head-up display.

FIGURE 24–26 The dash-mounted control for the head-up display on this Cadillac allows the driver to move the image up and down on the windshield for best viewing.

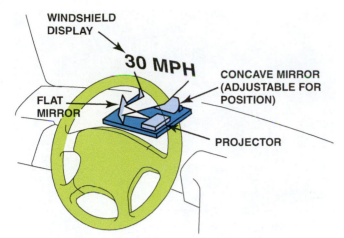

FIGURE 24–27 A typical head-up display (HUD) unit.

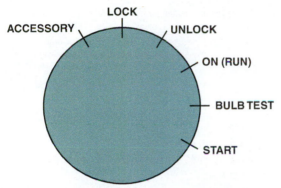

FIGURE 24–28 Typical ignition switch positions. Notice the bulb check position between "on" (run) and "start." These inputs are often just voltage signals to the body control module and can be checked using a scan tool.

FIGURE 24–29 Many newer vehicles place the ignition switch on the dash and incorporate antitheft controls. Note the location of the accessory position.

FIGURE 24–30 A night vision camera behind the grille of a Cadillac.

NIGHT VISION

PARTS AND OPERATION Night vision systems use a camera that is capable of observing objects in the dark to assist the driver while driving at night. The primary night viewing illumination devices are the headlights. The night vision option uses a HUD to improve the vision of the driver beyond the scope of the headlights. Using a HUD display allows the driver to keep eyes on the road and hands on the wheel for maximum safety.

Besides the head-up display, the night vision camera uses a special thermal imaging or infrared technology. The camera is mounted behind the grill in the front of the vehicle. ● SEE FIGURE 24–30.

CAUTION: Becoming accustomed to night vision can be difficult, and it may take several nights to get used to looking at the head-up display.

ELECTRONIC SPEEDOMETERS

OPERATION Electronic dash displays ordinarily use an electric vehicle speed sensor driven by a small gear on the output shaft of the transmission. These speed sensors contain a permanent magnet and generate a voltage in proportion to the vehicle speed. These speed sensors are commonly called **permanent magnet (PM) generators**. ● SEE FIGURE 24–31.

(a)

FIGURE 24–31 A vehicle speed sensor located in the extension housing of the transmission. Some vehicles use the wheel speed sensors for vehicle speed information.

(b)

FIGURE 24–32 (a) Some odometers are mechanical and are operated by an electric stepper motor. (b) Many vehicles are equipped with an electronic odometer.

ELECTRONIC ODOMETERS

PURPOSE AND FUNCTION An odometer is a dash display that indicates the total miles a vehicle travels. Some dash displays also include a trip odometer that can be reset and used to record total miles traveled on a trip or the distance traveled between fuel stops. Electronic dash displays can use either an electrically driven mechanical odometer or a digital display odometer to indicate miles traveled. On vehicles with electronic odometers, because the total miles traveled must be retained when the ignition is turned off or the battery is disconnected, a special electronic chip must be used that will retain the miles traveled. ● **SEE FIGURE 24–32.**

ELECTRONIC FUEL LEVEL GAUGES

OPERATION Electronic fuel level gauges ordinarily use the same fuel tank sending unit as that used on conventional fuel gauges. The tank unit consists of a float attached to a variable resistor. As the fuel level changes, the resistance of the sending unit also changes. As the resistance of the tank unit changes, the dash-mounted gauge also changes. The only difference between a digital fuel-level gauge and a conventional needle type is in the display. Digital fuel-level gauges can be either numerical (indicating gallons or liters remaining in the tank) or a bar graph display. ● SEE FIGURE 24–33.

  REAL-WORLD FIX

Electronic Devices Cannot Swim

The owner of a Dodge minivan complained that after the vehicle was cleaned inside and outside, the temperature gauge, fuel gauge, and speedometer stopped working. The vehicle speed sensor was checked and found to be supplying a signal that changed with vehicle speed. A scan tool indicated a speed, yet the speedometer displayed zero all the time. Finally, the service technician checked the body computer to the right of the accelerator pedal and noticed that it had been wet, from the interior cleaning. Drying the computer did not fix the problem, but a replacement body computer fixed all the problems. The owner discovered that electronic devices do not like water and that computers cannot swim.

NAVIGATION AND GPS

PURPOSE AND FUNCTION The **global positioning system (GPS)** uses 24 satellites in orbit around the earth to provide signals for navigation devices. GPS is funded and controlled by the U.S. Department of Defense (DOD). While the system can be used by anyone with a GPS receiver, it was designed for and is operated by the U.S. military. ● SEE FIGURE 24–34.

COMPONENTS Navigation systems include the following components.

1. Screen display
2. GPS antenna
3. Navigation control unit, usually with map information on a DVD. ● SEE FIGURE 24–35.

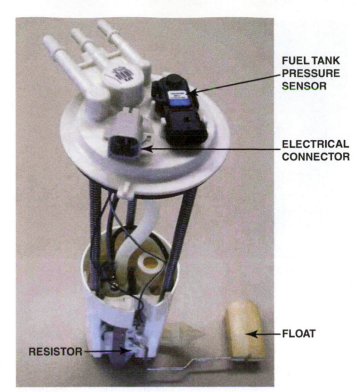

FUEL TANK PRESSURE SENSOR

ELECTRICAL CONNECTOR

FLOAT

RESISTOR

FIGURE 24–33 A fuel tank module assembly that contains the fuel pump and fuel-level sensor in one assembly.

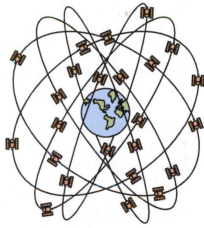

FIGURE 24–34 Global positioning systems use 24 satellites in high earth orbits whose signals are picked up by navigation systems. The navigation system computer then calculates the location based on the position of the satellite overhead.

 **TECH TIP**

Window Tinting Can Hurt GPS Reception

Most factory-installed navigation systems use a GPS antenna inside the rear back glass or under the rear package shelf. If a metalized window tint is applied to the rear glass, the signal strength from the GPS satellites can be reduced. If the customer concern includes inaccurate or nonfunctioning navigation, check for window tint.

FIGURE 24–35 A typical GPS display screen showing the location of the vehicle.

INFORMATION AVAILABLE The GPS unit usually uses internal memory that has the current street names and the following information.

1. Points of interest (POI), including automated teller machines (ATMs), restaurants, schools, colleges, museums, shopping complexes, and airports, as well as vehicle dealer locations.

2. Business addresses and telephone numbers, including hotels and restaurants. (If the telephone number is listed in the business telephone book, it can usually be displayed on the navigation screen. If the telephone number of the business is known, the location can be displayed.)

NOTE: Private residences or cellular telephone numbers are not included in the database of telephone numbers stored on the navigation system DVD.

3. Turn-by-turn directions to addresses that are:
   - Selected by points of interest
   - Typed in using a keyboard shown on the display

The navigation unit then often allows the user to select the fastest way to the destination, as well as the shortest way, or to avoid toll roads. ● **SEE FIGURE 24–36.**

FIGURE 24–36 A typical navigation display showing various options. Some systems do not allow access to these functions if the vehicle is in gear and/or moving.

<table>
<tr><td>**?**</td><td>**FREQUENTLY ASKED QUESTION**</td></tr>
</table>

Does the Government Know Where I Am?

No. The navigation system uses signals from the satellites and uses the signals from three or more to determine position. If the vehicle is equipped with OnStar, then the vehicle position can be monitored by the use of the cellular telephone link to OnStar call centers. Unless the vehicle has a cellular phone connection to the outside world, the only people who will know the location of the vehicle are the persons inside the vehicle viewing the navigation screen.

ONSTAR

PARTS AND OPERATION OnStar is a system that includes the following functions:

1. Cellular telephone
2. Global positioning antenna and computer

OnStar is standard or optional on most General Motors vehicles and selected other brands and models to help the driver in an emergency or to provide other services. Advisors at service centers use the cellular telephone to communicate with the driver. The advisor at the service center is able to see the location of the vehicle as transmitted from the GPS antenna and computer system in the vehicle on a display. OnStar does not display the location of the vehicle to the driver unless the vehicle is also equipped with a navigation system.

Unlike most navigation systems, the OnStar system requires a monthly fee. OnStar was first introduced in 1996 as an option on some Cadillac models. Early versions used a handheld cellular telephone, while later units used a group of three buttons mounted on the inside rearview mirror and a hands-free cellular telephone. ● **SEE FIGURE 24–37.**

- **Automatic notification of airbag deployment.** If the airbag is deployed, the advisor is notified immediately and attempts to call the vehicle. If there is no reply, or if the occupants report an emergency, the advisor will contact emergency services and give them the location of the vehicle.

- **Emergency services.** If the red button is pushed, OnStar immediately locates the vehicle and contacts the nearest emergency service agency.

- **Stolen vehicle location assistance.** If a vehicle is reported stolen, a call center advisor can track the vehicle.

- **Remote door unlock.** An OnStar advisor can send a cellular telephone message to the vehicle to unlock the vehicle if needed.

- **Roadside assistance.** When called, an OnStar advisor can locate a towing company or locate a provider who can bring gasoline or change a flat tire.

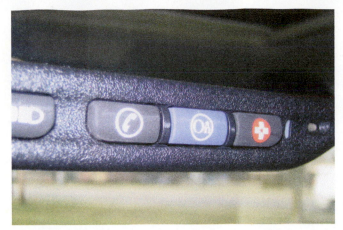

FIGURE 24–37 The three-button OnStar control is located on the inside rearview mirror. The left button (telephone handset icon) is pushed if a hands-free cellular call is to be made. The center button is depressed to contact an OnStar advisor and the right emergency button is used to request that help be sent to the vehicle's location.

- **Accident assistance.** An OnStar advisor is able to help with the best way to handle an accident. The advisor can supply a step-by-step checklist of the things that should be done plus call the insurance company, if desired.
- **Remote horn and lights.** The OnStar system is tied into the lights and horn circuits so an advisor can activate them if requested to help the owner locate the vehicle in a parking lot or garage.
- **Vehicle diagnosis.** Because the OnStar system is tied to the PCM, an OnStar advisor can help with diagnosis if there is a fault detected.

FIGURE 24–38 A typical view displayed on the navigation screen from the backup camera.

FIGURE 24–39 A typical fisheye-type backup camera usually located near the center on the rear of the vehicle near the license plate.

BACKUP CAMERA

PARTS AND OPERATION A **backup camera** is used to display the area at the rear of the vehicle in a screen display on the dash when the gear selector is placed in reverse. Backup cameras are also called *reversing cameras* or *rearview cameras*. Backup cameras are different from normal cameras because the image displayed on the dash is flipped so it is a mirror image of the scene at the rear of the vehicle. This reversing of the image is needed because the driver and the camera are facing in opposite directions. Backup cameras were first used in large vehicles with limited rearward visibility, such as motor homes. Many vehicles equipped with navigation systems include a backup camera for added safety while backing. ● **SEE FIGURE 24–38.**

The backup camera contains a wide-angle or fisheye lens to give the largest viewing area. Most backup cameras are pointed downward so that objects on the ground, as well as walls, are displayed. ● **SEE FIGURE 24–39.**

BACKUP SENSORS

COMPONENTS Backup sensors are used to warn the driver if there is an object behind the vehicle while backing. The system used in General Motors vehicles is called **rear park assist (RPA),** and includes the following components:

Ultrasonic object sensors built into the rear bumper assembly.

- A display with three lights usually located inside the vehicle above the rear window and visible to the driver in the rearview mirror.
- An electronic control module that uses an input from the transmission range switch and lights the warning lamps needed when the vehicle gear selector is in reverse.

OPERATION The three-light display includes two amber lights and one red light. The following lights are displayed depending on the distance from the rear bumper. ● **SEE FIGURE 24–40.**

FIGURE 24–40 A typical backup sensor display located above the rear window inside the vehicle. The warning lights are visible in the inside rearview mirror.

FIGURE 24–41 The small round buttons in the rear bumper are ultrasonic sensors used to sense distance to an object.

System uses sensors and different colored lamps or an alarm to provide the driver with information about distance to objects as the vehicle backs up. ● **SEE FIGURE 24–41.**

LANE DEPARTURE WARNING SYSTEM

PARTS AND OPERATION The **lane departure warning system (LDWS)** uses cameras to detect if the vehicle is crossing over lane marking lines on the pavement. Some systems use two cameras, one mounted on each outside rearview mirror. Some systems use infrared sensors located under the front bumper to monitor the lane markings on the road surface. The system names also vary according to vehicle manufacturer, including:

Honda/Acura: lane keep assist system (LKAS)
Toyota/Lexus: lane monitoring system (LMS)
General Motors: lane departure warning (LDW)
Ford: lane departure warning (LDW)
Nissan/Infiniti: lane departure prevention (LDP) system

If the cameras detect that the vehicle is starting to cross over a lane dividing line, a warning chime will sound or a vibrating mechanism mounted in the driver's seat cushion is triggered on the side where the departure is being detected. This warning will not occur if the turn signal is on in the same direction as detected. ● **SEE FIGURE 24–42.**

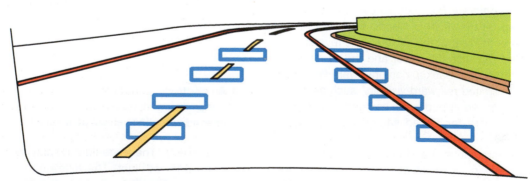

FIGURE 24–42 A lane departure warning system often uses cameras to sense the road lines and warns the driver if the vehicle is not staying within the lane, unless the turn signal is on.

SUMMARY

1. Most digital and analog (needle-type) dash gauges use variable-resistance sensors.
2. Dash warning lamps are called telltale lamps.
3. Fuel-level gauges use a sensor located inside the fuel tank.
4. Navigation systems and warning systems are part of the driver information system on many vehicles.

REVIEW QUESTIONS

1. How does a GPS navigation system know where the vehicle is located?
2. What can cause the red brake warning lamp to turn on?
3. How does a head up display work?

CHAPTER QUIZ

1. Technician A says that a navigation system uses cell phone tower information to locate the vehicle on streets and highways. Technician B says the system uses satellites. Which technician is correct?
   a. Technician A only
   b. Technician B only
   c. Both technicians A and B
   d. Neither technician A nor B

2. OnStar uses _____.
   a. GPS information
   b. Digital cellular phone service
   c. Automatic airbag deployment notification
   d. All of the above

3. When the oil pressure drops to between _____ and _____ PSI, the oil pressure lamp lights up.
   a. 3 and 7   b. 10 and 30
   c. 30 and 50   d. 50 and 70

4. A brake warning lamp on the dash remains on whenever the ignition is on. Technician A says that there could be a fault in the hydraulic brake system. Technician B says that the problem could be due to a stuck parking brake switch. Which technician is correct?
   a. Technician A only
   b. Technician B only
   c. Both technicians A and B
   d. Neither technician A nor B

5. A lane departure warning system uses _____.
   a. Radar to determine where the road is located
   b. Cameras or infrared sensors
   c. GPS to determine the location of the vehicle on the road
   d. All of the above are used

6. A dash warning light that looks like a battery means _____.
   a. A fault with the battery
   b. A fault with the alternator
   c. A fault with the electrical system
   d. Any of the above

7. If the maintenance reminder light comes on, this means that the owner should _____.
   a. Change oil
   b. Replace tires
   c. Replace air filter
   d. Any of the above depending on the vehicle make and model

8. Technician A says that metal-type tinting can affect the navigation system. Technician B says most navigation systems require a monthly payment for use of the GPS satellite. Which technician is correct?
   a. Technician A only
   b. Technician B only
   c. Both technicians A and B
   d. Neither technician A nor B

9. What should the driver do if the TPMS warning lamp comes on steady?
   a. Check the inflation pressures of all tires
   b. Use the pressure printed on the decal near the driver's door for the specified pressure
   c. Some vehicles need to have the spare tire checked
   d. All of the above

10. How does changing the size of the tires affect the speedometer reading?
    a. A smaller diameter tire causes the speedometer to read faster than actual speed and more than actual mileage on the odometer.
    b. A smaller diameter tire causes the speedometer to read slower than the actual speed and less than the actual mileage on the odometer.
    c. A larger diameter tire causes the speedometer to read faster than the actual speed and more than the actual mileage on the odometer.
    d. A larger diameter tire causes the speedometer to read slower than the actual speed and more than the actual mileage on the odometer.

chapter 25

LIGHTING SYSTEMS

OBJECTIVES: **After studying Chapter 25, the reader will be able to:** • Prepare for ASE Electrical/Electronic Systems (A6) certification test content area "E" (Lighting System Diagnosis and Repair). • Determine which replacement bulb to use on a given vehicle. • Describe how interior and exterior lighting systems work. • Describe how HID lights work. • Read and interpret a bulb chart.

KEY TERMS: • Brake lights 242 • Candlepower 239 • CHMSL 242 • Composite headlight 243 • Courtesy lights 246 • DRL 244 • Hazard warning 243 • HID 244 • Trade number 239 • Xenon headlights 244

INTRODUCTION

A vehicle has many different lighting and signaling systems, each with its own specific components and operating characteristics. The major light-related circuits and systems covered include the following:

- Exterior lighting (parking, tail lights, license plate, and high mounted stop light)
- Headlights (sealed beam, halogen, and HID)
- Bulb trade numbers
- Brake lights
- Turn signals and flasher units
- Interior lighting
- Light-dimming rearview mirrors

EXTERIOR LIGHTS

HEADLIGHT SWITCH CONTROL In vehicles in which exterior lighting is not controlled by the body computer, it is controlled by a headlight switch, which is connected directly to the battery. Therefore, if the light switch is left on accidentally, the lights could drain the battery. Older headlight switches contained a built-in circuit breaker. If excessive current flows through the headlight circuit, the circuit breaker will momentarily open the circuit, then close it again. The result is headlights that flicker on and off rapidly. This feature allows the headlights to function, as a safety measure, in spite of current overload. The headlight switch controls the following lights on most vehicles, usually through a module:

1. Headlights
2. Tail lights
3. License plate light
4. Side-marker lights
5. Front parking lights
6. Dash lights
7. Interior (dome) light(s)

COMPUTER-CONTROLLED LIGHTS Because exterior lights can easily drain the battery if accidentally left on, many newer vehicles control these lights through computer modules. The computer module, usually the body control module (BCM), keeps track of the time the lights are on with the engine off and can turn them off if the time is excessive. The computer can control either the power side or the ground side of the circuit.

For example, a typical computer-controlled lighting system usually includes the following steps:

STEP 1 The driver depresses or rotates the headlight switch.

STEP 2 The signal from the headlight switch is sent to the nearest control module.

STEP 3 The BCM then sends a request to the headlight control module to turn on the headlights as well as the front parking and side-marker lights. Through the data lines, the rear control module receives the lights on signal and turns on the lights at the rear of the vehicle.

STEP 4 All modules monitor current flow through the circuit and will turn on a bulb failure warning light if it detects an open bulb or a fault in the circuit.

STEP 5 After the ignition has been turned off, the modules will turn off the lights after a time delay to prevent the battery from being drained.

BULB NUMBERS

TRADE NUMBER   The number used to identify automotive bulbs is called the bulb **trade number,** as recorded with the American National Standards Institute (ANSI). The number is the same regardless of the manufacturer. ● **SEE FIGURE 25–1.**

CANDLEPOWER   The trade number also identifies the size, shape, number of filaments, and amount of light produced, measured in **candlepower.** For example, the 1156 bulb, commonly used for backup lights, is 32 candlepower. A 194 bulb, commonly used for dash or side-marker lights, is rated at only 2 candlepower. The amount of light produced by a bulb is determined by the resistance of the filament wire, which also affects the amount of current (in amperes) required by the bulb. It is important that the correct trade number of bulb always be used for replacement to prevent circuit or component damage. The correct replacement bulb for a vehicle is usually listed in the owner or service manual. ● **REFER TO CHART 25–1** for a listing of common bulbs and their specifications used in most vehicles.

BULB NUMBER SUFFIXES   Many bulbs have suffixes that indicate some feature of the bulb, while keeping the same size and light output specifications. Typical bulb suffixes include the following:

- NA: natural amber (amber glass)
- A: amber (painted glass)
- HD: heavy duty
- LL: long life

DOUBLE CONTACT
1157/2057 BULBS

SINGLE CONTACT
1156 BULBS

WEDGE
194 BULB

FIGURE 25–1 Dual-filament (double-contact) bulbs contain both a low-intensity filament for tail lights or parking lights and a high-intensity filament for brake lights and turn signals. Bulbs come in a variety of shapes and sizes. The numbers shown are the trade numbers.

- IF: inside frosted
- R: red
- B: blue
- G: green ● **SEE FIGURE 25–2.**

TESTING BULBS   Bulbs can be tested using two basic tests.

1. Perform a visual inspection of any bulb. Many faults, such as a shorted filament, corroded connector, or water, can cause weird problems that are often thought to be wiring issues. ● **SEE FIGURES 25–3 AND 25–4** on page 242.

2. Bulbs can be tested by checking the resistance of the filament(s) using an ohmmeter. Most bulbs will read low

FIGURE 25–2 Bulbs that have the same trade number have the same operating voltage and wattage. The NA means that the bulb uses a natural amber glass ampoule with clear turn signal lenses.

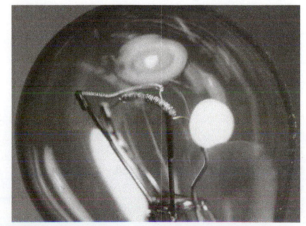

FIGURE 25–3 Close-up of a 2057 dual-filament (double-contact) bulb that failed. Note that the top filament broke from its mounting and melted onto the lower filament. This bulb caused the dash lights to come on whenever the brakes were applied.

BULB NUMBER	FILAMENTS	AMPERAGE LOW/HIGH	WATTAGE LOW/HIGH	CANDLEPOWER LOW/HIGH
Headlights				
1255/H1	1	4.58	55.00	129.00
1255/H3	1	4.58	55.00	121.00
6024	2	2.73/4.69	35.00/60.00	27,000/35,000
6054	2	2.73/5.08	35.00/65.00	35,000/40,000
9003	2	4.58/5.00	55.00/60.00	72.00/120.00
9004	2	3.52/5.08	45.00/65.00	56.00/95.00
9005	1	5.08	65.00	136.00
9006	1	4.30	55.00	80.00
9007	2	4.30/5.08	55.00/65.00	80.00/107.00
9008	2	4.30/5.08	55.00/65.00	80.00/107.00
9011	1	5.08	65.00	163.50
Headlights (HID—Xenon)				
D2R	Air Gap	0.41	35.00	222.75
D2S	Air Gap	0.41	35.00	254.57
Tail lights, Stop, and Turn Lamps				
1156	1	2.10	26.88	32.00
1157	2	0.59/2.10	8.26/26.88	3.00/32.00
2057	2	0.49/2.10	6.86/26.88	2.00/32.00
3057	2	0.48/2.10	6.72/26.88	1.50/24.00
3155	1	1.60	20.48	21.00
3157	2	0.59/2.10	8.26/26.88	2.20/24.00
4157	2	0.59/2.10	8.26/26.88	3.00/32.00
7440	1	1.75	21.00	36.60
7443	2	0.42/1.75	5.00/21.00	2.80/36.60
17131	1	0.33	4.00	2.80
17635	1	1.75	21.00	37.00
17916	2	0.42/1.75	5.00/21.00	1.20/35.00
Parking, Daytime Running Lamps				
24	1	0.24	3.36	2.00
67	1	0.59	7.97	4.00
168	1	0.35	4.90	3.00
194	1	0.27	3.78	2.00
889	1	3.90	49.92	43.00
912	1	1.00	12.80	12.00
916	1	0.54	7.29	2.00
1034	2	0.59/1.80	8.26/23.04	3.00/32.00
1156	1	2.10	26.88	32.00
1157	2	0.59/2.10	8.26/26.88	3.00/32.00
2040	1	0.63	8.00	10.50

CHART 25–1

Bulbs that have the same trade number have the same operating voltage and wattage. The NA means that the bulb uses a natural amber glass ampoule with clear turn signal lenses.

BULB NUMBER	FILAMENTS	AMPERAGE LOW/HIGH	WATTAGE LOW/HIGH	CANDLEPOWER LOW/HIGH
2057	2	0.49/2.10	6.86/26.88	1.50/24.00
2357	2	0.59/2.23	8.26/28.54	3.00/40.00
3157	2	0.59/2.10	8.26/26.88	3.00/32.00
3357	2	0.59/2.23	8.26/28.54	3.00/40.00
3457	2	0.59/2.23	8.26/28.51	3.00/40.00
3496	2	0.66/2.24	8.00/27.00	3.00/45.00
3652	1	0.42	5.00	6.00
4114	2	0.59/2/23	8.26/31.20	3.00/32.00
4157	2	0.59/2.10	8.26/26/88	3.00/32.00
7443	2	0.42/1.75	5.00/21.00	2.80/36.60
17131	1	0.33	4.00	2.80
17171	1	0.42	5.00	4.00
17177	1	0.42	5.00	4.00
17311	1	0.83	10.00	10.00
17916	2	0.42/1.75	5.00/21.00	1.20/35.00
68161	1	0.50	6.00	10.00
Center High-Mounted Stop Lamp (CHMSL)				
70	1	0.15	2.10	1.50
168	1	0.35	4.90	3.00
175	1	0.58	8.12	5.00
211-2	1	0.97	12.42	12.00
577	1	1.40	17.92	21.00
579	1	0.80	10.20	9.00
889	1	3.90	49.92	43.00
891	1	0.63	8.00	11.00
906	1	0.69	8.97	6.00
912	1	1.00	12.80	12.00
921	1	1.40	17.92	21.00
922	1	0.98	12.54	15.00
1141	1	1.44	18.43	21.00
1156	1	2.10	26.88	32.00
2723	1	0.20	2.40	1.50
3155	1	1.60	20.48	21.00
3156	1	2.10	26.88	32.00
3497	1	2.24	27.00	45.00
7440	1	1.75	21.00	36.60
17177	1	0.42	5.00	4.00
17635	1	1.75	21.00	37.00
License Plate, Glove Box, Dome, Side Marker, Trunk, Map, Ashtray, Step/Courtesy, Underhood				
37	1	0.09	1.26	0.50
67	1	0.59	7.97	4.00
74	1	0.10	1.40	.070
98	1	0.62	8.06	6.00

CONTINUED

BULB NUMBER	FILAMENTS	AMPERAGE LOW/HIGH	WATTAGE LOW/HIGH	CANDLEPOWER LOW/HIGH
105	1	1.00	12.80	12.00
124	1	0.27	3.78	1.50
161	1	0.19	2.66	1.00
168	1	0.35	4.90	3.00
192	1	0.33	4.29	3.00
194	1	0.27	3.78	2.00
211-1	1	0.968	12.40	12.00
212-2	1	0.74	9.99	6.00
214-2	1	0.52	7.02	4.00
293	1	0.33	4.62	2.00
561	1	0.97	12.42	12.00
562	1	0.74	9.99	6.00
578	1	0.78	9.98	9.00
579	1	0.80	10.20	9.00
PC579	1	0.80	10.20	9.00
906	1	0.69	8.97	6.00
912	1	1.00	12.80	12.00
917	1	1.20	14.40	10.00
921	1	1.40	17.92	21.00
1003	1	0.94	12.03	15.00
1155	1	0.59	7.97	4.00
1210/H2	1	8.33	100.00	239.00
1210/H3	1	8.33	100.00	192.00
1445	1	0.14	2.02	0.70
1891	1	0.24	3.36	2.00
1895	1	0.27	3.78	2.00
3652	1	0.42	5.00	6.00
11005	1	0.39	5.07	4.00
11006	1	0.24	3.36	2.00
12100	1	0.77	10.01	9.55
13050	1	0.38	4.94	3.00
17036	1	0.10	1.20	0.48
17097	1	0.25	3.00	1.76
17131	1	0.33	4.00	2.80
17177	1	0.42	5.00	4.00
17314	1	0.83	10.00	8.00
17916	2	0.42/1.75	5.00/21.00	1.20/35.00
47830	1	0.39	5.00	6.70

Instrument Panel

BULB NUMBER	FILAMENTS	AMPERAGE LOW/HIGH	WATTAGE LOW/HIGH	CANDLEPOWER LOW/HIGH
37	1	0.09	1.26	0.50
73	1	0.08	1.12	0.30
74	1	0.10	1.40	0.70

BULB NUMBER	FILAMENTS	AMPERAGE LOW/HIGH	WATTAGE LOW/HIGH	CANDLEPOWER LOW/HIGH
PC74	1	0.10	1.40	0.70
PC118	1	0.12	1.68	0.70
124	1	0.27	3.78	1.50
158	1	0.24	3.36	2.00
161	1	0.19	2.66	1.00
192	1	0.33	4.29	3.00
194	1	0.27	3.78	2.00
PC194	1	0.27	3.78	2.00
PC195	1	0.27	3.78	1.80
1210/H1	1	8.33	100.00	217.00
1210/H3	1	8.33	100.00	192.00
17037	1	0.10	1.20	0.48
17097	1	0.25	3.00	1.76
17314	1	0.83	10.00	8.00

Backup, Cornering, Fog/Driving Lamps

BULB NUMBER	FILAMENTS	AMPERAGE LOW/HIGH	WATTAGE LOW/HIGH	CANDLEPOWER LOW/HIGH
67	1	0.59	7.97	4.00
579	1	0.80	10.20	9.00
880	1	2.10	26.88	43.00
881	1	2.10	26.88	43.00
885	1	3.90	49.92	100.00
886	1	3.90	49.92	100.00
893	1	2.93	37.50	75.00
896	1	2.93	37.50	75.00
898	1	2.93	37.50	60.00
899	1	2.93	37.50	60.00
921	1	1.40	17.92	21.00
1073	1	1.80	23.04	32.00
1156	1	2.10	26.88	32.00
1157	2	0.59/2.10	8.26/26.88	3.00/32.00
1210/H1	1	8.33	100.00	217.00
1255/H1	1	4.58	55.00	129.00
1255/H3	1	4.58	55.00	121.00
1255/H11	1	4.17	55.00	107.00
2057	2	0.49/2.10	6.86/26.88	1.50/24.00
3057	2	0.48/2.10	6.72/26.88	2.00/32.00
3155	1	1.60	20.48	21.00
3156	1	2.10	26.88	32.00
3157	2	0.59/2.10	8.26/26.88	3.00/32.00
4157	2	0.59/2.10	8.26/26/88	3.00/32.00
7440	1	1.75	21.00	36.00
9003	2	4.58/5.00	55.00/60.00	72.00/120.00
9006	1	4.30	55.00	80.00
9145	1	3.52	45.00	65.00
17635	1	1.75	21.00	37.00

CONTINUED

FIGURE 25–4 Corrosion caused the two terminals of this dual filament bulb to be electrically connected.

FIGURE 25–5 This single-filament bulb is being tested with a digital multimeter set to read resistance in ohms. The reading of 1.1 ohms is the resistance of the bulb when cold. As soon as current flows through the filament, the resistance increases about 10 times. It is the initial surge of current flowing through the filament when the bulb is cool that causes many bulbs to fail in cold weather as a result of the reduced resistance. As the temperature increases, the resistance increases.

resistance at room temperature, between 0.5 and 20 ohms depending on the bulb. Test results include the following:

- **Normal resistance.** The bulb is good. Check both filaments if it is a two-filament bulb. ● **SEE FIGURE 25–5.**
- **Zero ohms.** It is unlikely but possible for the bulb filament to be shorted.
- **OL (electrically open).** The reading indicates that the bulb filament is broken.

BRAKE LIGHTS

OPERATION **Brake lights,** also called stop lights, use a separate brake light bulb or the high-intensity filament of a double-filament bulb. (The low intensity filament is for the tail

lights.) When the brakes are applied, the brake switch is closed and the brake lamps light. The brake switch receives current from a fuse that is hot all the time. The brake light switch is a normally open (NO) switch, but is closed when the driver depresses the brake pedal. Since 1986, all vehicles sold in the United States have a third brake light commonly referred to as the **center high-mounted stop light (CHMSL).**

The brake switch is also used as an input switch (signal) for the following:

1. Cruise control (deactivates when the brake pedal is depressed)
2. Antilock brakes (ABS)
3. Brake shift interlock (prevents shifting from park position unless the brake pedal is depressed)

TURN SIGNALS

OPERATION The turn signal circuit is supplied power from the ignition switch and operated by a lever and switch. ● **SEE FIGURE 25–6.**

When the turn signal switch is moved in either direction, the corresponding turn signal lamps receive current through the flasher unit. The flasher unit causes the current to start and stop as the turn signal lamp flashes on and off with the interrupted current. Turn signal circuits have instrument panel indicators to alert the driver if the turn signals are functioning properly.

FLASHER UNITS Turn signal flasher unit is a metal or plastic can containing a switch that opens and closes the turn signal circuit. Vehicles can be equipped with many different types of flasher units. ● **SEE FIGURE 25–7.**

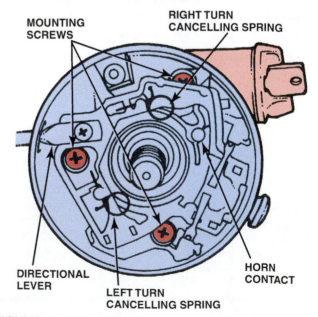

FIGURE 25–6 The typical turn signal switch includes various springs and cams to control the switch and to cause the switch to cancel after a turn has been completed.

FIGURE 25–7 Two styles of two-prong flasher units.

FIGURE 25–8 A hazard warning flasher uses a parallel resistor across the contacts to provide a constant flashing rate regardless of the number of bulbs used in the circuit.

HAZARD WARNING FLASHER

The **hazard warning** flasher is a device installed in a vehicle lighting system with a primary function of causing both the left and right turn signal lamps to flash at the same time when the hazard warning switch is activated. Secondary functions may include visible dash indicators for the hazard system and an audible signal to indicate when the flasher is operating. A typical hazard warning flasher is also called a *parallel* or *variable-load* flasher because there is a resistor in parallel with the contacts to provide a control load and, therefore, a constant flash rate, regardless of the number of bulbs being flashed. ● **SEE FIGURE 25–8.**

COMBINATION TURN SIGNAL AND HAZARD WARNING FLASHER

The combination flasher is a device that combines the functions of a turn signal flasher and a hazard warning flasher into one package, which often uses three electrical terminals.

HEADLIGHTS

SEALED BEAM HEADLIGHTS A sealed beam headlight consists of a sealed glass or plastic assembly containing the bulb, reflective surface, and prism lenses to properly focus the light beam. Low-beam headlights contain two filaments and three electrical terminals.

- One for low beam
- One for high beam
- One for ground

High-beam headlights contain only one filament and two terminals. Because low-beam headlights also contain a high-beam filament, the entire headlight assembly must be replaced if either filament is defective. ● **SEE FIGURE 25–9.**

COMPOSITE HEADLIGHTS **Composite headlights** are constructed using a replaceable bulb and a fixed lens cover that is part of the vehicle. ● **SEE FIGURE 25–10.**

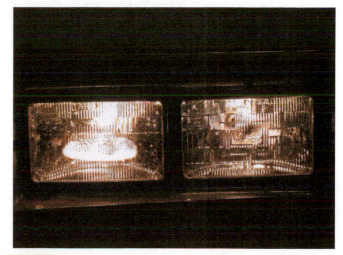

FIGURE 25–9 A typical four-headlight system using sealed beam headlights.

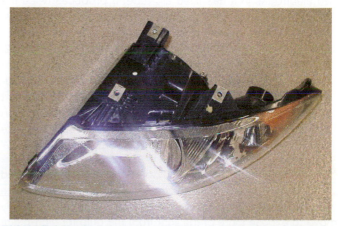

FIGURE 25–10 A typical composite headlamp assembly. The lens, housing, and bulb sockets are usually included as a complete assembly.

FIGURE 25–11 Handle a halogen bulb by the base to prevent the skin's oil from getting on the glass.

The replaceable bulbs are usually bright halogen bulbs. Halogen bulbs get very hot during operation, between 500°F and 1,300°F (260°C and 700°C). It is important never to touch the glass of any halogen bulb with bare fingers because the natural oils of the skin on the glass bulb can cause the bulb to break when it heats during normal operation. ● SEE FIGURE 25–11.

HIGH-INTENSITY DISCHARGE HEADLIGHTS

PARTS AND OPERATION **High-intensity discharge (HID)** headlights produce a distinctive blue-white light that is crisper, clearer, and brighter than light produced by a halogen headlight. High-intensity discharge lamps do not use a filament like conventional electrical bulbs, but contain two electrodes about 0.2 in. (5 mm) apart. A high-voltage pulse is sent to the bulb, which arcs across the tips of electrodes producing light. It generates light from an electrical discharge between two electrodes in a gas-filled arc tube. It produces twice the light with less electrical input than conventional halogen bulbs. The HID lighting system consists of the discharge arc source, igniter, ballast, and headlight assembly. ● SEE FIGURE 25–12.

The two electrodes are contained in a tiny quartz capsule filled with xenon gas, mercury, and metal halide salts. HID headlights are also called **xenon headlights.** The lights and support electronics are expensive, but they should last the life of the vehicle unless physically damaged. HID headlights produce a white light giving the lamp a blue-white color. ● SEE FIGURE 25–13.

BI-XENON HEADLIGHTS Some vehicles are equipped with bi-xenon headlights, which use a shutter to block some of the light during low-beam operation and then mechanically move to expose more of the light from the bulb for high-beam operation. Because xenon lights are relatively slow to start working, vehicles equipped with bi-xenon headlights use two halogen lights for the "flash-to-pass" feature.

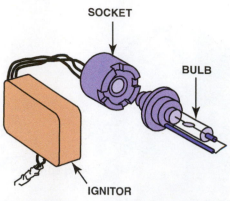

FIGURE 25–12 The igniter contains the ballast and transformer needed to provide high-voltage pulses to the arc tube bulb.

FIGURE 25–13 HID (xenon) headlights emit a whiter light than halogen headlights and usually look blue compared to halogen bulbs.

HEADLIGHT AIMING

According to U.S. federal law, all headlights, regardless of shape, must be able to be aimed using headlight aiming equipment. Older vehicles equipped with sealed beam headlights used a headlight aiming system that attached to the headlight itself. ● SEE FIGURES 25–14 AND 25–15. Also see the photo sequence on headlight aiming later in the chapter.

DAYTIME RUNNING LIGHTS

PURPOSE AND FUNCTION Some vehicles are equipped with **daytime running lights (DRLs).** These can involve operation of any of the following depending on the make and model of vehicle:

- Front parking lights
- Separate DRL lamps
- Headlights (usually at reduced current and voltage) when the vehicle is running

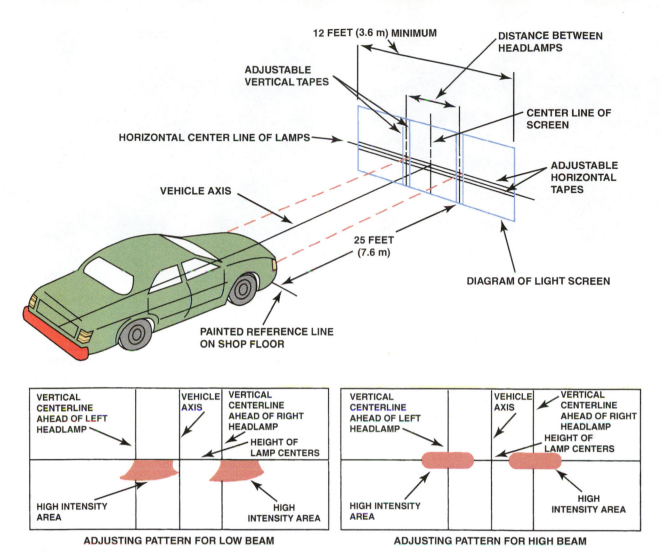

FIGURE 25–14 Typical headlight aiming diagram as found in service information.

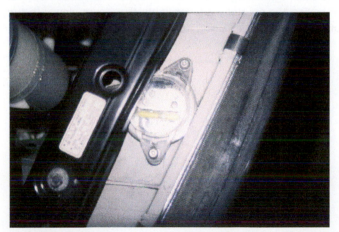

FIGURE 25–15 Many composite headlights have a built-in bubble level to make aiming easy and accurate.

Canada has required daytime running lights on all new vehicles since 1990. Studies have shown that DRLs have reduced accidents where used. Daytime running lights primarily use a control module that turns on either the low- or high-beam headlights or separate daytime running lights. The lights on some vehicles come on when the engine starts. Other vehicles will turn on the lamps when the engine is running but delay their operation until a signal from the vehicle speed sensor indicates that the vehicle is moving. To avoid having the lights on during servicing, some systems will turn off the headlights when the parking brake is applied and the ignition switch is cycled off then back on. Others will only light the headlights when the vehicle is in a drive gear. ● **SEE FIGURE 25–16.**

CAUTION: Most factory daytime running lights operate the headlights at reduced intensity. These are *not* designed to be used at night. Normal intensity of the headlights (and operation of the other external lamps) is actuated by turning on the headlights as usual.

DIMMER SWITCHES

The headlight switch controls the power or hot side of the headlight circuit. The current is then sent to the dimmer switch, which allows current to flow to either the high-beam or the low-beam filament of the headlight bulb.

FIGURE 25–16 Daytime running lights are available on many makes and models, and vehicles use either separate lights or connect the high beams in series to provide a reduced level of light intensity.

An indicator light illuminates on the dash when the high beams are selected. The dimmer switch is usually hand operated by a lever on the steering column and is made as an integral part of the multifunction switch. Some steering column switches are actually attached to the *outside* of the steering column and are spring loaded. To replace these types of dimmer switches, the steering column needs to be lowered slightly to gain access to the switch itself.

COURTESY LIGHTS

Courtesy light is a generic term primarily used for interior lights, including overhead (dome) and under-the-dash (courtesy) lights. These interior lights are controlled by operating switches located in the doorjambs of the vehicle doors or by a switch on the dash. ● **SEE FIGURE 25–17.**

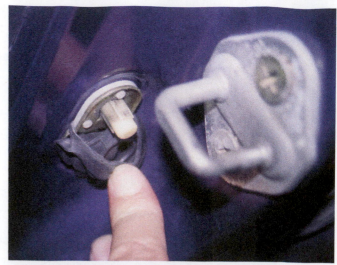

FIGURE 25–17 A typical courtesy light doorjamb switch. Newer vehicles use the door switch as an input to the vehicle computer and the computer turns the interior lights on or off. By placing the lights under the control of the computer, the vehicle engineers have the opportunity to delay the lights after the door is closed and to shut them off after a period of time to avoid draining the battery.

Many Ford vehicles use the door switches to open and close the power side of the circuit, while most other vehicles use door jamb switches to complete the ground side of the circuit. Many newer vehicles operate the interior lights through the vehicle computer or through an electronic module. Because the exact wiring and operation of these units differ, consult the service literature for the exact model of the vehicle being serviced. Courtesy lights often are designed to stay on for a programmed amount of time to allow illuminated vehicle entry and exit. "Theater lighting" is a term used to describe an option of having the courtesy interior lights dim down slowly to turn off, instead of simply being just turned off.▶

1 The driver noticed that the tail light fault indicator (icon) on the dash was on any time the lights were on.

2 A visual inspection at the rear of the vehicle indicated that the right rear tail light bulb did not light. Removing a few screws from the plastic cover revealed the tail light assembly.

3 The bulb socket is removed from the tail light assembly by gently twisting the base of the bulb counterclockwise.

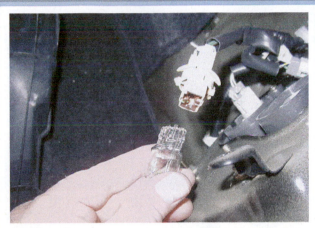

4 The bulb is removed from the socket by gently grasping the bulb and pulling the bulb straight out of the socket. Many bulbs required that you rotate the bulb 90° (1/4 turn) to release the retaining bulbs.

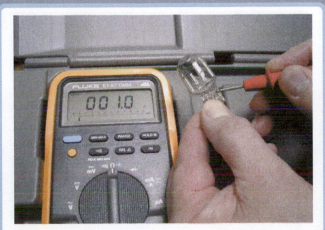

5 The new 7443 replacement bulb is being checked with an ohmmeter to be sure that it is okay before it is installed in the vehicle.

6 The replacement bulb in inserted into the tail light socket and the lights are turned on to verify proper operation before putting the components back together.

OPTICAL HEADLIGHT AIMING

1 Before checking the vehicle for headlight aim, be sure that all the tires are at the correct inflation pressure, and that the suspension is in good working condition.

2 The headlight aim equipment will have to be adjusted for the slope of the floor in the service bay. Start the process by turning on the laser light generator on the side of the aimer body.

3 Place a yardstick or measuring tape vertically in front of the center of the front wheel, noting the height of the laser beam.

4 Move the yardstick to the center of the rear wheel and measure the height of the laser beam at this point. The height at the front and rear wheels should be the same.

5 If the laser beam height measurements are not the same, the floor slope of the aiming equipment must be adjusted. Turn the floor slope knob until the measurements are equal.

6 Place the aimer in front of the headlight to be checked, at a distance of 10 to 14 inches (25 to 35 cm). Use the aiming pointer to adjust the height of the aimer to the middle of the headlight.

7 Align the aimer horizontally, using the pointer to place the aimer at the center of the headlight.

8 Lateral alignment (aligning the body of the aimer with the body of the vehicle) is done by looking through the upper visor. The line in the upper visor is aligned with symmetrical points on the vehicle body.

9 Turn on the vehicle headlights, being sure to select the correct beam position for the headlight to be aimed.

10 View the light beam through the aimer window. The position of the light pattern will be different for high and low beams.

11 If the first headlight is aimed adequately, move the aimer to the headlight on the opposite side of the vehicle. Follow the previous steps to position the aimer accurately.

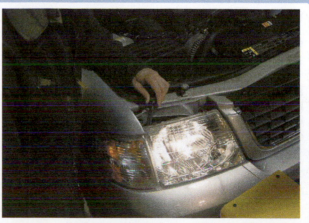

12 If adjustment is required, move the headlight adjusting screws using a special tool or a 1/4-in. drive ratchet/socket combination. Watch the light beam through the aimer window to verify the adjustment.

SUMMARY

1. Automotive bulbs are identified by trade numbers.
2. The trade number is the same regardless of manufacturer for the exact same bulb specification.
3. Daytime running lights (DRLs) are used on many vehicles.
4. High-intensity discharge (HID) headlights are brighter and have a blue tint.
5. Turn signal flashers come in many different types and construction.

REVIEW QUESTIONS

1. Why should the exact same trade number of bulb be used as a replacement?
2. Why is it important to avoid touching a halogen bulb with your fingers?
3. What lights can be used as daytime running lights?

CHAPTER QUIZ

1. Technician A says that the bulb trade number is the same for all bulbs of the same size. Technician B says that a dual-filament bulb has different candlepower ratings for each filament. Which technician is correct?
   a. Technician A only
   b. Technician B only
   c. Both technicians A and B
   d. Neither technician A nor B

2. Technician A says that HID headlights give a bluish-colored light. Technician B says the high beam lights can be used as daytime running lights in some vehicles. Which technician is correct?
   a. Technician A only
   b. Technician B only
   c. Both technicians A and B
   d. Neither technician A nor B

3. Interior overhead lights (dome lights) are operated by doorjamb switches that _____.
   a. Complete the power side of the circuit
   b. Complete the ground side of the circuit
   c. Move the bulb(s) into contact with the power and ground
   d. Complete either a or b depending on application

4. The letters "NA" on a light bulb trade number means _____.
   a. Not available
   b. Natural amber
   c. Not applied
   d. Any of the above depending on the bulb

5. A bulb is being measured using an ohmmeter and the meter display shows OL. This means that the bulb is _____.
   a. Good
   b. Bad
   c. Normal for a tail light bulb but not a brake light bulb
   d. Partially bad (will be dimmer than normal)

6. Which type of headlight has a blue color?
   a. Halogen   b. Sealed beam
   c. HID (xenon)   d. None of the above

7. Which bulb uses natural amber glass?
   a. 194   b. 168
   c. 194NA   d. 1157

8. If a 2057 bulb is burned out, which bulb should be used to replace it?
   a. 1157   b. 2057
   c. 2057 NA   d. 3057

9. A technician replaced a 1157NA with a 1157A bulb. Which is the most likely result?
   a. The bulb is brighter because the 1157A candlepower is higher.
   b. The amber color of the bulb is a different shade.
   c. The bulb is dimmer because the 1157A candlepower is lower.
   d. Both b and c

10. What is used for daytime running lights?
    a. The high beam headlights at reduced intensity
    b. Parking lights
    c. Separate daytime running lights (DRL)
    d. Any of the above

chapter 26

SAFETY BELT AND AIRBAG SYSTEMS

OBJECTIVES: **After studying Chapter 26, the reader will be able to:** • Prepare for ASE Electrical/Electronic Systems (A6) certification test content area "H" (Accessories Diagnosis and Repair). • Describe how an airbag system works. • List the appropriate safety precautions to be followed when working with airbag systems. • Explain how the passenger presence system works. • Discuss the purpose and function of safety belts.

KEY TERMS: • Airbag 252 • Arming sensor 253 • Clockspring 255 • Deceleration sensor 254 • Integral sensor 254 • Occupant detection systems (ODS) 256 • Passenger presence system (PPS) 256 • Pretensioners 252 • SAR 253 • Side airbags 257 • SIR 253 • Squib 253 • SRS 253

SAFETY BELTS

PURPOSE AND FUNCTION Safety belts are used to keep the driver and passengers secured to the vehicle in the event of a collision. Most safety belts include three-point support and are constructed of nylon webbing about 2 in. (5 cm) wide. The three support points include two points on either side of the seat for the belt over the lap and one crossing over the upper torso, which is attached to the "B" pillar or seat back. Every crash consists of three types of collisions.

Collision 1: The vehicle strikes another vehicle or object.

Collision 2: The driver and/or passengers hit objects inside the vehicle if unbelted.

Collision 3: The internal organs of the body hit other organs or bones, which causes internal injuries.

If a safety belt is being worn, the belt stretches, absorbing a lot of the impact, thereby preventing collision with other objects in the vehicle and reducing internal injuries. ● **SEE FIGURE 26–1.**

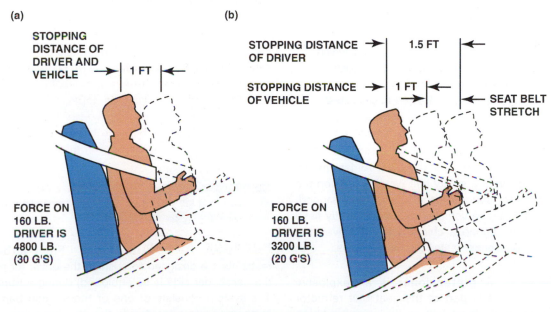

(a)

STOPPING DISTANCE OF DRIVER AND VEHICLE

1 FT

FORCE ON 160 LB. DRIVER IS 4800 LB. (30 G'S)

(b)

STOPPING DISTANCE OF DRIVER — 1.5 FT

STOPPING DISTANCE OF VEHICLE — 1 FT

SEAT BELT STRETCH

FORCE ON 160 LB. DRIVER IS 3200 LB. (20 G'S)

CRASH SCENARIO WITH VEHICLE STOPPING IN ONE FOOT DISTANCE FROM A SPEED OF 30 MPH.

FIGURE 26–1 (a) Safety belts are the primary restraint system. (b) During a collision the stretching of the safety belt slows the impact to help reduce bodily injury.

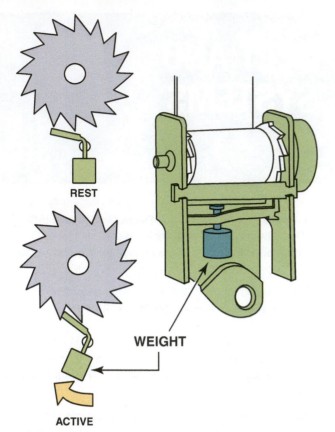

FIGURE 26–2 Most safety belts have an inertia-type mechanism that locks the belt in the event of rapid movement.

REST

WEIGHT

ACTIVE

FIGURE 26–3 A typical safety belt warning light.

SEAT BELT
PRETENSIONER
CABLE

EXPLOSIVE CHARGE

TUBE

FIGURE 26–4 A small explosive charge in the pretensioner forces the end of the seat belt down the tube, which removes any slack in the seat belt.

BELT RETRACTORS

Safety belts are also equipped with one of the following types of retractors.

- Nonlocking retractors, which are used primarily on recoiling.
- Emergency locking retractors, which lock the position of the safety belt in the event of a collision or rollover.
- Emergency and web speed-sensitive retractors, which allow freedom of movement for the driver and passenger but lock if the vehicle is accelerating too fast or if the vehicle is decelerating too fast. ● SEE FIGURE 26–2 for an example of an inertia-type seat belt–locking mechanism.

SAFETY BELT LIGHTS AND CHIMES

All late-model vehicles are equipped with a safety belt warning light on the dash and a chime that sounds if the belt is not fastened. ● SEE FIGURE 26–3. Some vehicles will intermittently flash the reminder light and sound a chime until the driver and sometimes the front passenger fasten their safety belts.

PRETENSIONERS

A **pretensioner** is an explosive (pyrotechnic) device that is part of the seat belt retractor assembly and tightens the seat belt as the airbag is being deployed. The purpose of the pretensioning device is to force the occupant back into position against the seat back and to remove any slack in the seat belt. ● SEE FIGURE 26–4.

CAUTION: The seat belt pretensioner assemblies must be replaced in the event of an airbag deployment. Always follow the vehicle manufacturer's recommended service procedure. Pretensioners are explosive devices that could be ignited if voltage is applied to the terminals. Do not use a jumper wire or powered test light around the wiring near the seat belt latch wiring. Always follow the vehicle manufacturer's recommended test procedures.

FRONT AIRBAGS

PURPOSE AND FUNCTION

Front **airbag** passive restraints are designed to cushion the driver (or passenger, if the passenger side is so equipped) during a frontal collision. The system consists of one or more nylon bags folded up in compartments located in the steering wheel, dashboard, interior panels, or side pillars of the vehicle. During a crash of sufficient force, pressurized gas instantly fills the airbag and then deploys out of the storage compartment to protect the occupant from serious injury. These airbag systems may be known by many different names, including the following:

1. **Supplemental restraint system (SRS)**
2. **Supplemental inflatable restraints (SIR)**
3. **Supplemental air restraints (SAR)**

Most airbags are designed to supplement the safety belts in the event of a collision, and front airbags are meant to be deployed only in the event of a frontal impact within 30° of the center. Front (driver and passenger side) airbag systems are *not* designed to inflate during side or rear impact. The force required to deploy a typical airbag is approximately equal to the force of a vehicle hitting a wall at over 10 mph (16 km/h). The force required to trigger the sensors within the system prevents accidental deployment if curbs are hit or the brakes are rapidly applied. The system requires a substantial force to deploy the airbag to help prevent accidental inflation.

PARTS INVOLVED ● **SEE FIGURE 26–5** for an overall view of the parts included in a typical airbag system.

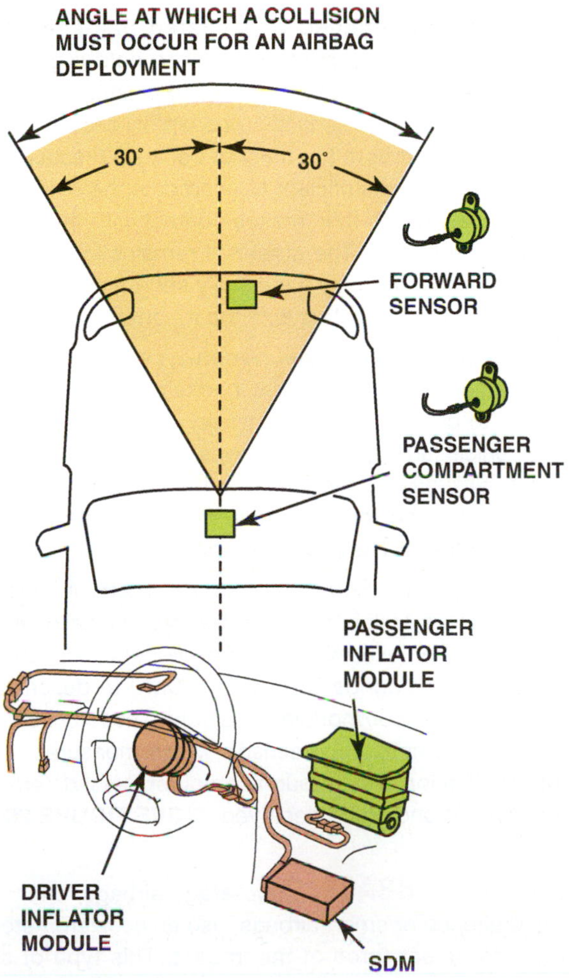

FIGURE 26–5 A typical airbag system showing many of the components. The SDM is the "sensing and diagnostic module" and includes the arming sensor as well as the electronics that keep checking the circuits for continuity and the capacitors that are discharged to deploy the air bags.

The parts include the following:

1. Sensors
2. Airbag (inflator) module
3. Clockspring wire coil in the steering column
4. Control module
5. Wiring and connectors

OPERATION   To cause inflation, the following events must occur:

- To cause a deployment of the airbag, two sensors must be triggered at the same time. The **arming sensor** is used to provide electrical power, and a *forward* or *discriminating sensor* is used to provide the ground connection.
- The arming sensor provides the electrical power to the airbag heating unit, called a **squib,** inside the inflator module.
- The squib uses electrical power and converts it into heat for ignition of the propellant used to inflate the airbag.
- Before the airbag can inflate, however, the squib circuit also must have a ground provided by the forward or the discriminating sensor. In other words, two sensors (arming and forward sensors) *must* be triggered *at the same time* before the airbag is deployed.

? **FREQUENTLY ASKED QUESTION**

When Do Side Airbags Deploy?

Side and curtain airbags are included in many newer vehicles to help the vehicle manufacturers meet crash safety standards. The side airbags will deploy during a collision from the side or if the airbag computer detects a possible roll-over condition. The side and/or curtain airbags will inflate within a few thousandths of a second, providing protection for the chest and shoulder areas of the driver and/or passengers. During minor collisions, front collisions, and rear collisions, the side airbags will *not* deploy.

TYPES OF AIRBAG INFLATORS   There are two different types of inflators used in airbags.

1. **Solid fuel.** This type usually uses sodium azide pellets, which, when ignited, generate a large quantity of nitrogen gas that quickly inflates the airbag. This was the first type used and is still commonly used in driver- and passenger-side airbag inflator modules. The squib is the electrical heating element used to ignite the gas-generating material. ● **SEE FIGURE 26–6.**

2. **Compressed gas.** Commonly used in passenger-side airbags and roof-mounted systems, the compressed gas system uses a canister filled with argon gas, plus a small percentage of helium at 3,000 PSI (435 kPa). A small igniter

FIGURE 26–6 The inflator module is being removed from the airbag housing. The squib, inside the inflator module, is the heating element that ignites the pyrotechnic gas generator that rapidly produces nitrogen gas to fill the airbag.

ruptures a burst disc to release the gas when energized. The compressed gas inflators are long cylinders that can be installed inside the instrument panel, seat back, door panel, or along any side rail or pillar of the vehicle. ● SEE FIGURE 26–7.

Once the inflator is ignited, the nylon bag quickly inflates (in about 30 ms or 0.030 second) with nitrogen gas generated by the inflator. During an actual frontal collision accident, the driver is being thrown forward by the driver's own momentum toward the steering wheel. The strong nylon bag inflates at the same time. Personal injury is reduced by the spreading of the stopping force over the entire upper-body region. The normal collapsible steering column remains in operation and collapses in a collision when equipped with an airbag system. The bag is equipped with two large side vents that allow the bag to deflate immediately after inflation, once the bag has cushioned the occupant in a collision.

TIMELINE FOR AIRBAG DEPLOYMENT Following are the times necessary for an airbag deployment, in milliseconds (each millisecond is equal to 0.001 second or 1/1,000 of a second).

1. Collision occurs: 0.0 ms
2. Sensors detect collision: 16 ms (0.016 second)
3. Airbag is deployed and seam cover rips: 40 ms (0.040 second)
4. Airbag is fully inflated: 100 ms (0.100 second)
5. Airbag deflated: 250 ms (0.250 second)

In other words, an airbag deployment occurs and is over in about a quarter of a second.

SENSOR OPERATION All three sensors are basically switches that complete an electrical circuit when activated. The sensors are similar in construction and operation, and the *location* of the sensor determines its name. All airbag sensors are rigidly mounted to the vehicle and *must* be mounted with the arrow pointing toward the front of the vehicle to ensure

FIGURE 26–7 This shows a deployed side curtain airbag on a training vehicle.

that the sensor can detect rapid forward deceleration. There are three basic styles (designs) of airbag sensors.

1. **Magnetically retained gold-plated ball sensor.** This sensor uses a permanent magnet to hold a gold-plated steel ball away from two gold-plated electrical contacts. If the vehicle (and the sensor) stops rapidly enough, the steel ball is released from the magnet because the inertia force of the crash was sufficient to overcome the magnetic pull on the ball, which then makes contact with the two gold-plated electrodes. The steel ball remains in contact with the electrodes for only a relatively short time because it is drawn back into contact with the magnet.

2. **Rolled up stainless-steel ribbon-type sensor.** This sensor is housed in an airtight package with nitrogen gas inside to prevent harmful corrosion of the sensor parts. If the vehicle (and the sensor) stops suddenly, the stainless-steel roll "unrolls" and contacts the two gold-plated contacts. Once the force is stopped, the stainless-steel roll will roll back into its original shape.

3. **Integral sensor.** Some vehicles use electronic **deceleration sensors** built into the inflator module, called **integral sensors**. For example, General Motors uses the term *sensing and diagnostic module (SDM)* to describe their integrated sensor/module assembly. These units contain an accelerometer-type sensor, which measures the rate of deceleration and, through computer logic, determines if the airbags should be deployed. ● SEE FIGURE 26–8.

TWO-STAGE AIRBAGS Two-stage airbags, often called advanced airbags or smart airbags, use an accelerometer type of sensor to detect force of the impact. This type of sensor measures the actual rate of deceleration of the vehicle, which is then used to determine whether one or both elements of a two-stage airbag should be deployed.

■ **Low-stage deployment.** This lower-force deployment is used if the accelerometer detects a low-speed crash.

FIGURE 26–8 A sensing and diagnostic module that includes an accelerometer. This assembly is shown with the cover removed showing the electronic circuits. This assembly is usually located under the center console.

CONNECTORS TO EACH STAGE   INFLATOR MODULE

FIGURE 26–9 A driver's side airbag showing two inflator connectors. One is for the lower-force inflator and the other is for the higher-force inflator. Either can be ignited or both at the same time if the deceleration sensor detects a severe impact.

- **High-stage deployment.** This stage is used if the accelerometer detects a high-speed crash or a more rapid deceleration rate.
- **Both low- and high-stage deployment.** Under severe high-speed crashes, both stages can be deployed.
  ● **SEE FIGURE 26–9.**

WIRING Wiring and connectors are very important for proper identification and long life. Airbag-related circuits have the following features.

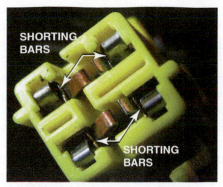

SHORTING BARS

SHORTING BARS

FIGURE 26–10 The terminals used in airbag circuits are gold plated to keep them from corroding. Shorting bars are used in most airbag connectors. These spring-loaded clips short across both terminals of an airbag connector when it is disconnected to help prevent accidental deployment of the airbag.

- All electrical connectors and conduit for airbags are colored yellow.
- To ensure proper electrical connection to the inflator module in the steering wheel, a coil assembly is used in the steering column. This coil is a ribbon of copper wires that operates much like a window shade when the steering wheel is rotated. As the steering wheel is rotated, this coil, usually called a **clockspring,** prevents the lack of continuity between the sensors and the inflator assembly that might result from a horn-ring type of sliding conductor.
- Inside the yellow plastic airbag connectors are gold-plated terminals, which are used to prevent corrosion.
  ● **SEE FIGURE 26–10.**

Most airbag systems also contain a diagnostic unit that often includes an auxiliary power supply, which is used to provide the current to inflate the airbag if the battery is disconnected from the vehicle during a collision. This auxiliary power supply normally uses capacitors that are discharged through the squib of the inflation module. When the ignition is turned off, these capacitors are discharged. Therefore, after a few minutes of the ignition being turned off, an airbag system will not deploy if the vehicle is hit while parked.

PRECAUTIONS Take the following precautions when working with or around airbags:

1. Always follow all precautions and warning stickers on vehicles equipped with airbags.
2. Maintain a safe working distance from all airbags to help prevent the possibility of personal injury in the unlikely event of an unintentional airbag deployment.
   - Side impact airbag: 5 in. (13 cm) distance
   - Driver front airbag: 10 in. (25 cm) distance
   - Passenger front airbag: 20 in. (50 cm) distance
3. In the event of a collision in which the bag(s) is deployed, the inflator module *and* all sensors usually must be replaced to ensure proper future operation of the system.

4. Avoid using a self-powered test light around the yellow airbag wiring. Even though it is highly unlikely, a self-powered test light could provide the necessary current to accidentally set off the inflator module and cause an airbag deployment.

5. Use care while handling the inflator module section when it is removed from the steering wheel. Always hold the inflator away from your body.

6. If handling a deployed inflator module, always wear gloves and safety glasses to avoid the possibility of skin irritation from the sodium hydroxide dust, which is used as a lubricant on the bag(s), that remains after deployment.

7. Never jar or strike a sensor. The contacts inside the sensor may be damaged, preventing the proper operation of the airbag system in the event of a collision.

8. When mounting a sensor in a vehicle, make certain that the arrow on the sensor is pointing toward the front of the vehicle. Also be certain that the sensor is securely mounted.

DISARMING   The airbags should be disarmed (temporarily disconnected) whenever performing service work on any of the following locations:

- Steering wheel
- Dash or instrument panel
- Glove box (instrument panel storage compartment)

Check service information for the exact procedure, which usually includes the following steps:

STEP 1   Disconnect the negative battery cable.

STEP 2   Remove the airbag fuse (has a yellow cover).

STEP 3   Disconnect the yellow electrical connector located at the base of the steering column to disable the driver's side airbag.

STEP 4   Disconnect the yellow electrical connector for the passenger side airbag.

This procedure is called "disabling air bags" in most service information. Always follow the vehicle manufacturer's specified procedures.

DIAGNOSTIC AND SERVICE PROCEDURE

SELF-DIAGNOSIS   All airbag systems can detect system electrical faults, and if found, will disable the system and notify the driver through an airbag warning lamp in the instrument cluster. Depending on circuit design, a system fault may cause the warning lamp to fail to illuminate, remain lit continuously, or flash. Some systems use a tone generator that produces an audible warning when a system fault occurs or if the warning lamp is inoperative. The warning lamp should illuminate with the ignition key on and engine off as a bulb check. If not, the diagnostic module is likely disabling the system.

If the airbag warning light remains on, the airbags may or may not be disabled, depending on the specific vehicle and the fault detected. Some warning lamp circuits have a timer that extinguishes the lamp after a few seconds. The airbag system generally does not require service unless there is a failed component. However, a steering wheel–mounted airbag module is routinely removed and replaced in order to service switches and other column-mounted devices.

OCCUPANT DETECTION SYSTEM

PURPOSE AND FUNCTION   The U.S. Federal Motor Vehicle Safety Standard 208 (FMVSS) specifies that the passenger-side airbag be disabled or deployed with reduced force under the following conditions. This system is referred to as an **occupant detection system (ODS)** or the **passenger presence system (PPS)**.

- When there is no weight on the seat and no seat belt is fastened, the passenger-side airbag will not deploy and the passenger airbag light should be off. ● **SEE FIGURE 26–11.**

- The passenger-side airbag will be disabled and the disabled airbag light will be on if only 10 to 37 lb (4.5 to 17 kg) is on the passenger seat, which would generally represent a seated child.

- If 38 to 99 lb (17 to 45 kg) is detected on the passenger seat, which represents a child or small adult, the airbag will deploy at a decreased force.

- If 99 lb (45 kg) or more is detected on the passenger seat, the airbag will deploy at full force, depending on the severity of the crash, speed of the vehicle, and other factors that may result in the airbag deploying at a reduced force.

FIGURE 26–11 The passenger-side airbag "on" lamp will light if a passenger is detected on the passenger seat.

SIDE AIRBAGS

Side and/or *curtain airbags* use a variety of sensors to determine if they need to be deployed. **Side airbags** are mounted in one of two general locations.

- In the side bolster of the seat. ● **SEE FIGURE 26–12.**
- In the door panel.

FIGURE 26–12 A typical seat (side) airbag that deploys from the side of the seat.

Most side airbag sensors use an electronic accelerometer to detect when to deploy the airbags, which are usually mounted to the bottom of the left and right "B" pillars (where the front doors latch) behind a trim panel on the inside of the vehicle.

CAUTION: Avoid using a lockout tool (e.g., a "slim jim") in vehicles equipped with side airbags to help prevent damage to the components and wiring in the system.

SIDE CURTAIN AIRBAGS

Side curtain airbags are usually deployed by a module based on input from many different sensors, including a lateral acceleration sensor and wheel speed sensors. For example, in one system used by Ford, the ABS controller commands that the brakes on one side of the vehicle be applied, using down pressure, while monitoring the wheel speed sensors. If the wheels slow down with little brake pressure, the controller assumes that the vehicle could roll over, thereby deploying the side curtain airbags.

SUMMARY

1. Airbags use a sensor(s) to determine if the rate of deceleration is enough to cause bodily harm.
2. All airbag electrical connectors and conduit are yellow and all electrical terminals are gold plated to protect against corrosion.
3. Always follow the manufacturer's procedure for disabling the airbag system prior to any work performed on the system.
4. Frontal airbags operate only within 30° from the center and do not deploy in the event of a rollover, side, or rear collision.
5. Two sensors must be triggered at the same time for an airbag deployment to occur. Many newer systems use an accelerometer-type crash sensor that actually measures the amount of deceleration.
6. Pretensioners are explosive (pyrotechnic) devices which remove the slack from the seat belt and help position the occupant.
7. Occupant detection systems use sensors in the seat to determine whether the airbag will be deployed and with full or reduced force.

REVIEW QUESTIONS

1. What are the safety precautions to follow when working around an airbag?
2. What sensor(s) must be triggered for an airbag deployment?
3. How should deployed inflation modules be handled?
4. What is the purpose of pretensioners?

1. A vehicle is being repaired after an airbag deployment. Technician A says that the inflator module should be handled as if it is still live. Technician B says rubber gloves should be worn to prevent skin irritation. Which technician is correct?
   a. Technician A only
   b. Technician B only
   c. Both technicians A and B
   d. Neither technician A nor B

2. A seat belt pretensioner is _____.
   a. A device that contains an explosive charge
   b. Used to remove slack from the seat belt in the event of a collision
   c. Used to force the occupant back into position against the seat back in the event of a collision
   d. All of the above

3. What conducts power and ground to the driver's side airbag?
   a. Twisted-pair wires
   b. Clockspring
   c. Carbon contact and brass surface plate on the steering column
   d. Magnetic reed switch

4. Two technicians are discussing dual-stage airbags. Technician A says that a deployed airbag is safe to handle regardless of which stage caused the deployment of the airbag. Technician B says that both stages ignite, but at different speeds depending on the speed of the vehicle. Which technician is correct?
   a. Technician A only
   b. Technician B only
   c. Both technicians A and B
   d. Neither technician A nor B

5. When will side or curtain airbags be deployed?
   a. In the event of a hard impact into the side of the vehicle
   b. If the vehicle rolls over
   c. In the event of a frontal impact
   d. In the event of an impact to the rear of the vehicle

6. Technician A says that a deployed airbag can be repacked, reused, and reinstalled in the vehicle. Technician B says that a deployed airbag should be discarded and replaced with an entirely new assembly. Which technician is correct?
   a. Technician A only
   b. Technician B only
   c. Both technicians A and B
   d. Neither technician A nor B

7. What color are the airbag electrical connectors and conduit?
   a. Blue   b. Red
   c. Yellow   d. Orange

8. Driver and/or passenger front airbags will deploy only if a collision occurs how many degrees from straight ahead?
   a. 10°   b. 30°
   c. 60°   d. 90°

9. How many sensors must be triggered at the same time to cause an airbag deployment?
   a. One   b. Two
   c. Three   d. Four

10. The electrical terminals used for airbag systems are unique because they are _____.
    a. Solid copper
    b. Tin-plated heavy-gauge steel
    c. Silver plated
    d. Gold plated

HEATING AND AIR CONDITIONING SYSTEMS

OBJECTIVES: After studying Chapter 27, the reader should be able to: • Prepare for ASE Heating and Air conditioning (A7) certification test content area "A" (Air Conditioning System Diagnosis and Repair) and content area "C" (Heating and Engine Cooling Systems Diagnosis and Repair). • Describe how the heater functions. • Describe how the refrigeration cycle functions. • List the parts of a typical air conditioning system. • Explain how the air conditioning system removes heat from the passenger compartment. • Describe how to check for refrigerant leaks. • Check for proper heater operation. • Describe how to measure air conditioning outlet temperature.

KEY TERMS: • Blower motor 260 • Boiling point 261 • British Thermal Units (BTUs) 261 • Calorie (c) 261 • CFC-12 263 • Desiccant 263 • Condenser 262 • Condensation point 261 • Electromagnetic clutch 262 • Evaporator 262 • Freon 263 • Heat 261 • Heater core 259 • Heater hoses 259 • Heating, ventilation, and air conditioning system (HVAC) 259 • HFC-134a 263 • Liquid 261 • R-12 263 • R-134a 263 • Solid 261 • Vapor 261

HEATING, VENTILATION, AND AIR CONDITIONING SYSTEM

PURPOSE AND FUNCTION Driver and passenger comfort is the primary purpose of the **heating, ventilation, and air conditioning system (HVAC).** The heater is also needed in cold climates to provide comfort and to prevent freezing or death due to cold temperatures.

PARTS INVOLVED The parts involved include the following:

1. Heater system
2. Blower motor
3. Ducts and airflow control valves
4. Air conditioning compressor, related components and control systems

HEATING SYSTEM

PURPOSE AND FUNCTION The purpose and function of the heater system is to provide heat to the passenger compartment in cold weather and to defrost the windshield.

PARTS AND OPERATION All automotive and light-truck heater systems use the hot coolant from the engine to produce heat. The engine coolant (antifreeze and water) flows through

heater hoses and a **heater core.** The engine water pump supplies the force necessary to circulate the engine coolant through the heater core. The heater core is a small radiator with tubes and fins that help transfer the heat from the coolant to the air flowing through the heater core. ● **SEE FIGURE 27–1.**

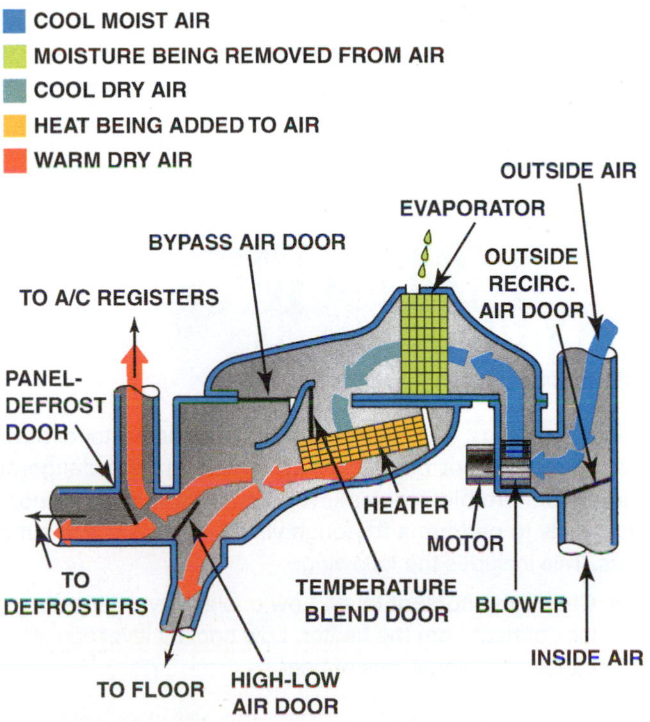

■ COOL MOIST AIR
■ MOISTURE BEING REMOVED FROM AIR
■ COOL DRY AIR
■ HEAT BEING ADDED TO AIR
■ WARM DRY AIR

FIGURE 27–1 Typical flow of air through an automotive heat, ventilation, and air conditioning system when placed in the heat position.

FIGURE 27–2 A typical blower motor assembly with attached squirrel-cage blower is used to move air into the passenger compartment through ducts, hoses, and vents located under the dashboard.

A **blower motor** with a squirrel cage–type fan is usually used to force air through the heater core and into the passenger compartment. ● **SEE FIGURE 27–2.**

 FREQUENTLY ASKED QUESTION

What Is an Auxiliary Electric Water Pump?

Some vehicles are equipped with an auxiliary electric water pump. The purpose and function of this pump is to help warm the interior of the vehicle by circulating coolant from the engine through the heater core when the engine is at idle speed. At idle speed, the water pump does not circulate a sufficient quantity of coolant through the heater core to warm the interior in freezing weather.

HEATER OPERATION DIAGNOSIS

ITEMS TO CHECK A lack of heat from the heater or having airflow coming out of the wrong vents can be a dangerous and uncomfortable problem. The first step in the diagnostic process is to perform a thorough visual inspection and simple tests. This includes the following:

- **Check the coolant level.** Low coolant level can cause a lack of heat from the heater. Low coolant level can also cause occasional loss of heat.

  CAUTION: Do not remove the radiator cap when the engine is hot. Allow the vehicle to sit several hours before removing the pressure cap to check the radiator coolant level.

FIGURE 27–3 Heater hoses are the smaller coolant hoses that run from and back to the engine.

- **Carefully touch the upper radiator hose with the engine running.** In most vehicles, the temperature of the hose should be so hot that you cannot keep your hand on it (between 190°F to 220°F [88°C to 104°C]).

  NOTE: An infrared pyrometer can be used to measure the temperature of the upper radiator hose and the area around the thermostat housing.

  Results: If the upper radiator hose is not too hot to hold, then the engine thermostat is defective. If the radiator hose is too hot to handle, then the lack of heat from the heater is not due to a lack of hot water in the engine.

- **Carefully touch the heater hoses.** Both heater hoses should also be too hot to the touch. This test confirms that the engine coolant is able to flow from the engine to and through the heater core and return to the engine. ● **SEE FIGURE 27–3.**

RESULTS The results of the inspection include:

a. If neither heater hose is hot to the touch, it is likely there is an air pocket in the heater that is preventing the flow of coolant into the heater core.

b. If only one heater hose is hot to the touch, then the heater core is likely to be clogged or partially clogged. A clogged heater core would prevent enough hot coolant from circulating through the heater core to provide adequate heat to the passenger compartment.

AIR CONDITIONING SYSTEM

PRINCIPLES The basic principle of the refrigeration cycle is that as a liquid changes into a gas, heat is absorbed. The heat that is absorbed by an automotive air conditioning system is the heat from inside the vehicle.

What Can Cause the Heat from the Heater to Go from Warm to Cold?

If heat from the heater seems to go from warm to cold while driving, it is an indication of low coolant level. When the engine speed is higher, such as during acceleration, the coolant will be flowing through the engine which will tend to keep if from flowing through the heater core. But when the engine speed is lower such as when the vehicle is stopped at a traffic light, coolant again flows through the heater core and warm air is felt inside the passenger compartment. If this condition is being reported by the driver, then visually check for proper coolant level and if low, check for a possible leak in the cooling system.

A **solid** is a substance that cannot be compressed and has strong resistance to flow. The molecules of a solid attract each other strongly, and resist changes in volume and shape.

A substance is solid at any temperature below its melting point. The melting point is a characteristic of a substance and is related to the temperature at which a solid turns to a liquid. For water, the melting point is 32°F (0°C), which means that the changes between liquid water and ice can be observed under normal weather conditions.

A **liquid** is a substance that cannot be compressed. A substance in a liquid state has a fixed volume, but no definite shape.

The **boiling point** is the temperature at which a solid or liquid turns to vapor. For water at normal sea-level conditions, the boiling point is 212°F (100°C).

A **vapor** is a substance that can be easily compressed, has no resistance to flow, and no fixed volume. Since vapor flows, it is considered a fluid just like liquids are. ● **SEE FIGURE 27–4.**

A substance changes to a vapor if the temperature rises above its boiling point. A vapor condenses to liquid if its

FIGURE 27–4 Water is a substance that can be found naturally in solid, liquid, and vapor states.

Why Is Liquid Sprayed from a Can Cold?

If you spray a can of liquid continuously, the can becomes cold, and the liquid being sprayed becomes cold. The can becomes cold because the pressure in the can is reduced while spraying, allowing the liquid propellant inside the can to boil and absorb heat. The liquid being sprayed has also been cooled by the liquid propellant. The propellant vapor is further cooled as it decompresses when it hits the open air. Rapid decompression results in a rapid temperature drop.

temperature falls below its boiling point. Just like melting and freezing, the boiling point and **condensation point** are the same temperature. Again, the difference is simply whether heat is being added or taken away. Boiling point and condensation point temperatures are not fixed; they vary with pressure.

HEAT AND TEMPERATURE   Molecules in a substance tend to vibrate rapidly in all directions, and this disorganized energy is called **heat.** The level of this energy is measured as temperature.

Heat and temperature are not the same. Heat is measured in **calories (c).** The calorie is a metric unit that expresses the amount of heat needed to raise the temperature of 1 gram of water 1°C. Heat is also measured in **British Thermal Units (BTU).** One BTU is the heat required to raise the temperature of one pound of water 1°F at sea level. One BTU equals 252 calories.

PRESSURE–TEMPERATURE RELATIONSHIPS   There are two aspects of the relationship between pressure and temperature that are important to understanding the operation of an HVAC system.

- The temperature at which a liquid boils (and vapor condenses) increases and decreases with the pressure.

- Pressure in a sealed system that contains both liquid and vapor increases and decreases with the temperature.

AIR CONDITIONING REFRIGERATION CYCLE

BASIC OPERATION   The air conditioning system is a closed system where refrigerant is forced to move through the system by a compressor. Along the way, the refrigerant changes its state from liquid to gas and back to liquid.

HIGH-PRESSURE VAPOR
HIGH-PRESSURE LIQUID
LOW-PRESSURE VAPOR
LOW-PRESSURE LIQUID

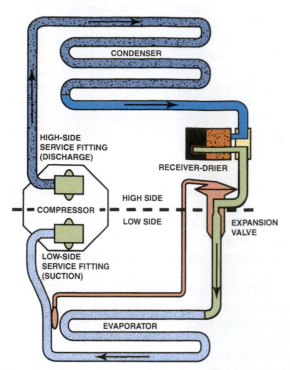

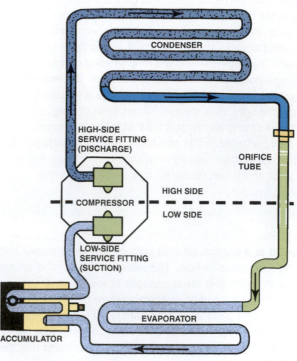

FIGURE 27–5 The evaporator serves to allow the liquid refrigerant to evaporate and absorb heat from the passenger compartment. The evaporator is located inside the passenger compartment in the dash area usually behind the glove compartment.

EVAPORATOR

The liquid refrigerant evaporates in a small radiator-type unit called the **evaporator.** As the refrigerant evaporates, it absorbs heat as it changes from liquid to gas. As the heat is absorbed by the refrigerant, the evaporator becomes cold. A blower motor equipped with a squirrel cage–type fan circulates air through the evaporator and forces the cooler air into the passenger compartment. Because the evaporator is cold (usually just above the freezing point of 32°F [0°C]), any moisture in the air condenses on its cool surface. This removes the moisture from the air and lowers the relative humidity. The moisture that condenses out of the air then becomes water that is allowed to flow out of the evaporator housing drain and onto the ground. ● **SEE FIGURE 27–5.**

COMPRESSOR

After the refrigerant has evaporated in the evaporator, the refrigerant (as a low pressure gas) flows into the engine-driven compressor. Most compressors use an **electromagnetic clutch** that is used to engage the compressor when cooling is required. The compressor compresses the low-pressure refrigerant gas into a high-pressure gas and forces the refrigerant through the system. The compressor performs the following functions:

- Compresses the low-pressure gas refrigerant from the evaporator into a high-pressure gas that is then sent to the condenser.

- Raises the temperature of the gas so that there is a difference in temperature between the outside (ambient) air and the refrigerant in the condenser.
- Acts as the pump used to circulate the refrigerant throughout the system.
- Often switches on and off (cycles) to control evaporator temperatures.
- The oil in the refrigerant lubricates the moving parts of the compressor. ● **SEE FIGURE 27–6.**

CONDENSER

The high-pressure gas flows into the condenser located in front of the cooling system radiator. The **condenser** looks like another radiator, and its purpose and function is the same as the cooling system radiator, to remove heat from the high-pressure gas. In the condenser, the high-pressure gas changes (condenses) to form a high-pressure liquid as the heat from the refrigerant is released to the air. When the refrigerant leaves the compressor and enters the condenser, it is over 300°F (150°C). Even on a hot 100°F (38°C) day, there is a difference in temperature between the outside air around the condenser and the temperature of the refrigerant inside the condenser. Heat always travels hot to cold. Therefore, the heat in the hot refrigerant has a natural tendency to radiate into the outside air. As the heat travels into the air, the high-pressure gas

FIGURE 27–6 A typical air conditioning compressor that is belt driven.

refrigerant changes state and becomes a high-pressure liquid. This is the reason the condenser is called by that name: as the heat leaves the refrigerant, it condenses from a gas (vapor) to a liquid. ● SEE FIGURE 27–7.

REFRIGERATION CYCLE OPERATION

1. The high-pressure liquid then flows through a device (orifice tube or thermal expansion valve) that meters the flow into the evaporator. When the high pressure of the liquid drops, it causes the refrigerant to vaporize.

2. Air is blown through the evaporator by the blower motor. The air is cooled as heat is removed from the air and transferred to the refrigerant in the evaporator. This cooled air is then directed inside the passenger compartment through vents. ● SEE FIGURE 27–8 on page 265.

 FREQUENTLY ASKED QUESTION

How Does the Inside of the Vehicle Get Cooled?

The underlying principle involved in air conditioning or refrigeration is that "cold attracts heat." Therefore, a cool evaporator attracts the hot air inside the vehicle. Heat always travels toward cold and when the hot air passes through the cold evaporator, the heat is absorbed by the cold evaporator, which lowers the temperature of the air. The cooled air is then forced into the passenger compartment by the blower through the air conditioning vents.

REFRIGERANTS

R-12 An air conditioning refrigerant is used to transfer heat from the inside of the vehicle to the condenser located in the front of the vehicle. A refrigerant absorbs heat when it changes its state from liquid to gas. One of the first refrigerants was **CFC-12,** commonly referred to as **R-12** or by its brand name **Freon,** a registered trade name of the DuPont Corporation. R-12 was phased out by the mid-1990s because of concerns that R-12 depletes the atmosphere's ozone layer.

R-134A Another refrigerant, **HFC-134a,** also called **R-134a,** has been selected by vehicle manufacturers to replace the ozone-harming CFC. Its chemical name is tetrafluoroethane, and Dupont calls it Suva®. The boiling points and therefore the operation characteristics of R-12 and R-134a are similar. ● SEE FIGURE 27–9 on page 265.

 FREQUENTLY ASKED QUESTION

What Will Be Used in the Future?

The refrigerant that holds the best promise for widespread use is R-1234yf. While expensive, this refrigerant is less reactive and more environmental friendly than R-134a. In Europe, some vehicles started to use carbon dioxide (R-144) but this requires a much higher pressure and the cost is higher. While carbon dioxide (CO_2) is being used on prototype vehicles, such as the Toyota Fuel Cell Hybrid Vehicle (FCHV), it requires extremely high pressures, up to 2,000 PSI, and is not as efficient as a refrigerant as R-134a. ● SEE FIGURE 27–10 on page 265.

REFRIGERANT OILS

PURPOSE AND FUNCTION The oil carried by the refrigerant through the various components is often the only source of lubrication for the compressor. The oil used must be able to mix without separating in the refrigerant. If the refrigerant charge is too low, the compressor can be damaged because it is the refrigerant that carries and moves the oil through the system.

RECEIVER-DRIER

PURPOSE AND FUNCTION A drier is needed to remove moisture from the system. The drier contains a **desiccant** (usually silica alumina or silica gel). A desiccant is a drying agent that absorbs any moisture (water) that gets into the air conditioning refrigerant system. Moisture can combine with the refrigerant to form an acid. Water can also freeze and form ice in the system. ● SEE FIGURE 27–11 on page 266.

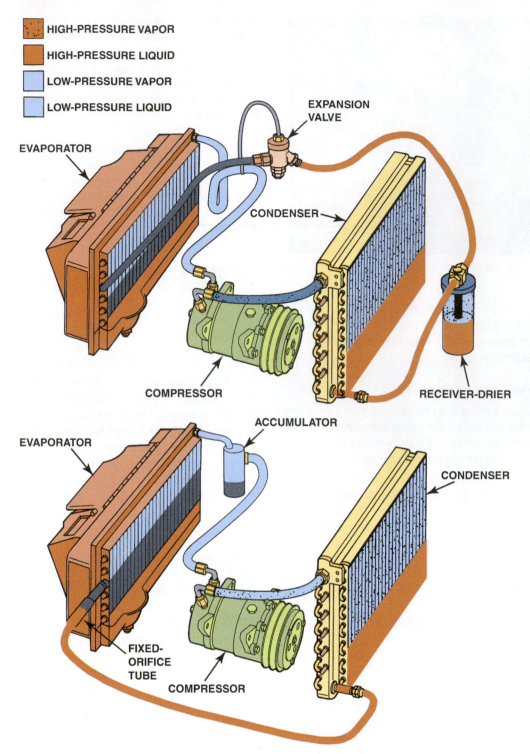

HIGH-PRESSURE VAPOR

HIGH-PRESSURE LIQUID

LOW-PRESSURE VAPOR

LOW-PRESSURE LIQUID

EVAPORATOR

EXPANSION VALVE

CONDENSER

RECEIVER-DRIER

COMPRESSOR

EVAPORATOR

ACCUMULATOR

CONDENSER

FIXED-ORIFICE TUBE

COMPRESSOR

FIGURE 27–7 The evaporator serves the same function for both the orifice-tube and the expansion valve–type air conditioning system and that is to allow the liquid refrigerant to evaporate and absorb heat from the passenger compartment.

REFRIGERANT LINES AND HOSES

Aluminum tubing is used to connect many stationary items together like the condenser to the receiver-drier and the receiver-drier to the evaporator. Rubber lines are usually used to and from the compressor. Because the compressor is attached to the engine and the engine is mounted on flexible rubber mounts, there is movement between the compressor and the other air conditioning components that are attached to the body of the vehicle. These flexible refrigerant hoses are constructed from many layers of rubber and fabric. ● **SEE FIGURE 27–12** on page 266.

FIGURE 27–8 Air flows through the vent to the passenger compartment. Above this vent on the driver's side is another smaller vent used to demist the driver's door glass.

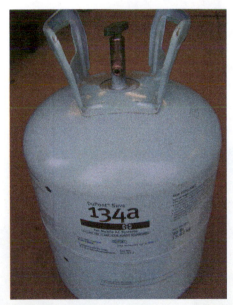

FIGURE 27–9 R-134a is available in 12-oz cans as well as larger 30-lb containers.

FIGURE 27–10 The label on a Toyota Fuel Cell Hybrid Vehicle (FCHV) showing that CO_2 is being used as the refrigerant.

AIR CONDITIONING SYSTEM CHECKS

VERIFY THE CUSTOMER CONCERN The first step in any diagnosis is to verify the customer concern. If a customer complains that the air conditioning system is not functioning properly, check that the controls are set correctly for air conditioning and verify that the system is not functioning correctly.

TEMPERATURE MEASUREMENTS The first step in the diagnosis of any cooling system problem is to verify the complaint (concern).

STEP 1 Start the engine and turn the air conditioning system to maximum, with the engine operating between 1,500 and 2,000 RPM with the doors open. Operate the system for 5 to 10 minutes.

STEP 2 Verify by visual inspection that the air conditioning compressor clutch is engaged.

HINT: If the air conditioning compressor clutch cannot be observed, have an assistant turn the air conditioning on and then off and listen for the "click" of the air conditioning compressor clutch.

STEP 3 Place an air conditioning thermometer in the air conditioning vent near the center of the vehicle. Wait several minutes to allow the system to reach maximum output and observe the thermometer.
- *if 35°F to 45°F (2°C to 7°C)*, the system is functioning okay.
- *If over 45°F (7°C)*, it indicates that there is a concern with the system and more detailed diagnosis will be needed to find the root cause and to correct it. ● SEE FIGURE 27–13.

LEAK DETECTION If the air conditioning system is not functioning correctly, it could be low on a charge of refrigerant and the sources of the leak should be found and corrected.

🔧 **TECH TIP**

Water on the Carpet? Check the Evaporator Water Drain

If the evaporator water drip tube becomes clogged with mud, leaves, or debris, water will build up inside the evaporator housing and spill out onto the carpet on the passenger side. Customers often think that the windshield or door seals are leaking. Most evaporator water drains are not visible unless the vehicle is hoisted.

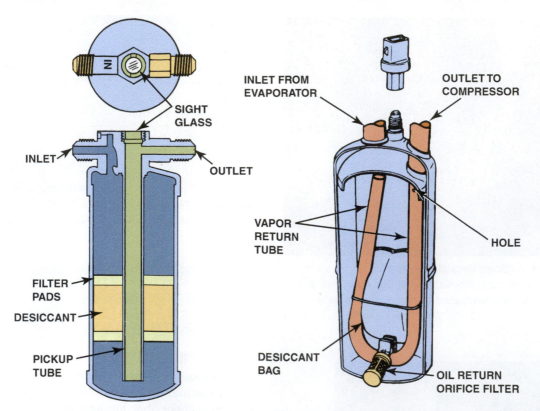

SIGHT GLASS

INLET

OUTLET

FILTER PADS

DESICCANT

PICKUP TUBE

INLET FROM EVAPORATOR

OUTLET TO COMPRESSOR

VAPOR RETURN TUBE

HOLE

DESICCANT BAG

OIL RETURN ORIFICE FILTER

FIGURE 27–11 Some systems store excess refrigerant in a receiver-drier, which is located in the high-side liquid section of the system, whereas other systems (orifice-tube systems) store excess refrigerant in an accumulator located in the low-side vapor section of the system.

FIGURE 27–12 Aluminum tubing lines and the accumulator have service valves that are used to test system pressures and to evacuate and recharge the system using a recovery and recharging machine.

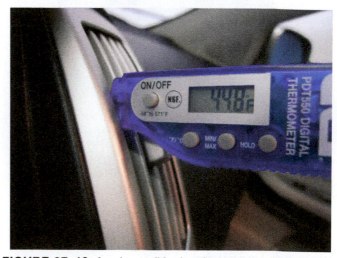

FIGURE 27–13 An air conditioning thermometer being used to check the discharge temperature at the center vents.

Several different methods of leak detection are available, including the following:

- **Visual inspection.** Look for oily areas that are formed when refrigerant leaks and some refrigerant oil is lost. It is this oil that indicates a refrigerant leak.
- **Electronic leak detector.** Many of these units can detect both R-12 and R-134a. The detector will

sound a tone if a leak is detected. ● **SEE FIGURE 27–14.**

- **Soap solution.** Mix a few drops of liquid soap or detergent into a small glass of water. Using a small brush or a small spray bottle, apply the soapy solution to all fittings and other areas such as the condenser and compressor, which often are sources of leaks.

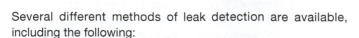

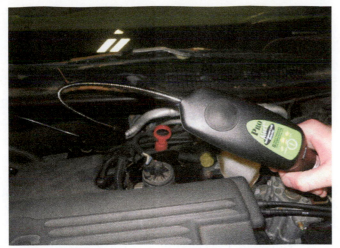

FIGURE 27–14 An electronic leak detector being used to check for leaks at the hoses and connections of an air conditioning system.

? FREQUENTLY ASKED QUESTION

What's Wrong When the Air Conditioning Compressor Clutch Cycles On and Off Rapidly?

This is a common occurrence on a vehicle equipped with a cycling clutch orifice tube (CCOT) system that is low on refrigerant charge. With a normal charge, the low-side pressure should be 15 to 35 PSI and the clutch should be on for 45 to 90 seconds and be off for only about 15 to 30 seconds.

SUMMARY

1. Engine coolant flows through heater hoses and through a heater core to provide heat to the inside of the vehicle.

2. The refrigeration cycle uses a compressor to circulate a refrigerant through a closed system.

3. Refrigerant expands in the evaporator. When the refrigerant expands, both its pressure and temperature drop. The air from inside the vehicle is cooled as it passes through the evaporator.

4. The compressor forces the refrigerant through the closed system and raises the temperature of the refrigerant so that the refrigerant will condense back into liquid in the condenser.

5. Air flow through the condenser removes heat from the hot refrigerant, which condenses back into liquid.

6. The expansion valve (or orifice tube) causes the refrigerant to expand. When the refrigerant expands, its pressure and temperature both drop, thereby cooling the evaporator.

7. A desiccant is used either in the receiver-drier or accumulator to remove any moisture that may get into the system.

8. The air flow through the heater core and the evaporator help condition the air by removing humidity and directing the air flow where needed.

9. The upper radiator hose and both heater hoses should be hot to the touch on a warm engine.

10. Normal air-vent temperature for a properly operating air conditioning system is 35°F to 45°F (2°C to 7°C).

11. Refrigerant leaks can be detected by visual inspection, an electronic leak detector, or a soap solution.

REVIEW QUESTIONS

1. How does the air conditioning system remove moisture from the air?

2. What is the operation of the typical automotive air conditioning system?

3. Why is a desiccant needed in automotive air conditioning systems?

4. How do you diagnose the lack of heat from the heater?

CHAPTER QUIZ

1. Technician A says that heat is measured in degrees. Technician B says that temperature is measured in degrees. Which technician is correct?
   a. Technician A only
   b. Technician B only
   c. Both technicians A and B
   d. Neither technician A nor B

2. The heater uses _____ to heat the air inside the vehicle on most vehicles.
   a. Hot coolant from the engine run through a heater core
   b. Warm air created by the air conditioning system run in reverse
   c. An electrically heated coil
   d. Heat from the exhaust system

3. Where in the air conditioning system is the refrigerant a low-pressure gas?
   a. Condenser outlet
   b. Evaporator outlet
   c. Evaporator inlet
   d. Condenser inlet

4. Where in the air conditioning system is the refrigerant a high-pressure liquid?
   a. Condenser outlet
   b. Evaporator outlet
   c. Evaporator inlet
   d. Condenser inlet

5. Clear water is observed dripping out from beneath the evaporator. Technician A says that is normal. Technician B says that the evaporator housing is defective and should be replaced. Which technician is correct?
   a. Technician A only
   b. Technician B only
   c. Both technicians A and B
   d. Neither technician A nor B

6. The material used to absorb moisture from inside the air conditioning system is called:
   a. Drier
   b. Desiccant
   c. Ester
   d. PAG

7. A customer complains that the heater works generally, but sometimes only cold air comes out while driving. Technician A says that the air conditioning system may not have enough refrigerant in the system. Technician B says that the cooling system could be low on coolant. Which technician is correct?
   a. Technician A only
   b. Technician B only
   c. Both technicians A and B
   d. Neither technician A nor B

8. The first step in the diagnostic procedure when attempting to solve an HVAC customer problem is _____.
   a. Visual inspection
   b. Check for diagnostic trouble codes
   c. Check for technical service bulletins
   d. Verify customer concern

9. Technician A says that one heater hose should be hot and the other hose cool if the heater is functioning okay. Technician B says that both hoses should be hot to the touch. Which technician is correct?
   a. Technician A only
   b. Technician B only
   c. Both technicians A and B
   d. Neither technician A nor B

10. A properly operating air conditioning system should be able to provide air discharge airflow at the center vents at what temperature range?
    a. 65°F–72°F (18°–22°C)
    b. 55°F–64°F (13°–18° C)
    c. 45°F–54°F (7°–12°C)
    d. 35°F–45°F (2°–7°C)?

chapter 28

GASOLINE AND ALTERNATIVE FUELS

OBJECTIVES: After studying Chapter 28, the reader should be able to: • Describe how the proper grade of gasoline affects engine performance. • List gasoline purchasing considerations. • Discuss how volatility affects driveability. • Explain how oxygenated fuels can reduce CO exhaust emissions. • Discuss safety precautions when working with gasoline. • Discuss the advantages and disadvantages of alternative fuels.

KEY TERMS: • AFV 273 • Anti-knock index (AKI) 270 • B20 276 • B5 276 • Biodiesel 275 • Cetane number 275 • Compressed natural gas (CNG) 273 • Diesohol 276 • Distillation 269 • E10 271 • E85 272 • E-diesel 276 • Ethanol 271 • Ethyl alcohol 272 • FFV 273 • Flex fuel 273 • Fungible 269 • Gasoline 269 • Grain alcohol 272 • Liquefied petroleum gas (LPG) 273 • LP gas 273 • Petrodiesel 276 • Propane 273

GASOLINE

DEFINITION **Gasoline** is a term used to describe a complex mixture of various hydrocarbons refined from crude petroleum oil for use as a fuel in engines. A mixture of gasoline and air burns in the cylinder of the engine and produces heat and pressure, which is transformed into rotary motion inside the engine and eventually powers the drive wheels of a vehicle. When the combustion process in the engine is perfect, all of the fuel and air are consumed and only carbon dioxide and water are released.

REFINING CRUDE OIL In the late 1800s, crude was separated into different products by boiling in a process called **distillation.**

Cracking is the process during which hydrocarbons with higher boiling points can be broken down (cracked) into lower boiling hydrocarbons by treating them to very high temperatures. Today, instead of high heat, cracking is performed using a catalyst and is called *catalytic cracking.* ● **SEE FIGURE 28–1.**

SHIPPING Gasoline is transported to regional storage facilities by tank railway car or through pipelines. In the pipeline method, gasoline from many refineries is often sent through the same pipeline and can become mixed. Gasoline is said to be **fungible,** meaning that it is capable of being interchanged because each grade is created to specification so there is no reason to keep the different gasoline brands separated except for grade. Regular grade, midgrade, and premium grades are separated by using a device, called a *pig,* in the pipeline and sent to regional storage facilities. ● **SEE FIGURE 28–2.**

It is at these regional or local storage facilities where the additives and dye (if any) are added and then shipped by truck to individual gas stations.

SEASONAL BLENDING Cold temperatures reduce the normal vaporization of gasoline; therefore, winter-blended gasoline is specially formulated to vaporize at lower temperatures for proper starting and driveability at low ambient temperatures.

- **Winter blend.** The *American Society for Testing and Materials (ASTM)* standards for winter-blend gasoline allow volatility of up to 15 pounds per square inch (PSI) RVP.

- **Summer blend.** At warm ambient temperatures, gasoline vaporizes easily. However, the fuel system (fuel pump, fuel-injector nozzles, etc.) is designed to operate

? FREQUENTLY ASKED QUESTION

Why Do I Get Lower Gas Mileage in Winter?

Several factors cause the engine to use more fuel in winter than in summer.

- Gasoline that is blended for use in cold climates is designed for ease of starting and contains fewer heavy molecules, which contribute to fuel economy. The heat content of winter gasoline is lower than summer-blend gasoline.
- In cold temperatures, all lubricants are stiff, causing more resistance. These lubricants include the engine oil, as well as the transmission and differential gear lubricants.
- Heat from the engine is radiated into the outside air more rapidly when the temperature is cold, resulting in longer run time until the engine has reached normal operating temperature.
- Road conditions, such as ice and snow, can cause tire slippage or additional drag on the vehicle.

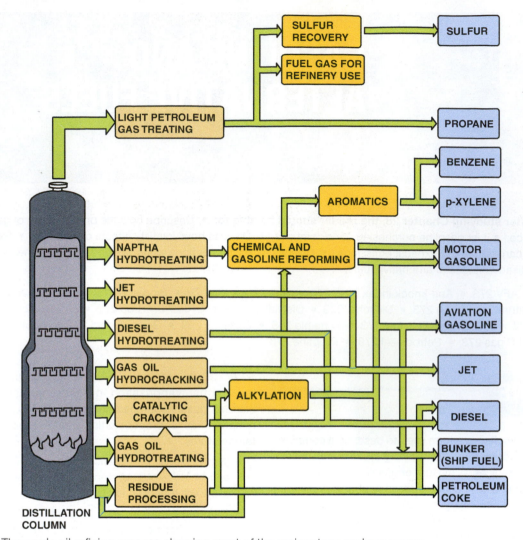

FIGURE 28–1 The crude oil refining process showing most of the major steps and processes.

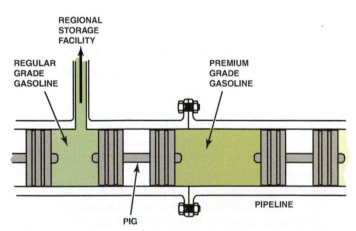

FIGURE 28–2 A pig is a plug-like device that is placed in a pipeline to separate two types or grades of fuel.

with liquid gasoline. The volatility of summer-grade gasoline should be about 7 PSI RVP. According to ASTM standards, the maximum RVP should be 10.5 PSI for summer-blend gasoline.

GASOLINE GRADES   Gasoline must to be able to operate knock-free in an engine. Most engines are designed to operate on regular grade gasoline whereas some high-performance engines are designed to operate on premium grade gasoline. Gasoline grades are based on octane rating, which is a measure of the gasoline to stop or prevent engine knocks and is often referred to as the **anti-knock index (AKI)**. If an engine is operating on a gasoline that has too low an octane rating, it will likely cause the engine to make a rattling sound during acceleration. This noise, which sounds like clattering valves or loose marbles in a metal can be called by any of the following names:

- Ping
- Spark knock
- Detonation

Hearing this rattling noise is rare because most engines today are equipped with a knock sensor that can signal the powertrain control module (PCM) to change the spark timing to stop this potentially engine-damaging condition. When spark knock occurs, the temperature and pressure inside the combustion chamber increases, which can cause severe engine damage if the spark knock continues for an extended duration

FIGURE 28–3 A pump showing regular with a pump octane of 87, plus rated at 89, and premium rated at 93. These ratings can vary with brand as well as in different parts of the country.

FIGURE 28–4 This refueling pump indicates that the gasoline is blended with 10% ethanol (ethyl alcohol) and can be used in any gasoline vehicle. E85 contains 85% ethanol and can be used only in vehicles specifically designed to use it.

of time. When the PCM retards the ignition timing, which is when the spark occurs in the cylinder, the engine power and the fuel economy are reduced. Therefore, for best results, always use the octane grade recommended for the vehicle. The specified octane level can be found in the owner's manual or sometimes inside the gas fill door.

The octane rating posted on pumps in the United States is the average of the two methods (Research and Motor) and is referred to as (R+M)/2.

- **Regular grade** = 87
- **Midgrade (Plus)** = 89
- **Premium grade** = 91 or higher
- ● SEE FIGURE 28–3.

ETHANOL-ENHANCED GASOLINE Also called ethyl alcohol, **ethanol** is drinkable alcohol and is usually made from grain. Adding 10% ethanol (ethyl alcohol or grain alcohol) increases the octane rating by three points. The oxygen content of a 10% blend of ethanol in gasoline, called **E10,** is 3.5% oxygen by weight. ● **SEE FIGURE 28–4.**

GENERAL GASOLINE RECOMMENDATIONS

The fuel used by an engine is a major expense in the operation cost of the vehicle. The proper operation of the engine depends on clean fuel of the proper octane rating and vapor pressure for the atmospheric conditions. To help ensure proper engine operation and keep fuel costs to a minimum, follow these guidelines.

1. Purchase fuel from a busy station to help ensure that it is fresh and less likely to be contaminated with water or moisture.

2. Keep the fuel tank above one-quarter full, especially during seasons in which the temperature rises and falls by more than 20°F between daytime highs and nighttime lows. This helps to reduce condensed moisture in the fuel tank and could prevent gas line freeze-up in cold weather.

   NOTE: Gas line freeze-up occurs when the water in the gasoline freezes and forms an ice blockage in the fuel line.

3. Do not purchase fuel with a higher octane rating than is necessary. Try using premium high-octane fuel to check for operating differences. Most newer engines are equipped with a detonation (knock) sensor that signals the vehicle computer to retard the ignition timing when spark knock occurs. Therefore, an operating difference may not be noticeable to the driver when using a low-octane fuel, except for a decrease in power and fuel economy.

4. Try to avoid using gasoline with alcohol in warm weather, even though many alcohol blends do not affect engine driveability. If warm-engine stumble, stalling, or rough idle occurs, change the brand of gasoline.

5. Do not purchase fuel from a retail outlet when a tanker truck is filling the underground tanks. During the refilling procedure, dirt, rust, and water may be stirred up in the underground tanks. This undesirable material may be pumped into your vehicle's fuel tank.

6. Do not overfill the gas tank. After the nozzle clicks off, add just enough fuel to round up to the next dime. Adding additional gasoline will cause the excess to be drawn into the charcoal canister. This can lead to engine flooding and excessive exhaust emissions.

7. Be careful when filling gasoline containers. Always fill a gas can on the ground to help prevent the possibility of static electricity buildup during the refueling process. ● **SEE FIGURE 28–5.**

FIGURE 28–5 Many gasoline service stations have signs posted warning customers to place plastic fuel containers on the ground while filling. If placed in a trunk or pickup truck bed equipped with a plastic liner, static electricity could build up during fueling and discharge from the container to the metal nozzle, creating a spark and possible explosion. Some service stations have warning signs not to use cell phones while fueling to help avoid the possibility of an accidental spark creating a fire hazard.

 TECH TIP

Do Not Overfill the Fuel Tank

Gasoline fuel tanks have an expansion volume area at the top. The volume of this expansion area is equal to 10% to 15% of the volume of the tank. This area is normally not filled with gasoline, but rather is designed to provide space for the gasoline to expand into, if the vehicle is parked in the hot sun and the gasoline expands. This prevents raw gasoline from escaping from the fuel system. A small restriction is usually present to control the amount of air and vapors that can escape the tank and flow to the charcoal canister. This volume area could be filled with gasoline if the fuel is slowly pumped into the tank. Since it can hold an extra 10% (2 gallons in a 20 gallon tank), some people deliberately try to fill the tank completely. When this expansion volume is filled, liquid fuel (rather than vapors) can be drawn into the charcoal canister. When the purge valve opens, liquid fuel can be drawn into the engine, causing an excessively rich air–fuel mixture. Not only can this liquid fuel harm vapor recovery parts, but overfilling the gas tank could also cause the vehicle to fail an exhaust emission test, particularly during an enhanced test when the tank could be purged while on the rollers.

FIGURE 28–6 A pump for E85 (85% ethanol and 15% gasoline). E85 is available in more locations every year.

WHAT IS E85? Vehicle manufacturers have available vehicles that are capable of operating on gasoline plus ethanol or a combination of gasoline and ethanol called **E85,** composed of 85% ethanol and 15% gasoline. Ethanol is also called **ethyl alcohol** or **grain alcohol,** because it is usually made from grain and is the type of alcohol found in alcoholic drinks such as beer, wine, and distilled spirits like whiskey. ● **SEE FIGURE 28–6.**

Pure ethanol has an octane rating of about 113. E85, which contains 35% oxygen by weight, has an octane rating of 100 to 105. This compares to a regular unleaded gasoline, which has a rating of 87.

NOTE: The octane rating of E85 depends on the exact percentage of ethanol used, which can vary from 81% to 85%. It also depends on the octane rating of the gasoline used to make E85.

TECH TIP

The Sniff Test

Problems can occur with stale gasoline from which the lighter parts of the gasoline have evaporated. Stale gasoline usually results in a no-start situation. If stale gasoline is suspected, sniff it. If it smells rancid, replace it with fresh gasoline.

NOTE: If storing a vehicle, boat, or lawnmower over the winter, put some gasoline stabilizer into the gasoline to reduce the evaporation and separation that can occur during storage. Gasoline stabilizer is frequently available at lawnmower repair shops or marinas.

HEAT ENERGY OF E85

E85 has less heat energy than gasoline. Gasoline: 114,000 BTUs per gallon; E85: 87,000 BTUs per gallon. This means that the fuel economy is reduced by 20% to 30% if E85 is used instead of gasoline.

Example: A Chevrolet Tahoe 5.3-liter V-8 with an automatic transmission has an EPA rating using gasoline of 15 mpg in the city and 20 mpg on the highway. If this same vehicle is fueled with E85, the EPA fuel economy rating drops to 11 mpg in the city and 15 mpg on the highway. The 15% gasoline in the E85 blend helps the engine start, especially in cold weather. Vehicles equipped with this capability are commonly referred to as:

- **Alternative fuel vehicles (AFVs)**
- **Flex fuels**
- **Flexible fuel vehicles (FFVs)**

Using E85 in a flex fuel vehicle can result in a power increase of about 5%. For example, an engine rated at 200 hp using gasoline or E10 could produce 210 hp if using E85.

NOTE: E85 may test as containing less than 85% ethanol if tested because it is often blended according to outside temperature. A lower percentage of ethanol with a slightly higher percentage of gasoline helps engines start in cold climates.

FLEX FUEL VEHICLE IDENTIFICATION

Flexible fuel vehicles (FFVs) can be identified by:

- Emblems on the side, front, and/or rear of the vehicle.
- Yellow fuel cap showing E85/gasoline. ● **SEE FIGURE 28–7.**
- Vehicle emission control information (VECI) label under the hood.
- Vehicle identification number (VIN).

NOTE: For additional information on E85 and for the location of E85 stations in your area, visit www.e85fuel.com.

FIGURE 28–7 A flex-fuel vehicle often has a yellow gas cap, which is labeled E85/gasoline.

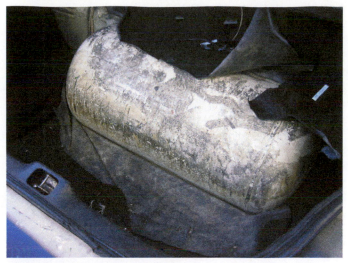

FIGURE 28–8 Propane fuel storage tank in the trunk of a Ford taxi.

PROPANE

Propane is the most widely used of all the alternative fuels mainly because of its use in fleets, which utilize a central refueling station. Propane is normally a gas but is easily compressed into a liquid and stored in inexpensive containers. When sold as a fuel, it is also known as **liquefied petroleum gas (LPG)** or **LP gas,** because the propane is often mixed with about 10% of other gases, including:

- Butane
- Propylene
- Butylenes
- Mercaptan, to give the colorless and odorless propane a smell. Propane is nontoxic, but if inhaled can cause asphyxiation because of lack of oxygen.

Propane is heavier than air and lays near the floor if released into the atmosphere. Propane is commonly used in forklifts and other equipment located inside warehouses and factories because the exhaust from the engine using propane is not harmful. Propane is a by-product of petroleum refining of natural gas. In order to liquefy the fuel, it is stored in strong tanks at about 300 PSI (2,000 kPa). The heating value of propane is less than that of gasoline; therefore, more propane is required, which reduces the fuel economy. ● **SEE FIGURE 28–8.**

COMPRESSED NATURAL GAS (CNG)

CNG VEHICLE DESIGN

Another alternative fuel that is often used in fleet vehicles is **compressed natural gas (CNG).** Vehicles using this fuel are often referred to as *natural gas vehicles*

(NGVs). Look for the blue CNG label on vehicles designed to operate on compressed natural gas. ● **SEE FIGURE 28–9.**

Because natural gas must be compressed to 3,000 PSI (20,000 kPa) or more, the weight and cost of the storage container are major factors when it comes to preparing a vehicle to run on CNG. The tanks needed for CNG are typically constructed of 0.5 in. (3 mm) thick aluminum reinforced with fiberglass. ● **SEE FIGURE 28–10.**

The octane rating of CNG is about 130 and the cost per gallon is roughly half of the cost of gasoline. However, the heat value of CNG is also less, and therefore more CNG is required to produce the same power; and the miles per gallon is less.

FIGURE 28–11 This CNG pump is capable of supplying compressed natural gas at either 3,000 PSI or 3,600 PSI. The price per gallon is higher for the higher pressure.

The CNG engine is designed to include:

- Increased compression ratio
- Strong pistons and connecting rods
- Heat-resistant valves
- Fuel injectors designed for gaseous fuel instead of liquid fuel

CNG FUEL SYSTEMS When completely filled, the CNG tank has 3,600 PSI of pressure in the tank. CNG vehicles are designed for use in fleets, which usually have their own refueling capabilities. One of the drawbacks of using CNG is the time that it takes to refuel a vehicle. The ideal method of refueling is the slow-fill method. The slow-filling method compresses the natural gas as the tank is being fueled. This method ensures that the tank will receive a full charge of CNG; however, this method can take three to five hours to accomplish. If more than one vehicle needs filling, the facility will need multiple CNG compressors to refuel the vehicles.

There are three commonly used CNG refilling station pressures.

P24: 2,400 PSI

P30: 3,000 PSI

P36: 3,600 PSI

Try to find and use a station with the highest refilling pressure. Filling at lower pressures will result in less-compressed natural gas being installed in the storage tank, thereby reducing the driving range. ● **SEE FIGURE 28–11.**

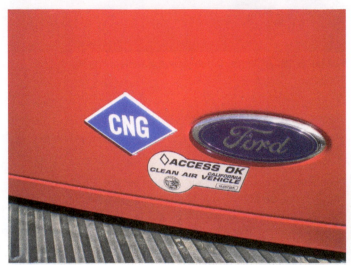

FIGURE 28–9 The blue sticker on the rear of this vehicle indicates that it is designed to use compressed natural gas. This Ford truck also has a sticker that allows it to be driven in the high occupancy vehicle (HOV) lane, even if there is just the driver, because it is a CNG vehicle.

FIGURE 28–10 A CNG storage tank from a Honda Civic GX shown with the fixture used to support it while it is being removed or installed in the vehicle. Honda specifies that three technicians be used to remove or install the tank through the rear door of the vehicle due to the size and weight of the tank.

DIESEL FUEL

FEATURES OF DIESEL FUEL Diesel fuel must meet an entirely different set of standards than gasoline. Diesel fuel contains 12% more heat energy than the same amount of gasoline. The fuel in a diesel engine is not ignited with a spark, but is ignited by the heat generated by high compression. The pressure of compression (400 to 700 PSI, or 2,800 to 4,800 kPa) generates temperatures of 1,200°F to 1,600°F (700°C to 900°C).

CETANE NUMBER The cetane number for diesel fuel is the opposite of the octane number for gasoline. The **cetane number** is a measure of the ease with which the fuel can be ignited. The cetane rating of the fuel determines, to a great extent, its ability to start the engine at low temperatures and to provide smooth warm-up and even combustion. The cetane rating of diesel fuel should be between 45 and 50. The higher the cetane rating, the more easily the fuel is ignited.

DIESEL FUEL COLOR Diesel fuel intended for use on the streets and highways is either clear or green. Diesel fuel to be used on farms and off-road is dyed red. ● **SEE FIGURE 28–12.**

GRADES OF DIESEL FUEL

Grade 1 This grade of diesel fuel has the lowest boiling point and the lowest cloud and pour points, as well as a lower BTU content (less heat per pound of fuel). As a result, grade 1 is suitable for use during low-temperature (winter) operation. Grade 1 produces less heat per pound of fuel compared to grade 2, and may be specified for use in diesel engines involved in frequent changes in load and speed, such as those found in city buses and delivery trucks.

Grade 2 This grade has a higher boiling point, cloud point, and pour point as compared with grade 1. It is usually specified where constant speed and high loads are encountered, such as in long-haul trucking and automotive diesel applications.

BIODIESEL

DEFINITION OF BIODIESEL **Biodiesel** is a domestically produced, renewable fuel that can be manufactured from vegetable oils, animal fats, or recycled restaurant greases. Biodiesel is safe, biodegradable, and reduces serious air pollutants such as particulate matter (PM), carbon monoxide, and hydrocarbons. Biodiesel is defined as mono-alkyl esters of long-chain fatty acids derived from vegetable oils or animal fats that conform to ASTM D6751 specifications for use in diesel engines. Biodiesel refers to the pure fuel before blending with diesel fuel. ● **SEE FIGURE 28–13.**

(a)

(b)

FIGURE 28–12 (a) Regular diesel fuel on the left has a clear or greenish tint, whereas fuel for off-road use is tinted red for identification. (b) A fuel pump in a farming area that clearly states the red diesel fuel is for off-road use only.

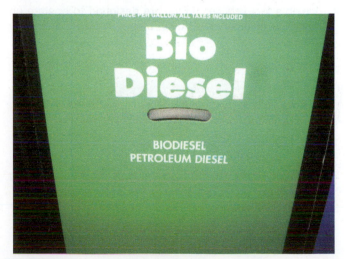

FIGURE 28–13 Biodiesel fuel is available at some locations only.

Biodiesel blends are denoted as BXX, with "XX" representing the percentage of biodiesel contained in the blend (i.e., **B20** is 20% biodiesel, 80% petroleum diesel). Blends of 5% biodiesel with 95% petroleum diesel, called **B5,** can generally be used in unmodified diesel engines. Some diesel-powered vehicles can use B20 (20% biodiesel). Dodge, for example, allows the use of B5 in all diesel vehicles and B20 only if the optional additional fuel filter is installed. Biodiesel can also be used in its pure form (B100), but it may require certain engine modifications to avoid maintenance and performance problems and may not be suitable for wintertime use. Users should consult their engine warranty statement for more information on fuel blends of greater than 20% biodiesel. In general, B20 costs 30 to 40 cents more per gallon than conventional diesel. Although biodiesel costs more than regular diesel fuel, often called **petrodiesel,** fleet managers can make the switch to alternative fuels without purchasing new vehicles, acquiring new spare parts inventories, rebuilding refueling stations, or hiring new service technicians.

NOTE: For additional information on biodiesel and the locations where it can be purchased, visit www. biodiesel.org.

E-DIESEL

DEFINITION   **E-diesel,** also called **diesohol** outside of the United States, is standard No. 2 diesel fuel that contains up to 15% ethanol. While E-diesel can have up to 15% ethanol by volume, typical blend levels are from 8% to 10%.

CETANE RATING OF E-DIESEL   The higher the cetane number, the shorter the delay between injection and ignition. Normal diesel fuel has a cetane number of about 50. Adding 15% ethanol lowers the cetane number. To increase the cetane number back to that of conventional diesel fuel, a cetane-enhancing additive is added to E-diesel. E-diesel has better cold-flow properties than conventional diesel. The heat content of E-diesel is about 6% less than conventional diesel, but the particulate matter (PM) emissions are reduced by as much as 40%, carbon monoxide by 20%, and oxides of nitrogen (NOx) by 5%. Currently, E-diesel is considered to be experimental and can be used legally in off-road applications or in mass-transit buses with EPA approval. For additional information, visit www.e-diesel.org.

SUMMARY

1. Gasoline is a complex blend of hydrocarbons. Gasoline is blended for seasonal usage to achieve the correct volatility for easy starting and maximum fuel economy under all driving conditions.

2. Abnormal combustion (also called detonation or spark knock) increases both the temperature and the pressure inside the combustion chamber.

3. Most regular grade gasoline today, using the (R+M)/2 rating method, is 87 octane; midgrade (plus) is 89 and premium grade is 91 or higher.

4. Flexible fuel vehicles (FFVs) are designed to operate on gasoline or gasoline–ethanol blends having up to 85% ethanol (E85).

5. E85 has fewer BTUs of energy per gallon compared with gasoline and will therefore provide lower fuel economy.

6. Propane is the most widely used alternative fuel. Propane is also called liquefied petroleum gas (LPG).

7. Compressed natural gas (CNG) is available for refilling in several pressures, including 2,400 PSI, 3,000 PSI, and 3,600 PSI.

8. Biodiesel is the blend of vegetable-based liquid with regular diesel fuel. Most diesel engine manufacturers allow the use of a 5% blend, called B5, without any changes to the fuel system or engine.

REVIEW QUESTIONS

1. What is the difference between summer-blend and winter-blend gasoline?

2. What does the (R+M)/2 gasoline pump octane rating indicate?

3. How is a flexible fuel vehicle identified?

4. What other gases are often mixed with propane?

5. Why is it desirable to fill a compressed natural gas (CNG) vehicle with the highest pressure available?

6. Biodiesel blends are identified by what designation?

1. Winter-blend gasoline _____.
   a. Vaporizes more easily than summer-blend gasoline
   b. Has a higher RVP
   c. Can cause engine driveability problems if used during warm weather
   d. All of the above

2. Technician A says that *spark knock*, *ping*, and *detonation* are different names for abnormal combustion. Technician B says that any abnormal combustion raises the temperature and pressure inside the combustion chamber and can cause severe engine damage. Which technician is correct?
   a. Technician A only
   b. Technician B only
   c. Both technicians A and B
   d. Neither technician A nor B

3. Technician A says that E10 contains 10% ethanol and 90% gasoline. Technician B says that the octane rating posted on fuel pumps is an average of the two ratings. Which technician is correct?
   a. Technician A only
   b. Technician B only
   c. Both technicians A and B
   d. Neither technician A nor B

4. Propane is also called _____.
   a. LPG
   b. Diesohol
   c. CNG
   d. LNG

5. A vehicle owner should _____.
   a. Purchase gasoline that has the octane rating recommended for use as stated in the owner's manual
   b. Use Plus grade for all gasoline engines
   c. Use premium grade for all engines for best performance
   d. Either b or c

6. E85 can be used _____.
   a. In a vehicle labeled "Flex fuel"
   b. Can harm the engine if used in non-flex fuel gasoline engine
   c. Can cause a conventional gasoline engine to not start if used
   d. All of the above

7. E85 means that the fuel is made from _____.
   a. 85% gasoline and 15% ethanol
   b. 85% ethanol and 15% gasoline
   c. Ethanol that has 15% water
   d. Pure ethyl alcohol

8. A flex fuel vehicle can be identified by _____.
   a. Emblems on the side, front, and/or rear of the vehicle
   b. VECI
   c. VIN
   d. All of the above

9. When refueling a CNG vehicle, why is it recommended that the tank be filled to a high pressure?
   a. The range of the vehicle is increased.
   b. The cost of the fuel is lower.
   c. Less of the fuel is lost to evaporation.
   d. Both a and c.

10. What color is diesel fuel dyed if it is for off-road use only?
    a. Red
    b. Green
    c. Blue
    d. Yellow

chapter 29

COMPUTERS AND SENSORS

OBJECTIVES: After studying Chapter 29, the reader should be able to: • Prepare for ASE Electrical/Electronic Systems (A6) certification test content area "A" (General Electrical/Electronic Systems Diagnosis). • Explain the purpose and function of onboard computers. • List input sensors. • List output devices (actuators) controlled by the computer. • Explain the purpose and function of the ECT, IAT, MAP, MAF, and oxygen sensors.

KEY TERMS: • Actuator 279 • Engine coolant temperature (ECT) 279 • Intake air temperature (IAT) sensor 279 • Input 278 • Manifold absolute pressure (MAP) sensor 280 • Mass airflow (MAF) sensor 280 • Oxygen (O2S) sensor 281 • Potentiometer 279 • Powertrain control module (PCM) 278 • Throttle position (TP) sensor 279 • Vehicle speed (VS) sensor 281 • Wideband oxygen sensor 281

POWERTRAIN CONTROL MODULE (PCM)

PURPOSE AND FUNCTION Modern automotive control systems consist of a network of electronic sensors, actuators, and computer modules designed to regulate the engine and transmission (powertrain). The onboard automotive computer has many names but **powertrain control module (PCM)** is the Society of Automotive Engineers (SAE) standardized name.

BASIC FUNCTIONS The operation of every computer can be divided into four basic functions.

- **Input.** Receives voltage signals from sensors
- **Processing.** Performs mathematical calculations
- **Storage.** Includes short-term and long-term memory
- **Output.** Controls an output device by either turning it on or off usually by providing a ground. ● **SEE FIGURE 29–1.**

INPUT FUNCTIONS First, the computer receives a voltage signal (input) from an input device. **Input** is a signal from a device that can be as simple as a button or a switch on an instrument panel, or a sensor on an automotive engine.

The PCM coordinates engine and transmission operation, processes data, maintains communications, and makes the control decisions needed to keep the vehicle operating. The PCM is constructed of many electronic components and programmed to function in a specific vehicle. ● **SEE FIGURE 29–2.**

Not only is it capable of operating the engine and transmission, but it is also able to do the following:

- Perform self-tests (40% of the computing power is devoted to diagnosis)
- Set and store diagnostic trouble codes (DTCs)
- Communicate with the technician using a scan tool

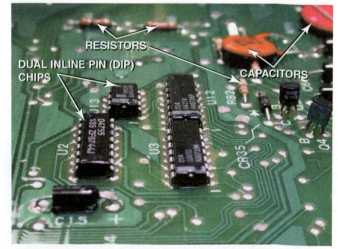

FIGURE 29–2 Many electronic components are used to construct a typical vehicle computer (PCM), including chips, resistors, and capacitors.

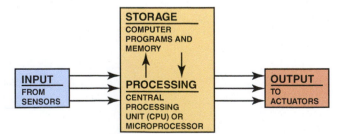

FIGURE 29–1 All computer systems perform four basic functions: input, processing, storage, and output.

FIGURE 29–3 The powertrain control module (PCM) is located under the hood on this Chevrolet pickup truck.

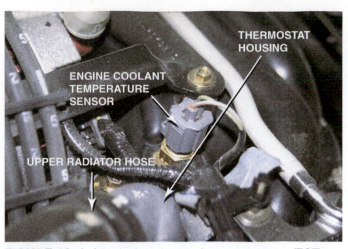

FIGURE 29–4 A typical engine coolant temperature (ECT) sensor. ECT sensors are located near the thermostat housing on most engines.

OUTPUT FUNCTIONS After the computer has processed the input signals, it usually provides a ground to devices in the system, such as actuators. An **actuator** is an electrical or mechanical output device that converts electrical energy into a mechanical action. Some actuators include:

- Engine idle speed device
- Fuel pump relay
- Fuel injectors
- Automatic transmission shift solenoids
- Electronic suspension system control valves

COMPUTER COMMUNICATION A typical vehicle can have many computers, also called *modules* or *controllers.*

Computers can also communicate with, and control, each other through their output and input functions. This means that the output signal from one computer system can be the input signal for another computer system through a data network. ● **SEE FIGURE 29–3.**

ENGINE SENSORS

PURPOSE AND FUNCTION The engine management system uses many different types of input sensors to monitor engine running conditions. Engines use sensors to measure what is happening to the engine so that the computer (PCM) can provide the correct amount of fuel at the correct time for best overall power and efficiency with the lowest possible exhaust emissions.

ENGINE COOLANT TEMPERATURE (ECT) The powertrain control module (PCM) uses an **engine coolant temperature (ECT)** sensor for engine temperature information.

The two-wire ECT sensors are located in the cooling system usually installed near the thermostat housing. ● **SEE FIGURE 29–4.**

The ECT sensor is used as an important input to the computer for the following:

- Idle speed
- Fuel calculations especially on a cold engine
- Transmission shifting
- Evaporative emission control operation

INTAKE AIR TEMPERATURE (IAT) SENSOR The IAT sensor is used to measure the temperature of the air entering the engine. These two-wire sensors can be located in one of the following locations:

- In the air cleaner housing
- In the air duct between the air filter and the throttle body. ● **SEE FIGURE 29–5.**
- Built into the mass airflow (MAF) or airflow sensor

The purpose and function of the intake air temperature sensor is to provide the engine computer (PCM) the temperature of the air entering the engine. The IAT sensor information is used for fuel control (adding or subtracting fuel) and spark timing, depending on the temperature of incoming air.

THROTTLE POSITION (TP) SENSOR The **throttle position (TP)** sensor measures the throttle opening and is used by the computer for engine control and to determine the shift points of the automotive transmission/transaxle. ● **SEE FIGURE 29–6.**

The TP sensor consists of a **potentiometer,** a type of variable resistor that has three wires. The computer uses their input to determine the amount of throttle opening and the rate of change. Engines that use an electronic throttle control (ETC) system also use a throttle position sensor and in this case, it is used to monitor that the electronic throttle is being opened to the correct angle as commanded by the controller or PCM.

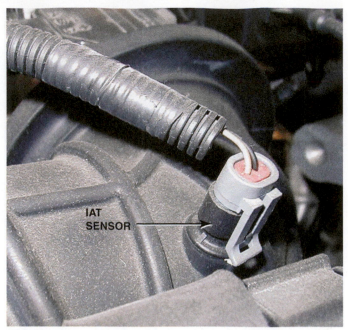

FIGURE 29–5 The IAT sensor on this General Motors 3800 V-6 engine is in the air passage duct between the air cleaner housing and the throttle body.

FIGURE 29–6 A typical TP sensor mounted on the throttle shaft on this port-injected engine.

MANIFOLD ABSOLUTE PRESSURE (MAP) SENSOR.

The MAP sensor detects engine load by using a signal from a sensor that measures the vacuum in the intake manifold. A **manifold absolute pressure (MAP)** sensor uses three wires and is used on many engines to determine the load on the engine.

- When the load on the engine is light (such as when cruising at a steady highway speed), the engine vacuum is high.
- When the load on the engine is heavy, such as during heavy acceleration, the engine vacuum is low.
- By monitoring the engine vacuum (manifold pressure), the PCM is able to determine the amount of load the engine is under. A heavy load requires that the PCM supply more fuel than when the engine is operating under a light load (higher vacuum). ● **SEE FIGURE 29–7.**

FIGURE 29–7 The MAP sensor uses three wires and is located on the intake manifold of the engine in most vehicles.

MASS AIRFLOW (MAF) SENSORS

A **mass airflow (MAF)** sensor measures the mass (weight and density) of the air flowing through the sensor and entering the engine. The MAF sensor takes into account relative humidity, altitude, and temperature of the air and most use three wires. Some MAF sensors have an intake air temperature (IAT) sensor built into them and, therefore, use five wires. ● **SEE FIGURE 29–8.**

The computer constantly monitors the change in current and translates it into a voltage signal that is used to determine how long the fuel injector stays on.

- The longer the injector stays on, the more fuel is delivered to the engine.
- The shorter the amount of time that the fuel injector is on results in less fuel delivered to the engine.
- The greater the amount of fuel delivered to the engine results in greater power from the engine.

FIGURE 29–8 The mass airflow (MAF) sensor is located between the air filter housing and the engine, where it can measure all of the air entering the engine.

OXYGEN SENSORS (O2S) Automotive computer systems use a sensor in the exhaust system to measure the oxygen content of the exhaust. These sensors are called **oxygen sensors (O2S).** Oxygen sensors can have one, two, three, or four wires. Oxygen sensors that use three or four wires are equipped with a heater used to keep the sensor working correctly even if the engine is cold.

The oxygen sensor is installed in the exhaust manifold or located downstream from the manifold in the exhaust pipe. ● SEE FIGURE 29–9.

There is another oxygen sensor located after the catalytic converter and it is the purpose of this sensor to monitor how well the converter is functioning as required by the second generation of on-board diagnosis (OBD-II). ● SEE FIGURE 29–10.

A conventional zirconia oxygen sensor (O2S) is only able to detect if the exhaust is richer or leaner than 14.7:1. A conventional oxygen sensor is therefore referred to as a *two-step or narrow-band sensor,* which informs the PCM whether the exhaust is rich or lean.

Wideband oxygen sensors are constructed using a reference chamber that allows the sensor to detect air–fuel ratios as rich as 12:1 and as lean as 23:1. This type of sensor is used to provide the PCM with accurate air–fuel ratios so it can precisely control exhaust emissions and provide the highest fuel economy and the lowest possible exhaust emissions.

VEHICLE SPEED (VS) SENSOR The **vehicle speed sensor** measures the vehicle speed using a sensor located at the output of the transmission/transaxle or by monitoring the wheel speed sensors. The vehicle speed sensors can be located on the case of the transmission. This sensor is used by the speedometer, cruise control, and the shifting of the automatic transmission/transaxle.

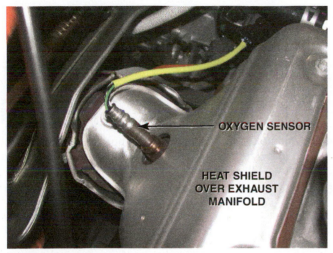

FIGURE 29–9 This oxygen sensor is mounted on the exhaust manifold, which is hidden behind a heat shield.

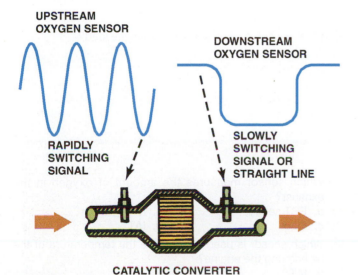

FIGURE 29–10 The OBD-II catalytic converter monitor compares the signals of the upstream and downstream oxygen sensor to determine converter efficiency.

OUTPUT CONTROLS

PURPOSE AND FUNCTION After the PCM has processed the input signals, it sends voltage signals or commands to other devices in the system, as follows:

- By **operating actuators.** An actuator is an electrical or mechanical device that converts electrical energy into heat, light, or motion to control engine idle speed, suspension height, ignition timing, and other output devices.
- **Network communication.** Computers can also communicate with another computer system through a network.

OPERATION A vehicle computer can do only two things usually by commanding a ground.

1. Turn a device on.
2. Turn a device off.

Typical outputs controlled by the computer include the following:

- **Fuel injectors.** The computer can vary the amount of time in milliseconds the injectors are held open, thereby controlling the amount of fuel supplied to the engine.
- **Blower motor control.** Many blower motors are controlled by the body computer by pulsing the current on and off to maintain the desired speed.
- **Transmission shifting.** The computer provides a ground to the shift solenoids and torque converter clutch (TCC) solenoid. The operation of the automatic transmission/transaxle is optimized based on vehicle sensor information.

FIGURE 29–11 A dash display showing that one of the computers has detected a fault in an electrical circuit. The service technician will then follow the specified test procedures to pinpoint the cause and to correct the fault.

- **Idle speed control.** The computer can control the idle air control (IAC) or electronic throttle control (ETC) to maintain engine idle speed and to provide an increased idle speed as needed.
- **Evaporative emission control solenoids.** The computer can control the flow of gasoline fumes from the charcoal canister to the engine and seal off the system to perform a fuel system leak detection test as part of the OBD-II system requirements.
- **Set diagnostic trouble codes (DTCs).** Each computer in the vehicle can set a DTC for the circuits that it is monitoring.
- **Communicates to the drivers.** The computers are also capable of sending messages to the driver information center (dash display) if a fault is detected. ● **SEE FIGURE 29–11.**

SUMMARY

1. A throttle position (TP) sensor is a three-wire variable resistor called a potentiometer.

2. The MAF sensor measures the amount of air entering the engine and the MAP sensor is used to determine he load on the engine.

3. Pressure below atmospheric pressure is called vacuum and is measured in inches of mercury.

4. A manifold absolute pressure sensor uses a perfect vacuum (zero absolute pressure) in the sensor to determine the pressure.

5. An oxygen sensor can detect if the exhaust is rich or lean.

REVIEW QUESTIONS

1. What is the purpose and function of the PCM?

2. What sensor can determine the air–fuel ratio of the exhaust?

3. What sensor is used to measure engine load?

CHAPTER QUIZ

1. What sensor measures the load on the engine?
   a. TP sensor
   b. MAP sensor
   c. Oxygen sensor
   d. IAT

2. A TP sensor is what type of sensor?
   a. Rheostat
   b. Voltage generating
   c. Potentiometer
   d. Piezoelectric

3. What sensor measures the temperature of the engine coolant?
   a. ECT sensor
   b. Oxygen sensor
   a. MAP sensor
   c. IAT

4. Which sensor measures the amount of oxygen in the exhaust?
   a. ECT sensor
   b. MAP sensor
   c. O2S
   d. IAT

5. Which sensor is used to measure the temperature of the air entering the engine?
   a. IAT
   b. ECT
   c. MAP
   d. MAF

6. Fuel injectors are _____.
   a. A computer sensor
   b. Output device (actuator) controlled by the computer
   c. Both a sensor and an output device
   d. Neither a sensor nor an output device

7. A conventional oxygen sensor can have how many wires?
   a. 1   b. 3
   c. 4   d. Any of the above

8. Which sensor is located between the air cleaner housing and the throttle body?
   a. MAF
   b. MAP
   c. Wide band oxygen sensor
   d. TP sensor

9. MAF sensors measure _____.
   a. The temperature of the air entering the engine
   b. The amount of oxygen entering the engine
   c. The mass of the air entering the engine
   d. The angle of the throttle plate

10. Vehicle speed (VS) sensors are used by what systems?
    a. Cruise control
    b. Speedometer
    c. Automatic transmission shifting
    d. all of the above

OBJECTIVES: After studying Chapter 30, the reader should be able to: • Prepare for ASE Engine Performance (A8) certification test content area "B" (Ignition System Diagnosis and Repair). • Explain how ignition coils create 40,000 volts or more. • Describe the operation of distributor, waste-spark, and coil-on-plug ignition systems. • Explain how to inspect and replace spark plugs. • Discuss what to inspect and look for during a visual inspection of the ignition system.

KEY TERMS: • Coil-on-plug (COP) ignition 284 • Distributor ignition (DI) 284 • Electronic ignition (EI) 284 • Firing order 285 • Ignition coil 284 • Iridium spark plugs 289 • Platinum spark plugs 288 • Spark plugs 288 • Spark tester 286 • Waste-spark system 284

IGNITION SYSTEM

PURPOSE AND FUNCTION   The ignition system includes components and wiring necessary to create and distribute a high voltage (up to 40,000 volts or more) that is sent to the spark plugs. A high-voltage arc occurs across the gap of a spark plug inside the combustion chamber. The spark raises the temperature of the air–fuel mixture and starts the combustion process inside the cylinder. ● **SEE FIGURE 30–1.**

ELECTRONIC IGNITION   Since the mid-1970s, sensors, such as a pickup coil and reluctor (trigger wheel), are used

to trigger or signal an electronic module that switches the primary ground circuit of the ignition coil. The **ignition coil** is a part where 12 volts from the battery is stepped up to a higher voltage (up to 40,000 volts). An ignition coil has two coils (called windings) inside:

1. A primary winding where battery voltage flows to create a magnetic field when the circuit is complete.

2. A secondary winding where a high voltage is produced when the primary circuit is turned off and the magnetic field collapses. It is the collapsing magnetic field that creates a high voltage pulse that is sent to the spark plug where it arcs across the electrodes and ignites the air–fuel mixture inside the cylinder.

   ■ **Distributor ignition (DI)** is the term specified by the Society of Automotive Engineers (SAE) for an ignition system that uses a distributor.

   ■ **Electronic ignition (EI)** is the term specified by the SAE for an ignition system that does not use a distributor. Electronic ignition system types include:

   1. **Waste-spark system**. This type of system uses one ignition coil to fire the spark plugs of two cylinders at the same time.

   2. **Coil-on-plug (COP) system**. This type of system uses a single ignition coil for each cylinder, with the coil placed above or near the spark plug.

OPERATION   The high voltage created in the secondary winding is high enough to jump the air gap at the spark plug. The electrical arc at the spark plug ignites the air–fuel mixture in the combustion chamber of the engine. For each spark that occurs, the coil must be charged with a magnetic field and then discharged.

FIGURE 30–1 A high-voltage pulse is sent to the spark plug to ignite the air–fuel mixture in the cylinder.

DISTRIBUTOR IGNITION

PURPOSE AND FUNCTION
The purpose of a distributor is to distribute the high-voltage spark from the output terminal of the ignition coil to the spark plugs of each cylinder. A gear or shaft drives the distributor that is connected to the camshaft and is driven at camshaft speed. Most distributor ignition systems also use a sensor to trigger the ignition control module (ICM). A spark is created when the ignition coil is triggered. These triggering devices used in distributor ignition systems include the following:

- Magnetic pulse generator, also called a pickup coil located in the distributor
- Hall-effect sensor located in the distributor
- Optical sensor located in the distributor
- **SEE FIGURE 30–2**

FIRING ORDER
Firing order refers to the order in which the spark is distributed to the correct spark plug at the right time. The firing order of an engine is determined by crankshaft and camshaft design and by the location of the spark plug wires in the distributor cap of an engine equipped with a distributor. The firing order is often cast into the intake manifold for easy reference. **SEE FIGURE 30–3.**

Service information also shows the firing order and the direction of the distributor rotor rotation, as well as the location of the spark plug wires on the distributor cap.

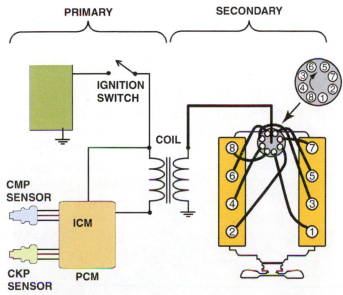

FIGURE 30–2 The primary ignition system is used to trigger and, therefore, create the secondary (high-voltage) spark from the ignition coil. The high-voltage spark is then sent to the spark plugs by the distributor and through spark plug wires.

FIGURE 30–3 The firing order is cast or stamped on the intake manifold on most engines that have a distributor ignition.

WASTE-SPARK IGNITION OPERATION
Both spark plugs fire at the same time (within nanoseconds of each other). When one cylinder (for example, cylinder number 6) is on the compression stroke, the other cylinder (number 3) is on the exhaust stroke.

- The spark that occurs on the exhaust stroke is called the waste spark, because it does no useful work and is only used as a ground path for the secondary winding of the ignition coil. The voltage required to jump the spark plug gap on cylinder 3 (the exhaust stroke) is only 2,000 to 3,000 volts.
- The voltage required in the cylinder during the compression stroke is 10,000 to 12,000 volts.
- **SEE FIGURE 30–4**

FIGURE 30–4 A Ford V-6 engine that uses a waste-spark-type ignition system. Note that each of the three coils has two spark plug wires. Both the cylinders fire at the same time.

FIGURE 30–6 This General Motors V-8 engine is equipped with a coil-near-plug ignition. Each cylinder has a coil and uses a short spark plug wire from the coil to the spark plug.

COIL-ON-PLUG IGNITION

TERMINOLOGY Coil-on-plug (COP) ignition uses one ignition coil for each spark plug. This system is also called *coil-by-plug, coil-near-plug,* or *coil-over-plug* ignition. ● **SEE FIGURES 30–5 AND 30–6.**

The coil-on-plug system eliminates the spark plug wires that are often the source of electromagnetic interference (EMI), which can cause problems to some computer signals. The vehicle computer controls the timing of the spark. Ignition timing can also be changed (retarded or advanced) on a cylinder-by-cylinder basis for maximum performance.

TESTING FOR SPARK

USING A SPARK TESTER In the event of a no-start condition, the first step should be to check for secondary voltage out of the ignition coil or to the spark plugs. On a distributor-equipped engine, remove the coil wire from the center of the distributor cap, install a **spark tester,** and crank the engine. A good coil and ignition system should produce a blue spark at the spark tester. ● **SEE FIGURES 30–7 AND 30–8.**

On engines equipped with distributorless (EI) ignition systems, disconnect any spark plug wire from a spark plug and, while cranking the engine, test for spark available at the spark plug wire, again using a spark tester.

NOTE: An intermittent spark should be considered a no-spark condition.

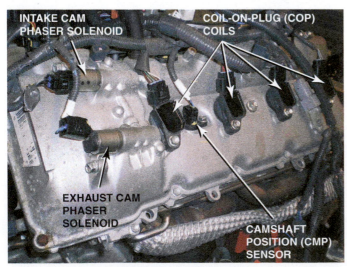

FIGURE 30–5 An overhead camshaft engine equipped with variable valve timing on both the intake and exhaust camshafts and the coil-on-plug ignition.

FIGURE 30–7 A spark tester looks like a regular spark plug with an alligator clip attached to the shell. This tester has a specified gap that requires at least 25,000 volts (25 kV) to fire.

FIGURE 30–8 A close-up showing the recessed center electrode on a spark tester. It is recessed 3/8 in. into the shell and the spark must then jump another 3/8 in. to the shell for a total gap of 3/4 in.

FIGURE 30–9 Spark plug wires carry high-voltage pulses from the ignition coil or distributor to the spark plugs. Always take the time to install spark plug wires back into the original holding brackets (wiring combs).

🔧 **TECH TIP**

Always Use a Spark Tester

A spark tester looks like a spark plug except it has a recessed center electrode and no side electrode. The tester commonly has an alligator clip attached to the shell so that it can be clamped on a good ground connection on the engine. A good ignition system should be able to cause a spark to jump this wide gap at atmospheric pressure. Without a spark tester, a technician might assume that the ignition system is okay, because it can spark across a normal, grounded spark plug. The voltage required to fire a standard spark plug when it is out of the engine and not under pressure is about 3,000 volts or less. An electronic ignition spark tester requires a minimum of 25,000 volts to jump the 3/4-in. gap. Therefore, never assume that the ignition system is okay because it fires a spark plug—always use a spark tester. *Remember that an intermittent spark across a spark tester should be interpreted as a no-spark condition.*

which is embedded in a nylon string. This conductive material is then covered with insulation. Spark plug wires should be visually inspected for cuts or defective insulation. Faulty spark plug wire insulation can cause hard starting or no starting during rainy or damp weather conditions.

When removing a spark plug wire, be sure to rotate the boot of the wire at the plug before pulling it off the spark plug. This will help prevent damaging the wire as many wires are stuck to the spark plug and are often difficult to remove.
● SEE FIGURE 30–9.

🔧 **TECH TIP**

Spark Plug Wire Pliers Are a Good Investment

Spark plug wires are often difficult to remove. Using good-quality spark plug wire pliers saves time and reduces the chance of harming the wire during removal. ● SEE FIGURE 30–10.

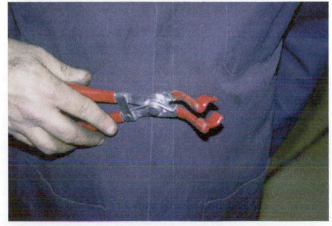

FIGURE 30–10 Spark plug wire boot pliers are a handy addition to any tool box.

SPARK PLUG WIRES

PURPOSE AND FUNCTION Spark plug wires conduct the high-voltage electricity from the ignition coil to the spark plug. Spark plug wires use carbon as the conducting material,

VISUAL INSPECTION A thorough visual inspection should include a look at the following items:

- Check all spark plug wires for proper routing. All plug wires should be in the factory wiring separators and be clear of any metallic object that could damage the insulation and cause a short-to-ground fault.

- Check that all spark plug wires are securely attached to the spark plugs and to the distributor cap or ignition coil(s).

- Check that all spark plug wires are clean and free from excessive dirt or oil. Check that all protective covers normally covering the coil and/or distributor cap are in place and not damaged.

- Carefully check the cap and distributor rotor for faults or coil secondary terminal on waste spark coils.

- Visually check the wires and boots for damage. ● **SEE FIGURE 30–11.**

Check all spark plug wires with an ohmmeter for proper resistance. Good spark plug wires should measure less than 10,000 ohms per foot of length. ● **SEE FIGURE 30–12.**

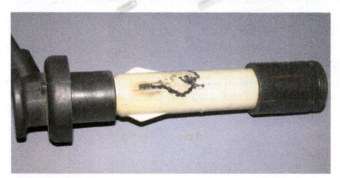

FIGURE 30–11 This spark plug boot on an overhead camshaft engine has been arcing to the valve cover causing a misfire to occur.

FIGURE 30–12 Measuring the resistance of a spark plug wire with a multimeter set to the ohms position. The reading of 16.03 kΩ (16,030 ohms) is okay because the wire is about 2-ft long. Maximum allowable resistance for a spark plug wire this long would be 20 kΩ (20,000 ohms).

SPARK PLUGS

SPARK PLUG CONSTRUCTION **Spark plugs** are manufactured from ceramic insulators inside a steel shell. The threads of the shell are rolled and a seat is formed to create a gas-tight seal with the cylinder head. ● **SEE FIGURE 30–13.**

The physical differences in spark plugs include the following:

- **Reach.** This is the length of the threads of the plug.

- **Heat range.** This refers to how rapidly the heat created at the tip is transferred to the cylinder head. A spark plug with a long ceramic insulator path will run hotter at the tip than one that has a shorter path, because the heat must travel farther.

- **Type of seat.** Some spark plugs use a gasket and others rely on a tapered seat to seal.

RESISTOR SPARK PLUGS Most spark plugs include a resistor in the center electrode, which helps to reduce electromagnetic noise or radiation from the ignition system. The closer the resistor is to the actual spark or arc, the more effective it becomes. The value of the resistor is usually between 2,500 and 7,500 ohms.

PLATINUM SPARK PLUGS **Platinum spark plugs** have a small amount of the precious metal platinum included on the end of the center electrode, as well as on the ground or side electrode. Platinum is a gray-white metal that does not react with oxygen and, therefore, will not erode away as can occur with conventional nickel alloy spark plug electrodes. Platinum is also used as a catalyst in catalytic converters, where it is able to start a chemical reaction without itself being consumed.

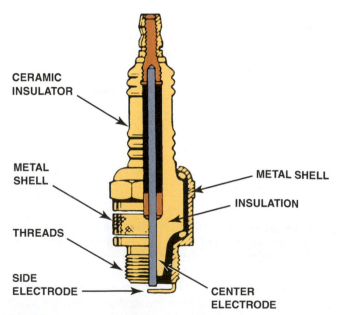

FIGURE 30–13 Parts of a spark plug.

IRIDIUM SPARK PLUGS Iridium is a white precious metal and is the most corrosion-resistant metal known. Most **iridium spark plugs** use a small amount of iridium welded onto the tip of a small center electrode, 0.015 to 0.020 in. (0.4 to 0.6 mm) in diameter. The small diameter reduces the voltage required to jump the gap between the center and the side electrode, thereby reducing possible misfires. The ground or side electrode is usually tipped with platinum to help reduce electrode gap wear.

FIGURE 30–14 When removing spark plugs, it is wise to arrange them so that they can be compared and any problem can be identified with a particular cylinder.

SPARK PLUG SERVICE

Spark plugs should be inspected when an engine performance problem occurs and should be replaced at specified intervals to ensure proper ignition system performance.

- Non-platinum spark plugs have a service life of over 20,000 miles (32,000 km).
- Platinum-tipped and Iridium spark plugs have a typical service life of 60,000 to 100,000 miles (100,000 to 160,000 km) or longer.

When replacing spark plugs, perform the following steps:

STEP 1 **Check service information.** Check for the exact spark plug to use and the specified instructions and/ or technical service bulletins (TSBs) that affect the number of plugs to be used or a revised replacement procedure.

STEP 2 **Allow the engine to cool before removing spark plugs.** This is true especially on engines with aluminum cylinder heads.

STEP 3 **Use compressed air or a brush to remove dirt from around the spark plug before removal.** This step helps prevent dirt from getting into the cylinder of an engine while removing a spark plug.

STEP 4 **Keep the spark plugs in order.** Keep them in order so that they can be inspected and if there is a fault, the cylinder where it was removed from can be identified. ● **SEE FIGURE 30–14.**

STEP 5 **Check the spark plug gap and correct as needed.** Be careful not to damage the tip on the center electrode if adjusting a platinum or iridium type of spark plug.

FIGURE 30–15 A spark plug thread chaser is a low-cost tool that hopefully will not be used often, but is necessary in order to clean the threads before installing new spark plugs.

CAUTION: Used platinum-tipped or iridium spark plugs should not be regapped! Using a gapping tool can break the platinum after it has been used in an engine. Engine heat makes the platinum or iridium brittle and using a gapping tool can cause the tip to break. Check service information regarding the recommended type of spark plugs and the specified service procedures.

STEP 6 **Install the spark plugs by hand.** After starting by hand, use a torque wrench to tighten the spark plugs to factory specifications. ● **SEE FIGURE 30–15.**

STEP 7 **Reinstall the spark plug wire.** To help avoid engine-operating problems, double-check that the correct spark plug wire is being installed on the correct plug.

SUMMARY

1. All inductive ignition systems supply battery voltage to the positive side of the ignition coil and pulse the negative side of the coil on and off to ground to create a high-voltage spark.

2. If an ignition system uses a distributor, it is a distributor ignition (DI) system.

3. If an ignition system does not use a distributor, it is an electronic ignition (EI) system.

4. A waste-spark ignition system fires two spark plugs at the same time.

5. A coil-on-plug ignition system uses an ignition coil for each spark plug.

6. A thorough visual inspection should be performed on all ignition components when diagnosing an engine performance problem.

REVIEW QUESTIONS

1. How can 12 volts from a battery be changed to 40,000 volts for ignition?

2. How does an ignition coil create up to 40,000 volts?

3. How does a waste-spark ignition system work?

4. Why should a spark tester be used to check for spark rather than a standard spark plug?

CHAPTER QUIZ

1. The ignition system creates a high voltage which is created in the _____.
   a. Spark plug
   b. Ignition coil
   c. Pickup coil
   d. Trigger wheel

2. What is used to ignite the air-fuel mixture in the cylinder of a gasoline engine?
   a. An arc at the spark plug
   b. Heat of compression
   c. Chemical reaction of the air-fuel mixture
   d. The primary winding of the ignition coil

3. Distributor ignition systems can be triggered by a _____.
   a. Hall-effect sensor
   b. Magnetic sensor
   c. Spark sensor
   d. Either a or b

4. A waste spark ignition _____.
   a. Uses two coils for each spark plug
   b. Uses one coil for two spark plugs
   c. Fires two spark plugs at the same time
   d. Both b and c

5. A spark tester is a _____.
   a. A tool that is used to check for spark
   b. Is calibrated to fire only if the spark voltage is higher than 25,000 volts
   c. One part is attached to a good ground and the other to the end of a spark plug wire
   d. All of the above

6. A coil-near-plug is what type of ignition?
   a. Distributor
   b. Coil-on-plug (COP)
   c. Waste spark
   d. All of the above

7. The high voltage is produced by _____.
   a. Using an ignition coil
   b. Supplying 12 volts from the battery to one side of the coil
   c. Using a module of the PCM to turn the primary current on and off
   d. All of the above

8. Two technicians are discussing coil-on-plug (COP) ignition systems. Technician A says that they can be called coil-near-plug or coil-by-plug ignition systems. Technician B says that in a COP system, an ignition coil is used for each spark plug. Which technician is correct?
   a. Technician A only
   b. Technician B only
   c. Both technicians A and B
   d. Neither technician A nor B

9. An engine equipped with a distributor-type ignition has the firing order located where?
   a. On the engine block
   b. On the intake manifold
   c. On the spark plugs
   d. On the ignition coil

10. The steps involved in replacing spark plugs includes _____.
    a. Allow the engine to cool
    b. Use compressed air to clean around the base of the plug
    c. Keep the spark plugs arranged so that they can be compared in case of a fault with one cylinder
    d. All of the above

chapter 31

FUEL-INJECTION SYSTEMS

OBJECTIVES: **After studying Chapter 31, the reader will be able to:** • Prepare for ASE Engine Performance (A8) certification test content area "C" (Fuel, Air Induction, and Exhaust Systems Diagnosis and Repair). • Describe how a port fuel-injection system works. • Discuss the purpose and function of the fuel-pressure regulator. • List the types of fuel-injection systems. • Describe the parts and operation of a gasoline direct injection system.

KEY TERMS: • Electronic fuel injection (EFI) 291 • Fuel injector 291 • Fuel-pressure regulator 291 • Port fuel-injection 291 • Throttle-body injection (TBI) 291

ELECTRONIC FUEL INJECTION

PURPOSE AND FUNCTION
The purpose and function of electronic fuel injection is to provide fuel mixed with air to the cylinders of the engine. Therefore, a fuel-injection system requires that clean fuel be supplied to the engine under pressure, where it can be easily mixed with filtered air.

PARTS INVOLVED
Electronic fuel-injection systems use the *powertrain control module (PCM)* to control the operation of fuel injectors and other functions based on information sent to the PCM from the various sensors. Most electronic fuel-injection systems share the following:

1. Electric fuel pump (usually located inside the fuel tank)
2. Fuel filter and fuel lines
3. Fuel-pump relay (usually controlled by the computer)
4. **Fuel-pressure regulator** (mechanically operated spring-loaded rubber diaphragm that maintains proper fuel pressure)
5. Fuel-injector nozzle or nozzles

● **SEE FIGURE 31–1.**

PCM CONTROL
Most electronic fuel-injection systems use the PCM for:

1. **Pulsing the fuel injectors on and off.** The longer the injectors are held open, the greater the amount of fuel that is injected into the cylinder.
2. **Operating the fuel-pump relay circuit.** The computer usually controls the operation of the electric fuel pump located inside (or near) the fuel tank by using an electric relay. The computer uses signals from the ignition switch and RPM signals from the ignition system to energize the fuel-pump relay circuit.

NOTE: This is a safety feature, because if the engine stalls and the tachometer (engine speed) signal is lost, the computer will shut off (de-energize) the fuel-pump relay and stop the fuel pump.

TYPES OF FUEL INJECTION
There are three types of electronic fuel-injection systems:

- **Throttle-body-injection (TBI)** type. A TBI system delivers fuel from a nozzle(s) into the air above the throttle plate. This type of system was used from the early 1980s until 1996, when the emission law required the use of a fuel-injection system that delivered fuel to each individual cylinder. ● **SEE FIGURE 31–2.**
- **Port fuel-injection** type. A port fuel-injection design uses a nozzle for each cylinder and the fuel is squirted into the intake manifold about 2 to 3 in. (70 to 100 mm) from the intake valve. ● **SEE FIGURE 31–3.**
- **Gasoline direct injection (GDI).** This type of fuel injection uses an injection nozzle that squirts fuel directly into each cylinder. ● **SEE FIGURE 31–4.**

FUEL INJECTORS

An **electronic fuel-injection (EFI)** injector is simply a specialized solenoid. It has an armature winding to create a magnetic field, and a needle (pintle), a disc, or a ball valve. A spring holds the needle, disc, or ball closed against the valve seat, and when energized, the armature winding pulls open the valve when it receives a current pulse from the PCM. When the solenoid is energized, it unseats the valve to inject fuel. Electronic

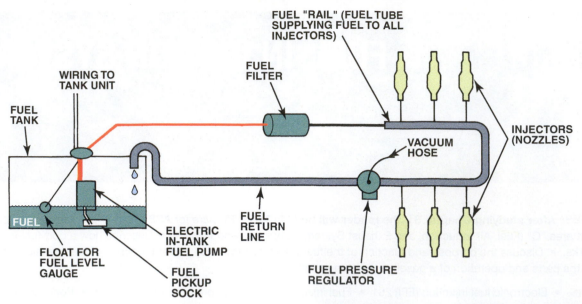

FIGURE 31–1 Typical port fuel-injection system, indicating the location of various components. Note that the fuel-pressure regulator is located on the fuel return side of the system. The computer does not control fuel pressure but does control the operation of the electric fuel pump (on most systems) and the pulsing on and off of the injectors.

FIGURE 31–2 A dual-nozzle TBI unit on a Chevrolet 4.3-L V-6 engine. The fuel is squirted above the throttle plate, where the fuel mixes with air before entering the intake manifold.

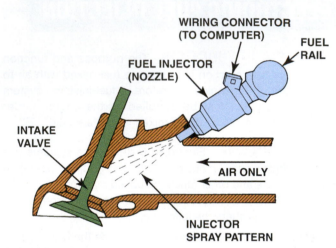

FIGURE 31–3 A typical port fuel-injection system squirts fuel into the low pressure area (vacuum) of the intake manifold, about 2 to 3 in. (70–100 mm) from the intake valve.

fuel-injection systems use a solenoid-operated injector to spray atomized fuel in timed pulses into the manifold or near the intake valve. ● **SEE FIGURE 31–5.**

FUEL-PRESSURE REGULATOR

PURPOSE AND FUNCTION   The pressure regulator and fuel pump work together to maintain the required pressure drop at the injector tips.

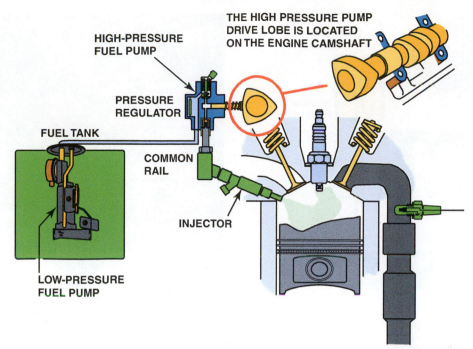

FIGURE 31–4 A typical direct-injection system uses two pumps—one low-pressure electric pump in the fuel tank and the other a high-pressure pump driven by the camshaft. The high pressure fuel system operates at a pressure as low as 500 PSI during light load conditions and as high as 2,900 PSI under heavy loads.

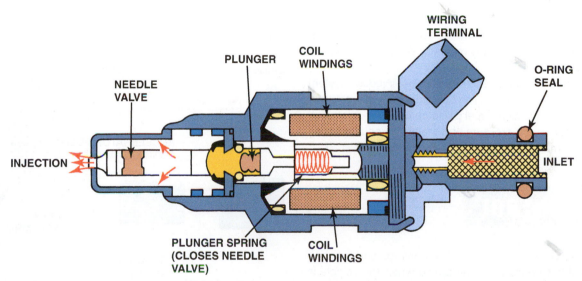

FIGURE 31–5 Cross-section of a typical port fuel-injection nozzle assembly. These injectors are serviced as an assembly only; no part replacement or service is possible except for replacement of external O-ring seals.

PARTS AND OPERATION The fuel-pressure regulator typically consists of a spring-loaded, diaphragm-operated valve in a metal housing. Fuel-pressure regulators on fuel-return-type fuel-injection systems are installed on the return (downstream) side of the injectors at the end of the fuel rail, or are built into or mounted upon the throttle-body housing. Downstream regulation minimizes fuel-pressure pulsations caused by pressure drop across the injectors as the nozzles open. It also ensures positive fuel pressure at the injectors at all times and holds residual pressure in the lines when the engine is off.

NOTE: On returnless systems, the pressure regulator is located in the fuel tank and is often part of the fuel-pump assembly.

In order for excess fuel (about 80% to 90% of the fuel delivered) to return to the tank, fuel pressure must overcome

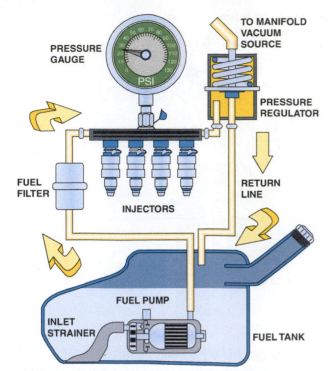

FIGURE 31–6 A typical port fuel-injected system showing a vacuum-controlled fuel-pressure regulator.

FIGURE 31–7 An idle control unit has four wires and it uses a reversible stepper motor to regulate the amount of air bypassing the throttle plate.

spring pressure on the spring-loaded diaphragm to uncover the return line to the tank. This happens when system pressure exceeds operating requirements. With TBI, the regulator is close to the injector tip, so the regulator senses the same air pressure as the injector.

The pressure regulator used in a port fuel-injection system has an intake manifold vacuum line connection on the regulator vacuum chamber. This allows fuel pressure to be modulated by a combination of spring pressure and manifold vacuum acting on the diaphragm. ● SEE FIGURE 31–6.

IDLE CONTROL

PURPOSE AND FUNCTION   The purpose and function of idle control is to control engine speed when the vehicle is stopped.

PARTS AND OPERATION   Port fuel-injection systems generally use an auxiliary air bypass to control idle speed. ● SEE FIGURE 31–7.

This air bypass or regulator provides needed additional airflow, and thus more fuel. The engine needs more power when cold to maintain its normal idle speed to overcome the increased friction from cold lubricating oil. When the engine stops, most *idle air control (IAC)* units will retract outward to get ready for the next engine start. When the engine starts, the engine speed is high to provide for proper operation when the engine is cold. Then, as the engine gets warmer, the computer reduces engine

idle speed gradually by reducing the number of counts or steps commanded by the PCM and sent to the IAC.

ELECTRONIC THROTTLE CONTROL   Since about 2000, most vehicles are equipped with an *electronic throttle control (ETC)* system. These systems use an electric motor to move the throttle valve. The PCM moves the throttle based on movement of the driver's foot as determined by an *accelerator pedal position (APP)* sensor, which is part of the accelerator pedal assembly. The use of an electronic throttle control system eliminates the need for an idle air control valve or any throttle linkage, as well as cruise control mechanisms. ● SEE FIGURE 31–8.

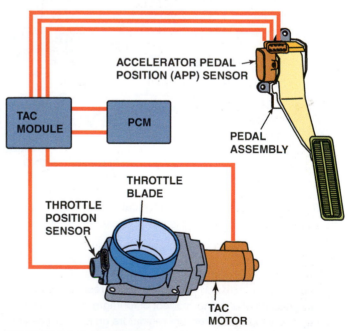

FIGURE 31–8 The throttle pedal is connected to the accelerator pedal position (APP) sensor. The electronic throttle body includes a throttle position sensor to provide throttle angle feedback to the vehicle computer. Some systems use a throttle actuator control (TAC) module to operate the throttle blade (plate).

1. A fuel-injection system includes the electric fuel pump, fuel-pump relay, fuel-pressure regulator, and fuel injectors (nozzles).

2. The three types of fuel-injection systems are the throttle body design, port fuel-injection design, and gasoline direct-injection systems.

3. The amount of fuel supplied by fuel injectors is determined by how long they are kept open.

4. The fuel-pressure regulator is usually located on the fuel return on return-type fuel-injection systems.

5. TBI-type fuel-injection systems do not use a vacuum-controlled fuel-pressure regulator, whereas many port fuel-injection systems use a vacuum-controlled regulator to monitor equal pressure drop across the injectors.

REVIEW QUESTIONS

1. What are the three basic types of fuel-injection systems?

2. What is the purpose of the vacuum-controlled fuel-pressure regulator?

3. How does an electronic throttle control system work?

CHAPTER QUIZ

1. Technician A says that the fuel-pump relay is usually controlled by the PCM. Technician B says that a TBI injector squirts fuel above the throttle plate. Which technician is correct?
   a. Technician A only
   b. Technician B only
   c. Both technicians A and B
   d. Neither technician A nor B

2. What is the difference between gasoline direct injection (GDI) and port fuel injection systems?
   a. GDI uses a low pressure and a high pressure fuel pump
   b. Port fuel injection uses just one fuel pump
   c. The GDI high pressure pump is driven by the camshaft
   d. All of the above

3. Where is the fuel squirted in an engine equipped with gasoline direct injection (GDI) fuel injection?
   a. Into the intake manifold
   b. Into the cylinder
   c. Above the throttle plate
   d. Under the throttle plate

4. What part turns the fuel injectors on and off?
   a. PCM
   b. MAF sensor
   c. MAP sensor
   d. Ignition system

5. The fuel pump is located where in TBI and port electronic fuel injection systems?
   a. Mounted to the engine
   b. Front of the engine belt driven from by an accessory drive belt
   c. Rear of the engine gear driven by the engine crankshaft or camshaft
   d. Inside the fuel tank

6. Where does a port-type fuel-injection system squirt fuel?
   a. Below the throttle place
   b. Above the throttle plate
   c. Into the cylinder
   d. In the intake port near the intake valve

7. What moves the throttle plate on an engine equipped with an electronic throttle control (ETC) system? _____.
   a. A cable from the accelerator pedal
   b. An electric motor
   c. A solenoid
   d. An electric plunger

8. Where can the fuel-pressure regulator be mounted?
   a. On the fuel rail
   b. Part of the fuel-pump module assembly
   c. Inside the engine under the intake manifold
   d. Either a or b

9. Idle speed is controlled by an _____.
   a. Ignition system
   b. Idle air control valve
   c. Electronic throttle control (ETC) system
   d. Either b or c

10. Which sensor is used to determine the position of the accelerator pedal on a system that uses an electronic throttle control (ETC) system?
    a. APP sensor
    b. TP sensor
    c. MAF sensor
    d. MAP sensor

OBJECTIVES: After studying Chapter 32, the reader will be able to: • Prepare for the ASE Engine Performance (A8) certification test content area "D" (Emission Control Systems). • Describe the purpose and function of the exhaust gas recirculation (EGR) system. • Describe the purpose and function of the positive crankcase ventilation (PCV). • Describe the purpose and function of the secondary air-injection (SAI) reaction system. • Describe the purpose and function of the catalytic converter. • Describe the purpose and function of the evaporative emission control system.

KEY TERMS: • Blowby 297 • Canister purge (CANP) 301 • Catalyst 299 • Catalytic converter 299 • Check valves 299 • EGR 296 • NOx 296 • Palladium 300 • PCV 297 • Platinum 300 • Rhodium 300 • SAI 298 • Smog 296 • Smog pump 298 • TWC 298

INTRODUCTION

Most of the major advances in engines are a direct result of the need to improve fuel economy and reduce exhaust emissions. It has been said that engine changes are due to the need to reduce three things.

1. Emissions
2. Emissions
3. Emissions

SMOG

DEFINITION AND TERMINOLOGY The common term used to describe air pollution is **smog,** a word that combines two words: *smoke* and *fog.* Smog is formed in the atmosphere when sunlight combines with unburned fuel (hydrocarbons, or HC) and oxides of nitrogen (NOx) produced during the combustion process inside the cylinders of an engine. Carbon monoxide (CO) is a poisonous gas. Smog is *ozone* (O_3), a strong irritant to the lungs and eyes. Ozone is located in two places.

1. Upper-atmospheric ozone is desirable because it blocks out harmful ultraviolet rays from the sun.
2. Ground-level ozone is considered to be unhealthy smog.

  Emissions that are controlled include:

  ■ **HC (unburned hydrocarbons).** Unburned hydrocarbons contribute to smog formation. Excessive HC emissions (unburned fuel) are controlled by the

evaporative system (charcoal canister), the positive crankcase ventilation (PCV) system, the secondary air-injection (SAI) system, and the catalytic converter.

  ■ **CO (carbon monoxide).** Carbon monoxide is a colorless, odorless, and deadly gas. Excessive CO emissions are controlled by the positive crankcase ventilation (PCV) system, the secondary air-injection (SAI) system, and the catalytic converter.

  ■ **NOx (oxides of nitrogen).** Oxides of nitrogen are considered to be a health hazard because they cause respiratory problems. Excessive NOx emissions are controlled by the exhaust gas recirculation (EGR) system and the catalytic converter. An oxide of nitrogen (NO) is a colorless, tasteless, and odorless gas when it leaves the engine, but as soon as it reaches the atmosphere and mixes with more oxygen, nitrogen oxides (NO_2) are formed, which appear as red-brown emissions. Both NO and NO_2 together are labeled NOx. **SEE FIGURE 32–1.**

EGR

INTRODUCTION **Exhaust gas recirculation** (EGR) is an emission control system that lowers the amount of **nitrogen oxides** formed during combustion. In the presence of sunlight, NO_x reacts with hydrocarbons in the atmosphere to form ozone (O_3) or photochemical smog, an air pollutant.

CONTROLLING NO$_X$ The most efficient method to control NO_x emissions generated above 2,500°F (1,370°C) without significantly affecting engine performance, fuel economy, and

FIGURE 32–1 Nitrogen oxides (NOx) create a red-brown haze that often hangs over major cities.

FIGURE 32–2 Typical vacuum-operated EGR valve. The operation of the valve is controlled by the PCM by pulsing the EGR control solenoid on and off.

other exhaust emissions is to use exhaust gas recirculation (EGR). The EGR system routes small quantities, usually between 6% and 10%, of exhaust gas into the intake manifold. The result is a lower peak combustion temperature. When the combustion temperature is lowered, the production of oxides of nitrogen is reduced. The EGR system has some means of interconnecting the exhaust and intake manifolds. ● **SEE FIGURES 32–2 AND 32–3.**

OBD-II MONITORING

PURPOSE AND FUNCTION In 1996, the US EPA began requiring OBD-II (On-Board Diagnosis-second generation) systems in all passenger cars and most light duty trucks. These

FIGURE 32–3 A General Motors electronic EGR valve.

systems include emissions system monitors that alert the driver and the technician if an emissions system is malfunctioning. The OBD-II system performs this test by opening and closing the EGR valve. The PCM monitors an EGR function sensor for a change in signal voltage. If the EGR system fails, a diagnostic trouble code (DTC) is set. If the system fails two consecutive times, the malfunction indicator light (MIL) is lit.

POSITIVE CRANKCASE VENTILATION

PURPOSE AND FUNCTION The problem of crankcase ventilation has existed since the beginning of the automobile, because no piston ring, new or old, can provide a perfect seal between the piston and the cylinder wall. When an engine is running, the pressure of combustion forces the piston downward. This same pressure also forces gases and unburned fuel from the combustion chamber, past the piston rings, and into the crankcase. **Blowby** is the term used to describe when combustion gases are forced past the piston rings and into the crankcase.

These combustion by-products, particularly unburned hydrocarbons (HC) caused by blowby, must be ventilated from the crankcase. However, the crankcase cannot be vented directly to the atmosphere, because the hydrocarbon vapors add to air pollution. **Positive crankcase ventilation (PCV)** systems were developed to ventilate the crankcase and recirculate the vapors to the engine's induction system so they can be burned in the cylinders. PCV systems help reduce HC and CO emissions.

All systems use the following:

1. PCV valve, calibrated orifice, or orifice and separator
2. PCV inlet air filter plus all connecting hoses

● **SEE FIGURE 32–4.**

FIGURE 32–4 A PCV valve and hose on a Ford 5.0-liter V-8. Many are hard to see as they are hidden from view under plastic covers.

An oil/vapor or oil/water separator is used in some systems instead of a valve or orifice, particularly with turbocharged and fuel-injected engines. The oil/vapor separator lets oil condense and drain back into the crankcase. The oil/water separator accumulates moisture and prevents it from freezing during cold engine starts. The air for the PCV system is drawn after the air cleaner filter, which acts as a PCV filter.

PCV VALVES

The PCV valve in most systems is a one-way valve containing a spring-operated plunger that controls valve flow rate. ● **SEE FIGURE 32–5.**

Flow rate is established for each engine and a valve for a different engine should not be substituted. The flow rate is determined by the size of the plunger and the holes inside the valve. PCV valves usually are located in the valve cover or intake manifold. The PCV valve regulates airflow through the crankcase under all driving conditions and speeds. When manifold vacuum is high (at idle, deceleration, cruising, and light-load operation), the PCV valve restricts the airflow to maintain a balanced air–fuel ratio.

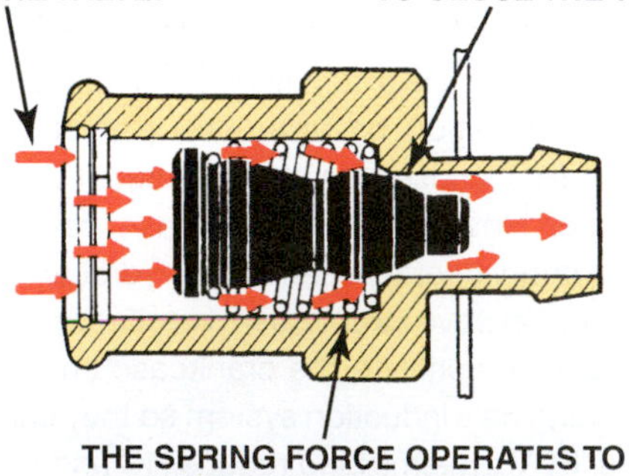

SECONDARY AIR INJECTION

PURPOSE AND FUNCTION The **secondary air-injection (SAI)** system provides the air necessary for the oxidizing process either at the exhaust manifold or inside the catalytic converter.

PARTS AND OPERATION The SAI pump, also called an air injection reaction (AIR) pump, a **smog pump,** or a *thermactor pump,* is mounted at the front of the engine and can be driven by a belt from the crankshaft pulley. It pulls fresh air in through an external filter and pumps the air under slight pressure to each exhaust port through connecting hoses or a manifold. The typical SAI system includes the following components:

- A belt-driven pump with inlet air filter (older models).
  ● **SEE FIGURE 32–6.**
- An electric air pump (newer models)
- One or more air distribution manifolds and nozzles
- One or more exhaust check valves
- Connecting hoses for air distribution
- Air management valves and solenoids on all newer applications

With the introduction of NOx reduction converters (also called dual-bed, **three-way converters,** or **TWC**), the output of the SAI pump is sent to the center of the converter, where

THIS END OF THE PCV VALVE IS SUBJECT TO CRANKCASE PRESSURE THAT TENDS TO CLOSE THE VALVE.

THIS END IS SUBJECT TO INTAKE MANIFOLD VACUUM THAT TENDS TO CLOSE THE VALVE.

THE SPRING FORCE OPERATES TO OPEN THE VALVE TO MANIFOLD VACUUM AND CRANKCASE PRESSURE.

FIGURE 32–5 Spring force, crankcase pressure, and intake manifold vacuum work together to regulate the flow rate through the PCV valve.

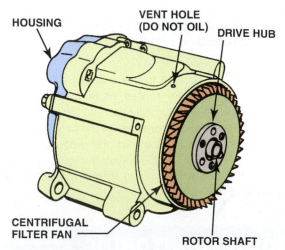

HOUSING · VENT HOLE (DO NOT OIL) · DRIVE HUB · CENTRIFUGAL FILTER FAN · ROTOR SHAFT

FIGURE 32–6 A typical belt-driven AIR pump. Air enters through the revolving fins behind the drive pulley. The fins act as an air filter because dirt is heavier than air, and therefore the dirt is deflected off of the fins at the same time air is being drawn into the pump.

the extra air can help oxidize unburned hydrocarbons (HC) and carbon monoxide (CO) into water vapor (H_2O) and carbon dioxide (CO_2). The computer controls the airflow from the pump by switching on and off various solenoid valves.

AIR DISTRIBUTION MANIFOLDS AND NOZZLES The secondary air-injection system sends air from the pump to a nozzle installed near each exhaust port in the cylinder head. This provides equal air injection for the exhaust from each cylinder and makes it available at a point in the system where exhaust gases are the hottest. Air is delivered to the exhaust system in one of the following two ways:

1. An external air manifold, or manifolds, distributes the air through injection tubes with stainless steel nozzles. The nozzles are threaded into the cylinder heads or exhaust manifolds close to each exhaust valve. This method is used primarily with smaller engines.

2. An internal air manifold distributes the air to the exhaust ports near each exhaust valve through passages cast in the cylinder head or the exhaust manifold. This method is used mainly with larger engines.

EXHAUST CHECK VALVES All air-injection systems use one or more one-way check valves to protect the air pump and other components from reverse exhaust flow. A **check valve** contains a spring-type metallic disc or reed that closes under exhaust backpressure. Check valves are located between the air manifold and the switching valve(s). If exhaust pressure exceeds injection pressure, or if the air pump fails, the check valve spring closes the valve to prevent reverse exhaust flow. ● **SEE FIGURE 32–7.**

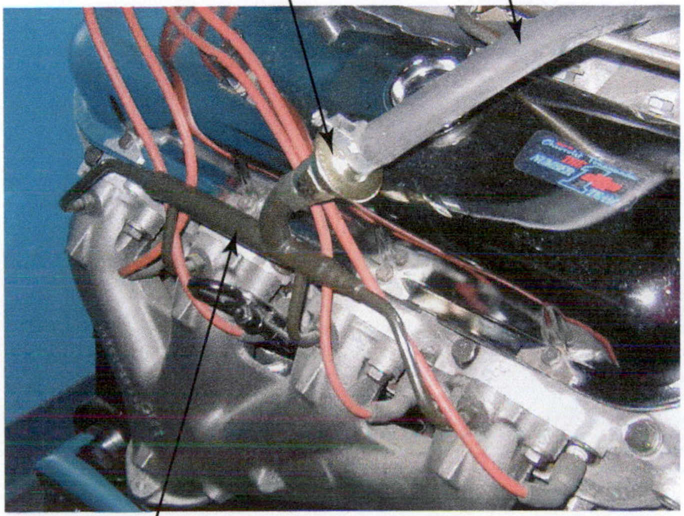

EXHAUST CHECK VALVE **AIR HOSE FROM AIR PUMP**

AIR MANIFOLD

FIGURE 32–7 The external air manifold and exhaust check valve on a restored muscle car engine.

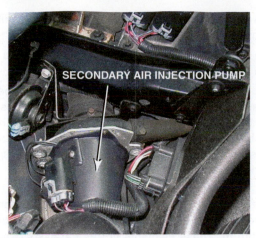
SECONDARY AIR INJECTION PUMP

FIGURE 32–8 A typical electric motor–driven SAI pump. This unit is on a Chevrolet Corvette and only works when the engine is cold.

BELT-DRIVEN AIR PUMPS The belt-driven air pump uses a centrifugal filter just behind the drive pulley. As the pump rotates, underhood air is drawn into the pump and is slightly compressed. The system uses either vacuum- or solenoid-controlled diverter valves to direct the air to the correct component as needed.

ELECTRIC MOTOR–DRIVEN AIR PUMPS The electric motor–driven air pump is generally used only during cold engine operation and is computer controlled. The secondary air-injection (SAI) system helps reduce hydrocarbon (HC) and carbon monoxide (CO). It also helps to warm the three-way catalytic converters quickly on engine start-up so that conversion of exhaust gases may occur sooner.

■ The SAI pump solenoids are controlled by the PCM. The PCM turns on the SAI pump by providing the ground to complete the circuit, which energizes the SAI pump solenoid relay. When air to the exhaust ports is desired, the PCM energizes the relay in order to turn on the solenoid and the SAI pump. ● **SEE FIGURE 32–8.**

■ The PCM turns on the SAI pump during start-up any time the engine coolant temperature is above 32°F (0°C). A typical electric SAI pump operates for a maximum of four minutes, or until the system commands it off.

CATALYTIC CONVERTERS

PURPOSE AND FUNCTION A **catalytic converter** is an after-treatment device used to reduce exhaust emissions outside of the engine. The catalytic converter uses a **catalyst,** which is a chemical that helps start a chemical reaction but does not enter into the chemical reaction.

■ The catalyst on the surface of the material inside the converter helps create a chemical reaction.

- The chemical reaction changes harmful exhaust emissions into nonharmful exhaust emissions.
- The converter, therefore, converts harmful exhaust gases into water vapor (H_2O) and carbon dioxide (CO_2).

This device is installed in the exhaust system between the exhaust manifold and the muffler, and usually is positioned beneath the passenger compartment. The location of the converter is important, since as much of the exhaust heat as possible must be retained for effective operation. The nearer it is to the engine, the better. ● **SEE FIGURE 32–9.**

CATALYTIC CONVERTER OPERATION The converter substrate contains small amounts of **rhodium, palladium, and platinum.** These elements act as catalysts, which, as mentioned, start a chemical reaction without becoming a part of the reaction, or being consumed in the process. In a three-way catalytic converter (TWC), all three exhaust emissions (NOx, HC, and CO) are converted to carbon dioxide (CO_2) and water (H_2O). As the exhaust gas passes through the catalyst, oxides of nitrogen are chemically reduced (i.e., nitrogen and oxygen are separated) in the first section of the catalytic converter. In the second section of the catalytic converter, most of the hydrocarbons and carbon monoxide remaining in the exhaust gas are oxidized to form harmless carbon dioxide (CO_2) and water vapor (H_2O). ● **SEE FIGURE 32–10.**

FIGURE 32–9 Most catalytic converters are located as close to the exhaust manifold as possible, as seen in this display of a Chevrolet Corvette.

canister, hoses, and valves. These vapors are routed into a charcoal canister and then into the intake airflow, where they are burned in the engine instead of being released into the atmosphere. ● **SEE FIGURE 32–11.**

COMMON COMPONENTS The fuel tank filler caps used on vehicles with modern EVAP systems are a special design. Most EVAP fuel tank filler caps have a pressure-vacuum relief valve built into them. When pressure or vacuum exceeds a calibrated value, the valve opens. Once the pressure or vacuum has been relieved, the valve closes. If a sealed cap is used on an EVAP system that requires a pressure-vacuum relief design, a vacuum lock may develop in the fuel system, or the fuel tank may be damaged by fuel expansion or contraction. ● **SEE FIGURE 32–12.**

EVAPORATIVE EMISSION CONTROL SYSTEM

PURPOSE AND FUNCTION The purpose of the evaporative (EVAP) emission control system is to trap and hold gasoline vapors, also called volatile organic compounds, or VOCs. The evaporative control system includes the charcoal

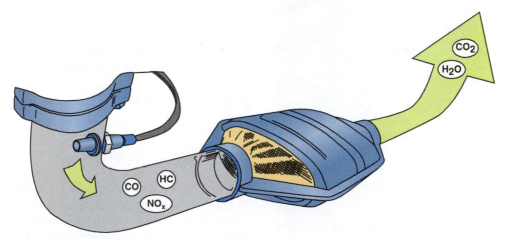

FIGURE 32–10 The three-way catalytic converter first separates the NOx into nitrogen and oxygen and then converts the HC and CO into harmless water (H_2O) and carbon dioxide (CO_2). The nitrogen (N) passes through the converter, exits the tailpipe, and enters the atmosphere, which is about 78% nitrogen.

FIGURE 32-11 A charcoal canister can be located under the hood or underneath the vehicle.

EVAPORATIVE CONTROL SYSTEM OPERATION

Gasoline fumes from the fuel system are trapped by the carbon canister. The canister traps and holds the vapors until the system applies engine vacuum to the canister to draw the fumes into the engine. The system opens the purge valve to allow the gas vapor to flow from the canister into the intake manifold. When the fumes enter the intake manifold, they are drawn into the cylinder and are burned.

NOTE: Some vehicles with large or dual fuel tanks may have dual canisters.

CANISTER VENT VALVE The canister vent valve is a *normally open* valve and is closed only when commanded by the PCM during testing of the system. The vent valve is closed only during testing by the PCM as part of the mandated OBD-II standards. The vent solenoid is located under the vehicle in most cases and is exposed to the environment, subjecting it to rust and corrosion.

CANISTER PURGE VALVE The purge valve, also called the **canister purge (CANP)** solenoid, is *normally closed* and is pulsed open by the PCM during purging. The purge valve is connected to the intake manifold vacuum and this line is used to draw gasoline vapors from the charcoal canister into the engine when the purge valve is commanded open. Most purge valves are pulsed on and off to better control the amount of fumes being drawn into the intake manifold.

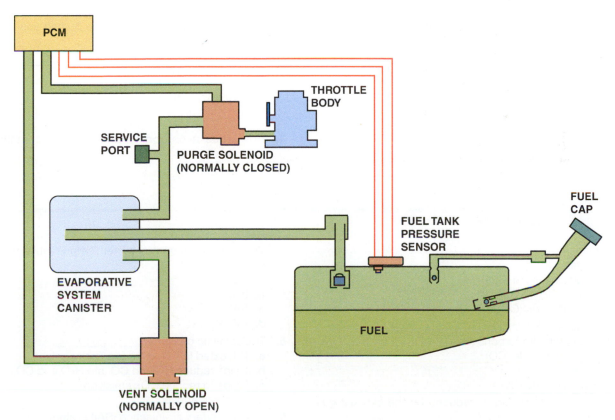

FIGURE 32-12 An enhanced EVAP system is able to perform system and leak detection diagnosis.

FIGURE 32–13 Some vehicles will display a message if an evaporative control system leak is detected that could be the result of a loose gas cap.

SUMMARY

1. Recirculating 6% to 10% exhaust gases back into the intake system by the EGR system reduces peak temperature inside the combustion chamber and reduces NOx exhaust emissions.

2. Positive crankcase ventilation (PCV) systems use a valve or a fixed orifice to control and direct the fumes from the crankcase back into the intake system.

3. A PCV valve regulates the flow of fumes depending on engine vacuum and seals the crankcase vent in the event of a backfire.

4. The secondary air-injection (SAI) system forces air at low pressure into the exhaust to reduce CO and HC exhaust emissions.

5. A catalytic converter is an after-treatment device that reduces exhaust emissions outside of the engine. A catalyst is an element that starts a chemical reaction but is not consumed in the process.

6. The catalyst material used in a catalytic converter includes rhodium, palladium, and platinum.

7. The purpose of the evaporative (EVAP) emission control system is to reduce the release of volatile organic compounds (VOCs) into the atmosphere.

8. A carbon (charcoal) canister is used to trap and hold gasoline vapors until they can be purged and run into the engine to be burned.

REVIEW QUESTIONS

1. What is smog?

2. How does a catalytic converter reduce NOx to nitrogen and oxygen?

3. How does a carbon (charcoal) canister help reduce emissions?

CHAPTER QUIZ

1. Smog is _____.
   a. Nitrogen (N)
   b. Carbon monoxide (CO)
   c. Ozone
   d. Carbon Dioxide (CO_2)

2. Which gas is poisonous?
   a. Unburned hydrocarbons (HC)
   b. Carbon monoxide (CO)
   c. Ozone
   d. Carbon Dioxide (CO_2)

3. Which gas is controlled or reduced by the exhaust gas recirculation (EGR) system?
   a. Unburned hydrocarbons (HC)
   b. Carbon monoxide (CO)
   c. Oxides of nitrogen (NOx)
   d. Carbon Dioxide (CO_2)

4. Which emission control system helps reduce the effect of engine blowby?
   a. PCV
   b. EGR
   c. SAI
   d. EVAP

5. The catalytic converter _____.
   a. Is located in the exhaust system
   b. Helps reduce HC and CO into H_2O and CO_2
   c. Helps to reduce NOx emissions
   d. All of the above

6. The secondary air-injection (SAI) system _____.
   a. Includes an air pump
   b. Includes valves and pipes
   c. Injects air into the exhaust to reduce exhaust emissions
   d. All of the above

7. At about what temperature does oxygen combine with the nitrogen in the air to form NOx?
   a. 2,500°F (1,370°C)
   b. 1,500°F (815°C)
   c. 750°F (400°C)
   d. 500°F (260°C)

8. Which EVAP valve(s) is (are) normally closed?
   a. Canister purge valve
   b. Canister vent valve
   c. Both canister purge and canister vent valves
   d. Neither canister purge nor canister vent valve

9. Which emission control device is located in the exhaust system (exhaust manifold or exhaust pipe)?
   a. SAI
   b. Catalytic converter
   c. EGR
   d. EVAP

10. Which emission control system can turn on a "check engine" light if the gas cap is loose?
   a. SAI
   b. EVAP
   c. EGR
   d. PCV

chapter 33

HYBRID ELECTRIC VEHICLES

OBJECTIVES: **After studying Chapter 33, the reader will be able to:** • Describe the different types of hybrid electric vehicles. • Explain how a hybrid vehicle is able to achieve an improvement in fuel economy compared to a conventional vehicle design. • Discuss the advantages and disadvantages of the various hybrid designs. • Describe HEV components, including motors, energy sources, and motor controllers. • Discuss the operation of a typical hybrid electric vehicle.

KEY TERMS: • BEV 304 • Full hybrid 305 • HEV 304 • Hybrid 305 • ICE 304 • Idle stop mode 304 • Medium hybrid 305 • Mild hybrid 305 • Motoring mode 304 • Power assist mode 304 • Strong hybrid 305

HYBRID ELECTRIC VEHICLES

DEFINITION OF TERMS A hybrid vehicle is one that uses two different methods to propel the vehicle. A hybrid electric vehicle, abbreviated **HEV** uses both an **internal combustion engine (ICE)** and an electric motor to propel the vehicle. Most hybrid vehicles use a high-voltage battery pack and a combination electric motor and generator to help or assist a gasoline engine. The internal combustion engine used in a hybrid vehicle can be either gasoline or diesel, although only gasoline-powered engines are currently used in hybrid vehicles. An electric motor is used to help propel the vehicle, and in some designs, is capable of propelling the vehicle alone without having to start the internal combustion engine.

BACKGROUND In the early years of vehicle development, many different types of propulsion systems were used, including the following:

- Steam engine powered
- Gasoline engine powered
- Electric motor powered

Early electric vehicles (EVs) were also called **battery electric vehicles (BEV).** These early electric vehicles used lead–acid batteries, an electric motor, and a mechanical controller. A traction motor is an electric motor used to rotate the drive wheels and propel the vehicle. The traction between the wheel and the road surface transmits the torque needed to move the vehicle. ● **SEE FIGURE 33–1.**

COMMON FEATURES OF HYBRID ELECTRIC VEHICLES

The following are the most common modes of operation that hybrid electric vehicles (HEV) use to improve fuel economy:

- **Idle stop.** The **idle stop mode** turns off the engine when the vehicle is stopped. When the brake is released, the engine immediately starts. This ensures that the vehicle is not using fuel, nor creating CO_2 emissions, when the engine is not required to propel the vehicle.

- **Regenerative braking.** When decelerating, the braking system captures the energy from the vehicle's inertia and converts it to electrical energy, which is stored in the battery for later use. Regenerative braking helps keep the batteries charged.

- **Power assist.** The electric motor provides extra power using electrical current drawn from the battery to assist the internal combustion engine during acceleration. This **power assist mode** enables the vehicle to use a smaller, more fuel-efficient engine without giving up vehicle performance.

- **Engine-off drive-electric vehicle mode.** The electric motor propels the vehicle at lower speeds. This mode is often called the **motoring mode.** Because the internal combustion engine is not being used during acceleration, no fuel is being used and no emissions are being released. When the hybrid is in this mode, it is essentially an electric vehicle.

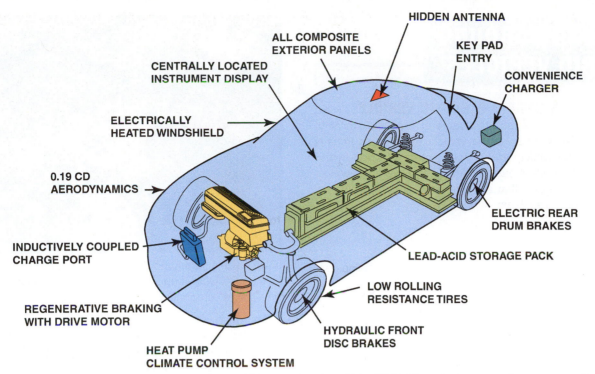

FIGURE 33–1 View of the components of the General Motors electric vehicle (EV1). Many features, such as regenerative braking, currently used on hybrid vehicles were first put into production on this vehicle.

LEVELS OF HYBRID ELECTRIC VEHICLES

The term **hybrid** refers to a type of vehicle. However, there are different levels of "hybridization" among hybrids on the market. Different vehicle manufacturers use different hybrid technologies.

MILD HYBRID   A **mild hybrid** will incorporate idle stop and regenerative braking but is not capable of using the electric motor to propel the vehicle on its own without help from the internal combustion engine. A mild hybrid system has the advantage of costing less, but saves less fuel compared to a full hybrid vehicle and usually uses a 42-volt electrical motor and battery package (36-volt batteries, 42-volt charging). An example of this type of hybrid is the General Motors Silverado parallel hybrid truck (PHT) and the Saturn VUE. The fuel savings for a mild type of hybrid design is about 8% to 15%.

MEDIUM HYBRID   A **medium hybrid** uses 144- to 158-volt batteries that provide for engine stop/start, regenerative braking, and power assist. Like a mild hybrid, a typical medium hybrid is not capable of propelling the vehicle from a stop using battery power alone. Examples of a medium hybrid vehicle include the Honda Insight, Civic, and Accord. The fuel economy savings are about 20% to 25% for medium hybrid systems.

FULL HYBRID   A **full hybrid**, also called a **strong hybrid**, uses idle stop regenerative braking, and is able to propel the vehicle

using the electric motor(s) alone. Each vehicle manufacturer has made its decision on which hybrid type to implement based on its assessment of the market niche for a particular model. Examples of a full or strong hybrid include the Ford Escape SUV, Toyota Highlander, Lexus RX400h, Lexus GS450h, Toyota Prius, and Toyota Camry. The fuel economy savings are about 30% to 50% for full hybrid systems. ● **SEE FIGURE 33–2.**

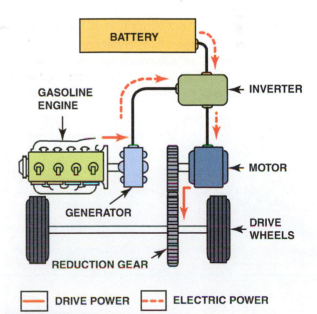

FIGURE 33–2 A full hybrid design allows the vehicle to operate in electric motor mode only or in combination with the internal combustion engine.

WORKING AROUND HYBRID VEHICLES

IDENTIFYING A HYBRID ELECTRIC VEHICLE Most hybrid electric vehicles look the same or are very similar to non-hybrid versions of the same vehicle. The Toyota Prius is a unique-looking vehicle and it does not have a non-hybrid version, so this vehicle is easy to identify as a hybrid. However, there are many models that are offered in both conventional and hybrid versions such as:

Ford Escape

Ford Fusion

BMW 7 series

Chevrolet Malibu

Chevrolet Silverado

Chevrolet Tahoe

Cadillac Escalade

Saturn AURA

Saturn VUE

Toyota Highlander

Toyota Camry

Lexus RX400h/450h

Lexus GS 450h

Lexus 600h

Mercury Mariner

Nissan Altima

Honda Civic

Honda Accord

To identify whether a vehicle is a hybrid electric vehicle or not, look for the following:

1. Emblems that state that it a hybrid. ● **SEE FIGURE 33–3.**

2. The presence of orange cables under the hood or orange shielding under the vehicle would identify the vehicle as an HEV. Electrical energy flows between the high-voltage battery module and the motor through either two or three

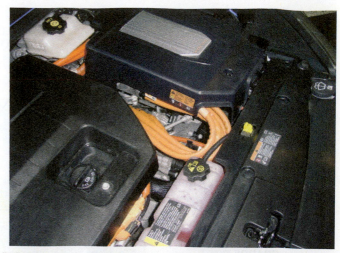

FIGURE 33–4 Orange-colored cable under the hood means that the vehicle is a hybrid or an electric vehicle that uses high-voltage components and circuits.

heavy-duty orange cables. In some hybrid vehicles, high-voltage cables also deliver current to the air conditioning (A/C) compressor (if equipped). The high-voltage cables are routed under the vehicle between the battery box and the engine compartment inside sturdy orange plastic protective shields. ● **SEE FIGURE 33–4.**

HIGH VOLTAGE COMPONENTS Most service work to be performed on hybrid electric vehicles does not require any special precautions or the need to disconnect the high-voltage circuits. However, if work is going to be performed on any of the following components, then factory-approved service procedures must be followed to prevent possible electrical shock and personal injury from:

- The high-voltage (HV) battery pack
- Any of the electronic controllers that use orange cables such as the inverter and converters
- The air conditioning compressor if electrically driven and has orange cables attached

To safely depower the vehicle always follow the instructions found in service information for the exact vehicle being serviced. The steps usually include the following:

STEP 1 Turn the ignition off and remove the key (if equipped) from the ignition.

CAUTION: If a push-button start is used, remove and store the key fob at least 15 feet (5 m) from the vehicle to prevent the vehicle from being powered up.

STEP 2 Remove the 12-volt power source to the HV controller. This step could involve the following:
- Removing a fuse or a relay
- Disconnecting the negative battery cable from the auxiliary 12-volt battery

STEP 3 Remove the HV fuse or service plug or switch. ● **SEE FIGURE 33–5.**

FIGURE 33–3 Look for an emblem that says "Hybrid" on the front, side, or rear of the vehicle.

Silence Is NOT Golden

Never assume the vehicle is shut off just because the engine is off. When working with a Toyota or Lexus hybrid electric vehicle, always look for the "READY" indicator status on the dash display. The vehicle is shut off when the "READY" indicator is off. The vehicle may be powered by the following:

1. The electric motor only
2. The gasoline engine only
3. A combination of both the electric motor and the gasoline engine

    The vehicle computer determines the mode in which the vehicle operates to improve fuel economy and reduce emissions. The driver cannot manually select the mode. ● **SEE FIGURE 33–6.**

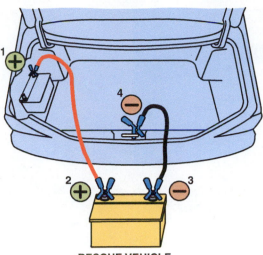

RESCUE VEHICLE

FIGURE 33–7 Jump-starting a 2001–2003 Toyota Prius using a 12-volt supply to boost the 12-volt auxiliary battery in the trunk.

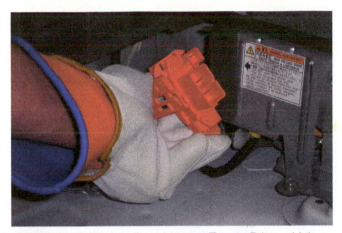

FIGURE 33–5 The service plug on a Toyota Prius, which is located in the trunk and is orange in color. Toyota recommends that the technician wear high-voltage gloves when removing the disconnect plug.

FIGURE 33–6 If the "Ready" light is on, then the gasoline engine can start at any time and the vehicle can be driven in electric mode for a short distance and limited speed.

JUMP STARTING

The 12-volt auxiliary battery may be jump-started if the vehicle does not start. The auxiliary battery is located under the hood or in the cargo (trunk) area of some HEVs. Using a jump box or jumper cables from another vehicle, make the connections to the positive and negative battery terminals. ● **SEE FIGURE 33–7.**

MOVING OR TOWING A HYBRID VEHICLE

TOWING If a disabled HEV needs to be moved a short distance (to the side of the road, for example) and the vehicle can still roll on the ground, the easiest way is to shift the transmission into neutral and manually push the vehicle. To transport a vehicle away from an emergency location, a flatbed truck should be used if the vehicle is repairable. If a flatbed is not available, the vehicle should be towed by wheel-lift equipment with the front wheels off the ground (FWD hybrid electric vehicles only). Do not use sling-type towing equipment. In the case of 4WD HEVs such as the Toyota Highlander, only a flatbed vehicle should be used.

HYBRID SERVICE PROCEDURES

OIL CHANGE Performing an oil change is similar to changing oil in any vehicle equipped with an internal combustion engine. However, there are several items to know

FIGURE 33–8 The high-voltage wiring on this Honda hybrid is colored orange for easy identification.

when changing oil on a hybrid electric vehicle, including the following:

- **Use the vehicle manufacturer's recommended lifting points.** Use caution when hoisting a hybrid electric vehicle and avoid placing the pads on or close to the orange high-voltage cables that are usually located under the vehicle. ● **SEE FIGURE 33–8.**

- **Always use the specified oil viscosity.** Most hybrid electric vehicles require either of the following:

  SAE 0W-20

  SAE 5W-20

  Using the specified oil viscosity is important because the engine stops and starts many times, and using the incorrect viscosity not only can cause a decrease in fuel economy but also could cause engine damage. ● **SEE FIGURE 33–9.**

- **Always follow the specified procedures.** Be sure that the ICE is off and that the "READY" lamp is also off. If

REAL-WORLD FIX

The Case of the Hybrid Vehicle Oil Change

The owner of a hybrid electric vehicle took it to a local shop for an oil change. When the vehicle was done, the owner noticed that the work order stated SAE 10W-30 and not SAE 0W-20, the oil specified in the owner's manual was used. When talking to the service manager, the manager said that it was acceptable to use the thicker oil in Ohio because it never gets cold enough to need the thinner engine oil. The hybrid owner left and had the oil changed at another shop, this time using the specified oil. Even though the cost of the oil change was higher to the customer, every shop should ALWAYS use the specified oil to meet the fuel economy and emissions levels that the vehicle was designed to meet.

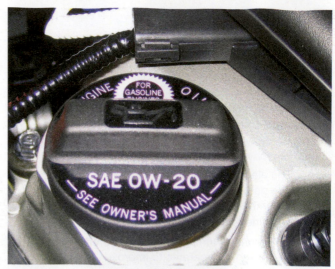

FIGURE 33–9 Always use the specified viscosity of oil in a hybrid electric vehicle not only for best fuel economy but also because of the need for fast lubrication due to the engine (idle) stop feature.

there is a smart key or the vehicle has a push-button start, be sure that the key fob is at least 15 feet (5 m) away from the vehicle to help prevent the engine from starting accidentally.

COOLING SYSTEM SERVICE Performing cooling system service on a hybrid is similar to performing this service on any vehicle equipped with an internal combustion engine. However, there are several points to know when servicing the cooling system on a hybrid electric vehicle, including the following:

- **Always check service information for the exact procedure to follow.** The procedure will include the following:

  1. **The specified coolant.** Most vehicle manufacturers will recommend using premixed coolant because using water (half of the coolant) that has minerals could cause corrosion issues.

  2. **The specified coolant replacement interval.** While this may be similar to the coolant replacement interval for a conventional vehicle, always check to be sure that this service is being performed at the specified time or mileage interval.

  3. **The specified precautions.** Some Toyota Prius HEVs use a coolant storage reservoir that keeps the coolant hot for up to three days. Opening a coolant hose could cause the release of this hot coolant and can cause serious burns to the technician.

  4. Always read, understand, and follow all of the service information instructions when servicing the cooling system on a hybrid electric vehicle.

AIR FILTER SERVICE Performing air filter service on a hybrid is similar to performing this service in any vehicle equipped with an internal combustion engine. However, there are several items to know when servicing the air filter on a hybrid electric vehicle, including the following:

1. Always follow the service information recommended air filter replacement interval.

2. For best results use the factory type and quality air filter.

BRAKING SYSTEM SERVICE   Performing braking system service on a hybrid is similar to performing this service on any vehicle equipped with an internal combustion engine. However, there are several points to know when servicing the braking system on a hybrid electric vehicle, including the following:

1. Check service information for any precautions that are specified to be followed when servicing the braking system.

2. All hybrid electric vehicles use a regenerative braking system, which captures the kinetic energy of the moving vehicle and converts it to electrical energy, which is sent to the high-voltage battery pack. The amount of current produced during hard braking can exceed 100 amperes. This current is stored in the high-voltage battery pack and is then used as needed to help power the vehicle.

3. The base (service) brakes used on hybrid electric vehicles are the same as any other conventional vehicle except for the master cylinder and related control systems. There is no high-voltage circuit associated with the braking system, as the regeneration occurs inside the electric drive (traction) motor and is controlled by the motor controller.

4. The standard hydraulic mechanical brakes on many hybrid vehicles are often found to be stuck or not functioning correctly because the brakes are not doing much work and can rust.

NOTE: Always check the base brakes whenever there is a poor fuel economy complaint from the owner of a hybrid vehicle. Often when a disc brake caliper sticks, the brakes drag but the driver is not aware of any performance problems, but the fuel economy drops.

TIRES   Performing tire-related service on a hybrid is similar to performing this service in any vehicle equipped with an internal combustion engine. However, there are several items to know when servicing tires on a hybrid electric vehicle, including the following:

1. Tire pressure is very important to not only the fuel economy but also the life of the tire. Lower inflation pressure increases rolling resistance and reduces load-carrying capacity and tire life. Always inflate the tires to the pressure indicated on the door jamb sticker or found in service information or the owner's manual.

2. All tires create less rolling resistance as they wear. This means that if new tires are installed, the owner may experience a drop in fuel economy.

3. Try to avoid using tires that are larger than used from the factory. The larger the tire, the heavier it is and it takes more energy to rotate, resulting in a decrease in fuel economy.

4. Follow normal tire inspections and tire rotation intervals as specified by the vehicle manufacturer.

12-VOLT AUXILIARY BATTERY TESTING AND SERVICE   Performing auxiliary battery service on a hybrid is similar to performing this service on any vehicle equipped with an internal combustion engine. However, there are several points to know when servicing the auxiliary battery on a hybrid electric vehicle, including the following:

1. Auxiliary 12-volt batteries used in hybrid electric vehicles are located in one of two general locations.
   - **Under the hood.** If the 12-volt auxiliary battery is under the hood, it is generally a flooded-type lead–acid battery and should be serviced similar to any conventional battery. ● SEE FIGURE 33–10.
   - **In the passenger or trunk area.** If the battery is located in the passenger or trunk area of the vehicle, it is usually of the absorbed glass mat (AGM) design. This type of battery requires a special battery charger that limits the charging voltage.

2. The auxiliary 12-volt battery is usually smaller than the battery used in a conventional vehicle because it is not normally used to actually start the engine. The 12-volt battery is used only to start Honda hybrids and then only under extreme conditions.

3. The 12-volt auxiliary battery can be tested and serviced similar to any battery used in a conventional vehicle.

4. Always read, understand, and follow all of the service information instructions when servicing the auxiliary battery on a hybrid electric vehicle.

FIGURE 33–10 This 12-volt battery under the hood on a Ford Fusion hybrid is a flooded cell-type auxiliary battery.

1. Hybrids use two different power sources to propel the vehicle.

2. A mild hybrid with a lower voltage system (36 to 42 volts) is capable of increasing fuel economy and reducing exhaust emissions but is not capable of using the electric motor alone to propel the vehicle.

3. A medium hybrid uses a higher voltage than a mild hybrid (140 to 150 volts) and offers increased fuel economy over a mild hybrid design but is not capable of operating using the electric motor alone.

4. A full or strong hybrid uses battery voltages of about 200 to 300 volts, is capable of operating using the electric motor(s) alone, and achieves the highest fuel economy improvement of all types of hybrids.

5. Early in vehicle history, electric vehicles were more popular than either steam- or gasoline-powered vehicles.

6. A hybrid vehicle is defined as having two power sources to propel the vehicle.

7. Electric motors are perfect for vehicle use because they produce torque at lower speed, whereas internal combustion engines need to have an increased speed before they produce maximum power and torque.

REVIEW QUESTIONS

1. Why do hybrid electric vehicles stop running when at idle?

2. What type of hybrid electrical vehicle is a Toyota Prius and Ford Escape hybrid?

3. What are the advantages and disadvantages of mild, medium, and full hybrid vehicles?

4. What are the four modes of operation of a typical hybrid vehicle?

CHAPTER QUIZ

1. The GM EV1 was what type of vehicle?
   a. Totally electric powered
   b. A first-generation hybrid electric vehicle (HEV)
   c. A series-type HEV
   d. A parallel-type HEV

2. Which type of hybrid uses 36 to 42 volts?
   a. Mild hybrid
   b. Medium hybrid
   c. Full hybrid
   d. Strong hybrid

3. Which type of hybrid is capable of propelling the vehicle using just the electric motor?
   a. 36-volt type
   b. Strong (full) hybrid
   c. Medium hybrid
   d. Mild hybrid

4. The gasoline engine of a hybrid electric stops running when the vehicle stops at a traffic light. Technician A says that it is normal for most hybrid electric vehicles. Technician B says that there is a fault with the engine. Which technician is correct?
   a. Technician A
   b. Technician B
   c. Both technicians A and B
   d. Neither technician A nor B

5. Which type of hybrid electric design costs the least?
   a. Strong hybrid design
   b. Full hybrid design
   c. Medium hybrid design
   d. Mild hybrid design

6. Which type of hybrid electric vehicle has idle stop operation?
   a. Strong hybrids only
   b. Strong, mild, and medium hybrids
   c. Mild hybrids only
   d. Medium hybrids only

7. Technician A says that most hybrids require that they be plugged into an electrical outlet at night to provide the electrical power to help propel the vehicle. Technician B says that the internal combustion engine in an HEV will often stop running when the vehicle is stopped. Which technician is correct?
   a. Technician A only
   b. Technician B only
   c. Both technicians A and B
   d. Neither technician A nor B

8. How can a hybrid electric vehicle be identified?
   a. By emblems on the front, side or rear of the vehicle
   b. By orange electrical cable under the hood
   c. Both a and b
   d. Neither a nor b

9. What routine service procedure could result in lower fuel economy, which the owner may discover?
   a. Using the wrong viscosity engine oil
   b. Replacing tires
   c. Replacing the air filter
   d. Either a or b

10. Hybrid electric vehicle usually use _____ engine oil.
   a. SAE 0W-20 or 5W-20
   b. SAE 5W-20 or 5W-30
   c. SAE 5W-30 or 10W-30
   d. SAE 10W-30 or 10W-40

chapter
34

SCAN TOOLS AND DIAGNOSTIC PROCEDURES

OBJECTIVES: **After studying Chapter 34, the reader will be able to:** • Prepare for the ASE computerized engine controls diagnosis (A8) certification test content area "E." • List the steps of the diagnostic process. • List six items to check as part of a thorough visual inspection. • Discuss the type of scan tools that are used to assess vehicle components.

KEY TERMS: • Data link connector (DLC) 313 • Pending code 314 • Technical service bulletin (TSB) 314

SCAN TOOLS

Scan tools are the most important tools for any diagnostic work on all vehicles. Scan tools can be divided into the following three basic groups:

1. **Factory scan tools.** These are the scan tools required by all dealers that sell and service a specific brand of vehicle. Examples of factory scan tools include:

   - **General Motors**—TECH 2. ● **SEE FIGURE 34–1**.
   - **Ford**—WDS (Worldwide Diagnostic System) and IDS (Integrated Diagnostic Software)
   - **Chrysler**—DRB-III, Star Scan, or WiTECH
   - **Honda**—HDS or Master Tech
   - **Toyota**—Master Tech and Tech Stream

All factory scan tools are designed to provide bidirectional capability, which allows the service technician the opportunity to operate components using the scan tool, thereby confirming that the component is able to work when commanded. Also, all factory scan tools are capable of displaying all factory parameters.

2. **Aftermarket scan tools.** These scan tools are designed to function on more than one brand of vehicle. Examples of aftermarket scan tools include the following:

   - **Snap-on** (various models, including the Ethos, Modis, and Solus).
   - **OTC** (various models, including Pegasus, Genisys, and Task Master). ● **SEE FIGURE 34–2**.
   - **AutoEnginuity** and other programs that use a laptop or handheld computer for display.

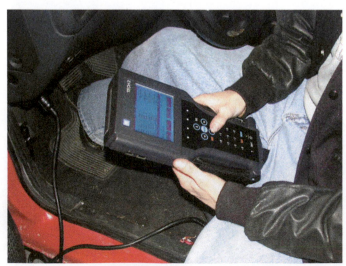

FIGURE 34–1 A TECH 2 scan tool is the factory scan tool used on General Motors vehicles.

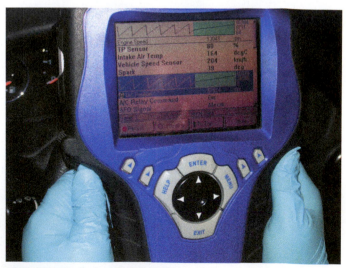

FIGURE 34–2 An OTC Genisys being used to troubleshoot a vehicle. This scan tool can be used on most makes and models of vehicles and is capable of diagnosing other computer systems in the vehicles such as the antilock braking system (ABS) and airbag systems.

While many aftermarket scan tools can display most if not all of the parameters of the factory scan tool, there can be a difference when trying to troubleshoot some faults.

3. **Global scan tools.** The vehicle diagnostic trouble codes (DTCs) and data can be acquired by looking at the global (generic) part of the PCM and does not need to have the vehicle information entered into the scan tool. All the global scan tools display only emission-related data stream information. The data displayed on this type of scan tool will be emission-related only and will not display faults or codes for any of the following systems:

- Airbag
- ABS brakes
- Traction control system
- Electronic stability control systems
- Chassis faults such as power windows

FIGURE 34–3 A typical malfunction indicator lamp (MIL) often labeled "check engine" or "service engine soon" (SES).

 TECH TIP

Check Engine Light On Means a Trouble Code Has Been Set

If the malfunction indicator light (check engine light) is on, this means that the computer has detected a fault and a diagnostic trouble code has been set. Therefore, one of the first things that should be done to determine what is wrong with the vehicle is to use a scan tool and determine what code or codes have been set. Knowing what circuit is involved will be the start of the procedure to find the exact cause. **SEE FIGURE 34–3.**

FIGURE 34–4 Connecting a scan tool to the data link connector (DLC) located under the dash on this vehicle.

HOW TO USE A SCAN TOOL

In order to get the most from a scan tool, the technician should read, understand, and follow the operating instructions. To use a scan tool follow these simple steps:

STEP 1 Locate the **data link connector (DLC).** This 16-pin connector is usually located under the dash on the driver's side. It can be located in the center console and may be covered by a panel that can be removed without the use of tools. Check service information for the exact location of the DLC for the vehicle being serviced.

STEP 2 Connect the scan tool to the DLC. **SEE FIGURE 34–4.**

STEP 3 Turn the ignition key on (engine off). In most cases, the scan tool will come on automatically because the DLC has power and ground connections for the scan tool.

STEP 4 If using a factory or factory-level scan tool, select the vehicle you are scanning and enter the information requested on the screen such as:
- Year (10th character of the VIN)
- Model (usually the 4th or 5th character of the VIN)
- Engine (usually the 8th character of the VIN
- Any options that may be on the vehicle

STEP 5 Follow the on-screen instructions. Read and record any stored diagnostic trouble codes (DTCs).

DIAGNOSTIC PROCEDURE

The diagnostic process is a strategy that eliminates known good components or systems in order to find the root cause of automotive engine performance problems. All vehicle manufacturers recommend a diagnostic procedure, and the plan suggested in this chapter combines most of the features of these plans plus additional steps developed over years of real-world problem solving. Many different things can cause an engine performance problem or concern. The service technician has to narrow the possibilities to find the cause of the problem and correct it.

The wide range of possible solutions must be narrowed to the most likely and these must eventually be further narrowed to the actual cause. The following six steps include the procedure that most vehicle manufactures recommend to find the root cause of a problem.

STEP 1 **Verify the Problem (Concern).** Before spending any time on diagnosis, be certain that a problem exists. If the problem cannot be verified, it cannot be solved or tested to verify that the repair was complete.

STEP 2 **Perform a Thorough Visual Inspection and Basic Tests.** Visual inspection is the most important aspect of diagnosis! Most experts agree that between 10% and 30% of all engine performance problems can be detected simply by performing a *thorough* visual inspection. The inspection should include the following steps:

- **Check for obvious problems (basics, basics, basics).**
  - Fuel leaks
  - Vacuum hoses that are disconnected or split
  - Corroded connectors, damaged or disconnected wiring
  - Unusual noises, smoke, or smell
  - Check the air cleaner and air duct (squirrels and other small animals can build nests or store dog food in them). ● **SEE FIGURE 34–5.**

STEP 3 **Retrieve the Diagnostic Trouble Codes (DTCs).** If a diagnostic trouble code (DTC) is present in the computer memory, it may illuminate the malfunction indi-

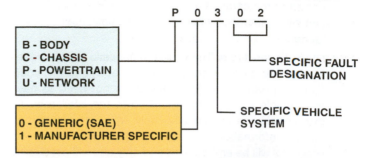

EXAMPLE: P0302 = CYLINDER #2 MISFIRE DETECTED

B - BODY
C - CHASSIS
P - POWERTRAIN
U - NETWORK

0 - GENERIC (SAE)
1 - MANUFACTURER SPECIFIC

SPECIFIC FAULT DESIGNATION

SPECIFIC VEHICLE SYSTEM

FIGURE 34–6 OBD-II DTC identification format.

cator lamp (MIL), commonly labeled "check engine" or "service engine soon." ● **SEE FIGURE 34–6.** Any code(s) that is displayed on a scan tool when the MIL is *not* on is called a **pending code.** Because the MIL is not on, this indicates that the fault has not repeated to cause the PCM to turn on the MIL. Although this pending code is helpful to the technician to know that a fault has, in the past, been detected, further testing will be needed to find the root cause of the problem.

STEP 4 **Check for Technical Service Bulletins (TSBs).** Check for corrections or repair procedures in **technical service bulletins (TSBs)** that match the symptoms. ● **SEE FIGURE 34–7.** According to studies performed by automobile manufacturers, as many as 30% of vehicles can be repaired following the information, suggestions, or replacement parts found in a service bulletin. DTCs must be known before searching for service bulletins, because bulletins often include information on solving problems that involve a stored diagnostic trouble code.

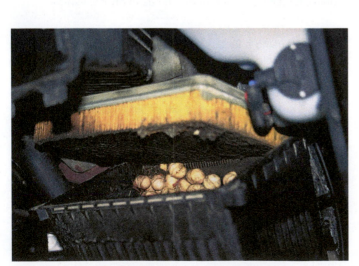

FIGURE 34–5 This is what was found when removing an air filter from a vehicle that had a lack-of-power concern. Obviously, the nuts were deposited by squirrels or some other animal, blocking a lot of the airflow into the engine.

FIGURE 34–7 After checking for stored diagnostic trouble codes (DTCs), the wise technician checks service information for any technical service bulletins that may relate to the vehicle being serviced.

STEP 5   **Determine the root cause and repair the problem.** The repair or part replacement must be performed following the vehicle manufacturer's recommendations and be certain that the root cause of the problem has been found.

STEP 6   **Verify the Repair and Clear any Stored DTCs.**
- Test drive to verify that the original problem (concern) is fixed.
- Verify that no additional problems have occurred during the repair process.
- Clear the diagnostic trouble codes (DTCs).
- Document the work order by stating what the "three Cs" (the complaint, the cause, and the correction) are.

SUMMARY

1. Scan tools are available from each vehicle manufacturer as well as independent companies that manufacture scan tools that work well on many makes and models of vehicles.

2. Some scan tools display only emission-related data and are called global OBD-II or generic scan tools.

3. The wise technician always follows the same troubleshooting procedure on each vehicle to make sure that steps are not skipped.

REVIEW QUESTIONS

1. What is the procedure to follow when diagnosing a vehicle?

2. What three things should be checked as part of a thorough visual inspection?

3. What are the three types of scan tools?

4. Why should a bulletin search be performed after stored DTCs are retrieved?

CHAPTER QUIZ

1. Technician A says that the first step in the diagnostic process is to verify the problem (concern). Technician B says the second step is to perform a thorough visual inspection. Which technician is correct?
   a. Technician A only
   b. Technician B only
   c. Both technicians A and B
   d. Neither technician A nor B

2. A global (generic) OBD-II scan tool is capable of displaying _____ data.
   a. Emission-related data only
   b. Emission-related DTCs
   c. All data
   d. Both a and b on most scan global scan tools

3. What is the factory scan tool for General Motors vehicles?
   a. WiTECH
   b. Snap-on
   c. Tech 2
   d. IDS

4. What is the factory scan tool for Ford vehicles?
   a. WiTECH
   b. Snap-on
   c. Tech 2
   d. IDS

5. What is the factory scan tool for Chrysler-Jeep vehicles?
   a. WiTECH
   b. Snap-on
   c. Tech 2
   d. IDS

6. What is the factory scan tool for Toyota vehicles?
   a. Techstream
   b. Snap-on
   c. Tech 2
   d. IDS

7. Which step should be performed *last* when diagnosing an engine performance problem?
   a. Checking for any stored diagnostic trouble codes
   b. Checking for any technical service bulletins (TSBs)
   c. Performing a thorough visual inspection
   d. Verify the repair

8. Where is the data link connector (DLC) located on OBD-II vehicles (1996 and newer)?
   a. Under the hood on the passenger side
   b. Under the dash
   c. In the glove box (instrument panel compartment)
   d. Can be either under the hood or under the dash.

9. Which scan tool can access detailed information on many different makes and models?
   a. Snap-on Solus
   b. OTC Genisys
   c. AutoEnginuity
   d. Any of the above

10. Which character of the vehicle identification number (VIN) represents the model year?
    a. 1st
    b. 4th
    c. 6th
    d. 10th

chapter 35

TIRES AND WHEELS

OBJECTIVES: **After studying Chapter 35, the reader will be able to:** • Prepare for ASE Suspension and Steering (A4) certification test content area "E" (Wheel and Tire Diagnosis and Repair). • Discuss how tires are constructed. • Discuss tire sizes and ratings. • Explain the construction and sizing of steel and alloy wheels and attaching hardware. • Discuss the correct lug nut tightening procedure and torque.

KEY TERMS: • Aspect ratio 318 • Bead 316 • Belt 317 • Body ply 317 • Carcass ply 317 • Center section 319 • DOT tire code 319 • Hydroplaning 316 • Inner liner 317 • Lug nuts 320 • Major splice 318 • Schrader valve 320 • Sidewall 316 • Speed ratings 318 • Tread 316 • UTQG 318 • Wear bars 316

PURPOSE OF TIRES

The friction (traction) between the tire and the road determines the handling characteristics of any vehicle. Think about the previous statement for a second. The condition of the tires is one of the most important aspects of the steering, suspension, alignment, and braking systems of any vehicle. A vehicle that handles poorly or that pulls, darts, jumps, or steers "funny" may be suffering from defective or worn tires.

FUNCTION OF TIRES

Tires are mounted on wheels that are bolted to the vehicle to provide the following:

1. Shock absorber action when driving over rough surfaces.
2. Friction (traction) between the wheels and the road. All tires are assembled by hand from many different component parts consisting of various rubber compounds, steel, and many types of fabric material. Tires are also available in many different designs and sizes.

PARTS OF A TIRE

TREAD   **Tread** refers to the part of the tire that is in contact with the ground. *Tread rubber* is chemically different from other rubber parts of a tire, and is compounded for a combination of traction and tire wear. *Tread depth* is usually 11/32 in. deep on new tires (this could vary, depending on manufacturer, from 9/32 to 15/32 in.).

NOTE: The tread depth gauge is used to measure the thickness of the tire tread. A tread depth is always expressed in 1/32s of an inch, even if the fraction can be reduced to 1/16s or 1/8s. ● **SEE FIGURE 35–1.**

The tire tread has wear indicators molded into the tread. These wear indicators are also called **wear bars.** When tread depth is down to the legal limit of 2/32 in., bald strips appear across the tread. ● **SEE FIGURE 35–2.**

Grooves are large, deep recesses molded in the tread, separating the tread blocks. These grooves help water escape from under the tread and help prevent a condition called hydroplaning. **Hydroplaning** occurs when the tire leaves the surface of the road and rides on a layer of water. Stopping and cornering is impossible when hydroplaning. Hydroplaning can occur at speeds as low as 30 mph when on wet roads. ● **SEE FIGURE 35–3.**

SIDEWALL   The **sidewall** is that part of the tire between the tread and the wheel. The sidewall contains all the size and construction details of the tire.

BEAD   The **bead** is the foundation of the tire and is located where the tire grips the inside of the wheel rim.

1. The bead is constructed of many turns of copper- or bronze-coated steel wire.
2. The main body plies (layers of material) are wrapped around the bead.

CAUTION: If the bead of a tire is cut or damaged, the tire must be replaced!

(a)

(b)

FIGURE 35–1 (a) A typical tire tread depth gauge. The center movable plunger is pushed down into the groove of the tire. (b) The tread depth is read at the top edge of the sleeve. In this example, the tread depth is 6/32 in.

BODY PLY
A tire gets its strength from the layers of material wrapped around both beads under the tread and sidewall rubber. This creates the main framework, or "carcass," of the tire; these **body plies** are often called **carcass plies.** ● SEE FIGURE 35–4.

FIGURE 35–2 Wear indicators (wear bars) are strips of bald tread that show when the tread depth is down to 2/32 in., the legal limit in many states.

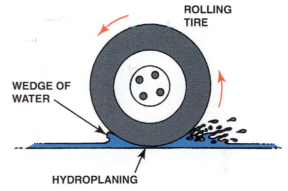

FIGURE 35–3 Hydroplaning can occur at speeds as low as 30 mph (48 km/h). If the water is deep enough and the tire tread cannot evacuate water through its grooves fast enough, the tire can be lifted off the road surface by a layer of water. Hydroplaning occurs at lower speeds as the tire becomes worn.

BELT
A tire **belt** is two or more layers of material applied over the body plies and under the tread area only, to stabilize the tread and increase tread life and handling.

INNER LINER
The **inner liner** is the soft rubber lining (usually a butyl rubber compound) on the inside of the tire that protects the body plies and helps provide for self-sealing of small punctures.

MAJOR SPLICE
When the tire is assembled by a craftsperson on a tire-building machine, the body plies, belts, and tread rubber are spliced together. The fabric is

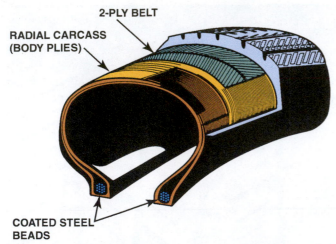

FIGURE 35–4 Typical construction of a radial tire. Some tires have only one body ply, and some tires use more than two belt plies.

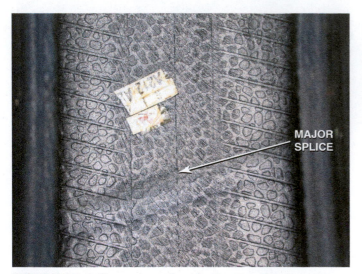

FIGURE 35–5 The major splice of a tire can often be seen and felt on the inside of the tire. The person who assembles (builds) the tire usually places a sticker near the major splice as a means of identification for quality control.

overlapped approximately five threads. The point where the majority of these overlaps occur is called the **major splice,** which represents the stiffest part of the tire. This major splice is visible on most tires on the inside, as shown in ● **FIGURE 35–5.**

NOTE: On most new vehicles and/or new tires, the tire manufacturer paints a dot on the sidewall near the bead, indicating the largest diameter of the tire. The largest diameter of the tire usually is near the major splice. The wheel manufacturer either marks the wheel or drills the valve core hole at the smallest diameter of the wheel. Therefore, the dot should be aligned with the valve core or marked for best balance and minimum radial runout.

LETTER	MAXIMUM RATED SPEED
S	112 MPH (180 km/h)
T	118 MPH (190 km/h)
H	130 MPH (210 km/h)
V	149 MPH (240 km/h)
W	168 MPH (270 km/h)
Y	186 MPH (300 km/h)
Z	The exact speed rating for a particular Z-rated tire is determined by the tire manufacturer and may vary according to size. For example, not all Brand X Z-rated tires are rated at 170 mph, even though one size may be capable of these speeds.

CHART 35–1

Speed ratings are based on continuous operation at the speed rating speed.

TIRE SIZE

P-METRIC DESIGNATION SERVICE DESCRIPTION

The size of tires is expressed with a series of numbers and letters. For example,

$$P205/60R \times 17\ 92H$$

- P = passenger vehicle
- 205 = mm cross-sectional width
- 60 = aspect ratio (The **aspect ratio** is the ratio of the height from the rim to the tread, compared to the width of the tire. The 60 means that the height is 60% of the width.)
- R = radial construction
- 17 = rim diameter in inches
- 92 = load index
- H = speed rating (130 mph/210 km/h)

A vehicle should never be driven faster than the **speed rating** of the tires. ● **SEE CHART 35–1.**

UNIFORM TIRE QUALITY GRADING SYSTEM

The U.S. Department of Transportation (DOT) and the National Highway Traffic Safety Administration (NHTSA) developed a system of tire grading, the **Uniform Tire Quality Grading (UTQG)** system, to help customers better judge the relative performance of tires. The three areas of tire performance are tread wear, traction, and temperature resistance, as shown in ● **FIGURE 35–6.**

NOTE: All tires sold in the United States must have UTQGS ratings molded into the sidewall.

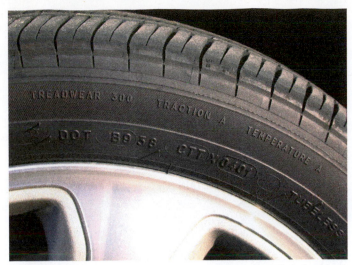

FIGURE 35–6 Typical "Uniform Tire Quality Grading System" (UTQGS) ratings imprinted on the tire sidewall.

TREAD WEAR

The tread wear grade is a comparison rating based on the wear rate of a standardized tire, tested under carefully controlled conditions, which is assigned a value of 100. A tire rated 200 should have a useful life twice the life of the standard tire.

The tread wear life of any tire is affected by driving habits (fast stops, starts, and cornering will decrease tread life), tire rotation (or lack of tire rotation), inflation, wheel alignment, road surfaces, and climate conditions.

TRACTION

Traction performance is rated by the letters AA, A, B, and C, with AA being the highest.

NOTE: The traction rating is for wet braking distance only! It does not include cornering traction or dry braking performance.

The traction rating is only one of many other factors that affect wet braking traction, including air inflation, tread depth, vehicle speed, and brake performance.

TEMPERATURE RESISTANCE

Temperature resistance is rated by the letters A, B, and C, with A being the highest rating. Tires generate heat while rotating and flexing during normal driving conditions. Grade C is the minimum level that all tires must be able to pass under the current Federal Motor Vehicle Safety Standard No. 109.

DOT CODE

All tires sold in the United States must be approved by the U.S. Federal Department of Transportation (DOT). The **DOT tire code** requirements include resistance to tire damage that could be caused by curbs, chuckholes, and other common occurrences for a tire used on public roads.

NOTE: Most race tires are *not* DOT-approved and must never be used on public streets or highways.

Each tire that is DOT-approved has a DOT number molded into the sidewall of the tire. The DOT code includes letters and numbers, such as *MJP2CBDX2609*.

The first two letters identify the manufacturer and location. For this example, the first two letters (MJ) mean that the tire was made by the Goodyear Tire and Rubber Company in Topeka, Kansas. The last four numbers are the build date code. The first two numbers represent the week of the year and the last two numbers indicate the year (2009). Therefore, the tire was built during the 26th week of 2009.

WHEELS

TERMINOLOGY The concept of a wheel has not changed in the last 5,000 years, but the style and materials used have changed a lot. Early automotive wheels were constructed from wood with a steel band as the tire. Today's wheels are constructed of steel or aluminum alloy. The **center section** of the wheel that attaches to the hub is also called the spider because early wheels used wooden spokes that resembled a spider's web. The rubber tire attaches to the rim of the wheel. The rim has two *bead flanges* where the bead of the tire is held against the wheel when the tire is inflated. The shape of this flange is very important and is designated by Tire and Rim Association letters. For example, a wheel designated 16 × 6 JJ means that the diameter of the wheel is 14 in. and the wheel is 6-in. wide measured from inside to inside of the flanges. The letters JJ indicate the *exact* shape of the flange area. ● **SEE FIGURE 35–7.**

This flange area shape and the angle that the rim drops down from the flange are important because of the following reasons:

- They permit a good seal between the rim and the tire.
- They help retain the tire on the rim in the event of loss of air.
- Run-flat tires (tires that are designed to operate without air for a limited distance without damage) often require a specific wheel rim shape.

WHEEL RIM CONTOUR

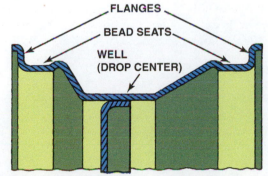

FIGURE 35–7 The wheel rim well provides a space for the tire to fit during mounting; the bead seat provides a tire-to-wheel sealing surface; the flange holds the beads in place.

What Does This Mark in a Wheel Mean?

The symbol **JWL,** for the Japan Wheel Light Metal Standard Mark, means that the wheel meets the technical standards for passenger-car light-alloy wheels. The manufacturer is responsible for conducting the inspections set forth in the technical standard, and the JWL mark is displayed on those products that pass the inspection. ● **SEE FIGURE 35–8.**

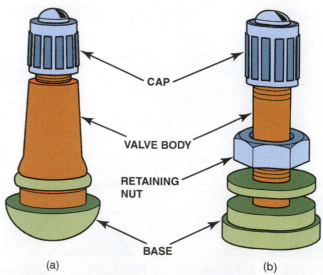

FIGURE 35–9 (a) A rubber snap-in–style tire valve assembly. (b) A metal clamp–type tire valve assembly used on most high pressure (over 60 PSI) tire applications such as is found on many trucks, RVs, and trailers. The internal Schrader valve threads into the valve itself and can be replaced individually, but most experts recommend replacing the entire valve assembly every time the tires are replaced to help prevent air loss.

ALUMINUM WHEELS

Forged and cast aluminum wheels are commonly used on cars and trucks. *Forged* is a term that means that the aluminum is hammered or forged under pressure into shape. A forged aluminum wheel is much stronger than a *cast* aluminum wheel. A cast aluminum wheel is constructed by pouring liquid (molten) aluminum into a mold. After the aluminum has cooled, the cast aluminum wheel is removed from the mold and machined. Aluminum wheels are usually thicker than steel wheels and require special wheel weights when balancing. Aluminum alloy wheels are often called alloy wheels.

Some racing wheels are made from a lighter-weight metal called magnesium. These wheels are called *mag* wheels (an abbreviation for *magnesium*). True magnesium wheels are not practical for production vehicles because their cost is excessive compared with steel or aluminum alloy wheels. The term *mag wheel*, however, is still heard when referring to alloy (aluminum) wheels.

SCHRADER VALVES
All wheels use a valve stem that contains a tire valve, called a **Schrader valve,** to hold air in the tire. The Schrader valve was invented in New York in 1844 by

August Schrader for the Goodyear Brothers: Charles, Henry, and Nelson. Today, Schrader valves are used not only as valves in tires but also on fuel-injection systems, air conditioning systems, and air-shock (ride control) systems. Most tire experts agree that the valve stem (which includes the Schrader valve) should be replaced whenever tires are replaced. A defective or leaking valve stem is a major cause of air loss. Low tire pressure can cause the tire to become overheated. Replacement of valve stems are, therefore, a wise investment whenever purchasing new tires. Aluminum (alloy) wheels often require special metal valve stems that use a rubber washer and are actually bolted to the wheel. ● **SEE FIGURE 35–9.**

LUG NUTS

PURPOSE AND FUNCTION **Lug nuts** are used to hold a wheel to the brake disc, brake drum, or wheel bearing assembly.

Most manufacturers use a stud in the brake or bearing assembly with a lug nut to hold the wheel. Some older models of VW, Audi, and Mazda use a lug *bolt* that is threaded into a hole in the brake drum or bearing assembly.

NOTE: Some aftermarket manufacturers offer a stud conversion kit to replace the lug bolt with a conventional stud and lug nut.

Typical lug nuts are tapered so that the wheel stud will center the wheel onto the vehicle. Another advantage of the taper of the lug nut and wheel is to provide a suitable surface to prevent the nuts from loosening. The taper, usually 60°, forms a wedge that helps ensure that the lug nut will not loosen. Steel wheels are deformed

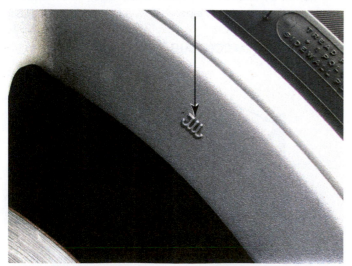

FIGURE 35–8 A typical JWL symbol for the Japan Wheel Light Metal standard mark.

WHEEL NUTS

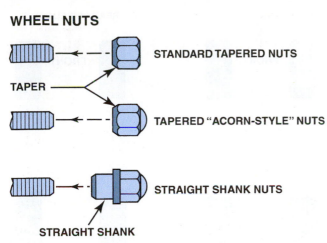

TAPER

STANDARD TAPERED NUTS

TAPERED "ACORN-STYLE" NUTS

STRAIGHT SHANK NUTS

STRAIGHT SHANK

FIGURE 35–10 Various styles of lug nuts.

slightly when the lug nut is torqued down against the wheel mounting flange; be certain that the taper is *toward* the vehicle.

TYPES Many alloy wheels use a *shank-nut* -type lug nut that has straight sides without a taper. This style of nut must be used with wheels designed for this nut type. If replacement wheels are used on any vehicle, check with the wheel manufacturer as to the proper type and style of lug nut. ● **FIGURE 35–10** shows several of the many styles of lug nuts that are available.

SIZES Lug nuts are sized to the thread size of the stud onto which they thread. The diameter and the number of threads per inch are commonly stated. Though most vehicles use right-hand (clockwise rotation to tighten) threads, some vehicles use left-hand threads on the driver's side. An "L" or an "R" may be stamped on the stud to indicate thread type.

A typical size is 7/16−20, where the 7/16 indicates the diameter of the wheel stud and 20 indicates that there are 20 threads per inch. Another common fractional size is 1/2−20. Metric sizes, such as M12 × 1.5, use a different sizing method. In this case, the number 12 indicates a diameter of 12 mm, and the 1.5 indicates the thread point distance from one point to the next thread point. Other commonly used metric lug sizes include M12 × 1.25 and M14 × 1.5. Obviously, metric wheel studs require metric lug nuts.

LUG STUDS Lug studs are usually installed in hubs or drums using a press fit. Serrations on the shoulder of the stud provide support. Most studs are replaceable and should be replaced if the treads are damaged.

TIRE AND WHEEL SERVICE

SPECIFIED TIRE PRESSURE The specified tire inflation pressure should always be used when checking or adjusting tire pressure. The specified inflation pressure is found in any of the following locations:

TIRE	SIZE	COLD TIRE PRESSURE
FRONT	P235/70R16	240 KPA, 35 PSI
REAR	P235/70R16	240 KPA, 35 PSI
SPARE	T165/80D17	415 KPA, 60 PSI

FIGURE 35–11 The tire pressure placard (sticker) on the driver's side door or door jamb indicates the specified tire pressure. The specified inflation pressure is when the tires are cold and the vehicle has not been driven for several hours.

- Door placard on the driver's door or on the jamb (post) of the driver's door. ● **SEE FIGURE 35–11.**
- In the owner's manual.
- In service information.

If the inflation pressure is lower than that specified, the tires will wear excessively and the tread will wear more on both outside edges. If the inflation pressure is too high, then the ride will be stiffer or harsh and the tread will wear more in the center.

NOTE: It is the law in some states such as California that the tire inflation pressure must be checked and corrected whenever any service is being performed on the vehicle.

Tire pressure should be checked and adjusted if necessary after a tire rotation has been completed because some vehicles require different inflation pressure for front and rear tires. Therefore, when the tires are rotated, the front and rear tire inflation pressure may need to be adjusted. The spare tire should also be checked at each oil change interval. Check service information for the exact inflation pressure.

TIRE INSPECTION All tires should be carefully inspected for faults in the tire itself or for signs that something may be wrong with the steering or suspension systems of the vehicle. The tires should be checked for the following conditions:

- Thread depth (2/32 of an inch is the standard minimum allowable tread depth in most states)
- Unequal tread wear which could be caused by a wheel alignment problem
- Cuts in the tread or sidewall
- Bulges or uneven sidewalls

Check the spare tire for proper inflation pressure as well as the condition of the tire and wheel.

How Much Does Tire Pressure Change with a Change in Temperature?

As the temperature of a tire increases, the pressure inside the tire also increases. The general amount of pressure gain (when temperatures increase) or loss (when temperatures decrease) is as follows:

10°F increase causes 1 PSI increase

10°F decrease causes 1 PSI decrease

For example, if a tire is correctly inflated to 35 PSI when cold and then driven on a highway, the tire pressure may increase 5 PSI or more.

CAUTION: DO NOT LET AIR OUT OF A HOT TIRE! If air is released from a hot tire to bring the pressure down to specifications, the tire will be *underinflated* when the tire has cooled. The tire pressure specification is for a cold tire.

Always check the tire pressures on a vehicle that has been driven fewer than 2 miles (3.2 km).

TIRE ROTATION To assure long life and even tire wear, it is important to rotate each tire to another location. Some rear-wheel-drive vehicles, for example, may show premature tire wear on the front tires. While some shoulder wear on front tires is normal, it can be reduced by proper inflation, alignment, and tire rotation.

The specified tire rotation method can include the following:

- Front to back and back to front.
- Cross rotation (X) meaning that the right front is moved to the left rear and the left rear is moved to the right front.

 TECH TIP

Three Quick Checks

If the vehicle is hoisted on a frame-contact lift, perform the following three quick checks (transmission in neutral):

1. Spin each wheel to check that the brakes are not dragging.
2. When spinning the tire, look over the top of the tire to check if it is round. An improperly mounted tire or a tire that is out-of-round due to a fault in the tire can be detected by watching for the outside of the tire to move up and down as it is being rotated.
3. Look at the tread of the tire while spinning it. The tread should be straight and should not be seen as moving left or right while it is being rotated.

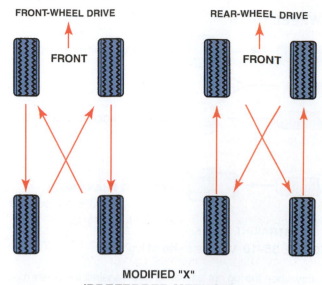

MODIFIED "X"
(PREFERRED METHOD)

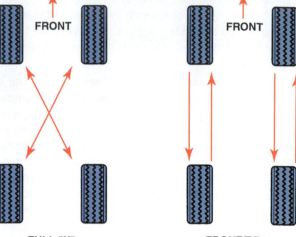

FULL "X"
(ACCEPTABLE)

FRONT/REAR
(ACCEPTABLE)

FIGURE 35–12 The method most often recommended is the modified X method. Using this method, each tire eventually is used at each of the four wheel locations. An easy way to remember the sequence, whether front-wheel drive or rear-wheel drive, is to say to yourself, "Drive wheels straight, cross the nondrive wheels."

- Modified X method is where the drive wheels are moved straight back (front-wheel drive) or straight forward (rear-wheel drive) and the non drive wheels are moved in an "X" method.
- Tire rotation should not be performed if the wheels/tires are different sizes front and rear and use directional tires or wheels. Directional tires or wheels are marked and should not be rotated to the opposite side of the vehicle. When a wheel or tire is moved from one side of the vehicle to the other, the direction of rotation is reversed. ● **SEE FIGURE 35–12.**

NOTE: Radial tires can cause a radial pull due to their construction. If the wheel alignment is correct, attempt to correct a pull by rotating the tires front to rear or, if necessary, side to side.

NOTE: To help remember when to rotate the tires, just remember that it should be done at every other oil change. Most manufacturers recommend changing the engine oil every 5,000 miles (8,000 km) or every six months and recommend tire rotation every 10,000 (16,000 km) miles or every year.

WHEEL MOUNTING TORQUE There are two commonly used methods to ensure proper tire lug nut torque.

- **Torque wrench.** Using a torque wrench is the preferred method to tighten the wheel lug nuts.
- **Torque sticks.** These tools, also called *torque-limiting adapters*, are calibrated to transmit a limited amount of torque to the lug nut when used according to factory instructions.

Make certain that the wheel studs are clean and dry and torqued to the manufacturer's specifications. Most vehicles specify a tightening torque of between 80 lb-ft and 100 lb-ft (108 and 136 N-m). ● **SEE FIGURE 35–13.**

CAUTION: Most manufacturers warn that the wheel studs should not be oiled or lubricated with grease because this can cause the wheel lug nuts to loosen while driving.

Always tighten lug nuts gradually, in the proper star pattern sequence (tighten one nut, skip one, and tighten the next nut), to prevent warping the brake drums or rotors, or bending a wheel. ● **SEE FIGURE 35–14.**

NOTE: Anytime you install a new set of aluminum wheels, retorque the wheels after the first 25 miles. The soft aluminum often compresses slightly, loosening the torque on the wheels.

FIGURE 35–13 A torque-limiting adapter (torque stick) for use with an air impact wrench still requires care to prevent over tightening. The air pressure to the air impact should be limited to 125 PSI (860 kPa) in most cases, and the proper adapter must be selected for the vehicle being serviced. The torque adapter absorbs any torque beyond its designed rating. Most adapters are color coded for easy identification as to the size of lug nut and torque value.

TORQUE SEQUENCE

FIGURE 35–14 Always tighten wheel lug nuts (or studs) in a star pattern to ensure even pressure on the axle flange, brake rotors or drums, and the wheel itself.

SUMMARY

1. Tires are constructed using many parts that are put together and then placed into a mold where it is cured.
2. Proper inflation is important for proper vehicle handling, traction, and tire life.
3. The proper pressure is found on the driver's door placard.
4. Tires should be inspected for unequal tire wear.
5. Tires should be rotated regularly and according to the manufacturer's recommended procedure.
6. Wheels are constructed of steel or aluminum alloy and are designed to keep a tire from falling off if all of the air pressure is lost.
7. Wheel lug nuts should always be tightened using a torque wrench or torque sticks.

REVIEW QUESTIONS

1. What are the three major areas of the Uniform Tire Quality Grading System?

2. How is the proper tire inflation pressure determined?

1. The part of the tire that is just under the tread of a radial tire is called the _____.
   a. Bead
   b. Body (carcass) ply
   c. Belt
   d. Inner liner

2. The aspect ratio of a tire means _____.
   a. Its width to diameter of a wheel ratio
   b. The ratio of height to width
   c. The ratio of width to height
   d. The ratio of rolling resistance

3. A tire is labeled 215/60RX17 92T; the T indicates _____.
   a. Its speed rating
   b. Its tread wear rating
   c. Its load rating
   d. Its temperature resistance rating

4. The 92 in the tire designation in question 3 refers to the tire's _____.
   a. Speed rating
   b. Tread wear rating
   c. Load rating
   d. Temperature resistance rating

5. Tire inflation is very important to the safe and economical operation of any vehicle. Technician A says that if the pressure is too high, the ride will be stiffer. Technician B says that if the pressure is too low, the tires will wear more on both outside edges. Which technician is correct?
   a. Technician A only
   b. Technician B only
   c. Both technicians A and B
   d. Neither technician A nor B

6. The proper tire inflation pressure is _____.
   a. The maximum pressure as shown on the sidewall of the tire
   b. As specified in the owner's manual
   c. As shown on the door placard
   d. Either b or c

7. Uneven tire wear can be caused by _____.
   a. Underinflation
   b. Overinflation
   c. Wheel alignment problem
   d. Any of the above

8. What is the minimum tread depth required on tires in most states?
   a. 1/32 in.
   b. 2/32 in.
   c. 3/32 in.
   d. 4/32 in.

9. Using the modified X tire rotation method on a front-wheel-drive vehicle, where would be the place for the right front tire?
   a. Left front
   b. Left rear
   c. Right rear
   d. Right front

10. Most vehicle manufacturers specify a lug nut (wheel nut) tightening torque specification of about _____.
    a. 80 lb-ft to 100 lb-ft
    b. 100 lb-ft to 125 lb-ft
    c. 125 lb-ft to 150 lb-ft
    d. 150 lb-ft to 175 lb-ft

chapter 36

BRAKES AND ANTILOCK BRAKING SYSTEMS

OBJECTIVES: After studying Chapter 36, the reader will be able to: • Prepare for the Brakes (A5) ASE certification test. • List the parts and terms for disc and drum brakes. • List the six brake system categories. • Describe the purpose and function of the antilock brake system (ABS). • Discuss the procedure recommended for brake drum removal. • List the items that should be checked during a visual inspection.

KEY TERMS: • Antilock braking system (ABS) 328 • Apply system 327 • Base brakes 325 • Boost system 327 • Brake balance control system 327 • Brake shoe clearance gauge 330 • Brake pedal 327 • Brake warning lights 327 • Disc brakes 325 • Drum brakes 325 • Foundation brakes 325 • Hydraulic system 327 • Parking brake 327 • Red brake warning lamp 327 • Service brakes 325 • Wheel brakes 327 • Speed nuts 328 • Tinnerman nuts 328 • Wheel speed sensor (WSS) 328

BRAKE SYSTEM FUNDAMENTALS

OVERVIEW Brakes are by far the most important mechanism on any vehicle because the safety and lives of those riding in the vehicle depend on proper operation of the braking system. It has been estimated that the brakes on the average vehicle are applied 50,000 times a year!

Brakes are an energy-absorbing mechanism that converts the kinetic energy of a moving vehicle into heat energy while stopping the rotation of the wheels. All braking systems are designed to reduce the speed and stop a moving vehicle and to keep it from moving if the vehicle is stationary.

SERVICE BRAKES Service brakes are the main driver-operated brakes of the vehicle. Service brakes are also called **base brakes** or **foundation brakes.** ● SEE FIGURE 36–1.

BRAKE SYSTEM PARTS To stop a wheel, the driver exerts a force on the brake pedal. The force on the brake pedal pressurizes brake fluid in a master cylinder. This hydraulic force (liquid under pressure) is transferred through steel lines and flexible brake lines to a wheel cylinder or caliper at each wheel. Hydraulic pressure to each wheel cylinder or caliper is used to force friction materials against the brake drum or rotor. The friction between the stationary friction material and the rotating

drum or rotor (disc) causes the rotating part to slow down and eventually stop. Because the wheels are attached to the drums or rotors, the wheels of the vehicle also stop. The heavier the vehicle and the higher the speed, the more heat the brakes have to be able to absorb. Long, steep hills can cause the brakes to overheat, reducing the friction necessary to slow and stop a vehicle.

DRUM BRAKES **Drum brakes** are used on the rear of many vehicles. When drum brakes are applied, brake shoes are moved outward against a rotating brake drum. The wheel studs for the wheels are attached to the drum. When the drum slows and stops, the wheels also slow and stop. Drum brakes are economical to manufacture, service, and repair. Parts for drum brakes are generally readily available and reasonably priced. On some vehicles, an additional drum brake is used as a parking brake on vehicles equipped with rear disc brakes. ● SEE FIGURE 36–2.

DISC BRAKES **Disc brakes** are used on the front of most vehicles built since the early 1970s and on the rear wheels of many vehicles. A disc brake operates by squeezing brake pads on both sides of a rotor or disc that is attached to the wheel. ● SEE FIGURE 36–3.

TYPE OF BRAKE, ROTATING PART, AND FRICTION PART The names used for brake parts depend on the type of brakes. ● SEE CHART 36–1.

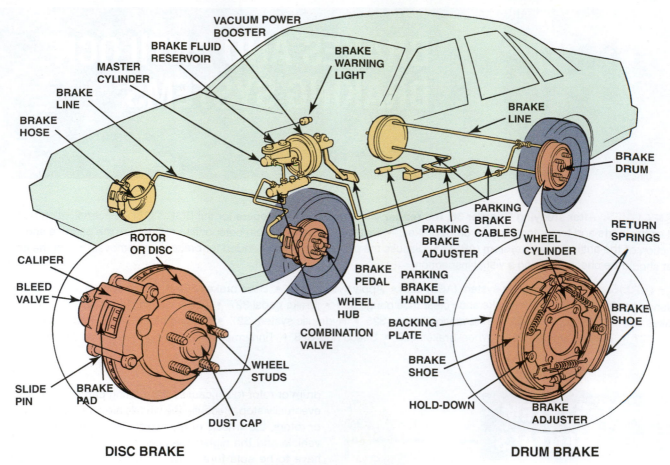

FIGURE 36–1 Typical vehicle brake system showing all typical components.

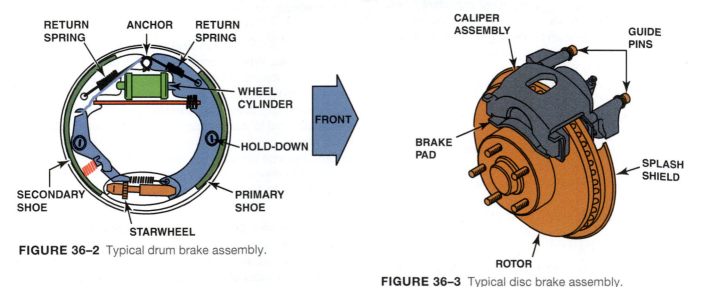

FIGURE 36–2 Typical drum brake assembly.

FIGURE 36–3 Typical disc brake assembly.

TYPE of BRAKE	ROTATING PART NAME	FRICTION MATERIAL NAME
Drum Brake	Brake Drum	Brake Shoes
Disc Brake	Brake Rotor (Disc)	Brake Pads

CHART 36–1

Terms used to describe disc and drum brake parts.

BRAKE SYSTEM CATEGORIES

Brake system components can be classified and placed into six subsystem categories, depending on their function. ● SEE FIGURE 36–4 for an overall view of the entire braking system.

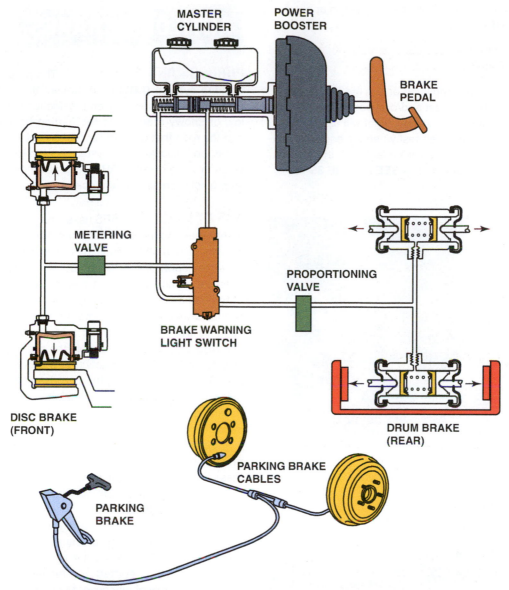

FIGURE 36–4 Typical brake system components.

1. **Apply System**. The driver starts the operation of the braking system by pressing on the **brake pedal** or applying the **parking brake**. The apply system includes all the levers, pedals, or linkages needed to activate a braking force.

2. **Boost System**. The boost (power brake) system is used on most vehicles to reduce the force that the driver must exert on the brake pedal.

3. **Hydraulic System**. The brake pedal force is transferred to the hydraulic system, where the force is directed through pipes and hoses to the wheel brakes. The hydraulic system includes the master cylinder, brake lines and hoses, wheel cylinders, and calipers.

4. **Wheel Brakes**. Hydraulic pressure from the hydraulic system moves a piston, in either a disc or drum brake system, and forces the friction material against a rotating drum

or rotor. The resulting friction slows the rotation of the wheels.

5. **Brake Balance Control System**. Mechanical, electrical, and hydraulic components are used to ensure that brakes are applied quickly and with balanced pressure for safe operation. Components in this category include metering valves, proportioning valves, and antilock braking system components.

6. **Brake warning lights**. There are two brake system-related warning lights.

   - The **red brake warning lamp (RBWL)** lights whenever a hydraulic system failure occurs. The red brake warning lamp lights when the ignition is turned on as a bulb check and then goes out unless a hydraulic fault has been detected. The red brake warning lamp

will also come on when the parking brake is applied.
● **SEE FIGURE 36–5.**

CAUTION: Do not test drive a vehicle if the red brake warning light is on.

■ The amber ABS warning lamp or dim red brake light indicates an ABS self-test and/or a possible problem in the ABS system. This warning light will usually flash several times during a self-test when the engine is first started and then go out unless a fault with the antilock braking system is detected. ● **SEE FIGURE 36–6.**

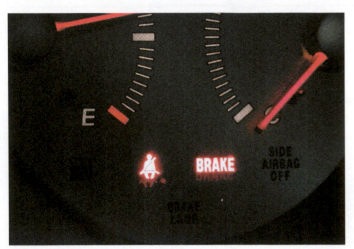

FIGURE 36–5 The red brake warning light will remain on after a bulb test if there is a fault with the hydraulic part of the brake system.

FIGURE 36–6 An amber ABS warning lamp.

PURPOSE AND FUNCTION   The purpose of an **antilock braking system (ABS)** is to prevent the wheels from locking during braking, especially on low-friction surfaces such as wet, icy, or snowy roads. It is the friction between the tire tread and the road that does the actual stopping of the vehicle. As a result, an antilock brake system is able to provide traction for steering while braking. ABS does not mean that a vehicle can stop quickly on all road surfaces.

ABS OPERATION   ABS uses **wheel speed sensors (WSS)** at the wheels to measure the wheel speed. If a wheel is rotating slower than the others, indicating possible lockup (for example, on an icy spot), the ABS computer will pulse the brake fluid pressure to that wheel for a fraction of a second. The pulsing of the brake fluid pressure momentarily reduces braking force to that wheel, which prevents wheel lockup. *A locked wheel has less traction to the road surface than a rotating wheel.* The ABS computer can reapply the pressure from the master cylinder to the wheel a fraction of a second later. Therefore, if a wheel starts to lock up, the purpose of the ABS system is to pulse the brakes on and off to maintain directional stability with maximum braking force. The pulsating brake pedal can be a cause for concern for some drivers.

Some ABS units use an isolator valve in the ABS unit to prevent brake pedal pulsations during ABS operation. With these types of systems, it is often difficult for the driver to know if and when the ABS unit is working to control a locking wheel. ● **SEE FIGURE 36–7.**

Another symptom of normal ABS unit operation is the operation of the hydraulic pressure pump used by many ABS units. In some ABS units, the hydraulic pump is run every time the vehicle is started and moved. Other types of units operate randomly or whenever the pressure in the system calls for the pump to operate.

DRUM BRAKE INSPECTION

BRAKE DRUM REMOVAL   Brake systems should be routinely inspected to determine component condition and potential problems. The drum has to be removed from a drum brake before inspection or repair can begin. There are two basic types of drums, and the removal procedure depends on which type is being serviced. With either type, it is usually recommended that the drums be marked with an "L" for left or an "R" for right so that they can be replaced in the same location.

The drums are secured to the axle flange by the wheel and lug nuts. New vehicles have **tinnerman nuts** (clips), also called **speed nuts,** on the stud when the vehicle is being assembled. These thin sheet-metal nuts keep the brake drum from falling

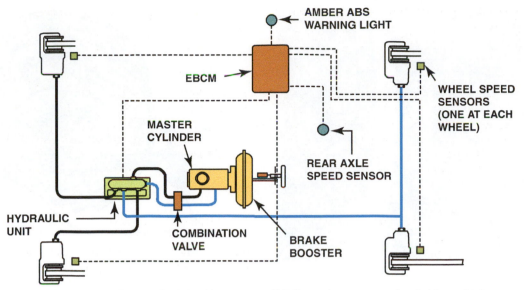

FIGURE 36–7 Typical components of an antilock braking system (ABS) used on a rear-wheel-drive vehicle.

off during the manufacturing process of the vehicle prior to installation of the rear wheels. ● **SEE FIGURE 36–8.**

The tinnerman nuts can be discarded because they are not needed after the vehicle leaves the assembly plant. After removing the wheels, the drum *should* move freely on the hub and slip off over the brake shoes.

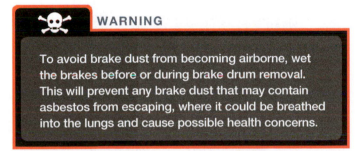

> ☠ **WARNING**
>
> To avoid brake dust from becoming airborne, wet the brakes before or during brake drum removal. This will prevent any brake dust that may contain asbestos from escaping, where it could be breathed into the lungs and cause possible health concerns.

BRAKE LINING INSPECTION Both primary (leading or front facing) and secondary (trailing or rear facing) lining material should be thicker than 0.060 in. (1.5 mm). To inspect the drum brake lining, follow these steps:

STEP 1 Some vehicles are equipped with holes in the backing plate that allow for a visual inspection of the thickness of the lining. Most vehicle and brake lining manufacturers recommend replacing worn brake lining when the thickness of the riveted lining reaches 0.060 in. or less. An American nickel is about 0.060 in. thick, so simply remember that you must always have at least "a nickel's worth of lining."

STEP 2 Most experts agree that the best possible inspection involves removing the brake drum and making a thorough visual inspection of the entire brake instead of just looking at the thickness of the remaining lining. If a riveted brake lining is cracked between the rivets, the lining must be replaced. ● **SEE FIGURE 36–9.**

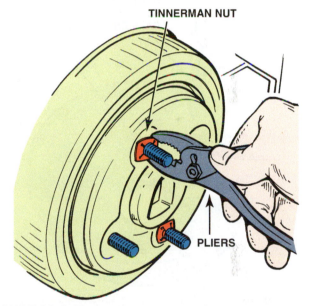

FIGURE 36–8 Tinnerman nuts are used at the assembly plant to prevent the brake drum from falling off until the wheels are installed.

ADJUSTING DRUM BRAKES

Most drum brakes are adjusted by rotating a starwheel or rotary adjuster. As the adjuster is moved in the correct direction, the brake shoes move toward the drum. If the brakes have been assembled correctly and with the parking brake released, both brake shoes should make contact with the anchor pin at the top.

If the clearance between the brake shoes and the brake drum is excessive, a lower than normal brake pedal is the

FIGURE 36–9 Cracked brake lining must be replaced.

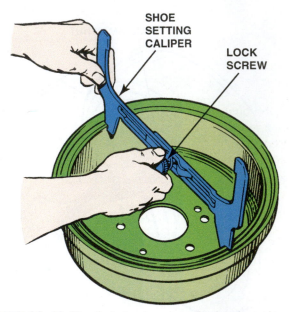

FIGURE 36–10 The first step in using a brake shoe clearance gauge is to adjust it to the drum inside diameter and tighten the lock screw.

most likely result. The wheel cylinder travel may not be adequate to cause the lining to contact the drums. Often, the driver has to pump the brakes to force enough brake fluid into the wheel cylinder to move it enough for braking action to occur.

Many technicians use a **brake shoe clearance gauge** to adjust the brake shoes before installing the drum. ● SEE **FIGURES 36–10 AND 36–11.**

CAUTION: Before installing the brake drum, be sure to clean any grease off the brake lining. Some experts warn not to use sandpaper on the lining to remove grease. The sandpaper may release asbestos fiber into the air. Grease on the linings can cause the brakes to grab.

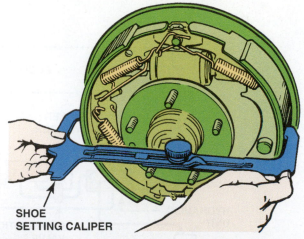

FIGURE 36–11 Place the gauge over the shoes and adjust the brakes until they contact the inside of the gauge.

DISC BRAKE INSPECTION

Most disc brake pads are equipped with a sensor that rubs against the rotor and makes a "chirping" or squealing noise if the pads are worn down to the thickness requiring replacement. The noise may occur only when driving and stop when the brakes are applied. This is normal and can lead vehicle owners to think that the noise is not brake related. ● SEE FIGURE 36–12.

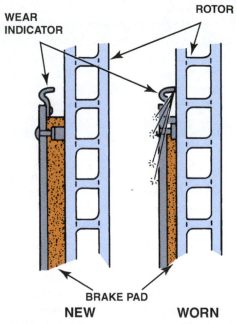

FIGURE 36–12 Typical pad wear sensor operation. It is very important that the disc brake pads are installed on the correct side of the vehicle to be assured that the wear sensor will make a noise when the pads are worn. If the pads with a sensor are installed on the opposite side of the vehicle, the sensor tab is turned so that the rotor touches it going the opposite direction. Usually the correct direction is where the rotor contacts the sensor before contacting the pads when the wheels are being rotated in the forward direction.

FIGURE 36–13 Most disc brake calipers have a brake inspection opening. For a thorough inspection, however, the caliper should be removed and the entire braking system thoroughly inspected.

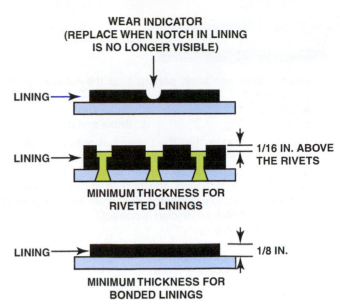

WEAR INDICATOR
(REPLACE WHEN NOTCH IN LINING
IS NO LONGER VISIBLE)

LINING →

LINING →   1/16 IN. ABOVE
            THE RIVETS

MINIMUM THICKNESS FOR
RIVETED LININGS

LINING →   1/8 IN.

MINIMUM THICKNESS FOR
BONDED LININGS

FIGURE 36–14 Minimum thickness for various types of disc brake pads. If the pads are worn, the pad wear sensors often make a "chirping" or squealing sound when the vehicle is moving. Do not confuse that noise for a defective wheel bearing or other fault.

A thorough visual inspection of the disc brake system is very important. This visual inspection should include the following steps:

1. Check the disc brake pads for wear to make sure that the lining thickness is greater than the minimum allowable. ● **SEE FIGURES 36–13 AND 36–14**.
2. Check the brake lines for cracking or leaks.
3. Check the caliper for excessive rust or leaks.

SUMMARY

1. Drum brakes are used on the rear of many vehicles.
2. Disc brakes are used on the front of most vehicles.
3. The six brake subsystems include: apply system, boost system, hydraulic system, wheel brakes, brake balance control system (which includes ABS), and instrument panel brake warning lights.
4. An antilock braking system (ABS) pulses the hydraulic force to the wheels to prevent the tires from locking up. A locked tire has lower friction than a rolling tire.
5. Use care to prevent getting grease on brake linings. It can cause the brake to grab.

REVIEW QUESTIONS

1. How do you remove a brake drum?
2. How do ABS units prevent wheel lockup?
3. What are the steps for inspecting brakes?

1. Drum brakes use what part to stop the rotation of the brake drum?
   a. Brake pad
   b. Brake shoe
   c. Axle housing
   d. Brake pedal

2. Technician A says that the tinnerman nuts are used to hold the brake drum on and should be reinstalled when the drum is replaced. Technician B says that before the brake drum is removed, the brakes should be wetted to prevent possible asbestos dust from being released into the air. Which technician is correct?
   a. Technician A only
   b. Technician B only
   c. Both technicians A and B
   d. Neither technician A nor B

3. Technician A says that the vehicle should not be driven on public streets or highways if the red brake warning light is on. Technician B says that the vehicle should not be driven on public streets or highways if the amber antilock brake warning light is on. Which technician is correct?
   a. Technician A only
   b. Technician B only
   c. Both technicians A and B
   d. Neither technician A nor B

4. Most brake experts and vehicle manufacturers recommend replacing brake lining when the lining thickness is _____.
   a. 0.030 in. (0.8 mm)
   b. 0.040 in. (1.0 mm)
   c. 0.050 in. (1.3 mm)
   d. 0.060 in. (1.5 mm)

5. Technician A says that the power brake system (boost system) helps reduce the force required by the driver to apply the brakes. Technician B says the brake boost system is used to reduce stopping distance. Which technician is correct?
   a. Technician A only
   b. Technician B only
   c. Both technicians A and B
   d. Neither technician A nor B

6. Disc brakes are used _____.
   a. On the front only
   b. On the rear only
   c. On both front and rear
   d. None of the above

7. A "chirping" or squealing noise is heard while the vehicle is moving forward, but stops when the brakes are applied. Technician A says that the noise is likely caused by the disc brake pad wear sensors. Technician B says the noise is likely a wheel bearing because the noise stops when the brakes are applied. Which technician is correct?
   a. Technician A only
   b. Technician B only
   c. Both technicians A and B
   d. Neither technician A nor B

8. Technician A says that disc brake pads should be replaced when worn to minimum allowable thickness. Technician B says the wear indicator will start making a noise when the brake pads are worn down to the thickness requiring replacement. Which technician is correct?
   a. Technician A only
   b. Technician B only
   c. Both technicians A and B
   d. Neither technician A nor B

9. The primary purpose of antilock brakes is to _____.
   a. Allow the front wheels to be steering during braking
   b. Allow for a shorter stopping distance under all road conditions
   c. Reduce brake pad/lining wear
   d. All of the above

10. Power-assisted brakes are used to _____.
    a. Allow the front wheels to be steering during braking
    b. Allow for a shorter stopping distance
    c. Reduce brake pad/lining wear
    d. Reduce the force required by the driver on the brake pedal

chapter 37

SUSPENSION AND STEERING SYSTEMS

OBJECTIVES: After studying Chapter 37, the reader will be able to: • Prepare for ASE Suspension and Steering (A4) certification test content area "A" (Steering System Diagnosis and Repair). • Describe how a suspension system works. • Describe the various types of suspensions. • Discuss steering columns and intermediate shafts. • Describe how a rack-and-pinion steering gear works. • Identify steering linkage components. • Describe how the movement of the steering wheel causes the front wheels to turn.

KEY TERMS: • A-arm 335 • Center link 340 • Collapsible column 338 • Cradle 333 • Grease fitting 341 • Idler arm 340 • Independent suspension 334 • Parallelogram linkage 340 • Pinion gear 339 • Pitman arm 339 • Pitman shaft 339 • Rack 339 • Rack-and-pinion 339 • Sector gear 338 • Short/long-arm (SLA) 335 • Steering knuckle 341 • Steering shaft 338 • Steering stops 341 • Strut suspension 335 • Telescope 338 • Telescoping steering column 338 • Tie rod ends 340 • Tie rods 340 • Tilt steering column 338 • Unit-body 334 • Universal joint 338 • Worm gear 338 • Zerk fitting 341

SUSPENSIONS

PURPOSE AND FUNCTION Street-driven cars and trucks use a suspension system to keep the tires on the road. A vehicle with a solid suspension, or no suspension, would bounce off the ground when the tires hit a bump. If the tires are off the ground, even for a fraction of a second, loss of control is possible.

The purpose of the suspension is to provide the vehicle with the following:

1. A smooth ride
2. Accurate steering
3. Responsive handling
4. Support for the weight of the vehicle
5. Provide acceptable tire wear

VEHICLE FRAMES

PURPOSE AND FUNCTION Vehicle frame construction usually consists of channel-shaped steel beams welded and/or fastened together. The frame of a vehicle supports all the "running gear" of the vehicle, including the engine, transmission, rear axle assembly (if rear-wheel drive), and all suspension components.

TYPES OF FRAMES

- **Full frame** construction is so complete that most vehicles can usually be driven without the body. Most trucks and larger rear-wheel-drive cars use a full frame.

- **Ladder frame** is a common name for a type of perimeter frame where the transverse (lateral) connecting members are straight across. ● SEE FIGURE 37–1. When viewed with the body removed, the frame resembles a ladder. Most pickup trucks are constructed with a ladder-type frame.

- **Perimeter frame** consists of the body. This means that the frame members provide support underneath the sides as well as for the suspension and suspension components.

- **Stub-type frame** is a partial frame often used on unit-body vehicles to support the power train and suspension components. It is also called a **cradle** on many front-wheel-drive vehicles. ● SEE FIGURE 37–2.

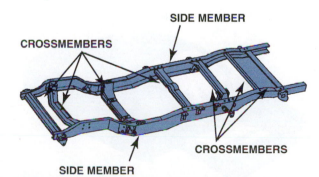

FIGURE 37–1 A typical truck frame is an excellent example of a ladder-type frame. The two side members are connected by a crossmembers.

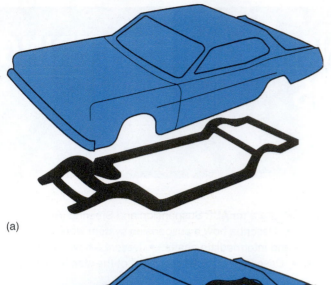

(a)

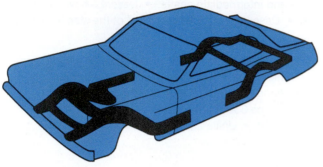

(b)

FIGURE 37–2 (a) Separate body and frame construction; (b) Unitized construction: The small frame members are for support of the engine and suspension components. Many vehicles attach the suspension components directly to the reinforced sections of the body and do not require the rear frame section.

UNIT-BODY CONSTRUCTION **Unit-body** construction (sometimes called *unibody*) is a design that combines the body with the structure of the frame. The body supports the engine and driveline components, as well as the suspension and steering components. The body is composed of many individual stamped steel panels welded together. The strength of this type of construction lies in the *shape* of the assembly. The typical vehicle uses 300 separate and different stamped steel panels that are spot-welded to form a vehicle's body. ● **SEE FIGURE 37–3.**

UNIT-BODY CONSTRUCTION

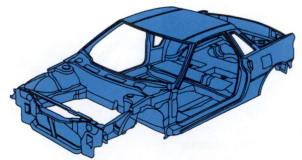

FIGURE 37–3 Welded metal sections create a platform that combines the body with the frame using unit-body construction.

NOTE: A typical vehicle contains about 10,000 individual parts.

SUSPENSION SYSTEM

BACKGROUND Early suspension systems on old horse wagons, buggies, and older vehicles used a solid axle for front and rear wheels. If one wheel hit a bump, the other wheel was affected. ● **SEE FIGURE 37–4.**

INDEPENDENT SUSPENSIONS Most vehicles today use a separate control-arm type of suspension for each front wheel, which allows for movement of one front wheel without affecting the other front wheel. This type of front suspension is called **independent suspension.** ● **SEE FIGURE 37–5.**

Many rear suspensions also use independent-type suspension systems. Regardless of the design type of suspension, all suspensions use springs in one form or another.

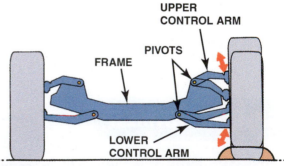

FIGURE 37–4 Most early vehicles used single straight axles.

SHORT/LONG-ARM (SLA) SUSPENSION

FIGURE 37–5 An independent suspension means that if one wheel hits a bump, only that wheel moves upward and allows the opposite wheel to remain unaffected by the bump. This type of suspension allows for smoother ride and is used in most front suspensions and many rear suspensions.

SPRINGS

PURPOSE   A suspension spring serves two purposes:

1. It acts as a buffer between the suspension and frame to absorb vertical wheel and suspension movement without passing it on to the frame.

2. Each spring transfers part of the vehicle weight to the suspension component it rests on, which transfers it to the wheels.

Most springs are made of a tempered steel alloy known as spring steel. Spring resilience is the ability of the metal to return to, or spring back to, its original shape after being twisted or compressed.

The basic method by which springs absorb road shocks varies according to the type of spring.

- **Coil springs**. ● **SEE FIGURE 37–6.**
- **Leaf springs**. ● **SEE FIGURE 37–7.**
- **Torsion bars**. ● **SEE FIGURE 37–8.**

What all springs have in common is that they give way to absorb the vertical force of the moving wheel when the vehicle hits a bump or rise in the road, then release that force during rebound as they return to their original shape and position.

FRONT SUSPENSIONS

SLA TYPE   The short/long-arm suspension uses a short upper control arm and a longer lower control arm and usually is referred to as the *SLA-type suspension*. The two main links in a **short/long-arm (SLA)** suspension are the upper control arm and the lower control arm. ● **SEE FIGURE 37–9.**

This type of suspension system goes by a variety of names, including:

- Unequal-arm suspension,
- Double-wishbone suspension, or
- **A-arm** suspension.

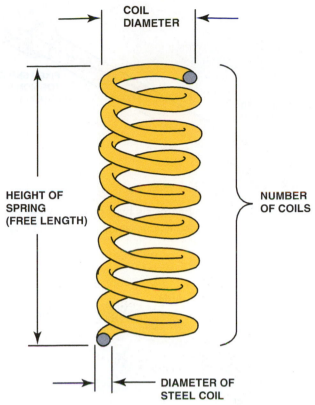

FIGURE 37–6 The spring rate of a coil spring is determined by the diameter of the spring and the diameter of the steel used in its construction plus the number of coils and the free length (height).

STRUT SUSPENSIONS

Strut suspension have the following features:

- A MacPherson strut includes the suspension spring that transfers the weight of the body to the wheel.
- A MacPherson strut is a structural part of the vehicle.

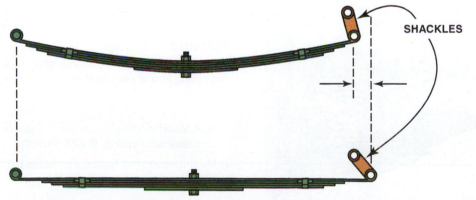

FIGURE 37–7 When a leaf spring is compressed, the spring flattens and becomes longer. The shackles allow for this lengthening. Rubber bushings are used in the ends of the spring and shackles are used to help isolate road noise from traveling into the passenger compartment.

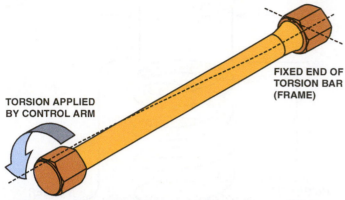

FIGURE 37–8 A torsion bar resists twisting and is used as a spring on some cars and many four-wheel-drive pickup trucks and sport utility vehicles.

TORSION APPLIED BY CONTROL ARM

FIXED END OF TORSION BAR (FRAME)

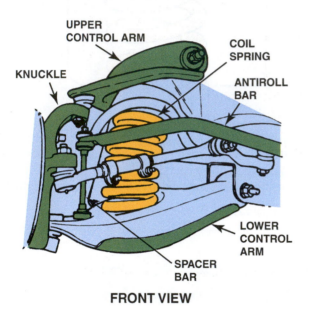

UPPER CONTROL ARM

COIL SPRING

KNUCKLE

ANTIROLL BAR

LOWER CONTROL ARM

SPACER BAR

FRONT VIEW

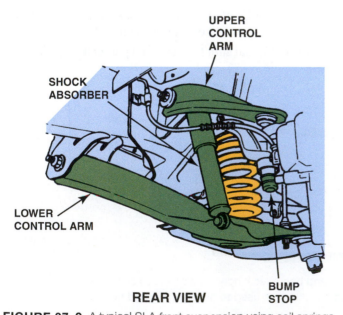

UPPER CONTROL ARM

SHOCK ABSORBER

LOWER CONTROL ARM

BUMP STOP

REAR VIEW

FIGURE 37–9 A typical SLA front suspension using coil springs.

MACPHERSON STRUT SUSPENSION

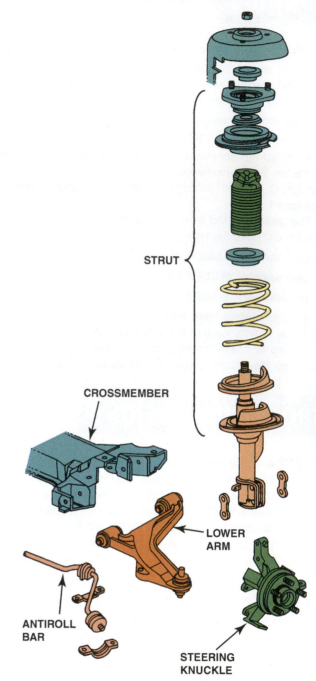

STRUT

CROSSMEMBER

LOWER ARM

ANTIROLL BAR

STEERING KNUCKLE

FIGURE 37–10 A typical MacPherson strut showing all of the components of the assembly. A strut includes the shock and the spring in one structural assembly.

- A MacPherson strut contains the main load-carrying suspension spring. ● **SEE FIGURE 37–10.**

A MacPherson strut typically includes the following:

- An upper and a lower spring seat
- A hydraulic shock absorber
- A dust cover for the piston rod
- A bump stop

STRUT/SLA SUSPENSION

MAZDA

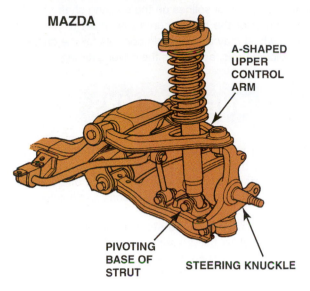

A-SHAPED UPPER CONTROL ARM

PIVOTING BASE OF STRUT

STEERING KNUCKLE

HONDA

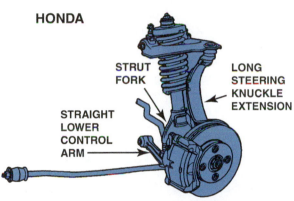

STRUT FORK

LONG STEERING KNUCKLE EXTENSION

STRAIGHT LOWER CONTROL ARM

NISSAN

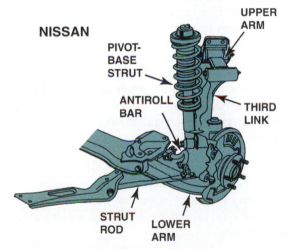

UPPER ARM

PIVOT-BASE STRUT

ANTIROLL BAR

THIRD LINK

STRUT ROD

LOWER ARM

FIGURE 37–11 Multilink front suspension design varies depending on the vehicle manufacturer.

The upper mount secures the upper spring seat to the strut tower. A rubber bushing at the top of the strut absorbs vibrations. A bearing on the top of a front-wheel strut allows it to rotate when the steering wheel is turned. There are several other types of front suspension that use various designs of control arms and are often called multilink-type suspensions. ● **SEE FIGURE 37–11.**

SUSPENSION SYSTEM INSPECTION

SYMPTOMS OF WORN SUSPENSION PARTS If a component in the suspension system is worn, the following symptoms may be noticed by the driver:

- Uneven or excessive tire wear
- Noises when driving over rough or uneven pavement
- Pulling to one side when driving straight on a straight road
- Excessive play in the steering

VISUAL INSPECTION All suspension components should be carefully inspected for signs of wear or damage. A thorough visual inspection should include checking all of the following:

1. Shock absorbers. ● **SEE FIGURE 37–12.**
2. Springs
3. Upper and lower shock absorber mounting points
4. Bump stops
5. Body-to-chassis mounts and other components under the vehicle
6. Engine and transmission (transaxle) mounts
7. Suspension arm bushings ● **SEE FIGURE 37–13.**

While an assistant bounces the vehicle up and down, check to see if there is any free play in any of the suspension components.

FIGURE 37–12 A leaking strut. Either a cartridge insert or the entire strut will require replacement. If a light film of oil is seen, this is to be considered normal. If oil is dripping, then this means that the rod seal has failed.

FIGURE 37–13 It is easy to see that this worn control arm bushing needed to be replaced. The new bushing is shown next to the original.

WITNESS MARK

FIGURE 37–14 The exhaust was found to be rubbing on the frame rail during a visual inspection. Rubber exhaust system hangers are used to isolate noise and vibration from the exhaust system from entering the interior. These rubber supports can fail, causing the exhaust system to be out of proper location.

 **TECH TIP**

Check for Witness Marks

Witness marks are places where two parts have come into contact and left a mark. A visual inspection should include looking for places where two parts have rubbed together, which will often lead to where there is a fault or worn part. ● **SEE FIGURE 37–14.**

STEERING WHEELS

PARTS AND OPERATION The steering wheel, which consists of a rigid rim and a number of spokes connecting the rim to a center hub, attaches to the top of the steering shaft

at its center. Most steering wheel hubs have internal splines that fit over external splines on the steering shaft. A bolt or nut at the center of the hub secures the wheel to the shaft. The steering wheel may also contain controls for the cruise control and audio controls, as well as the driver's airbag.

STEERING COLUMNS

The steering shaft transmits rotary motion from the steering wheel to the steering gear, while the column jacket that encases it attaches to the vehicle body and offers a stationary mounting point for a number of switches and mechanisms.

STEERING SHAFT The **steering shaft** extends from the steering wheel to the steering gear. A bolt or nut secures the shaft to the steering wheel, and a flexible coupling joins it to the steering gear input shaft.

UNIVERSAL JOINT A **universal joint,** or U-joint, consists of two yokes with a steel crosspiece joining them together. Universal joints allow changes in the angle between two rotating shafts. In a steering shaft, U-joints allow transfer of rotary motion between the steering wheel and the steering gear even though the steering shaft meets the steering gear input shaft at an angle. In some models, the steering shaft itself is assembled in sections that are connected by U-joints. This permits the steering shaft to bend around obstacles between the steering wheel and the steering gear. ● **SEE FIGURE 37–15.**

COLLAPSIBLE COLUMN Federal law requires that all vehicles sold in the United States have steering columns and shafts that collapse, called **collapsible columns,** during a head-on collision to absorb some of the energy of the crash and lessen the danger of injury to the driver.

TILT MECHANISMS Many steering columns have tilt mechanisms, which allow the driver to adjust the angle of the steering wheel relative to the steering column. In a typical **tilt steering column,** the steering shaft has a short section at the top joined to the rest of the steering shaft either by a U-joint or gears.

TELESCOPING STEERING COLUMNS Some steering columns are designed to **telescope,** which means that the top of the steering shaft and jacket can be pulled out toward the driver or pushed in toward the dashboard, and then locked into the new position.

CONVENTIONAL STEERING GEARS

PURPOSE AND FUNCTION Steering gears are used primarily on rear-wheel-drive vehicles. All steering gears consist of an input gear usually called a **worm gear,** and an output gear usually called a **sector gear.** The worm and sector gears are

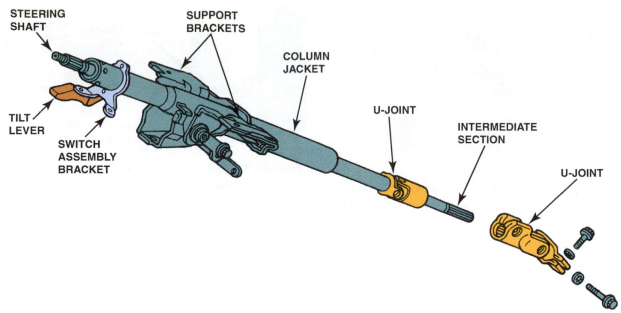

FIGURE 37–15 The steering shaft links the steering wheel to the steering gear while the column jacket, which surrounds part of the shaft, supports the brackets and switches. This steering shaft has a small intermediate section between the main section and the steering gear.

meshed together. The worm gear is connected to the steering wheel and the sector gear is connected to the **pitman shaft,** which is part of the steering linkage. ● **SEE FIGURE 37–16.**

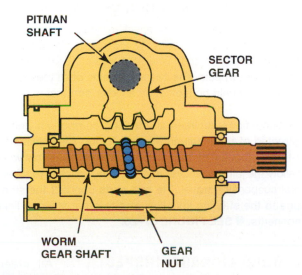

FIGURE 37–16 As the steering wheel is turned, the nut moves up or down on the threads, shown using a bolt to represent the worm gear and the nut representing the gear nut that meshes with the teeth of the sector gear.

As the steering wheel is turned, the movement is transmitted through the steering gear to an arm attached to the bottom end of the pitman shaft. This arm is called the **pitman arm.** Whenever the steering wheel is turned, the pitman arm moves.

RACK-AND-PINION STEERING GEARS

PARTS AND OPERATION The term "rack-and-pinion" is simply a description of the basic design of this type of steering gear. Rack-and-pinion gears are used primarily on front-wheel-drive vehicles. The **rack-and-pinion** steering gear is widely used because it is light in weight and takes less space than a conventional steering gear.

A typical rack-and-pinion assembly consists of **pinion gear** attached to the steering shaft and steering wheel by using either a flexible coupling or universal joint. The pinion gear meshes with a long straight gear called a **rack.** The rack has teeth that match the pinion gear. ● **SEE FIGURE 37–17.**

When the pinion gear rotates, the rack moves either one direction or the other based on the rotation of the pinion gear. The ends of the rack are connected with steering linkage to the front tires/wheels.

The rack is encased in the long, tubular steering gear housing with a mounting flange on the pinion end. Rubber bushings fit into the mounting flange bolt holes to absorb vibration and isolate the assembly from the frame. ● **SEE FIGURE 37–18.**

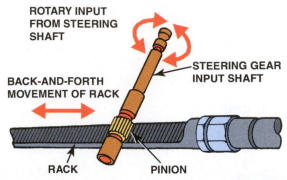

FIGURE 37–17 Rack-and-pinion steering gear operation is simple, direct, and the rack is in a straight line to the front wheels.

FIGURE 37–18 A typical rack-and-pinion steering gear as viewed from under the vehicle. A small air tube is used to transfer air between the boots as they extend and compress during turns.

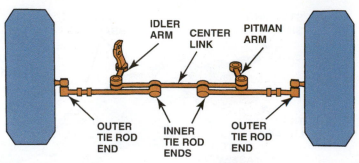

FIGURE 37–19 Steering movement is transferred from the pitman arm that is splined to the sector shaft (pitman shaft), through the center link and tie rods, to the steering knuckle at each front wheel. The idler arm supports the passenger side of the center link and keeps the steering linkage level with the road. This type of linkage is called a parallelogram-type design.

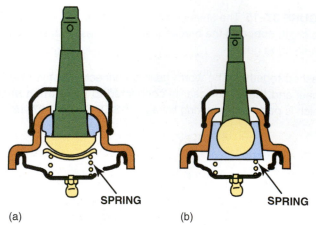

FIGURE 37–20 Two different styles of tie rod ends. (a) A dual bearing design with a preload spring. (b) The nylon wedge bearing type allows for extended lube intervals. Wear is automatically compensated for by the tapered design and spring-loaded bearing.

STEERING LINKAGE

PARTS AND OPERATION The steering linkage relays steering forces from the steering gear to the front wheels. Most conventional steering gear linkages use the **parallelogram**-type design. A **parallelogram** is a geometric box shape where opposite sides are parallel and at equal distance. A parallelogram-type linkage uses four **tie rods,** two inner and two outer (left and right), a **center link** (between the tie rods), an **idler arm** on the passenger side, and a pitman arm attached to the steering gear output shaft (pitman shaft). ● SEE FIGURE 37–19.

As the steering wheel is rotated, the pitman arm is moved. The pitman arm attaches to a center link. At either end of the center link are inboard (inner) tie rods, adjusting sleeves, and outboard (outer) tie rods connected to the steering arms, which

move the front wheels. The passenger side of all these parts is supported and held horizontal by an idler arm that is bolted to the frame.

Connections between all steering component parts are constructed of small ball-and-socket joints. These joints allow side-to-side movement to provide steering of both front wheels, and allow the joints to move up and down, which is required for normal suspension travel. **Tie rod ends** connect the steering linkage to the steering knuckles and to other steering linkage components. ● SEE FIGURE 37–20.

STEERING LINKAGE INSPECTION All steering components should be checked for wear and damage. After safely hoisting the vehicle, check that all steering components are tight without any vertical or end-to-end movement. ● SEE FIGURE 37–21.

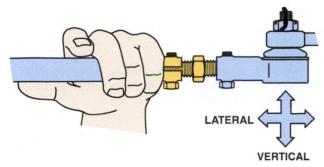

FIGURE 37–21 All joints should be checked by hand for any lateral or vertical play.

STEERING LINKAGE LUBRICATION

It is important that all of these joints be lubricated with chassis grease through a **grease fitting,** also called a **zerk fitting or alemite fitting,** named for a company that manufactures grease fittings, at least every six months or as per the vehicle manufacturer's specifications. Most vehicles come equipped with sealed joints and do not require periodic servicing. Some vehicles come from the factory with plugs that need to be removed and replaced with grease fittings and then lubricated.

Keeping all joints equipped with a grease fitting properly greased is necessary for long life and ease of steering. ● **SEE FIGURE 37–22.**

During chassis lubrication, do not forget to put grease on the *steering stop,* if so equipped. **Steering stops** are the projections or built-up areas on the control arms of the front suspension designed to limit the steering movement at full lock. ● **SEE FIGURE 37–23.**

When the steering wheel is turned as far as it can go, the steering should *not* stop inside the steering gear! Forces exerted by the power steering system can do serious damage to the steering gear if absorbed by the steering gear rather than the steering stop.

NOTE: Many rack-and-pinion steering units are designed with a rack-travel-limit internal stop and do not use an external stop on the steering knuckle or control arm.

FIGURE 37–22 Greasing a tie rod end. Some joints do not have a hole for excessive grease to escape, and excessive grease can destroy the seal.

FIGURE 37–23 Part of steering linkage lubrication is applying grease to the steering stops. If these stops are not lubricated, a grinding sound may be heard when the vehicle hits a bump when the wheels are turned all the way in one direction or the other. This often occurs when driving into or out of a driveway that has a curb.

SUMMARY

1. Suspension designs include a straight or solid-axle, two-control-arm type called an SLA or a MacPherson strut.

2. The suspension can be checked for visual signs or faults such as looking for witness marks that may indicate a problem when two parts have come into contact.

3. Many rear-wheel-drive vehicles use a steering gear, and front-wheel vehicles and many rear-wheel-drive vehicles use a rack-and-pinion-type steering gear.

REVIEW QUESTIONS

1. What are the types of suspensions and what are the names of their component parts?

2. What components are included in a typical steering column assembly?

3. When the driver turns the steering wheel, how is the motion transferred to the front wheels through a conventional steering gear?

CHAPTER QUIZ

1. The types of frames used include _____.
   a. Full frame
   b. Ladder frame
   c. Stub-type frame
   d. Any of the above depending on the vehicle

2. The steering gear rotates which part on a system using a conventional type steering gear?
   a. Idler arm
   b. Pitman arm
   c. Center link
   d. Intermediate shaft

3. Which type of suspension uses two control arms?
   a. Strut
   b. SLA
   c. Leaf spring
   d. All of the above

4. A witness mark is _____.
   a. A person who witnesses an accident
   b. A type of suspension
   c. A type of steering system
   d. A mark made when two parts touch each other and leave a mark

5. A MacPherson strut is a structural part of the vehicle.
   a. True
   b. False

6. Which part in the steering column allows for changes in the angle between the upper and lower shafts?
   a. Flexible coupling
   b. Column cover
   c. Universal joint
   d. Collapsible section

7. The rotation of the steering wheel causes which part to move the actual steering linkage in a rack-and-pinion steering gear?
   a. Sector shaft
   b. Rack which is connected to the front wheel through tie rods
   c. Worm gear
   d. Gear nut

8. In a rack-and-pinion steering gear, which part is the rack?
   a. The part that is rotated by the driver
   b. The part that is bolted to the frame
   c. The part that is moved side to side when the steering wheel is turned
   d. The steering wheel itself

9. Which is a type of spring?
   a. Coil
   b. Leaf
   c. Torsion bar
   d. All of the above

10. The fitting that is used to install grease into a steering or suspension part is called _____.
    a. Grease fitting
    b. Zerk fitting
    c. Alemite fitting
    d. Any of the above

OBJECTIVES: After studying Chapter 38, the reader will be able to: • Prepare for ASE Manual Drive Train and Axles (A3) certification test content area "A" (Clutch Diagnosis and Repair). • List the parts that are included in the clutch system. • Describe how the clutch works. • Explain how to calculate gear ratios. • Name the parts of a typical manually shifted transmission/transaxle. • Describe how the synchronizer assembly allows for smooth, clash-free shifting. • Describe the different types of lubricants that may be used in a manual transmission/transaxle. • Explain the purpose and function of driveshafts. • Describe the operation of CV joints. • Determine the rear axle ratio. • Describe the difference between four-wheel drive and all-wheel drive.

KEY TERMS: • Axle ratio 351 • Bell housing 347 • Cardan joints 349 • Clutch disc 343 • Counter gears 347 • Countershaft 347 • CV joints 350 • Drive gear 347 • Driven gear 347 • Driveshaft 348 • Extension housing 347 • Final drive assembly 347 • Input shaft 347 • Locking hubs 353 • Low range 352 • Main shaft 347 • Mode shift 352 • Output shaft 347 • Part-time four-wheel drive 352 • Pilot bearing 345 • Pressure plate 343 • Propeller shaft 348 • Range shift 352 • Release bearing 345 • Rzeppa joint 350 • Slave cylinder 345 • Spider 349 • Synchronizer assemblies 347 • Throwout bearing 345 • Transmission case 347 • Trunnions 349 • Universal joints 348

CLUTCHES

PURPOSE AND FUNCTION The clutch assembly is located between the engine and the transmission/transaxle. The purpose and function of a clutch includes the following:

- To disconnect the engine from the transmission/ transaxle to permit the engine to remain running when the vehicle is stopped and to permit the transmission/ transaxle to be shifted

- To connect and transmit engine torque to the transmission/transaxle

  NOTE: The term *transmission* refers to rear-wheel-drive vehicles and the term *transaxle* usually refers to front-wheel-drive vehicles that have a differential built into the unit. A separate differential is used with a transmission.

- To dampen and absorb engine impulses and drivetrain vibration

- To provide a smooth engagement and disengagement between the engine and the transmission/ transaxle

● SEE FIGURE 38–1

PARTS AND OPERATION

A clutch assembly consists of a **clutch disc** that is splined to the input shaft of the transmission/transaxle.

The **pressure plate** is bolted to and rotates with the flywheel and clamps the friction disc between the pressure plate and the flywheel. ● SEE FIGURE 38–2.

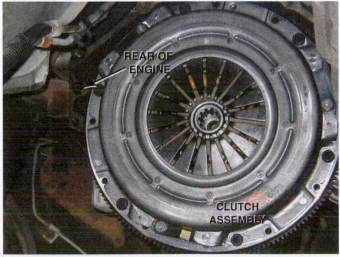

FIGURE 38–1 A clutch assembly attached to the engine crankshaft at the rear of the engine.

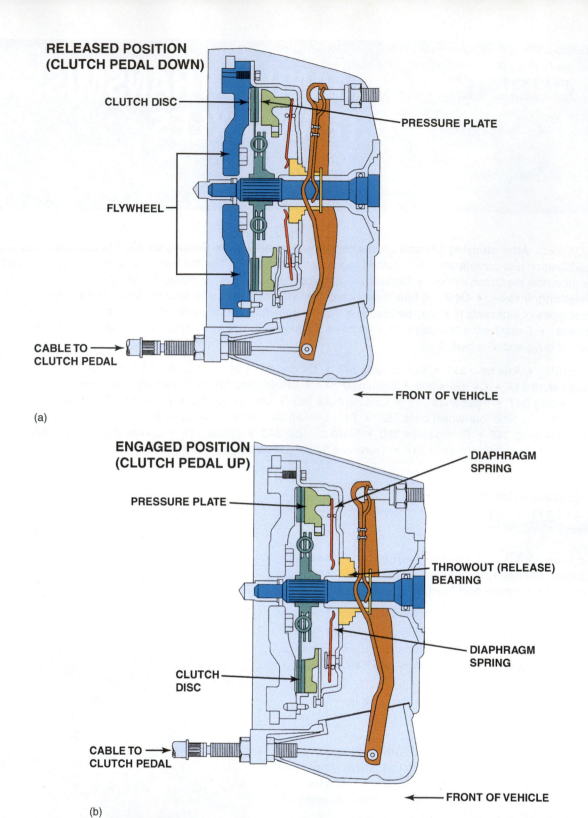

**RELEASED POSITION
(CLUTCH PEDAL DOWN)**

CLUTCH DISC

PRESSURE PLATE

FLYWHEEL

CABLE TO
CLUTCH PEDAL

FRONT OF VEHICLE

(a)

**ENGAGED POSITION
(CLUTCH PEDAL UP)**

DIAPHRAGM
SPRING

PRESSURE PLATE

THROWOUT (RELEASE)
BEARING

DIAPHRAGM
SPRING

CLUTCH
DISC

CABLE TO
CLUTCH PEDAL

FRONT OF VEHICLE

(b)

| | CLUTCH FORK | | DIAPHRAGM SPRING | | CLUTCH PLATE |
| | THROWOUT (RELEASE) BEARING | | PRESSURE PLATE | | FLYWHEEL |

FIGURE 38–2 (a) When the clutch is in the released position (clutch pedal depressed), the clutch fork is applying a force to the throwout (release) bearing, which pushes on the diaphragm spring, releasing the pressure on the friction disc. (b) When the clutch is in the engaged position (clutch pedal up), the diaphragm spring exerts force on the clutch disc, holding it between the flywheel and the pressure plate.

The clutch disc is "squeezed" between the flywheel and pressure plate by springs contained within the pressure plate. This connection allows power flow from the engine flywheel to the transmission input shaft. When the clutch pedal is pushed down, the **throwout bearing (release bearing)** pushes against the pressure plate fingers, causing the clutch disc to be released, and the engine power flow is interrupted for the purpose of shifting. When the clutch pedal is allowed to come up, the springs in the pressure plate reapply pressure to the pressure plate and the clutch disc is squeezed again between the flywheel and the pressure plate.

Additional related parts include the **pilot bearing (or bushing)** that supports the front of the transmission input shaft. To summarize

- When the clutch pedal is up, the clutch is engaged.
- When the clutch pedal is down, the clutch is disengaged.

CLUTCH PEDAL LINKAGE
There are three methods of transferring the force of the driver's foot to the throwout (release) bearing, including the following:

- **Levers and rods.** Older vehicles used a series of levers and rods to operate the release fork, which was forced against the throwout bearing.
- **Cable operation.** A cable is used similar to a brake cable used on a bicycle.
- **Hydraulic.** This is the most commonly used type of clutch operation device. A small master cylinder and a **slave cylinder** located near the throwout bearing is a very common method of connecting the clutch pedal to the release fork on vehicles equipped with a manual transmission. ● **SEE FIGURES 38–3 AND 38–4.**

FIGURE 38–4 A typical clutch master cylinder and reservoir mounted on the bulkhead on the driver's side of the vehicle. DOT 3 brake fluid is used in the hydraulic system to operate the slave cylinder located on the bell housing.

RELEASE BEARING
The release (throwout) bearing is attached to the clutch fork and rides on the fingers of the pressure plate. The clutch operating system moves the clutch release bearing when the driver presses or releases the clutch pedal. ● **SEE FIGURE 38–5.**

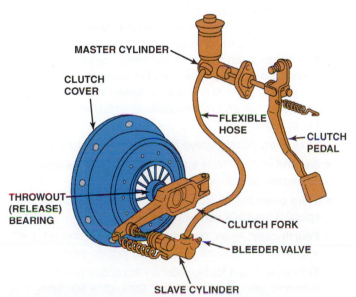

FIGURE 38–3 A hydraulic clutch linkage uses a master cylinder and a slave cylinder.

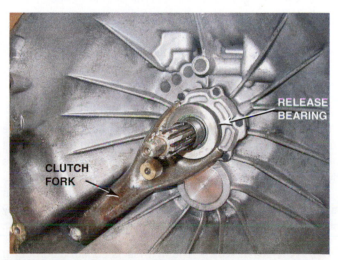

FIGURE 38–5 The clutch pedal linkage moves the clutch fork, which then applies a force against the release bearing, which then releases the clamping force the pressure plate is exerting on the clutch disc.

FIGURE 38–6 A typical clutch friction disc that uses coil spring torsional dampers that absorb the initial shock of engagement and help dampen engine firing in pulses being transmitted into and through the transmission/transaxle.

CLUTCH DISC The clutch disc is round with a splined center hole that slips over the splines of the input shaft of the transmission/transaxle. Friction material is riveted to both sides of the clutch disc—one side touches the flywheel of the engine and the other side touches the friction surface of the pressure plate. ● **SEE FIGURE 38–6.**

For many years, asbestos was the most common material used in both clutch and brake linings. However, it is no longer used because inhaling tiny particles of asbestos causes lung damage. Today, clutch friction material may contain paper, cotton, and bits of copper or brass wire with resin holding the mixture together.

FLYWHEELS

PURPOSE AND FUNCTION The engine flywheel serves four basic purposes:

- Smoothes out or dampens engine power pulses.
- Absorbs some of the heat created by clutch operation.
- Provides the connection point for the starter motor to crank the engine.
- Provides the application surface for the clutch friction disc.

A flywheel is heavy, or has a large mass, which creates inertia. This inertia acts upon crankshaft rotation to smooth out or dampen engine power pulses. The inertia provided by the flywheel mass tends to keep crankshaft speed more constant.

Whenever friction exists between two moving parts, heat is generated. The flywheel absorbs some of the heat created by clutch operation by acting as a heat sink for the clutch friction disc.

FRICTION SURFACE The flywheel is constructed of cast iron and attaches to the end of the engine crankshaft.

The face on the transmission side of the flywheel has a smooth, machined area that creates the application surface for the clutch friction disc.

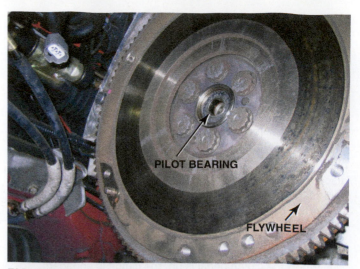

FIGURE 38–7 The flywheel has a friction surface for the clutch and has gear teeth that are used by the starter motor to rotate the engine for starting.

RING GEAR An external ring gear is pressed or welded onto the flywheel along its outer circumference. When the starter motor is engaged, the starter-drive gear meshes with the flywheel ring gear. ● **SEE FIGURE 38–7.**

MANUAL TRANSMISSIONS

PURPOSE AND FUNCTION A vehicle requires a lot of torque to start off and to climb hills, yet it does not require as much torque to move on level ground. The source of the torque is the engine. Torque is a twisting or turning force that is exerted on the input shaft of a transmission/transaxle. An engine produces increasing torque as its speed increases up to a certain point where the torque output starts to decrease. Therefore, to get a vehicle moving or to accelerate up a hill, it is desirable to use a transmission that allows the engine speed to be increased even though the vehicle speed may be low. Using gears allows the engine speed to increase at low vehicle speeds, yet still permits the engine speed to drop at higher speeds to save fuel and reduce exhaust emissions.

For example,

- **First gear:** Vehicle speed is low, engine speed is high.
- **Second gear:** Vehicle speed increases, engine speed decreases as shift is made.
- **Third gear:** Vehicle speed continues to increase, engine speed is kept in a narrow range.
- **Fourth gear:** Again, the vehicle speed is increasing, yet engine speed is about the same as in third gear.
- **Fifth gear:** Used for highway driving and is usually an overdrive ratio. This means that the engine is rotating slower in this gear than any other gear, which provides improved fuel economy.

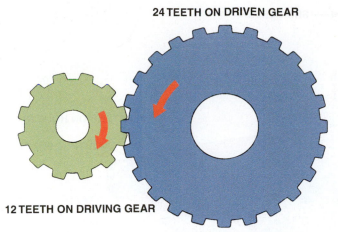

24 TEETH ON DRIVEN GEAR

12 TEETH ON DRIVING GEAR

FIGURE 38–8 Gear ratio is determined by dividing the number of teeth of the driven (output) gear (24 teeth) by the number of teeth on the driving (input) gear (12 teeth). The ratio illustrated is 2:1.

GEAR RATIOS When one gear turns another, the speed that the two gears turn in relation to each other is the gear ratio. Gear ratio is expressed as the number of rotations the **drive gear** must make in order to rotate the **driven gear** through one revolution. To obtain a gear ratio, simply divide the number of teeth on the driven gear by the number of teeth on the drive gear. Gear ratios, which are expressed relative to the number one, fall into three categories:

1. Direct drive
2. Gear reduction

   Number of teeth on the driven gear (24)

   Number of teeth on the driving gear (12) = 2:1

3. Overdrive
   ● **SEE FIGURE 38–8.**

TRANSMISSION PARTS A transmission is usually constructed of cast aluminum machined to accept the internal parts and strong enough to be a structural member of the drivetrain. The front of the transmission attaches to a separate **bell housing** or includes the bell housing as part of the casting of the transmission itself. The rear of the transmission usually includes a separate casting called the **extension housing.** The center housing is usually referred to as the **transmission case.**
● **SEE FIGURE 38–9.**

The **input shaft** is splined to the clutch disc. The **main shaft,** also called the **output shaft,** is splined at the backend and transmits engine torque to the drive shaft (propeller shaft) through a yoke and universal shaft. All manual transmissions/transaxles use a **countershaft** to provide the other set of gears necessary to achieve the changes in gear ratio. The gears on the countershaft are called **cluster gears or counter gears.**
● **SEE FIGURE 38–10.**

The shifting lever moves either shift fork directly. Inside the transmission/transaxle are shift forks that control shifts between two gears, such as first and second or second and third. Interlocks either in the shifter linkage itself

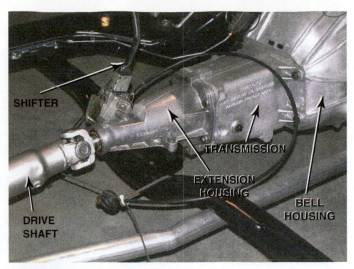

FIGURE 38–9 A manual transmission on a restored muscle car showing the bell housing, transmission, extension housing, and shifter.

or inside the transmission/transaxle prevent the accidental selection of reverse gear except when shifting from neutral and also prevent selecting two gears at the same time.
● **SEE FIGURE 38–11.**

Synchronizers are used in manual transmissions/transaxles to make shifting easier. To synchronize means to make two or more events occur at the same time.

The real "shifting" in a synchromesh transmission takes place in the **synchronizer assemblies,** not the gears. Most synchronizer assemblies ride on the output shaft between two gears. A synchronizer assembly is named for the gears on either side of it, which are the two speeds that it engages. For example, a five-speed transmission with constant-mesh reverse uses a 1–2 synchronizer, 3–4 synchronizer, and a 5–reverse synchronizer. ● **SEE FIGURE 38–12.**

MANUAL TRANSAXLES A manually shifted transaxle includes an input shaft, an output shaft, and a differential assembly all in one case. The input shaft is attached to the clutch, which transfers engine torque from the engine flywheel to the input shaft when the clutch is engaged.

The differential assembly, also called a **final drive assembly,** attaches to the output shaft and splits the torque to both front drive axles. ● **SEE FIGURE 38–13** on page 349.

MANUAL TRANSMISSION/TRANSAXLE LUBRICATION
After the installation of the transmission/transaxle, the unit should be filled with the correct lubricant. The specified fluid may include one of the following:

- SAE 80W-90 (GL-4) gear lube
- STF (synchromesh transmission fluid), but with friction characteristics designed for manual transmissions.
  ● **SEE FIGURE 38–14** on page 349.
- ATF (automatic transmission fluid)
- Engine oil (usually SAE 5W-30)

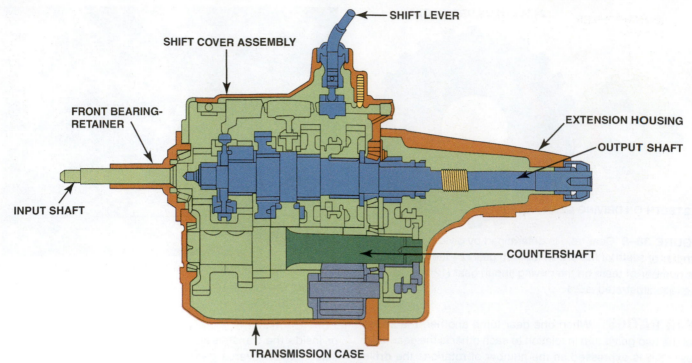

FIGURE 38–10 Cross-section of a five-speed manual transmission showing the main parts.

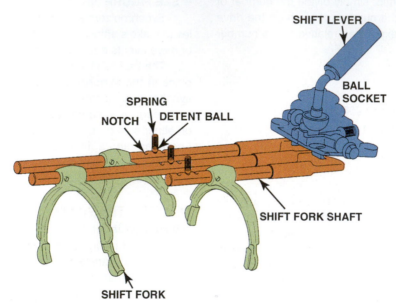

FIGURE 38–11 A typical shift mechanism is designed not only to give the driver a solid feel when shifting but also to prevent two gears from being selected at the same time. The shifter mechanism also prevents shifting into reverse except from the neutral position.

CAUTION: Failure to use the specified manual transmission/transaxle lubricant could cause hard shifting and possible severe transmission damage.

DRIVE SHAFTS

TERMS AND CONSTRUCTION **Driveshaft** is the term used by the Society of Automotive Engineers (SAE) to describe the shaft between the transmission and the rear axle assembly on a rear-wheel-drive vehicle. The driveshaft is also called a **propeller shaft** or *prop shaft*. A typical driveshaft is a hollow steel tube. A splined end yoke is welded onto one end that slips over the splines of the output shaft of the transmission. ●**SEE FIGURE 38–15.**

An end yoke is welded onto the other end of the driveshaft. Some two-piece drive shafts use a center support bearing.

U-JOINTS **Universal joints (U-joints)** are used at both ends of a driveshaft. U-joints allow the wheels and the rear axle to move up and down, remain flexible, and still transfer

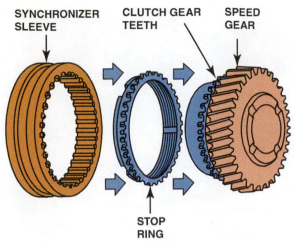

FIGURE 38–12 The shifter fork fits into the groove of the synchronizer sleeve. When a shift is made, the sleeve is moved toward the speed gear. The sleeve presses the stop ring (synchronizer ring) against the cone area of the speed gear. The friction between the stop ring and the speed gear causes the speed of the two to become equal, permitting the sleeve to engage the gear clutch teeth of the speed gear. When this engagement occurs, the shift is complete.

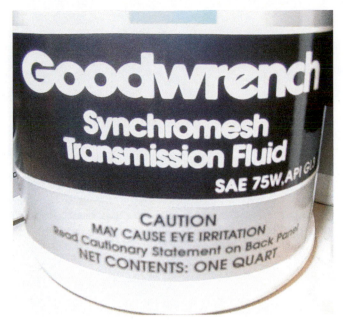

FIGURE 38–14 Some manual transmissions/transaxles require synchromesh transmission fluid.

FIGURE 38–13 A partially disassembled manual transaxle showing the final drive assembly and some of the bearings and gears.

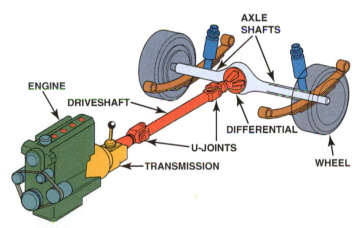

FIGURE 38–15 Typical rear-wheel-drive power train arrangement. The engine is mounted longitudinal (lengthwise).

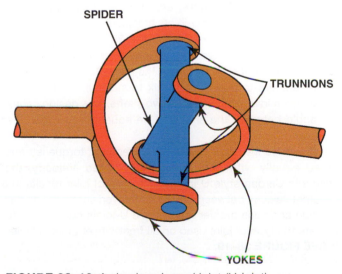

FIGURE 38–16 A simple universal joint (U-joint).

torque to the drive wheels. A simple universal joint can be made from two Y-shaped yokes connected by a crossmember called a cross or **spider**. The four arms of the cross are called **trunnions.** ● SEE FIGURE 38–16.

Most U-joints are called cross-yoke joints or **Cardan joints.** *Cardan* is named for a sixteenth-century Italian mathematician who worked with objects that moved freely in any direction. Torque from the engine is transferred through the U-joint. ● SEE FIGURE 38–17.

FIGURE 38–17 A Cardan U-joint used on the drive shaft on a rear-wheel-drive vehicle.

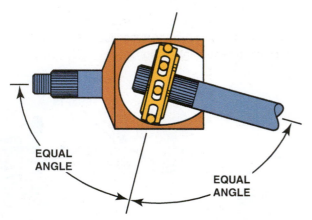

FIGURE 38–18 A constant velocity (CV) joint can operate at high angles without a change in velocity (speed) because the joint design results in equal angles between input and output.

EQUAL ANGLE

EQUAL ANGLE

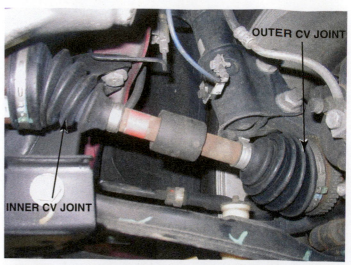

OUTER CV JOINT

INNER CV JOINT

FIGURE 38–19 A drive axle shaft (also called a *half shaft*) on a front-wheel-drive vehicle showing the inner and outer CV joints. The rubber boots that cover the joints and hold in the grease should be inspected for tears or other faults due to road debris.

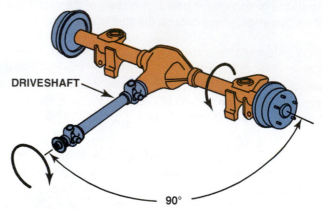

DRIVESHAFT

90°

FIGURE 38–20 The differential assembly changes the direction of engine torque and increases the torque to the drive wheels.

CONSTANT VELOCITY JOINTS Constant velocity joints, commonly called **CV joints,** are designed to rotate without changing speed. Regular U-joints are usually designed to work up to 12° of angularity. ● SEE FIGURE 38–18.

The first constant velocity joint was designed by Alfred H. Rzeppa (pronounced shep'pa) in the mid-1920s. The **Rzeppa joint** transfers torque through six round balls that are held in position midway between the two shafts. This design causes the angle between the shafts to be equally split regardless of the angle.

Because the angle is always split equally, torque is transferred equally without the change in speed (velocity) that occurs in Cardan-style U-joints. This style of joint results in a constant velocity between driving and driven shafts. It can also function at angles greater than simple U-joints can, up to 40°, and are the type of joint used on all front-wheel-drive vehicles. ● SEE FIGURE 38–19.

DRIVE AXLES AND DIFFERENTIALS

PURPOSE AND FUNCTION The differential allows engine torque to be applied to both drive axles, which rotate at varying speeds during cornering and while traveling over bumps and dips in the road. The differential also changes the direction of engine torque 90° from the rotation of the driveshaft lengthwise with the vehicle. These two purposes of a differential can be summarized as follows:

- To change the direction of engine torque. ● SEE FIGURE 38–20.
- To allow the drive wheels to rotate at different speeds. ● SEE FIGURE 38–21.

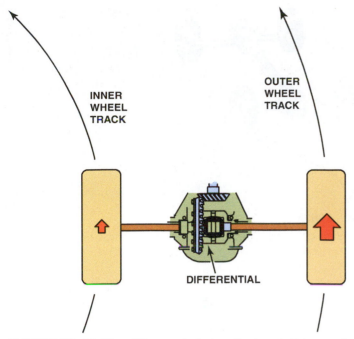

FIGURE 38-21 The difference between the travel distance of the drive wheels is controlled by the differential.

A differential is a mechanical addition and subtraction assembly. By splitting the engine torque to the drive wheels when the vehicle is turning a corner, the torque forces cause the side gear and pinion gears to subtract torque from one side and add torque to the opposite side. ● **SEE FIGURE 38-22.**

AXLE RATIO The final gear reduction in the drivetrain occurs in the differential assembly. The amount of torque a gear set delivers depends on the gear ratio between the drive pinion gear and the driven ring gear. The gear ratio of the final drive (differential) is called the **axle ratio.** To determine the axle ratio, divide the number of teeth of the ring gear (driven gear) by the number of teeth of the drive pinion gear (driving gear):

Ring gear (41 teeth)

Pinion gear (10 teeth)

= 4.10 (Axle ratio)

The higher the axle ratio number, the faster the engine rotates for each rotation of the drive wheels. To determine the axle ratio of a differential without having to remove the axle housing cover, simply follow these steps:

STEP 1 Hoist the vehicle safely.

STEP 2 Mark the rear tires with masking tape at 12 o'clock position.

STEP 3 Mark the driveshaft with masking tape.

STEP 4 Have an assistant hold one drive tire to keep it from moving and slowly rotate the other drive tire exactly 10 times while the assistant counts the driveshaft revolutions.

STEP 5 Multiply the driveshaft revolutions by 2 (except for a limited-slip differential), and then move the decimal

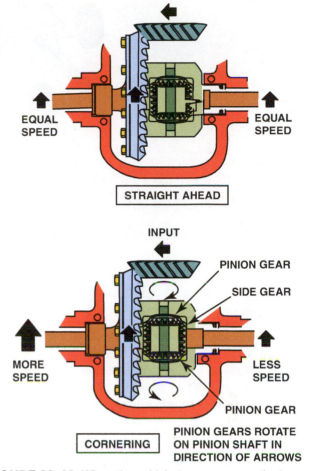

FIGURE 38-22 When the vehicle turns a corner, the inner wheel slows and the outer wheel increases in speed to compensate. This difference in rotational speed causes the pinion gears to "walk" around the slower side gear.

point one place to the left. For example, if 10 turns of the tire result in 18.5 turns of the driveshaft, that multiplied by 2 equals 37.0; then, moving the decimal point to the left one place equals a 3.70:1 gear ratio.

LIMITED SLIP DIFFERENTIALS When a vehicle equipped with a standard differential spins a tire, the opposite wheel does not receive enough torque to move the vehicle. A limited-slip differential distributes torque to both wheels equally or unequally, allowing the wheels to turn at the same or at different speeds. ● **SEE FIGURE 38-23.**

DIFFERENTIAL LUBRICANT All differentials use a hypoid gear set, which is a special design gear set and requires a lubricant that allows the gears to both roll and slide between their meshed teeth.

NOTE: Differential lubricant is called EP and contains sulfurized esters and organic sulfur phosphorous compounds, which gives the lubricant a strong pungent smell.

NOTE: Always check the *exact* specification before adding or replacing rear axle lubricant.

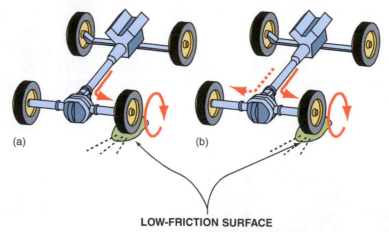

LOW-FRICTION SURFACE

FIGURE 38–23 (a) A two-wheel-drive vehicle equipped with a standard differential. (b) A two-wheel-drive vehicle equipped with a limited-slip differential.

FOUR-WHEEL DRIVE

PURPOSE AND FUNCTION Two-wheel-drive vehicles use engine torque to turn either the front or the rear wheels. A differential is required to allow the drive wheels to travel different distances and speeds while cornering or driving over bumps or dips in the road.

NOTE: The term 4 × 4 means a four-wheeled vehicle that has engine torque applied to all four wheels (four-wheel drive). A 4 × 2 means a four-wheeled vehicle that has engine torque applied to only two wheels (two-wheel drive).

Four-wheel-drive vehicles require more than just differentials at the front and rear axles. The front and the rear wheels of a four-wheel-drive vehicle also travel different distances and speeds whenever cornering or running over dips or rises in the road. A third center differential is used to allow for front-to-rear driveline speed variation.

TRANSFER CASE Engine torque from the transmission is applied directly to the rear differential through the transfer case. ● **SEE FIGURE 38–24.**

The transfer case permits the driver to select a low-speed, high-torque gear ratio inside the transfer case while in four-wheel drive. These positions and their meanings include:

- 4H four-wheel drive with no gear reduction in the transfer case.
- 4L four-wheel drive with gear reduction. Use of this position is usually restricted to low speeds on slippery surfaces.
- 2H two-wheel drive (rear wheels only) in high range

MODE SHIFT Either two-wheel drive or four-wheel drive may be selected. Many transfer cases also have a neutral position. The mode shift is achieved by the use of a floor-mounted lever to engage and disengage a clutch inside the transfer case. This shift is usually performed when the vehicle

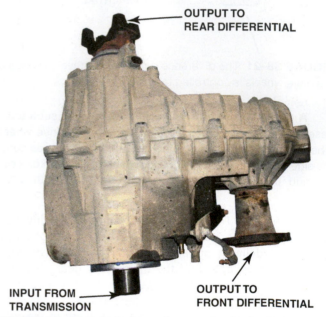

OUTPUT TO REAR DIFFERENTIAL

INPUT FROM TRANSMISSION

OUTPUT TO FRONT DIFFERENTIAL

FIGURE 38–24 A typical transfer case is attached to the output of the transmission and directs engine torque to the rear or to the front and rear differentials.

is stopped. However, new designs allow the mode shift to be performed under most driving conditions.

CAUTION: If the neutral position is selected, the vehicle can move even if the transmission is in the park position. Use the neutral position only when towing the vehicle. Check the owner's manual for details.

RANGE SHIFT A **low range** may be selected to deliver high torque at low speeds to the drive wheels. Low range usually provides a 2:1 to 3:1 gear reduction. High range (usually 1:1) simply transfers engine torque at the same speed as the output shaft of the transmission.

PART-TIME FOUR-WHEEL DRIVE In a part-time four-wheel vehicle, the front wheels must be able to be disengaged from the transfer case so they can be driven on hard surfaces (pavement) yet be locked when traveling on loose gravel or snow.

There are several different methods used to allow four-wheel drive on a part-time basis, including the following:

- **METHOD 1—Locking Hubs.** The transfer case also applies power to the front differential. Power is then applied to the front wheels through the drive axles to the **locking hubs.** In normal 4H driving on hard surfaces, the front hubs *must* be in the unlocked position. The front hubs are locked whenever driving on loose road surfaces to absorb and allow for the different tire speeds front to rear.

CAUTION: Failure to unlock the front wheel hubs while driving on a hard road surface can cause serious driveline vibrations and damage to driveshafts, U-joints, and bearings, as well as to the transfer case, transmission, and even the engine.

- **METHOD 2—Autolocking Hubs.** Another method of locking the hubs on a part-time four-wheel-drive system is with a clutch arrangement built into the hub assembly. Whenever driving on smooth, hard road surfaces, the hubs "free wheel" and allow the front wheels to rotate at different speeds from the rear wheels. When the speed difference between the wheels and the front drive axle is great, the hubs will automatically lock and allow engine torque to be applied to the front wheels. Automatic-locking hubs are unlocked by disengaging four-wheel drive at the transfer case and driving in reverse for several feet.

FULL-TIME FOUR-WHEEL DRIVE

This method uses a center differential to allow front and rear wheels to travel at different speeds under all operating conditions. Although this drivetrain design is the easiest to operate both on and off the road, the center differential can cause the vehicle to get stuck in mud or snow even though it is a four-wheel-drive vehicle. This is why many vehicles spin just one wheel when stuck on ice or snow. But if one rear wheel starts to spin, the vehicle may not move forward at all. ● SEE FIGURE 38–25.

ALL-WHEEL DRIVE

Some cars and light trucks are equipped with an all-wheel-drive system that uses a transfer case with a center differential and only one speed (high). Low-range gear reduction is not used. A viscous coupling is usually incorporated into the center differential to provide superior all-weather traction. Combined with a limited-slip differential in the rear, and sometimes also in the front, an all-wheel-drive system can provide ideal road traction under all driving conditions without any action by the driver.

TRANSFER CASE INSPECTION

All transfer cases require lubrication and the fluid level should be checked as part of routine service. Most transfer cases require automatic transmission fluid (ATF), but the correct fluid needed will depend on the exact make and model of the transfer case. Always check the identification tag on the transfer case itself. ● SEE FIGURES 38–26 AND 38–27.

FIGURE 38–26 An identification tag on the housing of a transfer case. This identification information is often needed to be sure that the correct parts or fluids are purchased.

FIGURE 38–25 The controls for the transfer case on a Chevrolet four-wheel-drive pickup truck.

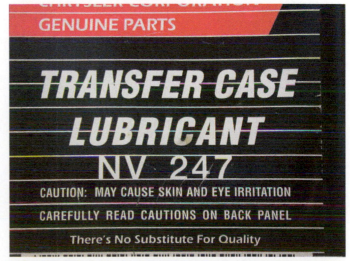

FIGURE 38–27 Some transfer cases require the use of special fluids. Always check service information for the exact fluid needed.

1. The clutch is used to connect and disconnect engine power to the transmission.
2. The clutch is needed to shift gears because engine power has to be stopped to change gears.
3. A transmission is used on a rear-wheel-drive vehicle and a transaxle is used in the front-wheel-drive vehicle.
4. A transaxle includes a final drive assembly, which is the name of the differential used in a transaxle.
5. Gear ratio is determined by dividing the number of teeth of the driven (output) gear by the number of teeth on the driving (input) gear.
6. Drive shafts use universal joints (U-joints) at the both ends to allow for the up and down movement of the rear axle during suspension movement.
7. Drive axle shafts use constant velocity joints (CV joints) that allow engine torque to be applied when the front wheels are being turned.
8. The differential allows engine torque to be applied to both drive axles, which rotate at varying speeds during cornering and while traveling over bumps and dips in the road.
9. Four-wheel-drive vehicles use three differentials; one each at the front and rear axles and one in between.

REVIEW QUESTIONS

1. What are the parts of a typical clutch assembly?
2. What happens when the driver depresses the clutch pedal?
3. If the driven gear has 36 teeth and the driving gear has 12 teeth, what is the gear ratio?
4. How do you determine the axle ratio without removing the housing cover?
5. What is the difference between four-wheel drive and all-wheel drive?

CHAPTER QUIZ

1. Which part is clamped between the pressure plate and the flywheel?
   a. Clutch disc
   b. Pilot bearing
   c. Throwout bearing
   d. Release bearing
2. The driving gear has 15 teeth and the driven gear has 29 teeth. Technician A says that the output gear will be going faster than the input gear. Technician B says the ratio is 3.86:1. Which technician is correct?
   a. Technician A only
   b. Technician B only
   c. Both technicians A and B
   d. Neither technician A nor B
3. Which part is splined to the clutch disc?
   a. Input shaft
   b. Countershaft (lay shaft)
   c. Cluster shaft
   d. Main gear
4. Which type of lubricant is usually *not* used in a manual transmission/ transaxle?
   a. Automatic transmission fluid (ATF)
   b. High-temperature chassis grease
   c. SAE 80W-90 gear lube
   d. Engine oil
5. The name most often used to describe the universal joints on a conventional rear-wheel-drive vehicle driveshaft is
   _____.
   a. Trunnion
   b. Cardan
   c. CV
   d. Spider
6. Which type of system uses a one-speed transfer case and a center differential with a viscous coupling?
   a. Part-time four-wheel drive
   b. Full-time four-wheel drive
   c. Full-time four-wheel drive with automatic locking front hubs
   d. All-wheel drive
7. What is the function of a clutch?
   a. To disconnect the engine from the transmission/transaxle to permit the engine to remain running when the vehicle is stopped
   b. To permit the transmission/transaxle to be shifted
   c. To connect and transmit engine torque to the transmission/transaxle
   d. All of the above
8. What is the purpose of a differential?
   a. To change the direction of engine torque
   b. To allow the drive wheels to rotate at different speeds
   c. Both a and b
   d. Neither a nor b
9. A drive shaft is also called a _____.
   a. Propeller shaft
   b. Prop shaft
   c. CV shaft
   d. Either a or b
10. What type of lubricant is used in transfer cases?
    a. Automatic transmission fluid or a special fluid
    b. Wheel bearing grease
    c. SAE 80W-90 gear lube
    d. Any of the above

chapter 39
AUTOMATIC TRANSMISSION AND TRANSAXLES

OBJECTIVES: After studying Chapter 39, the reader will be able to: • Prepare for the ASE Automatic Transmission/Transaxle (A2) certification test content area "A" (General transmission/transaxle service). • Describe the purpose of a torque converter clutch. • Explain the shift modes and when each is used. • Describe the operation of a planetary gearset. • Discuss how to replace the automatic transmission filter and pan gasket.

KEY TERMS: • Automatic transmission fluid (ATF) 360 • Creep 357 • Impeller 355 • Planet carrier 359 • Ring (annulus) gear 359 • Stator 355 • Sun gear 359 • Torque converter clutch (TCC) 358 • Turbine 355

BACKGROUND

Automatic transmissions were first used on a large scale in the early 1950s, and now about 85% of the vehicles in North America are so equipped. Unlike manual transmissions, most automatic transmissions do not actually "shift gears," but apply clutches (or bands) to hold or drive various elements of two or more planetary gear sets that provide different gear ratios. The history of automatic transmission goes back over 100 years. ● **SEE CHART 39–1** for a timeline for automatic transmissions. ● **SEE FIGURE 39–1.**

INTRODUCTION

Automatic transmissions and transaxles are constructed using many different components such as the following:

- Torque converter
- Fluid pump
- Gear sets
- Clutches and bands
- Speed sensors
- Shift control solenoids
- Valve body assembly

All of the above components are located on or inside an aluminum housing that attaches to the engine.

TORQUE CONVERTERS

PURPOSE AND FUNCTION The torque converter is located between the engine and the transmission/transaxle and performs the following functions:

1. Transmits and multiplies engine torque.
2. Acts as a clutch between the engine and the transmission/transaxle.
3. Allows slippage, which makes it possible for the transmission to be engaged in gear even when the vehicle and wheels are stopped.

PARTS OF A TORQUE CONVERTER A torque converter is a doughnut-shaped assembly that is located between the engine and the automatic transmission or transaxle. ● **SEE FIGURE 39–2.**

The three major parts of the torque converter include:

1. **Impeller.** The **impeller** is the driving member inside the torque converter housing and is driven by the engine.
2. **Turbine.** The **turbine** is located on the engine side of the converter. The impeller vanes pick up fluid in the converter housing and direct it toward the turbine. Fluid flow drives the turbine, and when the flow between the impeller and the turbine is adequate, the turbine rotates and turns the transmission input shaft.
3. **Stator.** A torque converter also contains the **stator**, or reactor, which is a reaction member mounted on a one-way clutch. ● **SEE FIGURE 39–3.**

YEAR	BRAND NAME	NUMBER OF FORWARD SPEEDS	DESCRIPTION
1904	Sturtevant Brothers	2	2 forward speeds. Gear ratios automatically shifted by flyweights
1908	Ford	2	Model T (2 speeds plus reverse using a planetary gear set shifted with foot pedals)
1934	REO & GM[a]	2	A semiautomatic transmission with a foot clutch
1939	Chrysler Corp[b]	3	First to use "fluid coupling" (Hy-drive) with a manual three speed transmission
1940	Oldsmobile	4	Hydra-Matic unit used a fluid coupling plus three planetary gear sets giving four forward speeds plus reverse. (Other vehicles that used this transmission are: Nash, Cadillac, Pontiac, Bentley, Mercedes Benz, and Rolls-Royce)
1948	Buick	2	First transmission to use a fully automatic torque converter (with fluid coupling and a planetary gear set). Named the "DynaFlow" (1949–1967)
1949	Packard	2	First vehicle to have a lock-up torque converter (Ultramatic transmission)
1950	Chevrolet	2	Powerglide (1950–1973)
1950	Borg-Warner	3	Developed 3-speed torque converter transmissions for American Motors[c], Ford Motors (Ford-O-Matic), and Studebaker (1950–1968)
1953	Chrysler Corp[b]	2	First 2-speed torque converter transmission called the Power-Flite (1953–1961).
1956	Chrysler Corp[b]	3	First 3-speed torque converter transmission called the Torque-Flite (1956–1977). First was a cast iron case, then changed to aluminum in 1962
1956	General Motors[a]	4	Introduced the "Jet-A-Way" unit. Used two fluid couplings to improve shift quality. First transmission to use a "Park" position (1956–1969)
1964	General Motors[a]	2	2-Speed transmission (Jet-A-Way) (1964–1969)
1979	General Motors[a]	3	First transmission to use an electronically activated torque converter clutch (lock-up torque converter) (THM-200C)(1979–1987)
1980	Ford[d]	4	First overdrive transmission (AOD)(1980–1992)
1989	Chrysler Corp	4	First computer-controlled transmission (A604/41TE) (1989–Current)
2002	BMW	6	First to introduce a 6-speed transmission. (2001–Current)
2003	Mercedes	7	First to introduce a 7-speed transmission (2003–Current)
2007	Lexus	8	First to introduce an 8-speed transmission (2007–Current)
2007	Mercedes	7	Introduced an automatic transmission that replaced the torque converter with a lock-up clutch

[a] General Motors Corp. includes: Chevrolet, Oldsmobile, Buick, Cadillac, Pontiac, and Chevrolet/GMC trucks.
[b] Chrysler Corp. includes: Dodge, Plymouth, Chrysler, DeSoto, Jeep, and Dodge/Plymouth Trucks.
[c] American Motors Corp. includes: Nash, Rambler, Jeep, and Pacer.
[d] Ford Motor Co. includes: Ford, Lincoln, Mercury, and Ford Trucks.

CHART 39–1

Automatic transmission use, while available in some models much sooner, really increased in numbers in the 1950s.

The vanes used in each of the three elements of a torque converter are curved to increase the angle of the fluid flow. This also increases the force exerted by the fluid and improves the hydraulic advantage. The outlet side of the impeller vanes accelerates the fluid as it leaves the impeller to increase torque transfer to the turbine.

OPERATION OF A TORQUE CONVERTER

Inside a torque converter are two elements facing each other, which act like two fans pointing toward each other. Air pushed by the powered fan causes the blades of the nonpowered fan to rotate. The powered fan is the converter impeller and the nonpowered fan is the converter turbine. The transmission fluid is the air that is being forced to turn the nonpowered fan.

● **SEE FIGURE 39–4.**

The fluid-only connection between the impeller and the turbine allows for absorption of sudden and harsh shocks in speed and/or torque. The curve of the stator vanes is opposite in direction to the curve of the impeller and turbine vanes. Since the stator is located between the impeller and turbine, it changes the direction of the fluid as it leaves the turbine, and thereby multiplies the torque from the impeller. Torque converters are single-piece, welded and balanced assemblies.

A torque converter is capable of transferring some engine torque to the transmission with the engine at idle speed,

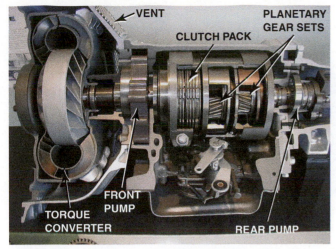

FIGURE 39-1 A cutaway of a Chrysler Power Flight 2-speed automatic transmission used in the 1950s.

FIGURE 39-2 A torque converter looks like a metal doughnut and takes the place of a clutch in an automatic transmission or transaxle.

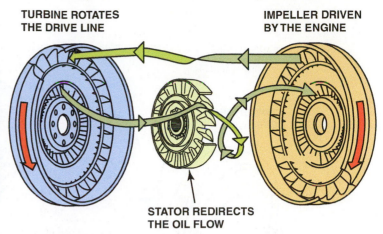

FIGURE 39-3 A torque converter is made from three parts: The impeller is located at the transmission end, attached to the housing, and is driven by the engine. The turbine is located at the engine side and is driven by the fluid flow from the impeller and drives the input shaft of the transmission. The stator redirects the flow to improve efficiency and multiply torque.

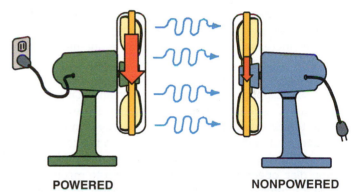

FIGURE 39-4 Two fans can be used to show how fluid, or air in the case of fans instead of automatic transmission fluid, can be used to transfer energy. If one fan is operating, the blades of a second fan will be rotated by the flow of air past the fan that is unplugged, causing the blades to rotate.

which results in some vehicle movement when the brakes are released. This slight movement is called **creep.**

TORQUE CONVERTER FLEXPLATE

The torque converter is typically bolted to a thin metal disc called a flexplate. The center of the flexplate often has a pilot indention for the nose of the converter, and the flexplate itself is bolted to the rear flange of the engine's crankshaft.

The flexplate replaces the heavy flywheel used with a manual transmission. An important function of a flywheel is to smooth out engine pulsations and dampen vibrations. An automatic transmission does not require a conventional flywheel because the weight of the torque converter provides enough mass to dampen engine vibrations. ● SEE FIGURE 39-5.

LOCKUP TORQUE CONVERTER

Even the most efficient torque converters slip 8% to 12% during operation.

FIGURE 39-5 A torque converter is bolted to the flexplate, which is attached and rotates with the engine crankshaft (TCC).

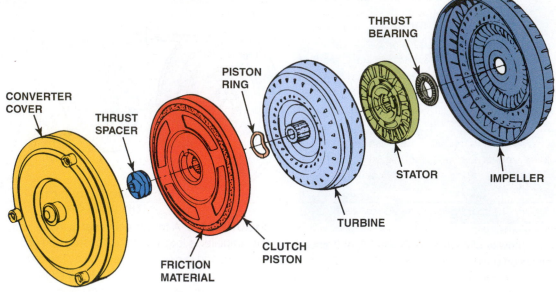

FIGURE 39–6 An expanded view of a typical torque converter assembly showing the torque converter clutch (TCC).

Eliminating torque converter slippage can improve fuel economy approximately 4% to 5% during freeway cruising. With the increased emphasis on fuel economy and low exhaust emissions for late model vehicles, this became an important goal for automotive engineers. An additional benefit to reducing slippage is a reduction of transmission operating temperature, which increases transmission life expectancy. Lockup torque converters reduce slippage by using a **torque converter clutch (TCC)** to lock the turbine to the cover (shell). Similar to a clutch for a manual transmission, a TCC uses a friction disc operated by a hydraulic piston to mechanically couple the turbine to the converter (cover/shell). Engaging the clutch creates mechanical connection between the engine and transmission, resulting in a direct 1:1 drive ratio without slippage. ● **SEE FIGURE 39–6.**

- **Neutral.** In the neutral position, no torque is being transmitted through the automatic transmission/transaxle. In this position the engine can be started by the driver.

- **Overdrive (OD).** The OD is the normal position for the shift selector for most driving conditions. This position allows the transmission or transaxle to shift through all forward gears as needed for the best fuel economy and lowest exhaust emissions.

- **Drive (D).** The D position includes the overdrive ratios in most vehicles. If there is an overdrive shift mode, however, then D is used to provide all forward gears except overdrive. Use this position when driving in hilly areas or when towing with a vehicle equipped with an overdrive selection.

SHIFT MODES

Most automatic transmissions and transaxles include the following shift modes. ● **SEE FIGURE 39–7.**

- **Park.** In the park position, the output shaft is locked to the case of the transmission/transaxle, which keeps the vehicle from moving. No power is transmitted through the unit so the engine can remain running while the vehicle is held stationary. In the park position:
  1. The engine can be started by the driver.
  2. To move the shifter out of the park position on a late-model vehicle, the brake pedal must be depressed to release the transmission shift interlock.

- **Reverse.** The reverse gear selector position is used to move the vehicle in reverse. Reverse usually uses a lower gear ratio than any of the forward gears.

FIGURE 39–7 The gear selector is often called the "PRNDL," pronounced "prindle," regardless of the actual letters or numbers used.

- **Third (3).** In third position the transmission/transaxle will upshift normally to third gear but will not upshift to a higher gear. When the third (3) position is selected while driving in a higher gear, the transmission will downshift into third if the vehicle speed is low enough to prevent the engine from being overrevved. This gear selection is used for the gentle grades at a moderate vehicle speed.
- **Second (2).** The second position is used for slowing the vehicle while descending long grades. In this gear selection, the vehicle speed is controlled and the engine speed is increased to provide engine compression braking. This gear selection is used for the gentle grades at a slower vehicle speed.
- **First (1 or Low).** The first (or low) position is used for slowing the vehicle while descending long grades. In this gear selection, the vehicle speed is controlled and the engine speed is increased to provide engine compression breaking. This gear selection is used for the steepest grades at the lowest possible speed.

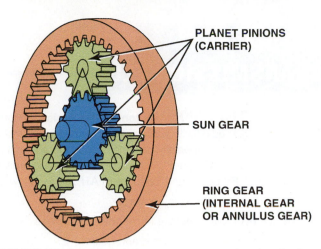

FIGURE 39–8 A typical planetary gear set showing the terms that are used to describe each member.

PLANETARY GEAR SETS

PURPOSE AND FUNCTION In a manual transmission, different gear ratios are obtained by sliding the gears into mesh. However, torque flow must be momentarily interrupted (accomplished by using a clutch) before the gears are shifted. With an automatic transmission there is no driver-operated clutch, so gear shifts are not made by sliding gears into mesh. Most automatic transmissions use a planetary gear set system that does not require manual gear shifting or an interruption of torque flow to change gear ratios.

PARTS OF A PLANETARY GEAR SET A simple planetary gear set consists of three primary components.

- Sun gear
- Planet carrier (including planet pinion gears)
- Ring (annulus) gear

The **sun gear** gets its name from its position at the center of the gear set. The **planet carrier** holds the pinion gears, also known as planet gears, which revolve around the sun gear. The planet carrier assembly is commonly referred to simply as "the carrier." The outermost member of the gear set is the **ring gear,** the internal type with teeth inside. The ring gear is sometimes called an annulus or internal gear. The pinion gears are in simultaneous mesh with both the sun gear and the ring gear.

OPERATION OF A PLANETARY GEAR SET Different gear ratios are obtained in automatic transmissions by either holding or driving the three elements of the planetary gear sets in various combinations. Transmission clutches and bands provide the driving and holding effects for the planetary gear set. ● **SEE FIGURE 39–8.**

? FREQUENTLY ASKED QUESTION

What Do All the Letters and Numbers Mean in Transmission Designations?

The numbers and letters usually mean the following:

- **Number of forward speeds.** The number of forward speeds may include four, five, or six (such as GM 4T60-E four speed unit).
- **Front-wheel drive or rear-wheel drive.** The letter **T** usually means *transverse* (front-wheel-drive transaxle) such as the Chrysler 41-TE; the **L** means *longitudinal* (rear-wheel-drive transmission) such as the General Motors 6L80; and the **R** means *rear-wheel drive* such as the Ford 5R55E.
- **Electronically controlled.** The letter **E** is often used to indicate that the unit is electronically controlled, and **M** or **H** is used to designate older mechanically (hydraulically) controlled units. All automatic transmissions built since the early 1990s are electronically controlled; therefore, **E** is often included in the designation of newer designs of transmission or transaxles.
- **Torque rating.** The torque rating is usually designated by a number where the higher the number, the higher the amount of torque that the unit is designed to handle. The transmission torque ratings are "relative" specifications. For example, in a GM 6L80-E used in trucks and vans equipped with a V-8 engine, the torque rating is 80, whereas the much smaller transmission/transaxle used with four-cylinder engines might have a torque rating of 40. Always check service information for the exact transmission designation for the vehicle being studied or serviced.

AUTOMATIC TRANSMISSION FLUID

FIGURE 39–10 The "add" mark on most automatic transmission dipsticks indicates the level is down 0.5 quart (0.5 liter). Always follow the instructions stamped or printed on the dipstick.

PURPOSE AND FUNCTION

Automatic transmission fluid (ATF) is a highly refined oil with a viscosity similar to SAE 20W-20 oil. It is red in color and specially designed for use in automatic transmissions. Newer ATFs are lower in viscosity and are similar to SAE 0W-10 oil. Purposes and functions of ATF are as follows:

- Transfers power in torque converter
- Provides hydraulic pressure in clutches and servos
- Lubricates bearings, bushings, and gears
- Transfers heat to cool transmission parts
- Provides the correct friction for clutch and band application
- Acts as the medium to control transmission shifting by traveling through passageways, acting on valves, and being directed by solenoids

FLUID CHECK

The first step in diagnosing any problem is to test drive the vehicle and verify the customer complaint (concern). Before test driving the vehicle, check the level and condition of the automatic transmission/transaxle fluid. Follow the procedure for checking the level as published in the owner's manual or factory information. ● **SEE FIGURES 39–9 AND 39–10.**

The typical procedure for checking automatic transmission fluid level includes the following steps: (Check service information for the exact procedure to be followed.)

STEP 1 Start the engine, except for Honda/Acura vehicles which specify that the ATF be checked with the engine off.

STEP 2 Be sure that the ATF is at normal operating temperature. This may require that the vehicle be driven for several miles.

FIGURE 39–9 A typical automatic transmission dipstick (fluid level indicator). Many use a clip to keep it from being forced upward due to pressure changes inside the automatic transmission. A firm seal also helps keep water from getting into the fluid, which can cause severe damage to the clutches and bands.

STEP 3 Park the vehicle on a level surface. Start the engine and shift the transmission through each gear, allowing engagement in each gear, then place back into the park position.

STEP 4 Clean the area around the dipstick to help prevent dirt from falling into the filler tube when the dipstick is removed.

CAUTION: Be sure any transmission filler cap, plug, or dipstick is installed tightly. Water contamination of the transmission fluid will eventually destroy frictional linings of apply devices.

STEP 5 Remove the dipstick and wipe it off with a shop cloth.

STEP 6 Reinsert the dipstick and then remove it again. Check the level. The "add" mark indicates that the level is a half quart (liter) low. Results and possible causes include the following:

- If the fluid level is low, add the specified fluid until the proper level is achieved before test driving the vehicle.
- If the level is too high, this can cause the fluid to become aerated, meaning that the fluid becomes filled with air bubbles. When the fluid is aerated, the transmission or transaxle cannot shift properly. The fluid should be red, although some highly friction-modified ATFs are normally light brown, which is normal and not a cause for alarm.
- If the color of the fluid is dark brown or black, then the fluid has been overheated.
- Smell the fluid. It should have a "clean petroleum" smell. If it smells "burned" or rancid, then this indicates that the fluid has been overheated and will require replacement.
- If the fluid is milky, this usually means that engine coolant has entered the fluid, usually through a fault with the ATF cooler located in the radiator.

STEP 7 Insert the dipstick into the transmission/transaxle and remove. Allow a few drops to fall onto a paper towel. Then take the end of the dipstick and place it into a container of new ATF and allow the same number of drips to fall onto another section of the paper towel. Allow to sit for ten minutes.

- If the fluid expands to the same size as the new fluid, then it has maintained its lubricity and viscosity.
- If the fluid fails to expand to the same diameter as the new fluid, this means that the fluid has lost some of its lubricity and has increased in viscosity. A fluid change would then be indicated.

- If a dark stain shows on the white paper towel, this means that it is contaminated with clutch material or varnish from oxidized fluid and requires further diagnosis.
- If the stain is a foamy pink, then this may indicate engine coolant in the transmission/transaxle.

STEP 8 Shut the engine off and replace the dipstick, being sure it is fully seated.

NOTE: Many newer transmissions/transaxles do not use a dipstick. The fluid level is usually checked similar to how the fluid in a manual transmission/transaxle is checked by removing a plug in the side of the case. In some vehicles the fluid level can be checked using a scan tool. Check service information for the exact methods to use to check the ATF level.

FLUID LEAK CHECK

VISUAL INSPECTION To locate a leak from an automatic transmission/transaxle, the first step is to perform a thorough visual inspection. Start by checking the fluid level.

Perform a visual inspection using the following steps.

STEP 1 Use a trouble light and start the visual inspection under the hood and look for signs of fluid leakage on the top of the unit. Because fluids flow downward due to gravity, the fluid will be most likely seen from underneath the vehicle; however, the source could be at or the near the top.

STEP 2 Hoist the vehicle safely and look for the highest and most forward place where fluid is seen. ● **SEE FIGURE 39–11.**

FIGURE 39–11 Sometimes the location of a transmission fluid leak is easy to see, but with others it can be difficult to find the exact location. Look closely at places where O-rings seals or gaskets are used, as these are the most common areas where fluid leaks occur.

FIGURE 39–12 A black light being used to locate the source of an automatic transmission fluid leak.

DYE TESTING Often the exact location of a fluid leak is difficult to locate. Using a dye designed for ATF and a black light is an effective method to locate ATF leaks. To check for leaks using a dye, perform the following steps:

STEP 1 Add a small bottle of dye that is designed for use in ATF into the dipstick tube using a transmission funnel.

CAUTION: Do not use dye designed for use in coolant or air conditioning systems or severe harm can occur to the automatic transmission/transaxle.

STEP 2 Drive the vehicle until the fluid has reached normal operating temperature.

STEP 3 Safely hoist the vehicle.

STEP 4 Using a black light, look for the highest and most forward place where a greenish stain appears. This is the source of the leak. ● **SEE FIGURE 39–12.**

IN-VEHICLE SERVICE

PAN REMOVAL Check service information for the exact procedure to follow when removing the pan. Some transaxles are equipped with a side pan that may or may not need to be removed when serving the assembly.

CAUTION: Always wear protective rubber gloves to protect the hands from the effects of used automatic transmission fluid, which can affect the skin. Also, always wear eye protection.

The usual procedure includes the following steps:

STEP 1 Hoist the vehicle safely.

STEP 2 Place a large drain pan under the transmission/transaxle pan.

STEP 3 Loosen all of the fasteners except for those at one end. Allow the pan to drop down slightly at one end

FIGURE 39–13 Draining the fluid from an automatic transaxle by allowing the fluid to flow into a container after most of the retaining bolts have been removed.

allowing fluid to drain into the drain pan. ● **SEE FIGURE 39–13.**

STEP 4 After the fluid has stopped flowing from the pan, carefully remove the last retaining bolts, slowly lower the pan, and allow any remaining fluid to flow into the drain pan.

STEP 5 Dispose of or recycle the used automatic transmission fluid according to state or local laws.

STEP 6 Inspect the inside of the pan for excessive friction material and wear metals (such as lead and copper from bushings). Use a magnet to check for steel particles, which would indicate serious wear to major components. ● **SEE FIGURE 39–14.**

NOTE: The presence of metal particles in the pan of an automatic transmission/transaxle does not necessarily mean that a part(s) has failed or needs to be replaced. Some wear is normal. If there are a lot of metallic particles in the pan, then this may be an indication of severe

FIGURE 39–14 This is a normal amount of wear material in the bottom of an automatic transmission pan. Use a magnet and check for any steel particles which could indicate serious transmission wear or damage.

gear failure that may require replacement. Use a magnet to check for steel particles. Ask the advice of an experienced transmission expert if in doubt about whether the wear should be considered "normal."

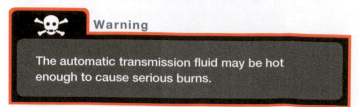

☠ Warning

The automatic transmission fluid may be hot enough to cause serious burns.

FILTER REPLACEMENT Check service information for the exact procedure to follow when replacing the filter. Most are retained by a clip or a bolt. ● **SEE FIGURE 39–15.** After the filter assembly has been installed, clean the pan and install a new pan gasket. ● **SEE FIGURE 39–16.** Lower the vehicle and refill the unit with the specified fluid to the correct level.

FILTER RETAINING CLIP

FIGURE 39–15 Always check that the filter is secured by a clip or other fastener to keep it from dropping out of location.

FIGURE 39–16 In this case, the cork-rubber gasket is glued to the pan and is ready to be installed. The retaining bolts need to be tightened in sequence, but be aware that overtightening will cause a leak. Also, some manufacturers recommend using only an RTV sealer, but never use an RTV sealer and a gasket together.

1. Most automatic transmissions do not actually "shift gears," but apply clutches or bands to hold a part of a planetary gear set to achieve different ratios.

2. The torque converter is located between the engine and the transmission/transaxle and transmits and multiplies engine torque, plus acts as a clutch between the engine and the transmission/transaxle.

3. The shift modes include park, reverse, neutral, drive, and one or more other gear selections depending on the vehicle.

4. The three elements of a planetary gear set include the sun gear, planet carrier, and ring gear.

5. Fluid leaks can be detected by visual inspection or by using a dye and a black light.

6. Automatic transmission service includes draining the automatic transmission fluid and replacing the filter and the pan gasket.

REVIEW QUESTIONS

1. What is the purpose of the torque converter?
2. What are the three members of a planetary gear set?
3. What are the shift modes (gear selector positions) for most automatic transmissions?
4. What steps are involved in draining the automatic transmission and filter replacement?

CHAPTER QUIZ

1. A typical automatic transmission includes:
   a. Planetary gear sets
   b. Clutches or bands
   c. Torque converter
   d. All of the above

2. Which part takes the place of a clutch in an automatic transmission?
   a. Planetary gear sets
   b. Clutches or bands
   c. Torque converter
   d. All of the above

3. The torque converter _____.
   a. Rotates at the same speed as the engine
   b. Allows the vehicle to creep when the brakes are released
   c. Includes a clutch to improve fuel economy
   d. All of the above

4. A planetary gear set includes a _____.
   a. Torque converter
   b. Sun gear
   b. Clutch
   c. Band

5. What does the "T" mean in the designation 41TE?
   a. Transmission
   b. Transverse
   c. Torque
   d. Tough

6. What color is new automatic transmission fluid (ATF)?
   a. Red
   b. Blue
   c. Yellow
   d. Clear (like water)

7. The "add" mark on an automatic transmission dipstick means _____.
   a. Two quarts (two liters)
   b. One quart (one liter)
   c. One-half quart (half liter)
   d. Quarter of a quart (quarter liter)

8. Automatic transmission fluid leaks can be found using a black light if _____.
   a. The fluid level is overfilled
   b. The fluid level is at least a quart (liter) low
   c. Dye is added to the fluid
   d. A rear-wheel-drive automatic transmission is being checked

9. What has to be removed to replace the filter on most automatic transmission/transaxles?
   a. Transmission pan
   b. Torque converter
   c. Drive shaft or drive axle shaft
   d. All of the above

10. Two technicians are discussing inspection of the transmission pan. Technician A says that some friction material at the bottom of the pan is normal. Technician B says that if any metal parts stick to a magnet then further investigation is needed to determine the cause. Which technician is correct?
    a. Technician A only
    b. Technician B only
    c. Both technicians A and B
    d. Neither technician A nor B

USED VEHICLE AND PRE-DELIVERY INSPECTIONS

OBJECTIVES: **After studying Chapter 40, the reader should be able to:** • Discuss the condition ratings used by many used-vehicle information websites. • Describe how to carefully inspect a used vehicle. • Explain how to purchase a used vehicle. • Describe how to best sell your used vehicle. • Describe the steps and procedures used to prepare a new vehicle for delivery to the customer.

KEY TERMS: • Detailing 365 • Dealer retail value 364 • Halderman's Laws 365 • Reconditioning 365 • Pre-delivery inspection (PDI) 368 • Trade-in (wholesale) value 364

VEHICLE VALUE RATINGS

NEW VEHICLE COST A new vehicle can be expensive, but a buyer can select the exact model, color, and options desired. The cost of a new vehicle to a dealer is generally 10% to 20% less than the "sticker price." However, the price of a used vehicle can vary by thousands of dollars depending upon the vehicle's condition, its age, accessories, and true value. These values include the following.

DEALER RETAIL VALUE The highest value of a vehicle is called the **dealer retail value.** This price is usually paid at a dealer and usually includes a warranty. The listed retail book value is average, which means that as many vehicles are sold above the indicated price as below.

PRIVATE PARTY VALUE This value reflects the price that a buyer is willing to pay to a willing private owner of a vehicle. Because a private individual cannot offer service or any guarantee, this value is less than dealer retail value and usually higher than the price that the owner could receive from a dealer as a trade-in.

TRADE-IN (WHOLESALE) VALUE The **trade-in value,** also called **wholesale price,** is generally 60% to 80% of the retail value and is the price that dealers pay for used vehicles. These vehicles usually need some repairs and/or cleaning and the difference between retail and wholesale reflects the cost of repairs and a profit for the selling dealer. Dealers always want to buy vehicles as low as possible and sell for as much money as possible.

These values are average, which means that some vehicles will sell for more or less than listed values. All of these values assume that the vehicles are in clean condition without major mechanical or body damage. If a vehicle needs mechanical or body repair, the value is reduced by the amount of these needed items.

Values are available at:

- www.edmunds.com
- www.kbb.com
- Other websites and forums

? FREQUENTLY ASKED QUESTION

How Much Does Condition Affect the Value?

The condition of a vehicle is a major part of the value. This is the reason why it is important to carefully inspect any used vehicle to check for any and all damage or faults. The value difference between outstanding and poor can be many thousands of dollars.

Condition is often expressed in the following categories:

- **Excellent (Outstanding)** This means that the vehicle is free of any body or mechanical faults and is clean both inside and outside.
- **Good (Clean)** Some normal wear, and may need a light reconditioning.
- **Fair** May need mechanical or appearance reconditioning.
- **Poor** Several mechanical or appearance problems.
- ● **SEE FIGURE 40–1**

FIGURE 40–1 A vehicle in poor condition may not be worth purchasing regardless of the price. The wise vehicle owner uses a car cover or tries to keep the vehicle in a garage to help prevent damage to the paint and interior due to the effect of the sun and other hazards.

FIGURE 40–2 Rain tends to make all vehicles look shiny and new even though the paint may be faded.

HALDERMAN'S LAWS

It is important that a buyer know the condition of the vehicle because it is very important to the overall value of a vehicle. Based on years of experience buying and selling vehicles, consider the following to get a good vehicle for the least amount of money. I call these items **Halderman's Laws:**

1. **Try to avoid buying a vehicle at night.** Bright lights often hide differences in paint, and therefore, would hide evidence of accident damage. Bright lights make every vehicle look good because the shadows tend to hide rusted areas and the reflected lights make the paint shiny.

2. **Try to avoid buying a vehicle when it is raining.** Rain water on any vehicle usually makes the paint look shinier than it is and any differences in paint color are difficult to detect. For example, if a door had been repainted as a result of an accident, the rain would tend to hide this difference in paint color. ● **SEE FIGURE 40–2.**

3. **Buy dirty—sell clean.** No one wants other people's dirt; therefore, a clean vehicle can be worth hundreds of dollars more than a dirty vehicle. If buying a dirty used vehicle, remember that you should pay less to allow for cleaning supplies and time or expense to have it cleaned. If selling your vehicle, be certain it is clean inside and out. Cleaning a vehicle is called **detailing** (cleaning every detail of the inside and outside of the vehicle). Another term used is reconditioning. **Reconditioning** means that the vehicle is completely cleaned inside and out including under the hood and in the trunk, plus a complete mechanical condition restoration to industry standards.

4. **Buy as loaded as possible.** Items such as antilock brakes (ABS), navigation system, heated seats, and other accessories add to the value of a vehicle and make owning and driving more enjoyable, plus adding to its resale value. You may or may not want or need some of the features, but the next owner might, making the vehicle easier to sell.

5. **Check everything.** Open and close all windows, work every accessory.

6. **Try not to get emotional!** This is the most difficult. If you get emotional over a particular vehicle, you are more likely to overlook its faults and end up paying too much.

STEPS TO FOLLOW

When shopping to purchase a used vehicle, include the following steps:

STEP 1   Determine what price range and type of vehicle meets your needs and wants (your wants are not necessarily what you need).

STEP 2   Become familiar with prices and values by checking average asking prices on websites, newspapers, or used-vehicle guides.

STEP 3 Shop for the best or newest vehicle in your price range.

STEP 4 Have your selected vehicle inspected by a competent technician, after leaving a deposit.

STEP 5 Note any suggested work to the seller and try to convince the seller to do any necessary repairs.

QUESTIONS TO ASK THE SELLER When calling or looking at a vehicle being offered for sale by a private owner, ask the following questions:

- Why are they selling the vehicle? (This may be because they did not want to fix a major problem.)
- How long have they owned the vehicle? (Maybe they just buy and sell vehicles to make money.)
- Ask if they know of any faults.
- Ask to see that the title is clear of any liens (loans on the vehicle).
- Ask who the driver was. (Maybe this is not an adult-owned vehicle and knowing this might lead to seeing if it has been abused or modified.)
- Ask if it has been in an accident or has had any body repairs.

INSPECTION ITEMS TO CHECK For most buyers, having a professional service technician look over a vehicle is a wise decision. While this is an expense, the cost involved is a good investment because buying a vehicle that needs a lot of work to correct hidden faults can be even more expensive.

- **Body** Look at the vehicle from a distance to detect waves in the body panels (evidence of major body repairs caused by accidents or severe rust). Start at the front of the vehicle and look closely (high and low) for chips, rust, and scratches. You may not wish to purchase the vehicle after this close inspection.
  ● **SEE FIGURE 40–3.**
- **Under Hood** There should be no visible oily areas or excessive corrosion on the battery. For further checks, consult a competent technician. Watch out for a spotlessly clean and shiny engine compartment area. This may mean the engine has been repainted and then sprayed with clear lacquer (a method used by some dealers to make the engines look better than new). Therefore, looks alone do not tell the whole story. Start the engine. You should not hear or see anything unusual such as knocking or smoke.
- **Interior** Check the following inside the vehicle:
  - Sit behind the wheel, start the engine, and turn the steering wheel. If the steering wheel moves more than 2" (1" in either direction from the center) without moving the front tires, major steering components may be need to be replaced.
  - Check the condition of the seats and carpet (front and rear) and the pedal pads on the brake and/ or clutch pedals. Does the wear seem excessive for the mileage?

(a)

(b)

FIGURE 40–3 (a) The left side of a lift gate on an SUV shows a wide gap. (b) The right side of the same lift gate on the passenger side shows a very small gap. This shows that this vehicle may have been in an accident and not properly repaired.

- Check that all of the following work correctly:
  1. Seat belts
  2. Lighter or 12-volt outlets (you may want to plug in a cell phone or MP3 player)
  3. Heater and air conditioning
  4. Rear defogger
  5. Cruise control
  6. All windows roll up and down

 TECH TIP

Look as if You Were Waxing a Vehicle
Remember the last time you washed or waxed your vehicle and noticed all the new dents and rust you hadn't noticed before?

Look at the Lower Part of the Body

Most used-vehicle dealers know that many inexperienced vehicle buyers will tend to look at the upper parts on the vehicle such as the roof top of the hood and trunk. An experienced vehicle buyer will look down low on the body panels behind the wheels, looking for rust, stone chip damage, and other faults. Always check all parts of the vehicle or have someone else help you look it over.

7. Door locks, radio, and CD player
8. All lights (inside and out) and turn signals
9. Windshield wipers and washers
10. Horn

- **Trunk** The general condition of the trunk usually reflects the general condition of the vehicle. Check for the spare tire condition, the jack and the jack handle (everything necessary to change a tire), and the trunk lock. If the trunk area is dirty then it is likely that the other aspects of vehicle maintenance and care have not been routinely performed.

TEST DRIVING

Any vehicle should be test driven before purchase. During the test drive observe the following:

1. Drive past parked vehicles or buildings with the vehicle's windows down. Any abnormal or strange noises are more easily heard reflected from solid objects during driving, turning, and braking.
2. Drive the vehicle on as many different road surfaces as possible checking for noises or handling problems.
3. Drive the vehicle at both low and highway speeds.
4. Test the brakes from both low and highway speeds.
5. Turn around into a driveway noticing any unusual noises from the suspension while driving up and over raised driveway approaches.
6. Test all accessories while driving, including cruise control, wipers, and washers.
7. Check the shift points of the automatic transmission. The transmission should shift smoothly and quickly at both low and higher speeds.
8. While driving at highway speeds, check for excessive wind noise around the doors and windows with the radio or sound system off.

When to Buy or Sell?

Unfortunately, the best time of the year to buy is not the best time to sell and vice versa. An interesting point—most people tend to "think" about six weeks ahead. Therefore, "spring" and "winter" come early to vehicle buyers. The general trends are as follows:

1. Thanksgiving through about February 15th—The lowest vehicle prices because of the lowest demand.
2. February 15th through April (depending on the "break" in the weather)—Rapidly rising demand as prices peak due to high school graduation and vacation plans. (Remember, six weeks ahead.)
3. May through August—Generally steady or slight decease in price as models become older.
4. Labor Day through Thanksgiving—Steady decline in price as new models are introduced and winter nears.

COMPLETING THE PURCHASE

Before completing the purchase, double-check that everything is working as designed. Before signing a check, a lease, or a loan application, consider performing the following:

- Consider checking the vehicle through a vehicle identification research company such as Car Fax (www.carfax.com) to see if the vehicle has been involved in a serious accident or other conditions that could reduce its value.
- Ask for a written receipt for the amount of the deposit and the remaining balance due.
- Verify that the title to the vehicle is clear of any loans or liens.
- Get the owners full name and address and contact information.
- Record the vehicle identification number (VIN). This can be used to verify the model year.
- Check that the title is clear and able to be transferred into your name.
- Make arrangements to when change of ownership will take place and where. Be prepared to have license plates to be able to legally drive the vehicle after taking possession.

HOW TO SELL YOUR OLD VEHICLE

GET THE VEHICLE READY TO SELL Before trying to sell a vehicle yourself or even thinking about trading it to a dealer for a new or newer vehicle, be sure that the vehicle is clean. Some repairs may not be worth having repaired and in this case let the buyers know what is wrong and then reduce the price accordingly. If the vehicle needs new tires, consider not replacing them and instead let the buyers know that it needs new tires.

Some items to consider include the following:

- Wash the vehicle inside and outside.
- Remove all personal items such as sun glasses and MP3 players.
- Remove everything from the trunk or rear area except what came with the vehicle. This would include road safety items or sports equipment.
- Have the engine compartment cleaned. Prospective buyers may not know what they are looking at under the hood but they do not like seeing dirt.
- Consider having the vehicle professionally cleaned.

RESEARCH THE MARKET Check websites and newspapers to help determine the value of your vehicle. Try to price your vehicle right the first time to help ensure a faster sale. Overpricing the vehicle is a common reason why owners have problems selling their vehicle.

PLACING AN AD Many vehicles are purchased by acquaintances. Let everyone know your vehicle will be for sale (say in December), and try to get several prospective buyers to agree to a price (when prices are high) for sale later (when prices are lower).

After you've tried to sell your old vehicle to acquaintances and cannot do it (or do not want to do it), advertising in your local daily paper is the next step if you keep in mind these guidelines:

1. The odds are greatest of selling a vehicle on Saturday or Sunday. Remember, if you receive calls, the callers are interested in your vehicle; therefore, the condition of the vehicle and your address are the only questions they should ask.

2. Suggested newspaper ad:

   2006 Chevrolet Impala, 4-dr., blue, V-6, auto, low miles, asking $7,850. 555-888-8888.

3. The reason for the wording of the ad:

   Year—(2006) Always list the year. This is very important to the value of the vehicle.

   Make—(Chevrolet) Necessary information.
   Model—(Impala four door.) Necessary information, this tells most people the size of the vehicle.
   Color—(blue) This helps eliminate unnecessary calls and if a person does call, then you know the prospective buyer likes or will accept a blue vehicle.
   Engine type—(V-6) A person wishing a four-cylinder engine will not call.
   Transmission type—(auto) Necessary information.
   Mileage—(low miles)—If normal or high miles, do not mention the mileage in the paper. (Normal mileage is 12,000 miles per year to 15,000 miles per year.)
   Asking price—($7,850) By using the word *asking*, you are informing the buyers that the price is not firm, but you are not begging someone to take it off your hands. Try to avoid using "Or Best Offer (OBO)" or "must sell." Try to end the price in $50 increments ($7,850) and then drop your price only $50 at a time—but never over the telephone. Remember, if you can talk five minutes to prevent the buyer from making you drop $50, you are earning $10 per minute.
   Telephone number—(555-888-8888) Place an ad in the paper to run over a weekend if possible for best results. Be sure you are available to show the vehicle during the time the ad is running or find someone who can help. If the weather is bad, wait a week or two and place the same ad again.

TECH TIP

Remove the Floor Mats

Most people purchase floor mats to protect the carpet. Dealers often remove these mats entirely to show off the good carpet that was protected by the previous owner and it makes the vehicle look more expensive. If the carpet is torn or discolored, the floor mats should be left in the vehicle.

TECH TIP

Use Newspaper to Clean Windows

Wash the windows with glass cleaner and newspapers (black and white). The newspaper will easily remove any film on the window glass better than paper towels or a soft cloth.

NEW VEHICLE PRE-DELIVERY INSPECTION

PURPOSE The purpose of the **pre-delivery inspection (PDI)** is to prepare the vehicle for customer use after a new vehicle has shipped from the assembly plant to the selling dealer. When the vehicle leaves the assembly plant, it is prepared for shipment with the following:

- The interior is covered in protective plastic.
- The exterior flat surfaces are covered to help protect the painted surfaces from acid rain and other elements such as bird droppings when being transported to the dealer.
- The tires are overinflated to reduce the amount of tire deflection during transport
- Some of the exterior brackets or accessories are in the trunk or storage area to be installed at the dealer.

CHECKLIST Most vehicle manufacturers provide a checklist to be used by the person designated to prepare the vehicle for delivery to the customer. While this list varies according to the make and model of the vehicle, most include the following:

- Removal of the exterior and interior plastic coverings. This process is commonly referred to as "pulling plastic." ● **SEE FIGURE 40–4.**
- Install all equipment including exterior antenna, cargo net, license plate bracket, wheel trim, and floor mats.
- Set the clock to the correct local time.
- Adjust the tire inflation pressure to the specified pressure.

FIGURE 40–4 Plastic protective covering is used on all surfaces that may be touched by others during transport from the assembly plant to the selling dealer. This plastic is removed at the dealer before the vehicle is delivered to the customer.

NOTE: Not adjusting the tire pressures down to the specified pressures causes a very common complaint of harsh riding. If the tire pressures are set at the correct pressure, then customer satisfaction is improved and saves the customer from having to make a service appointment to address the harsh ride concern.

SUMMARY

1. The three values that are often quoted on websites include the following:
   - Trade-in
   - Private Party
   - Dealer Retail
2. The value of any vehicle varies widely and is based on its condition, the number of miles, and other factors.
3. The condition of the vehicle is often stated as:
   - Excellent
   - Good
   - Fair
   - Poor

4. Before purchasing any vehicle, a thorough inspection and test drive should be performed.
5. Before selling a vehicle, be sure that it is clean and all personal items have been removed from the interior and trunk area.
6. When placing an ad, be sure to include all of the important information about the vehicle, including year, make, model, color, and miles, as well as the asking price.
7. When looking at a used vehicle, use a checklist to record information so that the details can be remembered or recalled later.

REVIEW QUESTIONS

1. What are the commonly used values found on vehicle-purchasing websites?
2. What are the commonly used terms to describe the condition of a vehicle?
3. What are the six Halderman's laws?

4. What should be done to insure a smooth purchase of a used vehicle?
5. What items should be checked when looking at a used vehicle being considered for purchase?

1. What is the price that is often the highest?
   a. Private party
   b. Dealer retail
   c. Trade-in
   d. Loan value

2. Which vehicle condition rating is the highest?
   a. Excellent
   b. Good
   c. Fair
   d. Poor

3. Why not look at a vehicle to purchase when it is raining?
   a. The wet paint can hide fading or paint differences
   b. The rain will wash away the paint
   c. The rain will cause starting problems
   d. Any of the above

4. Which vehicle condition means that there is need for major mechanical or bodywork?
   a. Excellent
   b. Good
   c. Fair
   d. Poor

5. What questions should a buyer ask the seller?
   a. Why are they selling the vehicle?
   b. What is wrong with the vehicle?
   c. Is the title clear of any loans or liens?
   d. All of the above

6. Why drive next to a building or a wall during the test drive?
   a. To hear noises from the vehicle
   b. To see the vehicle in the reflection of windows
   c. To check for a bad radio antenna
   d. Both b and c

7. Why check the trunk on a used vehicle?
   a. To see if there is a spare tire
   b. Check if there is a jack to lift the vehicle in case needed to replace a flat tire
   c. General condition
   d. All of the above

8. What does turning into and out of a driveway test?
   a. The body for rust
   b. The suspension
   c. The engine
   d. The transmission

9. What is considered to be normal amount of miles driven per year?
   a. 6,000 miles to 9,000 miles
   b. 10,000 miles to 12,000 miles
   c. 12,000 miles to 15,000 miles
   d. 15,000 miles to 20,000 miles

10. What should be done as part of a new vehicle pre-delivery inspection?
    a. Adjust the air pressure in all tires
    b. Install parts that are shipped inside the vehicle for installation at the selling dealer
    c. Removing all protective plastic
    d. All of the above

ENGINE REPAIR (A1) 8 TASKS

TASK NUMBER AND DESCRIPTION	PRIORITY	TEXT PAGE NUMBER	TASK SHEET PAGE NUMBER
A. GENERAL ENGINE DIAGNOSIS; REMOVAL AND REINSTALLATION (R & R)			
1. Complete work order to include customer information, vehicle identifying information, customer concern, related service History, cause, and correction.	P-1	Pages 14; 32–33	P. 6
3. Research applicable vehicle and service information, such as internal engine operation, vehicle service history, service precautions, and technical service bulletins.	P-1	Page 14	P. 20; P. 21; P. 22; P. 30; P. 38
4. Locate and interpret vehicle and major component identification numbers.	P-1	Pages 124–126	P. 1; P. 23; P. 24; P. 25; P. 26; P. 27
5. Inspect engine assembly for fuel, oil, coolant, and other leaks; determine necessary action.	P-1	Page 189–191	P. 40
D. LUBRICATION AND COOLING SYSTEMS DIAGNOSIS AND REPAIR			
3. Perform cooling system pressure tests; check coolant condition; inspect and test radiator, pressure cap, coolant recovery tank, and hoses; determine necessary action.	P-1	Pages 167–169	P. 31; P. 32; P. 35
4. Inspect, replace, and adjust drive belts, tensioners, and pulleys; check pulley and belt alignment.	P-1	Pages 169–170	P. 39
7. Test coolant; drain and recover coolant; flush and refill cooling system with recommended coolant; bleed air as required.	P-1	Pages 167–169	P. 29
13. Perform oil and filter change.	P-1	Pages 187; 192–194	P. 42

AUTOMATIC TRANSMISSION AND TRANSAXLES (A2) 5 TASKS

TASK NUMBER AND DESCRIPTION	PRIORITY	TEXT PAGE NUMBER	TASK SHEET PAGE NUMBER
A. GENERAL TRANSMISSION AND TRANSAXLE DIAGNOSIS			
1. Complete work order to include customer information, vehicle identifying information, customer concern, related service history, cause, and correction.	P-1	Pages 14; 32–33	P. 6
3. Research applicable vehicle and service information, such as transmission/transaxle system operation, fluid type, vehicle service history, service precautions, and technical service bulletins.	P-1	Page 14	P. 20; P. 21; P. 22
4. Locate and interpret vehicle and major component identification numbers.	P-1	Pages 124–126	P. 1; P. 23; P. 118
B. IN-VEHICLE TRANSMISSION/TRANSAXLE MAINTENANCE AND REPAIR			
6. Service transmission; perform visual inspection; replace fluid and filters.	P-1	Page 360–361	P. 119
C. OFF-VEHICLE TRANSMISSION AND TRANSAXLE REPAIR			
23. Describe the operational characteristics of a hybrid vehicle drive train.	P-3	Page 305	P. 123

MANUAL DRIVETRAIN AND AXLES (A3) 3 TASKS

TASK NUMBER AND DESCRIPTION	PRIORITY	TEXT PAGE NUMBER	TASK SHEET PAGE NUMBER
A. GENERAL TRANSMISSION AND TRANSAXLES DIAGNOSIS			
1. Complete work order to include customer information, vehicle identifying information, customer concern, related service history, cause, and correction.	P-1	Pages 14; 32–33	P. 6
3. Research applicable vehicle and service information, such as drivetrain system operation, fluid type, vehicle service history, service precautions, and technical service bulletins.	P-1	Page 14	P.20; P.21; P. 22
4. Locate and interpret vehicle and major component identification numbers.	P-1	Pages 124–126	P.1; P. 23

SUSPENSION AND STEERING (A4) 14 TASKS

TASK NUMBER AND DESCRIPTION	PRIORITY	TEXT PAGE NUMBER	TASK SHEET PAGE NUMBER
A. GENERAL SUSPENSION AND STEERING SYSTEMS DIAGNOSIS			
1. Complete work order to include customer information, vehicle identifying information, customer concern, related service history, cause, and correction.	P-1	Pages 14; 32–33	P. 6
3. Research applicable vehicle and service information, such as suspension and steering system operation, vehicle service history, service precautions, and technical service bulletins.	P-1	Page 14	P. 20; P.21; P. 22; P. 89
4. Locate and interpret vehicle and major component identification numbers.	P-1	Pages 124–126	P. 1; P. 23
B. STEERING SYSTEMS DIAGNOSIS AND REPAIR			
1. Disable and enable supplemental restraint system (SRS).	P-1	Page 256	P. 105
10. Determine proper power steering fluid type; inspect fluid level and condition.	P-1	Pages 170–171	P. 108
11. Flush, fill, and bleed power steering system.	P-2	Page 341	P. 108
C. RELATED SUSPENSION AND STEERING SERVICE			
6. Lubricate suspension and steering systems.	P-2	Pages 187–189	P. 43
F. WHEEL AND TIRE DIAGNOSIS AND REPAIR			
1. Inspect tire condition; identify tire wear patterns; check and adjust air pressure; determine necessary action.	P-1	Page 321	P. 91
3. Rotate tires according to manufacturer's recommendations.	P-1	Page 322	P. 92
6. Dismount, inspect, and remount tire on wheel; Balance wheel and tire assembly (static and dynamic).	P-1	Check tire machine/ balancer instructions	P. 94
7. Dismount, inspect, and remount tire on wheel equipped with tire pressure monitoring system sensor.	P-2	Pages 319–320	P. 94
8. Reinstall wheel; torque lug nuts.	P-1	Page 323	P. 93
9. Inspect tire and wheel assembly for air loss; perform necessary action.	P-1	N.A.	P. 91
10. Repair tire using internal patch.	P-1	N.A.	P. 95

BRAKES (A5) 9 TASKS

TASK NUMBER AND DESCRIPTION	PRIORITY	TEXT PAGE NUMBER	TASK SHEET PAGE NUMBER
A. GENERAL BRAKE SYSTEMS DIAGNOSIS			
1. Complete work order to include customer information, vehicle identifying information, customer concern, related service history, cause, and correction.	P-1	Pages 14; 32–33	P. 6
3. Research applicable vehicle and service information, such as brake system operation, vehicle service history, service precautions, and technical service bulletins.	P-1	Page 14	P. 20; P. 21; P. 22; P. 96; P. 99; P. 101
4. Locate and interpret vehicle and major component identification numbers.	P-1	Pages 124–126	P. 1; P. 23
B. HYDRAULIC SYSTEM DIAGNOSIS AND REPAIR			
13. Test brake fluid for contamination.	P-1	Page 163	P. 98
C. DRUM BRAKE DIAGNOSIS AND REPAIR			
2. Remove, clean, inspect, and measure brake drums; determine necessary action.	P-1	Pages 328–329	P. 99
7. Install wheel, torque lug nuts, and make final checks and adjustments.	P-1	Page 323	P. 100
D. DISC BRAKE DIAGNOSIS AND REPAIR			
12. Install wheel, torque lug nuts, and make final checks and adjustments.	P-1	Page 323	P. 100
E. MISCELLANEOUS (WHEEL BEARINGS, PARKING BRAKES, ELECTRICAL, ETC.) DIAGNOSIS AND REPAIR			
5. Check operation of brake stop light system; determine necessary action.	P-1	-	P. 97

ELECTRICAL/ELECTRONIC SYSTEMS (A6) 14 TASKS

TASK NUMBER AND DESCRIPTION	PRIORITY	TEXT PAGE NUMBER	TASK SHEET PAGE NUMBER
A. GENERAL ELECTRICAL SYSTEM DIAGNOSIS			
1. Complete work order to include customer information, vehicle identifying information, customer concern, related service history, cause, and correction.	P-1	Pages 14; 32–33	P. 6
3. Research applicable vehicle and service information, such as electrical/electronic system operation, vehicle service history, service precautions, and technical service bulletins.	P-1	Page 14	P. 20; P. 21; P. 22; P. 51
4. Locate and interpret vehicle and major component identification numbers.	P-1	Pages 124–126	P. 1; P. 23
18. Identify location of hybrid vehicle high voltage circuit disconnect (service plug) location and safety procedures	P-2	Pages 306–307	P. 84
B. BATTERY DIAGNOSIS AND SERVICE			
1. Perform battery state-of-charge test; determine necessary action.	P-1	Pages 219–220	P.52
3. Maintain or restore electronic memory functions.	P-1	N.A.	P. 53
4. Inspect, clean, fill, and/or replace battery, battery cables, connectors, clamps, and hold-downs.	P-1	Page 218	P. 54
5. Perform battery charge.	P-1	Page 221	P. 55

(continued)

TASK NUMBER AND DESCRIPTION	PRIORITY	TEXT PAGE NUMBER	TASK SHEET PAGE NUMBER
6. Start a vehicle using jumper cables or an auxiliary power supply.	P-1	Page 221	P. 56
7. Identify high voltage circuits of electric or hybrid electric vehicle and related safety precautions.	P-3	Pages 306–307	P. 85
8. Identify electronic modules, security systems, radios, and other accessories that require re-initialization or code entry following battery disconnect.	P-1	N.A.	P. 57
C. CHARGING SYSTEM DIAGNOSIS AND REPAIR			
3. Inspect, adjust, or replace generator (alternator) drive belts, pulleys, and tensioners; check pulley and belt alignment.	P-1	Pages 169–170	P. 60
D. LIGHTING SYSTEMS DIAGNOSIS AND REPAIR			
2. Inspect, replace, and aim headlights and bulbs.	P-2	Pages 244–245	P. 62
F. ACCESSORIES DIAGNOSIS AND REPAIR			
6. Disarm and enable the airbag system for vehicle service.	P-1	Page 256	P. 63

HEATING AND AIR CONDITIONING (A7) 7 TASKS

TASK NUMBER AND DESCRIPTION	PRIORITY	TEXT PAGE NUMBER	TASK SHEET PAGE NUMBER
A. A/C SYSTEM DIAGNOSIS AND REPAIR			
1. Complete work order to include customer information, vehicle identifying information, customer concern, related service history, cause, and correction.	P-1	Pages14; 32–33	P. 6
3. Research applicable vehicle and service information, such as heating and air conditioning system operation, vehicle service history, service precautions, and technical service bulletins.	P-1	Page 14	P. 20; P. 21; P. 22
4. Locate and interpret vehicle and major component identification numbers.	P-1	Pages 124–126	P. 1; P. 23; P. 64
B. REFRIGERATION SYSTEM COMPONENT DIAGNOSIS AND REPAIR			
5. Identify hybrid vehicle A/C system electrical circuits, service and safety precautions.	P-3	Page 306–307	P. 65
C. HEATING, VENTILATION, AND ENGINE COOLING SYSTEMS DIAGNOSIS AND REPAIR			
2. Perform cooling system pressure tests; check coolant condition, inspect and test radiator, cap (pressure/vacuum), coolant recovery tank, and hoses; perform necessary action.	P-1	N.A.	P. 34; P. 35
3. Inspect engine cooling and heater system hoses and belts; perform necessary action.	P-1	Pages 167–170	P. 68
5. Determine coolant condition and coolant type for vehicle application; drain and recover coolant.	P-1	Pages 167–168	P. 29
D. OPERATING SYSTEMS AND RELATED CONTROLS			
7. Inspect A/C-heater ducts, doors, hoses, cabin filters and outlets; perform necessary action.	P-2	Page 162	Check service information

TASK NUMBER AND DESCRIPTION	PRIORITY	TEXT PAGE NUMBER	TASK SHEET PAGE NUMBER
A. GENERAL ENGINE DIAGNOSIS			
1. Complete work order to include customer information, vehicle identifying information, customer concern, related service history, cause, and correction.	P-1	Pages 14; 32–33	P. 6
3. Research applicable vehicle and service information, such as engine management system operation, vehicle service history, service precautions, and technical service bulletins.	P-1	Page 14	P. 20; P. 21; P. 22; P. 69; P. 72; P. 73
4. Locate and interpret vehicle and major component identification numbers.	P-1	Pages 124–126	P. 1; P. 23; P. 28; P. 83
5. Inspect engine assembly for fuel, oil, coolant, and other leaks; determine necessary action.	P-2	Pages 190–191	P. 40
15. Perform cooling system pressure tests; check coolant condition; inspect and test radiator, pressure cap, coolant recovery tank, and hoses; perform necessary action.	P-1	Pages 167–169	P. 31
B. COMPUTERIZED ENGINE CONTROLS DIAGNOSIS AND REPAIR			
6. Access and use service information to perform step-by-step diagnosis.	P-1	Pages 313–315	P. 88
D. ENGINE RELATED SERVICE			
5. Perform common fastener and thread repairs, to include: remove broken bolt, restore internal and external threads, and repair internal threads with a threaded insert.	P-1	Pages 75–76	P. 11
6. Perform engine oil and filter change.	P-1	Pages 187; 192–194	P. 42
7. Identify hybrid vehicle internal combustion engine service precautions.	P-3	Pages 307–308	P. 86

GLOSSARY

4 × 2 The term used to describe a two-wheel-drive truck. The "4" indicates the number of wheels of the vehicle and the "2" indicates the number of wheels that are driven by the engine.

4 × 4 The term used to describe a four-wheel-drive vehicle. The first "4" indicates the number of wheels of the vehicle and the second "4" indicates the number of wheels that are driven by the engine.

4WAL Four-wheel antilock.

720° cycle The number of degrees of crankshaft rotation required to complete the four-stroke cycle.

A-arm Another name for a control arm because it often looks like the letter A.

ABS Antilock brake system.

AC/DC clamp-on DMM A type of meter that has a clamp that is placed around the wire to measure current.

AC See Alternating current.

Ackerman Principle The angle of the steering arms causes the inside wheel to turn more sharply than the outer wheel when making a turn. This produces toe-out on turns (TOOT).

ACM Active Control Engine Mount. ACMs are computer controlled and are designed to dampen unusual vibrations during ICE start/stop.

Actuator An electromechanical device that performs mechanical movement as commanded by a controller.

Additive package A group of chemicals engine oil, protect the oil or to protect the engine.

Adjustable wrench A wrench that has a moveable jaw to allow it to fit many sizes of fasteners.

Advisor A role played by a mentor.

Advocate A role played by a mentor.

Aftermarket parts Parts that are used in the repair of vehicles that are made by a company other than the same company who made the original factory-installed part.

AFV Alternative fuel vehicle.

AGM battery Absorbed glass mat. AGM batteries are lead–acid batteries, but use an absorbent material between the plates to hold the electrolyte. AGM batteries are classified as valve-regulated lead-acid (VRLA) batteries.

AGST Above ground storage tank, used to store used oil.

Ah Ampere-hour. A battery capacity rating.

Air compressor A piece of shop equipment that uses an electric motor to power an air compressor, which is stored in a pressure tank for use in the shop.

Air drill A drill powered by compressed air.

Air Filter An element usually constructed of pleated paper that filters dirt from the air entering the engine. Most air filters are designed to trap dirt particles that are larger than 20 microns in size.

Air management system The system of solenoids and valves that control the flow of air from the secondary air-injection system.

Air ratchet An air-operated hand tool that rotates a socket.

Airbag An inflatable fabric bag that deploys in the event of a collision that is severe enough to cause personal injury.

Air-blow gun A handheld nozzle attached to a compressed air hose to apply air pressure to a component or device.

AKI Antiknock index. The octane rating posted on a gas pump, which is the average of the RON and MON octane ratings.

ALB Antilock brakes.

Alemite fitting See Zerk.

Algorithm A computer program that is used to process information from sensors to determine what action needs to be taken.

Alloy A metal that contains one or more other elements usually added to increase strength or give the base metal important properties.

Alternating current (AC) An electrical signal in which current and voltage vary in a repeating sequence.

Alternator An electric generator that produces alternating current; also called an *AC generator*.

Altitude Elevation as measured in relationship to the earth's surface at sea level.

Amber ABS warning lamp The dash warning lamp that lights if a fault in the antilock braking system (ABS) is detected.

Ammeter An electrical test instrument used to measure amperes (unit of the amount of current flow).

Ampere The unit of the amount of current flow. Named for André Ampère (1775–1836).

Analog A type of dash instrument that indicates values by use of the movement of a needle or similar device. An analog signal is continuous and variable.

Anchor pin A steel stud firmly attached to the backing plate. One end of the brake shoe is either attached to or rests against it.

ANSI American National Standards Institute, an organization that publishes safety standards for safety glasses and other personal protective equipment.

Anti-drain-back valve A value usually built into oil filters that prevent the oil from draining from the filter when the geometry of the engine is not running.

Antifreeze A liquid such as ethylene glycol or propylene glycol that is used to lower the freezing point of the ICE coolant. Antifreeze also raises the coolant boiling point and contains inhibitors to prevent rust and corrosion inside the cooling system.

Antiknock index A measure of a fuel's ability to resist engine knock, stated as a number, that is called the octane number.

Antilock braking system A system that is capable of pulsing the wheel brakes if lockup is detected to help the driver maintain control of the vehicle.

API Gravity An arbitrary scale expressing the specific gravity or density of liquid petroleum products, usually diesel fuel.

API American Petroleum Institute.

APP Accelerator pedal position sensor. Also known as an accelerator pedal sensor (APS).

Apply system The part of a brake system that starts the operation of the brakes, including the brake pedal and levers, as well as the parking brake.

Apprentice program A program where a person enrolls to learn a trade under the direction of a journeyman plus includes classroom training in addition to on-the-job training.

Arming sensor A sensor used in an airbag circuit that is most sensitive and completes the circuit first of two sensors that are needed to deploy an airbag.

Asbestosis A health condition where asbestos causes scar tissue to form in the lungs, causing shortness of breath.

ASE Certified Master Automobile Technician A person who has taken and passed ASE certification tests for A1 through A8 and has had the specified work experience.

ASE Abbreviation for the National Institute for Automotive Service Excellence, a nonprofit organization for the testing and certification of vehicle service technicians.

Aspect ratio The ratio of height to width of a tire. A tire with an aspect ratio of 60 (a 60 series tire) has a height (from rim to tread) of 60% of its cross-sectional width.

Association des Constructeurs Européens d'Automobiles (ACEA) The organization that rates engine oil in Europe.

ASTM American Society for Testing Materials.

Atmospheric pressure Pressure exerted by the atmosphere on all things based on the weight of the air (14.7 pounds per square inch at sea level).

Atom An atom is the smallest unit of matter that still retains its separate unique characteristic.

AT-PZEV Advanced Technology Partial-Zero-Emission Vehicle.

Automatic transmission fluid An oil specifically designed for use in automatic transmissions that can vary according to make, model, and year of vehicle. Abbreviated ATF.

Auxiliary battery The 12-volt battery in a hybrid electric vehicle.

Aviation tin snips Cutters designed to cut sheet metal.

Axle ratio The gear ratio in the drive axle (differential).

B20 A blend of 20% biodiesel with 80% petroleum diesel.

B5 A blend of 5% biodiesel with 95% petroleum diesel.

Backing plate A steel plate upon which the brake shoes are attached. The backing plate is attached to the steering knuckle or axle housing.

Backlight Light that illuminates the test tool's display from the back of the LCD.

Backlight The rear window of a vehicle.

Backup camera A camera mounts on the rear of the vehicle that is used to display what is behind a vehicle when the gear selector is placed in reverse.

Ball bearings An antifriction bearing that uses steel balls between the inner and outer race to reduce friction.

Ball joints A ball and socket joint used in the front suspension to allow up and down and turn motion of the front wheel.

Ball socket assembly An inner tie rod end assembly that contains a ball and socket joint at the point where the assembly is threaded on to the end of the steering rack.

Ballast resistor A variable resistor used to control the primary ignition current through the coil.

Barrel A part of a micrometer, which has 40 threads per inch.

Base brakes See Service brakes.

Battery cables Cables that attach to the positive and negative terminals of the battery.

Battery A chemical device that produces a voltage created by two dissimilar metals submerged in an electrolyte.

BCI Battery Council International.

Bead The part of a tire that is made of wire that the body plies are wrapped around.

Beam-type torque wrench A type of wrench that displays the torque being applied to a fastener by the position of a deflective pointer and a scale, indicating the amount of torque.

Bearing splitter A two-part steel device used between a bearing and a gear or other component, which is used to remove the bearing using a hydraulic press.

Bell housing A bell-shaped housing attached between the engine and the transmission.

Belt Fabric or woven steel material over the body plies of a tire, and just under the tread area, to help keep the tread from squirming.

Bench grinder An electric motor with a grinding stone and/or wire brush attached at both ends of the armature and mounted on a bench.

Bench vise A vise mounted to a bench

BEV Battery electric vehicle.

BIN number A U.S. federal rating of emissions. The lower the BIN number, the cleaner the exhaust emission is.

Biodiesel A renewable fuel manufactured from vegetable oils, animal fats, or recycled restaurant grease.

Block The foundation of any engine. All other parts are either directly or indirectly attached to the block of an engine.

Blowby gases Combustion gases that leak past the piston rings into the crankcase during the compression and combustion strokes of the engine.

Blower motor An electric motor and squirrel-cage type of fan that moves air inside the vehicle for heating, cooling, and defrosting.

Body ply A layer of cloth that gives a tire its strength.

Body The steel structure of the vehicle that includes the doors, hood, fenders, and rear section.

Body-on-frame A type of vehicle construction that uses a steel frame to support the drivetrain (engine, transmission, and drive axle assembly), a separate body that is attached to the frame.

Boiling point The temperature that a liquid changes to a gas.

Bolts A threaded fastener that is used to hold two parts together with a nut on the other end of the threaded end. If installed into a threaded hole, then a bolt is often called a *cap screw.*

Boost system The component in the brake system used to increase the brake pedal force.

Boost An increase in air pressure above atmospheric. Measured in pounds per square inch (PSI).

Bore The inside diameter of the cylinder in an engine.

Bottom dead center (BDC) The lowest position in the cylinder that a piston can travel without reversing its direction.

Box-end wrench A type of wrench that has the end enclosed so that it can grip around the head of a bolt or nut.

Boxer A type of engine design that is flat and has opposing cylinders. It is called boxer because the pistons on one side resemble a boxer during engine operation. Also called a *pancake engine.*

Brake Balance control system The component in a brake system that ensures that the wheel brakes are applied quickly and balanced among all four wheels for safe operation.

Brake fluid level sensor   A sensor used in the brake fluid reservoir to detect when brake fluid is low and turns on the red brake warning light on the dash.

Brake fluid   A non-petroleum-based fluid called polyglycol used in hydraulic brake systems.

Brake light switch   A switch located on the brake pedal linkage used to turn on the rear brake lights.

Brake lines   Steel tubes used to transmit brake fluid pressure.

Brake lining   A friction material fastened to the brake shoes. It is pressed against the rotating brake drum to accomplish braking.

Brake pad   The brake friction material used in disc brakes.

Brake pedal   The pedal depressed by the driver to operate the wheel brakes.

Brake shoe clearance gauge   A tool used to set the brake shoes adjustment which is first set to the size of the brake drum.

Brake shoe hold-down   Springs or clips used to hold brake shoes against the backing plate.

Brake shoe   The part of the brake system upon which the brake lining is attached.

Brake shoes   The part of the brake system upon which the brake lining is attached.

Brake warning lights   Include the red brake warning light and the amber ABS warning light.

Brake   Any device that is designed to slow or stop a mechanism or component.

Breaker bar   A handle used to rotate a socket; also called a *flex handle*.

Breaker bar   A long-handled socket drive tool.

Breather tube   A tube that connects the left and right bellows of a rack-and-pinion steering gear.

British thermal unit (BTU)   The amount of heat required to raise 1 pound of water 1°F at sea level.

BTU   See British thermal unit.

Bulb test   A test to check the operation of certain circuits controlled by the ignition switch.

Bulkhead   The panel between the engine compartment and the passenger compartment.

Bump cap   A hat that is plastic and hard to protect the head from bumps.

Bump stop   A rubber or urethane stop to limit upward suspension travel. Also called a strikeout bumper, suspension bumper, or compression bumper.

Bypass Value   A value usually built into an oil filter that allows oil to bypass the filter if it becomes clogged.

CA   Cranking amperes. A battery rating.

CAA   Clean Air Act. Federal legislation passed in 1970 that established national air quality standards.

Cabin filter   A filter located in the air intake of the HVAC system.

Calendar year (CY)   A calendar year is from January 1 through December 31 each year.

Calibration codes   Codes used on many powertrain control modules.

California Air Resources Board (CARB)   A state of California agency which regulates the air quality standards for the state.

Caliper   The U-shaped housing that contains the hydraulic pistons and holds the pads on disc brake applications.

Calorie (c)   A metric unit of the amount of heat.

Cam-in-block design   An engine where the crankshaft is located in the block rather than in the cylinder head.

Camshaft   A shaft with lobes that open valves when being rotated through a chain, belt, or gear from the crankshaft.

Candlepower   Measures the amount of light produced by a bulb.

Canister purge (CANP)   A valve used to allow gasoline vapor to be drawn from the charcoal canister into the engine where it is then burned in the cylinders.

Cap screw   A bolt that is threaded into a casting.

Capacity test   A test performed on a battery to determine if it can perform according to specification. Also called a *battery load test*.

Capillary action   The movement of a liquid through tiny openings or small tubes.

CARB   See California Air Resources Board.

Carbon dioxide (CO_2)   A colorless, odorless, nonflammable gas produced during the combustion process. The amount (%) in the exhaust can be used to evaluate the efficiency of an engine's combustion process.

Carbon monoxide (CO)   A colorless, odorless, and highly poisonous gas. It is formed by the incomplete combustion of gasoline.

Carcass ply   Plies of fabric in a tire that covers the entire tire from bead to bead.

Cardan joint   A type of universal joint named for a sixteenth-century Italian mathematician.

Casting number   An identification code cast into an engine block or other large cast part of a vehicle.

Castle nut   A nut with notches cut out around the top to allow the installation of a cotter key to keep the nut from loosening.

Catalyst   A chemical that is used to start a chemical reaction but does not enter into the chemical reaction so it is not consumed in the process.

Catalytic converter   An emission control device located in the exhaust system that changes HC and CO into harmless H_2O and CO_2. A three-way catalyst NOx is also divided into harmless separate nitrogen (N_2) and Oxygen (O_2).

Catalytic cracking   Breaking hydrocarbon chains using heat in the presence of a catalyst.

CCA   Cold Cranking Amperes. A rating of a battery tested at 0°F.

CCR   Computer Command Ride.

Cd   Coefficient of drag. A measure of the aerodynamic efficiency of a vehicle.

Celsius   A temperature scale where 0° is the freezing point of water (32°F) and 100° is the boiling point of water (212°F).

Center link   The center part of a parallelogram-type steering linkage.

Center section   The section of a wheel that attaches to the hub. Also called the spider.

Center support bearing   A bearing used to support the center of a long drive shaft on a rear-wheel-drive vehicle. Also called a *steady bearing*.

Cetane number   A diesel fuel rating that indicates how easily the fuel can be ignited.

CFC-12 A refrigerant used until the mid-1990s for use in vehicle air conditioning systems. Also called R-12.

CFR Code of Federal Regulations.

Change of state The process where a material absorbs or releases heat energy to change between solid, liquid, and gaseous states.

Charge indicator A hydrometer built into one battery cell that gives a visual indication of the state of charge.

Charging circuit Electrical components and connections necessary to keep a battery fully charged.

Chassis ground In electrical terms, a ground is the desirable return circuit path.

Chassis The frame, suspension, steering, and machinery of a motor vehicle.

Cheater bar A pipe or other object used to lengthen the handle of a ratchet or breaker bar. Not recommended to be used as the extra force can cause the socket or ratchet to break.

Check engine light A dashboard warning light that is controlled by the vehicle computer. Also called the *malfunction indicator light (MIL)*.

Check valves Valves used to allow flow in only one direction.

Chisel A sharpened tool used with a hammer to separate two pieces of an assembly.

CHMSL Centrally High Mounted Stop Light. Also called the third brake light.

Christmas tree clips Plastic clips used to hold interior panels in place. The end that goes into a hole in the steel door panel is tapered and looks like a Christmas tree.

Circuit A circuit is the path that electrons travel from a power source, through a resistance, and back to the power source.

Clock in The act of recording the time when a technician reports for work or when work is started on a vehicle.

Clock time The time charged to complete a service procedure, which is determined by the actual time spent.

Clockspring A flat ribbon of wire used under the steering wire to transfer airbag electrical signals. May also carry horn and steering wheel control circuits depending on make and model of vehicle.

Close end An end of a wrench that grips all sides of the fastener.

Clutch disc The part of a clutch used in a vehicle equipped with a manual transmission that is splined to the input shaft of the transmission or transaxle.

CNG Compressed natural gas.

CO Carbon monoxide.

Coach A role played by a mentor.

Coefficient of drag (Cd) A calculation of the amount of aerodynamic drag created by a vehicle's body. A higher coefficient of drag indicates more wind resistance created by the vehicle.

Coil spring A spring steel rod wound in a spiral (helix) shape. Used in both front and rear suspension systems.

Coil-on-plug ignition system An ignition system without a distributor, where each spark plug is integrated with an ignition coil.

Cold chisel A type of chisel used to remove rivets or to break off fasteners.

Cold-cranking amperes (CCA) The rating of a battery's ability to provide battery voltage during cold-weather operation. CCA is the number of amperes that a battery can supply at 0°F (−18°C) for

30 seconds and still maintain a voltage of 1.2 volt per cell (7.2 volt for a 12-volt battery).

Collapsible column A steering column that collapses in the event of a front impact to the vehicle to help prevent injury to the driver.

Combination wrench A type of wrench that has an open end at one end and a closed end at the other end.

Combination wrench A wrench that is open ended at one end and has a box end at the other end.

Combustion chamber The space left within the cylinder when the piston is at the top of its combustion chamber.

Combustion The rapid burning of the air–fuel mixture in the engine cylinders, creating heat and pressure.

Commission pay Income to a service technician determined by the number of hours that a flat-rate manual states in the time it should take multiplied by the hourly rate of the technician.

Complete circuit A type of electrical circuit that has continuity and current would flow if connected to power and ground.

Composite headlights A type of headlight that uses a separate, replaceable bulb.

Compression ratio (CR) The ratio of the volume in the engine cylinder with the piston at bottom dead center (BDC) to the volume at top dead center (TDC).

Computer Any device that can perform high-speed mathematical or logical calculations and otherwise process data.

Condensation point The point (temperature) where a gas changes back to a liquid.

Condenser (electrical) Also called a capacitor; stores an electrical charge.

Condenser An A/C system component located in front of the radiator in most vehicles that removes heat from the refrigerant and causes it to change from a gas to a liquid.

Conductance The plate surface area in a battery that is available for chemical reaction. Battery condition can be assessed using a measurement of its conductance.

Conductor A material that conducts electricity and heat. A metal that contains fewer than four electrons in its atom's outer shell.

Connecting rod An engine part that connects the piston to the crankshaft.

Constant velocity joint Commonly called CV joints. CV joints are driveline joints that can transmit engine power through relatively large angles without a change in the velocity as is usually the case with conventional Cardan-type U joints.

Continuity Instrument setup to check wiring, circuits, connectors, or switches for breaks (open circuit) or short circuits (closed circuit).

Control arms A suspension link that connects a knuckle or wheel flange to the body or frame of the vehicle.

Control module An electronic device used to control the operation of activities.

Conventional theory The theory that electricity flows from positive (+) to negative (−).

Coolant The liquid mixture in the engine cooling system.

Cooperative education A training program that includes on-the-job plus classroom training.

COP Coil-on-plug. This term describes ignition systems in which each spark plug has its own coil assembly mounted directly over the top of it. Also known as *coil-over-plug*, *coil-by-plug*, or *coil-near-plug* ignition.

Core charge An amount of money paid when a rebuildable part is purchased and refunded when the worn or defective part is returned to the parts store.

Core The name of a used part that is to be returned to a supplier to be rebuilt.

Cotter pin A metal loop used to retain castle nuts by being installed through a hole. Size is measured by diameter and length (for example, 1/8" × 1 1/2"). Also called a cotter key. Named for the old English verb meaning "to close or fasten."

Coulomb A measurement of electrons. A coulomb is 6.28 × 101 (6.28 billion billion) electrons.

Counter gears The gears that are located under the main shaft in a manual transmission.

Country of origin The first number of the vehicle identification number (VIN), which identifies where the vehicle was assembled.

Courtesy light General term used to describe all interior lights.

CR See Compression ratio.

Cracking A refinery process in which hydrocarbons with high boiling points are broken into hydrocarbons with low boiling points.

Cradle A structural support for the engine and transaxle on a front-wheel-drive vehicle.

Cranking amperes A battery rating tested at 32°F (0°C).

Cranking circuit Electrical components and connections required to crank the engine to start. Includes starter motor, starter solenoid/relay, battery, neutral safety switch, ignition control switch, and connecting wires and cables.

Crankshaft An engine part that rotates and converts the up and down motion of the pistons to rotary motion.

Creeper A small platform mounted on short casters designed for a service technician to lie down and maneuver under a vehicle.

Crest The outside diameter of a bolt measured across the threads.

Critical thinking A term used to describe the thought process used to help make sound decisions.

Crowfoot socket A type of socket that slips onto the side of the bolt or nut. Used where direct access from the top is restricted.

CRT Cathode ray tube.

Cunife A magnetic alloy made from copper (Cu), nickel (Ni), and iron (Fe).

Cup Rubber seals that have a lip which faces toward where pressure is increased.

Cup The outer race or ring of a bearing.

Cuppy tire wear Scalloped tire wear usually on the inside or outside edges caused by defective or worn shock absorbers or other faults in the suspension system.

Current Electron flow through an electrical circuit; measured in amperes.

Customer pay CP) The amount that the customer pays for a repair.

CV joint boot The covering over a constant velocity joint made from rubber, thermoplastic, or urethane.

CY See Calendar year.

Cycle A series of events such as the four-stroke engine cycle.

Cylinder block The foundation of any engine. The cylinder block contains the cylinders and is where most engine parts are attached.

Cylinder The part of an engine that is cylinder and has a piston inside that moves up and down in the cylinder during engine operation. Sometimes called the cylinder bore.

Data link connector (DLC) The connector usually located under the dash used to communicate with scan tool during diagnosis.

dB An abbreviation for decibel, a measure of relative noise level.

DC Direct current.

Dead-blow hammer A type of hammer that has lead shot (small pellets) inside a steel housing, which is then covered with a plastic covering. Used to apply a blunt force to an object.

Dealer retail value The price often posted on used vehicles at dealers.

Deceleration sensor A sensor mounted to the body of frame of a vehicle that detects and measures the deceleration of the vehicle. Used to control the activation of the airbags and vehicle stability systems.

Decibel (dB) A unit of the magnitude of sound.

Deflection A bending or distorting motion. Usually applied to a brake drum when it is forced out-of-round during brake application.

Degrees A degree is 1/360th of a circle.

Desiccant An ingredient, such as silica gel used to remove moisture from air. Used in electronic systems that use air shocks or springs.

Detailing A term used to describe the cleaning and restoration of a used vehicle to make it look as new as possible.

DI Distillation index. A rating of the volatility of a fuel and how well it evaporates in cold temperatures.

Diagnostic trouble code (DTC) An alphanumeric or numeric sequence indicating a fault in a vehicle operating system. Each sequence corresponds to a specific malfunction.

Diagonal pliers Pliers designed to cut wire and to remove cotter keys. Also called *side cuts* or *dike pliers*.

Die grinder A handheld air-operated tool used with a grinding stone or a wire brush.

Die A tool used to create external threads on round bar stock.

Diesel exhaust fluid (DEF) A mixture of urea and demineralized water used to reduce oxides of nitrogen exhaust emissions in newer diesel engines.

Diesel exhaust particulate filter (DPF) A trap in the exhaust system of 2007 and newer diesel engines used to reduce particulate matter (PM) emissions.

Diesel oxidation catalyst (DOC) A unit located in the exhaust system of newer diesel engines used to reduce exhaust emission.

Diesohol Standard #2 diesel fuel combined with up to 15% ethanol.

Differential A mechanical unit containing gears that provides gear reduction and a change of direction of engine power and permits the drive wheels to rotate at different speeds as is required when turning a corner.

Digital A method of display that uses numbers instead of a needle or similar device.

Dimmer switch An electrical switch used to direct the current to either bright or dim headlight filaments.

Diode trio A group of three diodes grouped together with one output used to put out the charge indicator lamp and provide current for the field from the stator windings on many alternators.

Diode An electrical device that allows current to flow in one direction only.

Dipstick A long thin piece of metal used to determine the level of engine oil or automatic transmission fluid.

Direct current (DC) A constant electric current that flows in one direction only.

Direct injection (DI) A diesel engine design where diesel fuel is injected directly into the combustion chamber.

DIS Distributorless ignition system; also called *direct-fire ignition system*.

Disc brakes A type of wheel brake that squeezes two brake pads on both sides of a rotor or disc.

Discs Another name for brake rotors.

Displacement The total volume displaced or swept by the cylinders in an internal combustion engine.

Distillation The process of purification through evaporation and then condensation of the desired liquid.

Distracter An answer on a multiple choice test that is not the correct answer.

Distributor Electromechanical unit used to help create and distribute the high voltage disturb the function of the signal when it exceeds a certain electrical level.

Division A specific segment of a waveform, as defined by the grid on the display.

DMM Digital multimeter. A digital multimeter is capable of measuring electrical current, resistance, and voltage.

DOT 3 Rating of the most commonly specified brake fluid.

DOT 4 A brake fluid rating for polyglycol.

DOT 5.1 The highest rated polyglycol brake fluid.

DOT 5 Silicone brake fluid rating.

DOT tire code The Department of Transportation.

DOT Abbreviation for the Department of Transportation.

Double overhead camshaft (DOHC) An engine design with two camshafts above each line of cylinders—one for the exhaust valves and one for the intake valves.

Double-cut file A file that has two rows of teeth that cut at an opposite angle.

Drive gear The gear that is applying torque to another gear.

Drive shaft A shaft that transfers engine torque from the output of the transmission to the rear axle (differential) assembly.

Drive size The size in fractions of an inch of the square drive for sockets.

Driveability The general evaluation of an engine's operating qualities, including idle smoothness, cold and hot starting, throttle response, and power delivery.

Drive-end (DE) housing The end of a starter motor that has the drive pinion gear.

Driven gear The gear that is being driven or rotated by the drive gear.

DRL Daytime Running Lights. Lights that are located in the front of the vehicle and come on whenever the ignition is on. In some vehicles the vehicle has to be moving before they come on. Used as a safety device on many vehicles and required in many countries such as Canada since 1990.

Drum brakes A type of wheel brake that uses expanding brake shoes inside a brake drum.

DVOM Digiatl volt-ohm-milliammeter.

E10 A fuel blend of 10% ethanol and 90% gasoline.

E85 A fuel blend of 85% ethanol and 15% gasoline.

Easy out A tool used to extract a broken bolt.

E-diesel Standard #2 diesel fuel combined with up to 15% ethanol. Also known as *diesohol*.

EFI Electronic fuel injection.

EGR Exhaust gas recirculation. An emission control device to reduce NOx (oxides of nitrogen).

EI Electronic ignition. An SAE term for an ignition system that does not use a distributor.

Electrical load Applying a load to a component such as a battery to measure its performance.

Electrical potential Another term to describe voltage.

Electricity The movement of free electrons from one atom to another.

Electromagnet An electromagnet consists of a soft iron core surrounded by a coil of wire. Electrical current flowing through the coiled wire creates a magnetic field around the core.

Electromagnetic clutch A clutch on the air conditioning compressor used to engage and disengage the compressor as needed.

Electromagnetic interference (EMI) An undesirable electronic signal. It is caused by a magnetic field building up and collapsing, creating unwanted electrical interference on a nearby circuit.

Electromotive force (EMF) The force (pressure) that can move electrons through a conductor.

Electron theory The theory that electricity flows from negative (−) to positive (+).

Electron A negative charged particle: 1/1,800 the mass of a proton.

Electronic ignition General term used to describe any of various types of ignition systems that use electronic instead of mechanical components, such as contact points.

Element Any substance that cannot be separated into different substances.

E-metric A tire designation for electric vehicles, which have low rolling resistance.

EMF Electromotive force.

EMI Electromagnetic interference. An undesirable electronic signal. It is caused by a magnetic field building up and collapsing, creating unwanted electrical interference on a nearby circuit.

Emissions Gases and particles left over after the combustion event of an engine. The primary emissions of concern are hydrocarbons, carbon monoxide, and oxides of nitrogen.

Emitter The name of one section of a transistor. The arrow used on a symbol for a transistor is on the emitter and the arrow points toward the negative section of the transistor.

Endplay The movement in line with the centerline of an assembly.

Energy Capacity for performing work.

Engine coolant temperature (ECT) A sensor used to measure the temperature of the coolant of the engine.

Engine stand   A floor mounted-frame usually equipped with casters on which an engine can be attached and rotated.

Entrepreneur   A person who owns a business.

Environmental Protection Agency (EPA)   A federal government agency that oversees the enforcement of laws related to the environment. Included in these laws are regulations on the amount and content of automotive emissions.

EPA   Environmental Protection Agency.

EPS   Electric Power Steering.

ETC   Electronic throttle control. The intake system throttle plate is controlled by a servo motor instead of a mechanical linkage. Also known as *drive-by-wire*.

Ethanol (grain alcohol)   An octane enhancer added, at a rate of up to 10%, to gasoline; will increase the octane rating of the fuel by 2.5 to 3.0. Ethanol is a fuel oxygenate.

Ethyl alcohol   See Ethanol.

Ethylene glycol   Used with water for use as a coolant.

Evaporative (EVAP) emissions   Control system used to prevent fuel vapors in the tank from entering the atmosphere as HC emissions.

Evaporator   An A/C system component that absorbs heat from the air in the vehicle's passenger compartment.

Exhaust gas recirculation (EGR)   The process of passing a small, measured amount of exhaust gas back into the engine to reduce combustion temperatures and formation of NOx (oxides of nitrogen).

Exhaust valve   The value that opens to allow exhaust gases to escape from the cylinder as the piston moves upward.

Experience-based questions   A type of question asked on the ASE certification tests that requires the technician to determine the correct answer based on experience rather than on book knowledge.

Extension housing   The part of a transmission that is at the output end of the transmission.

Extension   A socket wrench tool used between a ratchet or breaker bar and a socket. When using a scope, an external trigger is used to start the recording of an event based on a voltage changed in another (external) circuit.

External combustion engine   An engine such as a steam engine where the fuel is burned outside of the engine.

Eye wash station   A water fountain designed to rinse the eyes with a large volume of water.

Fade   To grow weak; brakes becoming less effective.

Fahrenheit   A temperature scale developed by Gabriel Fahrenheit (1686–1736), a German physicist.

Federal tax   A payroll deduction.

Feedback   The reverse flow of electrical current through a circuit or electrical unit that should not normally be operating. This feedback current (reverse-bias current flow) is most often caused by a poor ground connection for the same normally operating circuit.

Feeler gauge   A set of precision thickness steel blades used to measure a gap. Also called a *thickness gauge*.

FFV   Flex-fuel vehicle. Flex-fuel vehicles are capable of running on straight gasoline or gasoline/ethanol blends.

FICA   A payroll deduction (Federal Insurance Contribution Act, also known as Social Security).

Files   A metal smoothing tool.

Final drive assembly   The differential assembly inside a transaxle.

Fire blanket   A fire-proof wool blanket used to cover a person who is on fire and smother the fire.

Fire extinguisher classes   The types of fires that a fire extinguisher is designed to handle is referred to as fire class.

Firing order   The sequence of firing of the spark plugs.

Fitting wrench   A wrench that is used to remove the fitting holding a brake line or other line. Also called a *line wrench* or *flare-nut wrench*.

Flagging   The act of recording the time and the description of the work completed on a vehicle.

Flare nut wrench   A type of wrench used to remove brake lines.

Flat rate   Pay based on the amount of time published in a labor guide rather than using the actual amount of time spent on the repair.

Flathead   A type of older engine design where the valves were placed in the block next to the cylinders instead of overhead in the cylinder heads as in modern engines.

Flat-tip screwdrivers   A screwdriver used to remove and insert screws that have a single slot. Also called a *straight blade screwdriver*.

Flex fuel   A vehicle designed to be able to use gasoline or E85.

Flex handle   See Breaker bar.

Flooded cell   A battery cell with electrodes immersed in liquid electrolyte.

Floor jack   A hydraulic jack mounted on casters or steel wheels and used to lift a vehicle.

FMVSS   Federal Motor Vehicle Safety Standard.

Foot-pound   A measurement of torque. A one-pound pull, one foot from the center of an object.

Force   Energy applied to an object.

Force   The amount of effort measured in pounds or Newtons.

Formal evaluation   Usually a written evaluation conducted by a supervisor that tries to identify areas of strengths as well as areas of an employee that may need to be improved as part of continuous improvement of the shop or dealer.

Forward bias   Current flow in normal direction.

Forward steer   See Front steer.

Foundation brakes   See Service brakes.

Four-stroke cycle   An internal combustion engine design where four strokes of the piston (two crankshaft revolutions) are required to complete one cycle of events. The four strokes include intake, compression, power, and exhaust.

Fractions   A measurement in parts of an inch, such as 1/2, 1/4, and 1/8.

Frame   The structural part of a vehicle that uses a frame to support the drivetrain and the body.

Freon   A trade name of R-12 air conditioning refrigerant.

Fuel cell   An electrochemical device that converts the energy stored in hydrogen gas into electricity, water, and heat.

Fuel injector   An electric solenoid used to inject a fuel in a spray pattern into the intake manifold (port-type fuel injection) or into the combustion chamber (direct fuel injection).

Fuel pressure regulator   A device used to control the fuel pressure in a fuel-injection system.

Fuel rail The term used to describe the tube or housing that sends fuel to the individual injectors.

Fuel trim A computer function that adjusts fuel delivery during closed-loop operation to bring the air–fuel mixture to as close to 14.7:1 as possible.

Full frame A frame of a vehicle that extends the entire length and width of the vehicle.

Full hybrid A hybrid electric vehicle that utilizes high voltages (200 volts and above) and is capable of propelling the vehicle using "all-electric" mode at low speeds. Also known as a "strong" hybrid.

Fungible Term used to describe that similar liquids such as gasoline can be mixed.

Fuse An electrical safety unit constructed of a fine tin conductor that will melt and open the electrical circuit if excessive current flows through the fuse.

FWD Front-wheel drive.

Gallery Passages in an engine where engine oil flows.

Gasoline Refined petroleum product that is used primarily as a fuel.

GAWR Gross axle weight rating. A rating of the load capacity of a vehicle and included on placards on the vehicle and in the owner's manual.

GDI Gasoline direct injection. A fuel injection system design in which gasoline is injected directly into the combustion chamber.

Gear ratio For a transmission or drive axle, the number of turns of the input shaft required to produce one turn of the output shaft.

Generator A device that converts mechanical energy into electrical energy.

Glow plug A heating element used in diesel engine to aid in starting in cold weather.

GPS Global Positioning System. A government program of 24 satellites that transmit signals and used by receivers to determine their location.

Grade The strength rating of a bolt.

Grain alcohol See Ethanol.

Gram A metric unit of weight measurement equal to 1/1,000 kilogram (1 oz. × 28 = 1 gram). An American dollar bill or paper clip weighs about 1 gram.

Grease fitting A metal replaceable fitting shaped to hold the end of a grease gun in place and equipped with a spring-loaded valve.

Grease Oil with thickener.

Grid The lead-alloy framework (support) for the active materials of an automotive battery.

Gross pay Total amount of income earned before deductions.

Ground (return) path The electrical return path that the current flows through in a complete circuit.

Ground The lowest possible voltage potential in a circuit. In electrical terms, a ground is the desirable return circuit path. Ground can also be undesirable and provide a shortcut path for a defective electrical circuit.

GVW Abbreviation for gross vehicle weight. GVW is the weight of the vehicle plus the weight of all passengers and cargo up to the limit specified by the manufacturer.

GVWR Gross vehicle weight rating. The total weight of the vehicle, including the maximum cargo.

Hacksaw A saw that uses a replaceable blade and is used to cut a variety of materials depending on the type of blade used.

Halderman's laws A series of principles that help avoid making a wrong decision when purchasing or selling a vehicle.

Half shaft Drive axles on a front-wheel-drive vehicle or from a stationary differential to the drive wheels.

Hammer A hand tool used to deliver a force to a concentrated place.

Hazard warning A sticker or decal warning that a hazard is close.

Hazardous waste material Chemicals such as waste oil and solvents that are no longer being used by a shop and may pose a danger to environment or people.

HC Hydrocarbons (unburned fuel); when combined with NOx and sunlight, they form smog.

Heat of compression When air is compressed, its temperature increases. In a diesel engine the hot air created by compression is used to ignite the diesel fuel that is injected into the combustion chamber when the piston is close to the top of the cylinder on the compression stroke.

Heat A measure of the amount of thermal energy usually expressed in BUTs.

Heater core A cooling system component that is responsible for transferring heat from the engine coolant to the passenger compartment.

Heater hoses Hoses used to transfer engine coolant from the engine to the heater core and back to the engine.

Heating, ventilation, and air conditioning system (HVAC) The term used to describe the entire system in a vehicle used to heat and cool the passenger areas.

Height sensor A height sensor determines the vertical relationship between the suspension component and the body of a vehicle.

Height-sensing proportioning valve A valve connected to the rear suspension that limits the brake pressure sent to the rear brakes if the rear of the vehicle is high (unloaded).

Helical insert A steel insert used to repair damaged threads.

Helicoil A brand name for a helical insert.

Helper springs Auxiliary or extra springs used in addition to the vehicle's original springs to restore proper ride height or to increase the load carrying capacity of the vehicle.

HEPA vacuum High efficiency particulate air filter vacuum used to clean brake dust.

HEPA High Efficiency Particulate Air filter.

Hertz A unit of measurement of frequency. One Hertz is one cycle per second, abbreviated Hz. Named for Heinrich R. Hertz, a nineteenth-century German physicist.

HEV Hybrid electric vehicle. Describes any vehicle that uses more than one source of propulsion, such as internal combustion engine (ICE) and electric motor(s).

HFC-134a A refrigerant used in the A/C systems of most domestic vehicles built since the mid-1990s. Also called R-134a.

HID High Intensity Discharge. A type of headlight that uses high voltage to create an arc inside the arc tube assembly, which then produces a blue-white light.

High energy ignition (HEI) The brand name for the electronic ignition used in General Motors vehicles.

High impedance meter   A digital meter that has at least 10 million ohms of internal resistance as measure between the test leads with the meter set to read volts.

High pressure common rail (HPCR)   A type of diesel engine where high pressure fuel is sent to all the injectors through a common tube called a rail.

High resistance   A type of electrical fault that causes a decrease in current flow of electricity in the circuit.

HOAT   Hybrid Organic Acid Technology. A corrosion inhibitor additive with reduced silicate content.

Horsepower   A unit of power; 33,000 foot-pounds per minute. One horsepower equals 746 Watts.

Housing expense   Includes rent or mortgage payment, plus heat, light, and other utility expenses.

HP   Horsepower.

HUD   Head up display.

HV battery   High-voltage battery. Hybrid electric vehicles use NiMH battery packs that are rated up to 330 volts DC.

HV   High voltage. Applies to any voltage above 50 volts.

Hybrid   Something (such as a battery) made from more than one different element; abbreviated version of hybrid electric vehicle (HEV); a type of vehicle that uses two types of propulsion.

Hydraulic press   A piece of shop equipment usually mounted on the floor, which uses a hydraulic cylinder to remove and install pressed-on components, such as bearings.

Hydraulic system   The base brake system containing the master cylinder, wheel cylinders, calipers, and brake fluid lines.

Hydraulic   The force exerted by pressurized liquid in a closed system.

Hydrocarbons (HC)   Any of a number of compounds of carbon and hydrogen used as fuel, such as gasoline. High levels of hydrocarbons in tailpipe emissions are a result of unburned fuel. When combined with NOx and sunlight, they form smog.

Hydrometer   An instrument used to measure the specific gravity of a liquid. A battery hydrometer is calibrated to read the expected specific gravity of battery electrolyte.

Hydroplaning   Condition that occurs when driving too fast on wet roads where the water on the road gets trapped between the tire and the road, forcing the tire onto a layer of water and off the road surface. All traction between the tire and the road is lost.

Hz   An abbreviation for Hertz, cycles per second.

IAT   Inorganic Additive Technology. The corrosion inhibitor used in most green-colored coolants.

ICE   Internal combustion engine.

Idle stop mode   A phase in hybrid electric vehicle operation in which the internal combustion engine shuts off during idle operation.

Idler arm   The pivot point and support arm of a parallelogram-type steering linkage located on the passenger side of the vehicle.

Ignition circuit   Electrical components and connections that produce and distribute high-voltage electricity to ignite the air–fuel mixture inside the engine.

Ignition control module (ICM)   The electronic control module that controls the charging and discharging of the ignition coil(s).

ILEV   Inherently low-emission vehicle. One category of emission standards set by the state of California.

ILSAC   International Lubricant Standardization and Approval Committee. Responsible for development of the ILSAC standard for motor oil performance.

Impact wrench   An air-operated hand tool used to install and remove threaded fasteners.

Impeller   The mechanism in a water pump that rotates to produce coolant flow.

Incandescent light   A type of light that uses an incandescent rather than a fluorescent or LED light source.

Incentive pay   See Commission pay.

Inches of Mercury   A measurement of vacuum, abbreviated as in. Hg.; pressure below atmospheric pressure.

Included angle   SAI angle added to the camber angle of the same wheel.

Independent suspension   A suspension system that allows a wheel to move up and down without undue effect on the opposite side.

Indirect injection (IDI)   A type of diesel engine design where the fuel is injected into a pre-combustion chamber instead of directly into the combustion chamber.

Inductive ammeter   A type of ammeter that is used as a Hall effect senor in a clamp that is used around a conductor carrying current.

Informal evaluation   A process of evaluation that is usually not written but instead is based on observation and verbal communications of an employer of an employee.

Injection pump   A high pressure pump used to create high fuel pressures in a diesel engine.

Inlet port   See Replenishing port.

Inner liner   The inner layer of rubber inside a tire.

Input shaft   The shaft that is connected to the clutch in a manual transmission or transaxle.

Input   Information on data from sensors to an electronic controller is called input. Sensors and switches provide the input signals.

Insulator   A material that does not readily conduct electricity and heat. A nonmetal material that contains more than four electrons in its atom's outer shell.

Insulators   Thin strips of plastic or hard rubber used to separate the leaves of a leaf spring.

Intake air temperature (IAT) sensor   Measures the air temperature of the air entering the engine.

Intake manifold   The part that delivers air to all of the individual cylinders from one throttle body unit.

Intake valve   The valve that opens in an engine to allow air into the cylinders as the piston moves downward.

Integral sensor   A term used to describe a crash sensor that is built into the airbag control module.

Inter-Provincial (IP) Certificate   A certificate required to work on vehicles in all Canadian provinces except Quebec and British Columbia.

IP   Abbreviation for instrument panel.

Iridium spark plugs   A type of spark plug that uses a thin iridium metal center electrode.

Iron   Refined metal from iron ore (ferrous oxide) in a furnace. (Also see Steel.)

ISC   Idle speed control.

Jack stand See Safety stand.

Jam nut A second nut used to prevent the first nut from loosening.

Job shadowing A term used to describe when someone is observing a person at work to see what is involved in the trade during a course of a day.

Jobber A name used to describe a store where automotive parts are sold to shops and individuals.

Julian date The number of the day of the year. Also called *JD*.

JWL Japan Wheel Light Metal Standard Mark.

Key fob A decorative unit attached to keys. Often includes a remote control to unlock/lock vehicles.

Kinetic energy The energy in any moving object. The amount of energy depends on the weight (mass) of the object and the speed of the object.

Labor guides A book or service information that provides the time that is needed to perform a service or repair operation.

Ladder frame A steel frame for a vehicle that uses cross braces along the length, similar to the rungs of a ladder.

LDWS Lane departure warning system.

Leaf spring A spring made of several pieces of flat spring steel.

Least likely questions A type of question asked on the ASE certification tests.

LED Light-emitting diode. A high-efficiency light source that uses very little electricity and produces very little heat.

LEV Low emission vehicle.

Lift pump A pump used in a diesel engine to move diesel fuel from the fuel tank to the high pressure pump.

Liquid crystal display (LCD) A display that uses liquid crystals to display waveforms and text on its screen.

Liquid A substance that is a readily flowing fluid.

Load test A type of battery test where an electrical load is applied to the battery and the voltage is monitored to determine the condition of a battery.

Load A term used to describe a device when an electrical current is flowing through it.

Locking hubs Assemblies found on the front wheels of some vehicles equipped with part-time four-wheel drive.

Locking pliers Pliers that can be used to grasp an object and then be locked into position. Often called by a popular brand name VISE-GRIPS®.

LOF An abbreviation for lube oil and filter. A routine service performed on vehicles usually every six months or every 6,000 miles or according to vehicle manufacturers' recommended interval.

Low range A gear reduction built into the transfer case of a four-wheel-drive vehicle.

LPG Liquefied petroleum gas. Another term for *propane*.

LSD An abbreviation commonly used for limited slip differentials.

LSD Low side driver.

LT Light truck.

Lug nuts Nuts used on wheel studs to attach wheels to hubs.

M85 Internal combustion engine fuel containing 85% methanol and 15% gasoline.

MacPherson strut A type of front suspension with the shock absorber and coil spring in one unit, which rotates when the wheels are turned. Assembly mounts to the vehicle body at top and to one ball joint and control arm at the lower end. Named for its inventor, Earle S. MacPherson.

Main shaft The shaft inside a manual transmission or transaxle that is in line with the clutch.

Magnetic pulse generator A type of sensor usually used to determine crankshaft or camshaft position.

Magnetism A form of energy that is recognized by the attraction it exerts on other materials.

Major splice A place in a tire where the tread rubber and one or more body plies are spliced during tire construction.

Malfunction indicator lamp (MIL) This amber dash board warning light may be labeled "check engine" or "service engine soon."

Manifold absolute pressure (MAP) Sensor used to measure the pressure inside the intake manifold compared to a perfect vacuum.

MAP Manifold absolute pressure.

Mass air flow (MAF) The volume of air passing into the engine. Varies with temperature and humidity. Used in calculating injector operation and spark timing.

Master certified technician A technician who has successfully passed all eight ASE certification tests and has completed at least two years of experience.

Master cylinder The part of the brake hydraulic system where the pressure is generated.

MCA Marine cranking amps. A battery specification.

Mechanical force The force of combustion in the engine cylinder creates the mechanical force that is then used to propel the vehicle.

Mechanical power Mechanical force created by the expanding gases inside the heat expansion cylinders of an engine are converted into useful mechanical power by the crankshaft.

Medium hybrid A hybrid electric vehicle design that utilizes "medium" voltage levels (between 50 and 200 volts). Medium hybrids use regenerative braking and idle stop but are not capable of starting the vehicle from a stop using electric mode.

Mentor An experienced technician who offers to help a beginning technician learn all aspects of the trade.

Mercury A heavy metal.

Mesothelioma A fatal type of cancer of the lining of the chest or abdominal cavity, which can be caused by asbestos inhalation.

Methanol (wood alcohol) Typically manufactured from natural gas. Methanol content, including cosolvents, in unleaded gasoline is limited by law to 5%.

Methyl alcohol See Methanol.

Metric bolts Bolts manufactured and sized in the metric system of measurement.

Microbe A microorganism that is too small to be seen by the human eye.

MIL See Malfunction indicator lamp.

Mild hybrid A hybrid electric vehicle design that utilizes regenerative braking and idle stop but cannot propel the vehicle in electric-only mode. Also called an assist hybrid and typically operates below 50 volts.

Millisecond One-thousandth of one second (1/1,000).

Minutes A unit of measure of an angle. Sixty minutes equal one degree.

Miscible A term used to describe the mixing of oils without causing any harm.

Misfire When complete combustion does not occur in one or more cylinders due to fuel, ignition, or cylinder compression.

Mode shift A shift made in a four-wheel-drive vehicle into one either four-wheel drive or two-wheel drive.

Mode A particular state of operation.

Model year (MY) The year of a vehicle, which may be different from the calendar year when it is sold.

Modified X A method of tire rotation.

Module A group of electronic components functioning as a component of a larger system.

Moly grease Grease containing molybdenum disulfide.

Morning sickness A slang term used to describe temporary loss of power steering assist when cold caused by wear in the control valve area of a power rack-and-pinion unit.

Most likely A type of test question used on ASE certification tests.

Motor An electromechanical device that converts electrical energy into mechanical movement.

Motoring mode A phase of BAS hybrid vehicle operation where the motor-generator cranks the ICE to start it.

MSDS Material safety data sheets.

MTBE Methyl tertiary butyl ether. MTBE is an oxygenated fuel that is used as a gasoline additive to enhance its burning characteristics being phased out due to ground water contamination concerns.

Multigroove adjustable pliers Pliers that are capable of grasping a wide range of object sizes; also called *water pump pliers* or by a popular brand name of Channel Locks®

Multiple choice The type of questions used on the ASE certification tests.

MY Model year.

N.C. Normally closed.

N.O. Normally open.

National Institute for Automotive Service Excellence The formal name of ASE, the company that gives technician certification tests.

Naturally aspirated An engine that uses atmospheric pressure to draw air into the cylinder compared to using a supercharger or a turbocharger to force air into the cylinders.

Needle–nose pliers Pliers that are equipped with pointed jaws, which allow use in restricted areas or for small parts.

Net pay Amount earned minus deductions. Also called *take home pay*.

Network A communications system used to link multiple computers or modules.

Neutral charge An atom that has the same number of electrons as protons.

Neutral safety switch A switch connected in series in the starter control circuit that allows operation of the starter motor to occur only when the gear selection is in neutral (N) or park (P).

Newton A unit of force in the metric system.

NHTSA Abbreviation for the National Highway Traffic Safety Administration.

Nitrile A type of rubber that is okay for use with petroleum.

Nitrogen An inert gas that comprises approximately 78% of the earth's atmosphere.

NLEV National Low-Emission Vehicle.

NLGI National Lubricating Grease Institute. Usually associated with grease. The higher the NLGI number, the firmer the grease. #000 is very fluid whereas #5 is very firm. The consistency most recommended is NLGI #2 (soft).

Noise Noise is the vibration of air caused by a body in motion.

NOx Oxides of nitrogen; when combined with HC and sunlight, form smog.

NTC Negative temperature coefficient. Usually used in reference to a temperature sensor (coolant or air temperature). As the temperature increases, the resistance of the sensor decreases.

Nucleus The central part of an atom, which has a positive charge and contains almost all the mass of the atom.

Nut splitter A hand tool designed to break a nut that is rusted onto a bolt or stud.

Nuts A female threaded fastener to be used with a bolt or stud.

NVH Abbreviation for noise, vibration, and harshness.

O₂ sensor Oxygen sensor; also called O2S.

OAT Organic Acid Technology. A corrosion inhibitor additive containing no silicates or phosphates. Used in DEX-COOL and some other extended-life coolants.

OBD-II On-Board Diagnosis, second generation. The standard used for all emissions-related systems of the engine since 1996 on all vehicles sold in the United States.

Occupant detection systems An airbag system that includes a sensor in the passenger seat used to detect whether or not a passenger is seated in the passenger side and the weight range of that passenger.

OE Original equipment.

Offset aviation snip A tin snip that has curved jaws allowing it to make curved cuts either left or right.

Offset The distance the center section (mounting pad) is offset from the centerline of the wheel.

Ohm's Law An electrical law that requires 1 volt to push 1 ampere through 1 ohm of resistance.

Ohm The unit of electrical resistance. Named for Georg Simon Ohm (1787–1854).

Ohmmeter An electrical test instrument used to measure ohms (unit of electrical resistance).

Oil filter A filter usually constructed of pleated paper in a sheet metal container that filters dirt from the engine oil.

Oil galleries A name used to describe the oil passages in an engine where pressurized oil flows to lubricate the moving parts.

Oil pan The lower part of an engine were oil is stored, usually made from stamped steel or cast aluminum.

Oil pump A pump inside an engine used to send pressurized oil to the moving parts of the engine.

Oil sump Another name for an oil pan.

OL Overload or over limit.

Omega The last letter of the Greek alphabet; a symbol for ohm, (Ω) the unit for electrical resistance.

On-the-job (OTJ) A term used to describe training that occurs when the worker is actually working on the job and learns from others who are doing the same or similar work.

Open circuit battery voltage test   An electrical test of the battery using a voltmeter attached to the battery terminals used to help determine the state-of-charge of the battery.

Open circuit   Any circuit that is not complete and in which no current flows.

Open end wrench   The end of a wrench that is open to allow the wrench to be inserted onto a fastener from the side.

OSHA   Occupational Safety and Health Administration. OSHA is the main federal agency responsible for enforcement of workplace safety and health legislation.

Out-of-round   A fault with a brake drum, which is not perfectly round.

Output shaft   The shaft that sends engine torque from the transmission to the drive wheels.

Output   The command from an electronic control module.

Overhead camshafts   An engine design where the camshaft(s) are located above the valves in the cylinder head.

Overhead valve (OHV)   An engine design where the camshaft is located in the engine block (cam in block design) and the valves are in the cylinder head over the pistons.

Oxidation catalysts   Platinum and palladium used in the catalytic converter to combine oxygen (O_2) with hydrocarbons (HC) and carbon monoxide (CO) to form nonharmful tailpipe emissions of water (H_2O) and carbon dioxide (CO_2).

Oxides of nitrogen (NOx)   A primary emission produced in the combustion chamber under high temperatures when nitrogen combines with oxygen. Oxides of nitrogen contribute to the formation of smog (ground level ozone [O_3]) when combined with HC and sunlight.

Oxygen   A colorless, odorless gas that is a direct supporter of combustion. Earth's atmosphere contains approximately 21% oxygen.

Ozone   Oxygen rich (O_3) gas created by sunlight reaction with unburned hydrocarbons (HC) and oxides of nitrogen (NOx); also called smog.

Pal nut   See Jam nut.

Palladium   One of the chemicals used inside a catalytic converter.

Pancake engine   See Boxer.

Parallelogram linkage   A type of steering linkage used with a conventional steering gear that uses a pitman arm, center link, idler arm, and tie rods.

Parallelogram   A geometric box shape where opposite sides are parallel (equal distance apart).

Parking brake   Components used to hold a vehicle on a 30° incline. Formerly called an emergency brake before 1967 when dual master cylinders and split braking systems became law. The parking brake is also called the hand brake.

Parts counter person   A term used to describe the person who works at a parts store or the parts department at a shop or dealer who gets parts for technicians or customers.

Part-time employment   A term used to describe working at a job for less than the normal 40 hours per week.

Part-time four-wheel drive   A system that uses a transfer case and locking hubs to provide four-wheel drive.

PASS   A word used to help remember how to use a fire extinguisher; pull pin, aim, squeeze the lever, and sweep the nozzle from side to side.

Passenger presence system (PPS)   An airbag system that includes a sensor in the passenger seat used to detect whether or not a passenger is seated in the passenger side and the weight range of that passenger.

Pending code   A diagnostic trouble code that has been set the first time but has not matured because a second failure has not been detected by the PCM.

Penetrating oil   A thin oil that is designed to penetrate through rust and provide lubrication for the threads of a fastener.

Penetration   A test for grease where the depth of a standard cone is dropped into a grease sample and its depth is measured.

Perimeter frame   A steel structure for a vehicle that supports the body of the vehicle under the sides, as well as the front and rear.

Petrodiesel   Another term *for petroleum diesel*, which is ordinary diesel fuel refined from crude oil.

Petroleum   Another term for *crude oil*. The literal meaning of petroleum is "rock oil."

PHT   Parallel hybrid truck. A term used to describe the Chevrolet Silverado/GMC Sierra hybrid pickup truck.

Pillars   A term used to describe the supporting vertical member of the body used to support the roof.

Pilot bearing   A bearing or bushing used to support the end of the input shaft and located in the end of the engine crankshaft.

Pinion gear   A small gear on the end of the starter drive that rotates the engine flywheel ring gear for starting.

Piston assemblies   A part of a master cylinder where the sealing cups and the piston are replaceable as an assembly.

Piston stroke   The distance the piston moves from the top of the cylinder to the bottom of the cylinder.

Pitch   The pitch of a threaded fastener refers to the number of threads per inch.

Pitman arm   A short lever arm that is splined to the steering gear cross shaft. It transmits the steering force from the cross shaft to the steering linkage.

Pitman shaft   See Sector shaft.

Planet carrier   The part of a planetary gear set that houses the planet pinions.

Planetary gear set   A simple mechanism made up of a ring gear, a planet carrier, and a sun gear. A single planetary gear set can be used to achieve a reduction, a direct drive, an overdrive, or a reverse.

Platform   The platform of a vehicle includes the basic structure (frame and/or major body panels), as well as the basic steering and suspension components. One platform may be the basis for several different brand vehicles.

Platinum spark plugs   A type of spark plug that uses platinum for the center electrode.

Platinum   One of the chemicals used inside a catalytic converter.

Pliers   A hand tool with two moveable jaws.

PM generator   A sensor that has a permanent magnet and a coil of wire and produces an analog voltage signal if a metal wheel with notches passes close to the sensor.

PM   Particulate matter. PM can be made up of any airborne liquid or solid, and its concentration is regulated by both the CARB and the EPA.

Polarity   The condition of being positive or negative in relation to a magnetic pole.

Polyglycol   A term used to describe brake fluid.

Pop rivet   A type of fastener that uses a rivet gun to pull out the rivet until the end deforms and thereby creates a light clamping form.

Port fuel injection   A type of fuel injection where the fuel is squirted into the intake manifold near the intake valve.

Portable crane   A piece of shop equipment that is used to lift and move heavy pieces of equipment, such as an engine.

Positive crankcase ventilation (PCV)   System used to prevent corrosive blowby gases (by-products of combustion) in the crankcase from entering the atmosphere.

Potentiometer   A 3-terminal variable resistor that varies the voltage drop in a circuit.

Pound foot   A measurement of torque. A 1-pound pull, 1 foot from the center of an object.

Pour point   The low temperature where oil can flow.

Power assist mode   A phase of hybrid vehicle operation in which the ICE is assisted by the electric motor(s) to propel the vehicle.

Power path   The part of an electrical circuit that is located from the power source to the electrical load device.

Power side   The wires leading from the power source (battery) to the resistance (load) of a circuit.

Power source   In electrical terms the battery or generator (alternator).

Power train   An engine and transmission in combination.

Power   The rate of doing work, measured in horsepower as kilowatts. In electrical terms, is amperes × volts (Power = $I \times E$).

PPE   Personal protective equipment, which can include gloves, safety glasses, and other items.

PPM   Parts per million.

Predelivery inspection (PDI)   The inspection and preparation of a new vehicle to get it ready to deliver to the customer.

Preload   A term used to describe a tightening of a nut or bolt to provide a force.

Pressure cap   A device used to maintain and limit pressure in the cooling system.

Pressure differential   A difference in pressure from one brake circuit to another.

Pressure plate   The part of a clutch that exerts a clamping force on the clutch disc located between the engine flywheel and the pressure plate.

Pressure regulator   A regulating device that maintains a specified pressure in a system.

Pressure   A force applied to a surface divided by its area.

Pretensioners   An explosive device used to remove the slack from a safety belt when an airbag is deployed.

Prevailing torque nut   A special design of nut fastener that is deformed slightly or has other properties that permit the nut to remain attached to the fastener without loosening.

Preventative maintenance (PM)   Operations and fluid changes performed on a vehicle as part of normal maintenance to help prevent faults or worn parts.

Processing   The act of a computer when input data is run through computer programs to determine what output is needed to be performed.

Prop shaft   An abbreviation for propeller shaft.

Propane   See LPG.

Propeller shaft   A term used by many manufacturers for a drive shaft.

Proportioning valve   Valve installed between the master cylinder and rear brakes that limits the amount of pressure to the rear wheels to prevent rear wheel lock-up.

Protection   A term used to describe a fuse or other electrical device that protects an electrical circuit from damage in the event of an electrical problem such as short circuit.

Proton   A positive-charged particle; one of the basic particles of the nucleus of an atom.

PSI   Pounds per square inch.

Pull   Vehicle tends to go left or right while traveling on a straight, level road.

Pulse generators   An electromagnetic unit that generates a voltage signal used to trigger the ignition control module that controls (turns on and off) the primary ignition current of an electronic ignition system.

Pulse width   The amount of "on" time of an electronic fuel-injector.

Pulse   A voltage signal that increases or decreases from a constant value, then returns to the original value.

Punch   A hand tool designed to be used with a hammer to drive out pins.

Push rod   The link rod connecting the brake pedal to the master cylinder piston.

Pushrod engine   A type of engine design that uses a camshaft located in the block and then operates the values using pushrods up to the cylinder head.

R.O.   An abbreviation for repair order.

R-12   A refrigerant used until the mid-1990s for use in vehicle air conditioning systems. Also called CFC-12.

R-134a   A refrigerant used in the A/C systems of most domestic vehicles built since the mid-1990s. Also called HFC-134a.

Race   Inner and outer machined surface of a ball or roller bearing.

Rack support   A spring-loaded unit that is used to hold the rack part of a rack-and-pinion steering gear assembly in proper position.

Rack-and-pinion   A type of lightweight steering unit that connects the front wheels through tie rods to the end of a long shaft called a *rack*. When the driver moves the steering wheel, the force is transferred to the rack-and-pinion assembly. Inside the rack housing is a small pinion gear that meshes with gear teeth, which are cut into the rack.

Radial runout   A measure of the amount a tire or wheel is out of round. Excessive radial runout can cause a tramp-type vibration.

Radial tire   A tire whose carcass plies run straight across (or almost straight across) from bead to bead.

Radiator hose   A flexible hose used to transfer coolant between the various cooling system components.

Radiator   A cooling system component used to dissipate heat from the coolant to the surrounding air.

Range shift   A selection on a four-wheel-drive vehicle that is used to select high or low range in the transfer case.

Range   The distance a vehicle can travel on a full charge or full-fuel tank without recharging or refueling. Range is measured in miles or kilometers.

Ratchet   A handle used to rotate a socket, which is reversible and allows the socket to be rotated in one direction and then free movement in the opposite direction of rotation.

Ratio The expression for proportion. For example, in a typical rear axle assembly, the drive shaft rotates three times faster than the rear axles. Expressed as a ratio of 3:1 and rear as "three to one." Power train ratios are always expressed as driving divided by driven gears.

RBS Regenerative braking system. A hybrid electric vehicle system that allows vehicle kinetic energy to be converted into electrical energy for charging the high-voltage battery.

RBWL Red brake warning lamp.

RCRA Resource Conservation and Recovery Act.

Rebuilt See Remanufactured.

Recall A notification to the owner of a vehicle that a safety issue needs to be corrected.

Receiver-drier An A/C system component used to filter and remove moisture from liquid refrigerant on the high side of the system.

Reconditioning A term used to describe the cleaning and restoration of a used vehicle to make it look as new as possible.

Red brake warning lamp The dash-mounted warning lamp that lights if a hydraulic system fault is detected.

Reduction A drivetrain mechanism designed to decrease speed and increase torque. A gear ratio of 3.56:1 would be considered to be a reduction because the input shaft must turn 3.56 times in order to achieve 1 turn of the output shaft.

Reference voltage A voltage applied to a circuit. Battery plus and ground are examples of reference voltages.

Reference A term used to describe the name of a person who knows you and can speak to others about your knowledge and skills.

Refractometer A device used to measure battery state-of-charge by allowing light to pass through an electrolyte sample.

Refrigerant A fluid used in A/C systems to absorb, transfer, and release heat energy.

Regen An abbreviation for *regenerative braking*.

Regeneration A process of taking the kinetic energy of a moving vehicle and converting it to electrical energy and storing it in a battery.

Regenerative braking A hybrid vehicle function that recovers kinetic energy while the vehicle is decelerating and stores it for later use.

Reid vapor pressure (RVP) A method of determining vapor pressure of gasoline and other petroleum products. Widely used in the petroleum industry as an indicator of the volatility of gasoline.

Relay An electromagnetic switch that uses a movable arm.

Release bearing The bearing assembly that rides on the pressure plate of a clutch assembly and is used to release the clamping force of the pressure plate on the clutch disc. Also called a *throw-out bearing.*

Remanufactured A term used to describe a process where a component is disassembled, cleaned, inspected, and reassembled using new or reconditioned parts. According to the Automotive Parts Rebuilders Association (APRA), this same procedure is also called *rebuilt.*

Remove and inspect (R&I) The term used to describe what a service technician does to check on the condition of a part. The part is removed from the vehicle and inspected to judge its condition to determine if it can be repaired or needs to be replaced with a new part.

Remove and replace (R&R) The term used to describe the replacement of a component or a part.

Removers This term is used to describe hand tools, which are designed to remove broken studs, bolts, and other fasteners.

Renewal parts The term used to referring to parts used to replace the original parts that came on the vehicle when it was new just as tires.

Renewal A part built to be used as a replacement for the original equipment (OE) part.

Repair order Also called an *R.O* or *work order*. Contains all vehicle and customer information and the list of service work that is to be completed.

Reserve capacity The number of minutes a battery can produce 25 A and still maintain a battery voltage of 1.75 volts per cell (10.5 volts for a 12-volt battery).

Resistance The opposition to current flow measured in ohms.

Resume A statement of your background and experience submitted to a potential employer.

Revolutions per minute (RPM) A measure of how fast an object is rotating around an axis.

RGB Regenerative braking.

Rheostat A two-terminal variable resistor.

Rhodium One of the chemicals used inside a catalytic converter.

Right-to-know laws Laws that state that employees have a right to know when the materials they use at work are hazardous.

RIM Reaction injection molded.

Ring gear The large gear inside a differential assembly, which meshes with the drive pinion gear.

Riveted linings Brake lining that is held to the brake shoe using rivets.

Role model A role played by a mentor.

Roller bearings Antifriction bearings that use hardened steel rollers between the inner and outer races.

Rolling circumference The distance a tire travels when rotated one revolution.

ROM Read-only memory.

Root mean square (RMS) Conversion of AC voltages to the effective DC value.

Rosin-core solder A type of solder for use in electrical repairs. Inside the center of the solder is a rosin that acts as a flux to clean and help the solder flow.

Rotary engine An engine that does not use piston that moves up and down in a cylinder but instead uses a rotor that rotates inside a complex combustion chamber. Also called a Wankel engine after its inventor.

Rotor The rotating part of a generator where the magnetic field is created.

RPA Rear Park Assist. The General Motors term to describe the system used to detect objects and warn the driver when backing.

RPM Engine speed expressed in revolutions per minute of the crankshaft.

RTV Room-temperature vulcanization.

Rubber coupling A flexible connection between the power seat motor and the drive cable.

RVP Reid vapor pressure. A measure of the volatility at exactly 100°F.

RWD Rear-wheel drive.

Rzeppa joint A type of constant velocity (CV) joint named after its inventor, Alfred H. Rzeppa.

SAE Society of Automotive Engineers.

Safety stand A metal device with an adjustable vertical support that is designed to support a vehicle after it has been raised off the ground. Also called a *jack stand*.

SAI Steering axis inclination (same as KPI).

Sample A reading taken from an electrical signal. A waveform is created from a successive number of samples.

SAR Supplemental Air Restraints. Another term used to describe an airbag system.

Scan tool An electronic unit that plugs into a data link connector of a vehicle and is used to retrieve diagnostic trouble codes and engine information.

Schrader valve A type of valve used in tires, air conditioning, and fuel injection systems. Invented in 1844 by August Schrader.

SCR Silicon Controller Rectifier.

Screwdriver A hand tool designed to remove or insert screws.

Seal driver A hand tool used with a mallet or hammer to seat seals into a seal groove.

Seal puller A hand tool designed to remove seals.

Secondary winding The high voltage winding inside an ignition coil.

Sector gear A section of a gear inside a steering gear that is attached to the sector shaft. Also called the pitman shaft.

Sector shaft The output shaft of a conventional steering gear. It is a part of the sector shaft in a section of a gear that meshes with the worm gear and is rotated by the driver when the steering wheel is turned. It is also called a *pitman shaft.*

Selective catalytic reduction (SCR) An emission control system used in newer engines to reduce oxides of nitrogen emissions. Uses diesel exhaust fluid (urea) injected into the exhaust to achieve the reduction in exhaust emissions.

Self-energizing A brake shoe, which when applied, develops a wedging action that assists the braking force applied by the wheel cylinder.

Self-propelled vehicles A term used to describe the first vehicles that used a motor or engine to propel the vehicle instead of using a horse to provide the power.

Self-tapping screw A screw that has a tapered tip that allows the screw to form threads in the metal.

SEMA Specialty Equipment Manufacturers Association.

Semiconductor A material that is neither a conductor nor an insulator; there are exactly four electrons in the atom's outer shell.

Separators In a battery, nonconducting, porous thin materials used to separate positive and negative plates.

Serial data Data that are transmitted by a series of rapidly changing voltage signals.

Series circuit An electrical circuit that provides only one path for current to flow.

Series–parallel hybrid A hybrid vehicle design that can operate as a series hybrid, a parallel hybrid, or both series and parallel at the same time.

Serpentine (poly V) belt A type of accessory drive belt that is used to power several accessories from the crankshaft of the engine.

Service advisor A person who talks to the customer about a vehicle service and completes the work order.

Service bay A work area for a vehicle, with or without a lift. Also called a *stall*.

Service brake The main driver-operated vehicle brakes.

Service consultant Another name for a service advisor.

Service information Includes service manuals, owner's manuals, CD ROM discs, Internet sites, or other sources where vehicle information is found.

Service manager The person in charge of a shop or dealer service department.

Service plug A high-voltage electrical disconnect device on hybrid electric vehicles. The service plug should always be disconnected whenever working on a hybrid electric vehicle's high-voltage circuits.

Service writer Another name for a service advisor.

Servomotor The actuator in an electronic throttle control (ETC) system.

Shackle A mounting that allows the end of a leaf spring to move forward and backward as the spring moves up and down during normal operation of the suspension.

Shock absorbers A suspension component that links and controls the action and reaction of the springs.

Shop foreman A journeyman service technician who helps solve technical problems and helps service technicians.

Short circuit A circuit in which current flows but bypasses some or all the resistance in the circuit. A connection that results in a "copper-to-copper" connection.

Short to ground A short circuit in which the current bypasses some or all the resistance of the circuit and flows to ground. Because ground is usually steel in automotive electricity, a short to ground (grounded) is a "copper-to-steel" connection.

Short/long arm suspension Abbreviated SLA. A suspension system with a short upper control arm and a long lower control arm. The wheel changes very little in camber with a vertical deflection. Also called *double-wishbone-type suspension.*

Shorted A condition of being shorted such as a short circuit.

Short-to-voltage A circuit in which current flows, but bypasses some or all the resistance in the circuit in the power side of the circuit. A connection that results in a "copper-to-copper" connection.

Side gears The gears inside a differential that attach to the axles.

Sidewall The side of a tire.

Silicon A semiconductor material.

Silicone brake fluid A type of brake fluid that is purple and does not absorb moisture.

Single cut file A file that has just one row of cutting teeth.

Single overhead camshaft (SOHC) A type of engine design that uses a single overhead camshaft per bank of cylinder to operate both the intake and the exhaust valves.

SIR Supplemental inflatable restraints. Another term for *airbags*.

SLA Abbreviation for short/long arm suspension.

Slave cylinder A hydraulic cylinder used to transfer the force of the driver's foot to the release (throw-out) bearing in a clutch system.

Sleeve A part of a micrometer that has the major measurement designations.

SLI battery The battery that is responsible for starting, charging, and lighting in a vehicle's electrical system.

Slip-joint pliers A hand tool that has two positions allowing the use of two different ranges of sizes.

Slip-ring end (SRE) The end of a generator (alternator) that has the brushes and the slip rings.

Small-hole gauge A handheld measuring tool that is adjustable to fit inside small holes. A micrometer is then used to measure the gauge to determine the inside diameter of the hole. Also called a *split-ball gauge*.

Smog pump An electric or engine-driven pump used to supply low pressure air to the exhaust system to help reduce exhaust emissions on some engines. Also called an AIR pump.

Smog The term used to describe a combination of *smoke* and *fog*. Formed by NOx and HC with sunlight.

SMR System main relay. The high-voltage disconnect relays used in most hybrid electric vehicles.

Snap ring pliers A hand tool that is designed to install or remove snap rings.

Snap ring A spring steel clip that is used to retain an object in a bore by being inserted into a groove.

Snips A hand tool designed to cut sheet metal.

SOC State-of-charge. Expressed as a percentage, this refers to the charge level of a battery.

Society of Automotive Engineers (SAE) A professional organization made up of automotive engineers and designers that establishes standards and conducts testing for many automotive-related functions.

Socket adapter An adapter that allows the use of one size of driver (ratchet or breaker bar) to rotate another drive size of socket.

Socket A tool that fits over the head of a bolt or nut and is rotated by a ratchet or breaker bar.

Soft skills A term used to describe skills needed to get along with others in the work place that are not included in the technical skills needed to actually perform the work.

Solenoid valves Valves that are opened and closed using an electromagnetic solenoid.

Solenoid An electromagnetic switch that uses a movable core.

Solid axle A solid supporting axle for both front or both rear wheels. Also referred to as a straight axle or nonindependent axle.

Solid Matter that is firm and does not move or flow.

Solvent Usually colorless liquids that are used to remove grease and oil.

Soot Particulate matter emitted by diesel engines.

Space frame A type of vehicle construction that uses the structure of the body to support the engine and drivetrain, as well as the steering and suspension. The outside body panels are nonstructural.

Spark plugs Removal plugs that have a gap where a high voltage spark is used to ignite the air–fuel mixture inside the cylinders of an engine.

Spark tester A tool used to check for spark.

Speakers A device consisting of a magnet, coil of wire, and a cone, which reproduces sounds from the electrical signals sent to the speakers from a radio or amplifier.

Speed nuts Also called Tinnerman nuts. Used to keep the brake drum on at the assembly plant. Can be removed and discarded when servicing drum brakes for the first time.

Speed rating A letter on most tires that indicates the maximum speed at which the tire is designed to perform.

Spider Center part of a wheel. Also known as the *center section*.

Spindle nut Nut used to retain and adjust the bearing clearance of the hub to the spindle.

Spindle The part of a micrometer that moves and contacts the object being measured.

Splice pack A central point where many serial data lines jam together, often abbreviated SP.

Split-ball gauge See Small hole gauge.

Spoke angle The angle of the steering wheel.

Spongy pedal When there is air in the brake lines, the pedal will have a springy or spongy feeling when applied.

Spontaneous combustion A condition that can cause some materials, such as oily rags, to catch fire without a source of ignition.

Spring rate The spring rate is the amount of weight it takes to compress a spring a certain distance, such as 200 pounds per inch.

Springs Used as a buffer between the suspension and the frame or body and used to absorb wheel movement plus support the weight of the vehicle.

Squeal A high pitched noise caused by high-frequency vibrations when brakes are applied.

Squib The heating element of an inflator module, which starts the chemical reaction to create the gas that inflates an airbag.

Squirrel-cage rotor A rotor design utilized in AC induction motors. The conductors in the rotor are made in the shape of a squirrel cage.

SRS Supplemental Restraint System. Another term for an *airbag system*.

Stabilizer links Usually consists of a bolt, spacer, and nut to connect (link) the end of the stabilizer bar to the lower control arm.

Stall See Service bay.

Star wheel A notched wheel with a left-or right-hand threaded member for adjusting brake shoes.

Starter drive A term used to describe the starter motor drive pinion gear with overrunning clutch.

Starter solenoid A type of starter motor that uses a solenoid to activate the starter drive.

State tax A typical payroll deduction.

State-of-health (SOH) A signal sent by modules to all of the other modules in the network indicating that it is well and able to transmit.

Stator A name for three interconnected windings inside an alternator. A rotating rotor provides a moving magnetic field and induces a current in the windings of the stator.

Steel Refined iron metal with most of the carbon removed.

Steering arms Arms bolted to or forged as a part of the steering knuckles. They transmit the steering force from the tie rods to the knuckles, causing the wheels to pivot.

Steering gear Gears on the end of the steering column that multiply the driver's force to turn the front wheels.

Steering knuckle The inner portion of the spindle that pivots on the king pin or ball joints.

Steering shaft The part of the steering that connects the steering wheel to the steering gear assembly.

Steering stop The location where the steering linkage stops at the extreme left and right end of travel.

Stone wheel A grinding stone attached to a grinder used for cleaning, sharpening, or other similar operations.

Storage The process inside a computer where data is stored before and after calculations have been made.

Straight axle See Solid axle.

Straight cut aviation snip A tin snip that is designed with curved jaws that allow a straight cut through sheet metal.

Straight time The amount of time actually spent performing a service operation.

Straightedge A precision ground measuring gauge that is perfectly straight.

Stroke The distance the piston travels in the cylinder.

Strong hybrid Another term for "full hybrid." See Full hybrid.

Strut suspension A type of suspension system that uses struts.

Struts A structural part of a suspension that includes the shock absorber.

Stub-type frame A type of vehicle frame that only supports the front suspension and engine.

Stud removal tool A hand tool used with a breaker bar or ratchet to remove what is left of a broken stud.

Stud A short rod with threads on both ends.

SULEV Super-Ultra-Low-Emission Vehicle.

Sump Another name for an oil pan that holds engine oil at the bottom of the engine.

Sun gear The center member of a planetary gearset. The other members (planet carrier and ring) rotate around the sun gear, thus the term *planetary*.

Supercharger An engine-driven air pump that is used to force air into the engine to help the engine produce more power.

Surge tank A reservoir mounted at the highest point in the cooling system.

Suspension bumper See Jounce bumper.

Suspension Parts or linkages by which the wheels are attached to the frame or body of a vehicle. These parts or linkages support the vehicle and keep the wheels in proper alignment.

SUV Sport utility vehicle.

SVR Sealed Valve Regulated. A term used to describe a type of battery that is valve-regulated lead acid or sealed lead acid.

Sway bar Shortened name for anti-sway bar. See Stabilizer bar.

Switches and controls Parts of an electrical circuit that is used to control the flow of electricity.

Synchromesh transmission fluid (STF) A fluid specified for use in some manual transmissions.

Synchronizer assemblies The parts needed to mesh gears during a shift in a manual transmission or transaxle.

Tachometer (tach) Instrument or gauge used to measure RPM (revolutions per minute).

Tap A metal cutting tool used to create threads in metal after a hole of the proper size has been drilled.

TBI Throttle body injection.

TCC Torque converter clutch. Used to lock the turbine to the housing, thus producing a direct drive through the torque converter assembly.

TDC Top dead center.

Teacher A role played by a mentor.

Team leader An experienced technician who helps advise a small group of technicians who are paid according to the total amount of work completed by all members of the team.

Technical service bulletin When a problem has a correction, the vehicle manufacturer releases a technical service bulletin (TSB), which details the repair. Also called *technical service bulletin information (TSBI)*.

Technician A and B questions A type of question used on ASE certification tests.

Technician A person who performs diagnosis and service work to a vehicle.

Telescoping steering column A steering column that can be adjusted toward and away from the driver.

Tell-tale light Dash warning light (sometimes called an *idiot light*).

Tensile strength The maximum stress used under tension (lengthwise force) without causing failure.

Terminal The metal end of a wire that fits into a plastic connector and is the electrical connection part of a junction.

Test light A light used to test for voltage. Contains a light bulb with a ground wire at one end and a pointed tip at the other end.

Thermostat A device that controls the flow in a system such as the engine cooling system based on temperature.

Thickness gauge See Feeler gauge.

Thimble The part of a micrometer that is rotated to move the spindle.

Threaded insert A type of thread repair where the original threads are replaced by an insert that contains the same size threads as the original on the inside of the insert.

Three Cs Technicians need to complete the work order by informing the customers of the three Cs—complaint (concern), cause, and the correction.

Throttle body A housing containing a valve to regulate the airflow through the intake manifold.

Throttle position (TP) sensor Signals the computer as to the position of the throttle.

Throw-out bearing The bearing assembly that rides on the pressure plate of a clutch assembly and is used to release the clamping force of the pressure plate on the clutch disc. Also called a *release bearing*.

Throws The term used to describe the number of output circuits there are in a switch.

Tie rods A rod connecting the steering arms together.

Tier A level of environmental regulation created by the EPA. Tier 1 is gradually being phased out in favor of stricter Tier 2 regulations.

Tilt steering column A type of steering column that can be moved upward or downward to fit the driver.

Tin snips A hand tool used to cut sheet metal, thin cardboard, or similar material.

Tinnerman nuts Used to keep the brake drums on at the assembly plant. Can be removed and discarded when servicing the drum brake for the first time.

Tire rotation   A term used to describe moving wheel/tire assemblies from one position on a vehicle to another.

Tire slip   The difference between the actual speed and the rate at which the tire tread moves across the road surface.

TLEV   Transitional Low-Emission Vehicle.

Top dead center (TDC)   The highest point in the cylinder that the piston can travel. The measurement from bottom dead center (BDC) to TDC determines the stroke length of the crankshaft.

Torque converter clutch   A clutch located inside the torque converter that locks the turbine and the impeller together to prevent any slippage. Also called a *lockup torque converter*.

Torque converter   A special form of fluid coupling in which torque is increased.

Torque prevailing nut   A type of nut that does not loosen, but rather retains its holding torque.

Torque wrench   A wrench that registers the amount of applied torque.

Torque   A twisting force measured in pounds-feet (lb-ft) or Newton-meters (N-m), which may result in motion.

Torsion bar   A type of spring in the shape of a straight bar. One end is attached to the frame of the vehicle, and the opposite end is attached to a control arm of the suspension. When the wheels hit a bump, the bar twists and then untwists.

Torx   A type of fastener that features a star-shaped indentation for a tool. A registered trade mark of the Camcar Division of Textron.

TP   Throttle position sensor. The sensor that provides feedback concerning the position of the throttle plate.

TPMS   Tire pressure monitoring system.

Trace   The displayed waveform that shows the variations of the input signal as a function of time.

Track   The distance between the centerline of the wheels as viewed from the front or rear.

Traction control   The electromechanical parts used to control wheel slip during acceleration.

Traction motor   A motor-generator in a hybrid electric vehicle that is responsible for propelling or assisting the internal combustion engine.

Traction   The friction (traction) between tires and the pavement.

Trade number   The number stamped on an automotive light bulb. All bulbs of the same trade number have the same candlepower and wattage, regardless of the manufacturer of the bulb.

Trade-in (wholesale) value   The value of a used vehicle usually paid to the owner who is purchasing a new or newer vehicle.

Trainee   The term used to describe a person being trained.

Trainer   A beginning service technician just learning about the trade.

Tramp   An up and down vibration of a tire/wheel assembly usually due to out-of-round tire or out-of-balance condition.

Transaxle   A transmission used in front-wheel-drive vehicles that include the final drive (differential) within the assembly.

Transducer   An electrical and mechanical speed sensing and control unit used on cruise control systems.

Transfer case   A unit containing gears used to transfer engine power to the rear wheels or to both the front and rear wheels on a vehicle equipped with four-wheel drive.

Transistor   A semiconductor device that can operate as an amplifier or an electrical switch.

Transmission case   The housing of a transmission where most of the parts are assembled inside.

Tread   The rubber part of a tire that touches the road.

Trigger   Determines the beginning point of a waveform.

Trouble light   A light used for close viewing of dark areas. Also called a *work light*.

Trunnions   The four arms of a typical universal joint.

TSB   Technical service bulletin.

TSBi   See Technical service bulletin.

Tube-nut wrench   See Fitting wrench.

Turbocharger   An exhaust-powered supercharger.

TV   Thickness variation.

TWC   Abbreviation for three-way catalytic converter used to control HC, CO, and NOx emissions.

Twisted pair   A pair of wires that are twisted together from 9 to 16 turns per foot of length. Most are twisted once every inch (12 per foot) to help reduce electromagnetic inference from being induced in the wires as one wire would tend to cancel out any interference pickup up by the other wire.

U joints   Universal joints.

ULEV II   Ultra Low-Emission Vehicle certified under the Phase II LEV standard.

ULEV   Ultra-Low-Emission Vehicle.

UNC   Unified national coarse.

Underinflation   A term used to describe a tire with too little tire pressure (less than minimum allowable pressure).

UNF   Unified national fine.

Unibody   Another name used to describe a unit body vehicle.

Unit body   A type of vehicle construction first used by the Budd Company of Troy, Michigan, that does not use a separate frame. The body is built strong enough to support the engine and the power train, as well as the suspension and steering system. The outside body panels are part of the structure. Also see Space frame construction.

Universal joint   A joint in a steering or drive shaft that allows torque to be transmitted at an angle.

Urea   A chemical used in the reduction oxides of nitrogen in exhaust emissions in a diesel engine equipped with selective catalytic reduction (SCR) system.

Used oil   Any petroleum-based or synthetic oil that has been used.

UST   Underground storage tank.

Utility knife   A handheld knife that uses replaceable blades.

UTQGS   Uniform Tire Quality Grading System.

Vacuum   Any pressure less than atmospheric pressure (14.7 PSI).

Valence ring   The outermost ring or orbit of electrons around a nucleus of an atom.

Valve train   The collection of parts that make the valves operate. The valve train includes the camshaft(s), related drive components, the various parts that convert the camshaft's rotary motion into reciprocating motion, and the valves and their associated parts.

Vapor   Visible particles of a liquid floating in the air. The change of a liquid to a gas.

VECI Vehicle emission control information. This sticker is located under the hood on all vehicles and includes emission-related information that is important to the service technician.

Vehicle identification number (VIN) Alphanumeric number identifying vehicle type, assembly plant, power train, etc.

VI Viscosity index. An index of the change in a motor oil's viscosity between hot and cold extremes.

Vibration An oscillation, shake, or movement that alternates in opposite directions.

VIN Vehicle identification number.

Viscosity The thickness or the resistance to flow of a liquid.

VISE GRIPS® A brand name for locking pliers.

VOC Volatile organic compounds. These compounds include gases emitted from paints, solvents, glass, and many other products.

Volt The unit of measurement for the amount of electrical pressure; named for Alessandro Volta (1745–1827).

Voltage drop Voltage loss across a wire, connector, or any other conductor. Voltage drop equals resistance in ohms times current in amperes (Ohm's law).

Voltage regulator An electronic or mechanical unit that controls the output voltage of an electrical generator or alternator by controlling the field current of the generator.

Voltmeter An electrical test instrument used to measure volts (unit of electrical pressure). A voltmeter is connected in parallel with the unit or circuit being tested.

VSC Vehicle stability control.

VSS Vehicle speed sensor.

VTF Vacuum-tube fluorescent.

Wankel engine See Rotary engine.

Warehouse distributor (WD) A company that purchases parts from the manufacturer and sells the parts to automotive parts stores.

Warning light A light on the instrument panel to alert the driver when one half of a split hydraulic system fails as determined by the pressure differential switch.

Washers Flat or shaped pieces of round metal with a hole in the center used between a nut and a part or casting.

Waste spark system A type of ignition system that uses one ignition coil to fire two spark plugs at the same time.

Wate–fuel separator Used in the fuel system of a diesel engine to remove water from the fuel before it is sent to the engine.

Water jacket The coolant passages around the cylinders that are used to absorb and transfer heat away from the ICE assembly.

Water pump pliers See Multiple-groove adjustable pliers.

Water pump A mechanical device responsible for circulating coolant through a liquid cooling system.

Watt An electrical unit of power; 1 watt equals current (amperes) × voltage (1/746 hp). Named after James Watt, a Scottish inventor.

Ways Places where the disc brake caliper contacts on a sliding-type caliper design.

Wear bars See Wear indicators.

Wear Indicators Bald area across the tread of a tire when only 2/32" or less of tread depth remains.

Web The stiffening member of the shoe to which the shoe table is attached.

Weight transfer The movement of weight forward during braking.

Wheel brakes Brakes at each wheel of a vehicle that slows and stops the rotation of that wheel.

Wheel cylinder The part of the hydraulic system that receives pressure from the master cylinder and applies the brake shoes to the drums.

Wheel mounting torque The amount of torque applied to the lug nuts.

Wheel speed sensors Sensors used to detect the speed of the wheels. Used by an electronic controller for antilock brakes (ABS) and/or traction control.

Wheelbase The distance between the centerline of the two wheels as viewed from the side.

WHMIS Workplace Hazardous Materials Information Systems.

Wide-band oxygen sensor An oxygen sensor design that is capable of detecting actual air–fuel ratios. This is in contrast to a conventional oxygen sensor that only changes voltage when a stoichiometric air–fuel ratio has been achieved.

Windage tray A sheet metal tray located under the crankshaft of an engine used to help prevent the aeration of the oil during engine operation.

Window regulator A mechanical device that transfers the rotating motion of the window hand crank or electric motor to a vertical motion to raise and lower a window in a vehicle.

Windshield wipers The assembly of motor, motor control, operating linkage, plus the wiper arms and blades that are used to remove rain water from the windshield.

Wire brush wheel A wire brush wheel is often mounted on one end of a grinder and is used for cleaning parts and other similar operations.

Wishbone suspension See SLA.

Witness mark A mark made by an object which indicates where a noise or vibration could be located.

Wood alcohol See Methanol.

Work experience Two years of work experience as a service technician is needed plus passing one or more tests to be certified by ASE.

Work light See Trouble light.

Work order Contains all vehicle and customer information plus what service work is requested by the customer. Also called a *repair order*.

Work The transfer of energy from one physical system to another. Actually moving an object is work.

Worm and sector A steering gear that uses a worm gear that engages a sector gear on the cross shaft.

Worm gear A type of gear used in an older type of steering gear, which is attached to the steering shaft.

WOW display A dash display when it first comes on and lights all possible segments. Can be used to test the dash display for missing lighted segments.

Wrench A hand tool used to grasp and rotate a threaded fastener.

WSS Wheel speed sensor.

Xenon headlights Headlights that use an arc tube assembly that has a xenon gas inside which produces a bright bluish light.

Yaw rate sensor An input sensor usually located in the center of the vehicle that detects yaw as part of an electronic suspension system.

Zerk fitting A name commonly used for a grease fitting. Named for its developer, Oscar U. Zerk, in 1922, an employee of the Alemite Corporation. Besides a Zerk fitting, a grease fitting is also called an Alamite fitting.

ZEV Zero-Emission Vehicle. This rating is typically only achieved by battery-powered vehicles or those powered by fuel cells.

Zinc dialkyl dithiophosphate (ZDDP or ZDP) An engine oil additive used to reduce sliding friction in an engine.

INDEX

Bulb numbers (continued)
   testing bulbs, 239–242
   trade number, 239
Bulb test, 225
Bump cap, 49
Bushing, 345
Business meetings, 35
Butane-powered soldering iron, 92
Bypass valve, 185

C

CA. See Cranking amperes (CA)
CAA. See Clean Air Act (CAA)
Cabin filter, 162
Cable operation, 345
Cadillac, 1
Calibration codes, 128
California Air Resources Board (CARB), 125
Calorie (c), 261
Cam-in-block design, 135
Camshaft bearing, 111
Camshaft measurement, 109
Canada's Automotive Apprenticeship Program (Red Seal), 46
Candlepower, 239
Canister purge (CANP), 301
Capacity test, 220
Capillary action, 75
Cap screws, 67
Carbon dioxide fire extinguisher, 53
Carbon monoxide (CO), 5, 296
Carcass plies, 317
Cardan joints. See Cross-yoke joints
Cardan U-joint, 350
Castellated nut, 74
Casting numbers, 128
Catalyst, 299
Catalytic converter, 5, 299
   operation, 300
Cathode ray tube (CRT), 229
CCA. See Cold-cranking amperes (CCA)
Center high-mounted stop light (CHMSL), 242
Center link, 335
Center section, 319
Cetane number, 275
CFC-12, 263
Chain hoist, 100
Charcoal canister, 301
Charging circuit, 217
   alternator construction, 222–223
   charging system voltmeter test, 223
Charging system fault, 226
Charging system voltage specifications, 223
Charging system voltmeter test, 223
Chassis faults, 313
Chassis lubrication, 187
   grease fittings, 187
   need for, 187
   steering stops, 188
   steering system inspection, 188
Chassis system, 2–3
Cheater bar, 93
Check engine, 226
Check engine light, 226
Check valves, 299
Chemical/microbe cleaning, 51

Chevrolet Impala with a 5.3 liter V-8, 184
"Chirping," 330–331
Chisels, 88
CHMSL. See Center high-mounted stop light (CHMSL)
Christmas tree clips, 73
Chronic test syndrome, 44
Chrysler CAP, 20
Circuit, 202
   breaker, 204
   complete circuit, 202
   definition, 202
Circuit faults
   high resistance, 204
   open circuits, 203
   short-to-ground, 203–204
   short-to-voltage, 203
Clamp mount, 113
Clean Air Act (CAA), 57
Cleaning methods and processes, 51
   abrasive cleaning, 51
   chemical/microbe cleaning, 51
   power washing, 51
   thermal ovens, 51
Clicker-type torque wrench, 81
Clips. See Tinnerman nuts
Clock-in, 22
Clockspring, 255
Clock time, 22
Clogged, shorted, or leaking fuel injectors, 120
Clogged oil pump, 153
Close end, 79
Clutches, 343
   clutch disc, 346
   parts and operation, 343–345
   pedal linkage, 345
   release bearing, 345–346
Clutch pedal linkage, 345
   cable operation, 345
   hydraulic, 345
   levers and rods, 345
Coach, 35
Code of Federal Regulations (CFR), 56
Coil-on-plug (COP) ignition, 284, 286
Cold chisel, 88
Cold-cranking amperes (CCA), 217
Collapsible column, 338
Combination wrench, 79
Combustion, 130
   chamber, 130
Commission pay, 23
Communicates to drivers, 282
Communications, 28
   listening, 28
   nonverbal, 28
   reading, 29–30
   telephone, 28–29
   verbal, 28
   writing, 29
Complete circuit, 202
Completion of apprenticeship, 41
Composite headlight, 243
Compressed air safety, 51
Compressed gas, 253–254
Compressed natural gas (CNG), 273
   vehicle design, 273–274